AN
INTRODUCTION
TO THINKING
LIKE A
SOCIOLOGIST

Core Eighth Edition

You May Ask Yourself

AN INTRODUCTION TO THINKING LIKE A SOCIOLOGIST

Core Eighth Edition

You May Ask Yourself

AN INTRODUCTION TO THINKING LIKE A SOCIOLOGIST

Dalton Conley

PRINCETON UNIVERSITY

W. W. NORTON & COMPANY
Celebrating a Century of Independent Publishing

W. W. Norton & Company has been independent since its founding in 1923, when William Warder Norton and Mary D. Herter Norton first published lectures delivered at the People's Institute, the adult education division of New York City's Cooper Union. The firm soon expanded its program beyond the Institute, publishing books by celebrated academics from America and abroad. By midcentury, the two major pillars of Norton's publishing program—trade books and college texts—were firmly established. In the 1950s, the Norton family transferred control of the company to its employees, and today—with a staff of five hundred and hundreds of trade, college, and professional titles published each year—W. W. Norton & Company stands as the largest and oldest publishing house owned wholly by its employees.

Editor: Michael Moss
Senior Project Editor: Rachel Mayer
Editorial Assistant: Emma Freund
Senior Managing Editor, College: Marian Johnson
Managing Editors, College: Carla Talmadge and Kim Yi
Production Manager: Brenda Manzanedo
Media Editor: Eileen Connell
Associate Media Editor: Alexandra Park
Assistant Media Editor: Caleb Wertz
Ebook Producer: Mica Clausen
Marketing Director, Sociology: Julia Hall
Book Designer: Kiss Me I'm Polish LLC, New York
Design Director: Jillian Burr
Director of College Permissions: Megan Schindel
Photo Editor: Thomas Persano
College Permissions Associate: Patricia Wong
Composition: Six Red Marbles
Manufacturing: Transcontinental

Permission to use copyrighted material is included on page A-46.

ISBN: 978-1-324-06251-6

W. W. Norton & Company, Inc., 500 Fifth Avenue, New York, NY 10110
wwnorton.com
W. W. Norton & Company, Ltd., 15 Carlisle Street, London W1D 3BS
1 2 3 4 5 6 7 8 9 0

Brief Contents

Contents

124 CHAPTER 4: SOCIALIZATION AND THE CONSTRUCTION OF REALITY

164 CHAPTER 5: GROUPS AND NETWORKS

202   CHAPTER 6: SOCIAL CONTROL AND DEVIANCE

Preface

I came to sociology by accident, so to speak. During the 1980s, there were no sociology courses at the high-school level, so I entered college with only the vaguest notion of what sociology—or even social science—was. Instead, I headed straight for the pre-med courses. But there was no such thing as a pre-med major, so I ended up specializing in the now defunct "humanities field major." This un-major major was really the result of my becoming a junior and realizing that I was not any closer to a declared field of study than I had been when arriving two years earlier. So I scanned a list of all the electives I had taken until then—philosophy of aesthetics, history of technology, and so on—and marched right into my adviser's office, declaring that it had always been my lifelong dream to study "art and technology in the twentieth century." I wrote this up convincingly enough, apparently, because the college allowed me to write a senior thesis about how the evolution of Warner Brothers' cartoon characters—from the stuttering, insecure Porky Pig to the militant Daffy Duck to the cool, collected, and confident Bugs Bunny—reflected the self-image of the United States on the world stage during the Depression, World War II, and the postwar period, respectively. Little did I know, I was already becoming a sociologist.

After college, I worked as a journalist but then decided that I wanted to continue my schooling. I was drawn to the critical stance and reflexivity that I had learned in my humanities classes, but I knew that I didn't want to devote my life to arcane texts. What I wanted to do was take those skills—that critical stance—and apply them to everyday life, to the here and now. I also was rather skeptical of the methods that humanists used. What texts they chose to analyze always seemed so arbitrary. I wanted to systematize the inquiry a bit more; I found myself trying to apply the scientific method that I had gotten a taste of in my biology classes. But I didn't want to do science in a lab. I wanted to be out in the proverbial real world. So when I flipped through a course catalog with these latent preferences somewhere in the back of my head, my finger landed on the sociology courses.

Once I became a card-carrying sociologist, the very first course I taught was Introduction to Sociology. I had big shoes to fill in teaching this course at Yale. Kai Erikson, the world-renowned author of *Wayward Puritans* and

Everything in Its Path and the son of psychologist Erik Erikson, was stepping down from his popular course, The Human Universe, and I, a first-year assistant professor, was expected to replace him.

I had a lot of sociology to learn. After all, graduate training in sociology is spotty at best. And there is no single theory of society to study in the same way that one might learn, for example, the biochemistry of DNA transcription and translation as the central dogma of molecular biology. We talk about the sociological imagination as an organizing principle. But even that is almost a poetic notion, not so easily articulated. Think of sociology as more like driving a car than learning calculus. You can read the manual all you want, but that isn't going to teach you how to do it. Only by seeing sociology in action and then trying it yourself will you eventually say, "Hey, I've got the hang of this!" The great Chinese philosopher Confucius said about learning: "By three methods we may learn wisdom: First, by reflection, which is noblest; second, by imitation, which is easiest; and third by experience, which is the bitterest." Hopefully you can skip the bitterness, but you get the general idea. For example, by trying to fix a local problem through appealing to your elected officials, you might better grasp sociological theories of the state.

Hence the title of this book. In *You May Ask Yourself*, I show readers how sociologists question what most others take for granted about society, and I give readers opportunities to apply sociological ways of thinking to their own experiences. I've tried to jettison the arcane academic debates that become the guiding light of so many intro books in favor of a series of contemporary empirical (gold) nuggets that show off sociology (and empirical social science more generally) in its finest hour. Most students who take an introductory sociology class in college will not end up being sociology majors, let alone professional sociologists. Yet I aim to speak to both the aspiring major and the student who is merely fulfilling a requirement. So rather than having pages filled with statistics and theories that will go out of date rather quickly, *You May Ask Yourself* tries to instill in the reader a way of thinking—a scientific approach to human affairs that is portable, one that students will find useful when they study anything else, whether history or medicine.

To achieve this ambitious goal, I tried to write a book that was as "un-textbook"-like as possible, while covering all the material that a student in sociology needs to know. In this vein, each chapter is organized around a motivating paradox, meant to serve as the first chilling line of a mystery novel that motivates the reader to read on to find out (or rather, figure out, because this book is not about spoon-feeding facts) the nugget, the debate, the fundamentally new way of looking at the world that illuminates the paradox. Along with a paradox, each chapter begins with a profile of a relevant person who speaks to the core theme of the chapter. These range from myself to Issa Rae to Satoshi Nakamoto, the pseudonym for whoever created Bitcoin. In addition, to show the usefulness of sociological knowledge in shaping the world around us, each chapter culminates in a Policy discussion and a Practice activity for students.

WHAT'S NEW IN THE EIGHTH EDITION

Higher education is in rapid transition, with online instruction expanding in traditional institutions, in the expanding for-profit sector, and in the new open-courseware movement. With these changes, textbooks must also reinvent and reorient themselves. Students now expect, I believe, an entire multimedia experience when they purchase a textbook.

To that end, the Eighth Edition ebook includes a "Check Your Understanding" question accompanying each chapter-opening "Paradox" animation. "Check Your Understanding" questions also follow each major section within chapters as well as select data figures and Q&A videos, providing a low-stakes opportunity to test comprehension and aid retention through recall and immediate feedback. Every chapter in the ebook also concludes with a short interactive activity focused on developing sociological skills by exploring research, analyzing data, or applying key concepts to our social world.

In this edition, racial and ethnic categorizations are considered proper nouns and thus are capitalized. As Temple University journalism professor Lori Tharps notes, "Black with a capital B refers to people of the African diaspora. Lowercase black is simply a color" (Tharps, 2014). In the same way, "White" as a racial category acknowledges the functions of this socially constructed label in society. Racial designations are not neutral markers of skin tone but socially constructed categories whose meanings and boundaries shift over time and place. Treating these categories as proper nouns recognizes them as such (Appiah, 2020).

There is an alternative school of thought that claims that capitalization leads to reification of those somewhat arbitrary and historically contingent categories and thus argues for capitalizing neither label. Indeed, some languages do not even capitalize nationalities. Yet another line of reasoning says that Black should be capitalized but white should not be on the grounds that there is a common experience of structural racism among the African diaspora while there is no unifying experience of white people and that capitalizing it only lends legitimacy to those who seek a "white nationalism." But this, in turn, denies the commonness of White privilege, for example, as a shared referent. Of course, it also denies the folk usage of White as a socially constructed term that conveys a tacit understanding of membership in a particular identity group. To those who say the White experience is too diverse to deserve such a label, the same can be said for the Black experience. In short, there is no perfect choice, but I feel that capitalizing all racial labels is the best option.

Then there is the issue of how to call those who might be referred to as Hispanic or of Hispanic origin or Latino. Over the last couple of decades, Latino has become a preferred way to reference the diverse category of people that includes those of Cuban, Puerto Rican, Mexican, Guatemalan, and Colombian descent—to name a few. It also includes those from Latin America who hail from non-Spanish-speaking countries, such as people of Brazilian descent (who typically speak Portuguese) or those from Belize (where English is an official language). Meanwhile, the term *Hispanic* is a language-based category that also included people from Spain but excluded those whose origin was in Latin American countries that were not Spanish-speaking (e.g., Brazil). Never mind that significant populations from some "Spanish-speaking" countries speak indigenous languages (and not Spanish) such as Quechua.

While most people who would fit into either of these categories actually prefer to use their specific national origin to denote their identity (such as Mexican or Mexican American), the terms remain in common usage for a variety of reasons—not least of which is that Hispanic has been an official U.S. government category since 1977 (a development that was pursued thanks to the wishes of some [pro-assimilationist, conservative] Mexican American political groups). The term *Latino*, meanwhile, gained usage currency starting in the 1990s. Today, however, there is increasing recognition that—as for terms in other Latin-derived languages—the male designation stands in for a mixed-gendered category. Some activists see its assimilation into English as an opportunity to change that gender dynamic and prefer to use the term *Latinx*—the "x" removing any gendered connotation from the group. This is the term that is used in the present edition. Some readers may object to this choice on the basis that strong majorities of Latinx individuals, when surveyed, reject the term. However, linguistic innovations often start among a highly engaged, highly informed minority to whom the issue is of paramount importance. Such is the case with Latinx. Of course, like all terms for social groups, this one may fade or further evolve, in which case, look out for new usage in the future editions! (This is, of course, true for all the categories discussed herein.) All of these decisions are highly political and sociological, and my own subject position as a cis-White male should be acknowledged in my role as the author who has had to make these decisions (in conjunction with, of course, the editor/publisher and in consideration of reviewer/reader feedback).

In addition, new learning objectives build additional transparency into the learning process and highlight the big picture concepts and applications in each chapter. Every chapter in the book has been thoroughly updated to include fresh examples, research, and data throughout. Here are some of the highlights:

CHAPTER 1: THE SOCIOLOGICAL IMAGINATION: AN INTRODUCTION

To clarify the discussion of the merits of a college degree, data on the true costs and returns of college has been updated and calculations streamlined.

There is an expanded discussion of college admissions and the newer trend of elite schools opting out of the *U.S. News & World Report* ranking. A new paragraph was added to foreshadow and sharpen the concepts of education as learning versus education as the acquisition of knowledge or skills. In the Doing Theory section, Table 1.2 (Applying Theory to the Question of Educational Attainment) distinguishes three main sociological paradigms' approaches to educational attainment, or the question of who goes to college and why. The section dedicated to explaining the divisions within sociology clarifies differences between quantitative and qualitative methods as well as the distinction between positive and interpretive sociology.

CHAPTER 2: METHODS

The section on Causality Versus Correlation has been updated to reflect the potential mistakes one may make while trying to establish causality in social science research. To investigate the various ways in which sociologists utilize the scientific method in their work, a new section called Designing a Study has been created. A revised section on Researcher Responsibility and Ethics of Social Research explores the moral quandaries that sociologists work with and through every day. In the Experimentation section, a new study where some low-income mothers were given money, while others weren't, is used as an example of experimentation to track how their children were affected. In a similar vein, the section on social research ethics has been expanded to discuss the ethical lessons of the Tuskegee Syphilis Study, the Tearoom Trade, and various psychology experiments.

CHAPTER 3: CULTURE AND MEDIA

This chapter includes a new chapter opener on the intersection of culture and media in actor Issa Rae's rise to fame. A section on counterculture has been added to highlight the growth potential of various subcultures, as well as how the counterculture's and mainstream culture's battle for the soul of society can result in culture wars. A new section on social media examines the impact of new forms of digital communication in our world today. The coverage on the intersection between sexism and the media discusses the book *Fearing the Black Body* by Sabrina Strings, which connects fat phobia with anti-Black racism.

CHAPTER 4: SOCIALIZATION AND THE CONSTRUCTION OF REALITY

In the section on the development of the self and the other, a discussion of the "Free the Nipple" movement leads to an examination of intentional violations of social norms in the modern-day world. The section on family units includes updated research on the intersections between race and class. In the school section, research on class and education has been streamlined for clarity. It also includes new coverage of how the COVID-19 pandemic has affected education. New paragraphs on adolescent peer pressure and risk-taking behavior have been added to the section on peer relationships. Older research in the adult socialization section and outdated examples of symbolic interactionism in the social construction of reality section have been omitted. In the section on new technologies and how the internet has impacted interaction, a new graph on impression management has been introduced.

CHAPTER 5: GROUPS AND NETWORKS

The chapter opener includes a new paragraph on cryptocurrency. In the United States and Social Capital section, data and research on recent election cycles and online fund-raising have been updated, and in the section on the Social Structure of Teen Sex, data has been brought up to speed with current trends in today's youth population. Updated research on interlocking directorates in pharmaceutical companies and health-care nonprofits has been added to the Organizational Structure and Culture section. In the Institutional Isomorphism: Everybody's Doing It section, a new paragraph on anti-isomorphism and *Moneyball* expands the discussion of theory.

CHAPTER 6: SOCIAL CONTROL AND DEVIANCE

In the Social Deviance section, research on COVID-19 and mask-wearing has been updated. The sections in this chapter have been rearranged for clearer development of chapter concepts. A new section, Conflict Theory, has been added to explore how conflict theorists understand deviance. Data has been updated in the Interpreting the Crime Rate section, with new material on the variation in murder rates over the long and short run.

CHAPTER 7: STRATIFICATION

This chapter has been reorganized for clearer development of key concepts. In the Income Versus Wealth box, a new explanation of the difference between income (as a steady stream of money) and wealth (as a pool of money collected over time) has been included. Data in the section on the upper class has been updated, including new research on the effect of COVID-19 on income. The section covering the expansion and retrenchment of the middle and working classes includes updated research on income gaps between CEOs and typical wage workers. In the section about modern theories of inequality, a new paragraph on Weber's expansion of Marxist thought has been added. The section on the caste system features updated research on the legacy of the caste system in rural India as well as Isabel Wilkerson's analysis of the racial caste system in the United States. A new paragraph has been added to the Elite–Mass Dichotomy System section on elite networks within Wall Street. Lastly, the section about global inequality includes a new discussion of the explanation for and legacy of unequal economic starting places.

CHAPTER 8: GENDER

The chapter opener includes updates on bathroom bills and gender policing. The Sexed Bodies in the Premodern World section includes new material highlighting how sex and gender affect each other mutually. In the section They Goes to College, the term "ze" has been changed to "they" with updated coverage of protections for transgender students and the Biden administration. In the section on gender differences over time, updated research on race and hegemonic masculinity has been added. The Inequality at Work section includes updated research and data in Figure 8.2 on women in the workforce as well as a new paragraph on emotional labor. The Motherhood Penalty is a new section that has been added to explore the motherhood wage penalty and cognitive labor. The theories explored in the Theories of Gender Inequality section have been consolidated for clearer, more concise development of chapter concepts.

CHAPTER 9: RACE

In this chapter, sections have been reorganized for clearer development of important concepts, including discussing the differences between race and ethnicity earlier in the chapter. Critical Race Theory: What's All the Fuss About? is a new feature box that explores the basic principles of CRT and some of its associated controversies. In the Prejudice, Discrimination, and the New Racism section, new material on individual racism, the Implicit Association Test, and Devah Pager's audit study on racism and job applications has been added. Sections on institutional racism and how structural racism impacts wealth have been updated with new research on institutional racism in policing as well as updated data on household wealth according to race. The section on Whites includes new coverage of responses to Peggy McIntosh's research on White privilege and Robin DiAngelo's concept of "white fragility."

CHAPTER 10: FAMILY

Sections on families of specific races, such as African American families and Latinx families, have been refreshed with current research, which carries over into a new section on Asian American families and the patterns of family dynamics in these households (such as the eldest child acting as the "language broker" for the rest of the family). Sections on the unique experience of gay, lesbian, and transgender families have been revised to include current research. Lastly, the section on how policies impact the expansion of marriage has itself expanded to reflect the most current data on the topic.

ACKNOWLEDGMENTS

You May Ask Yourself originated in the Introduction to Sociology course that I have taught on and off since the mid-1990s at New York University, Yale University, and Columbia University. However, the process of writing it made me feel as if I were learning to be a sociologist all over again. For example, I never taught religion, methodology, or the sociology of education. But instructors who reviewed the manuscript requested that these topics be covered, so with the assistance of an army of graduate students who really ought to be recognized as co-authors, I got to work. The experience was invaluable, and in a way, I finally feel like a card-carrying sociologist, having acquired at last a bird's-eye view of my colleagues' work. I consider it a great honor to be able to put my little spin (or filter) on the field in this way, to be able not just to influence the few hundred intro students I teach each year, but also to excite (I hope) and instill the enthusiasm I didn't experience until graduate school in students who may be just a few months out of high school (if that).

I mentioned that the graduate students who helped me create this book were really more like co-authors, ghostwriters, or perhaps law clerks. Law clerks do much of the writing of legal opinions for judges, but only a judge's name graces a decision. I asked Norton to allow more co-authors, but they declined—perhaps understandably, given how long such a list would be—so I will take this opportunity to thank my students and hope that you are still reading this preface.

The original transcription of my lectures that formed the basis of this text was completed by Carse Ramos, who also worked on assembling the glossary and drafted some parts of various chapters, such as sections in the economic sociology chapter, as well as some text in the chapters on authority and deviance. She also served as an all-around editor. Ashley Mears did the heavy lifting on the race, gender, family, and religion chapters. Amy LeClair took the lead on methods, culture, groups and networks, socialization, and health. Jennifer Heerwig cobbled together the chapter on authority and the state and deviance (a nice combo), while her officemate Brian McCabe whipped up the chapter on science, technology, and the environment and the one on social movements. Melissa Velez wrote the first draft of the education chapter (and a fine one at that). Michael McCarthy did the same for the stratification chapter. Devyani Prabhat helped revise the social movements chapter. My administrative assistant, Amelia Branigan, served as fact-checker, editor, and box drafter while running a department, taking the GREs, and writing and submitting her own graduate applications. When Amelia had to decamp for Northwestern University to pursue her own doctorate, Lauren Marten took over the job of chasing down obscure references, fact-checking, and proofreading. Alexandre Frenette drafted the questions and activities in the practice sections at the end of each chapter.

For the Second Edition, much of the work to integrate the interview transcripts and update material based on reviewer feedback fell to a great extent on the shoulders of Laura Norén, a fantastic New York University graduate student who has worked on topics as far-ranging as public toilets (with my colleague Harvey Molotch) and how symphonies and designers collaborate (as part of her dissertation). I hope Laura will find her crash-course overview of sociology useful at some point in what promises to be a productive and exciting scholarly career.

When it was time to begin the Third Edition, the updating of all the statistics, fact-checking, and so on that is the bread and butter of a revision fell upon the capable shoulders of Emi Nakazato who, although trained as a social worker in graduate school, adeptly pivoted to that field's cousin, sociology.

For the Fourth and Fifth Editions, Laura Norén returned as the research assistant. With her prior experience she picked up the task ably without dropping a beat. For the Sixth and Seventh Editions, I turned to Thomas Laidley, a graduate student at the time, who did a more than thorough job of not only updating facts and figures but questioning them as well.

In addition to the students who have worked with me on the book, I need to give shout-outs to all the top-notch scholars who found time in their busy schedules to sit down with me and do on-camera interviews: Julia Adams, Andy Bichlbaum, danah boyd, Andrew Cherlin, Nitsan Chorev, Susan Crawford, Adam Davidson, Matthew Desmond, Stephen Duncombe, Mitchell Duneier, Paula England, John Evans, Michael Gaddis, David Grusky, Fadi Haddad, Michael Hout, Jennifer Jacquet, Shamus Khan, Annette Lareau, Jennifer Lee, Ka Liu, Amos Mac, Douglas McAdam, Ashley Mears, Steven Morgan, Alondra Nelson, Devah Pager, Nathan Palmer, C. J. Pascoe, Frances Fox Piven, Allison Pugh, Adeel Qalbani, Marc Ramirez, Asha Rangappa, Jen'nan Read, Victor Rios, Jeffrey Sachs, Jennifer Senior, Mario Luis Small, Zephyr Teachout, Duncan Watts, and Robb Willer.

For the interview videos, the filmmaking, editing, and postproduction were done in earlier editions by Erica Rothman at Nightlight Productions with the assistance of Jim Haverkamp, Kevin Wells, Saul Rouda, Dimitriy Khavin, and Arkadiy Ugorskiy, and then in this new Eighth Edition by Elizabeth Audley and Ragnar Freidank. This was no easy task, because we wanted a bunch of cuts ranging from 30-second sound bites to television-show-length segments of 22 minutes. Although a bunch of interviews with academic social scientists on topics ranging from estimating the effects of Catholic schools on student outcomes to the political economy of global trade to the social contagion of autism are not likely to win any Emmys or rock the Nielsens (with the possible exception of the one on college sex), it has certainly been one of the most exciting highlights in my sociological career to host this makeshift talk show on such a wide range of interesting topics. (If only more of our public discourse would dig into issues in the way that we did in these interviews, our society and governance would be in better shape—if I do say so myself!)

When I began work on the Eighth Edition's updates and revisions, I knew I could use some expert help. I relied on a number of scholars who generously read chapters of this book and offered valuable feedback, criticisms, and suggestions:

REVIEWERS FOR THE EIGHTH EDITION

Amy August, San José State University

Monica Bibxy Radu, Southeast Missouri State University

Alicia Brunson, Georgia Southern University

Angie Carter, Michigan Technological University

Cindy Epperson, St. Louis Community College

Meredith P. Field, Alfred University

Jared Fitzgerald, Oklahoma State University

Daniel Harrison, Lander University

AnneMarie Hassan, Los Angeles Valley College

Devin Heyward, Saint Peter's University

Sarah Jakub, Bucks County Community College

Kyle Knight, University of Alabama in Huntsville

Pawel Maciag, Mercy College

Stephen Merino, Colorado Mesa University

Kathryn Nutter-Pridgen, Concord University

Nels Paulson, University of Wisconsin—Stout

Gregory Peter, University of Wisconsin Oshkosh

Hayley Pierce, Brigham Young University

Jeffrey Sacha, American River College

Elizabeth Scheel-Keita, Saint Cloud State University

Evan Shenkin, Western Oregon University

Yongren Shi, University of Iowa

Anna M. Sorensen, State University of New York at Potsdam

Craig Upright, Winona State University

Susan Vorsanger, Mount Saint Mary College

Elena Windsong, Colorado State University

Paige Sweet, University of Michigan

Nicole D. Jenkins, Ph.D., Howard University

Adia Harvey Wingfield, Washington University in St. Louis

Norah MacKendrick, Rutgers University

In addition to these formal reviewers, a number of readers wrote in with comments and suggestions, all of which made the book better. These include Craig Upright, L Tonkovich, and Leah Washburn-Moses. Beyond the important formal and informal feedback I received. I couldn't have completed this version of the book without the great research assistance and editorial advice ably provided by Princeton University recent sociology alumna Emma Daugherty, who I am happy to report, is now part of the W.W. Norton family, having taken a job as an Editorial Assistant.

As you can see, it took a village to raise this child. But that's not all. At Norton, I need to thank, first and foremost, Michael Moss, the editor into whose lap this project landed (after having passed through the hands of Justin Cahill, Steve Dunn, Melea Seward, and most notably Karl Bakeman, who got promoted onward and upward). Michael deserves great credit for bringing a fresh set of eyes and a powerful brain to help me sociologically question my own assumptions about the book, which, in turn, led to this edition's overhaul. In addition, I am grateful to Michael's editorial assistants Allen Chen and Emma Freund, project editor Rachel Mayer, and production manager Brenda Manzanedo, who handled every stage of the manuscript and managed to keep the innumerable pieces of the book moving through production. Agnieszka Gasparska and her team at Kiss Me I'm Polish are responsible for the terrific book design. I also must thank Norton's sociology marketing director Julia Hall and the social science sales and market development specialists Julie Sindel, Carrie Polvino, and Susan Hood. Much of *You May Ask Yourself*'s success is due to their boundless energy and enthusiasm. Finally, I owe a special thanks to Eileen Connell, Alexandra Park, and Caleb Wertz. They are responsible for putting together all of the video and electronic resources that accompany *You May Ask Yourself*. Those who develop new digital products to help instructors teach in the classroom or teach online are the most creative and resourceful folks working in college publishing today.

CORRELATION WITH PSYCHOLOGICAL, SOCIAL, AND BIOLOGICAL FOUNDATIONS OF BEHAVIOR SECTION OF THE MCAT®

In 2015, the Association of American Medical Colleges revised the Medical College Admissions Test (MCAT) to include fundamental concepts from sociology. To help students prepare for the test, here is a correlation guide for *You May Ask Yourself*, Core Eighth Edition.

FOUNDATIONAL CONCEPT 7

Biological, psychological, and sociocultural factors influence behavior and behavior change.

CHAPTER	HEADING/DESCRIPTION	PAGE
3	Cultural Effects: Give and Take	89
4	Agents of Socialization	133
4	Peers	140
5	Group Conformity	175
6	What Is Social Deviance?	205
6	Social Control	206
6	Functions of Deviance	208
6	A Normative Theory of Suicide	213
6	Symbolic Interactionist Theories	220

FOUNDATIONAL CONCEPT 8

Psychological, sociocultural, and biological factors influence the way we think about ourselves and others as well as how we interact with others.

CHAPTER	HEADING/DESCRIPTION	PAGE
3	Ethnocentrism	85
3	Cultural Relativism	92
4	Me, Myself, and I: Development of the Self and the Other	130
4	Agents of Socialization	133
4	Social Interaction	143
4	Dramaturgical Theory	148
5	Social Groups	167
5	From Groups to Networks	177
5	Network Analysis in Practice	190
5	Organizations	195
6	Stigma	227
9	Prejudice, Discrimination, and the New Racism	358
9	Institutional or Structural Racism	361
9	Inter-Group Relations	365

FOUNDATIONAL CONCEPT 9

Cultural and social differences influence well-being.

FOUNDATIONAL CONCEPT 10

Social stratification and access to resources influence well-being.

PARADOX

1

A SUCCESSFUL SOCIOLOGIST
MAKES THE FAMILIAR STRANGE.

The Sociological Imagination: An Introduction

If you want to understand sociology, why don't we start with you? Why are you taking this class and reading this textbook right now? Self-reflection is as good a place to start as any—after all, sociology is the study of human society, and that society is made up of people just like you. There is the sociology of sports, of religion, of music, of medicine, even the sociology of sociologists. So why not start, by way of example, with the sociology of an introduction to sociology?

So, go ahead and reflect. Why are you bent over this page? Take a moment to write down the reasons. Maybe you have heard of sociology and want to learn more about it. Maybe you are following the suggestion of a parent, a guidance counselor, or an academic adviser. The course syllabus probably indicates that you should read this chapter for the first week of class, so maybe you want to be a good student and follow your professor's instructions. Already, there are a few good reasons for reading this introduction to sociology.

One question always leads to a hundred more: Why are you taking this course? Why are you paying tuition? Why did you decide to go to college? You could just grab one of the course schedules at a local college, decide which courses to take, and show up! Most introductory classes are so large that nobody would notice if an extra student attended. In all my years of

SOCIOLOGY

the study of human society.

teaching, I have never known a faculty member who checks that all class attendees are legitimate students enrolled at the college—we're just happy when students actually do show up to class.

You know the rest of the drill: Complete your course readings (you can usually access the required texts for free at the library), do your homework, and participate in class discussion. The only thing you won't get out of the course is a grade, but you can give yourself one. As a matter of fact, once you have compiled enough free credits and written a senior thesis, award yourself a diploma. Why not? If you are willing and able to stick to this plan, you will probably have received a better education than most students—certainly better than I did in college.

But what does your homemade diploma mean? Even if you know that you're more educated than you were last year, a "real" diploma serves as evidence that others trust and understand. The fact that you're now asking yourself these "why" questions (questions about things you may have previously taken at face value) is the first step in thinking like a sociologist. Thinking like a sociologist means analyzing something you have always done without much conscious thought, like opening this book or enrolling in this class. It requires you to reconsider your assumptions about society and ask questions about ordinary life in order to better understand the world around you. In other words, thinking like a sociologist means *making the familiar strange*.

This chapter introduces you to a sociological approach to the world. Specifically, you will learn about the *sociological imagination*, a term introduced by C. Wright Mills. We'll return to the question "why go to college?" and apply our sociological imaginations to find some answers. You will also learn about social institutions and the sociology of sociology—that is, the history of sociology itself and where the discipline fits within the social sciences.

By the end of this chapter you'll be able to:

- Identify elements of everyday life that seem natural at first but might seem strange from an outside perspective.
- Understand how social narratives shape and reinforce social identities of individuals, groups, and organizations.
- Recognize influential, foundational scholars in the field of sociology and their social theories.
- Define sociology in contrast to history, anthropology, the psychological and biological sciences, economics, and political science.
- Describe the major differences between macro and micro approaches to sociological research.

The Sociological Imagination

I Identify elements of everyday life that seem natural at first but might seem strange from an outside perspective.

More than 50 years ago, sociologist C. Wright Mills argued that thinking critically about the social world around us required a sociological imagination, the ability to see the connections between our personal experiences and larger historical forces. When we question this textbook, this course, and college in general, we are starting to use our sociological imaginations. In *The Sociological Imagination* (1959), Mills describes the concept this way: "The first fruit of this imagination—and the first lesson of the social science that embodies it—is the idea that the individual can understand his own experience and gauge his own fate only by locating himself within his period, that he can know his own chances in life only by becoming aware of those of all individuals in his circumstances. In many ways it is a terrible lesson; in many ways a magnificent one." The terrible part of the lesson is to make our own lives ordinary—that is, to see our intensely personal, private life experiences as typical of the period and place in which we live. This realization can also serve as a source of comfort, though, by helping us understand we are not alone in our struggles. Mills writes that this mental framework also "enables [us] to take into account how individuals, in the welter of their daily experience, often become falsely conscious of their social positions," thus allowing us to see the veneer of social life for what it is and to gain perspective on rapid historical change as social foundations may shift right beneath our feet. As Mills wrote after World War II, a time of enormous political, social, and technological evolution, "The sociological imagination enables us to grasp history and biography and the relations between the two within society. That is its task and its promise. To recognize this task and this promise is the mark of the classic social analyst."

In the mid-nineteenth century, Mills presented his readers with a way to stop and take stock of their lives in light of all that had happened in the previous decade. Of course, we too feel that the world is constantly changing and continually getting ahead of us.

Sociologist C. Wright Mills smoking his pipe in his office at Columbia University. How does Mills's concept of the sociological imagination help us make the familiar strange?

HOW TO BE A SOCIOLOGIST ACCORDING TO QUENTIN TARANTINO: A SCENE FROM *PULP FICTION*

Have you ever felt like a fish out of water? Traveling to a foreign country or attending the worship service of a different denomination—or a different religion altogether—can reveal certain aspects of our own social environment that we view as "normal." If you have experienced that fish-out-of-water feeling, then you have, however briefly, engaged your sociological imagination. By shifting your social environment enough to consciously recognize your position or status, you are forced to notice the parts of your daily life that you normally accept as given. You may, for instance, wonder why there are bidets in most European bathrooms and not in American ones, why people waiting in lines in the Middle East typically stand closer to each other than they do in Europe or America, or why, in some rural Chinese communities, many generations of a single family sleep in the same bed. An essential sociological understanding emerges here: Other people's lifestyles are no more or less sensible than your own, and some aspects of your own life can seem abnormal to others.

In the following excerpt of dialogue from Quentin Tarantino's 1994 film *Pulp Fiction*, the character Vincent tells Jules about the "little differences" between life in the United States and life in Europe.

VINCENT: It's the little differences. A lotta the same s—t we got here, they got there, but there they're a little different.

JULES: Example?

VINCENT: Well, in Amsterdam, you can buy beer in a movie theater. And I don't mean in a paper cup either. They give you a glass of beer, like in a bar. In Paris, you can buy beer at McDonald's. Also, you know what they call a Quarter Pounder with Cheese in Paris?

JULES: They don't call it a Quarter Pounder with Cheese?

Vincent Vega (John Travolta) describes his visit to a McDonald's in Amsterdam to Jules Winnfield (Samuel L. Jackson).

VINCENT: No, they got the metric system there, they wouldn't know what the f—k a Quarter Pounder is.

JULES: What'd they call it?

VINCENT: Royale with Cheese.

VINCENT: [Y]ou know what they put on french fries in Holland instead of ketchup?

JULES: What?

VINCENT: Mayonnaise. [. . .] And I don't mean a little bit on the side of the plate, they f—in' drown 'em in it.

JULES: Uuccch!

Your job as a sociologist is to recognize that mayonnaise on french fries, though it might seem disgusting at first, is not strange after all. Mayonnaise is certainly no stranger than ketchup.

Let's return to our first question: "Why go to college?" Sociologists and economists have found that the financial benefits of education—particularly higher education—appear to be increasing with time. They refer to this as the "returns to schooling." In today's economy, 4 out of every 10 adults with a bachelor's degree fall in the highest income tier, as contrasted with about 1.5 out of every 10 adults without a bachelor's degree (Pew Research Center, 2022b). Four out of every 10 adults with only a high-school diploma fall in the lowest income tier (Pew Research Center, 2022b). If a college degree can launch you into a higher income bracket, does that make paying high tuition rates worth it in the long run? Let's shift gears and do a little math.

WHAT ARE THE TRUE COSTS AND RETURNS OF COLLEGE?

Now that you are starting to think like a sociologist, let's compare the cost of going to college for about four years to calling the whole thing off and taking a full-time job immediately after high school. In terms of price, we obviously need to consider tuition. Four years at a public state college (private universities are a completely different ball game) would cost you $38,000 (National Center for Education Statistics, 2021a). But these aren't your only costs. There are also what economists call "opportunity costs." Opportunity costs represent the amount of time you devote to school when you could have been doing other things like earning money. For the sake of simplicity, let's say you cannot work at all while going to school full-time (obviously not true for many who hold down a job while going to school, but there surely is some cost to the time you devote to school). Taking into account the typical wage for a high-school graduate, we can calculate that if you worked full-time instead of going to college, you would make about $42,000 per year (Bureau of Labor Statistics, 2021c). If you are out of the labor market for four years, that's $168,000 of forgone wages. Add these opportunity costs to the direct costs of tuition, and we get $206,000 of total costs to attend college full-time for four years.

Next, we need to calculate the "returns to schooling." Those who start working right out of high school begin earning income about four years earlier than those who spend that time in college (the average time to complete a bachelor's degree at a public university is actually 5.2 years [Shapiro et al., 2016], but we will stick to four). Assuming you retire at age 65, you will have worked 43 years, while high-school grads will have been in the workforce for 47 years because of that four-year head start. However, given your higher average earnings per year of work, when we compare your lifetime earnings to the lifetime earnings of someone who has only a high-school education, we find that with a college degree you will make about $2,900,000 (Bureau of Labor Statistics, 2021c) more than someone who went straight to work after high school (Figure 1.1). On top of this substantial financial return

FIGURE 1.1 Returns to Schooling

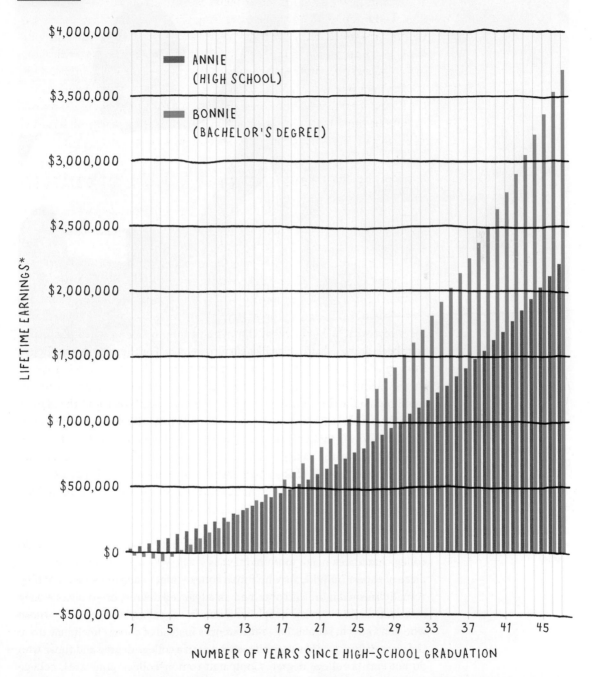

ANNIE
(HIGH SCHOOL)

BONNIE
(BACHELOR'S DEGREE)

LIFETIME EARNINGS*

NUMBER OF YEARS SINCE HIGH-SCHOOL GRADUATION

*This set of hypothetical women—Annie and Bonnie—live in a world that is not quite like reality. We did not flatten Annie's trajectory to account for the fact that high-school diploma holders are more likely to experience periods of forced part-time work and/or unemployment. We also assumed the same rate of income increase over time (i.e., raises) for these two, although high-school graduates are more likely to experience wage stagnation than college diploma holders.

SOURCE: Carnevale et al., 2014.

Two famous college dropouts. Facebook CEO Mark Zuckerberg (left) attended Harvard University but dropped out before graduating. Oprah Winfrey (right) left Tennessee State University as a sophomore to pursue a career in media.

to schooling, research also shows that people with college degrees tend to be healthier and less likely to engage in unhealthy behaviors like smoking, even after accounting for other indirect factors like the income boost (Heckman et al., 2016). For the sake of simplicity, these calculations do not take into consideration the fact that money now is worth more than money later, the changing economic returns to schooling, or many other complicating factors, but the bottom line is that, putting the fun of college aside, it seems like a "good deal" economically.

However, we've come to another important "why" question: Why do college graduates make more money? Is it the education itself, or is it the piece of paper? Individuals who finish college might earn more because they actually learned more and obtained an advanced degree, or—a *big* or—they might earn more because people who stay in school are different than those who don't stay in school. These differences instead of college itself may drive the wage differences between those who earn a college degree and those who do not earn a college degree. Compared to non-college graduates, college graduates may (1) be innately smarter, (2) know how to work the system, (3) come from wealthier families, (4) be able to delay gratification, (5) manage their time more efficiently, or (6) all of the above.

GETTING THAT "PIECE OF PAPER"

Even if college does affect outcomes rather than merely reflect the underlying differences between those who attend and those who do not, does higher education matter because of the actual learning that takes place there or because of the credentialist society that the degree aids and abets? The answer to this question has enormous implications for the role and meaning of education in our society. Imagine, for example, a society in which the route to becoming a doctor (instead of doing well in high school, going to college, taking premed courses, acing the MCATs, and then spending more time in the classroom) starts with emptying bedpans as a nurse's aide and working your way up through the ranks of registered nurse, apprentice physician, and so forth. Randall Collins has proposed this exact medical education system in his controversial book, *The Credential Society: A Historical Sociology of Education and Stratification* (1979), which argues that the expansion of higher education has merely resulted in a amplification of credentialism and expenditures on formal education rather than reflecting any practical need for more formal education or actually opening up opportunities to more people.

College bulletin boards are covered with advertisements like this one promoting websites that generate diplomas. Are these fake diplomas worth it?

If credentials matter most, as Collins proposes, then should there be a cheaper, faster way to get them? Newsflash: there is! In fact, all you need are $29.95 and some guts, and you can receive a diploma from one of the many websites that promise either actual degrees from nonaccredited colleges or a faux college diploma from any school of your choosing. If the piece of paper itself is your ticket to success, why not save four years and lots of money by obtaining your credentials immediately?

Obviously, universities have incentives to prevent such websites from undermining their exclusive authority over bestowing degrees. Despite universities' interests in protecting their reputations, I never had a university employer verify my education claims until I applied to teach at Princeton in 2015. Every other employer, including New York University (NYU), accepted my résumé without calling my graduate or undergraduate universities (although to its credit, NYU does check to make sure student applicants have completed high school). Are universities too lazy to care? Probably not.

Strong informal mechanisms protect universities' status. They rely on a wide range of social institutions, including but not limited to alumni networks, copyright laws, and magazines that publish national rankings. A university's alumni network functions as a sort of verification of your affiliation. Potential employers rarely call a university's registrar to make sure you graduated, but they may expect you to talk a bit about your college experience. If your interviewer is an alumnus/alumna or otherwise familiar with the institution, you might also be expected to talk about what dorm you lived in, to reminisce about a particularly dramatic homecoming game, or to gripe about an especially unreasonable professor. If you slip up on these details, suspicions will grow, and then people might call to check on your graduation status. These informal social checks serve as a first line of defense before the formal verifications take place. Perhaps there are a few good reasons not to opt for that immediate $29.95 degree after all (see Table 1.1).

On a more serious note, the powerful role of credentials in our society means that getting into college, especially into a wealthy school with plenty of need-based aid available, can make a huge difference for lower-income

TABLE 1.1 Over-credentialed? Workers with Bachelor's Degrees in 1970 and 2019

JOB TITLE	WORKERS AGES 25–64 IN 1970 WITH BACHELOR'S DEGREE (%)	WORKERS AGES 25 AND OLDER IN 2019 WITH BACHELOR'S DEGREE (%)	% CHANGE
Bartenders	3%	22%	633%
Photographers	10%	53%	430%
Electricians	2%	8%	300%
Accountants and auditors	42%	83%	98%
Writers and authors	47%	84%	6,796%
Dental hygienists	29%	38%	31%
Primary-school teachers	84%	95%	13%
Preschool teachers	53%	52%	−2%

A recent article in *The Economist* found that since the 1970s, more American workers in most professions have earned a bachelor's degree. In half of these professions, though, the authors found that wages have actually fallen. Do these examples support Collins's argument about over-credentialism? Have these jobs become more demanding or technologically complex over time, or are the people doing them simply more likely to have a diploma?

SOURCES: University of Minnesota IPUMS; *The Economist* (2018); Bureau of Labor Statistics (2021a).

students. I sat down with Asha Rangappa, the dean of admissions at Yale Law School (and a former FBI agent), who explained that by the time students are applying to law school, middle-class and upper-class students have already been granted all sorts of opportunities that bolster their applications, making them appear to be stronger candidates even if they do not have stronger aptitudes for law than less affluent applicants:

DIGITAL.WWNORTON.COM/YOUMAYASK8

To see my interview with Asha Rangappa, go to digital.wwnorton.com/youmayask8

> I read anywhere from three thousand, four thousand applications a year, and I do a kind of character and personality assessment. I decide who gets in. . . . I think that there's a meritocracy at the point where I'm doing it, but I think accessing the good opportunities that allow you to take advantage of the meritocracy is limited. I think that's the problem. When twenty-two to twenty-five years of someone's life are behind them, it is too late to correct the disparity in access that really needed to have been corrected from like zero to five years, zero to ten years. (Conley, 2015a)

Furthermore, average LSAT scores of incoming classes impact law schools' rankings in magazines like *U.S. News & World Report*. Rangappa's school, Yale, has such a long history of elite status that its high rankings are not affected by a slight dip in LSAT scores; however, for other programs, a drop in LSAT scores leads to a drop in rankings—and then a decline in high-quality applicants and a more drastic drop in rankings. From Rangappa's perspective:

> To me, the LSAT is one number, and I can look at the rest of the file. There may very well be somebody who has a crappy LSAT score, but . . . I can tell in the totality of the application that the applicant is going to be a better person at the school. I have the luxury of taking that person because it's Yale Law School and the way the *U.S. News* formula is created, we're not going to suffer a consequence if our median LSAT drops one point.

Rangappa's account reveals the balancing act performed by elite educational institutions, whereby they seek to broaden the population benefitting from their status and opportunities while at the same time maintaining their own rank in the hierarchy of similar institutions. That is, even when such organizations want to level the playing field, they themselves remain trapped in a highly competitive environment, perpetuating a vicious cycle that does not allow them to counteract preexisting inequalities without facing their own limitations. Social institutions thus have a tendency to reinforce existing social structures and the inequalities therein. College is no exception.

This cynical analysis is not to say that higher education does not provide important knowledge and skills to its students that might be difficult to impart through other means. Or that college is not a really important vehicle for upward mobility for students from disadvantaged backgrounds. It is all these things and more. If a sociologist knows one thing, it's that social institutions are complex. Moreover, institutions can try to change. A few years after I spoke with Rangappa, Yale Law School took the bold move of removing itself from the *U.S. News & World Report* rankings. Given Yale Law's top-dog status, several other elite schools immediately followed. Some schools are thinking of pulling out of the undergraduate rankings as well. Whether any of this makes a difference to the role of elite schools in our society remains to be seen, however.

What Is a Social Institution?

Understand how social narratives shape and reinforce social identities of individuals, groups, and organizations.

The university, then, is much more than a printing press churning out diplomas. For that matter, it also does more than impart formal knowledge to its students before sending them on their way. It fulfills a variety of roles and provides links to many other societal institutions. For example, a college acts as a gatekeeper to "legitimate" forms of educational advantage by certifying certain types of knowledge as "legitimate." It segregates great swaths of the population by age. (You won't find a more age-segregated environment than a four-year college; it even beats a retirement home in having the smallest amount of age variation in its client population.) A college name is a proprietary brand marketed through sweatshirts and mugs and televised sporting events. The college's reputation also exists as an informal set of stories shared within social networks of students, faculty, administrators, alumni, and other members of the community.

You've read the word "institution" quite a few times now, so you've probably gotten a sense of what it means. This last part of the definition is key to understanding the social institution, one of sociology's most important concepts. A social institution is a complex group of interdependent positions that, together, perform a social role and reproduce themselves over time. One way to think of these social positions is as a set of stories we tell ourselves: Social relations are a network of ties, and the social role is a grand narrative that unifies these stories within the network. In order to think sociologically about social institutions, you need to think of them not as uniform, stable entities—things that "just are"—but as dynamic systems embedded in dense networks of other social organizations and meanings. Sound confusing? Bear with me as I provide an example: I teach at Princeton University. What exactly is the social institution known as Princeton? It is not the collection of buildings I frequent, because we could move campuses and we'd still be Princeton. And it certainly cannot be the people who work there or even the students because those individuals change over time, shifting in and out through recruitment and retirement, admission and graduation. We might thus conclude that a social institution is just the name "Princeton" itself. However, an institution can change its name and still retain its social identity. Duke University was once called Normal College and then Trinity College, yet it remains the same institution. How?

Of course, all such transitions involving a change of name, location, mission, and so on require a great deal of effort and agreement among involved parties. In some cases, changes in personnel, function, or location may be too much for a social institution to sustain, resulting in its diminishment and replacement with a new resource. Sometimes institutions even try to intentionally rupture a compromised identity. Tobacco company Philip Morris received such bad press as a cigarette manufacturer for so long that it changed its name to Altria, hoping to start fresh and shake the negative connotations of its previous embodiment. For that effort to succeed, the

Tobacco company Philip Morris changed its name to Altria at a stockholders' meeting in January 2003.

narrative of Philip Morris circulating in social networks had to die out without being connected to Altria.

The sum of individual stories told between pairs of individuals constitutes the grand narrative of social identity. Think about your relationship with your parents. You may have a particular story that you tell if asked to describe your relationship with your mother. She also has a story about you. Your story may change slightly depending on who you are talking to; you may add some details or leave out others. Your other relatives have stories about your mother and her relationship to you too. So do her friends and yours. Anyone who knows your mother contributes to her social identity. The sum total of stories about your mom is the grand narrative of who she is.

All of this may seem like a fairly flimsy notion of how the social world operates. Although any social identity boils down to, on the simplest level, a set of stories shared within a social network, that narrative is still complex, hearty, and robust. Imagine the effort and energy required to change an identity. Let's say your mom is 50 years old, and you want to make her 40 instead. You would not only have to convince her to refer to herself as 10 years younger but also convince other relatives and friends to abide by this change. And it wouldn't stop there. You'd have to change official documents, such as her driver's license, passport, and so on. Even though your mother's identity (in this case, her age, but the same logic applies to her name, ethnicity, and other aspects of her identity) is essentially a local-scale understanding involving everyone who knows her and the formal authorities as well as herself, the matter is a complicated one. Now think about trying to change the identity of a major institution such as your university. The scale of the social network grows significantly. You'd have to convince the board of directors, alumni, faculty, students, and everyone else who has a relationship to the school of the need for a change. Altering an identity is difficult, even if it is ultimately nothing more than a collective idea understood by a group of people.

I mentioned that if you wanted to change your mother's age, name, or race, you'd have to convince not only her friends but also the formal authorities, which are social institutions with their own logics and inertias. Let's take the example of college once again. Colleges themselves are comprised of series of stories within social networks, but other than the stories and informal ties of people with relationships to the grand narrative of a particular college, a number of social structures make the existence of colleges possible:

1. The *legal system* enforces copyright law, making fake diplomas illegitimate.

2. The *primary and secondary educational system* (i.e., K–12 schooling) prepares students both academically and culturally for college, as

well as acting as an extended screening and sorting mechanism to help determine who goes to college and to which one.

3. The *Educational Testing Service* and *ACT* are private companies that have a duopoly on the standardized tests that screen for college admission.

4. The *wage labor market* encompasses the entire economy that allows your teachers to be paid, as well as the administrators, staff, and other outside contractors who maintain the intellectual, fiscal, and physical infrastructure of the school you attend.

5. *English*, although not the official language of the United States (there isn't one!), is the language in which instruction takes place at the majority of U.S. colleges. Language itself is a social phenomenon, and some would argue that it is the basis for all of social life. But a given language is a particular outcome of political boundaries and historical struggles among various populations in the world. It is often said that the only difference between a language and a dialect is that a language has an army to back it up; in other words, deciding whether a spoken tongue is a language or merely a dialect is fundamentally a question of power and legitimacy.

Trying to understand social institutions such as the education system, the legal system, the labor market, or language itself lies at the heart of sociological inquiry. Although social institutions shape every aspect of our behavior, they are not monolithic, and they are not static. In fact, every day we construct and change social institutions through ordinary interactions and the meanings we ascribe to them. By becoming aware of the intersections between social institutions and your life, you are already thinking like a sociologist.

The Sociology of Sociology

Recognize influential, foundational scholars in the field of sociology and their social theories.

Now that we have an idea of how sociologists approach their analyses of the world, let's turn that lens, the sociological imagination, to sociology itself. What social conditions gave rise to the field? Who is celebrated as its founders, and who tends to be excluded? Sociology is a relatively young

POSITIVISM

the approach to sociology that emphasizes the scientific method as an approach to studying the objectively observable behavior of individuals irrespective of the meanings those actions have for the subjects themselves.

discipline. A wide range of fields of inquiry exists, from molecular genetics to radio astronomy to computer science, that could not have emerged until a certain technology had been invented, and the specific "technology" we rely on to study society is the lens of the sociological imagination. The sociological imagination is a frame of reference that could have developed only in a certain historical context. That time was, arguably, the nineteenth century, when French scholar Auguste Comte (1798–1857) invented "social physics" or positivism.

AUGUSTE COMTE AND THE CREATION OF SOCIOLOGY

According to Comte, positivism arose from a need to develop a secular basis for morality and social order in a time of declining religious authority. Comte argued that human society had gone through three historical stages with

TWO CENTURIES OF SOCIOLOGY

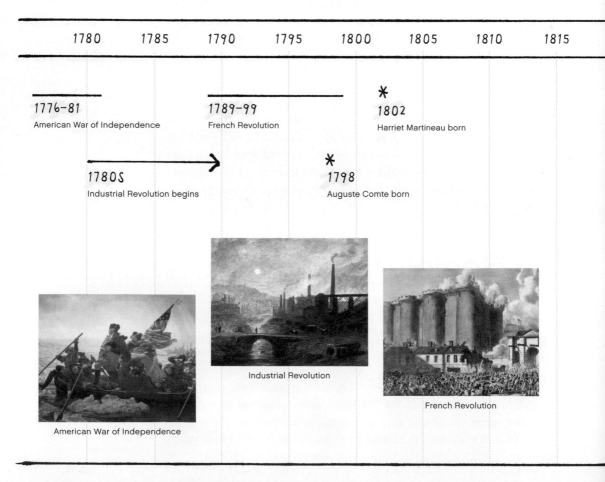

| 1780 | 1785 | 1790 | 1795 | 1800 | 1805 | 1810 | 1815 |

1776–81
American War of Independence

1789–99
French Revolution

1802
Harriet Martineau born

1780S
Industrial Revolution begins

1798
Auguste Comte born

Industrial Revolution

French Revolution

American War of Independence

respect to our understanding of morality. In the first, which he referred to as the theological stage, societal structures existed as a result of divine will. If you wanted to understand why kings ruled, why Europe used a feudal and guild system of labor, or why colonialism took root, the answer was that these processes were part of God's plan. To better understand God's plan and thus comprehend the logic of social life, scholars in the theological stage might have consulted the Bible or other ecclesiastical texts. During the second stage, which Comte called the metaphysical stage, Enlightenment thinkers such as Jean-Jacques Rousseau, John Stuart Mill, and Thomas Hobbes saw human behavior as governed by natural, biological instincts. To understand the nature of society—why things were the way they were—we needed to strip away the influences of society to better analyze how our basic drives and natural instincts established the foundation for and governed the social world. Comte deemed the third and final stage of historical

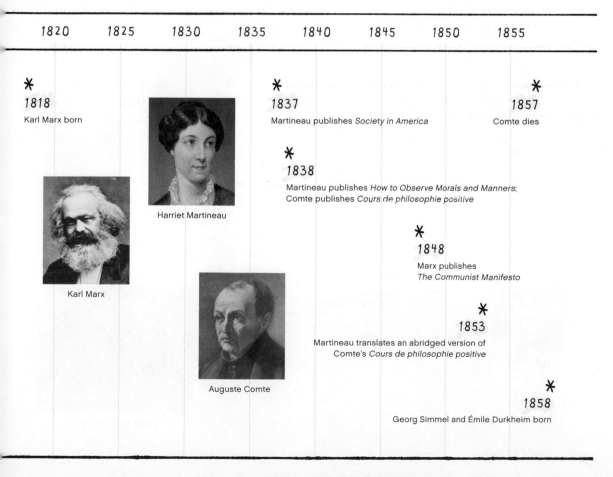

1820   1825   1830   1835   1840   1845   1850   1855

✳
1818
Karl Marx born

✳
1837
Martineau publishes *Society in America*

✳
1857
Comte dies

Harriet Martineau

✳
1838
Martineau publishes *How to Observe Morals and Manners*; Comte publishes *Cours de philosophie positive*

Karl Marx

✳
1848
Marx publishes
The Communist Manifesto

✳
1853
Martineau translates an abridged version of
Comte's *Cours de philosophie positive*

Auguste Comte

✳
1858
Georg Simmel and Émile Durkheim born

development the scientific stage. In this era, he predicted, we would develop a sort of social physics to identify a set of scientific laws that determine human behavior. The analogy here is not theology or biology but rather physics. Comte believed we could understand how social institutions worked (and didn't work), how we relate to one another (whether on an individual or group level), and the overall structure of societies if we merely ascertained their "equations" or underlying logic. These concepts of society as systemic and scientifically based laid the foundations for sociological study today.

Harriet Martineau Harriet Martineau (1802–1876), an English social theorist, wrote important works like *Society in America* (1837) that describe society's physical and social aspects. She addressed topics ranging from the way we educate children (which, she attests, affords parents too much control and fails to ensure quality) to the relationship between the federal

TWO CENTURIES OF SOCIOLOGY

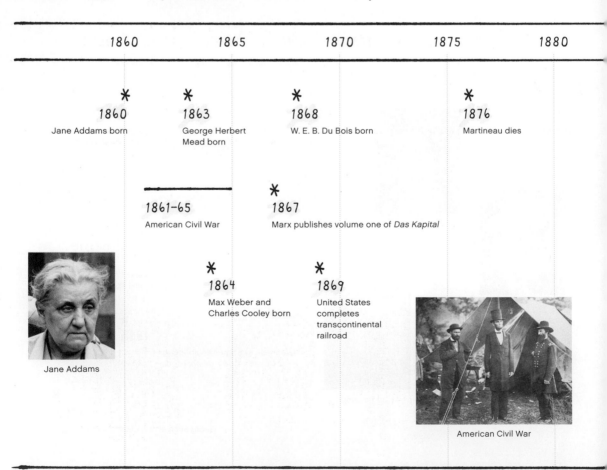

| 1860 | 1865 | 1870 | 1875 | 1880 |

1860
Jane Addams born

1863
George Herbert Mead born

1868
W. E. B. Du Bois born

1876
Martineau dies

1861–65
American Civil War

1867
Marx publishes volume one of *Das Kapital*

1864
Max Weber and Charles Cooley born

1869
United States completes transcontinental railroad

Jane Addams

American Civil War

and state governments. She also authored the first methods book in what would become sociology, *How to Observe Morals and Manners* (1838), which analyzed the institution of marriage, claiming that the practice relied on an assumption of women as inferior. This critique, among other writings, positioned Martineau as one of the earliest feminist social scientists writing in the English language. She also translated Comte into English. In fact, Comte assigned his students to read her translations, claiming that they were better than the original.

CLASSICAL SOCIOLOGICAL THEORY

Although Comte and Martineau laid the initial groundwork for sociology as a field, Karl Marx, Max Weber, and Émile Durkheim typically receive credit as the founding fathers of the sociological discipline. Some add a

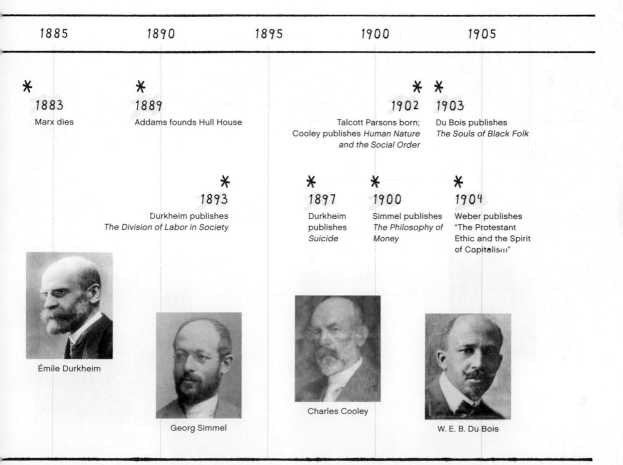

| 1885 | 1890 | 1895 | 1900 | 1905 |

* 1883
Marx dies

* 1889
Addams founds Hull House

* 1902
Talcott Parsons born; Cooley publishes *Human Nature and the Social Order*

* 1903
Du Bois publishes *The Souls of Black Folk*

* 1893
Durkheim publishes *The Division of Labor in Society*

* 1897
Durkheim publishes *Suicide*

* 1900
Simmel publishes *The Philosophy of Money*

* 1904
Weber publishes "The Protestant Ethic and the Spirit of Capitalism"

Émile Durkheim

Georg Simmel

Charles Cooley

W. E. B. Du Bois

fourth classical sociological theorist, Georg Simmel, to the triumvirate. A brief overview of each of their paradigms follows. We will return to the paramount work of these pivotal thinkers throughout the book.

Karl Marx Karl Marx (1818–1883) is probably the most famous of the three early sociologists; the term *Marxism* (an ideological alternative to capitalism) derives from his surname, and his writings provided the theoretical basis for Communism. As a young man, Marx edited a newspaper suppressed by the Prussian government for its radicalism. Forced into exile, Marx settled in London, where he wrote his most important works. Marx was essentially a historian, and he elaborated a theory of the factors that drive history, now coined historical materialism. Marx saw history as an account of man's struggle to gain control of and later dominate his natural

TWO CENTURIES OF SOCIOLOGY

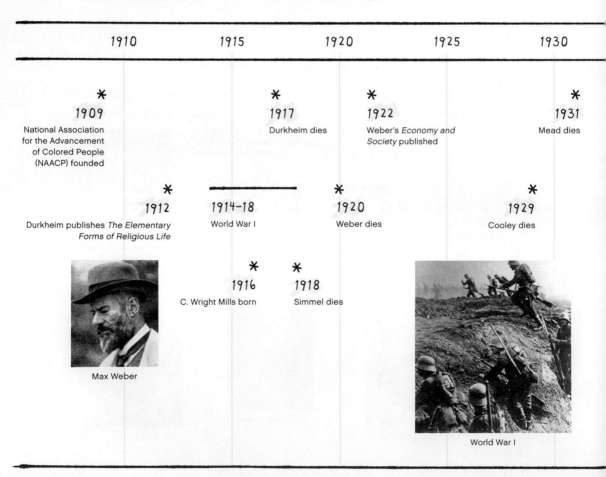

| 1910 | 1915 | 1920 | 1925 | 1930 |

✳
1909
National Association for the Advancement of Colored People (NAACP) founded

✳
1917
Durkheim dies

✳
1922
Weber's *Economy and Society* published

✳
1931
Mead dies

✳
1912
Durkheim publishes *The Elementary Forms of Religious Life*

1914–18
World War I

✳
1920
Weber dies

✳
1929
Cooley dies

✳
1916
C. Wright Mills born

✳
1918
Simmel dies

Max Weber

World War I

environment, attributing historical and social change to conflict between economic classes. However, at a certain point with the Industrial Revolution and the emergence of modern capitalism, the very tools and processes that humans embraced to survive and to manage their surroundings came to dominate humankind. Instead of using technology to master the natural world, people became slaves to industrial technology in order to make a living. In Marx's version of history, each economic system, whether small-scale farming or large-scale factory capitalism, had its own fault lines of conflict; in the current epoch, that fault line divided society into a small number of owners (the capitalists) and a large number of workers (the proletariat) whose interests were opposed. The political struggle, along with escalating crises within the economic system itself, would eventually produce social change through a Communist revolution. The ensuing Communist society would

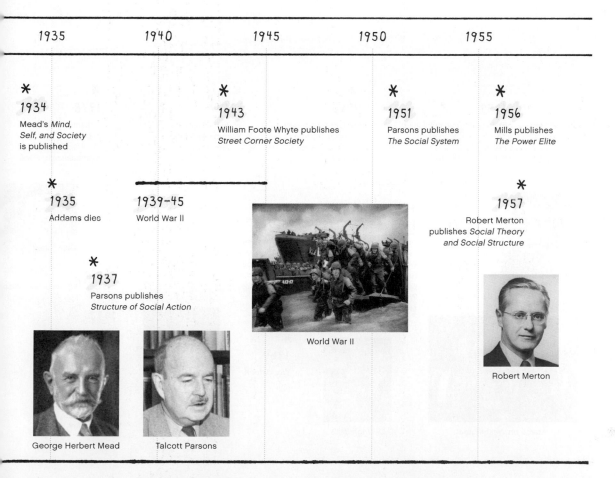

1935   1940   1945   1950   1955

* 1934
Mead's *Mind, Self, and Society* is published

* 1943
William Foote Whyte publishes *Street Corner Society*

* 1951
Parsons publishes *The Social System*

* 1956
Mills publishes *The Power Elite*

* 1935
Addams dies

1939–45
World War II

* 1957
Robert Merton publishes *Social Theory and Social Structure*

* 1937
Parsons publishes *Structure of Social Action*

World War II

Robert Merton

George Herbert Mead   Talcott Parsons

abolish private property and accept a new economy structured around an ideology of "from each according to his abilities, to each according to his needs" (Marx & Engels, 1848/1998). We will explore Marx's theories on social stratification in depth in Chapter 7.

Max Weber Writing shortly after Marx, Max Weber (1864–1920) believed Marx went too far in seeing culture, ideas, religion, and the like as merely an effect of economic relations and not a cause of how societies evolve. Ideas also drove history and shaped the essence of societies, according to Weber. Specifically, Weber criticized Marx for his exclusive focus on the economy and social class, advocating sociological analysis to accommodate the multiple influences of culture, economics, and politics. Weber is most famous for his two-volume work *Economy and Society* (published posthumously in 1922),

TWO CENTURIES OF SOCIOLOGY

1960	1965	1970	1975	1980

* 1959
Erving Goffman publishes *The Presentation of Self in Everyday Life*; Mills publishes *The Sociological Imagination*

* 1966
Equality of Educational Opportunity (the Coleman Report) published

* 1972
Ann Oakley publishes *Sex, Gender, and Society*

* 1978
William Julius Wilson publishes *The Declining Significance of Race*

* 1962
Mills dies

* 1963
Du Bois dies; the March on Washington; Betty Friedan publishes *The Feminine Mystique*

* 1967
Elliot Liebow publishes *Tally's Corner*; Peter M. Blau and Otis Dudley Duncan publish *The American Occupational Structure*

* 1973
Daniel Bell publishes *The Coming of the Post-Industrial Society*

Erving Goffman

William Julius Wilso

* 1977
Paul Willis publishes *Learning to Labor*

* 1969
Woodstock

Ann Oakley

* 1979
Parsons dies

March on Washington

C. Wright Mills

as well as for a lengthy essay titled "The Protestant Ethic and the Spirit of Capitalism" (1904/2003). In the latter, he argued that the religious transformation that occurred during the Protestant Reformation in the sixteenth and early seventeenth centuries laid the groundwork for modern capitalism by upending the medieval ethic of virtuous poverty and replacing it with an ideology that saw riches as a sign of divine providence. *Economy and Society* also provided the theories of authority, rationality, the state (i.e., government), and status, and a host of other concepts that sociologists still cite today.

One of Weber's most important contributions was the concept of *Verstehen* ("understanding" in German). By emphasizing *Verstehen*, Weber suggested that sociologists should approach social behavior from the perspective of those engaging in that behavior. In other words, to truly understand why people act in the ways they do, a sociologist must understand the

VERSTEHEN

German for "understanding." The concept of *Verstehen* comes from Max Weber and is the basis of interpretive sociology.

| 1985 | 1990 | 1995 | 2000 | 2005 | 2010 | 2015 | 2020 |

1984
Pierre Bourdieu publishes *Distinction*; Anthony Giddens publishes *The Constitution of Society*

Anthony Giddens

1989
Arlie Hochschild publishes *The Second Shift: Working Parents and the Revolution at Home*

1991
James Coleman publishes *Foundations of Social Theory*

1993
Douglas S. Massey and Nancy A. Denton publish *American Apartheid*

Arlie Hochschild

James Coleman

1999
Duncan Watts publishes *Small Worlds*; Mary Pattillo publishes *Black Picket Fences*

Duncan Watts

Mary Pattillo

2016
Matthew Desmond publishes *Evicted: Poverty and Profit in the American City*

Matthew Desmond

2022
Alondra Nelson appointed director of the White House Office of Science and Technology Policy

Alondra Nelson

**INTERPRETIVE
SOCIOLOGY**

a type of scholarship
in which researchers
imagine themselves
experiencing the life
positions of the people
they want to understand
rather than treating
them as objects to be
examined.

ANOMIE

a sense of aimlessness
or despair that arises
when we can no longer
reasonably expect life
to be predictable; too
little social regulation;
normlessness.

**POSITIVIST
SOCIOLOGY**

the approach to sociology
that emphasizes the
scientific method
as an approach to
studying the objectively
observable behavior of
individuals irrespective
of the meanings of those
actions for the subjects
themselves.

meanings people attach to their actions. Weber's emphasis on subjectivity is the foundation of interpretive sociology, the study of social meaning.

Émile Durkheim Across the Rhine in France, the work of Émile Durkheim (1858–1917) focused on themes similar to those studied by German colleagues like Weber. He wished to understand how society holds itself together, along with how modern capitalism and industrialization have transformed the ways people relate to one another. Durkheim's sociological writing began with *The Division of Labor in Society* (1893/1997). The division of labor refers to the degree to which jobs are specialized in any particular society. A community of hunter-gatherers or small-scale farmers has a low division of labor (each household essentially carries out the same set of tasks to survive); today, the United States has a high degree of division of labor with many extremely specialized occupations. What made Durkheim's analysis of work sociological was that he claimed the division of labor affected not only economic productivity but also the social and moral character of a society. Specifically, the division of labor in any given society determines its form of social solidarity—that is, the way social cohesion is maintained among individuals. Durkheim followed this work with *Suicide* (1897/1951), in which he showed how the seemingly individual act of taking one's own life is, in reality, conditioned by social forces like the degree to which someone is integrated into group life (or not) and the degree to which individual lives follow routines. Durkheim argued that a sense of normlessness resulting from drastic changes in living conditions or arrangements, which he called anomie, often leads to suicidal thoughts. He also wrote about the methods of social science as well as religion in *The Elementary Forms of Religious Life* (1917/1995). Although the concept originated with Comte, Durkheim is often considered the founding practitioner of positivist sociology, a strain within sociology that proposes the social world can be described and predicted by certain observable relationships.

Georg Simmel Until recently, Georg Simmel (1858–1918) received less credit as one of the founders of sociology. However, in a series of important lectures and essays Simmel established what we today refer to as formal sociology—that is, the sociology of pure numbers. (Formal sociology is an antecedent of network theory, which emerged in the latter half of the twentieth century, which we will discuss in Chapter 5.) Among the many issues he addressed were the fundamental differences between a group of two and a group of three or more—irrespective of who made up the group. His work significantly influenced the development of urban sociology and cultural sociology, and his theories of small-group interactions served as the intellectual foundation for later sociologists to study microinteractions.

He provided working definitions for small and large groups, such as a party, a stranger, and the poor, many of which are still used today.

AMERICAN SOCIOLOGY

In the short history of sociology, the pendulum has swung back and forth between large-scale, sweeping theories of society and more narrow, specific types of empirical research on particular social phenomena. Early American sociology emerged from the latter focus: an applied perspective best embodied by the Chicago School, named for many of its proponents' affiliation with the University of Chicago. If the Chicago School had a shared, basic premise, it was that social and physical environments shape humans' behaviors and personalities, a concept known as social ecology.

Chicago, which had grown from a midsize city in 1860 to a major metropolis by the time these scholars were writing at the beginning of the twentieth century, served as the main laboratory for the Chicago School's studies. The city functioned as fertile ground for studying urbanism and its many discontents. Immigration, race and ethnicity, politics, and family life became popular topics of study, primarily through a community-based approach (i.e., interviewing people and spending time with them). Robert Park (1864–1944), for example, exhorted scholars to "go and get the seat of [their] pants dirty in real research" (Duneier et al., 2014).

Thanks to a high rate of foreign immigration and the Great Migration of African Americans away from the rural South, the North experienced rapid growth and urbanization in the early twentieth century. The researchers of the Chicago School analyzed the evolving racial and ethnic divisions in the city, asking themselves how Polish peasants and African American share-croppers adapted to life in a new industrialized world. They also wondered how and why the anonymity of the city itself contributed to creativity and freedom on the one hand, while also leading to the breakdown of traditional communities and higher rates of social conflict on the other. For example, in the classic Chicago School essay "Urbanism as a Way of Life" (1938), Louis Wirth, who was himself an immigrant from a small village in Germany, described how the city broke down typical forms of social solidarity while promoting tolerance, rationality (which led to scientific advances), and individual freedom. Much of their work fell into the category of cultural sociology by today's terminology. For example, in their studies of ethnicity, Park and others challenged the notion inherited from Europe that ethnicity relied on bloodlines, instead showing ethnicity "in practice" to relate more to the maintenance of cultural traditions passed down through generations. Likewise, stages of immigrant assimilation into American society (contact, then competition, and finally assimilation), today regarded as common knowledge and part of our national ideology, were first identified and described by Park.

If there was a single theoretical paradigm that undergirded much of the research of the Chicago School, it would be the theory of the "social self" that emerged from the work of the social psychologists Charles Horton Cooley (1864–1929) and George Herbert Mead (1863–1931). Cooley and Mead adapted the Chicago School's conception of the relationship between the individual and the social environment to include key pillars of the pragmatist school of philosophy, which argues that inquiry and truth cannot be understood outside their environment (i.e., that environment inherently affects meaning). Cooley, who taught at the University of Michigan, developed the concept of the "looking-glass self." He argued that the self emerges from an interactive social process. We envision how others perceive us, and then we gauge the outside responses to our presentation of self. By refining our vision of how others perceive us, we create a self-concept that constantly interacts with the surrounding social world. Much of Cooley's work described the important role that group dynamics play in this process of defining and redefining. (See Chapter 5 on groups and networks.)

In his book *Mind, Self, and Society* (1934) Mead described how the "self" itself (i.e., the perception of consciousness as a tangible object) develops over the course of childhood as the individual learns to consider other points of view in certain contexts (such as games) and eventually internalizes what Mead calls the "generalized other," a view of the perspective of society as a whole that transcends individuals or particular situations. (Chapter 4 discusses Mead's theories on socialization in depth.) Key to both Cooley's and Mead's work is the notion that meaning emerges through social interaction. Another Chicago scholar, W. I. Thomas, summarized this concept in stating that "if men define situations as real they are real in their consequences" (Thomas & Thomas, 1928, p. 572). This statement provided an important foundation to theories of the social construction of reality.

DOUBLE CONSCIOUSNESS

a concept conceived by W. E. B. Du Bois to describe the use of two behavioral scripts, one for moving through the general social world and the other incorporating the external opinions of prejudiced onlookers. These two scripts are constantly maintained by African Americans.

W. E. B. Du Bois Even as the Chicago School questioned essentialist concepts of race, ethnicity, and the self itself, White men still dominated this community of scholars. The most important Black sociologist of the time and the first African American to receive a PhD from Harvard, W. E. B. Du Bois (1868–1963) did not receive the recognition he deserved during his lifetime. (For a discussion of the capitalization of racial and ethnic terms, see the preface.) The first sociologist to undertake ethnography in the African American community, Du Bois made manifold contributions to scholarship and social causes. He developed the concept of double consciousness, a process in which African Americans constantly maintain two separate behavioral scripts. The first represents the behavior of any American moving through the world; the second accounts for the external opinions of an often

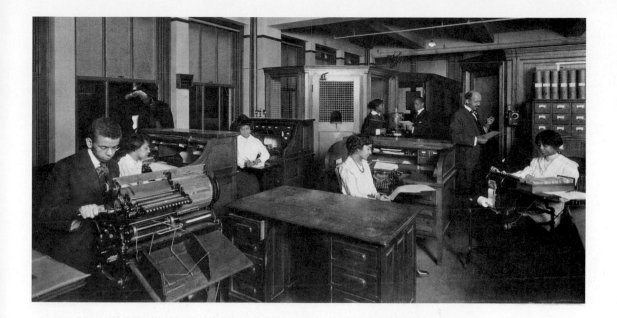

W. E. B. Du Bois (second from right) at the office of the NAACP's *Crisis* magazine.

racially prejudiced onlooker. The double consciousness is a "sense of always looking at one's self through the eyes of others, of measuring one's soul by the tape of a world that looks on in amused contempt and pity" (1903, p. 2). Without a double consciousness, a person shopping for groceries moves through the store trying to remember everything on the list, maybe taste-testing the grapes, impatiently scolding children begging for the latest sugary treat, or snacking on some cookies before paying for them at the register. With a double consciousness, an African American shopping for groceries remains aware of a store security guard's gaze and cognizant of stereotypes, making an effort to shop efficiently and to leave quickly. Unconscious actions for others, like lingering in back corners out of the gaze of shopkeepers or reaching into a pocket, could be perceived as evidence of shoplifting for an African American customer. Snacking on a bag of chips before reaching the register or sampling a tasty morsel from the bulk bins are totally out of the question. Du Bois was also interested in criminology, using Durkheim's theory of anomie to explain crime rates among African Americans. Specifically, Du Bois theorized that the breakdown of norms resulting from the former slaves' sudden and newfound freedom caused high crime rates among Blacks (at least in the South). He emphasized that those operating with a double consciousness risk conforming to others' negative perceptions of them. He also analyzed the social stratification among Philadelphia's Black population and argued that such class inequality led to progress in the Black community. He coined the term "the talented tenth," an elite of highly educated professionals that would inspire growth in the community. In addition to his work as a major academic sociologist, Du Bois worked to advance a civil rights agenda in the United States, co-founding the National Association for the Advancement of Colored People (NAACP) in 1909.

Jane Addams Women didn't always receive the respect they deserved among sociologists. Like Du Bois, Jane Addams (1860–1935) inspired a number of the movement's thinkers with her applied work, but she did not receive the high praise and status that she deserved. In Chicago, Addams founded Hull House, the first American settlement house that attempted to link the ideas of the university to the poor through a full-service community center, staffed by students and professionals, which offered educational services and aid along with promoting sports and the arts. Hull House put into practice and tested the ideas of the Chicago School. Although many of Addams's observations and experiences at Hull House influenced the development of the Chicago School's theories and Addams herself worked as a prolific author on both the substance and methodology of community studies, the majority of her contemporaries regarded her as a social worker. This label, which she rejected, partly resulted from the applied style of her work, but gender also played a significant role in her marginalization. Many of the men of the Chicago School also engaged in social activism yet retained their academic prestige and titles.

MODERN SOCIOLOGICAL THEORIES

Functionalism Although American sociology evolved out of a tradition of community studies that avoided grand theory and drew its insights from the careful observation of people in their environments, the discipline was also largely characterized by the concept of functionalism for much of the twentieth century. Drawing on writings by Durkheim and best embodied by the work of Talcott Parsons (1902–1979), functionalism derived its name from the notion that the best way to analyze society was to identify the roles that different groups, institutions, or other social phenomena play. These functions may be manifest (explicit) or latent (hidden). This lens is really just an extension of a nineteenth-century theory called *organicism*, or the idea that society functions like a living organism, with each part serving an important role in keeping society together. The state or government was seen as the brain, industry was the muscular system, media and mass communications were the nervous system, and so on.

Twentieth-century sociologists had moved beyond such simplistic biological metaphors, yet the essential notion that social institutions existed for a reason persisted. Hence, analysis by Parsons and others sought to describe how the various parts of the whole were integrated with, but also articulated against, one another. Functional analysis interrogated almost every social phenomenon with respect to its societal "reason" for existing:

FUNCTIONALISM

the theory that various social institutions and processes in society exist to serve some important (or necessary) function to keep society running.

What is the function of schooling? What function does the health-care system provide? Even crime and the Mafia came to play a theoretical role in a functioning society. For example, functionalists view social inequality as a "device by which societies ensure that the most important positions are conscientiously filled by the most qualified persons" (Davis & Moore, 1945).

Although associated with mid-twentieth-century sociology, the functionalist impulse originated in the nineteenth century, most notably in the work of Durkheim, who in 1893 (1972) wrote, "For, if there is nothing which either unduly hinders or favours the chances of those competing for occupations, it is inevitable that only those who are most capable at each type of activity will move into it. The only factor which then determines the manner in which work is divided is the diversity of capacities." Functionalism was still being applied late into the twentieth century by Richard J. Herrnstein and Charles Murray, who argued in *The Bell Curve* that "no one decreed that occupations should sort us out by our cognitive abilities, and no one enforces the process. It goes on beneath the surface, guided by its own invisible hand" (1994, p. 52).

Female textile workers struggle with a national guardsman during a 1929 strike in Gastonia, North Carolina. How might a functionalist interpret protest? How might a conflict theorist interpret labor unrest in a different way?

Conflict Theory Even though functionalism continues to reappear in many guises, its fundamental assertions have not gone unchallenged. Sociologists such as C. Wright Mills (remember the creator of sociological imagination?), writing from 1948 through 1962, criticized Parsons and functionalist theory for reinforcing the status quo and the unequal class structures of a dominant economic system instead of challenging how such systems evolved and offering potential alternatives. Functionalism also took a beating in the turbulent 1960s from a number of theories frequently subsumed under the label of Marxist theory or conflict theory. Whereas functionalists painted a picture of social harmony as the well-oiled parts of a societal machine working together (with some friction and the occasional breakdown), conflict theorists viewed society from a different perspective. Drawing on the ideas of Marx, the theory expressed by Ralf Dahrendorf, Lewis Coser, and others stated that conflict among competing interests serves as the basic, animating force of any society. Competition, not consensus, is the name of the game, and this conflict at all levels of analysis (from individuals to the family to the tribe to the nation-state), in turn, drives social change. Rather than occurring through evolution or gradual baby steps, social change primarily occurs through revolution and war according to conflict theory.

According to conflict theorists, inequality exists as a result of political struggles among different groups (classes) in a particular society. Although functionalists conceptualize inequality as a necessary and beneficial aspect of society, conflict theorists argue that inequality exists at the expense of less powerful groups. Today, most sociologists take a more complex approach to the functionalist-conflict debate, seeing societies as demonstrating characteristics of both consensus and conflict and believing that social change does result from both revolution and evolution.

Symbolic Interactionism Another strain of thought that developed in the 1960s was symbolic interactionism, which eschewed big theories of society (macrosociology) and instead focused on how face-to-face interactions create the social world (microsociology). Exemplified most notably by the work of Herbert Blumer, one of George Herbert Mead's students, this paradigm operates on the basic premise of a cycle of meaning—namely, the idea that people act in response to signs and social signals that hold particular meanings for them (e.g., a red light means stop). By acting on perceptions of the social world in this way and by regarding these meanings as *sui generis* (i.e., appearing to be self-constituting or quasi-natural rather than flimsily constructed by ourselves or others), we then collectively define their existence to create shared understandings. Think about red lights again. Red does not signify "stop" for any intrinsic or natural reason, just like green does not automatically mean "go." Over time, we assigned these meanings based on a collective thinking and practice; in other words, we (tacitly) have come to a

CONFLICT THEORY

the idea that conflict between competing interests is the basic, animating force of social change and society in general.

SYMBOLIC INTERACTIONISM

a micro-level theory in which shared meanings, orientations, and assumptions form the basic motivations behind people's actions.

social agreement on what these things signify in the context of driving. We then act in ways that reify, or make consequential, this consensus and arrive at our calculations based on the supposed objectivity or automatic nature of this "fact." We are all then socialized with these meanings and become agents in projecting them back out onto the world, thereby maintaining the status quo (think back to changing your mother's age or the name of your college).

Erving Goffman's dramaturgical theory of social interaction laid the groundwork for symbolic interactionism. Goffman used the language of theater to describe the social facade we create through devices such as tact, gestures, frontstage (versus backstage) behavior, props, and scripts. In *The Presentation of Self in Everyday Life* (1959), Goffman explored how our every-day personal encounters shape and reinforce notions of class and social status. According to Goffman, we make judgments about class and social status based on how people speak, what they wear, and the other specific details of how they present themselves to others. At the same time, they rely on similar aspects of our everyday interactions with them to classify us too.

Postmodernism

If symbolic interactionism emphasizes the mean-ings negotiated through local-scale interactions between individuals, postmodernism refers to the notion that these shared meanings have eroded with time. A red light, for instance, may have multiple meanings to different groups or individuals in twenty-first-century society. There is no longer one version of history that is objectively correct. Everything is up for interpre-tation within this framework; even "facts" can be debated. Postmodernists may not feel compelled to act on supposedly objective, shared meanings because the meanings aren't, in fact, objective. The term itself derives from the idea that the grand narratives of history are over (hence, "after" modern-ism, *postmodernism*), leading to a new understanding of social constructions and the breakdown of collective, organizing narratives.

Midrange Theory

Although many sociologists have taken to the post-modernist project of deconstructing social phenomena (i.e., showing how they are arbitrarily created by social actors with varying degrees of power), as the pendulum swings yet again, most sociologists are returning to what sociologist Robert Merton called for in the middle of the twentieth century: midrange theory.

Midrange theory exists somewhere in between macrosociology and microsociology, neither attempting to explain all of society nor its tiny, specific sections. Rather, midrange theory attempts to predict how cer-tain social institutions tend to function. For example, a midrange theorist might develop a theory of democracy (under what political or demographic conditions does this specific type of government arise?), a theory of the household (when do households expand to include extended kin or nonkin

---

POSTMODERNISM

a condition characterized by the questioning of the notion of progress and history, the replacement of narrative with pastiche (i.e., a collage of existing ideas) or imitation of other work in the service of satire or subversion, and multiple, perhaps even conflicting, identities resulting from unconnected affiliations.

SOCIAL CONSTRUCTION

an entity that exists because people behave as if it exists and whose existence is perpetuated as people and social institutions act in accordance with widely agreed-upon formal rules or informal norms of behavior associated with that entity.

MIDRANGE THEORY

a theory that attempts to explain generalizable patterns of behavior that are neither all-encompassing of society as a whole nor focused on very particular groups or individuals.

Las Vegas, the ultimate postmodern city, borrows from various regions, times, and cultures to shape its constantly changing landscape.

and when do they contract to the nuclear family unit or the individual?), or a theory explaining the relationship between the educational system and the labor market. The key to midrange theory is the generation of falsifiable hypotheses—that is, predictions that can be tested by analyzing the real world. (Chapter 2 covers hypothesis generation in greater detail.)

Feminist Theory Emerging from the women's movement of the 1960s and 1970s, feminist theory shares many ideas with Marxist theory—in particular, the Marxist emphasis on conflict and political reform. Feminism is not one isolated idea but a catchall term for a number of theories, all of which share an emphasis on women's experiences and a belief that sociology as a discipline and society in general subordinate women. Feminist theorists emphasize equality between men and women, working to see women's lives and experiences represented in sociological studies. Early feminist theory focused on defining concepts such as sex and gender, and in the process challenged conventional wisdom by questioning the conventional meanings assigned to these concepts. In *Sex, Gender, and Society* (1972), sociologist Ann Oakley argued that much of what we attribute to biological sex differences correlates with behaviors learned and internalized through socialization processes (see Chapter 8 on gender).

In addition to defining terms like *sex* and *gender*, much feminist research focuses on inequalities perpetuated through gender categories. Feminist theorists have studied women's experiences at home and in the workplace, along with researching gender inequality in social institutions such as schools, the family, and the government. In each environment, feminist sociologists remain interested in the definition, shaping, and reproduction of power relationships on the basis of gender differences.

DOING THEORY

Theories are not something to which sociologists should be beholden. That is, a sociologist can pick and choose, finding a Marxian approach fruitful in understanding one question but then turning to feminist theory when attempting to answer another. Rather than functioning as one-size-fits-all grand narratives, theories serve as useful lenses through which to view various parts of the social world. Think of them as different tints that you can overlay onto your sociological goggles. Sometimes, when we approach a problem, these distinct shades of analysis bring social dynamics into sharp focus. At other times, the lens of a given theory may reveal a layer of a complex issue that had previously gone unnoticed. They help make the familiar strange. Table 1.2 provides a particular example of how a few foundational social theories may address the same phenomenon. Theories are like the ancient Indian parable of the blind men and the elephant: One thinks the beast is like a fan

TABLE 1.2 Applying Theory to the Question of Educational Attainment (Or: Who Goes to College, Who Doesn't Go to College, and Why?)

FUNCTIONALISM	CONFLICT THEORY	SYMBOLIC INTERACTIONISM
Posits that educational institutions like universities provide stability in society by instilling core values and distinct social positions within a complex system; different levels of educational attainment reduce strain by socializing individuals into their social roles in the labor market and other domains of society.	Studies the role of schools in reproducing existing social boundaries and inequalities, along with the exclusionary divisions of power that allow some members of society to access higher education while others face obstacles that exclude them from the positions of power associated with a college degree.	Illustrates the arbitrary roles (not dictated by any natural laws) that individuals occupy based on their social positions; analyzes the rituals constructed by educational institutions (in other words, the ways that a college education might teach individuals to act in certain social spaces, providing them with the tacit skills necessary for particular types of interactions).

because he is touching its ear; another a snake, for he is grasping its trunk; a third a rope, for he is feeling the tail; and so on. Theories alone cannot tell us the whole story, but they are helpful tools for piecing together the puzzle.

Sociology and Its Cousins

| Define sociology in contrast to history, anthropology, the psychological and biological sciences, economics, and political science.

We have already noted that a sociology of sports exists, as can a sociology of music, of organizations, of economies, of science, and even of sociology itself. What then, if anything, distinguishes sociology from other disciplines? Overlap with other fields certainly occurs, but at the same time, the discipline occupies a distinctive position in academia, transcending the sociological imagination discussed earlier. Sociology often involves comparisons across cases (e.g., individuals, groups, institutions, societies), so perhaps the best way to conceptualize its role in the landscape of knowledge is by drawing comparisons to a few other fields.

Italian dictator Benito Mussolini (on the left) and Nazi despot Adolf Hitler at a 1937 rally in Munich. What tools does history provide to analyze the rise of fascism under these leaders? Does sociology offer a different toolbox, and how might a sociological perspective change your analysis?

HISTORY

Let's start with history. History focuses on the *idiographic* (from the Greek *idio*, "unique," and *graphic*, "depicting"), meaning that historians have traditionally been concerned with explaining unique cases. Why did Adolf Hitler rise to power? What conditions led to the Haitian slave revolt 200 years ago (the first such rebellion against European chattel slavery)? How did the Counter-Reformation affect the practices of lay Catholics in France? What was the impact of the railroad on civilization's sense of time? How did adolescence arise as a meaningful stage of life? Historians' research questions center on the core concept that an understanding of the particularity of certain past events, individual people, or intellectual concepts leads to a better understanding of the world in which we live today.

Sometimes, historians use comparative frameworks to situate their analyses—for example, comparing how Hitler and Mussolini

rose to power in order to examine why the Third Reich pursued a genocidal agenda, whereas the Italian fascists had no such agenda (and, in fact, somewhat resisted cooperating with Germany's deportation of Italian Jews). Historians also use a strategy, although sometimes controversial, called the counterfactual, asking questions like "what *would have* happened if Hitler had been killed rather than wounded in World War I?" "Would World War II have been inevitable even if the victors in World War I had not pursued such a punitive reparations policy after defeating Germany?"

DIGITAL.WWNORTON.COM/YOUMAYASK8

To see my interview with Julia Adams, go to
digital.wwnorton.com/youmayask8

The preceding description is, of course, a summary and an oversimplification of a diverse field. The practice of history runs a wide gamut. There are "great man" histories, which study powerful figures like Hitler. By contrast, there is a strand of history called "people's histories" that focuses on the lives of anonymous, disempowered people in various epochs or on groups traditionally given short shrift in historical scholarship, such as women, African Americans, and those who have been colonized. There is also historiography, which constitutes metahistory examining the intellectual assumptions and constraints on knowledge entailed by the subjects and methods used in the discipline. Sociology, by contrast, generally focuses not on the uniqueness of phenomena but on commonalities present across multiple cases. Whereas the unique case is the staple of the historian, the comparative method is the staple of sociologists. Historical comparative sociologist Julia Adams explained the difference between her work and a historian's: "If you define the difference according to whether one is engaged in primary archival research or not, I would . . . also be an historian as well as a sociologist," but the big difference is that historical sociologists are "consciously theoretical" and "very keen to explain and illuminate" historical patterns (Conley, 2013a). Whether looking at contemporary American life, the formation of city-states in medieval Europe, or the origins of unequal economic development thousands of years ago, historical sociologists formulate hypotheses and theorems about how social life worked (or still works) by identifying commonalities (and differences) and reoccurring systems.

How does anthropologist Natasha Dow Schüll's research on slot-machine gamblers challenge the historical boundaries between anthropology and sociology?

Therefore, instead of inquiring why Hitler rose to power, sociologists might ask which common element allowed fascism to arise during the early to mid-twentieth century in Germany, Italy, Spain, and Japan but not in other countries such as France, Great Britain, or the Scandinavian nations. Of course, sociologists recognize that no one-size-fits-all hypothesis can explain all these cases perfectly, but the exercise of considering common factors illuminates the role of certain environmental features in creating a certain type of social world. Instead of asking what specific conditions led to the Haitian slave revolt in 1791, the sociologist might look to other uprisings among indentured populations to identify those commonalities and patterns. Instead of asking how the Counter-Reformation affected the practices of lay Catholics in one region of Europe, the sociologist might ask what aspects of the conditions in various regions of Europe made the reaction to the Catholic Church's reforms different. This is a subtle but important difference in perspective.

ANTHROPOLOGY

The field of anthropology includes both physical anthropologists, who resemble biologists more than sociologists, and cultural anthropologists, who study human relations in a similar way to sociologists. Traditionally, sociologists studied "us" (Western society and culture), whereas anthropologists studied "them" (other societies or cultures). This distinction was helpful in the early to mid-twentieth century, when anthropologist Margaret Mead studied rites of passage in Samoa while sociologists interviewed Chicago residents, but it plays a less salient role today. Sociologists increasingly study both Western and non-Western social relations, while anthropologists tackle domestic and international social issues.

Take two recent examples that confound this division from either side of the metaphorical aisle: Caitlin Zaloom is a cultural anthropologist whose "tribe" (she likes to joke) is the group of commodities traders who work in the Chicago Mercantile Exchange. Natasha Dow Schüll, another anthropologist, studies gamblers in Las Vegas and how they lose themselves (and their money) in the slot-machine zone. Meanwhile, recent sociological scholarship includes Stephen Morgan's study of African status attainment and patronage relations. Another project, spearheaded by business school professor Doug Guthrie in 2006, investigated the way informal social connections facilitate business in China. The twenty-first-century era of globalization has appropriately diminished divisions on the basis of "us" and "them." Many scholars now question the legitimacy of such a distinction in the first place, questioning its roots in colonialism and the reproduction of dominant, exclusionary social relations, accomplishing on an intellectual level what European imperialism did on the military, political, and economic fronts.

What, then, distinguishes sociology from cultural anthropology? Nothing, some would argue. However, although certain aspects of sociology overlap significantly with those of cultural anthropology, sociology as a whole has a wider array of methods to answer questions, such as experimentation and statistical data analysis. Sociology also tends more toward comparative case study, whereas anthropology mirrors history in its focus on unique and particular circumstances. A wider range of methods does not indicate sociology's superiority as a discipline; in fact, varying methodologies can lead to irreconcilable differences within the field. For example, demographic and ethnographic studies of the family may employ different working definitions of a household, making meaningful dialogue between two subfields within sociology challenging.

THE PSYCHOLOGICAL AND BIOLOGICAL SCIENCES

Social, developmental, and cognitive psychology often addresses many of the same questions that sociologists do: How do people react to stereotypes? What explains racial differences in educational performance? How do individuals respond to authority in various circumstances? Ultimately, however, psychologists focus on the individual, whereas sociologists focus on the supra-individual (above or beyond the individual) level. In other words, psychologists use individual-level evidence and observations to explain the phenomenon under consideration, examining how urges, drives, instincts, and the mind itself can account for human behavior, whereas sociologists examine the group-level dynamics and social structures that influence individuals.

Biology, especially evolutionary biology, increasingly attempts to explain phenomena that once would have fallen into the exclusive dominion of social scientists. Biological (evolutionary) theories now attempt to explain many aspects of gender relations—even rape and high-heeled shoes (Posner, 1992). Medical science has identified genes that potentially explain some aspects of social behavior, such as aggressiveness, shyness, and even thrill seeking. Increasingly, diagnoses such as attention-deficit hyperactivity disorder (ADHD) and disorders on the autism spectrum medicalize social differences. The distinction between these areas of biology and the social sciences lies not so much in the topic of study (or even the scientific methods in some cases) but rather in the underlying variation or causal mechanisms with which the disciplines are concerned. Sociology addresses supra-individual-level dynamics that affect our behavior; psychology addresses individual-level dynamics; and biology typically deals with the intra-individual-level factors (those within the individual) that affect our lives, such as biochemistry, genetic makeup, and cellular activity. If a group of biologists would attempt to explain differences in culture across continents, they would typically analyze local ecological effects or the distribution of genes across subpopulations, while sociologists would focus on the external, observable behaviors that represent and explain these cultural distinctions.

ECONOMICS AND POLITICAL SCIENCE

The quantitative side of sociology shares many methodological features with economics and political science. Economics traditionally focused on market exchange relations (or, more simply put, on money). More recently, though, economics has expanded to include social realms such as culture, religion, and the family—the traditional stomping ground of sociologists. Given this overlap, some argue that a different underlying view of human behavior is what distinguishes economics from sociology. According to this view, economics assumes that people are rational utility maximizers: They always aim to get the best deals for themselves. Sociology, on the other hand, has a more open and fluid view of human motivation that includes selfishness, altruism, and simple irrationality. (New branches of economics, however, account for many forms of motivation even including the realm of the "irrational." See, for example, behavioral economics.) Another difference is methodological: Economics is a fundamentally quantitative discipline, exclusively basing its findings on numerical data, while sociology leaves room for a wide variety of methods.

Another very close relative to sociology, political science, focuses on mainly one aspect of social relations—namely, power. Of course, power relations take many forms. Political scientists study state relations, legal structures, and the nature of civic life. Like sociologists, political scientists deploy a variety of methods, ranging from historical case studies to abstract statistical models. Increasingly, political science has adopted the rational actor model implicit in economics in an attempt to explain everything from how lobbyists influence legislators to the recruitment of suicide bombers by terrorist groups.

Having examined these distinctions, we should keep in mind that disciplinary boundaries evolve constantly. For example, Stanford English professor Franco Moretti statistically analyzes thousands of books by thematic and linguistic patterns, which might seem more like quantitative social science than humanities. Economist Steven Levitt has explored how teachers teach to the test (and sometimes cheat) and how stereotypically African American names may or may not disadvantage their holders. Historian Zvi Ben-Dor Benite has assembled a global, comparative history of how different societies execute criminals. Maybe I'm biased, but it all sounds like sociology to me! For now, let's just remember that significant overlap exists between various arenas of scholarship, making any divisions simultaneously meaningful and arbitrary.

Divisions within Sociology

I Describe the major differences between macro and micro approaches to sociological research.

Even if all sociologists tend to leverage comparisons of some sort, significant fault lines still persist within the discipline. One important split exists between theorists and empiricists. Theorists develop high-level explanations from the top down, which may or may not then get tested. Meanwhile, empiricists test explanations for social life based on collected evidence and revise explanations accordingly. These are superficial dichotomies, though; they merely act as shorthand for the deeper intellectual divisions for which they are poor proxies.

Many observers perceive a division between those who deal in numbers (statistical or quantitative researchers) and those who deal in words (qualitative researchers). Quantitative sociologists collect and analyze data that can be represented numerically. For example, a quantitative sociologist might calculate how much income or social prestige each additional year of education confers in society and how that has varied across time and place. Qualitative researchers might describe the social norms of a street corner, a private country club, or a Fortune 500 company through observation and note-taking.

Often "quant" and "qual" labels act as an imprecise shorthand for a much more significant cleavage between "interpretive" and "positivist" sociology. Positivist sociology stems from the mission of Comte—that mission being to reveal the "social facts" (to use the term Durkheim later coined) that affect, if not govern, social life. It is akin to uncovering the laws of "social physics," although today most positivist sociologists would shun the implications of an overly deterministic sense of unwavering, time-transcendent laws in Comte's phrasing.

To this end, the standard practice is to first form a theory about how the social world works—for instance, that minority groups have a high degree of group solidarity. The second task is to generate a hypothesis based on this theory, perhaps that minority groups should demonstrate a lower level of intragroup violence than majority groups. Next, we make predictions based on our hypotheses. Both the hypotheses and predictions have to be falsifiable by an empirical, or experimental, test; in this case, the methodology might involve examining homicide rates among different groups in a given society or in multiple societies. Finally comes the acceptance or rejection of the hypothesis, along with the revision or extension of the theory in the face of contradictory or confirming evidence. These scientific methods mirror those used in any basic science. For that reason, positivism is often called the "normal science" model of sociology.

The normal science approach of positivism stands in contrast to interpretive sociology, which prioritizes the meanings of social phenomena to individuals (remember Weber's *Verstehen*). Rather than make a prediction about suicide rates based on the social cohesion of minority and majority groups, the interpretive sociologist will likely seek to understand the experience of solidarity among minority and majority groups in various contexts. An interpretive sociologist might object to the notion that we can make worthwhile predictions about human behavior—or more precisely, might question whether such an endeavor is worth the time and effort. It is a sociology predicated on the idea that situation matters so much that the search for social facts that transcend time and place may be futile. For example, does the role of a "friend" transcend modes of social interaction? Does what we expect out of friends and the way we interact with them change depending on whether that relationship is primarily face-to-face, via social media, or direct messaging? The interpretive sociologist would be more concerned with the meaning of friendship across these domains and less concerned with measuring how friends influence us across domains.

MICROSOCIOLOGY AND MACROSOCIOLOGY

A similar cleavage involves the distinction between *microsociology* and *macrosociology*. Microsociology seeks to understand local interactional contexts—for example, the reasons that people stare at the numbers in an elevator and avoid making eye contact in this setting. Microsociologists focus on face-to-face encounters and the types of interactions between individuals. They primarily rely on data gathered through participant observations and other qualitative methodologies (for more on these methods, see Chapter 2).

Macrosociology prioritizes social dynamics at a higher level of analysis—that is, across the breadth of a society (or at least a large swath of it). A macrosociologist might investigate immigration policy, gender norms, or how the educational system interacts with the labor market. Statistical analysis is the most typical manifestation of this strain of research, but this method is by no means the only one. Macrosociologists also use qualitative methods such as historical comparisons and in-depth interviewing. They may also rely on large-scale experimentation. That said, a perfect overlap between methodological divisions and level of analysis does not exist. Macro- and microsociologists use many of the same methods. For example, microsociologists might use an experimental design such as varying the layout of a room to see how people react, or they might use statistical methods such as conversation analysis, which measures turn-taking, pausing, and other quantifiable aspects of social interaction in localized settings.

MICROSOCIOLOGY

a branch of sociology that seeks to understand local interactional contexts; its methods of choice are usually ethnographic, generally including participant observation and in-depth interviews.

MACROSOCIOLOGY

a branch of sociology generally concerned with social dynamics at a higher level of analysis—that is, across the breadth of society.

Conclusion

The bottom line is that anything goes (almost). As long as you engage your sociological imagination, you will be asking important questions and seeking the best ways to answer them. As you read the subsequent chapters, keep in mind that a sociologist "makes the familiar strange."

SEEING SOCIOLOGICALLY

TRY IT!

Much of what we accept as "natural" in our daily lives is actually agreed-on social norms. Identify any mistakes here. For example, notice that the shopping cart has square wheels. Which are violating laws of nature, and which are sociological?

Now, do it for real: Go out and about today with your sociological notebook and note how many "rules" of social life you have been taking for granted.

SOCIAL NORM	WHERE YOU SAW IT
LINING UP AT THE CASHIER	GROCERY STORE
STRANGER NODDING HELLO	ELEVATOR AT WORK
STAYING QUIET IN A STUDY SPACE	CAMPUS LIBRARY

THINK ABOUT IT

What was the most surprising aspect of daily life that you now realize is social in origin rather than natural? Is this social norm unique to your community or does it apply pretty much any-where? Is it a recent development (like smartphone etiquette) or has it been around since humans first tamed fire? What is an annoying social norm you wish would go away, and why?

2 PARADOX

IF WE SUCCESSFULLY ANSWER ONE QUESTION, IT ONLY SPAWNS OTHERS. THERE IS NO MOMENT WHEN A SOCIAL SCIENTIST'S WORK IS DONE.

Animation at digital.wwnorton.com/youmayask8

Methods

danah boyd (yes, all lowercase) grew up in Lancaster, Pennsylvania, as the region attempted to adapt to the decline of the farming economy by reinventing itself as an industrial center. The bad news for central Pennsylvania was that factory employment in the United States had already had its heyday, so by the time Lancaster tried to invigorate its economy with manufacturing, the odds were stacked against it. Though Lancaster would later find its economic footing, other towns in the region would not be as lucky.

Raised by a single mother, danah saw her own financial fortunes ebb and flow with the transformation of the American economic landscape. For example, her mother supported herself by running a local franchise of the direct-mail coupon company Valpak. Of course, direct mail has also now been largely displaced by online marketing.

danah's own intellectual trajectory reflects all the subtleties of this background. Though she was taught some computer programming as a young child in school, her interest in this new technology really took off thanks to her brother's hogging of the home phone line. Back in the days of dial-up connections, her brother would take over the family phone line to communicate with other users on various online bulletin boards. Little is more annoying to a teenage girl, danah says, than a younger brother bogarting the telephone, but once she realized that there were actually other people whose computers were deciphering the clicks, beeps, and screeches that were emanating from her line, the die was cast. Computing was social, and it was cool.

At Brown University, danah combined her varied interests by concocting a hybrid concentration: computational gender studies. Her senior thesis research involved studying how sex hormones affect depth-cue prioritization in virtual reality spaces by investigating the changes experienced by transgender people undergoing hormone therapy. Evidently, the retina of the eye has the most sex hormone receptors outside of our reproductive

DIGITAL.WWNORTON.COM/YOUMAYASK8

To see my interview with danah boyd, go to
digital.wwnorton.com/youmayask8

system (who knew?), so how we see the world—quite literally—is shaped by sex.

danah continued her cross-disciplinary studies at MIT's Media Lab, where she graphed the social networks of individuals without ever seeing their electronic communications, instead only observing those of their friends. During a gap year between completing her master's degree and starting her PhD studies at the University of California, she bluffed her way into conducting her first real independent qualitative study. Her subject was early Friendster adopters. (Friendster was among the first social network sites, followed later by Myspace and more recently Facebook and Instagram.)

As an early adopter herself, she managed to gain incredible access to both Friendster and Myspace. Although many researchers study youth culture ethnographically by talking to kids and hanging out in spaces where teenagers congregate, and others perform "content analysis" of online interactions such as Twitter feeds, blogs, and so on, few have combined the two so deftly as danah. Access to online social networks allows her to draw samples of users to contact both online and offline in order to make sure that her interviews and participant observation are not only deep but also broad. She can cover not only different groups based on race, class, gender, and sexuality, but also different cliques that are not so easily categorized by demographers. This dual online–offline approach makes her work more generalizable than the typical approach that solely studies online data or offline socializing.

ETHNOGRAPHY

a qualitative method of studying people or a social setting that uses observation, interaction, and sometimes formal interviewing to document behaviors, customs, experiences, social ties, and so on.

The face-to-face ethnography that danah does is critical to understanding the social lives of teens. For example, although some teens talk about racial integration and cross-race friendships, online she observes very segregated social networks. Understanding those excluded from social networks can be just as important as mapping those included in them.

As more and more social life takes place across digital platforms, we need more researchers like danah who carefully stitch together the domains of our fragmented lives and help us make sense of them.

As scientists, we follow the scientific method: That is, we observe the world, form a theory about an aspect of it, generate hypotheses (testable predictions based on that theory) about our subject matter, and set up an experiment or systematic observations to test those hypotheses. After conducting our analysis, we accept or reject our hypotheses and revise our theory, if necessary. Rinse and repeat.

In everyday speech, we use the word *theory* as a synonym for "idea" or "hunch." But in science, a theory is a systematic, generalized model of how some aspect of the world works. A theory is more abstract and general than a specific hypothesis and in fact may generate multiple, testable hypotheses. A theory articulates a system of relationships between facts, suggesting causes and effects emerging out of those relationships. One scientific theory with which you may be familiar is Darwin's theory of evolution by natural selection. Now fundamental to the way evolutionary biologists see the world, this theory wasn't just an idea that popped into Darwin's head, but rather it was the product of many years of hypothesis, revision, and further hypothesis: the scientific method at work.

As social scientists, we sociologists have a set of standard approaches that we follow in investigating our curiosities. We call these rules research methods. These methods provide us with tools to describe, explore, and explain various social phenomena in an ethical fashion. There are two general categories of methods for gathering sociological data: quantitative and qualitative.

Quantitative methods seek to obtain information about the social world that is already in or can be converted to numeric form and then use statistical analysis to describe the social world that those data represent. Researchers often acquire such information through surveys but may also include data collected by other means, ranging from sampling bank records to weighing people on a scale to hanging out with teens at the mall. For example, had danah boyd coded her field notes and then tested whether the frequency of references to social media varied to a statistically significant extent whether she was observing her subjects in a mall or a private setting (such as someone's home), she would have been deploying quantitative methods.

Qualitative methods, of which there are many, attempt to collect information about the social world that cannot be readily converted to numeric form. The information gathered with this approach often documents the meanings that actions engender in social participants or describes the mechanisms by which social processes occur. Researchers collect qualitative data in a host of ways, from spending time with people and recording what they say and do (participant observation) to interviewing them in an open-ended manner to reviewing archives. danah did, in fact, rely on qualitative methods

SCIENTIFIC METHOD

a procedure involving the formulation, testing, and modification of hypotheses based on systematic observation, measurement, and/or experiments.

THEORY

an abstracted, systematic model of how some aspect of the world works.

RESEARCH METHODS

approaches that social scientists use to investigate the answers to research questions.

QUANTITATIVE METHODS

methods that seek to obtain information about the social world that is already in or can be converted to numeric form.

QUALITATIVE METHODS

methods that attempt to collect information about the social world that cannot be readily converted to numeric form.

in her study—she interviewed her subjects on occasion, but mostly she hung out and took notes, which she later analyzed to draw out patterns and themes without resorting to counting them explicitly.

Both quantitative and qualitative research approaches provide ways to establish a causal relationship between social elements. Researchers using quantitative approaches hope to state with some certainty that one condition causes another by eliminating all other possibilities through their study's design. Qualitative methodology describes social processes in such detail as to rule out competing possibilities.

This chapter gives examples of sociological research conducted using different methods, starting with the various theoretical viewpoints from which social scientists approach research. We'll then examine some techniques used by researchers to tell causal stories and give examples of specific studies that have employed these methods. Finally, we'll talk about the ways that social research can do more than fill textbooks and keep sociologists busy.

By the end of this chapter you'll be able to:

- Define key terms essential to sociological research and methods.
- Develop a sociological research question, a testable hypothesis, and a set of variables.
- Justify the most effective sociological method of data collection for a particular research question.
- Articulate researcher responsibilities and the ethical implications of the researcher–subject power dynamic.

Research 101

❚ Define key terms essential to sociological research and methods.

The general goal of sociology is to see how our individual lives intimately relate to (and, in turn, affect) the social forces that exist at higher levels. Good sociological research begins with a puzzle or paradox, asking, "What causes such and such a thing to happen?" Once you pick a question, there are two ways to investigate: *deductively* and *inductively*. A deductive approach starts with a theory, forms a hypothesis, makes empirical observations, and then analyzes the data to confirm, reject, or modify the original theory. Conversely, an inductive approach starts with empirical observations and then works to form a theory. The research cycle shown in Figure 2.1 represents these different approaches.

FIGURE 2.1 The Research Cycle

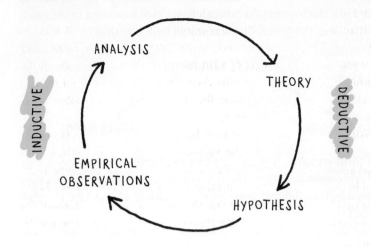

CAUSALITY VERSUS CORRELATION

Regardless of which method we use, social research is about telling a story. The goal is to recount the story as completely as possible so we're fairly certain it can't be told any other way. Let's use the relationship between income and health as an example. We know that a correlation (or association) exists between income and health—that is, they tend to vary together. For example, people with higher levels of income typically enjoy better overall health. However, correlation is very different from causation. In fact, a few different causal stories might explain the relationship between income and health. First, we might reasonably assert that bad health causes you to have a lower income—because when you get sick, you can't work, you lose your job, and so forth. If we drew a diagram of such a scenario, it would look like this:

CORRELATION OR ASSOCIATION

when two variables tend to track each other positively or negatively.

POORER HEALTH ⟶ LOWER INCOME

We could just as easily tell the opposite story—that is, higher income leads to better health because you can afford better doctors; you have access to fresh, healthful foods in your upscale neighborhood; and there's a gym at the office. The diagram of this story would look like this:

POORER HEALTH ⟵ LOWER INCOME

We could also conclude that a third factor causes both income and health to vary in the same direction. For the sake of argument, we will call this factor "reckless tendencies"—a love of fast cars, wine, and late nights.

Such shortsighted behavior could negatively affect our health (especially the wine), and it could also affect our income. Maybe we fail to get to work on time or spend too much money on fast cars instead of investing in the stock market. In that case, the causal diagram would look like this:

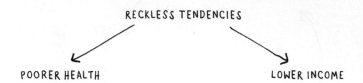

In this third scenario, if we merely observe health and income, it may appear as if one causes the other. The truth of the matter would be that they are not related in the slightest apart from an indirect connection through an outside factor.

How can we unpack the health–income correlation? We can't randomly assign people to different jobs at various pay levels and see what happens, nor can we independently affect people's health and (ethically) observe what happens to their income. It is certainly difficult to curb or instill reckless tendencies on a random basis. What we can do is rule out many outside factors by measuring them and comparing individuals who are similar in a particular respect (like education level) but differ in other key regards (say, income). Some researchers have used lottery winnings as a natural experiment—that is, an event or change in the real world that affects the factor we believe causes an outcome but does not affect the outcome in any way other than through that factor—comparing the health of winners who won a significant sum with those who won only a token amount. The assumption is that the amount won is not determined by the winner's health, but that subsequent changes in health may well be driven by the money won.

Although few certain answers exist in social science, we can safely conclude that low income does contribute to poor health, at least to some extent in specific contexts. (We can also be fairly sure that bad health has a negative effect on income.) However, we don't know the causal mechanism, that is, the specific reasons that low income hurts health. Is it because low-wage jobs are stressful? (It is well known that certain types of chronic stress are bad for you.) If so, does such stress cause low-wage workers' behavior to change, perhaps by increasing their consumption of fast food, smoking rates, or alcohol intake? Or is there a more direct, psychobiological pathway—say, the stress of a verbally abusive boss that can cause higher corticosteroid levels in the bloodstream? Or is it all of these factors and more? The more dots we can connect, the stronger our causal story becomes.

Remember, asserting causality—that change in one factor induces a change in another—is much harder than finding a correlation, which just means that we observe related changes in both. As we've seen, health and

NATURAL EXPERIMENT

something that takes place in the world that affects people in a way that is unrelated to any other preexisting factors or their characteristics, thereby approximating random assignment to treatment or control groups.

CAUSALITY

the notion that a change in one factor results in a corresponding change in another.

How did studying lottery winners help sociologists understand the relationship between income and health?

income have a definite correlation and potential causal relationship. We can also talk about the associated variation in nutrition and average height in certain populations: Countries with less food availability tend to have shorter people. But can we say that better nutrition *causes* some populations to be taller? Maybe, but maybe not. Let's examine this correlation further and try to establish a causal relationship.

Establishing causality requires three factors: correlation, time order, and ruling out alternative explanations. We've already covered correlation. We have noted that variation in food availability is associated with different average heights, but let's spell it out here with respect to specific cases. On average, people in country Gianterica have more food availability (i.e., better nutrition) and are taller than people in country Shortovia. Of course, some people in Shortovia are taller than some people in Gianterica. The tallest person in the world may even come from Shortovia, but the average height is still greater in Gianterica. Unlike, say, chemistry, a cause-and-effect relationship in social science does not always rely on the outcome caused by an "on" factor (like a light turning on at the flip of a switch). Rather, we sociologists focus on the likelihood or probability of that outcome occurring, which is why we pay so much attention to averages.

To continue our causal investigation about nutrition and height in Gianterica and Shortovia, we need to establish time order. Have people in Gianterica always been taller than those in Shortovia? And have people in Gianterica always had better nutritional resources? If there is no change over time, it becomes hard to say that nutrition, in part, causes the height differences between the populations (though it does not rule out that possibility). However, if nutrition levels used to be equal in the two countries (or better in Shortovia) and heights were still greater in Gianterica back then, that fact casts doubt on a causal role for height.

But what if changes in nutrition occurred before increases (or decreases) in height? We can imagine a situation where a drought, flood, frost, or some other environmental factor destroyed a main food source in Shortovia, leading to dramatic changes in people's diet and lowering average heights in that nation. Then we might be on firmer ground saying that nutritional differences caused the height differences between the two countries. However, time order does not guarantee accuracy. People may alter current behavior based on future expectations. Perhaps, for example, I feel extremely healthy today; in fact, I feel so darn healthy that I plan to work well into my eighties or nineties; thus, I don't need to earn a lot at age 50 to save money for retirement. So, I work less. I earn less. My income remains low. If I am indeed hale and hearty at age 85, then a researcher who measured my income when I was age 50 and predicted my health at age 85 (relying on time order to establish causality) would come to exactly the wrong answer. Although lower income at age 50 appears to predict better health at age 85, that interpretation would be false; in reality, my health at age 50 predicted both my income and my health at age 85. If it sounds confusing and difficult, it is! Even if a conclusion seems clear, we always have to consider alternative explanations for our initial reactions to our data.

Going back to our nutrition-height example, we must rule out alternative explanations for the fact that Shortovia has short people and Gianterica has tall people. Is a third factor responsible for differences in both height and nutrition across the two nations? The groundwater supply perhaps? Groundwater supply could lead to better nutrition through higher crop yields (which turns out not to matter for height, let's say), but it could also lead to cleaner drinking water and thus less infection (which does, in fact, matter for height). With enough evidence for the influence of groundwater on both height and nutrition, the relationship between nutrition and height might be termed spurious or false, suggesting that there might be a true causal

FIGURE 2.2 The Charge of Spuriousness

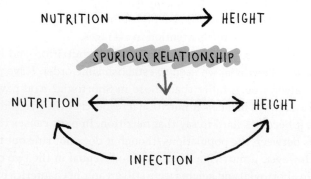

Why is the correlation between nutrition and height spurious?

relationship between infection and height. (In actuality, there is a pretty good consensus that both water quality [i.e., disease burden] and nutrition matter for stature.) Figure 2.2 illustrates this possibility.

The Problem of Reverse Causality Reverse causality is just what it sounds like: You think A causes B when, in fact, B causes A. Let's look at the relationship between income and health. We know that people who are sick often have less income, but which one causes the other? Is it that when you're sick, you tend to miss lots of school, don't receive as much education, must take off more time from work, may be passed over for promotions, and ultimately remain stuck in a lower-level job and, therefore, have a lower income than your comparatively healthy neighbor? Or is it that when you're employed in a lower-paying job, you may experience more on-the-job stress and more stress as a result of worrying about money, which has a negative impact on your health by putting you at higher risk for cardiovascular disease? On top of that, you may not be able to afford good health care, a gym membership, or fresh, nutritious food. The challenge of reverse causality makes establishing time order important. If a person's income drops only after getting sick, we can more confidently identify sickness as the cause of the decline in income.

Establishing a causal relationship based on a correlation is tough. The ideal way to say X causes Y is simply to run an experiment where we give X to some randomly selected people and withhold X (or better, give a fake or placebo X) to other randomly selected people. If the group that received the real treatment X has more or less of Y, then we can reasonably conclude that X causes Y. This experiment is called a randomized controlled trial (RCT), the bread and butter of medical studies. However, since sociologists generally study free-range humans, we cannot experiment on them to test factors of interest. We cannot randomly assign some people to get more education or to get divorced, for example, and wait to see how it affects their lives. In a complex, real world, sociologists must become detectives, finding ways to separate out the wheat of causal relationships from the chaff of spurious correlations and reverse causality. As Neil de Grasse Tyson once tweeted, "That's why Physics is easy and Sociology is hard."

REVERSE CAUSALITY
a situation in which the researcher believes that A results in a change in B, but B is actually causing A.

Designing a Study

Develop a sociological research question, a testable hypothesis, and a set of variables.

Given how hard it seems to establish that one thing causes another in social science, you might think that we should all just give up and rely on our intuitions about the social world. But sociologists and other social scientists refuse to concede defeat, and indeed, this entire textbook is testament to the fact that through using the scientific method, we have made progress in understanding human behavior and group dynamics. When we talk about how the scientific method is applied to understanding the social world, it all starts with deciding what we want to study and then figuring out how to measure that object of inquiry. In other words, it starts with variables.

VARIABLES

In research, we talk a great deal about variables. Simply put, you should always have one dependent variable, which represents the outcome you are trying to explain (say, height), and one or more independent variables (say, nutrition), which represent the measured factors that you believe have a causal impact on the dependent variable. Because more than one independent variable can exist, we will call the most important one the *key independent variable*. A change in your dependent variable depends on a change in your independent variable. Knowing the difference between your dependent and independent variables allows for the establishment of causality. Often, when we establish correlation but cannot establish causality, we don't know which variable causes change in the other—for example, we can't establish time order, so we don't know which variable is independent and which is dependent.

In high-school science class, you may have learned that a hypothesis is an educated guess. In social research, we use the term *hypothesis* to refer to a proposed relationship between two variables, usually with a stated direction. The *direction* of the relationship refers to whether your variables move in the same direction (positive) or in opposite directions (negative).

In our example case, we are hypothesizing that better nutrition increases height in a population. We also hypothesize that higher income leads to better health and, finally, that better health leads to higher income. Our study should aim to test these causal statements.

HYPOTHESIS TESTING

Are you starting to see how the pieces fit together in the design of a research project? Perhaps we are interested in the income–health relationship but have a special interest in the poor. Poverty is a broad concept, so we need to specify what we mean by poverty in this particular study and who qualifies for that label. The process of assigning a precise definition for measuring a concept being examined in a particular study is called operationalization. When you read a study, it's important to understand how the author is operationalizing their concepts. If I conduct a study on poverty and health by measuring the number of Americans who fall below the official U.S. poverty

DEPENDENT VARIABLE

the outcome the researcher is trying to explain.

INDEPENDENT VARIABLE

a measured factor that the researcher believes has a causal impact on the dependent variable.

HYPOTHESIS

a proposed relationship between two variables, usually with a stated direction.

OPERATIONALIZA-TION

how a concept is defined and measured in a given study.

line and someone else completes a study examining poverty using the United Nations' definition of it (i.e., subsistence on less than $2.00 per day), we're discussing two very different concepts. As the old adage says, we're comparing apples and oranges. Once I decide how I'm defining poverty, I can begin to consider the variables related to my concept. In the case of poverty, we might take a look at variables like education, employment status, race, or gender.

It's time to make some decisions. First of all, is poverty my dependent or independent variable? Am I thinking about poverty as the cause of something else (bad health) or its result (lack of formal education, or again, bad health)? Let's say I want to examine the effects of poverty, and I'm especially interested in the effect of parental poverty (i.e., growing up poor) on adult health. Assuming that I've defined poverty level and that I've also defined health (e.g., self-rated health on a scale of 1 to 5, overall health as rated by a professional, diagnosis of a particular disease, or number of hospitalizations), I'm now ready to pose my research question: What effect does parental poverty status during childhood have on children's health as adults? Based on this question, I can form a hypothesis:

> Hypothesis: Children who grew up with poor parents have a greater chance of experiencing poor health as adults.

For each hypothesis, an equal and opposite alternative hypothesis exists:

> Alternative hypothesis: There is a positive relationship between growing up poor and health in adulthood.

Parental poverty is my key independent variable, but I also believe that race and family structure may affect how my independent variable matters. In this example, race and family structure would be moderating variables—that is, they affect the relationship between my independent and dependent variables. (Children's education or test scores in this example would be mediating variables that are positioned between the independent and dependent variables but do not affect the relationship between them.)

I am not quite ready to test my hypotheses, however. First, I need to tell stories—that is, causal stories about why I would expect the hypotheses to be true. In support of my main hypothesis, I might say that non-poor parents can afford healthier food (like organic fruit) for their children, provide regular preventative medical care, and are more likely to live in housing without hazards like mold, cockroaches, lead paint, and so on; therefore, their kids are more likely to grow up healthy. In support of my alternative hypothesis, parents who are poor may feed their children healthier food because simple whole grains are actually cheaper than some less healthy food like processed, premade meals or meats. Establishing the groundwork for a reasonably "fair fight" between main and alternative hypotheses means less time spent rediscovering well-known trivialities (e.g., low-income individuals tend to be poor). Before we do any testing, which hypothesis do you put your money on, so to speak?

VALIDITY, RELIABILITY, AND GENERALIZABILITY

Validity, reliability, and generalizability are important concepts. To say a measure has validity means that it measures what you intend it to measure. If you step on a scale and it measures your body fat percentage but not your weight, it's not valid for weight. Likewise, if I ask you how happy you are with your life in general, and you tell me how happy you are with school in particular, my question does not elicit a valid measure of your life satisfaction. Reliability refers to how consistently you obtain the same result using the same measure multiple times. A scale that's off by 10 pounds might not be totally valid (i.e., it will not give me my actual weight), but the scale is reliable if every time I step on it, it reads exactly 10 pounds less than my true weight. Likewise, a clock that runs five minutes fast is reliable but not valid. Ideally, we'd like our measures to be both valid and reliable, but sometimes we have to make trade-offs between the two. Keep this in mind as we discuss the various methods of data collection.

Finally, generalizability is the extent to which we can apply our findings to a group beyond the one we studied. Can we generalize our findings to a larger population? And how do we determine whether we can?

VALIDITY

the extent to which an instrument measures what it is intended to measure.

RELIABILITY

the likelihood of obtaining consistent results using the same measure.

GENERALIZABILITY

the extent to which we can claim our findings inform us about a group beyond the one we studied.

Choosing Your Method

Justify the most effective sociological method of data collection for a particular research question.

In Chapter 1, I described the differences between positivist and interpretive sociology. As distinct as they are in their focus, they also lend themselves to different methodological approaches to research. Because positivists are concerned with the factors that influence social life, they tend to rely more heavily on quantitative measures. If, however, you're more concerned with the meanings actors attach to their behavior, as interpretive sociologists are, then you'll likely be drawn to more qualitative measures.

Ultimately, the distinction between quantitative and qualitative methods is a false dichotomy: The most important thing is to determine what you want to learn and then contemplate the best possible way to collect the empirical data that would answer your question—that is, deploy whatever tool or set of tools is called for by the present research problem. Research questions allow for the precise operationalization of particular factors, leading to an obvious method for answering your question. That's why the entire endeavor depends on getting the research question right. If the question still could be approached in several ways, then you probably haven't refined it enough. Figure 2.3 gives an overview of the entire process.

DATA COLLECTION

Remember that social science research largely focuses on collecting empirical evidence to generate or test empirical claims. So how do we go about collecting the evidence needed to support those claims? Let's use case studies—that is, particular examples of good research—and see what these researchers wanted to know, how they obtained their data, and what they found.

Participant Observation Neighborhoods rise and fall and (sometimes) rise again. Often racially tinged dynamics accompany these changes in fortune: White flight in one direction and, when the tides turn again, (White) gentrification. But sometimes class dynamics within racial groups can reshape neighborhoods. With the rise of a Black professional class since the civil rights era, gentrification—that is, the movement of higher-income individuals into once-distressed inner-city neighborhoods—can be an entirely Black affair. But does that create the same tensions as cross-race urban transitions? Or does it provide its own set of unique problems? Let's take a look at a sociologist who studied this phenomenon.

Sociologist Mary Pattillo (2007) studied the Chicago neighborhood of North Kenwood–Oakland to ask what happens when same-race gentrification occurs. Patillo found that unlike in typical cross-race situations of gentrification, the middle-class Blacks who revitalized the area occupied a "middleman" status. They offered social resources to their lower-class neighbors by helping them navigate systems like city politics and bureaucracy. The role came with costs and conflicts as well: Residents of different classes disagreed about the proper use of certain spaces, such as whether the front porch was a proper hangout or where barbecuing should take place (in the front yard or back yard). In the end, Pattillo's combination of historical analysis and time spent "hanging out" in the neighborhood painted a rich portrait of class and race as it plays out on Chicago's South Side.

The proper term for Pattillo's "hanging out" is participant observation. This research method aims to uncover the meanings people attach to their own social actions (and those of others) by observing their behavior in practice, in contrast to asking them about it after the fact. This strategy is predicated on the notion that surveys, interviews, and other approaches are more easily "managed" by the respondents. That is, studying racial attitudes by surveying respondents, for instance, may lead to subjects telling the researcher what they think is the "right" answer and what the researcher

PARTICIPANT OBSERVATION

a qualitative research method that seeks to uncover the meanings people give their social actions by observing their behavior in practice.

FIGURE 2.3 The Research Process

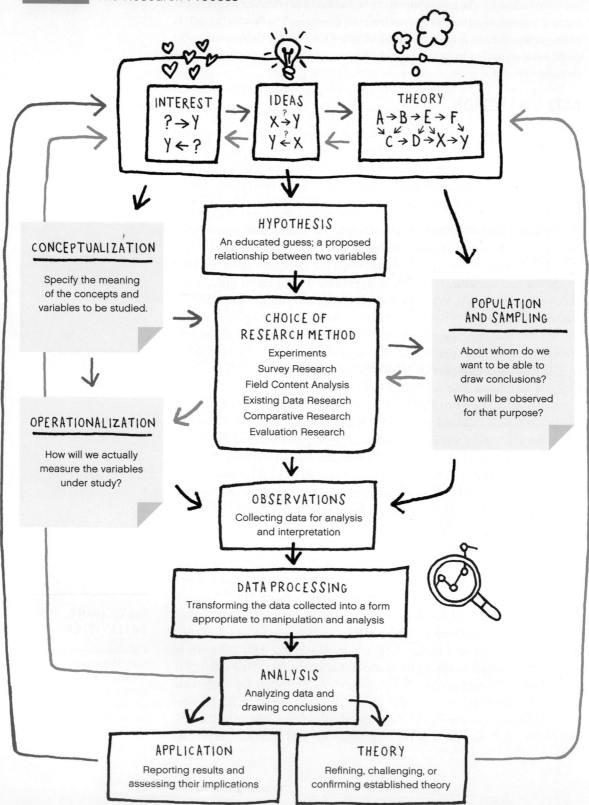

wants to hear. By hanging out in a given community over a long period, integrating into its daily fabric, and letting the dramas of everyday life unfold with minimal intrusion, participant observers are more likely to capture what folks actually think, feel, and do rather than what they would like to think they do.

This type of sociology involves a significant time investment (even years) because the participant observer must gain access to a given community, learn its local norms and logic of behavior, and then watch social dynamics unfold. In Pattillo's case, she moved into the community right when other professional Blacks were moving in. She attended local community board meetings, went to block parties, socialized with neighbors—basically she hung out like everyone else. But the difference was that she was engaging her sociological imagination and took extensive field notes about what was unfolding around her.

Interviews Want to know how and why someone does something? Why not just ask them to tell you all about it? Interviews are another common form of gathering qualitative data. For her book *Money, Morals, and Manners*, sociologist Michèle Lamont (1992) interviewed upper-middle-class men in France and the United States about their tastes. She chose the men in her sample based on their social status—for example, they were employed as managers, professionals, and entrepreneurs—arguing that these people hold enormous power in their jobs and communities and, consequently, their tastes shape the culture around them. Lamont (1992) conducted more than 160 interviews, trying to determine how the people in her sample defined a "worthy person" and analyzing "the relative importance attached to religion, honesty, low moral standards, cosmopolitanism, high culture, money, [and] power." The comparative aspect of her research design allowed her to identify some of the cultural differences between American and French tastes. For example, she ascertained that the French men valued art more than their American counterparts, whereas the Americans cared more about money than their French counterparts.

By using unstructured, open-ended interviews, Lamont allowed her subjects to go off on tangents, to vent, and to share intimacies that might not appear at first glance to be related to the study. But she also probed—that is, she pushed subjects past their initial, comfortable answers on somewhat delicate, controversial issues. Knowing how and when to probe and when to back off is part of the art of interviewing that results from practice.

Other researchers may rely on semistructured or structured interviews—that is, interviews in which the researchers have more than just a set of topics to cover in no preset order; rather, here the researchers develop a specific set of questions to address with all respondents in a relatively fixed sequence. If an interview becomes very structured, it could fall into the next category: survey research.

SURVEY

an ordered series of
questions intended to
elicit information from
respondents.

Survey Research Chances are you've filled out a survey at some point. Surveys are an ordered series of questions intended to elicit information from respondents, and they can be powerful methods of data collection. Survey research differs from interviews in that a set questionnaire exists, typically with set answers to choose from (like a multiple-choice test). Surveys may be done anonymously and distributed widely, so you can reach a much larger sample than if you relied solely on interviews. Response rates also matter. Out of all the surveys you distributed, how many were actually completed and returned to you? Lately, we have been bombarded with more and more surveys soliciting our opinions about everything from what soap we prefer to how to stop global warming. It has become increasingly difficult for researchers to get survey answers amid the din of our information society, and response rates, in general, continue to fall.

Why does response rate matter? If those who answered your survey or tore it up were truly random, then the only concern would be the cost in time and money to obtain, say, 200 completed surveys. As it turns out, who responds and who doesn't is usually not random. As a researcher, you need to consider the ways that response bias can enter your sample. Are the people who completed the survey different in some significant way from the people who didn't complete it? If your survey focuses on the sacrifices respondents would make to slow global warming and the only folks who bother to respond are passionate environmentalists, your results will likely indicate a much higher rate of sacrifice than the entire population would make. In fact, the nonrespondents did not even sacrifice the 10 minutes required to take the survey. Surveys are generally converted into quantitative data for statistical analysis—everything from simple estimates (how many gay policemen are there in America?) to comparisons of averages across groups (what proportion of gay policemen support abortion rights, and what proportion of retired female plumbers do?) to complex techniques such as multiple regression, where one measured factor (such as education level) remains constant, or is statistically removed from the picture, to pin down the effect of another factor (such as total family income) on, say, reported levels of happiness.

REPRESENTATIVE SAMPLE

the idea that a
particular slice of social
observation—a sample
of survey respondents,
an ethnographic
research site such as
an organization, or a
batch of social media
posts—captures in an
accurate way the larger
set (or universe) of those
phenomena that it is
meant to stand in for.

The General Social Survey (GSS) run by the National Opinion Research Center of the University of Chicago is one of the premier surveys in the United States, now conducted every other year. Since 1972, the GSS has asked a nationally representative sample of respondents a battery of questions about their social and demographic characteristics and their opinions on a wide range of subjects. This consistency has allowed researchers to track American attitudes about a range of important issues, from race relations to abortion politics to beliefs about sexual orientation, and to see how the beliefs of different demographic subgroups have converged or diverged over decades. The GSS is an example of a repeated cross-sectional survey.

A cross-sectional study stands in contrast to a panel survey, also known as a longitudinal study, which tracks the same individuals, households, or other social units over time. One such survey, the Panel Study of Income Dynamics (PSID), run by the Institute for Social Research at the University of Michigan, has followed 5,000 American families each year since 1968, even tracking family members who have split off and formed their own households. (Recently, the PSID had to trim back to every other year because of budget cutbacks.) In this way, the survey has taken on the structure of a family tree. The PSID has contributed to important research on questions about how families transition in and out of poverty, what predicts whether marriages will last, and how much economic mobility exists in the United States across generations.

Historical Methods, Comparative Research, and Content Analysis

How do we study the past? We can't interview or survey dead people, and we certainly can't observe institutions or social settings that no longer exist. Researchers employing historical methods collect data from written reports, newspaper articles, journals, transcripts, television programs, diaries, artwork, and other artifacts dating back to the period of interest. Researchers often study social movements using historical methods, because the full import of the movement may not be apparent until after it has ended.

How did America end up with a relatively weak welfare state and a high tolerance for inequality (particularly in the context of race) compared to other industrialized democracies? To answer this question, sociologist Jill Quadagno (1996) went back to the archives to research official statements (in regulations and other government documents) and unofficial statements (in the press) about the passage and implementation of the New Deal in the 1930s and the War on Poverty in the 1960s.

Quadagno took into account various explanations: timing (the United States industrialized early, before the adequate development of protective political institutions), institutions (the United States has one of the most fragmented political systems in the developed world, making it comparatively difficult to marshal large-scale government programs), and "American exceptionalism" (the notion that our culture, lacking a history of feudalism, was uniquely individualistic and nonpaternalistic).

Children of a plantation sharecropper preparing food on a woodstove in a sparsely furnished shack in 1936. How did Jill Quadagno use historical methods to analyze the ways in which children like these were excluded from the benefits of the New Deal?

SAMPLES:
THEY'RE NOT JUST THE FREE TASTES AT THE SUPERMARKET

POPULATION

an entire group of individual persons, objects, or items from which samples may be drawn.

SAMPLE

the subset of the population from which you actually collect data.

The word *sample* has a very specific and important meaning in social research. As a sociologist, you are always studying a population. It could be the entire U.S. population, gay fathers, public schools in the rural South, science textbooks, gangs, Fortune 500 companies, or middle-class, Caucasian, single mothers. Most of the time, collecting information about an entire population is too time-consuming and expensive, so you focus on a smaller sample. Your sample, then, is the subset of the population from which you actually collect data. (If you do collect information on the entire population, it's called a *census*.)

How you go about obtaining your sample determines, in part, the general applicability of your research. Let's say I want to study attitudes toward underage drinking in the United States, so I hand out a survey to your sociology class. Based on the findings of that one survey, I claim that the entire U.S. population is in favor of underage drinking. Would you believe my conclusions? I hope not! Your sociology class probably doesn't

Volunteer Phyllis Evans (center) questions a homeless man about his living situation and encourages him to seek help while conducting a survey with team members in New York City.

represent the U.S. population as a whole. Age would be the most important factor, but population differences in socioeconomic status, education, race, and the like would also exist. In other words, the results I would obtain from a survey of a college sociology class would not be generalizable to the U.S. population and probably not even to college students as a whole—maybe not even to students at your school (the students next door in organic chemistry might have very different thoughts about underage drinking). I would be "speaking beyond my data."

Although the issues of generalizability are always at play, they become particularly acute when social scientists use case studies. A case study, often used in qualitative research, is an in-depth look at a specific phenomenon in a particular social setting. If we wanted to understand the social dynamics of underage drinking in the United States, we might focus on your sociology class. How representative of all 18- to 20-year-olds do you think your class is? Does your class have a higher or lower aver-

Census conductor talking with Charles F. Piper as he works on his car.

age household income than the United States as a whole? Are the students particularly extraverted (i.e., like to party)? Is yours a commuter college whose students travel long distances to attend class? All of these factors— these variables—are important, and if your class isn't typical (statistically speaking), we would have more room to question the usefulness and wider import of the findings. The high specificity and low generalizability of case studies are perhaps the main drawback. One benefit, however, is that we typically obtain very detailed information. In this way, there is often a trade-off between breadth (i.e., generalizability) and depth (i.e., amount of information and nuanced detail), and high specificity can serve as a useful starting point for exploring new topics. For example, researchers often use case studies to develop initial hypotheses and to refine survey questions that the researchers will then administer to a much larger sample. Likewise, qualitative case studies can help researchers understand causal mechanisms reflected in large-scale survey studies.

CASE STUDY

an intensive investigation of one particular unit of analysis in order to describe it or uncover its mechanisms.

Greek miners seeking work in the German Ruhr Basin in 1960 after West Germany began a guest-worker program. What did Rogers Brubaker's comparative research about European immigration policies reveal about definitions of citizenship?

COMPARATIVE RESEARCH

a methodology by which two or more entities (such as countries), which are similar in many dimensions but differ on the one in question, are compared to learn about the dimension that differs between them.

Finally, Quadagno focused her research on the looming shadow of racism in America. According to Quadagno, in order to prevent Blacks from participating fully in the American social contract, authority devolved from the federal government to state and local authorities, which could then exclude Blacks overtly or covertly. The result was a much weaker safety net and one that excluded minorities disproportionately. For example, to ensure that congressional committees controlled by racist Southern Democrats passed Social Security, President Franklin D. Roosevelt had to agree to exclude agricultural and domestic workers when the system was established in 1935. This exception purposely excluded African Americans, who were employed in these two sectors at higher rates. Thus, by conducting historical, archival research, Quadagno and others can show the relevance of race in explaining the particularities of the social safety net in the United States.

Whereas the example just discussed focuses on one case, sometimes sociologists compare two or more historical societies; we call this "comparative historical" research. For example, Rogers Brubaker (1992) compared the conceptions of citizenship and nationhood in France and Germany. Comparative research is a methodology by which a researcher compares two or more entities with the intent of learning more about the factors that differ between them. By examining official documents and important texts written over a period of many years leading up to, during, and after the formation of the German and French states, Brubaker showed that their historical circumstances led to very different visions of citizenship in each nation. France was formed from a loosely knit group of powerful duchies and principalities, so no preexisting French nation or nationality existed before the creation of the French government. The idea of nationhood—that is, of French identity—was forged by the state itself leading to a very inclusive notion of citizenship. Germany, by contrast, grew out of a well-defined, tribal sense of Prussian nationality. Thus Germany's citizenship policy was based on excluding others rather than including them.

The most typical approach to comparative research focuses on finding cases that match on many potentially relevant dimensions but vary on the one of interest, allowing researchers to observe the effect of that particular dimension. This method is known as Mill's method of difference, named after philosopher John Stuart Mill. For example, in studying the effects of gun control laws on deaths from firearms, comparing the United States (which has one of the most hands-off approaches to gun regulations and a high degree of gun ownership) to Australia (which was very much like the United States with respect to gun culture—as well as other aspects of culture—but which changed its gun control policy drastically in 1996 in response to a mass shoot-

Fans line up outside a bookstore in Tel Aviv, Israel, in anticipation of the release of the final book in the Harry Potter series by J. K. Rowling. How can we explain the massive success of this cultural product?

ing) would be more fruitful than comparing Yemen (which, like the United States, has a heavily armed population) with Sweden (which doesn't). The latter two countries do indeed differ on gun control policies as do the United States and Australia, but they are significantly different from each other on too many other economic and cultural dimensions for us to conclude that any differences in gun violence between them were due to the differences in gun control laws.

One distinct subtype of historical methods research, content analysis, is a systematic analysis of the content in written or recorded material. Race scholar Ann Morning (2004) used content analysis to investigate depictions and discussions of race in American textbooks across academic disciplines over time. Morning analyzed both manifest and latent content on race in a sample of 92 high-school textbooks published in the United States between 1952 and 2002 in the fields of biology, anthropology, psychology, sociology, world culture, and world geography. *Manifest content* refers to what we can observe; Morning's study included overt discussions and definitions of race and images of different races. *Latent content* refers to what is implied but not stated outright; Morning looked for sections of the texts where race was directly implied, even if the word *race* wasn't used. Ultimately, Morning's analysis showed that social sciences texts employed constructivist approaches (i.e., the belief that race is a social construct), whereas biology books reinforced essentialist conceptualizations (i.e., the belief that race is innate and genetically determined).

CONTENT ANALYSIS

a systematic analysis of the content rather than the structure of a communication, such as a written work, speech, or film.

Experimentation Unlike other strains of science, social scientists often cannot take advantage of the tightly controlled environment of a laboratory-based experiment due to ethical constraints. Some sociologists do use experimental methods, however. One recent study by a team of social scientists raised money to conduct an experiment in which they gave some low-income mothers a significant amount of extra money each month (the treatment group) while to others (the control group) they only gave a token amount. They followed the children of both groups of mothers and studied their brain development, health, and a number of other outcomes to infer the effect of income on children's development. Because children were randomly assigned to the treatment and control groups, we can be sure that the income—and not other factors or reverse causation—was causing the observed differences. In this manner, experimentation, though very difficult, is one of the most powerful tools in the researchers' toolbox.

Researcher Responsibility and Ethics of Social Research

Articulate researcher responsibilities and the ethical implications of the researcher–subject power dynamic.

ROLE OF THE RESEARCHER

Experimenter Effects   Unlike in many other sciences (think astronomy or chemistry), social research often induces "white coat" effects—that is, the effects that researchers have on the very processes and relationships they are studying by virtue of being there. Often, subjects change their behavior, consciously or not, just because they are part of a study. Have you ever been in a classroom when the teacher is being observed? Think about how your teacher's behavior or demeanor might have changed in front of the observer.

When we do qualitative fieldwork (e.g., interviews, ethnography, or participant observation), we talk about reflexivity, which means analyzing and critically considering the white coat effects of our research process. What is our relationship to our research subjects? Frequently, research focuses on groups in disadvantaged positions relative to the researcher in one way or another. How does that shape the interactions between the researcher and the study participants and, ultimately, the findings?

Sociologist Shamus Khan, now a faculty member at Princeton University, attended an exclusive, private boarding school called St. Paul's. Khan has used his alumnus status to gain access to the institution to study how elites are groomed and trained (and whether kids on scholarships end up doing just as well as everyone else). He notes that the degree of privilege in his upbringing is not "so rare" among sociologists working in elite universities. He admits, "A lot of sociologists . . . obscure their class backgrounds. They tend [to act] as if they were middle class, but if you looked at the

DIGITAL.WWNORTON.COM/YOUMAYASK8

To see my interview with Shamus Khan, go to
digital.wwnorton.com/youmayask8

backgrounds of a lot of the people at elite departments, they would be from relatively advantaged class backgrounds" (Conley, 2014a). It is important to consider how researchers' class backgrounds might (unintentionally) influence what they choose to study and how they present their findings.

In a different setting, urban ethnographer Mitchell Duneier spent five years hanging out with booksellers in Manhattan's Greenwich Village. During the course of his research about street vendors' social positions in the community, Duneier became friends with many of his participants, which was apparent when he and I talked about how he made sure he was not exploiting them. Duneier's firm belief in the researcher's responsibility toward their participants is not always easy for him. He told me, "In the process of doing my research, before I publish my work, I make an effort to try to show the research that I'm going to publish to the people who are depicted in it. . . . Doing this is a very stressful process. Sometimes you have to read people things that are very unflattering to them. And for me, it has taken a lot of courage to sit in a room with someone, with a manuscript, and to read those things to them. Sometimes I can be shaking when I do it because I'm so afraid of the way people are going to respond. But I feel that if I am going to be writing something about people, and I'm going to be putting it out there for the public to read, whether it's with their name on it or not, then they deserve the basic respect of hearing it from me in advance." Even after the private reading and scrutiny of the work for its most important audience—namely, the subjects or informants—Duneier notes that the researcher must show ongoing respect for subjects:

> One of the most basic things that one can do is to try really hard to make sure that people don't feel used by you, after you leave the field. It's very easy given the constraints of our lives and the academy, and the great pressures we are under within our own universities, running departments, engaging in teaching, supervising students in research, it's very possible that given those demands that when we leave the field site that we can walk away from our subjects' lives and not stay in touch with them. Not ever send them any acknowledgment of the time that they spent with us. Not ever send them the results of the research. Especially if we end up moving to other parts of the country from where they live, and it's hard to stay in touch with them. It's very easy for them to get the impression that we have just walked away, benefited at their expense. They have given us their emotions; we have appropriated their lives for our sociological purposes, and then have gone on with ours. (Conley, 2009a)

As researchers, we're supposed to remain objective, but objectivity is not always possible. One day, an incident occurred between the police and the street vendors when Duneier was present (with his tape recorder running in his shirt pocket, unbeknownst to the police). He defended his friends to the officers. Because he was a White, well-spoken, and highly educated professional, his interactions with the police differed significantly from those between African American street vendors and the police. Duneier could speak his mind with less fear of arrest and the knowledge that he could afford a competent lawyer to defend himself. How did Duneier's presence change the interaction that transpired? Most social scientists would argue that once subjects become accustomed to the researcher's presence, they again behave as normal, but we don't have any guarantees. When we're engaged in qualitative research, we may find ourselves in situations where we must choose between objectivity and standing up for what we believe is right. At these times, we need to take a step back and think about our own role as both researcher and participant, because our perception and experience of events eventually become the data from which we make our claims. Duneier acknowledges that ethnographers are not perfect observer-reporters whose presence has absolutely no effect on subjects' attitudes and behavior. The ethnographer, like any other scientist, has a responsibility to readers to make their data collection methods public. Furthermore, readers "have to have a sense for how the conclusions were drawn . . . by [researchers] making the lens through which the reality is being refracted apparent.

How is the white coat effect in play here? Sociologist Mitch Duneier (center), who studied sidewalk booksellers for his book *Sidewalk* (1999), talks with a police officer. To see an interview with Duneier, go to digital.wwnorton.com/ youmayask8.

That means telling them something about who we are, not only our race, not only our class or our gender, but a number of other fundamental things" (Conley, 2009a).

Power: In the Eyes of the Researcher, We're Not All Equal Along the same line, the following question is worth asking: What role does power play in research? As social researchers, we're not supposed to make value judgments; we should put aside our personal biases, strive for neutrality, and remain impartial and objective. Truthfully, though, we make judgments all the time, beginning at the most basic level of deciding what to study. What does the field in general deem worthy of scholarly attention? What topics am I sufficiently interested in to spend 2, 5, or 10 years, or my entire career, studying? What research do grant-making institutions regard as important enough to fund? What does the social scientific community more broadly view as problematic or interesting and in need of explanation?

Although sociology, like most sciences, has historically been male dominated, it's also a discipline founded on the idea of making the natural seem unnatural, so it's a good place from which change can percolate. Following the second-wave feminist movement of the late 1960s, a growing stream of thought within sociology sought to turn a critical feminist lens on the discipline itself. Because research ultimately forms the foundation of our work, methods became a key site of debate, and thus the concept of feminist methodology was born. Feminist researchers use the same techniques for gathering data as other sociologists, but they employ those techniques in ways that differ significantly from traditional methods. As Sandra Harding (1987) explains it, feminist researchers

> listen carefully to how women informants think about their lives and men's lives, and critically to how traditional social scientists conceptualize women's and men's lives. They observe behaviors of women and men that traditional social scientists have not thought significant. They seek examples of newly recognized patterns in historical data. (p. 2)

The feminist part doesn't lie in the method per se, or necessarily in having women as subjects. Rather, Harding proposes three ways to make research distinctly feminist. First, treat women's experiences as legitimate empirical and theoretical resources. Second, engage in social science that may bring about policy changes to help improve women's lives. Third, take into account the researcher as much as the overt subject matter. When we enter a research situation, an imbalance of power usually exists between the researcher and the research subjects, and we need to take this power dimension seriously. The point of adopting feminist methods isn't to exclude men or male perspectives. It's not *instead of*; it's *in addition to*. It means taking all subjects seriously rather than privileging one type of data, experience, or worldview over another.

Many professional associations have their own ethical standards; doctors, lawyers, journalists, psychologists, and sociologists all do. Colleges and universities, too, often have guidelines for research conducted with humans (as well as with animals, particularly vertebrates). As a professional sociologist, I am beholden to the ethical guidelines established by my peers and by the American Sociological Association. As a professor, I am also responsible to my home institution. And as a researcher, I am ultimately responsible to my research subjects. I work with previously collected statistical information (or secondary data) for the most part, which makes the process a little easier, but that doesn't mean I don't have to pay careful attention to the ethical standards of my discipline.

A few golden rules exist in research. The first is "do no harm." This policy may seem obvious; of course, you don't want to cause physical harm to your subjects, but what about psychological or emotional harm? What if you want to interview people on their attitudes toward gun violence, and respondents become very upset because their family recently experienced gun violence?

FEMINIST METHODOLOGY

a set of systems or methods that treats women's experiences as legitimate empirical and theoretical resources, that promotes social science for women (think public sociology, but for a specific half of the public), and that takes into account the researcher as much as the overt subject matter.

To account for such possibilities, the second rule is to obtain informed consent. Participants have a right to know they are part of a study, what the study is about, what they are expected to do, what potential risks and benefits may be associated with participating, and how the results will be used. If you're interviewing people or asking them to complete a survey, this makes sense. But how far do you take the rule of informed consent in participant observation? Generally, you have to obtain permission to be at your chosen site, but do you remind every person you bump into that you're doing research? Transparency is key, but some research questions require that subjects don't know the "why" of the study; in other words, researchers might have to deceive people in safe and mild ways to get accurate responses. If researchers deceive subjects, the deception must be absolutely necessary to the study and, above all else, the subjects must be safe.

The third rule is to ensure voluntary participation, which goes hand in hand with informed consent. People have a right to decide if they want to participate in your study, and they are allowed to drop out at any point with no penalty. If you're interviewing someone who doesn't want to answer a question, they can skip questions; if the interviewee wants to stop for whatever reason or for no reason, that's their prerogative. Ethically, the researcher cannot badger respondents into participating in the study or completing it once they have started. Certain protected populations, such as minors, prisoners and other institutionalized individuals, pregnant women and their unborn fetuses, and people with disabilities, require additional approval to study. As danah boyd's research with teens shows, it's not impossible to study these populations; it just requires additional effort and caution.

These rules have evolved over time and were not always followed in practice. For example, in 1932, the Public Health Service of the United States conducted a study in Tuskegee, Alabama, about the long-term effects of syphilis infection in men. They recruited 412 infected African American men and 204 uninfected controls. They followed them for decades and denied them treatment even once it became available in 1943, in the form of penicillin. The subjects were deceived about the nature of the study, and they were actively harmed by the withholding of appropriate medical care. In 1965, questions began to circulate about the ethics of the study. It wasn't until the publication of an investigative journalism report by the Associated Press in 1972 that the study was shut down.

Tuskegee was a medical study, but the same violations have occurred in sociological research. Between 1965 and 1968, Laud Humphreys studied anonymous male-to-male sexual encounters, a practice called "tea-rooming" in slang at the time. He did not reveal that he was conducting research. Instead, he offered to play the role of "watchqueen" or lookout and passed himself off as a voyeur, someone who derives pleasure from watching others' sex acts. This deception allowed him access to watch sex, the social interactions around it, and sometimes the monetary exchanges that took place. Not only did he take extensive field notes on what he observed, but also he often wrote down the license plate numbers of his research subjects.

Later, Humphreys disclosed his true role as a researcher to some of the men and interviewed them about their lives. To interview others, he changed his appearance and went to their homes by tracking down their addresses from their license plates. There, he pretended to conduct an anonymous public health survey to gather information about them. When he published his dissertation as a book in 1970, *Tearoom Trade: Impersonal Sex in Public Places,* his findings were at first welcomed by many in the gay community. But soon ethical alarm bells were sounded. Though he removed identifying information in his book, what if his field notes had been subpoenaed? Was the deception that he deployed to observe intimate acts adequately justified by the importance and benefits of the research study? Many thought not.

Research like the Tuskegee Syphilis Study, the Tearoom Trade, and a number of psychology experiments done in the 1960s, along with concerns that emerged from Nazi experimentation on humans during World War II, led to the establishment of the National Commission for the Protection of Human Subjects of Biomedical and Behavioral Research. In 1978, the commission issued the Belmont Report, which established the human subjects research guidelines that are almost universally accepted today and implemented by institutional review boards (IRBs) at hospitals, universities, and other research entities.

If your college or university has an institutional review board, review the requirements for gaining approval before you start your first research project and your budding career as a sociological researcher. With their stamp of approval, you are all set to question everything and make the familiar strange. Good luck!

THE POLITICAL BATTLE OVER THE CITIZENSHIP QUESTION

You might think that designing U.S. Census questions is the arcane and unsexy concern of nerdy researchers trying to eke out as much population data as they can. However, factors like survey length and question wording can lead to significantly different results. If a survey starts to get tedious, respondents tend to stop answering, or worse, they may just fill in random answers to speed through, thereby generating misleading data. If the people who choose not to answer a question are systematically different from those who do, that difference can also bias results.

In the case of the 2020 Census, there was no more hot-button, politically charged issue than whether or not to add a question about citizenship status. In 2018, Wilbur Ross, then secretary of commerce in the Trump administration, ordered the question "Is this person a citizen of the United States?" to be added to the household roster (the listing of everyone living in a given abode). Ross claimed that he needed to restore this question (last included in the 1950 Census) in order to gather information to help the Department of Justice better enforce

The battle over whether or not questions regarding citizenship status should be added to the U.S. Census show that the Census is far from being apolitical.

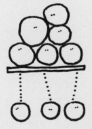

the 1965 Voting Rights Act. However, the American Community Survey, an ongoing survey of the U.S. population that replaced the long-form census, has already asked about citizenship status since 2005, so the U.S. government already has those figures.

As it turned out, the Justice Department never asked for this change to be implemented as Ross had testified. Investigation revealed that this rationale was a fig leaf for the true reason: to provide a political advantage to the Republican Party when the time came to redistrict based on the census results. This strategy was the brainchild of Republican strategist Thomas Hofeller. Households with undocumented persons would be more reluctant to share information for fear of deportation, thus not filling out the form. This is not an unfounded fear, as it turns out, since Ross testified before Congress in 2017 that he wanted to share census data so that they could be "strategically reused" by other government agencies and even private sector organizations. Indeed, in 2004, the Department of Homeland Security was able to locate Americans of Arab descent based on census data; back in 1940, census data were used to round up 120,000 citizens of Japanese descent for internment into detention camps, a crime for which the government later apologized and paid reparations.

It might seem obvious that the census should only count citizens; however, the purpose of the decennial census, as laid out in the Constitution, is to "enumerate" (i.e., count) all of the people living in the United States—citizen or not, documented or undocumented. Thus, the political motivations of the Commerce Department and misrepresentation of the real reasons for the change—in combination with the fact that it did not follow the proper procedure for instituting such a change (including providing a period for public comment) in violation of the Administrative Procedure Act— led to the Supreme Court blocking the administration's attempt to add the question. In July 2019, as the deadline for printing the census forms rapidly approached, the Trump administration gave up. As the end of Trump's presidency loomed, the administration rushed to finalize census results and assess the number of undocumented residents; without an explicit question about citizenship, though, they only came up with estimates (NPR, 2021a). In addition, questions arose about the accuracy of the results due to rapid and inconsistent analyses of the results (NPR, 2021).

Along with its political relevance, this issue also illustrates the importance of survey design in conducting research. Sociologists have long known that data are far from being apolitical, even if they are often portrayed as value-neutral.

Conclusion

Sociology deploys a variety of methodologies from survey research to participant observation to historical approaches. Our wide range of methods means that we often feel that we have to defend our identity as scientists, even to some of our colleagues within the discipline. In my opinion, sociology is a deceptively difficult science, since our methods usually lack the complete experimental control exercised by most bench science. Perhaps zoology, paleontology, and astronomy are other examples of fields in which the scientist pieces together observational data without the ability to run strictly designed experiments. Furthermore, sociologists also face the task of imputing causal processes, not just describing or classifying the social world; since we are, ourselves, social actors within that world, such a task can become doubly difficult to pull off.

Put another way: How does one assess causality with only observational data to go by, especially with so many factors interacting with one another? And add to that this complication: Reality changes as you study it and by virtue of the fact that you study it. Our basic units of analysis, such as the family, and our conceptual frameworks, such as race, class, and gender, shift even as we study them. On top of that, many of the topics we study (such as sexuality, family life, education, violence, and so on) are, by design, the most politically charged and personally sensitive topics in our society. From our wide range of research methods to these controversial topics, sociological research is never easy. We social scientists embrace the challenge, slowly inching our way toward causality.

SOCIOLOGY, WHAT IS
IT GOOD FOR?

You may think this chapter (indeed, this book) won't apply to your life after the semester is over. Think again! The research methods described in this chapter—the tools of a social scientist—can benefit many different jobs and careers.

TRY IT!

Let's say you're a brand-new marketing assistant at a cable company. You are given this draft of a customer survey. Don't forget your research question: You are hoping to figure out why an increasing number of consumers are dropping their cable subscription service (i.e., "cutting the cord"). Putting on your sociology cap, see if you can identify and fix some issues for your company:

Age: _____ **Gender:** _____ **Race/ethnicity:** _____

....

Do you currently subscribe to cable? ☐ Yes   ☐ No

....

If yes:

Have you considered "cutting the cord"?

☐ Yes   ☐ No

Do you agree that cable programming is superior to free video available on the internet?

☐ Yes   ☐ No

If no:

Do you not subscribe to cable because you can't afford it?

☐ Yes   ☐ No   ☐ refuse to answer

Do you watch cable programming illegally?

☐ Yes   ☐ No   ☐ refuse to answer

THINK ABOUT IT

Customer surveys are just one area of the economy that uses sociological tools. Using the pairings below, describe how each sociological method might be useful to the career with which it is matched.

SOCIOLOGICAL SKILL

Goffman's front stage (dramaturgical analysis)

Survey

Participant observation

Mill's method of difference

Social network analysis

Experimental methods

CAREER

Policy analyst for education department

Human resources manager

FAA crash site investigator

Real estate agent

Marketer for pharmaceutical company

Family therapist or social worker

DO MASS MEDIA CREATE SOCIAL NORMS
OR MERELY REFLECT THEM?
CULTURE IS LIKE TWO MIRRORS
FACING EACH OTHER:
IT SIMULTANEOUSLY REFLECTS AND
CREATES THE WORLD WE LIVE IN.

SOCIAL
NORMS

MASS
MEDIA

Animation at digital.wwnorton.com/youmayask8

Culture and Media

At Stanford University, Jo-Issa Rae Diop studied African and African American studies, but on the side, she created a mock reality show called *Dorm Diaries*. She also made music videos and wrote plays. When she graduated, she received a fellowship at New York City's prestigious Public Theater. While patching together a living from various jobs and aspiring to launch an artistic career, she started to produce online content. By age 26, she had launched a web series called *The Misadventures of Awkward Black Girl*, convincing a college friend to co-star alongside her. The web series gained a following for its realistic depiction of a young, Black female character. Beyond the experience of a particular Black nerd, the show gained traction for its universal depiction of uncomfortable moments many of us have experienced, like trying to have a conversation at a stop sign from one's car window or drinking a bit too much at an office party.

Despite a steadily growing number of viewers during the first season, Issa Rae—the professional name Diop had adopted—still struggled financially and needed a Kickstarter campaign to fund the remaining episodes. She added a White character by the name of White Jay, which broadened the viewing base, and eventually the singer Pharrell offered to host the series on his YouTube channel, giving the show even more exposure. Finally, she started getting some press. Katie Couric hosted Rae on her television show, CNN did a story, and *The New York Times* gave the show a great review. The number of viewers jumped, and soon she started working with Larry Willmore on a pilot for the HBO series *Insecure,* which debuted in 2016. In both 2018 and 2022, Rae was named one of *Time* magazine's 100 Most Influential People in the World.

Issa Rae at an event for entrepreneurs. What does it mean to be media-savvy? What does it mean to be a cultural icon?

Once artworks or artists become famous, we tend to think of their success as inevitable. Surely, Rae's comedic talent would have ensured her eventual discovery in Hollywood. Of course, the Mona Lisa is the greatest painting in the world and the Beatles are the greatest rock band in any world. All these cultural "facts" seem obvious after the fact. The hard truth about cultural markets, however, is that all hits are flukes. As much as producers would like to predict which band, book, movie, or show will be the next big thing, they cannot. Talent tells part of the story, as Duncan Watts shows in his book *Everything Is Obvious** (2011), but a lot of randomness influences who succeeds in the domain of culture.

In this way, Rae's story sounds like a standard Hollywood rags-to-riches story: the unemployed actor bartending until he gets his big break, the writer whose screenplay languishes in the slush pile of unsolicited manuscripts until it falls out of a stack on a messy desk and catches the producer's attention, or the singer who lands a record deal when a studio executive hears her set at a dive bar. But as much as both talent and luck matter, so does hard work. Since all hits are flukes, most successful producers of cultural products produce a lot of work, network with a lot of people, and hope that one of their creations goes viral (Stephens-Davidowitz, 2022). Rae didn't just post *Awkward Black Girl* and wait for Hollywood to come calling. She worked for it, navigating complex cultural systems in order to turn her dreams into reality. And how she worked it shows that social media content doesn't just "go" viral: Mainstream gatekeepers (such as Couric, Pharrell, *The New York Times*, etc.) still play a key role in deciding who rises to our attention in a glutted media market. As much as we would like to think of distinct pockets of culture that are separate, in actuality culture is one giant web, with certain nodes controlling the flow of ideas through the network.

By the end of this chapter you'll be able to:

- Define "culture" and the historical circumstances of its development.
- Explain the components of culture and how it shapes our lives.
- Describe the role of people in creating media and the role of media in reinforcing shared cultural meanings.

- Analyze the role of media in both perpetuating and modifying cultural biases.

- Describe the systemic forces behind consumer-centered culture.

What Is Culture?

❚ Define "culture" and the historical circumstances of its development.

We use the term *culture* to rationalize many behaviors and to describe all sorts of trends. We hear about a culture of poverty in the United States, corporate cultures and subcultures, culture wars, the clash of cultures, culture shock, and even cultural conflicts on a global scale. In a casual setting, culture can take on various meanings, ranging from innate biological tendencies to social institutions and everything in between.

CULTURE = HUMAN – NATURE

We might say that culture is the sum of the social categories and concepts we recognize in addition to our beliefs, behaviors (except the genetic ones), and practices. Culture has historically been defined in opposition to nature. The word *culture* derives from the Latin verb *colere* ("to cultivate or till"), suggesting the refinement of crops to meet human needs. (We still use *culture* as a verb in a similar sense, as when we culture bacteria in a petri dish.) The more common meaning of *culture* as a noun developed from the same kind of human control and domination over nature. In a sense, the concept of culture began when humans started acting as architects of nature by developing tools to hunt and gather and paint on the walls of caves, and then accelerated when some humans started growing crops and breeding livestock during the Neolithic revolution 10 to 12 thousand years ago, hence, the terms *agriculture* and *aquaculture* (growing fish and other aquatic organisms for human consumption). Dating back only a few centuries, the actual term *culture* has distinguished between what is natural—what comes directly from the earth and follows the laws of physics—and what is modified or created by humans and follows (or breaks) the laws of the state. That said, culture is both the technology used by humans to dominate nature and the belief systems, ideologies, and symbolic representations that constitute human existence.

Modern culture largely owes its creation to contacts between disparate groups of people, especially due to the Age of Exploration and colonialism. When, in the fifteenth century, European nations organized expeditions to extend commerce and establish colonies in North America, Africa, and Asia, Western peoples confronted non-Western peoples. The beliefs and behaviors

CULTURE

the sum of the social categories and concepts we operate within in addition to beliefs, learned behaviors, and practices; everything but the natural environment around us.

of the two groups served as foils to each other. Aspects of daily life that, until then, Europeans took for granted as the "natural way" of things turned out to be just one of many possible ways to organize society. Today, we recognize that culture is always relative. We cannot talk about culture without reference to the global world, but the definitions, practices, and concepts that we use in this chapter largely emanate from a Western viewpoint. Identifying cultural elements different from our own is relatively easy; the challenge in this chapter will be taking what is often seen as natural and viewing it as a product of culture. We'll also explore elements of media and the roles they play in the birth and dissemination of culture.

CULTURE = (SUPERIOR) MAN - (INFERIOR) MAN

Clockwise from top left: U.S. Capitol, Washington, D.C.; Lincoln Memorial, Washington, D.C.; Blue Mosque, Istanbul, Turkey; and Toltec columns, Tula, Mexico.

As colonialism led to increased interaction with non-Westerners, Europeans recognized that much of what they took as natural was not indeed so. Alternative ways of living existed, as manifested in a variety of living arrangements and marital rules, different styles of dress (or lack thereof), other ways of building cities, and other kinds of foodstuffs. Cultural differences may not

seem so striking to us now, but think about what it was like for Westerners who rarely came into contact with non-Westerners.

In the wake of these colonial encounters with the New World, philosophers began to define culture in contrast not just to nature but also to what other peoples did, realizing that the way they performed tasks or lived life was a historical product of specific cultural influences. People started to contemplate why their traditions, beliefs, styles of art, and other ways of living arose. There was nothing inevitable about them, and valid alternative approaches to interacting with the world existed. Coming face-to-face with these alternative practices caused Westerners to question aspects of society that they had thus far taken as natural. Philosophers such as Jean-Jacques Rousseau idealized non-Western "savages" in contrast to corrupt and debased Europeans, while others declared their own culture superior, with some actually claiming that non-Western peoples had no cultures. Ethnocentrism is a term that encapsulates the sense of taken-for-granted superiority in the context of cultural practices and attitudes. It represents both the belief that one's own culture or group is superior to others and the tendency to view all other cultures from the perspective of one's own. Some even believed that non-Westerners did not have souls and weren't human, and this notion was used to justify slavery, violence, and oppression. The long history of unjust racism and the development of racist systems of institutions with which we still struggle today stem from these cultural philosophies.

ETHNOCENTRISM

the belief that one's own culture or group is superior to others, and the tendency to view all other cultures from the perspective of one's own.

CULTURE = MAN – MACHINE

European imperialism also led to new technologies and forms of trade, which further upended European definitions of culture at home. Beginning in the eighteenth and nineteenth centuries, expensive, handcrafted goods began to be mass-produced and priced within the reach of the average European. New industries and a growing middle class of merchants and industrialists transformed the political and social climate of Europe, particularly in Great Britain. In response to these rapid social changes, the poet and cultural critic Matthew Arnold (1822–1888) redefined culture as the pursuit of perfection and broad knowledge of the world in contrast to narrow self-centeredness and material gain. Intellectual refinement became the "pursuit of our natural perfection by means of getting to know, on all the matters which most concern us, the best which has been thought and said in the world" (Arnold, 1869).

Arnold's definition of culture extended the ideas of Plato's *Republic*, which argues that culture is an ideal standing in opposition to the real world. A carpenter, for example, tries to construct a material embodiment of that ideal form. He starts with a vision, the divine vision of what a chair or table should look like, and he works his hardest to bring that vision to fruition,

A sixteenth-century Aztec's drawing of the conquistador Hernán Cortés. Why did Western definitions of culture change during the Age of Exploration?

Jean-Auguste-Dominique Ingres's *La Grande Odalisque* (1814).

knowing that the reality will always fall short of the "ideal type" of chair or table.

The artist's job, in contrast, is to *represent* the ideal within the realm of the real. When we see a chair in a painting, for example, it may not accurately represent the chairs we see in the real world. It may be quite abstract. But even abstract representations capture the essence of "chairness" and instill that feeling in the viewer, giving the consumer of the art a taste of the Platonic ideal. In fact, there's a long history of artists attempting to represent the ideal female in sculpture and painting, but in reality, no woman could ever exist as a flawless object, content to be gazed upon. Jean-Auguste-Dominique Ingres's *La Grande Odalisque* has an unrealistically long spine, allowing her to appear smooth, supple, and gracefully elegant as she shows us her backside but turns her face to meet the viewer's gaze with a hint of a smile.

Both the craftsman's physical chair and the artist's ideological depiction of a chair represent parts of culture. Culture, in this framework, is the aspiration toward the ideal forms, an objective perfection that lies beyond the material world in which we live. This conception, however, implies that there is one universal form of everything. There is a single, best example of any element in the world, from the ideal woman to the ideal form of government to the ideal citizen, which humanity ought to emulate. Arnold's conceptualization of culture lacks a recognition that no universal ideal form for cultural objects exists. What people consider the best family structure, chair, body type, and so on varies across time and place.

Material versus Nonmaterial Culture

▌ Explain the components of culture and how it shapes our lives.

Today, we tend to think of everything as a component of culture. We can divide culture into nonmaterial culture, which includes values, beliefs, social norms, and ideologies, and material culture, which represents everything that is a part of our constructed, physical environment, including technology. Well-known monuments, such as the Statue of Liberty or Mount Rushmore, are part of our culture, but so are modern furniture, books, movies, food, magazines, cars, and fashion. The relationship between nonmaterial culture and material culture takes on many forms. When someone conjures up a concept like a portable computer, such an invention flows directly from an idea into a material good. Other times, however, technology itself generates ideas, concepts, values, and beliefs that lead to a change in the material world. Before phones with cameras and apps such as Instagram, the word *selfie* did not exist, and before selfies there were no selfie sticks. The time it takes for culture to catch up with technological innovations is called cultural lag.

UNPACKING NONMATERIAL CULTURE: LANGUAGE, MEANING, AND CONCEPTS

Culture feels normal or natural to us but is, in fact, socially produced, like saying "Bless you" when someone—even a stranger—sneezes. As you might remember from using your sociological imagination, culture is what we do not notice at home but would spot in a foreign context (although remember that the sociologist's job is to notice these things at home too). In France, no one says "*Santé*" when a stranger sneezes in the grocery store. In Bosnia, they tell the cat to shoo when someone sneezes. Clearly, as reflexive and natural as it may feel to you, saying "Bless you" is a specific element of U.S. culture.

Along with determining our behaviors, culture also organizes our experiences. Take our symbols, for example. What does a red light mean? It could mean that an alarm is sounding. It could mean that something is X-rated (the "red-light" district in Amsterdam, for instance). It could also

NONMATERIAL CULTURE

values, beliefs, social norms, and ideologies.

MATERIAL CULTURE

everything that is a part of our constructed, physical environment, including technology.

CULTURAL LAG

the time gap between the appearance of a new technology and the words and practices that give it meaning.

CULTURE SHOCK

doubt, confusion, or anxiety arising from immersion in an unfamiliar culture.

CODE SWITCH

to flip fluidly between two or more languages and sets of cultural norms to fit different cultural contexts.

mean "stop." There is nothing natural about the meaning of the red light. It is embedded within our larger culture and therefore is part of a web of meanings, and those meanings differ in other cultural networks. Moving from one culture to another can induce feelings of culture shock—that is, confusion and anxiety caused by not knowing what words, signs, and other symbols mean. People who move fluidly from one cultural setting to another learn to code switch by swapping out one set of meanings, values, and/or languages on the fly. Elijah Anderson (1999) and others have pointed out how many minority groups, such as African Americans, learn to code switch in their daily lives by going back and forth between standard English and African American English as they move between predominantly White social contexts (perhaps their workplace) to environments in which they form the majority (such as at home or in a religious setting).

Language functions as an important pillar of culture. According to the Sapir-Whorf Hypothesis in linguistics, the language we speak directly influences (and reflects) the way we think about and experience the world. The Sapir-Whorf Hypothesis went a little too far in asserting that our language inherently limits the concepts we can understand. But its kernel idea that language shapes thought has proven to stand up. If you speak another language, you understand how certain meanings become lost in translation—you can't always say exactly what you want in every language. Language does directly reflect culture, and culture, in turn, reflects language. How many words do we have for college in English? What do "college," "university," and "postsecondary school" reveal about the central role of higher education in our society?

Just like the red light, more complex concepts like race, gender, class, and inequality are specific to certain cultures as well. If you try to explain the American understanding of racial differences to someone from another country, you might get frustrated because that person may struggle to relate. Meanings are embedded in a wider sense of cultural understanding; you cannot just extract singular concepts from their contexts and assume that

There are no inherent meanings behind a red light; its symbolism varies depending on context.

their meanings will retain lives of their own. In some cases, when opposing concepts come into contact, one will necessarily supplant the other. For example, when European colonization first reached the Americas, Native Americans viewed land as a free resource and largely understood property ownership as a collective responsibility. From a real estate perspective, the Europeans must have been very excited. ("All this land and *nobody* owns it?") The issue was not a language barrier: Native Americans had a social order that had nothing to do with assigning ownership to pieces of the earth. Acting on their concepts of ownership, Europeans thus began the process of displacing native peoples from their homelands and attacking them when they resisted.

CULTURAL EFFECTS: GIVE AND TAKE

Culture shapes our values, or our moral beliefs. The concept of equal opportunity is a good example of a moral value. The majority of us believe that everybody should have an equal shot at the "American dream": going to college, obtaining a job, and becoming economically self-sufficient. This belief is a relatively recent cultural conception. In England 600 years ago, culture took the form of a feudal system. If you had asked someone in the government of that period, a social elite, if he (and it would definitely have been a man) believed that everyone should have equal opportunity, he would probably have rejected such a claim. He would likely have insisted that the elite, the nobles, should have more rights, privileges, and opportunities than everybody else. Class mobility simply wasn't a desired goal. Similarly, the concept of equal opportunity in the contemporary United States has a particularly American flavor. We have a very individualistic culture, meaning that we hold dear the idea that everyone should have the opportunity to advance, but we believe that people should do it on their own—"pull yourself up by your bootstraps," as we say. Americans hold tightly to the rags-to-riches dream of triumph over adversity, of coming from nothing and becoming a success despite hardship. The problem with this cultural trope is that, as sociologists like to point out, the larger, structural, macro-level forces, such as general social stratification, racial segregation, sexism, differential access to health care, and education, make the concept of equal opportunity closer to fiction than reality. That is, our notion of equal opportunity often fails to account for the very unequal starting positions from which people set out to achieve their goals. Nonetheless, our rags-to-riches narrative has enough cultural influence to affect the kinds of policies we adopt in labor markets, the educational system, the welfare state, and so on.

If values are abstract cultural beliefs, norms are the ways that values are put into play. We value hygiene in our society, so washing your hands after going to the bathroom is a norm. At a young age, your parents and

VALUES
moral beliefs.

NORMS
how values tell us to behave.

teachers remind you because you haven't yet fully internalized this norm. Once you're an adult, others may still have to remind you of this norm by giving you a dirty look if you walk from a stall straight past the sinks and out the door of a public restroom. In an office, people might gossip about the guy who doesn't wash his hands, shaming him for not abiding by this norm. When you arrive at college, you enter a new culture with different norms and values, and you must adjust to that new environment. If you're attending a school with a major emphasis on partying, you might be reading this textbook secretly because the cultural norm in that kind of environment is not to buy the assigned books or even go to class on a regular basis.

IDEOLOGY

Nonmaterial culture, at its most abstract level, forms "ideology." Ideology is a system of concepts and relationships, an understanding of cause and effect. For example, generally on airplanes you're not allowed to use the toilets in the first-class cabin if you have a coach-class ticket. Why not? It's not as if the lavatories in first class are that much better. What's the big deal? We subscribe to an ideology that the purchase of an airline ticket at the coach, business, or first-class fare brings with it certain service expectations—that is, an expensive first-class ticket entitles a passenger to priority access to the lavatory, more leg room, and greater amenities, such as warm face towels. The ideology is embedded within an entire series of suppositions and, if you cast aside some of them, they will no longer hold together as a whole. If everyone flying coach started to hang out in first class, chatting with the flight attendants and using the first-class toilets, the system of class stratification (in airplanes at least) would break down. People would not be willing to pay extra for a first-class ticket; more airlines might go bankrupt, which would dramatically alter the industry itself.

A given society may have multiple ideological systems. Most of the time, these systems communicate with each other, but sometimes they can clash. Within Western culture, for example, both science and (Christian) religion are dominant ideological frameworks. They can, however, come into conflict. People once believed that the sun circled around the earth, and then, in the late fifteenth and early sixteenth centuries, along came Copernicus, Kepler, and Galileo, and this system of scientific beliefs changed. The earth no longer lay at the center of the universe but orbited the sun. This understanding represented a major shift in scientific ideology, one that led to tension with Christian ideology. In a geocentric universe, humans living on earth stand at its center, an idea that corresponds to popular Christian notions at the time that humans are the lords of the earth and the chosen children of God. However, if we view the earth as a rock orbiting the sun, just like seven other planets and countless subplanetary bodies, we may feel significantly less special and have to adjust the Christian notion of humanity's special role in the universe. People invest a lot in their belief systems, and those who go against the status quo and question the prevailing ideology may be severely punished, as was Galileo.

Ideologies can change over time and occasionally shatter. The fall of the former Soviet Union, for example, marked not just a transition in government but also the collapse of a particular brand of Communist ideology. Similarly, when apartheid was abolished in South Africa, more than just a few laws changed; a total reorganization of ideas, beliefs, and social relations followed. Often, ideological change comes more slowly. The fight for women's rights, including equal pay, continues today even though women won the right to vote in 1920.

In sum, ideologies organize a social world that encompasses us and everything around us, making the given order seem natural and inevitable. Yet ideologies evolve (think about ideologies around gender in many countries), and they also crack when they come into contact with competing ideologies (think about Galileo) or internal contradictions (such as corruption).

HEGEMONY: THE MOTHER OF ALL IDEOLOGIES

While all ideologies are systems of thought that help us organize the world around us, some ideologies are so entrenched and powerful that we don't even realize their power over us. We might not even realize that it's an ideology at all. Such an ideology is called "hegemonic." Antonio Gramsci, an Italian political theorist and activist, came up with the concept of hegemony to describe just that. Gramsci, a Marxist, was imprisoned by the Fascists in the 1920s and 1930s; while in jail, he attempted to explain why the working-class revolution Marx had predicted never came to pass in western Europe. He published his findings in his "prison notebooks" of 1929–35 (Gramsci, 1971). In this vein, then, hegemony "refers to a historical process in which a dominant group exercises 'moral and intellectual leadership' throughout society by winning the voluntary 'consent' of popular masses" (Kim, 2001). This concept of hegemony stands in contrast to another of Gramsci's ideas: *domination*. If domination means getting people to do what you want through the use of force, hegemony means getting them to go along with the status quo because it seems like the best course or the natural order of things. Although domination generally involves an action by the state (such as the Fascist leaders who imprisoned those who disagreed with them), "hegemony takes place in the realm of private institutions . . . such as families, churches, trade unions, and the media" (Kim, 2001). For example, if free-market capitalism is the hegemonic economic ideology of a given society, then the state does not have to explicitly work to inculcate that set of principles into its citizenry. Rather, private institutions, such as families, do most of the

HEGEMONY

a condition by which a dominant group uses its power to elicit the voluntary "consent" of the masses.

heavy lifting in this regard. Ever wonder why children receive an allowance for taking out the trash and doing other household chores? Gramsci might argue that this practice instills capitalist free-market ideology in individuals within the private realm of the family.

The concept of hegemony raises questions about the tension between macro-level structure and micro-level agency. Are people molded by the cultures in which they live, or do their everyday choices actively shape and reshape the world around them?

STUDYING CULTURE

Now that we have a sense of what culture is (and is not), how do we go about researching it? In the United States, the scholarly study of culture began in the field of anthropology. Franz Boas, who founded the first PhD program in anthropology at Columbia University in the early 1930s, had developed the concept of cultural relativity in 1887, though he was not the first to coin the term. Boas's student, Ruth Benedict, formalized the term *cultural relativism* in her book *Patterns of Culture* (1934; although it was actually coined by a philosopher named Alain Locke in 1924). Cultural relativism means accounting for differences across cultures without passing judgment or assigning value. For example, in the United States, you should look someone in the eye when you have a conversation; in China, eye contact is considered rude, and you generally divert your gaze as a sign of respect. Neither practice is inherently right or wrong. By employing the concept of cultural relativism, we can understand difference for the sake of increasing our knowledge about the world.

But what should one's position be when local traditions conflict with universally recognized human rights? For example, should Western businesspeople condone the cutting of the clitoris in young girls as a local cultural practice, something to be respected, as they go about their business in parts of Africa? There are, of course, limits to cultural relativism. In some countries, it is both legal and socially acceptable for a man to beat his wife. Should we accept that wife beating is part of the local culture and therefore conclude that we are not in a position to judge those involved? In the United States, some Jehovah's Witnesses reject blood transfusions because they believe blood is sacred and not for "consumption" by Christians. When parents refuse a potentially lifesaving surgery for their child because it requires a transfusion, do we respect their right to religious freedom or arrest them for child neglect? Where we draw the lines is a difficult matter to decide and sparks a great deal of political debate on topics such as domestic violence, female genital mutilation, and medical practices versus religious beliefs in treating the critically ill.

Margaret Mead, Benedict's student, further elaborated ideas around cultural relativism when she wrote *Coming of Age in Samoa* (1928), which has become part of the canon of anthropology and cultural studies. Based

---

CULTURAL RELATIVISM

taking into account the differences across cultures without passing judgment or assigning value.

on her ethnographic fieldwork among a small group of Samoans, she concluded that women there did not experience the same emotional and psychological turmoil as their American counterparts in the transition from adolescence to adulthood. She found that young women engaged in and enjoyed casual sex before they married and reared children. The book, published in 1928, caused an uproar in the United States and eventually contributed to the feminist movement. The validity of Mead's findings has been disputed, but her work continues to be a landmark of early anthropology for introducing the idea that cultural scripts, modes of behavior and understanding that are not universal or natural, shape our notions of gender. This concept stands in opposition to the belief that such ideas derive from biological programming.

Cockfighting and Symbolic Culture Clifford Geertz, another American anthropologist, analyzed culture in Bali through studying the meaning surrounding cockfighting, which involves placing two roosters together in a cockpit, a ring especially designed for the event, and watching them fight. The meaning of cockfighting varies, however. Some see it as a base form of animal cruelty, while others attach positive religious and spiritual significance to the event. In the Balinese village where Geertz lived, cockfighting primarily served as a vehicle for gambling, but it was also an important cultural event. Only certain men were allowed to referee these fights, and their decisions were treated with more regard than the law. People bet a lot of money, often forming teams that pool their resources. Bettors professed themselves to be "cock crazy."

The owners of the prized cocks expend an enormous amount of time caring for them. They feed them special diets, bathe them with herbs and flowers, and insert hot peppers in their anuses to give them "spirit." The cock takes on larger symbolic meaning within Balinese society. According to Geertz (1973),

> The language of everyday moralism is shot through, on the male side of it, with roosterish imagery. *Sabung*, the word for cock, is used metaphorically to mean "hero," "warrior," "champion," "man of parts," "political candidate," "bachelor," "dandy," "lady-killer," or "tough guy." . . . Court trials, wars, political contests, inheritance disputes, and street arguments are all compared to cockfights. Even

Margaret Mead (center) with two Samoan women, 1926.

CULTURAL SCRIPTS

modes of behavior and understanding that are not universal or natural.

A cockfight in Bali, Indonesia. How are roosters central to Bali's symbolic culture?

the very island itself is perceived from its shape as a small, proud cock, poised, neck extended, back taut, tail raised, in eternal challenge to large, feckless, shapeless Java. (pp. 412, 454)

In the United States, cocks do not carry much symbolic meaning. A more central metaphor in American society is baseball. According to anthropologist Bradd Shore (1998), baseball's function in the United States is similar to cockfighting's function in Bali. We call baseball America's favorite pastime and regularly use baseball metaphors in our daily conversations. If you ask your friend how it went the other night at a party when she spoke to the smart guy from your sociology class, and she says she "struck out," you know not to ask, "So when's your first date?" We could learn a lot about American culture by studying baseball, how people watch the game, and what symbolic meanings they attach to it, just as Geertz learned such things about the Balinese by placing cockfights at the center of his analysis.

In *The Interpretation of Cultures* (1973), perhaps his most famous book, Geertz wrote, "Culture is a system of inherited conceptions expressed in symbolic forms by means of which people communicate, perpetuate, and develop their knowledge about and attitudes toward life" (p. 89). This definition contests a monolithic definition of culture, illustrating that for some, culture is watching players hit a small, hard ball into a field and run around a diamond, while for others, it's squatting down in the dust beside a ring and watching two roosters brawl. Putting aside the issue that one is cruel to chickens and one uses cowhide to construct the balls, Geertz argues that one pastime isn't inherently better than the other. They're both interesting and meaningful in their own right, and by understanding the significance of these events for the local people, we can better understand their lives and perspectives. Though sociologists and anthropologists don't agree on all fundamental concepts, most sociologists today would accept Geertz's definition of culture, and sociological ideas of culture have built on this anthropological foundation.

SUBCULTURE

Ideologies, values, and norms get passed on to us through socialization, but we are not passive vessels that simply receive the dominant culture in society. Culture in any society contains many dimensions and complexities. Any given individual may accept some ideologies, norms, and values that are prevalent in that society and reject others. One way of seeing this complexity is through studying subcultures. Historically, subcultures have been groups united by sets of concepts, values, symbols, and shared meaning specific to the members of that group. Unique features different from the dominant culture define subcultures. Accordingly, the dominant culture usually labels subcultures as vulgar or deviant, leading to their marginalization. Gaining a deeper understanding of specific subcultures provides insight into the beliefs and behaviors of groups and individuals who traditionally have been dismissed as weirdos at best and deviants at worst.

For example, many music genres have affiliated subcultures: hip-hop, hardcore, punk, Christian rock. High-school cliques verge on becoming subcultures—namely, the jocks, the band kids, the geeks—although these groups don't really go against the dominant society because athleticism, musical ambition, and academic diligence are fairly conventional values. But what about the group of kids who dress in black and wear heavy eyeliner? Maybe teachers simply see them as moody teenagers, with a penchant for dark fashion and extreme makeup, just seeking to annoy the adults in their life, but perhaps their style of self-presentation means more to them.

Goth culture has its roots in the United Kingdom of the 1980s, yet remains one of the most durable subcultures in a world where subcultures

SUBCULTURE

the distinct cultural values and behavioral patterns of a particular group in society; a group united by sets of concepts, values, symbols, and shared meanings specific to the members of that group and distinctive enough to distinguish it from others within the same culture or society.

Goths in Germany (left) and Japan (right). What characteristics of goth culture make it a subculture?

tend to come and go, according to Peter Hodkinson, author of *Goth: Identity, Style and Subculture* (2002). Goth originally emerged as an offshoot of post-punk music. Typified by a distinctive style of dress—namely, black clothing with a Victorian flair—and a general affinity for gothic and death rock, goth culture has evolved over the last three decades with many internal subdivisions. Some goths are more drawn to magical or religious aspects of the subculture, whereas others focus mainly on the music. Even the term *goth* has different meanings to people within the subculture. Some see it as derogatory, while some appropriate the moniker for their own personal meaning making. An internal struggle has grown over who has the right to claim and define the label.

What makes today's goths a subculture? They are not just a random group of people dressed in black listening to the same kind of music. (For example, classical musicians usually wear black when they perform, but we don't consider them goth.) Goth communities use unique slang and terminology, such as *baby bat* (young goth poseur) or *weekend goth* (someone who dresses up and enters the subculture only on the weekends). Goths in Germany may look very different from those in the United Kingdom, and norms even differ among U.S. cities, so each represents a distinct branch of the subculture. Yet as a whole, goths have their own shared symbols, especially with regard to fashion, which make them visible as a subculture. Not all subcultures, however, adopt characteristic styles of dress or other easily identifiable features.

COUNTERCULTURE

COUNTERCULTURE

a large cultural group defined in opposition to the ideologies, values, and norms of the mainstream culture.

Sometimes subcultures become large enough that they constitute a counterculture. A counterculture is a significant subcultural group that is defined in opposition to the mainstream culture. Whereas goths or disaster preppers or hackers may all make up cohesive subcultures, they are not defined in terms of their complete opposition to the ideologies, values, norms, and so on of the dominant or mainstream culture—even if they differ in specifics. Hence, the possibility of weekend goths exists, for example. Moreover, subcultures generally do not seek to revolutionize all of society. Countercultures, on the other hand, do.

A counterculture rejects most core aspects of mainstream culture and develops its own, incompatible narratives and ideologies. Sometimes that counterculture seeks to separate from the mainstream culture—think of the hippy phrase of "tune in, turn on, drop out." During the counterculture of the 1960s, hippies rejected mainstream society by forming and living on communes that organized themselves in a way that was explicitly noncapitalist, nonfamily based, and nonpatriarchal. Meanwhile, sociologist Alondra Nelson (2011) documented how the Black Panther Party not only resisted

Countercultural efforts can be geared toward justice too, like how the Black Panther Party aimed to connect Black folks with essential social services.

police violence but also provided essential social services like health clinics to urban Black communities.

While some countercultures simply reject mainstream ideologies in favor of their own, other countercultures want to impose their ideologies on the mainstream culture, changing society itself in favor of their own beliefs. Rather than stepping back from mainstream society, instead the counterculture and mainstream culture battle for the soul, so to speak, of society. When such political (or violent) conflict occurs, we call it a culture war; the term *culture war* originated in the late nineteenth century in Germany, where it was called a *Kulturkampf*.

In the United States, we often see a culture war between so-called red states (conservative areas) and blue states (liberal areas). In actuality, the divide falls more along the urban–rural axis. Rural areas of liberal-leaning states tend to be more conservative, and many cities within conservative states tend to be more liberal. A number of wedge issues divide the two cultures and demarcate the front lines of the culture war. In the contemporary United States, these issues include abortion, sexuality and gender identity, immigration, gun ownership, multiculturalism, and the role of religion in civic life. These topics, which at one time were not political, became polarized due to the warring cultures. For example, in the early 1990s, political affiliation did not predict attitudes about climate change. Before the COVID-19 pandemic, vaccines were not a front within the U.S. culture wars. In the twenty-first century, though, these beliefs influence our membership in a sharply split political divide, attaching us to cultures structured by distinct ideological affiliations.

CULTURE WAR

a conflict between distinct cultures within a given society.

the process by which
individuals internalize
the values, beliefs, and
norms of a given society
and learn to function as
members of that society.

**REFLECTION
THEORY**

the idea that culture
is a projection of
social structures and
relationships into the
public sphere, a screen
onto which the film of the
underlying reality of social
structures of a society is
projected.

REFLECTION THEORY

Culture affects us. Culture shapes us. Behaviors and beliefs are transmitted to us through different processes, with socialization—that is, our internalization of society's values, beliefs, and norms—being the main one. But how do we affect culture? Let's start with reflection theory, which states that culture is a projection of social structures and relationships into the public sphere, a screen onto which the film of the underlying reality or social structures of our society is shown. For example, some people criticize the violence in certain song lyrics, particularly in rap music. How do hip-hop artists often respond? "I live in a violent world, and I'm like a reporter. I'm telling it like it is; so if you want to fix that, then fix the problems of violence in my community. I'm just the messenger." They are invoking reflection theory.

A different version of reflection theory derives from the Marxist tradition (see Chapter 1), which says that cultural objects reflect the material labor and relationships of production that went into them. Earlier in this chapter, we discussed the distinction between material and nonmaterial culture. Karl Marx asserted that the relationship between the material and the ideological is a one-way street from technology and the means of production to belief systems and values. According to Marx's view of reflection theory, our norms, values, sanctions, ideologies, laws, and even language are outgrowths of the technology and economic means and modes of production. Likewise, for Marx, ideology had a very specific definition: culture that justifies given relations in production.

By way of example, consider the creation of limited liability partnerships. The concept of limited liability emerged in the nineteenth century during the Industrial Revolution, when new technologies enabled the growth of factories and long-distance travel. At the same time, European countries such as Great Britain were colonizing regions all over the world and establishing large global trade networks. As merchants and factory owners tried to expand, they needed more capital from investors. To attract the most money, they came up with the idea of limited liability partnerships. Limited liability means that when you invest money in a publicly traded corporation, you are not responsible for its debt (you can't lose more than what you paid for your shares) or its actions (unless you are on the board of directors). So if you have stock in a cereal company and it goes bankrupt, the farmers who supply the grain can't hit you up for unpaid bills. Likewise, if several small children choke on the prize included in their boxes of cereal, you cannot be held personally responsible for this tragedy. You only lose the money you invested in the shares. Even if you didn't know what limited liability meant before you read this paragraph, the legal concept is something we take as given, a common understanding of how capitalism works. Historically, however, it arose from a choice made in England in a specific context: Marx would argue that the combination of factory labor and global trade relations between England and its colonies necessitated and inevitably led to these kinds of legal structures.

Though culture truly is a projection of underlying social and economic forces, reflection theory has been rejected largely because it is too unidirectional; that is, it basically supports the rappers' defense that culture has no impact on society. Do we really believe that the media have no impact on the way we live or think? Do we really believe that ideologies have no effect on the choices we make? No. Most people now understand that an interactive process exists between culture and social structure, and most would agree that culture is not just an outcome. It is a causal agent in society as well.

Media

Describe the role of people in creating media and the role of media in reinforcing shared cultural meanings.

Among the most pervasive and visible forms of culture in modern societies are those produced by the mass media. We might define media as any formats or vehicles that carry, present, or communicate information. This definition would, of course, include newspapers, periodicals, magazines, books, pamphlets, and posters. But it would also include wax tablets, sky writing, web pages, and the children's game of telephone. We'll first discuss the history of the media and then tackle media theory and empirical studies of media in order to illustrate the reproduction and reinforcement of cultural trends through communication. We'll see how people create media, how the media shape the culture in which people live, how the media reflect the culture in which they exist, and how individuals and groups use the media as their own means to shape, redefine, and change culture.

MEDIA

any formats, platforms, or vehicles that carry, present, or communicate information.

Innovations in mass media include the invention of the printing press and movable type in the fifteenth century, the creation of moving pictures at the turn of the twentieth century, and the adoption of the scrolling ticker by today's 24-hour news channels.

FROM THE TOWN CRIER TO TIKTOK: A BRIEF HISTORY

When we talk about the media, we're generally talking about the mass media. Before the invention of the printing press, the media did exist—the town crier brought news, and royal messengers traveled by horseback, every now and then hopping off to read a scroll aloud—but they did not exactly reach the masses. Most information passed by word of mouth. After the 1440s, when Johannes Gutenberg developed movable type for the printing press, printing text became much easier. Books and periodicals were produced and circulated at much greater rates and began to reach large audiences, becoming the first form of mass media. Since that time the terms *media* and *mass media* have become virtually synonymous—at least until the rise of social media.

Media innovations obviously didn't stop with movable type. In the 1880s, along came another invention: the moving picture or silent film. In the 1920s, films started to include sound. For many, this represented an improvement over the radio, which had come along about the same time as the silent film. Television was invented in the 1930s, although this technology didn't make its way into most American homes until after World War II. During the postwar period, new forms of media technology quickly hit the market, and the demand for media exploded: glossy magazines; color televisions; blockbuster movies; Betamax videos, then VHS videos, then DVDs; vinyl records, then 8-track tapes, then cassette tapes, then CDs—and

In 1963, for the first time, televisions beamed images such as this photo of police officers attacking a student in Birmingham, Alabama. How did television influence the reaction to events such as the civil rights movement?

once the internet came along, the sky was the limit! In 2021, 77 percent of the American population had broadband internet at home, with access clustered among the younger, wealthier, and better educated, while 15 percent used their smartphones in place of high-speed internet service (Pew Research Center, 2021c).

You're well aware of the numerous forms of media, but let's stop for a minute and contemplate the impact certain forms, such as television, have had on society. Again, televisions didn't become household staples in the United States until after World War II. From 1950, the year President Harry S Truman first sent military advisers to South Vietnam, to 1964, when Congress approved the Gulf of Tonkin Resolution calling for victory by any means necessary, the share of American households with television sets increased from 9 to 92 percent. During the Vietnam War, the American public witnessed military conflict in a way they never had before, and these images helped fuel the antiwar movement. Likewise, television played a large role in the civil rights movement of the 1950s and 1960s. Hearing about discrimination secondhand was very different than sitting with your family in the living room and watching images of police with attack dogs confronting peaceful protesters or turning fire hoses on little African American girls dressed up in their Sunday best.

TEXTS

Why do the adventures in fairy tales often begin once a mother dies? Are Blacks more often portrayed as professionals or criminals in television shows? How often are Asians the lead characters in mainstream films? Do men or women generally initiate conversation in U.S. (or Mexican) soap operas? These questions are all examples of textual analysis, analysis of the content of media in its various forms.

During the 1960s and 1970s, academic studies of culture focused largely on texts—for example, television talk shows, newspapers, and magazine pages. Scholars recognized the importance of finding out how people read and interpret and are influenced by these texts. These practices are called "audience studies." Sociologists have explored the way women read romance novels or how teenage girls interpret images of super-thin models in magazines. For example, in *Reading the Romance: Women, Patriarchy, and Popular Literature* (1987), Janice Radway argues that women exhibit a great deal of individual agency when reading romance novels, which helps them cope with their daily lives in a patriarchal society by providing both escapes from the drudgery of everyday life and alternative scripts. We do not just passively receive media; as readers or viewers, we experience texts through the lens of our own critical, interpretive, and analytical processes.

BACK TO THE BEGINNING: CULTURAL PRODUCTION

The media don't just spontaneously spring into being. They aren't organic; they're produced. You may have heard the expression "History is written by the winners." Well, before something becomes history, it first happens in the present. Who decides what the news is? How are decisions made about the content of television shows? To write his classic *Deciding What's News* (1979a), Herbert Gans went inside the newsrooms at *CBS Evening News*, *NBC Nightly News*, *Newsweek*, and *Time* in the late 1970s. He paid careful attention to the processes by which these news outlets made their decisions on editorial content, "writing down the unwritten rules of journalism," because rules, sociologists know, reflect values. Journalists strive for objectivity, but Gans illustrated the ways in which mainstream American values biased the finished product—that is, the news. The notion of "the facts, just the facts, and nothing but the facts" is a worthy idea but to a large degree a farce. Powerful boards of directors regulate the various media; writers, casting agents, directors, and producers decide what goes into sitcoms, soap operas, and after-school specials. Even the huge cache of secret government documents made available on the internet by WikiLeaks in 2010 (and in other dumps since then) was prescreened by individual hackers and researchers. The media are produced by human beings often working for organizations within which they can be influenced by market pressures to publish "fresh" stories rather than follow situations unfolding slowly over time (Usher, 2014).

Increasingly, however, human beings are only indirectly "deciding" what's news by designing the artificial intelligence algorithms that figure out which stories to put before our eyes (based on our past browsing behavior). The campaigns (and Russian operatives) gamed these algorithms in the 2016 and 2020 presidential elections, causing Facebook to alter its own software to try to better protect users against "fake news." Computers are even writing the news sometimes: Software writes simple stories like the recap of a sporting event, based on data from the game itself, and the bots get better and better with each passing day. Online activist and entrepreneur Eli Pariser (CEO of Upworthy) and others have become worried about what he calls the "filter bubble" or online echo chamber (Pariser, 2011). Since our newsfeed depends on our past clicks (or what our friends like), we risk never seeing new information that conflicts with our preexisting views—not a healthy algorithm for a robust, democratic society.

SOCIAL MEDIA

Just as when we talk about mass media, we lump together any technology that allows for the communication of ideas among a large number of people, such as television, radio, newspapers, and books. When we talk about

TikTok's interface shows an endless stream of short-form videos meant to capture the user's attention.

social media, we mean a whole variety of forms of communication including but not limited to TikTok, Instagram, Facebook, Twitter, and YouTube. Social media are technologies that allow users to create and share cultural content. They differ from mass media in the sense that users themselves primarily provide the content. Some people include electronic messaging apps such as Viber, WhatsApp, or Signal in the category of social media to the extent that they allow groups of people to communicate en masse and to share images, videos, and documents. The key distinction between social media and, say, telecommunications is the involvement of "content"—that is, communication that is not just ephemerally produced but rather stored and that can be accessed later.

Assuming your phone wasn't being tapped, when you hung up from a traditional landline, the conversation was no longer accessible. That's different than, say, a Zoom meeting recorded to your computer or to a remote storage service (i.e., the cloud). That's different than Instagram, where once you log off, people can still scroll through your posts from 10 minutes ago, yesterday, or even years ago. There are digital traces, either intentional as in the case of a Facebook or TikTok post or unintentional as in the case of messaging apps, that store our threads on their servers.

Although big corporations technically own social media platforms and do host content, they also exert much less editorial control than traditional media. The power of the individual on social media mimics the reconstruction of culture in the real world, allowing users to internalize norms and reinforce those norms through their own posts. However, the notion of a noisy town square of individuals voicing or amplifying opinions also has

SOCIAL MEDIA

technologies that allow users to produce, share, and consume media in a variety of formats.

its own complications. In recent years, we have seen how authoritarian governments can limit, control, and even secretly produce content online. They can also use social media accounts to identify and crack down on dissidents. Moreover, as much as we'd like to think that the cute video of our cat we tweeted out yesterday has just as good a chance as any of going viral if our friends like it and forward it on, research by Sharad Goel, Duncan Watts, and Daniel Goldstein (2012) showed that our chances are literally one in a million. Most chains of retweeting die out very fast. It usually still requires a big "broadcaster" to reach a lot of users. That broadcaster could be a celebrity with millions of followers or an established institution like *The New York Times*. That's all to say that even if they bill themselves as the return of the small town square, social media have many of the same dynamics as traditional mass media.

MEDIA EFFECTS

We now know that reflection theory is only half right. Culture does indeed reflect local-scale social relations within a society, but culture also affects society itself on a larger scale. In considering the media, mass culture, and subcultures, we can plot the media's effects in a two-dimensional diagram, as shown in Figure 3.1. The vertical dimension indicates whether the effect is intended (i.e., deliberate) or unintended. The horizontal axis depicts whether it is a short- or long-term effect. A short-term, deliberate media effect (section A in the illustration) would be advertising. A child today might see an ad for Cocoa Puffs on YouTube in the morning and that same afternoon still have the ad in mind while grocery shopping with their parents. The advertisers timed their content just right, with the pressure on Mom or Dad to buy that cereal. These days, advertising can be very short term. I search for symptoms of low vitamin D, wanting to know whether that might explain mysterious leg pains I've had lately. Before I can even read articles about vitamin D deficiency, I see ads for vitamin D supplements. When I scroll through a social media feed a half-hour later, vitamin advertisements start popping up everywhere. Eventually, I give in and click through to order one for delivery.

FIGURE 3.1 Media Effects

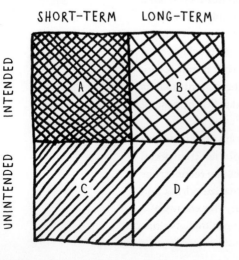

Section B of Figure 3.1, on the other hand, represents a deliberate, long-term media campaign. Here, a single theme is reinforced through repeated exposure, as in public service announcements (PSAs). Nonprofit organizations generally use PSA campaigns to educate the public. Some examples include Smokey the Bear (created in 1944, "Only you can prevent forest fires"),

Woodsy Owl (created in 1970, "Give a hoot, don't pollute"), and the "This is your brain on drugs" commercials from the Partnership for a Drug-Free America (the original fried egg aired in 1987, and the sequel frying-pan smash aired a decade later). A recent public service announcement about texting and driving states, "You don't want them responding to your text" next to an ambulance (Ad Council, 2018). Other recent campaigns focus on sexual harassment, suicide prevention, and health problems like type 2 diabetes.

Section C of Figure 3.1 represents media with short-term, unintended consequences. An example might be when teenagers play violent video games and then commit crimes almost identical to those portrayed in the game. You hear of such events every so often, and sometimes the media's creator will use the defense that the short-term response was not intended. In an interview, for example, the software producer or musician might be asked, "Did you know that your music is causing teenage boys to commit violent crimes?" And the response will be, "That is not my intention at all. I use violence as a metaphor." Scientific research hasn't yet ruled definitively one way or the other on this controversial subject, but many believe that the media occasionally have short-term, unintended effects. However, a controversial study of Facebook posts showed that social media can affect users' moods. The researchers manipulated the newsfeeds of 689,003 users, some of whom they showed primarily positive posts and some of whom they showed primarily negative posts. By following and analyzing the posting patterns of these users, they found that their moods changed significantly. Social media, then, impact us in ways of which we might not be consciously aware.

Finally, section D of the illustration represents the long-term, unintended effects of the media. Many people, not just cultural conservatives, argue that we have been desensitized to violence, sexual imagery, and other content that some people consider inappropriate for mass audiences. In the film industry, for example, the Production Code, also known as the Hays Code, was a set of standards created in 1930 (although it wasn't officially enforced until 1934) to protect the moral fabric of society. The fairly strict guidelines attested to the mainstream ideologies of the time (see the box on pages 106–7). Slowly, however, the power of the code began to erode because of the influence of television and foreign films, along with the realization that being condemned as immoral didn't prevent a film from becoming a success. In 1967, the movie rating system replaced the code. Over time, we have grown accustomed to seeing sexually explicit material in films, on television, and on the internet. Those who lament this desensitization seek to reinstitute controls over media content. But in an age of TikTok, YouTube, and myriad other forms of media distribution, it seems unlikely that the so-called genie can be put back in the bottle. It's not just in the realm of sex (or violence) that media have affected our sensibilities. Another example of the long-term, unintended consequences of media appears in the development and perpetuation of stereotypes, which we address next.

THE RACE AND GENDER POLITICS OF MAKING OUT

"When I'm good, I'm very good, but when I'm bad, I'm better." —ACTRESS MAE WEST

The movie industry's Production Code (1930) enumerated three "general principles":

1. No picture shall be produced that will lower the moral standards of those who see it. Hence the sympathy of the audience should never be thrown to the side of crime, wrongdoing, evil, or sin.
2. Correct standards of life, subject only to the requirements of drama and entertainment, shall be presented.
3. Law, natural or human, shall not be ridiculed, nor shall sympathy be created for its violation.

Specific restrictions were spelled out as "particular applications" of these principles:

- Nudity and suggestive dances were prohibited.

- The ridicule of religion was forbidden, and ministers of religion were not to be represented as comic characters or villains.
- The depiction of illegal drug use was forbidden, as well as the use of liquor, "when not required by the plot or for proper characterization."
- Methods of crime (e.g., safecracking, arson, smuggling) were not to be explicitly presented.
- References to "sex perversion" (such as homosexuality) and venereal disease were forbidden, as were depictions of childbirth.
- The language section banned various words and phrases considered to be offensive.
- Murder scenes had to be filmed in a way that would not inspire imitation in real life, and brutal killings could not be shown in detail. "Revenge in modern times" was not to be justified.
- The sanctity of marriage and the home had to be upheld. "Pictures shall not infer that low forms of sex relationship are the accepted or common thing." Adultery and illicit sex, although recognized as sometimes necessary to the plot, could not be explicit or justified; they were never to be presented as an attractive option.

Lucille Ball and Desi Arnaz in the hit television comedy of the 1950s, *I Love Lucy*. Even though their characters were married, they still did not share a bed.

- Portrayals of interracial relationships were forbidden.
- "Scenes of passion" were not to be introduced when not essential to the plot. "Excessive and lustful kissing" was to be avoided, along with any other physical interaction that might "stimulate the lower and baser element."
- The flag of the United States was to be treated respectfully, as were the people and history of other nations.
- "Vulgarity," defined as "low, disgusting, unpleasant, though not necessarily evil, subjects," must be treated "subject to the dictates of good taste." Capital punishment, "third-degree methods," cruelty to children and animals, prostitution, and surgical operations were to be depicted with similar sensitivity and discretion.

"Rules were made to be broken," the old saying goes. Filmmakers like Alfred Hitchcock pushed the boundaries of a 10-second time limit for kisses by filming a lip-lock for the maximum allotted time, panning away, and then returning to the couple still passionately embracing. Rules

such as this were slow to change, but not as slow as other conventions. For one thing, you can be sure that the people kissing were a man and a woman, and they were both White. In fact, in the beginning they would have been married, too, but that ideology—the sanctity of marriage—fell away more quickly on the silver screen than did notions about racial and gender hierarchies and stereotypes. The first on-screen interracial kiss, between Sidney Poitier and Katharine Houghton in *Guess Who's Coming to Dinner*, didn't occur until 1967, the same year the U.S. Supreme Court ruled that state laws preventing interracial marriage—known as antimiscegenation laws—were unconstitutional. And in a 1968 episode of *Star Trek*, William Shatner and Nichelle Nichols boldly ventured where no one had gone before with the first Black–White lip-lock televised in the United States. The first homosexual kiss between two women hit prime time in 1991 (on the television show *L.A. Law*, which received backlash from advertisers), while the first same-sex kiss between two men did not happen until 2001 on *Will and Grace*. Change in the media takes time; as society's ideologies about what constitutes good and bad love change, the media will reflect those changes by portraying more positive images of people loving whomever they choose.

Angel and Papi's romance on *Pose* provided representation for trans couples.

Mommy, Where Do Stereotypes Come From?

Analyze the role of media in both perpetuating and modifying cultural biases.

On December 22, 1941, two weeks after the Japanese attack on Pearl Harbor, *Time* magazine ran an article with the headline "How to Tell Your Friends from the Japs." Annotated photographs helped readers identify characteristics that would distinguish, for instance, friendly Chinese from the Japanese, America's enemies during World War II. The magazine offered the following rules of thumb, although it admitted that they were "not always reliable":

- Some Chinese are tall (average: 5 ft. 5 in.). Virtually all Japanese are short (average: 5 ft. 2½ in.).

- Japanese are likely to be stockier and broader-hipped than short Chinese.

- Japanese—except for wrestlers—are seldom fat; they often dry up and grow lean as they age. The Chinese often put on weight, particularly if they are prosperous (in China, with its frequent famines, being fat is esteemed as a sign of being a solid citizen).

- Chinese, not as hairy as Japanese, seldom grow an impressive moustache.

- Most Chinese avoid horn-rimmed spectacles.

- Although both have the typical epicanthic fold of the upper eyelid (which makes them look almond-eyed), Japanese eyes are usually set closer together.

- Those who know them best often rely on facial expression to tell them apart: The Chinese expression is likely to be more placid, kindly, open; the Japanese more positive, dogmatic, arrogant.

How can Gramsci's concept of hegemony, introduced earlier in the chapter, help us understand this piece from *Time*? Does this article tell us more about the physical differences between Japanese and Chinese or about the state of mind of the American public at the time? What values are reflected and projected? Are the descriptors empirical (based on fact) or normative (based on opinion)? This is what racism looks like in the media, and it clearly illustrates America's fear and hatred of the Japanese at that time. But most stereotypes in popular culture are not as purposive and blatant as those about the Japanese during World War II. In fact, modern media often subtly uphold discriminatory preconceptions, catering to the underlying beliefs historically reinforced by our cultural values.

Why do stereotypes matter? Even if you've never been the punchline of an offensive joke, you should know that they can evoke negative effects on the individual and institutional levels. For example, negative stereotypes about African American test performance can actually affect how Blacks score on tests. This phenomenon is called "stereotype threat," and experiments show that when test takers face negative stereotypes before taking a test, they perform more poorly (Steele & Aronson, 1995). Not surprisingly, positive stereotypes can have the opposite effect. In this way, stereotypes themselves contribute to the constant remaking of inequalities at an institutional level (i.e., college admissions). This trend also occurs in hiring practices, where employers internalize stereotyped notions of pools of applicants—say, Asians, older workers, women, and so on—and unconsciously (or even consciously) make decisions that perpetuate those very stereotypes. (We will discuss such dynamics in Chapter 9.) When lasting stereotypes permeate powerful institutions, we can say they have contributed to an ideology, an example of which might be White supremacy or patriarchy.

The controversial O. J. Simpson arrest photo. *Time* magazine was accused of darkening his features for its cover.

RACISM IN THE MEDIA

The media continue to reflect and perpetuate racist ideologies, even if less blatantly as those in the 1941 article in *Time*. Sometimes the racism is obvious, and these instances present us with the opportunity to discuss racism in the media. In early September 2005, just days after Hurricane Katrina had devastated the areas surrounding the Mississippi River basin, two photos quickly began to circulate on the internet amid discussion of racism and the role it played in the reaction (or inadequate government response) to the catastrophe. The first photo, published by the Associated Press, showed a young African American wading through chest-high water toting groceries; the caption proclaimed that the man had just been "looting a grocery store." The second photo pictured a White couple doing the same thing; the caption stated that the two were photographed "after finding bread and soda at a local grocery

The photo above, published by the Associated Press, shows a young Black man wading through chest-high water toting groceries; the caption proclaimed that the man had just been "looting a grocery store." The photo on the right pictures a White couple doing the same thing; the caption stated that the two were photographed "after finding bread and soda at a local grocery store."

store" (Ralli, 2005). The different analyses of these similar photos illustrated the idea that White looters, in their struggle to survive the catastrophe, were not committing a crime, whereas Blacks resorting to the same behavior were. Indeed, much of the coverage in the wake of Katrina focused on the looting, vandalism, and other criminal acts that took place. Critics have pointed out that these people did what most of us would logically do—that is, try to obtain food and water for our suffering families in the absence of competent government assistance and disaster relief. Because the city of New Orleans, which received the majority of the media attention, was 78 percent nonwhite, the victims were frequently portrayed as criminals.

The coverage of Hurricane Katrina, which received an exceptional amount of criticism publicly levied against such racially charged portrayals (unlike, for example, the December 1941 *Time* piece), supports the main thesis of Barry Glassner's *The Culture of Fear: Why Americans Are Afraid of the Wrong Things* (Glassner, 1999). Glassner asserts that, as a culture, we grossly exaggerate the frequency of rarely occurring events, often through amplification of a single instance through media repetition. We tend to divert or redirect our attention away from controversial or complex political, economic, and cultural issues and toward sensational but rare events. The media are the main vehicles through which this process occurs. In the case of Katrina, we blame the victims, the poorest of the poor, for not leaving the city, rather than ask how the government could leave its own citizens stranded like refugees without access to life's basic necessities.

Racial bias in the media goes far beyond major events like Hurricane Katrina. The skin tone of Black models is routinely lightened in postproduction, for example. What can be done about such practices, and who has the power to change them? According to a survey by *Publisher's Weekly* (an industry magazine), the percentage of Whites in the publishing industry has ranged from 86 to 89 percent. With White people making most of the decisions, Black media producers rarely receive the representation they deserve. Looking at the top 500 books used as "comps" over the period from 2013 to 2019, Stanford University researchers Laura McGrath and Jonathan Morales found that only 22 were written by nonwhite authors (of which 10 were Black authors). "Comps" are the successful books that agents, authors, and publishers use to compare their books to in order to make a case that they will sell, as in "It's *Harry Potter* meets *Lord of the Rings*." So, within book publishing at least, overwhelmingly White editors compare new books to other books by White writers. No wonder authors of color find it challenging to get a book out there.

SEXISM IN THE MEDIA

Gender affects both the quantity and quality of media representation. Women, for example, make up only 31 percent of speaking characters in films and 23 percent of protagonists (main characters) despite representing half the population. They make up less than a quarter of the people in the news media. They are underrepresented both as subjects of the news and as news anchors, reporters, and especially as experts. This trend is not benign; rather, it is a self-fulfilling prophecy. The lower the share of women as news subjects, the less likely are women willing to run for political office (Haraldsson & Wängnerud, 2019); the representation of women as experts—or lack thereof—has a particularly notable effect on how many female candidates stand for election in a given country. In this way, when women internalize messages that they do not belong in the public sphere, they are less likely to be heard as voices, perpetuating a vicious cycle of underrepresentation.

Media depictions of women often create highly skewed versions of femininity. For instance, U.S. media in particular and Western media more generally glamorize and perpetuate unrealistic ideals of feminine beauty. The feminine beauty ideal of slenderness is a relatively recent and racially tinged phenomenon. In centuries past, being plump was considered attractive. In periods and places where food is scarce, being heavier seems more attractive as a sign of wealth, but when food is abundant, slenderness becomes more of an ideal (particularly for women). However, as Sabrina Strings shows in *Fearing the Black Body* (2019), this story is too simple and ignores the role of race and imperialism. It is true that when sugar (called "white gold") started pouring into Europe during the sixteenth century from its colonies, and waistlines started expanding, anxiety over out-of-control bodies took hold. Thinness no

A depiction of Saartje Baartman, a Khoikhoi woman who was trafficked to London in 1810 and put on display for onlookers to scrutinize her figure.

longer was seen as an economic deficit but rather as a sign of moral worth, especially given the ascetic ethic of self-deprivation and self-regulation that came along with the Protestant Reformation. Soon, a large body was seen as a failing, a sign of weak character and lazy habits. This association was always interlaced with racialization.

At the start of the age of imperialism, Black Africans were depicted as emaciated servants in European paintings. But as the abovementioned cultural shift regarding fatness occurred, Blacks' iconography also shifted: As fatness took on the tarnish of gluttony and stupidity, it became increasingly associated with Black women in European art and pseudoscience of the late seventeenth and eighteenth centuries. By the nineteenth and twentieth centuries, a moral panic around fatness emerged, sanctified by the medicalization of obesity, which itself had racialized tones. In other words, for the past three centuries, body size and race have been inextricably linked, according to Strings (2019).

Some argue that the repetitive bombardment of images of idealized body types as well as those posted on social media by women who have internalized this ideal decreases girls' self-esteem and may contribute to eating disorders. Women's magazines have received heavy criticism, although some researchers (such as Angela McRobbie from the United Kingdom) have taken care to show that women who are active, critical readers still enjoy reading women's magazines. However, as the Canadian sociologist Dawn Currie (1999) points out, although girls can choose which magazines, if any, to read and how to read them critically, they can't control the images available to them in those and other texts.

Feminist media critiques also focus on images of violence against women. Jean Kilbourne has become one of the most popular lecturers at college and university campuses across America. In 1979, she released a film titled *Killing Us Softly: Advertising's Image of Women*, which examines the ways that women are maimed, sliced, raped, and otherwise deformed in advertising images. One classic example is a photo that shows the image of a woman's body in a garbage can, with only her legs and a fantastic pair of high heels on her feet visible. The message is clear: These shoes are, literally, to die for. Kilbourne's point is also clear: Such images help sustain a kind of symbolic violence against women. In this critique, advertising both reflects the underlying culture that produced it and creates desirable narratives that enter women's and men's lives with causal force.

Some girls (with the help of their parents) have responded by creating their own magazines that focus on topics other than makeup, clothing, and boys, as mainstream teenage magazines do. For example, *New Moon Girls* is written and edited by girls aged 8–13 and contains no advertisements. Likewise, magazines exist for adult women that have more pro-woman messages; *Ms. Magazine* was founded in 1971 during the feminist movement to give voice to women and explore women's issues. Because such magazines don't accept advertising from huge makeup companies and designer fashion houses, however, they are often less economically viable than mainstream women's magazines, which carry ads on as many as 50 percent of their pages. For example, *Bitch* magazine ("It's a noun; it's a verb; it's a magazine"), which was founded in 1996, is a self-declared feminist response to pop culture. It is supported by advertisers but is a not-for-profit publication. However, in 2022, *Bitch* could no longer make a go of it economically and said goodbye to its readership. Of course, magazines may be less relevant today in an era when teens and young adult influencers themselves post manipulated images on social media that perpetuate unrealistic images of women. Throughout this chapter, we've seen a transition from spoken to written to digital transfers of information, but the presentation and perpetuation of cultural values occur despite the format.

Political Economy of the Media

▌ Describe the systemic forces behind consumer-centered culture.

In the United States, we (politicians especially) spend a lot of time talking about freedom, particularly freedom of the press. The freedom to say whatever you want represents one of the great markers of the "land of the free." The press, however, is hardly free. Most broadcasting companies are privately owned in the United States, supported financially by advertising and, therefore, likely to reflect the biases of their owners and backers. (Compare this model with that in the United Kingdom, where the British Broadcasting Company [BBC] cannot accept private funding, households must pay fees for owning television sets, and these fees help cover the BBC's operating costs. This system is beginning to change, however, because of increasing economic pressures, such as competition from satellite television.)

In 2017, just two corporations—Alphabet, the parent company of Google, and Facebook—generated 20 percent of global advertising revenue

DIGITAL.WWNORTON.COM/YOUMAYASK8

To see my interview with Allison Pugh, go to
digital.wwnorton.com/youmayask8

(Zenith USA, 2018). Ownership alone does not equal censorship, but when the majority of the media lies in the hands of a few players, it is easier to ignore or purposely suppress messages that the owners of the media don't agree with or support. For example, Apple's App Store is the dominant player in the sales of apps for smartphones. Apple demands to review every app to ensure that the content does not cross "over the line," which they explain is a boundary that developers will just know when they reach it. This type of vague policy tends to promote a "chilling effect" whereby developers—not knowing where this mystical "line" is—choose to avoid any content they think might be at all objectionable. Receiving Apple's approval is important because once developers have made an app for Apple's iOS platform they cannot sell it anywhere but the App Store. Is Apple protecting its shoppers, or ruling the app developers through a combination of monopoly power and shadowy threats? As corporate control of the media becomes more and more centralized (owned by fewer and fewer groups), the range of opinions available will decrease and corporate censorship (the act of suppressing information that may reflect negatively on certain companies and/or their affiliates) will further compromise the already tarnished integrity of the mainstream media.

The internet, to some extent, has partially balanced out communications monopolies. It's much easier to put up a website expressing alternative views than it is to broadcast a television or radio program suggesting the same. Led by Ethan Zuckerman, the Center for Civic Media at MIT works to leverage the internet for the promotion of local activism. One of the MIT projects, VGAZA or Virtual Gaza, allowed Palestinians in the Gaza Strip to document crises and share local stories globally while under embargo. But the internet is not beyond the realm of political economy. Yelp.com, for example, reports that updates to Google's search algorithm place Google+ reviews higher in Google's search results than reviews for the same venues on other sites, shifting web traffic to Google+ at the expense of competing review sites like Yelp and Thrillist (Leswing, 2015). Moreover, the internet often acts as a force for reinforcing our prejudices, including extremist views, by creating a "filter bubble" in the words of Eli Pariser (2011), author of a book by that title. That is, the major corporations that own the backbones of how we interact with the internet, such as Alphabet, Meta, and so on, have a profit incentive to feed us news, posts, and so on that confirm our preexisting desires, beliefs, and viewpoints because we are more likely to click on such links.

CONSUMER CULTURE

America is often described as a consumer culture, and rightly so. In my interview with sociologist Allison Pugh, she pointed out that "corporate marketing to children is a 22 billion dollar industry." She then added, "Children 8 to 11 ask for between two and four toys [for Christmas], and they receive eleven on average!" (Conley, 2011a). Sales on major patriotic holidays (Veterans Day, Memorial Day, Presidents' Day) thrive based on the notion that our duty as American citizens is to be good shoppers. As Sharon Zukin points out in her book on shopping culture, *Point of Purchase: How Shopping Changed American Culture* (2003), 24 hours after the terrorist attacks of September 11, 2001, Mayor Rudy Giuliani urged New Yorkers to take the day off and go shopping. The term consumerism, however, refers to more than just buying merchandise; it refers to the belief that the acquisition of material possessions leads to happiness and fulfillment. Versace, J. Crew, and real estate agents in certain hip neighborhoods are not just peddling shoes, jeans, and apartments; they are also selling a self-image, a lifestyle, and a sense of belonging and self-worth. The media and advertising in particular play a large role in the creation and maintenance of consumerism.

CONSUMERISM
the steady acquisition of material possessions, often with the belief that happiness and fulfillment can thus be achieved.

ADVERTISING AND CHILDREN

The rise of the consumer-citizen has been met with increasing criticism, but how does our society produce these consumer-citizens? Canadian author and activist Naomi Klein published *No Logo: Taking Aim at the Brand Bullies* in 2000. In this book, Klein (2000) analyzes the growth of advertising in schools. Pepsi and Coca-Cola now bargain for exclusive rights to sell their products within schools, brand-name fast foods often appear in cafeterias, and company logos light up athletic fields as proud sponsors.

One striking example of in-school propaganda is Google Classroom. Google gives out low-cost Chromebook laptop computers to many schools and school districts, charging only a $30 annual management fee. The computers include a suite of web-based software applications ranging from Google Docs to Google Classroom (a learning management system). Going from basically nothing in 2012, Google had shipped almost 8 million devices to schools by 2016, with the trend line showing no signs of flattening out anytime soon. For example, the city of Chicago, the third-largest school district

These third-grade students at an elementary school in San Clemente, California, seem to be very concentrated on their Google Chromebook laptops. Do you think Google is doing a good thing by providing low-cost technology to school districts, or is the company creating millions of consumer-citizens?

in the country, saved about $1.6 million per year in technology costs by switching to Google (Singer, 2017). Sounds like a win for everyone from the company whose motto was "Don't be evil," right? Well it is, in some ways, but many parents worry about the data their children are providing the company whose financial model is based almost solely on advertising revenue. Since students will migrate their educational accounts over to their noneducational Google accounts, the company will have "watched" the developmental trajectory of these students throughout most of their childhood and now be able to better target them with ads.

All of this advertising creates a self-sustaining consumer culture among children, albeit one that plays out differently for low-income and high-income families. Let's hear Pugh discuss her research with me again on this point:

> I found, for low-income parents, a practice of what I ended up calling "symbolic indulgence." They couldn't afford everything that a middle-class family might consider part of an adequate resource to childhood. So, they might not have blocks, or a bike. They might not have those basics, but they would have the thing that kind of gave the child something to talk about at school [such as a Gameboy]. And so it would be these highly [socially] resonant items [that parents would purchase]. (Conley, 2011a)

In other words, these highly symbolic purchases of "in" toys or devices gave low-resource families an avenue to feel as though they were participating in the broader American consumer culture. Meanwhile, ironically, middle-class parents downplayed their consumerism:

> "I'm not materialistic. I'm not one of those bad parents you read about on TV . . . never being able to say no to my kids" [they would say]. So what I found for them is the systematic practice of "symbolic deprivation." The kid would have an enormous amount of stuff. There would be mostly yeses in that child's life. But there would be particular things that that child didn't have, so that they [the parents] could really kind of convince me, and convince themselves, that they were honorable people. (Conley, 2011a)

In other words, how consumer culture manifests depends not just on corporate advertising but also on the local social systems in which kids and their families find themselves.

CULTURE JAMS: HEY CALVIN, HOW 'BOUT GIVING THAT GIRL A SANDWICH?

People can take back the media or use the media for their own ends. In that sense, Issa Rae, whom we met at the beginning of the chapter, used her knowledge of cultural systems and networks to gradually gain an audience for her media and to launch her career. She found a neglected area of representation in the media (accurate portrayals of race), and she worked to fill it herself. Culture jamming (a term that evolved from radio jamming,

CULTURE JAMMING
the act of turning media against themselves.

Two satirical ads from *Adbusters* magazine. How do these ads critique or subvert the tobacco and fashion industries?

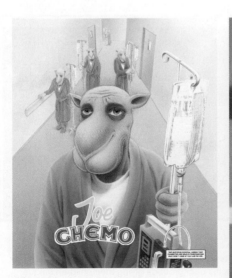
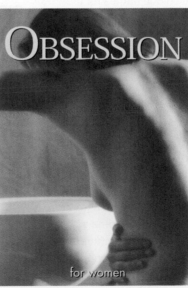

WHAT'S IN A NAME?

I named my first two kids E and Yo Xing Heyno Augustus Eisner Alexander Weiser Knuckles, so forgive me if I didn't understand all the fuss about Beyonce and Jay-Z naming their kids Blue Ivy, Rumi, and Sir Carter. After all, unlike in countries such as France or Japan, no U.S. laws constrain what we can name our offspring; only names that would be considered abusive can be stopped. Names present a unique measure of culture: There are few rules, and no institutions attempt to directly influence our choices, unlike almost every other aspect of culture from food to film to fashion. Thus trends in names are as close to a pure, unmediated, reflective mirror of societal culture as we can get.

In that light, it was almost inevitable that Beyonce and Jay-Z chose unique names for their children. There's a long tradition of celebrities marking their status by giving atypical names to their children. Perhaps you might have heard of Moon Unit Zappa? Born in 1967 to musician Frank Zappa, she was perhaps one of the first notable celebrity offspring given a "weird" moniker in the television age. The 1960s was the Age of Aquarius, after all. Besides her own siblings, she pioneered a trend followed by uncapitalized "america," the child of Abbie Hoffman; and Free, the spawn of Barbara Hershey and David Carradine, just to mention a few. Fast-forward to Gwyneth Paltrow's daughter, Apple Martin, and it should come as no surprise that celebrities still do things differently.

The more interesting sociological phenomenon that Blue Ivy, Rumi, and Sir Carter embody, as the children of African American parents, is the rise of unique Black names. Around the same time celebrities started thinking up names that otherwise served as nouns, verbs, or adjectives, African Americans began to abandon long-standing naming patterns. Until the civil rights movement, a typical Black name might have been Franklin or Florence, but after the Black Power movement, Blacks wanted to assert their individuality and break ties from the dominant society. The proportion of unique names—those that appear in birth records only once for that year—shot up.

Until about 1960, the proportion of unique names for girls in the United States hovered around

Beyonce and Jay-Z's choice of unique names for their children represents a larger sociological trend of parents from specific backgrounds giving their children unique names.

20 percent for Whites and 30 percent for Blacks. Throughout the decade, the number of White girls with unique names inched up to about 25 percent, but for Black girls, it skyrocketed, peaking around 1979 at more than 60 percent (based on Illinois data). Harvard sociologists Stanley Lieberson and Kelly S. Mikelson (1995) examined this trend in their paper following it only through the 1980s, but I'm willing to guess that the practice has continued at a similar rate. Even an apparently individual practice like unique naming can appear in patterns, illustrating the collective influence of culture and the environments in which we exist.

You might think that all this name coinage would lead to gender confusion in kindergarten. Though I am not advocating gender rigidity, there is some evidence that gender-ambiguous names can cause problems for boys. Economist David Figlio (2007) found that "boys named Sue" tend to get into more trouble at school around sixth grade when puberty hits.

But it turns out that even unique names are gendered. When Lieberson and Mikelson gave a list of unique names they found in the Illinois database to respondents, the vast majority identified the gender of the actual child—for example, Cagdas (boy) or Shameki (girl)—correctly. My own experience mirrors this. Nobody mistakes Yo for a girl's name. Meanwhile, three other Es, who heard about my daughter's name from my public musings, wrote to me. (So much for unique . . .) Two of them were female, bringing the total to 75 percent female. I only wish I had 25 other kids so I could test the gender of every letter in the alphabet. If you think I'm crazy, move to Paris.

another form of guerrilla cultural resistance that involves seizing control of the frequency of a radio station) means co-opting media in spite of themselves. Part of a larger movement against consumer culture and consumerism, it's based on the notion that advertisements are basically propaganda. Culture jamming differs from appropriating advertisements for the sake of art and sheer vandalism (where the sole goal is the destruction of property), although advertisers probably don't care too much about this latter distinction. Numerous anticonsumerist activist groups have sprung up, such as *Adbusters*, a Canadian magazine that specializes in spoofs of popular advertising campaigns. For example, it parodied a real Calvin Klein campaign (which advanced the career of Kate Moss and ushered in an age of ultra-thin, waiflike models) with a presumably bulimic woman vomiting into a toilet. *Adbusters* also sponsors an annual Buy Nothing Day (held, with great irony, on the day after Thanksgiving, known in retail as "Black Friday," the busiest shopping day of the year), which encourages people to do just that—buy nothing on this specific day of the year—so that they can reclaim their buying power and focus on the noncommercial aspects of the holiday, such as spending time with family and friends.

Another *Adbusters* spoof caricatured the legendary Joe Camel, the anthropomorphic advertising icon of Camel cigarettes from 1987 until 1997, when R. J. Reynolds, the tobacco firm that conjured up the character, voluntarily stopped using his image after receiving complaints from Congress and various public-interest groups that its ads primarily targeted children. (In 1991, a *Journal of the American Medical Association* study found that more 5- and 6-year-old kids recognized Joe Camel than they did Mickey Mouse or Fred Flintstone [Fischer et al., 1991].) In the *Adbusters* spoof, "Joe Chemo" walks down a hospital hallway with an IV, presumably dying of cancer caused by smoking.

Conclusion

The chapter opened with a description of Issa Rae's rise to the pinnacle of cultural success. Now perhaps you can see how she fits into a discussion of culture and media. She contravened media stereotypes of young Black women in the way she depicted characters in her show, *The Misadventures of Awkward Black Girl*. She leveraged new media and technologies—namely, YouTube.com and gofundme.com—to launch a career in an older form of media (television and film). CNN, the *Times*, and other media outlets picked up the story of *Awkward Black Girl* because their cultural gatekeepers—that is, reporters—learned about it through word of mouth.

But her show only went truly viral thanks to mainstream media like *The New York Times*. We may think of social media and mass media as two separate ecologies, but they very much articulate with each other, each amplifying the other's messages. In the case of the rise of Issa Rae, that relationship between new and old media can lift someone from obscurity to renowned cultural success. Rae's series brought people together to understand others' experiences of the world; however, when it comes to politics, we have also seen how media can further drive us apart, as social networks and conflicting ideologies increasingly sort us into two worlds with different values, narratives, and even facts. It may be no coincidence that the most politically partisan period of the modern era coincides with the rise of social media.

This chapter has presented some new ways of looking at culture: how we construct it, how it affects us, and what this means for understanding ourselves and the world in which we live. Do you now have a new understanding of culture? Can you now see your own culture through a critical lens? What have you previously taken for granted that you can now view as a product of our culture? Can you now look at the media in a different way? Don your critical thinking cap and put some of the tools you've just learned into practice.

PRACTICE

SUBCULTURE WARS

Some observers think the internet functions as a homogenizing force that drives all eyeballs to the latest meme and creates winner-take-all cultural markets. Others suggest that by allowing geographically dispersed individuals to organize around common interests, the internet and social media create a cultural garden where a thousand flowers can bloom. What do you think? Can it go both ways?

TRY IT!

How do subcultures appropriate and reinterpret mainstream cultural memes? Pick an interest from the list below and two subcultures. Search these combinations and see how these subcultures form unique communities and practices around that hacked theme—for example, Goth Cats versus Emo Cats. You're welcome to go to Google, YouTube, Reddit, Pinterest, or other online sites to research the combinations.

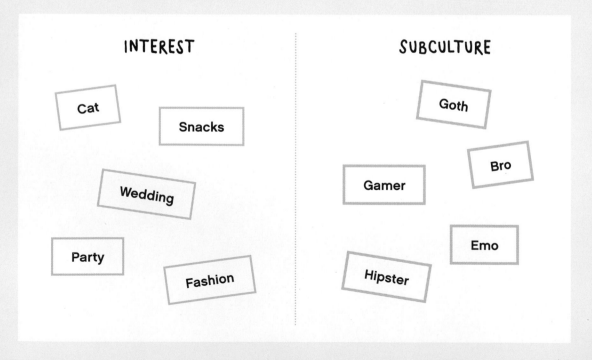

INTEREST

Cat
Snacks
Wedding
Party
Fashion

SUBCULTURE

Goth
Bro
Gamer
Emo
Hipster

How do the two subcultures put their unique stamps on something otherwise generic and mainstream? What are the chances that the subcultural interpretation will go viral and influence the mainstream?

PARADOX

4

THE MOST IMPORTANT ASPECTS OF SOCIAL LIFE ARE THOSE CONCEPTS WE LEARN WITHOUT ANYONE TEACHING US.

Socialization and the Construction of Reality

Think back to your first day of college. What did you do upon arriving at the classroom? Presumably, you sat in a chair. You probably opened a notebook or a laptop. When the professor walked in and called the class to attention, you stopped talking to the person next to you (or, if you didn't, you at least knew that you should). You did not sit on anyone's lap. A million dollars says that you wore clothes. Is all of this an accurate description of what occurred?

So how did you know what to do? Why did you sit in a chair and not on the floor? What if the room had no furniture? If a blackboard hung on one wall, you probably still sat facing it even in the absence of desks. Why? How did you know to bring paper or a computer? Did you receive an e-mail earlier in the week with explicit instructions telling you to do so? Why did you put on clothes this morning? You've internalized many unwritten rules about social behavior and public interaction. We call the process by which you learn how to become a functioning member of society socialization. Congratulations! You've been properly socialized.

SOCIALIZATION

the process by which individuals internalize the values, beliefs, and norms of a given society and learn to function as members of that society.

Imagine Mr. Spock, Tarzan, or an android trying to disguise himself as a college freshman. The droid would have to be programmed in minute detail with an endless list of possible reactions to potential situations. Think about your responses to the following situations versus the potential responses of our droid: You know how to answer when someone asks "What's up?"; you know to shift your knees when someone else needs to slip in or out of a row of seats in the lecture hall; you know to wait your turn when asking a question in lecture or discussion section; you know how to react when someone yells "Fire!" during class and then screams (versus a student shouting the same word during a final exam and then laughing). You know how to react to all of these scenarios, but the droid doesn't. He hasn't been socialized. Think how much you have needed to learn, how much knowledge you have internalized and processed, in order to understand that making direct eye contact with someone in a crowded elevator is inappropriate, whereas such behavior at a crowded party might be acceptable. The former might be considered creepy; the latter, flirting.

One famous test in the computer science field of artificial intelligence is the Turing Test, in which a subject has two parallel conversations, one with an actual human and one with a computer. Both occur via instant messaging or some other text-based platform. If the subject can't reliably distinguish the computer from the living human, then the computer passes the Turing Test (named for the scientist Alan Turing, who first proposed the test in a 1950 research paper). A computer did not pass the test until 2014 fooling 33 percent of judges for five minutes—Turing had set the threshold at 30 percent (*Guardian*, 2014). Now imagine adding facial expressions, body language, and other nonverbal communication cues to the test criteria. It quickly becomes clear why to be human is to be socialized and that true artificial intelligence is still a long way off.

By the end of this chapter you'll be able to:

- Identify examples of socialized behaviors in your own life.
- Explain the influential role of others in forming an individual's self-image.
- Identify social institutions and the processes used to mold functional members of society.
- Evaluate your own status set and its related conflicting responsibilities or expectations.
- Describe the shared meanings assigned to social scripts and how they impact social interactions.

Socialization: The Concept

▌ Identify examples of socialized behaviors in your own life.

Socialization, then, as defined by Craig Calhoun in the *Dictionary of the Social Sciences* (2002), is "the process through which individuals internalize the values, beliefs, and norms of a society and learn to function as its members" (p. 47). Starting from when you were born, your interactions with the rest of the world have shaped who you are. For babies, the primary unit of socialization is generally the family. At some point, you were potty-trained, presumably with the help of your parents or other family members. As children grow older and enter the educational system, school becomes a key location in their socialization. In school, you probably learned to sit facing the front of the classroom, to raise your hand before asking or answering a question, and not to talk when the teacher was speaking (and the punishment for failing to follow this rule). By the time you entered college, you probably did not need punishments to reinforce these behaviors because you had *internalized* the rules that govern situations in which students and teachers operate. As the examples that open this chapter illustrate, however, we learn more than explicit sets of rules. We learn how to interact on myriad levels in an endless number of situations.

New situations test the limits of your socialization. Have you ever been to a new place and felt unsure about how to behave? If you were shy and bookish in high school, you may not know what to wear or how to act when your new party-going college friends take you to a raucous fraternity party. You may take parties on television and in movies as models, but the party you are attending may not be quite the same. If, on the other hand, you've been going to similar parties, maybe even at the very same fraternity, with an older brother or sister for the past year or two, this particular party will

Early in elementary school you were taught to raise your hand to speak in class. Can you think of other examples of internalized behavior?

not present any sort of anxiety. You'll know what to wear, which bathroom to use, whether or not it is cool to post photos to Instagram, what music to like, and which songs deserve an eye-roll. Your previous experience as a tagalong may now make you a well-socialized leader among your freshman peers.

LIMITS OF SOCIALIZATION

While socialization is necessary for people to function in society, individuals are not simply blank slates onto which society transcribes its norms and values. Biology also plays an important role. Identical twins raised hundreds or even thousands of miles apart may experience the same pain in their right arms, love the same brand of beer, and fiddle with their keys when they feel nervous—score one point for nature. Take another set of twins, however, who were separated at birth in the early 1900s. One of them was raised as a Jew and the other became a Nazi—score one for nurture. So, which— nature or nurture—is correct? Both and neither. In sociology, we tend to think less about right and wrong and more about how certain theories help explain different aspects of our social world. The concept of socialization helps us understand how people become functioning members of society. Like most concepts, however, socialization can be limited in its explanatory power. Have you ever heard someone discussing a "problem child"? The conversation might go something like this: "I just don't know what's wrong with him. He comes from such a nice family. And his older brothers are such nice, respectful boys." How did this child go astray? The primary unit of socialization, the family, seems to have been functional. The other children in that unit went on to lead happy and productive lives. What else might explain the youngest son's delinquency? For starters, human beings have agency, meaning that despite our environmental limits (e.g., we cannot choose our parents or siblings, and U.S. law requires that all children receive schooling), we also make individual choices about how to interact with that environment. We can physically walk out of the school, fall asleep in class, or run away from home. Those choices stem from both the environmental (e.g., social) influences we have experienced and internalized as well as genetic dispositions that affect our behavior.

"HUMAN" NATURE

Does "human nature" really exist? Physiology prompts you to urinate, but socialization tells you where and when to do so. Interaction shapes us, such that without society the human part of human nature would not develop. We can observe this phenomenon in children who were raised by animals or denied human contact. These extreme and tragic examples demonstrate the power of socialization. Take the horrific case of "Anna," a young girl whose true age was unknown but estimated at about five years, who was found in torturous conditions, bound to a chair in an attic, where she had been left almost completely alone in the dark since birth. Her nutritional requirements had been minimally met, and it is believed that her only regular human contact was when her mother delivered these small meals. She could not properly speak or use her limbs, or even walk, when she was discovered. She did not respond to light or sounds the way children normally do. With some care and attention, the nurses at the treating hospital were able to provoke some giggles and coos by tickling her. Eventually, she was able to make speech-like sounds and gain more control of her body, but she never developed to the level of most children her age and died a few years later. Some of the doctors examining her wondered if she had been born mentally disabled, but ultimately, they opined that she could not have survived such an environment unless she had been healthy at birth.

The professionals who cared for Anna and followed her case reached five general conclusions:

1. Her inability to develop past an immature mental capacity "is largely the result of social isolation."

2. "It seems almost impossible for any child to learn to speak, think, and act like a normal person after a long period of isolation."

3. When compared with other cases of isolated children, the similarities in her case "seem to indicate that the stages of socialization are to some extent necessarily related to the stages of organic development."

4. "Anna's history . . . seems to demonstrate that human nature is determined by the child's communicative social contacts as much as by his organic equipment and that the system of communicative symbols is a highly complex business acquired early in life as the result of long and intimate training."

5. Theories of socialization are neither right nor wrong in this case "but simply inapplicable." (Davis, 1940, pp. 554−65)

This case illustrates that "human nature" is a blend of "organic equipment" (the raw materials we are physically made of) and social interaction (the environment in which we are raised). In what other ways can we look at the role of socialization (or lack thereof) and social structures in shaping our behaviors?

How does a small child playing peekaboo demonstrate the social process of creating the self?

Theories of Socialization

Explain the influential role of others in forming an individual's self-image.

Now that we have identified this process called socialization, we can turn to a few theories about how it works.

ME, MYSELF, AND I: DEVELOPMENT OF THE SELF AND THE OTHER

Have you ever seen a little girl cover her eyes with her hands and declare, "You can't see me now!"? She cannot distinguish between *I* and *you* and has not yet formed an idea of her individual self. How does the concept of the self develop? Sociologists argue that it emerges through a process of interaction. Perhaps the first full theory of the social self was developed by Charles Horton Cooley, who coined the term *the looking-glass self.* According to Cooley in *Human Nature and the Social Order* (1922), this sense of self results from our ability to assume the point of view of others and thereby imagine how they see us—that is, how we "look" in the mirror. We then test this "theory" of how we are perceived by gauging others' reactions and revise our theory by fine-tuning our "self-concept."

In the 1930s, George Herbert Mead further defined the process by which the social self develops (Figure 4.1). Infants only know the I—that is, one's sense of agency, action, or power. Through social interaction, however, they learn the me—that is, the self as a distinct object perceived by others (and by the I). Imagine, for example, that you are taking care of your two-year-old cousin Joey. He wants a cookie. You explain to him that you will happily give him a cookie just as soon as you go to the bathroom. He starts shouting, "I want cookie! I want cookie!" And you are ready to scream, "But I have to pee!" In a more rational moment, you might argue with your adorable cousin: "How would you feel if I demanded a cookie immediately when you entered the house after a six-hour car ride with no rest stops along the way and your bladder was about to explode?" Although such a line of logic might work with your cousin's seven-year-old sister, little Joey has yet to develop a sense of the other—that is, someone or something outside of oneself. In Joey's mind, there is no *other*, the *you* who hasn't seen a toilet in six hours;

SELF

the individual identity of a person as perceived by that same person.

I

one's subjective sense of having consciousness, agency, action, or power.

FIGURE 4.1 Mead's Stages of Social Development

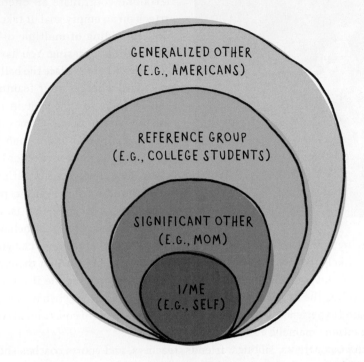

there is only the *self* who wants a cookie. We allow children a certain amount of leeway, but if your best friend behaved like this, you would accuse them of being childish, and you would be correct.

To function as fully adult members of society, we need to be able to recognize that other people also have wants, needs, and desires that are sometimes similar to and sometimes different from our own. Thus, imitation, play, and games are important components of childhood development. When a child imitates, they learn to recognize another. That's what peekaboo is all about. Eventually, kids understand that you are still there when they cover their eyes. They can then advance to play, according to Mead. During play, children make a distinction between the role of the self and the role of the other. Suppose that you are playing with your cousin Joey, who is now five years old, and he says, "Let's play school. I'll be the teacher and you be the student." He's recognizing you as the other, the student, who has a different set of motives, responses, and actions from the teacher. Eventually, children move beyond play to formal games.

Games involve a more complex understanding of multiple roles; indeed, you must recognize and anticipate what many other players are going to do in a given situation. Have you ever watched a swarm of toddlers try to play soccer? It's a mess. They're content to kick the ball; that's

ME

the self-perceived as an object by the "I"; the self as one imagines others perceive one.

OTHER

someone or something outside of oneself.

↑

Why are games an important part of child development? What do team sports like soccer teach us about multiple roles?

GENERALIZED OTHER

an internalized sense of the total expectations of others in a variety of settings—regardless of whether we've encountered those people or places before.

enough for them. They can't pass, let alone coordinate an offensive attack on an empty goal. It takes an understanding of multiple others to coordinate passing: You have to consider where to place the ball and calculate whether your teammate can make it to that spot in time for the pass to occur. Games such as soccer involve more than just hand—eye (or foot—eye) coordination. They involve a sophisticated understanding of the various positions others occupy—that is, they require a theory of social behavior, knowing how others are likely to react to different situations. The goalie is not likely to leave the box in front of the goal, even if I tempt them with the ball. But a defender or midfielder is likely to pursue me if I am not controlling the ball very well. We learn to anticipate these behaviors from repeated experience in the context of a particular sort of constrained social interaction—namely, a soccer game.

As our parents, siblings, friends, teachers, and sports coaches socialize us, we learn to think beyond the self to multiple others. According to Mead, however, that process brings us only halfway to being fully socialized. The final step is developing a concept of the generalized other, which represents an internalized sense of the total expectations of others in a variety of settings—regardless of whether we've encountered those people or places before. In this way, we should be able to interact and coexist with complete strangers in a wide range of social settings, not just in the constrained situation of a game with known rules. For example, the perception of the generalized other keeps you from taking off your pants to lounge more comfortably in the park on hot summer days, from singing loudly on the bus no matter how much you are enjoying the song on Spotify, and from picking a wedgie in public. We can, and do, continually update our internal sense of the generalized other as we gather new information about norms and expectations in different contexts.

For instance, as a child, your parents may have chided you for picking your nose. You had to be taught that this is unacceptable behavior, because otherwise it might seem perfectly reasonable. You have something in your nose, it's bothering you, you want to remove whatever is stuck there, and, lo and behold, your finger is just the right size. It's remarkably convenient. However, you learn not to pick your nose because it's a socially unacceptable action. But wait! Sometimes you might catch your dad picking his nose in the bathroom at home, so you revise the original lesson and realize what is most important: not to pick your nose in public. You may even have been taught explicitly that certain activities that are acceptable in private are unacceptable in public. The concept of the generalized other shapes our actions by our internalization of what is, and is not, acceptable in different social situations. Some of us may have internalized the notion that nose picking is inherently disgusting and should never be done anywhere. Some of us may have internalized the notion that nose picking is a little gross but believe it's okay when done in private. If you walked outside right now and saw a child picking his nose, you might think "Ew," but you could laugh because he is, after all, a child. On the other hand, if his mom was picking her nose too, you might give her a look of disapproval for violating an established social norm.

People may also intentionally violate established norms. Female members of the "Free the Nipple" movement participate in rallies in public settings wearing no top. This conscious violation of the U.S. social norm (and laws in some places) that prohibits women from exposing their breasts functions as a protest of the double standard that men can go shirtless in public while women cannot. Many adherents to the movement also refute the idea that a woman can display almost all of her breasts in a bikini top or low-cut dress, but not the nipple itself. While topless beaches and certain other venues now accept the values promoted by "Free the Nipple," this movement has not made a lot of progress as of yet in changing community norms as a whole.

Agents of Socialization

Identify social institutions and the processes used to mold functional members of society.

Socialization never reaches a stopping point; even as adults, we constantly experience socialization and resocialization in new situations and relationships. Learning new "appropriate" or accepted behaviors may occur when our partner kicks us under the table at dinner when we make an "inappropriate" comment or when we stream a favorite show and unconsciously take in the styles of dress, talking, and so on that we later find ourselves mimicking. Even just taking the bus on a random day contributes to our social selves. Despite the important influences of these everyday experiences, a few major institutions do a lot of the heavy lifting in terms of socialization. We already talked about the media in Chapter 3. The criminal justice system also attempts to serve as an agent of socialization. Next we will discuss some of these major institutions, starting with the family.

FAMILIES

For most individuals, the family is the primary unit of socialization. If you have siblings, you may develop the sense that parents treat older and younger children differently. The general impression is that the younger siblings get away with more. Parents, having already gone through the experience of child rearing, may relax their attitudes and behaviors toward later children (even if unconsciously). Note, too, that socialization is a two-way street. Information doesn't always flow from the older to the younger family members. For example, children of immigrants who are immersed in the U.S. school system may have parents who maintain less contact with mainstream American communities. These children often take on the role of an agent of socialization by teaching their parents the language and other tools of cultural assimilation instead of the other way around. In a similar vein, a study by economist Ebonya Washington (2008) showed that members of Congress who had daughters were more likely to vote for feminist measures. Perhaps daughters socialize their parents into being more sensitive to women's concerns. Alternatively, when legislators have their own daughters' future to worry about, they may vote for legislative changes that will help them (and, by extension, women in general). It's hard to say whether this is really socialization at work or merely a change in rational, selfish calculations. Meanwhile, sociologist Emily Rauscher and I found that, for the average American, daughters made parents more politically conservative, specifically with respect to views about sexuality (Conley & Rauscher, 2013).

Various demographics affect the socialization that occurs within the family. Parents from different social class backgrounds socialize their

According to Annette Lareau, how do working-class and middle-class families structure their children's free time differently? What are the results of these different socializing behaviors?

children differently. For example, when asked what values they want their children to have, middle-class parents are more likely to stress independence and self-direction, whereas working-class parents prioritize obedience to external authority (Kohn & Schooler, 1983). Indeed, sociologists have long recognized that the parents' social class matters, but how exactly this privilege is transmitted to children (beyond strictly monetary benefits) has been less clear. To better understand this process, ethnographer Annette Lareau spent time in both Black and White households with children approximately 10 years of age. She found that middle-class parents, both Black and White, are more likely to engage in what she calls "concerted cultivation." They structure their children's leisure time with formal activities (such as soccer leagues and piano lessons) and reason with them over decisions in an effort to foster their kids' talents.

Working-class and poor parents, in contrast, focus on the "accomplishment of natural growth." They give their children the room and resources to develop but let them to decide how they want to structure their free time. A greater division between the social life of children and that of the adults exists in such households (Lareau, 2002). Whereas middle-class parents send their kids off to soccer practice, music lessons, and myriad other after-school activities, kids in poor families spend a disproportionate amount of time "hanging out," as has been observed by Jason DeParle in *American Dream* (2004), his chronicle of three families on public assistance struggling through the era of welfare reform in Milwaukee. Likewise, a 2006 study by Annette Lareau, Eliot Weingarter, and this author shows the same statistical results: Outside of school, disadvantaged children spend 40 percent more time in unstructured activities than their middle-class counterparts.

Middle-class kids, on the other hand, spend their days learning how to interact with adult authority figures, how to talk to strangers, how to follow rules, and how to manage schedules. From a very young age, they learn to use logic and reason to support their choices by mirroring their parents' explanations of why they can or cannot get what they want. Low-income parents, Lareau found, were more likely to answer their children with "Because I said so," instilling respect for authority but missing an opportunity to help their children develop logical reasoning skills commonly used in adult interactions. Middle-class kids discover the confidence that comes with achievements such as learning to play the piano or mastering a foreign language. Whether they actually have fun is unknown, but they are certainly socialized into the same kind of lifestyles that their parents hope them to have as adult professionals. In fact, the rise of the "overscheduled" child comes during a period when, for the first time in history, higher-income Americans work more hours than lower-income Americans. If we flip the equation and look at leisure time, it seems that getting lots of education might limit your fun time. Those with advanced degrees reported the fewest hours of weekly leisure time (31.3) while those who didn't graduate high school reported the most (44.38; Bureau of Labor Statistics, 2019b), though half of the leisure gap stems from the difficulty men and women with less education have in finding full-time jobs (Attanasio et al., 2013). Professional parents familiarize their children with the kind of lives they expect them to lead as adults.

An important question, however, is how these different parenting strategies may or may not affect the long-term outcomes of kids. Indeed, work by Amy Hsin (2009), for example, has shown that the amount of time parents spend with their children, while highly correlated with social class, did not predict children's cognitive outcomes. Later work found that perhaps intensive parenting did have a delinquency-protective effect, but only in adolescence (Milkie et al., 2015). The problem with much of the work on parenting and how kids spend their time is that many parenting behaviors and decisions regarding a child's activities may be reactions to how the child is faring. For example, a child at risk of failing in school may garner extra attention and more intensive parenting than the child's sibling who is doing fine. This reactive nature of parenting, then, may obscure the true effects of certain styles. To try to address this concern, Thomas Laidley and I used random variation in weather patterns to study whether the ways kids spent their time affected their cognitive performance. We found that physical, outdoor activity had a positive influence on math test scores while indoor, sedentary behavior had the opposite effect. There may be something said, then, for the style of parenting common in the 1970s of just sending your kids outside to play (without phones) all day as compared to having them sit inside in front of a screen.

On the issue of even longer-term effects of different child-rearing patterns, I spoke to Annette Lareau upon the publication of her updated edition of *Unequal Childhoods* (2011), in which she followed up with many of the families she had originally studied. Here's what she told me:

> There really were no surprises. I would say it was sad. Many of the working-class and poor children had wanted to do well, their parents had wanted them to do well, but things had not worked out. Not one was in the professional sector. [For] the middle-class families, it wasn't always easy sailing [either]. Garrett Talinger got his heart broken. Melanie Hamlin had a friend killed in a car accident. It's not that bad things don't happen to middle-class kids; they do. But in terms of being launched, in terms of their life chances, they were much more likely to go to college, and their parents helped them and supervised them in college. So their parents helped them choose their college classes, they gave them advice on their majors, and so the parents continued to provide guidance and help as they went into adulthood. Alexander Williams, the middle-class African American boy, is now going to become a doctor. Garrett Talinger became a high-level manager. He has a suit and tie, his face is shining. (Conley, 2011b)

This was an interesting finding, so I probed further: What exactly happened in the poor and working-class families' lives that caused the kids, despite their high aspirations, to drop out of high school or go no further than a high-school diploma?

To go to college involves many, many steps. You've been through this process, so you can imagine (or maybe you experienced) the challenge of doing it on your own. If you wanted to go to college, did you pass all your courses and order a transcript to be sent where you were applying? Did you take the SAT and the ACT, if required by the school you wanted to attend, and also

DIGITAL.WWNORTON.COM/YOUMAYASK8

To see my interview with Annette Lareau about *Unequal Childhoods*, go to digital.wwnorton.com/youmayask8

have those results submitted to the admissions office? Did you fill out the application? And if you got in, did you have the ability to go? All of these steps are crossroads, potentially limiting students' future options based on current actions. Despite similar aspirations, students and their parents from different social class backgrounds may find themselves facing varying obstacles or challenges at each of these steps.

Lareau went on to provide a concrete example of these hurdles in the case of a working-class girl (who was not included in the book due to limitations on space):

> She applied to colleges, but she applied to colleges that were two and three hundred points above her SAT. Now, if she had been my daughter, could I have gotten her into a school? Probably. I would have found a school that would have taken a child who had a learning disability, or had low scores, and I could have placed her in college. It would have taken a lot of work. But in her system, her mother depended on the [high] school to help her daughter go to college. So, the mother didn't see the applications, and the mother had a car, but she didn't go on college tours. It was up to her daughter and the school. And that is a reasonable decision. Her daughter was rejected everywhere, and she ended up going to community college for a semester and dropping out. And [her experience follows] a very typical pattern for working-class families. (Conley, 2011b)

Although Lareau can't definitively discern cause and effect here (e.g., what if Tara's SAT scores had been higher or she lucked out with a fabulous guidance counselor?), things might have turned out differently for Tara, despite the "natural growth" strategy her mother followed. But by showing how social stratification actually worked on the ground, Lareau tells a pretty convincing, if depressing, story of how social background can limit individual choices.

SCHOOL

When children enter school, the primary locus of socialization shifts to include reference groups such as peers and teachers. In addition to helping you learn the three *R*s, one of the teacher's main goals is to properly socialize you—that is, teaching you to share, take turns, resolve conflict with words, be quiet when necessary, and speak when appropriate. Walk into any kindergarten classroom and compare it with a third-grade class. What differences would you observe? For starters, you probably notice a lot more order, and less noise, among the third-graders. When you were young and needed to leave the classroom as a group (whether for recess, gym, or music class), you probably had to line up and follow your teacher. It is highly unlikely you had to do this in high school because teenagers have learned how to navigate from one classroom to the next, whereas five-year-olds have not yet learned how to do so themselves.

Socialization does not always run smoothly. When students resist classroom behavior norms, many parents and teachers turn to a variety of strategies, including medication. Psychiatrist Fadi Haddad treats kids referred to him with signs of attention-deficit hyperactivity disorder (ADHD). He has identified four factors leading to the uptick in ADHD cases in the United States. Only one of them is the mental health of the kid; the rest have roots in the broader social context. He sees that "the demands of the schools are built on certain curricul[a]" that are "not very flexible . . . they want the kid to behave in a certain way." If a kid does not behave, "it's easy to say this kid has ADHD and that's why he is not successful in school rather than, oh, well,

DIGITAL.WWNORTON.COM/YOUMAYASK8

To see my interview with Fadi Haddad, go to
digital.wwnorton.com/youmayask8

maybe this kid, his brain is functioning a little bit different, and if we change the curriculum, he will be a brilliant kid and he will succeed" (Conley, 2014b).

A compounding parallel issue is the foundation of American culture on "work, work, work, work. So parents start work at 8:00 in the morning. They don't come home before 5:00 or 6:00 in the evening . . . and they want kids to do their homework. If the kid is not able because of many different reasons. . . . This kid might have symptoms of depression, and that's why he's not able to concentrate on his work. It's much easier for the parents to say, 'Well, my son has ADHD and he needs medication' rather than dealing with other issues that [are] affecting them." The school structure and the long hours of work that parents face run into a third concern. Even as a psychiatrist specializing in children's mental health, Haddad says:

> [A]ny doctor can prescribe medications for ADHD, and many people, because [of] the difficulty of accessing child psychiatrists and the expense—because child psychiatrists are very expensive—say, "well, I cannot afford going to a child psychiatrist. I will go to my pediatrician." And they'll sit with the pediatrician for five minutes, and the pediatrician gets convinced, "all right, you have ADHD, so let me give you medications for ADHD." So we see half of the kids taking ADHD medications, [although] many of them would benefit from something else. (Conley, 2014c)

Ultimately, Haddad says that medicating children to comply with socialization norms is easier than changing society. As he sums up the standardizing impact of socialization: "[A]nybody who's different, anybody who's functioning on [a] different level, we do not accommodate them." For active young kids, "we just claim that, 'okay, *you* have a problem. You need help.' And the easiest problem to have is ADHD because the medications are easy to prescribe" (Conley, 2014c). Socialization may not come easily for anyone, but it is especially difficult for those who find conformity a challenge for whatever reason.

Academic learning suffered due to the major disruptions that occurred to in-person schooling in many areas of the world during the COVID-19 pandemic. Still, we do not yet know how the pandemic has affected the socialization functions of schools. For example, interacting online with peers and teachers may not provide enough nonverbal social cues to cultivate norms of behavior. Even in-person mask wearing may drastically reduce subtle, but important, information communicated to children. When someone smiles while giving an instruction, for example, the words carry a very different meaning than the same instruction conveyed with a scowl. Navigating the subtleties of human interaction is hard, and doing it on a screen or behind a mask makes it even tougher.

PEERS

Once we reach school age, peers become an important part of our lives and function as agents of socialization. Adolescents, in particular, spend a great deal of their free time in the company of peers. Peers can reinforce messages taught in the home (even the most liberal of friends will probably expect you to wear clothing when you hang out with them after school) or contradict them. Either way, conformity is generally expected; hence, the term *peer pressure*. Walk into any high-school cafeteria and you'll observe the power of conformity among peer groups.

Research on adolescent peer pressure has asserted that friend groups provide an emotional waystation of sorts for teenagers seeking distance from their parents but not yet ready for complete autonomy (Steinberg & Monahan, 2007). Peer groups, in this way, provide normative regulation—that is, instructions on how to live in the social world. It works like this: People sort themselves into groups whose members regulate each other's values, style, actions, and so on. This tendency to conform to the group helps maintain solidarity and a distinctive collective identity when contrasted with other groups or cliques, providing an alternative to the family as the primary reference group for one's identity. In this framework, risk-taking behavior plays a particularly important role since the high cost of risky behavior demonstrates (and creates) identification with the group, solidifying the clique in the process.

If you have ever tried drugs or alcohol, did you do so by yourself? Probably not. Even deviance often occurs in the company (or by the suggestion) of others. Parents may have reason to worry about their children hanging out with the "wrong crowd." However, research by Ramina Sotoudeh, Kathy Harris, and myself in 2019 found that with adolescent smoking the entire grade matters more than the friend clique. We found that if a few kids in a grade have tobacco addictions, the entire grade's smoking behavior changes, not just the behavior of the smokers' friends. The dynamics of peer influence are complicated and cannot be contained just to the few friends who form a clique.

While peers may influence behavior, they also affect the transfer of information. Adolescents tend to glean the most information on sex and dating from their peers. A study of young adolescents aged 14–17 (Bleakley et al., 2018) found, on the one hand, that friends were the major source of information on dating and sex. If you think about it, this probably makes sense. No matter how cool your parents are (or try to be), when you're 15, you probably don't want to talk to them about your love life. On the other hand, most research tends to show that adolescents who do communicate more with their parents about sex tend to engage in safer sex behaviors than those who don't (i.e., using contraceptives; Widman et al., 2016). It seems as if some adolescents have already learned that they shouldn't believe everything they hear from their peers.

ADULT SOCIALIZATION

The socialization we receive as children can never fully prepare us for the demands that we will face as adults. *Adult socialization* simply refers to the ways in which we are continuously socialized as adults. For instance, when you work at a restaurant, you learn what your job responsibilities are, how to take orders and place them in the kitchen, and how to carry a tray full of drinks. As a result of your prior socialization, you probably already knew that you should not talk back to customers. Similarly, your plans upon graduation from college might include moving out of your parents' house, finding a job, and maybe starting a family. Right now, you may not know everything you need to in order to function in each of those situations, but you will learn. Some roles, like some jobs, take more preparation than others. For example, you have to go to law school to become an attorney and medical school to become a doctor. Did you ever wonder why parenting schools don't exist?

Resocialization is a more drastic form of adult socialization. When you change your environment, you may need some resocialization. If you plan to live in another country, you may have to learn a new language and new ways of eating, speaking, talking, listening, or dressing. If you went to a single-sex high school and then attend a co-ed college or university, this change will probably require some resocialization, depending on the extent to which you interacted with the opposite sex during your high-school years. The most drastic case of resocialization would be necessary if you had suffered a terrible accident and lost all of your memory. You would need to relearn everything—for example, how to hold a fork and knife, how to tie your shoes, how to engage in conversation. You would be completely childlike once again—and any inappropriate nose picking would be forgiven.

Adult socialization doesn't just occur when we move out of our parents' home or join the military or go to prison. As we navigate new challenges that come with each stage of development we are influenced by the people and institutions in our life.

Let's take early adulthood, the period when we seek intimate love and companionship. People tend to pick partners similar to themselves on a wide range of attributes from height to political ideology. However, partners also function as important socializing agents for each other; for example, sometimes one decides to convert to the other's religion.

As another example, a study on the effect of "trash television" shows that its effects on our political values and behavior are strongest among those age 55 and older. The authors of the study used the fact that in Italy

RESOCIALIZATION

the process by which one's sense of social values, beliefs, and norms are reengineered, often deliberately, through an intense social process.

a new network called Mediaset was rolled out gradually across the country, so some communities were exposed to its light fare of movies and entertainment (without as much news as the preexisting channels) for longer than others. Older viewers became more populist and angrier in their voting patterns when exposed to this television programming. (There were also effects on young children's test scores and civic views but no effect on young or middle-aged adults.) A similar effect of television viewing was seen in Indonesia, among 606 villages that got television at different times: Those who were more exposed to broadcasts became more distrustful and participated less in civic life.

The point is that we are not done being socialized at 18 or even 25 years old, like a Jell-O mold that has set. Our social environments, including our partners, children, peers, media, work, and so on, continue to shape who we are as we transition through life's stages.

TOTAL INSTITUTIONS

The term total institution refers to an institution that controls all the basics of day-to-day life. Members of the institution eat, sleep, study, play, and perhaps even bathe and pray together. Boarding schools, colleges, monasteries, the army, and prisons are all total institutions to varying degrees with prisons being the most extreme (see Chapter 6). Sociologist Gwynne Dyer's *War* (1985) provides some insight into the total institution of the U.S. Marine Corps. Marine boot camp strips down much of the prior socialization of recruits and resocializes them to become Marines. Think about how boot camp erases certain parts of new enlistees' identities. They receive uniforms and men shave their heads. They live, eat, sleep, bathe, exercise, and study together. Supervisors watch and critique their every move, from how they hold a weapon to how they tuck in the corners of their bedsheets. Basic training not only teaches recruits new skills, but it changes their mindsets as well so that they can perform tasks they wouldn't have dreamed of doing otherwise. It works by applying enormous physical and mental pressure on men and women who have been isolated from their normal civilian environment and constantly placed in situations where the only right way to think and behave is that espoused by the Marine Corps.

TOTAL INSTITUTION

an institution in which one is totally immersed and that controls all the basics of day-to-day life; no barriers exist between the usual sphere of daily life, and all activity occurs in the same place and under the same single authority.

Marines training at Parris Island. How is Marine boot camp an example of a total institution?

Social Interaction

Evaluate your own status set and its related conflicting responsibilities or expectations.

To talk about how institutions and society as a whole socialize us, we need a language to describe social interaction. Robert Merton's role theory provides just such a vocabulary. The first key concept for an understanding of role theory is status, which refers to a recognizable social position that an individual occupies. The person who runs your class and grades each student has the status of professor. Roles, then, refer to the duties and behaviors associated with a particular status. You can reasonably expect your professor to show up on time, clothed and prepared for class. You can also expect that they have a fair amount of education, often a PhD, and therefore have extensive knowledge about the material. Roles are complicated, however, and relatively few of them materialize with handbooks and clear sets of expectations. Sometimes we experience role strain, the incompatibility among roles corresponding to a single status. An example of this is the old dictum for university faculty, particularly young professors, to "publish or perish." On the one hand, they need to stay on top of their research, write articles, give lectures, and attend conferences to stay abreast of current topics and remain active in the academic world. On the other hand, they have to teach and perform the teaching roles associated with the status of professor, such as preparing lectures, running class sections, meeting with students, grading papers, and writing letters of recommendation.

When your professor arrives to class tomorrow morning with bags under her eyes and a look on her face that seems to say, "No amount of coffee will help me at this point," you may be tempted to conclude, "Oh, she's experiencing role strain." But what if her exhaustion results not from the time demands of simultaneously grading her midterms and preparing for an upcoming research conference, but rather from the turmoil that ensued last night when the family dog destroyed her daughter's biology project and she had to stay up all night helping her daughter redo it? In this case, role conflict is the culprit. It is not the roles within her status as professor that are the root of her problems, but rather the tensions between her role as professor and her role as mother. Whereas *role strain* refers to conflicting demands within the same status, *role conflict* describes the tension caused by competing demands between two or more roles within different statuses. Each one of us, at any given time, enjoys numerous statuses. These statuses (and their corresponding roles) can and do change over time and among places. When you started college, how did your status change? The obvious answer is that you went from being either a high-school student or perhaps

STATUS
a recognizable social position that an individual occupies.

ROLE
the duties and behaviors expected of someone who holds a particular status.

ROLE STRAIN
the incompatibility among roles corresponding to a single status.

ROLE CONFLICT
the tension caused by competing demands between two or more roles pertaining to different statuses.

an unskilled worker to becoming a college student. If you graduated from high school and went straight to college, you traded in one status for another. If you still maintain a full- or part-time job, you have added another status. The term status set refers to all the statuses you have at any given time.

To obtain a better sense of how roles and statuses function, try the following experiment: Write down as many answers to the question "Who am I?" as you can. Compare your answers with your classmates' answers. With remarkable similarity, the lists will include statuses such as brother, sister, daughter, boyfriend, student, lifeguard, babysitter, roommate, and so forth. These commonalities occur because we know ourselves in our social roles, in the ways in which we relate to others. You most likely will have listed the key components of your status set.

Sociologists also make a distinction between an ascribed status and an achieved status, which basically amounts to what you are born with versus what you become. Another way to think about this difference is in terms of involuntary versus voluntary status. Your age, race, and sex are all largely ascribed statuses, whereas your status as a juggler, drug dealer, peace activist, or reality television aficionado is an achieved status. Sometimes, one status within our status set stands out or overwhelms all the others. This is called a master status. Examples might include being unemployed, being

Who are you? What are the different roles in your status set? For example, singer Beyoncé's statuses include mother, daughter, and partner.

a lesbian, being disabled, or any status that overshadows other statuses. Master status roles can be ascribed, such as having a disability, or achieved, such as being an Olympic athlete. The key characteristic of a master status is that people tend to interact with you on the basis of that one status alone.

GENDER ROLES

One of the most popular lines of thought to evolve from role theory has been the concept of gender roles, sets of behavioral norms assumed to accompany one's identity as masculine, feminine, or other. In their critiques of role theory, gender theorists such as Candace West and Don Zimmerman (1987) have argued that the statuses of male/female have distinct power and significance that role theory doesn't adequately capture (you can read more about this in Chapter 8 on sex and gender). Gender plays an influential role in broader theories of socialization. Sometimes gendering starts before birth. One recent tradition is the gender-reveal party, where a baker is given the results of a sonogram or other test that reveals the biological sex of the fetus and then bakes a cake or cupcakes with either pink or blue filling. The family gathers around to celebrate the revealed sex by eating the sweet. Knowing the sex of a baby may influence how parents talk to them—for example, their tone of voice and what they say—even before the baby is born.

From the moment they are born, babies may be dressed in either pink or blue to designate their sex if their parents want to signal to the wider society that they should be treated as one gender (although many hospitals now offer gender-neutral blankets, hats, and so on to patients). These seemingly silly

GENDER ROLES

sets of behavioral norms assumed to accompany one's status as masculine, feminine, or other.

How do the displays at this New York City toy store serve as an example of the ways that we learn gender roles through socialization?

differences—babies don't care if they wear blue or pink—create a context for older kids and adults to treat babies not as an undifferentiated group of babbling incoherents but as boys and girls. Studies (Lewis et al., 1992) have shown that people interact with babies differently based on their biological sex, commenting on how "big" and "strong" baby boys are and how "pretty" baby girls are or closely snuggling with female babies and holding male babies facing outward so that they might see the world.

Not just family members but also people in the larger social world interact with boys and girls very differently and, consequently, socialize them into different roles and into the schema of a gender binary itself (the idea that one has to pick between two genders). Take a stroll through your local toy store, and you will glimpse the function of toys and play—both very important to the development of children—in creating and maintaining gender roles. The toys for playing house will likely be displayed in boxes showing images of little girls pushing and pulling pink irons and purple vacuum cleaners. The boxes for toy stoves will depict girls cooking. Baby dolls will be wrapped in pastel colors, and their packaging will show little girls cradling them. Now, meander through the section of the store displaying tool sets, workbenches, and toys related to outdoor activities. On the packages, you will note little boys dressed in bright primary colors, wielding hammers and fishing poles. The action-figure aisle will be similarly gendered (think Barbie versus G.I. Joe). (Admittedly, these are generalizations. Some images will show boys playing house and girls constructing a bridge, but the vast majority adheres to what we perceive as traditional gender roles.)

In high school, gender-role socialization continues as peers police each other. Sociologist C. J. Pascoe spent a year in a working-class high school in California finding out just how teens enforce gender norms on one another. She discovered what she calls "fag discourse," a term that describes the near-continuous use of the term *fag* or *faggot* as an insult teenage boys use against one another to curtail improper behavior. She explained in a recent interview how it worked. Someone could get called a fag if, as she said, "you danced, if you cared about your clothing, if you were too

DIGITAL.WWNORTON.COM/YOUMAYASK8

To see my interview with C. J. Pascoe about *Dude, You're a Fag*, go to digital.wwnorton.com/youmayask8

emotional, or if you were incompetent." Rather than associating the word with someone's sexuality, Pascoe explained: "What I came to realize was that they used *fag* as an insult to police the boundaries of masculinity. It wasn't about same-sex desire. In fact, when I asked them about same-sex desire, one boy said, 'Well, being gay is just a lifestyle; you can still throw a football around and be gay.'" This "masculinity policing" is no joking matter. A boy she called Ricky was "targeted so relentlessly that he dropped out of school" (Conley, 2009c).

If boys constantly police the boundaries of masculinity with homophobic insults, how are girls socialized into their gender roles? At the school in Pascoe's study, girls did not insult each other. Instead, they experienced constant sexual harassment from the boys. As the boys looked for behaviors that would prove their masculinity, they used girls as unwitting resources with which to perform aggressive sexuality by describing to one another either how they could "get" girls or the outlandish and often violent sexual escapades that would then follow. Further, they engaged in rituals of forceful touching, often physically constraining girls' movements. Pascoe describes one hallway scene in which she "watched one boy walk down the hallway jabbing a girl in the crotch with his drum-stick yelling, 'Get raped, get raped'" (Conley, 2009c). In this case, gender socialization looks a lot like gender-based assault. Do these scenes remind you of high school? Was your gender performance policed by your peers?

For some, constant gender-boundary policing has catastrophic effects. Ricky was subject to the steadiest, most virulent fag discourse in Pascoe's study and he dropped out. An 11-year-old in Massachusetts committed suicide after being relentlessly teased; many of the insults he received were part of fag discourse. And Pascoe points out that 90 percent of school shooters who go on rampage school shootings have been subject to homophobic harassment and teasing (Conley, 2009c). Extreme gender socialization during childhood may form the roots of adult gender performances, ranging from the fact that men are more likely to sexually harass women in the workplace than the reverse to the simple fact that men are 33 percent more likely to talk over or interrupt a woman than they are another man (Shore, 2017).

Recent evidence on adolescent socialization contains good and bad news. In a recent poll, 92 percent of the 10- to 18-year-old respondents believed in gender equality as a principle, and a majority agreed that sexism still persists and equality has yet to be achieved. Life goals were the same, overall, by gender, and boys and girls were equally represented in school leadership positions and were as likely to aspire to leadership positions in life as well as to value a career. Moreover, the survey found that it is now more socially acceptable for girls to violate traditional gender norms by adopting "male" interests, styles, and manners. That said, boys still felt very constrained by expectations for them to be stoic, strong, and athletic. Girls, by contrast, were uncomfortable with how much emphasis was placed on their looks by society (a finding that is echoed by adult women) and how sexualized they were by the boys. Finally, 3 percent of respondents identified as transgender, illustrating the breakdown of the entire gender-binary system to a certain extent (see Chapter 8 for more on gender fluidity). So, while the next generation (and women in particular) may view and adopt gender roles in a more fluid manner, there are still deeply ingrained ways of behaving with respect to sexuality and gender that persist. We should keep in mind that these overall numbers obscure significant variation by race, class, and region. Indeed, most roles still exist in an intersectional lens—that is, related to the specific individual's position of being, for example, a White woman from a wealthy, rural family—rather than based on universal categories (more on intersectionality in Chapter 8).

DRAMATURGICAL THEORY

All the world's a stage,
And all the men and women merely players.
> —William Shakespeare, *As You Like It*

DRAMATURGICAL THEORY

the view (advanced by Erving Goffman) of social life as essentially a theatrical performance, in which we are all actors on metaphorical stages, with roles, scripts, costumes, and sets.

If all this talk of roles has made you think that society sounds a bit like a movie or play we each star in—well, you're not alone. We might say that the dramaturgical theory of society has its roots in William Shakespeare, but we generally credit Erving Goffman with expounding this theory in *The Presentation of Self in Everyday Life* (1959). He argued that social life essentially functions as a play with a moral, of sorts. Goffman and social psychologists call this moral "impression management." That is, all of us actors on the metaphorical social stage want to make good impressions on our audience (who also happen to be other actors). What's more, we often actively work to ensure that others will believe they are making good impressions as well. This interactive performance helps keep society and social relations rolling smoothly (without the need for too many retakes).

For our acting roles, according to Goffman's dramaturgical theory, we also need scripts, costumes, and sets. Think again about your first day in this college classroom. You knew your role was the student, and presumably the professor understood their role as well. The professor handed out the syllabus (a prop), talked about the general outline of the class for the semester (a script), and maybe gave a short lecture (a performance). What if he had instead started talking about his love for Batman and all things related to Batman? You might have indulged him briefly, thinking that he seemed a bit loony but would eventually relate this tangent to sociology. If your professor, however, had spent the entire lecture talking about Batman, how would you feel? Shocked? Confused? The professor would have deviated from the script generally followed in a college classroom. Was anyone wearing a tuxedo or dressed like an action hero? Probably not, because those are not the costumes we wear to a sociology lecture. Think back to your status set for a minute and ask yourself what the stages, costumes, scripts, and other props associated with each of your roles are. For some, the answer seems fairly clear.

Some roles reflect dramaturgical theory more clearly than others such as competing as a member of a sports team. As a member of a basketball team, you play on a basketball court (the stage or set), wear a uniform (the costume), follow the rules of the game (the script), and play with a ball (a prop). Often, though, our roles are more complex, but very manageable. We play several roles simultaneously, and if we have been properly socialized and don't suffer from too much role conflict, we can transition in and out of roles with a certain amount of ease. Presumably, you understand that the classroom is not the appropriate stage on which to act out an intimate scene with your partner. If you did, one of your classmates might heckle you to "get a room." In dramaturgical theory, the translation would be: "This is the wrong stage. Find the right one."

Another important part of Goffman's theory is the distinction between front-stage and backstage arenas. If you've ever participated in a school play or some other type of performance, you know all about front stage and back-stage. In the theater, a curtain clearly delineates these two separate areas, making the distinction quite literal. If you've ever worked in a restaurant, you see a similar line of demarcation. As a waiter, you are all smiles out in the dining room, replying politely with a "yes, ma'am" or "right away, sir." Back in the kitchen, however, you might complain loudly to the rest of the staff, criticizing your customer's atrocious taste for ordering escargot with his cheeseburger.

For people in certain professions, the distinction between front stage and backstage is more literal. In the news, we sometimes hear about celebrities who have been caught saying something inappropriate because they thought the camera or microphone was off—they believed they were comfortably backstage. Whoops! The higher your profile, particularly if you have a master status such as a celebrity or politician, the greater the portion of your daily world that takes on the designation of front stage. Constant scrutiny means that others always expect you to perform your role. In other situations, the lines between front stage and backstage become more blurred. Has a professor ever caught you off guard while you were talking with friends about her class? You might have thought that you were backstage when joking with your friends in the student union, but the unfortunate, unexpected appearance of your professor turned the situation into a front-stage experience.

Face, according to Goffman, describes the esteem in which an individual is held by others. We take this notion very seriously; hence, the idea of saving face, which is essentially the most important goal of impression management. If your best friend walked into the classroom right now and sat down

FACE
the esteem in which an individual is held by others.

beside you with a big smear of chocolate on his face, you would tell him. If the professor walked in sporting the same chocolate smear, however, you might not say anything. Because of the difference in status (and therefore power) between you and the professor, you might decide it's not your place, your role, to say something. If few students are in the class and the professor is your adviser with whom you have a fairly amicable relationship, you might indicate to him that he's got a little something on his cheek. Have you ever encountered a stranger with toilet paper stuck to the bottom of her shoe or with the fly of his pants unzipped? Did you say something? If you did, you probably thought that, if it were you, you would want someone to say something. If you didn't, perhaps you thought calling attention to the toilet paper or exposed underwear would embarrass the person. Or maybe you just simply felt it wasn't any of your business to interfere with a stranger. So you can see how no absolute, fixed scripts exist. (That said, one common rule of thumb says to speak up if the person can do something about it. For example, you would tell a man that he has chocolate on his face because he can wipe his face and remove the chocolate. On the other hand, you would not tell him that his shirt is ugly, because he probably cannot change his shirt at that moment.)

Similarly, if your professor walked in tomorrow with a black eye, you might ask him what happened. Not wanting to admit he fell asleep grading papers and smacked his face on the desk, he might simply say, "You should see the other guy." Through this common joke, you understand the underlying implication that he wants to save face by not going into the details. No one explicitly told you what the saying meant, but like driving a car, we generally learn by doing and sometimes by making mistakes.

Indeed, mistakes, called breaches, are themselves an important part of the game. After a breach in an established script, we work hard to repair it and move forward. Humor is a useful tool in getting the script back in place. So, if your professor lets out an enormous belch in the middle of a lecture, how do you react? You might be horrified; you might laugh nervously. You might delight a little because she has been so arrogant all semester and you are pleased to see her off script, not the perfectly polished professor. If the professor manages to recover and says, "Note to self: skip the Mountain Dew before lecture next time!" it may smooth over the situation a little (but just a little,

After Sony Pictures Entertainment's internal computer system was hacked, executive Amy Pascal suffered from scandal when her e-mails and other personal information were released and her backstage life became public.

because let's face it, what happened was funny) and allow class to continue without a hitch. If the same thing happens during your next class, however, you are just going to assume that your professor has severe gastrointestinal problems, needs to scale back on carbonation, or is poorly socialized.

Sometimes, when facing high stakes or new situations, we seek explicit guidance. People can and do make careers out of negotiating social scripts and methods for saving face—for instance, think about Miss Manners, Emily Post, or Dear Abby. Not wanting to act inappropriately but unsure of how to behave in situations where we lack a script, we may appeal to professional etiquette experts to coach us through a scene and give stage directions. The truth is, however, that human social interaction is too complex for a single script to work universally.

For example, the art of tact even involves, on occasion, breaking the rules to make others feel comfortable. One particular fable tells the story of a peasant who receives an invitation to the palace for dinner. Unknowingly, she picks up the bowl of water meant for handwashing and begins to drink from it. Many of the nobles at the table chuckle and mutter disparaging comments under their breath. But the queen, who invited the poor woman to dine with her, instead picks up her own silver finger bowl and drinks the water from it. She breaks a formal rule to preserve the face of the invited guest. Moreover, the social situation dictates that only the queen herself, as the most powerful figure at the table, has the influence to repair the situation and save face for everyone.

Although social scripts cannot be written in stone, we can generalize in some ways. For example, we almost always begin our scripts in specific ways; we generally can't just plunge into our lines. (Imagine a colleague getting on the elevator, not saying hello or even looking directly at you, but launching straight into the story of what happened to her on the way to work that day while staring up at the floor number indicators.) Goffman uses the term *opening* to signal the start of an encounter as the first bracket. The closing bracket marks the end of an encounter. Sometimes, we need a nonverbal bracket to commence an encounter, a signal to cease our civil inattention. *Civil inattention* means refraining from directly interacting with someone, even someone you know, until an opening bracket has been issued. For example, you might clear your throat before speaking to somebody. You might catch their eye. You might stand up. You might purposely go to the bathroom first, so you can pass that person on the way back and start a conversation. You hope that you will bump into the person and catch their attention. We have to signal to people to warn them that we intend to break civil inattention and initiate an encounter.

Openings can seem awkward, but it may be even more difficult to end situations. How many times have you gotten off the phone saying, "I should get going." Where? To do what? Or you may say, "Well, I should let you go." Maybe you do hear sirens and screams in the background, so you feel genuinely concerned that the person on the phone has more pressing matters to attend to. Under less extreme circumstances, you may be phrasing your desire to end the conversation as a kind gesture to your interlocutor. Sometimes, we resort to formal closings. A ringing bell often indicates the end of a class period. In the absence of a bell, or even prior to its ringing, however, you may close your notebook, start to pack your books, and pick up your coat to signal to the professor that, although the lecture on socialization is fascinating, you have another class in 10 minutes that is a 15-minute walk away. *Given gestures* also signal closings, such as putting on your coat. Or, at the end of a meal, you may rub your stomach and say, "That was delicious. I'm stuffed!" to indicate that you have finished eating but did very much enjoy the food. However, *given-off gestures* also exist, unconscious signals of our true feelings. If you grimace every time your fork reaches your mouth, you communicate something else entirely regarding your thoughts about the meal. Many of our gestures and brackets are nonverbal. It is often more difficult to end a conversation on the phone or in a message thread than in person because much of our toolbox of visual cues is not available to us.

Which one of these paintings is a "real" Jackson Pollock? Does it matter? (For the record, the real one is on the right.) How is the controversy over the Pollock paintings an example of the social construction of reality?

The Social Construction of Reality

| Describe the shared meanings assigned to social scripts and how they impact social interactions.

In a *New York Times* op-ed essay titled "Mind over Splatter," Vassar professor Don Foster (2006) commented on the debate surrounding an allegedly fake Jackson Pollock painting. Is the painting any less artistic for not being a

real Pollock when it was, after all, good enough to fool so many people for so long? In a similar vein, Shakespeare's Juliet once inquired, "What's in a name? That which we call a rose by any other name would smell as sweet." The underlying implication is that something is what it is, apart from what we call it or who made it. But do we agree? This question speaks less to the essential nature of things and more to the social construction of reality. Something is real, meaningful, or valuable when society tells us it is.

So, what does "socially constructed" really mean? This question is less a debate about what is real versus fake and more an explanation of how we assign meanings to objects or ideas through social interaction. We can better understand how we socially construct our reality by either comparing one society over two different time periods or two contemporary societies. Let's look at some examples.

In U.S. society, we take for granted a common understanding of childhood as a critical and unique stage of life. This is a social construction, however natural it feels to us. In fact, childhood as a concept is a relatively recent historical occurrence. The idea of younger people going through a unique stage of life with characteristics and challenges different from other stages came about through a series of cultural, political, and economic changes. In preindustrial times, children cared for younger siblings and contributed to households in other ways as soon as they were physically capable. Toys specifically made for children, one of the recent cultural markers of childhood, did not exist. The early years of a child's life were not regarded as a time for play and education. They represented an introduction to adult work and responsibility, like most of life's course. However, the development of the industrial factory led to the need for schools, a place where children might spend their days, because parents now left home to go to work. This change in parents' lifestyles created a new necessity for a separate sphere for children. People's lives became more segregated by age and, because of this separation, childhood became a protected life stage (for example, through child labor laws that kept children from hazardous working conditions).

Adolescence has had a similar and even more recent history in terms of its social construction. The notion that a distinct phase exists between childhood and adulthood is relatively new. This important change evolved during the 1950s. After decades of financial hardship and war, America's booming economy led to a new freedom in the popular culture. Access to higher education broadened as well. For many Americans, this extension of educational opportunity delayed the onset of adult responsibilities, such as being employed and raising a family. With the possibility of an extended adolescence, teenagers (biologically able to reproduce but delayed in their assumption of adult sexual roles) emerged as a distinct social category. Concurrently, the advent of rock and roll, doo-wop, and other popular forms of music marked cultural changes. With more access to radios and, to a lesser extent, televisions and with more free hours after school, teens found the time and the means to consume this emerging music culture. Today we can see the life course becoming even further socially subdivided, with the construction of terms such as *tween*, which refers to the time between childhood and one's teenage years (roughly, ages 10 to 12) and *emerging adulthood*, which is between age 18 and the late twenties.

If dramaturgical theory laid out the roles and scripts we live our lives by, then the social construction of reality—and symbolic interaction in particular—tries to unpack those roles and scripts to understand where they come from and what implications they have for society. We can call the process by which roles, ideas, concepts, and values are socially constructed symbolic interactionism (see Chapter 1). This theory suggests that we interact with others using words and behaviors that have symbolic meanings and, in turn, make and reinforce those meanings through those very social interactions. It's a loop that socially constructs much of what we take for granted in society. This theory has three basic tenets:

SYMBOLIC INTERACTIONISM

a micro-level theory in which shared meanings, orientations, and assumptions form the basic motivations behind people's actions.

1. Human beings act toward ideas, concepts, and values on the basis of the meanings that those things have for them.

2. These meanings are the products of social interaction in human society.

3. These meanings are modified and filtered through an interpretive process that each individual uses in dealing with outward signs.

Symbolic interactionism can be very useful in understanding cultural differences in styles of social interaction. A classic example of this theory would be the distance two people stand from one another when conversing. In an interaction between a tourist and a local, standing too close or too far away may make one of the parties feel uncomfortable, but in an international business meeting or in peace talks between nations, symbolic interactions take on a greater level of importance. For example, people in the United States tend to keep greater interpersonal distance between each other than do people in Middle Eastern countries. And, of course, during periods of pandemic, how much social distance one maintains in face-to-face interaction transcends the symbolic and becomes a matter of, perhaps, life and death. However, even in such circumstances with serious biological consequences, social and cultural signaling becomes encoded with such choices on an everyday level. In the United States during the COVID-19 pandemic, for example, wearing protective masks and keeping 6 feet apart have been highly charged political issues, showing that the symbolic nature of interactional choices persists in both low-stakes and high-stakes scenarios.

How does symbolic interactionism help us understand the differences in greetings among various cultures? Pictured here (clockwise from bottom) are Bedouins touching noses, Malian men with their arms around each other, and the Belgian royal family celebrating the prince's eighteenth birthday.

In another example, in the United States, people generally believe that looking someone in the eye while talking to them indicates respect and sincerity. However, in some other cultures it is considered rude to look someone directly in the eye. When you raise your glass in a toast with others and say, "Cheers," you can generally focus your eyes wherever you want. In many European countries, however, it is highly impolite not to establish eye contact while touching glasses and may even be regarded as a sign of dishonesty.

Comprehending the three basic tenets of symbolic interactionism listed earlier is key to understanding the ongoing and deeply embedded process of social construction. Symbolic interactionism as a theory is a useful tool for understanding the meanings of symbols and signs and the way shared meanings—or a lack thereof—facilitate or impede everyday routine interactions.

ETHNOMETHODOLOGY

If dramaturgical theory reveals that all the world's a stage and we each play our required roles, while symbolic interactionism describes the processes by

ETHNO-METHODOLOGY

literally "the methods of the people"; this approach to studying human interaction focuses on the ways in which we make sense of our world, convey this understanding to others, and produce a shared social order.

which we create those roles, scripts, and other concepts that organize social life, then ethnomethodology throws a monkey wrench into the works to see what happens. In the 1950s and 1960s, Harold Garfinkel (1967) developed a method for studying social interactions called ethnomethodology, which involves *acting* critically about them. Ethnomethodology literally means "the methods of the people" (from *ethnos*, the Greek word for "people"). Garfinkel and his followers became famous for their "breaching experiments." They would send students into the social world to track others' reactions to breaching social norms. In one example, Garfinkel sent his students home for the weekend and told them to treat their parents' home like a rooming house where they paid rent. Imagine what would happen if you sat down at the kitchen table and demanded to know when dinner was typically served and what days of the week the bed linens were changed. Similarly, a New York City professor instructed his students to ask people on the subway for their seats without offering any reason. Some students simply could not take this action. Others did it, but they lied saying that they were not feeling well when they asked for the seat. Try your own breaching experiments. What do you normally do when you get in an elevator? You face forward and watch the numbers above the door. Next time you get into an elevator, face backward. See how the other people in the elevator react. A few weeks into a semester, students tend to sit in the same seats in the same class, particularly in a small group, even if they do not have assigned seats. The next time you are in such a situation, take someone else's usual seat and see how they react. (Come on, that's an easy one!)

Let's think through some of the reactions to breaches. Take the example of the student on the subway asking a stranger to give up his seat. What would you do if this happened to you? Would you give up your seat to the student? You might just get up and offer it to him because you assume he

A scene from the film *Borat*. What established scripts did Sacha Baron Cohen's character Borat violate by going on an elevator naked? How did the unsuspecting woman on the elevator try to cope with the breach?

would not ask for it without a good reason (even if you don't see a cast on his leg). If the stranger were elderly, on crutches, or pregnant or had a small child, you might be more willing to get up. Remember that some students simply could not bring themselves to breach social norms, while others lied, saying they were sick, because being ill provides a valid excuse to sit down. Why is that? What's the big deal in asking someone to give you a seat? Well, you might decide, you just don't typically do such a thing. It's not normal behavior. But note that as a society, we construct rules and meanings for what constitutes normal.

Now contemplate the previously mentioned elevator scenario. How would you react if you stepped into an elevator and the only other person inside was facing away from the door (assuming the elevator only opens on one side)? You might look at the wall to see if the person sees something there you can't see. You might try to stand farther away from that person. If someone else got on the elevator, maybe you would gauge her reaction. If she gave you a look that said, "What's this guy doing?" you might give a sympathetic look, even the hint of a smile, to indicate your agreement: "Yeah, crazy, huh?" Then you could breathe a little easier, knowing that the guy facing backward in the elevator is abnormal, and you, the other passenger, and anyone else who steps inside and faces forward are normal, although there's no social imperative to face forward rather than backward in an elevator.

If you walked into the classroom today and someone was sitting in the seat you consider "yours," how would you feel? Maybe you wouldn't think twice about it, but chances are you would notice, have an emotional reaction—be it annoyance, confusion, even anger—and get to class earlier the next time to claim what's rightfully yours.

NEW TECHNOLOGIES: WHAT HAS THE INTERNET DONE TO INTERACTION?

How do we approach entirely new situations? We have no rules, no scripts, no established social norms. How do people know what to do or what constitutes appropriate behavior? Usually, some continuity exists between situations, so we can draw on our previous knowledge (just as you could anticipate the norms of a college classroom even though you had never been in one before). But what about something like social media, something that humans created, which in turn creates social situations never before possible? Let's think about that sort of novelty.

Tinder, Reddit, Second Life, and other online forums provide an interesting test of the dramaturgical model. On the one hand, the potential anonymity of the internet allows us to portray ourselves however we choose. In Goffman's words, anonymity allows for a very sharp distinction between

ROOMMATES WITH BENEFITS

Eager to cast off my nerdy past and reinvent myself at college, I wrote "party animal" on my roommate application form. When I told my mother about this later, she laughed and bought me a T-shirt that sported the image of Spuds MacKenzie, the 1980s Budweiser beer mascot, under the words "the original party animal."

I ended up with Tony from Sacramento, a very quiet, Republican son of a judge. (I suppose it's good policy to separate the party animals from those who request them.) I learned to appreciate his taste in music (U2 and the Smiths, as opposed to my predilection for reggae and jazz), and we agreed to disagree about politics during the reelection campaign of Alan Cranston, then one of the most liberal members of the U.S. Senate. I had never met anyone like Tony, and I'm pretty sure he hadn't come across many half-Jewish, Democratic children of New York artists. We learned to get along that first year at Berkeley, and every now and then even tried on each other's values and beliefs, just to see how they fit.

Evidently, Tony and I did not have a unique experience as living with someone different expanded our worldviews. David R. Harris, a sociologist who now serves as the president of Union College, studied roommates and found that White students who were assigned a roommate of a different race ended up more open-minded about race (Harris & Sim, 2002). In another study, the economist Bruce Sacerdote (2001) found that randomly assigned roommates at Dartmouth affected each other's GPAs.

Of course, influences can sometimes be negative. Some minority students have to carefully navigate the roommate scene to avoid being stuck with racists. Furthermore, in 2003, researchers at four colleges discovered that male students who reported binge drinking in high school drank more in college if their first-year roommate also reported binge drinking in high school (Duncan et al., 2005; Eisenberg et al., 2013; Kremer & Levy, 2008), a case of bad behavior egging on more bad behavior.

These studies reinforce the idea that much education takes place outside the formal classroom curriculum and in the peer-to-peer learning that occurs in places like dorm rooms or student lounges. In nonresidential colleges, the people you meet in class or work with for group projects contribute just as much to your learning process as your professor.

Other than prison and the military, there are not many other institutions outside of residential colleges that shove two people into a 100-square-foot space and expect them to get along for nine months. Can you think of any better training for marriage? In fact, in my research with Jennifer A. Heerwig, we found that Vietnam-era military service actually lowered the risk of subsequent divorce (Conley & Heerwig, 2011). It's possible that the military teaches you how to subsume your individual desires for the good of the collective—in other words, how to get along well with others.

As illustrated by my freshman year roommate, Tony, getting to know someone different

Patti Kilroy, right, and Bliss Baek in their dorm room at New York University after first contacting each other through Facebook. Does this process of connecting online reduce the diversity and randomness of the college experience?

from yourself can expand your perspective. However, today, most students who attend a residential college and live on campus will not have the same experience that I did back when Meta CEO Mark Zuckerberg was still in diapers. While the internet allows us to reconnect with the lost Tonys of our lives years later, meeting our Tonys has become more difficult as social life becomes less random.

As soon as today's students receive their proverbial fat acceptance envelope, they get on social media to meet other potential classmates. By the time the roommate application forms arrive, many like-minded students with similar backgrounds have already connected and agreed to request one another as roommates. It's just one of many ways in which digital technologies now spill over into non-screen-based aspects of social experience. I know certain people who can't bear to eat in a restaurant they haven't researched on

Yelp. And Google and Facebook, of course, tailor content to exactly what they think you want to find.

Perhaps, then, all colleges should follow the lead of Hamilton College in New York, a residential college that does not permit roommate choice. And if you end up with the roommate from hell, you'll survive, and someday you'll have great stories to tell your future partner, with whom you'll probably get along better than you would have without the challenging experience of getting along with your first college roommate.

front stage and backstage. Online, I can play the role of a 57-year-old, stay-at-home mom who was an international college badminton champ and enters semiannual pesto-making competitions. Is that who I am? Some online dating and networking websites allow us to craft our own presentation of self, alter our identities, and thereby create new "realities." However, we've largely removed the costumes, props, vocal inflections, and other nonverbal cues that we use to play our roles (and to assess someone else's role performance), so we must depend entirely on the scripts with which we are presented. We even develop new ways of communicating—for example, using emojis to substitute for nonverbal cues to indicate tone (e.g., that we're joking in a text). 😊 😕

The internet has changed society in other ways, such as forcing us to develop new technologies to prevent identity theft and to create secure online transactions for shopping and banking. Certain aspects of the internet have also altered the nature and details of crime. We've probably all experienced someone trying to scam us out of money online by promising untold riches if we would just share our bank account information. We may have been phished or hacked or experienced full-fledged identity theft, where someone impersonates us online using biographic details acquired through a data breach. The hacker may simply charge some purchases to a credit card in our name or may go much farther and create a whole life with our identity. Without the face-to-face interactional cues that verify someone's identity, these crimes become easier to pull off and more common. Some of us, meanwhile, may have participated in online crime unwittingly. Some websites, such as eBay, allow for the sale of stolen goods in ways previously unforeseen. Intentionally or not, people may foster underground economies by purchasing stolen goods in a way not possible before the advent of online auctions. Clicking on an item and entering your credit card number is a completely different social interaction than walking into a dark alley and buying something that literally fell off the back of a truck.

Conclusion

In the nature-versus-nurture debate, sociologists have generally fallen firmly on the side of nurture. At least that's what most of us study. Socialization helps us understand and explain how babies—those wrinkled, sometimes alien-looking creatures newly emerged from their mothers' wombs—eventually become people who attend college. How much stake do we put in preserving normality, the status quo? We already talked about tact. Little children are tactless all the time. I once handed my grandfather a wrapped present from my mother and announced, "Happy Father's Day! It's a shirt!"

It was cute because I was 5, but what if I had done the same thing at 15? Would it have been cute? Somewhere along the way, we learn the unwritten rules.

On May 23, 1999, the World Wrestling Federation (WWF) aired a live pay-per-view event called *Over the Edge*. When a harness malfunctioned, wrestler Owen Hart, who was being lowered into the ring, fell 78 feet to his death. Although television viewers did not see the live footage of his death, once Hart was removed and sent to the hospital (he was pronounced dead on arrival), the program continued. The decision to go forward with the event sparked conversation and criticism far beyond the wrestling world. Some were shocked, even outraged, that the producers did not cancel the program, whereas others stood by the old adage "the show must go on." Why the radically different reactions? Well, for starters, we do not have a standardized social script for this type of incident. How should death be handled when it occurs on live television? We tend to seek a return to normalcy when things do not go as planned. Trying to quickly transition the situation back to normal (and probably to keep its paying customers happy), the WWF continued the live event. While some might have been appeased, others were disgusted by this apparent insensitivity. The following night, the association aired a two-hour tribute to the fallen wrestler.

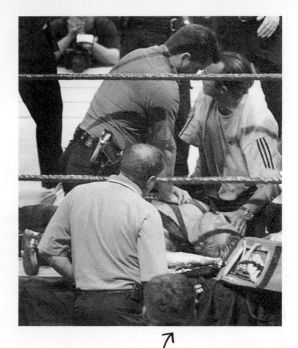

Paramedics try to resuscitate professional wrestler Owen Hart after a deadly fall in Kansas City, Missouri.

This is an extreme and tragic example, but we witness more mundane breaches of social scripts on a fairly regular basis. When things don't go according to plan, depending on the severity, nature, and context of the deviation, we must find some way to recover, and recover we usually do. From small breaches in our shared understanding of turn-taking etiquette to major ruptures in the fabric of society, people work hard to broker consensus with respect to shared meaning. A lack of agreed-upon socialization only leads to chaos and social insanity.

PRACTICE

ROLE CONFLICT AND ROLE STRAIN

Part of modern social life involves seamlessly managing the inevitable conflicts and strains that arise due to the many hats we wear. Sociologist Robert Merton identified two forms of this phenomenon: (1) role strain, where the tension is between two roles (i.e., duties or scripts) associated with a particular status; and (2) role conflict, which stems from competing demands arising from different statuses.

TRY IT!

Make a list of a few of your statuses (e.g., student, roommate, waitress). For each of the statuses, list three roles that each status entails. Here's one example:

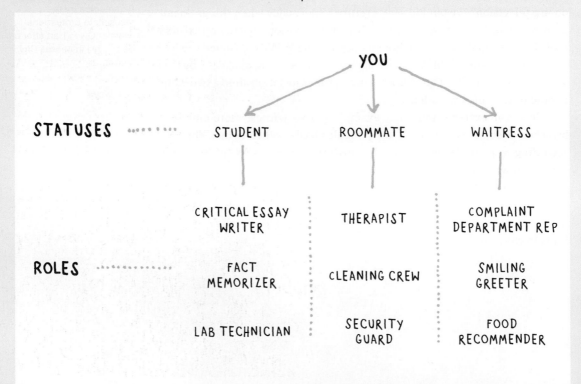

When you lay out these various roles, you can see that the role of "complaint department rep" conflicts with the role of "food recommender." You have to upsell the food and make it sound appealing, but then you have to take seriously complaints about the undercooked burger you just recommended.

ROLE STRAIN: COMPLAINT DEPARTMENT REP ⟷ FOOD RECOMMENDER

We can also see evidence of role strain. Let's say your essay is due by midnight. You're making progress, but suddenly, the door to your dorm room springs open and your roommate is weeping because her boyfriend just dumped her. What do you do?

ROLE CONFLICT: CRITICAL ESSAY WRITER ⟷ THERAPIST

How do you manage the role strains and conflicts that you've identified? Merton talked about compartmentalization, for example, in which you create a firewall between two conflicting statuses.

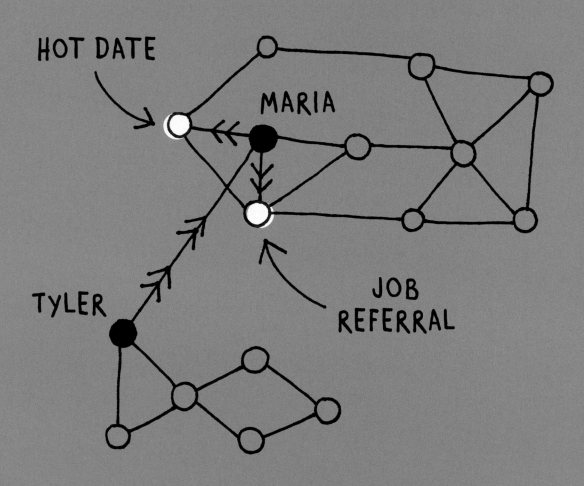

5

THE STRENGTH OF WEAK TIES:
IT IS THE PEOPLE WITH
WHOM WE ARE THE LEAST
CONNECTED WHO OFFER US
THE MOST OPPORTUNITIES.

HOT DATE

MARIA

TYLER

JOB
REFERRAL

Groups and Networks

Who is Satoshi Nakamoto? Nobody really knows for sure. Candidates have included a deceased extropian cryptographer on the West Coast of the United States named Hal Finney (extropians are a group of people dedicated to finding a way to live forever), a Hungarian American recluse, and an Australian academic. Whoever uses the pseudonym Satoshi Nakamoto is one of the richest people in the world due to the value of the bitcoin that person possesses (worth about $20 billion at the time of this writing). In late 2008, someone using the name Satoshi Nakamoto published a white paper online titled "Bitcoin: A Peer-to-Peer Electronic Cash System." The idea was bold: Instead of keeping financial records in a central system, like a bank, all financial transactions would appear on the "blockchain," a public shared ledger. In January 2009, at the depths of the financial crisis and the Great Recession, Nakamoto released the software to make the concept of a peer-to-peer anonymous form of currency operational. In the first "block" issued in the blockchain, Nakamoto embedded the following message: "The Times 3 January 2009 Chancellor on brink of second bailout for banks." And, voilà, the first major cryptocurrency was born.

Since the launch of Bitcoin, the number of cryptocurrencies has skyrocketed. New ones include Ethereum, Litecoin, and Tether. Once mainly used for the "dark web" (or online trade in illegal goods), a rapidly growing number of mainstream businesses now accept bitcoin as payment. Many residents of countries with unstable currencies who may have once tried to shift their assets to dollars or euros now use bitcoin to avoid the possibility that runaway inflation will decimate their savings. The CEO of America's largest bank, JPMorgan Chase, once scoffed at bitcoin, claiming that he would fire

bitcash

| 비트코인 (BTC) | ₩ 18,800,000 | 대시 (DASH) | ₩ 968,600 | 이더리움 클래식 (ETC) | ₩ 32,370 | 이더리움 (ETH) | ₩ 711,000 |

In Seoul, South Korea, monitors display exchange rates of cryptocurrencies including Bitcoin (top left), Ethereum, and Litecoin.

anyone who traded in it, but he now admits the power of the blockchain concept. Cryptocurrencies represent an amazing feat of technical savvy—specifically the use of digital signatures and hash functions—to make sure all transactions are on the up-and-up. (For a great overview on how they work from a technical perspective, see **youtube.com /watch?v=bBC-nXj3Ng4**). Along with an impressive financial feat, the rise of Bitcoin also represents the triumph of social networks.

All currency systems rely on trust within a social network. After all, if everyone suddenly decided not to accept British pounds sterling or Swiss francs, the value of these fancy pieces of paper would evaporate. Traditional currencies receive support from government organizations—usually central banks—that regulate the amount of currency in circulation and "guarantee" their authenticity. Even pseudo-currencies like airline points, which exceeded the total value of dollars or euros or pounds in 2005 (Clark, 2005), require a central authority to lend them value—namely, the airline. The authority and value of bitcoin and other cryptocurrencies uniquely rest in the social network itself by virtue of the fact that a coin is merely an entry into a public ledger (or blockchain) recorded multiple times across the entire network of users' computers. Yet the owners (and miners) of bitcoin can remain completely anonymous like our protagonist, Satoshi Nakamoto. Welcome to the power of social networks.

Cryptocurrency has gone mainstream. By 2021, almost one-third of Americans ages 18–29 have used crypto (Pew Research Center, 2021a). At least two governments—namely, El Salvador and the Central African Republic—have made bitcoin their official currency. However, as the stock market entered bear market territory in 2022 (losing more than 20 percent of its value from a prior peak), the market for crypto cratered even more. Big investors found opportunities to escape without losing their shirts (completely), but small investors, lured into crypto by promises of quick profits, generally got soaked. This disparate distribution of consequences illustrates another aspect of social networks: They are not necessarily equalizing forces.

This chapter explores some of the basic theories about group interaction and its influence on our social world. We'll look at the connections between groups: how size and shape matter, what roles group members play, and how the power of groups compares to the power of individuals and other institutions. We'll also discuss organizations, including how they both react to and create social structure.

By the end of this chapter you'll be able to:

- Describe groups based on size and their resulting social dynamics.
- Reflect on our most embedded social relationships and the potential influences of weak ties in our own lives.
- Identify various types of visual models of social networks.
- Consider the internal and external factors that affect organizational culture.

Social Groups

▌ Describe groups based on size and their resulting social dynamics.

Unless you live alone in the woods (and perhaps even then), you are a member of many social groups. Social groups form the building blocks of society and most social interaction. In fact, even the self evolves from groups. Let's start by talking about the various types and sizes of groups. In his classic work "Quantitative Aspects of the Group," sociologist Georg Simmel (1950) argues that, without knowing anything about the group members' individual psychology or the cultural or social context in which they are embedded, we can predict the ways people behave based solely on the number of members, or "social actors," in that group. This theory applies not just to groups of people but also to states, countries, firms, corporations, bureaucracies, and any number of other social forms.

JUST THE TWO OF US

For Simmel, the most important distinction in social groups is that between a relationship of two, which he calls a dyad, and a group of three, which he calls a triad. This fundamental distinction holds regardless of the individual characteristics of the group's members. Of course, personality differences do influence social relations, but there are numerous social dynamics about which we can make predictions that have nothing to do with the content of the social relations themselves.

    The dyad has several unique characteristics. For starters, it is the most intimate form of social life, partly because the two members of the dyad are mutually dependent on each other. That is, the continued existence of the

DYAD
a group of two.

TRIAD
a group of three.

Dyads are the foundation of all social relationships. Why are they the most intimate relationship, according to Georg Simmel?

group relies entirely on the willingness of both parties to participate in the group; if either person leaves, the dyad ceases to exist. The fact that no third person buffers the situation or mediates between the two only enhances the intimacy of the dyad. Meanwhile, the two members of a dyad don't need to be concerned about how a third group member might perceive their relationship to each other since there is no third party.

For example, we might consider a couple the most intimate social arrangement in our society. Both people must remain committed to being in the dyad. If one partner leaves, the couple no longer exists. Secrets rarely last long—if the last piece of chocolate cake disappears and you didn't eat it, you know who did. You could try to withhold a secret from your dyadic partner, but in terms of the actions of the group itself, no mystery lingers about who performs which role or who did what. Either you did it, or the other person did.

A dyad must maintain symmetry. There might be unequal power relations within a group of two to a certain extent, but Simmel would argue that in a group of two an inherent symmetry exists because of the earlier stipulation of mutual dependence: The group survives only if both members remain. Even in relationships where the power seems so clearly unequal—for example, think of a master and a servant or a prisoner and a captor—Simmel argues that there's an inherent symmetry. Yes, the servant may be completely dependent on the master for wages, sustenance, food, and shelter, but what happens to the master who becomes dependent on the labor that the servant performs? Of course, forcible relationships might develop in which one of two parties truly cannot leave the dyad, but the relationship in a pure dyad has to be voluntary. The knowledge that a dyad could fall apart at any moment heightens the underlying social intimacy.

The group itself exerts no collective influence over the individuals involved because the group exists only as long as the individuals voluntarily maintain it. In other words, blame and peer pressure hold much weaker influences. For example, whereas a child might claim, "She made me do it!" and shamelessly tattle on her older sister, a member of a dyad has less room to say, "I was just following orders" or "the whole group decided to go see *Mission: Impossible 7*, and I really didn't want to, but I went anyway." Unlike the symmetrical balance of a dyad, a group of three or more individuals carries a much stronger force.

Let's take the real-life example of a divorce to see how the characteristics of a dyad play out. In the typical marriage timeline, the divorce rate becomes especially high after the birth of the first child (and not just because of the parental sleep deprivation that a newborn brings). The nature of the relationship between the two adults changes from a dyad to a triad. Perhaps the parents feel a sudden lack of intimacy, even though the baby is not yet a fully developed social actor. On the flip side, a husband or wife might begin to feel trapped in a marriage specifically because of a child. Abruptly, group power exists. A couple has evolved into a family, and with that growth comes the newfound power (and pressure) of numbers.

AND THEN THERE WERE THREE

The growth of our hypothetical couple brings us to the triad. In a triad, the group itself holds a degree of collective power. In other words, in a group of three or four, I can say, "I'm really unhappy, I hate this place, I hate you, and I'm leaving," but the group will go on. The husband may walk out on his wife and children, but the family he abandons still exists. Even if he ends his participation in the group, the group outlasts his decision to leave it. Therefore, a triad does not depend on any one particular member.

Furthermore, secrets can exist in a triad. Who left the cap off the toothpaste? If more than two people live under the same roof, you can't be sure. Politics is another aspect inherent in a group of three or more. Instead of generating consensus between two individuals, now you have multiple points of view and preferences to balance. This need for compromise allows for power politics among the group's members. Simmel refers to three basic forms of political relations that can evolve within a triad depending on the role assumed by the entering third party (Figure 5.1). The first role is the mediator, who tries to resolve conflict between the other two and sometimes joins the group for that explicit purpose. A good example of a mediator would be a marriage counselor. Rather than going to therapy, couples having marital problems often start a family because they believe a baby will bring them back together. Unfortunately, as most couples realize sooner rather than later, a baby cannot play the role of a mediator. Rather, the dynamics of the unhappy family may turn into a game of chicken, spurring questions such as which parent is more devoted to the child. Which dyad forms the core of the group, and which person will be left out or can walk away more easily?

A second possible role for the incoming third member of a triad is *tertius gaudens* (Latin for "the third that rejoices"). This individual profits from the disagreement of the other two, essentially playing a role opposite to that of the mediator. Someone in this position might have multiple roles. In the previous example, the marriage counselor plays the part of the mediator but also earns wages from the conflict between the couple. The counselor may encourage continued therapy even after the couple appears to have resolved their issues, or perhaps the counselor suggests staying together even after they decide on a divorce.

The third possible role for a third party that Simmel identifies is *divide et impera* (Latin for "divide and conquer"). This person intentionally drives

MEDIATOR

the member of a triad who attempts to resolve conflict between the two other actors in the group.

TERTIUS GAUDENS

the member of a triad who benefits from conflict between the other two members of the group.

DIVIDE ET IMPERA

the role of a member of a triad who intentionally drives a wedge between the other two actors in the group.

FIGURE 5.1 Political Relations within a Triad

MEDIATOR

The mediator attempts to resolve conflict between the other two members of the triad and sometimes joins the group for that explicit purpose.

TERTIUS GAUDENS

Latin for "the third that rejoices." This individual profits from the disagreement of the other two actors, essentially playing the opposite role from the mediator.

DIVIDE ET IMPERA

Latin for "divide and conquer." This person intentionally drives a wedge between the other two parties.

a wedge between the other two parties. Although similar to *tertius gaudens* in that the third member benefits from the conflict between the other two, the difference lies in a matter of intent and whether the rift preexisted. (If you've ever seen or read Shakespeare's *Othello*, there is no better example of *divide et impera* than the way Iago, counselor to Othello, uses the Moor's insecurities to foster a rift between him and his wife, Desdemona, in order to strengthen Iago's own hand in court politics. The play ends tragically, of course.)

Let's return to the case of the triad formed when a romantic couple has a child but then they experience strife and separate. What happens when the couple divorces? What role does the child play? A child could play any of the roles mentioned above. In the original dyad of the biological parents, the child can serve as a mediator, forcing the parents to work together on certain issues pertaining to the child's care. A child can be "the third who rejoices" from the disagreement of the two, profiting from the fact that the child might receive two allowances or extra birthday presents because each parent wants to prove that they love the child more. A complicated *divide et impera* situation could develop if one of the child's parents enters into a second marriage, in which the child remains the biological child of one parent and becomes the stepchild of the other. In this case, all sorts of politics may arise because of the biological connection between the one parent and the child versus the marital-love relationship between the two adults. The relationship between the nonbiological parent and the stepchild, who have the weakest bond, could unfold in any number of ways. Many domestic comedies (think *The Parent Trap*) stem from the premise of a young, angst-ridden prankster playing the role of *divide et impera* between their parent and the new stepmother or stepfather.

When contemplating how these theoretical concepts work within actual social interaction, keep in mind that these groups—dyads and triads—don't exist in a vacuum in real life. In discussing the politics of a stepfamily, we're talking about a household where there's a stepparent, a biological parent, and a child. Beyond our textbook example, in real life this triad probably doesn't function so independently. Another biological parent likely lives elsewhere, possibly with another stepparent or even siblings. We need to take the complexity of social groups into consideration when we attempt to determine how they operate. As Simmel's purest forms of interaction, dyads and triads become the building blocks for those in much larger groups.

In what ways are triads more complex than dyads? What are the possible roles of triad members?

SIZE MATTERS: WHY SOCIAL LIFE IS COMPLICATED

As the number of people (nodes) in the group increases geometrically (2 + 1 = 3; 3 + 1 = 4; 4 + 1 = 5), the complexity that group's ties (edges) increases exponentially (2 · 2 = 4; 4 · 4 = 16; 16 · 16 = 256). A two-person group has only one possible and necessary relationship; a tie must exist between the two people for a group to exist. A sum of three relationships comprises a triad, with each person in the group having two ties. Each person in the triad must have two ties because breaking a single tie turns the triad into two dyads. Even if one of the ties between two members is weaker, the other two ties reinforce it, making it unlikely to fade. This support system among ties is known as the "iron law" of the triad, or more technically, "triadic closure." When you move beyond triads to groups of four or more, something different happens. To create a group of four, there must be at least four relationships, but you can have as many as six. Figure 5.2 shows this exponential rise in possible relationships graphically.

In a diagram with four people (A, B, C, and D), we can cross out the diagonals and the group will still exist. Everyone may have only two relationships

FIGURE 5.2 Relationship between Group Size and Complexity

ONE POSSIBLE RELATIONSHIP

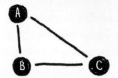

THREE POSSIBLE RELATIONSHIPS

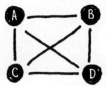

SIX POSSIBLE RELATIONSHIPS

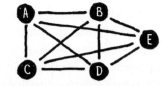

TEN POSSIBLE RELATIONSHIPS

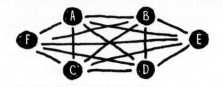

FIFTEEN POSSIBLE RELATIONSHIPS

as opposed to three (the number of possible relationships). Persons A and D might never have spoken to each other, but the group as a whole will continue to function. Trends show that these possible relationships often become actual relationships. You and your roommate are in separate chemistry classes, but your lab partners also happen to be roommates. If you both become friendly with your lab partners outside of class, you will eventually meet your roommate's lab partner and vice versa. Such social ties between friends of the same friend tend to form, for better or for worse. You may form a study group and, if your roommate's lab partner's boyfriend is a chemist, you (and everyone else) may benefit from his help. On the other hand, if the two break up and you start dating the chemist, future labs might feel a little uncomfortable for your roommate.

SMALL GROUP

a group characterized by face-to-face interaction, a unifocal perspective, lack of formal arrangements or roles, and a certain level of equality.

LET'S GET THIS PARTY STARTED: SMALL GROUPS, PARTIES, AND LARGE GROUPS

Groups larger than a dyad or triad, according to Simmel, fall into one of three classifications: small groups, parties, or large groups. Four factors characterize a small group. The first is *face-to-face interaction*; all the members of

the group are present and interact with one another. They are not spread out geographically. Second, a small group is *unifocal*, meaning that there is one center of attention at any given time. Speakers take turns sharing their thoughts. A classroom, except when students are engaged in small group work, should be unifocal.

Classes usually don't qualify as small groups because of the third characteristic of small groups: a *lack of formal arrangements or roles*. A study group, though, might qualify if you decide shortly before an exam to meet with some of your classmates. You need to agree on a place and time to meet, but otherwise, there is no formal arrangement. In the classroom, however, the professor, the teaching assistants, and the students all play official roles in the group.

The roles generally encountered in classrooms also contradict the fourth defining characteristic of a small group: *equality*. After all, you typically don't grade your professor, nor will your professor get into trouble (as you might) for arriving late to a scheduled lecture. Yours isn't a reciprocal and equal relationship. A small group, like a dyad, requires a certain level of equality. Only in a dyad can pure equality exist, because both members hold veto power over the group. However, in a small group, even if the group continues to exist beyond the membership of any particular member, no particular member has greater sway than the others. No one member can dissolve the group. If someone in your study group gets tired and falls asleep on his book, you and your classmates can continue to study without him.

When does a small group become a party? If you have ever hosted a party, you know that getting started is the hardest part. You're worried that people might not show up: The party has begun, only three people are there (everyone, after all, tends to arrive fashionably late), and you start to wonder, "Is this going to be it?" You have to keep a conversation going

What makes the study group on the left a small group, and how does it differ from the cocktail party on the right?

↑

How is this classroom an example of a large group?

among three people. You refill their glasses as soon as they take one sip (with alcohol only if you're all of legal drinking age, of course). When does your small gathering officially evolve into a party, so that you can relax and enjoy yourself? Simmel would say that a party, like a small group, relies on face-to-face interaction but also must be *multifocal*. Going back to the example of your sociology study group, if two people begin to talk about George Herbert Mead's theory of the self while the rest discuss the differences between role conflict and role strain, then your group becomes bifocal; if another subgroup splits off to deliberate on reference groups, then it is officially multifocal. According to Simmel, you've got yourself a party! So when you're hosting your next party, you'll recognize when it really gets started.

The last type of group that Simmel describes is the large group. Large groups must include a *formal structure* that mediates interaction and, consequently, *status differentiation*. When you enter a classroom, it should be clear who the teacher is, and you comprehend that the teacher has a higher status than you in that specific social context.

The professor works for your university, knows more than you know about an academic subject, and assigns you a grade based on your performance in the course. You might complete a teacher evaluation form at the end of the semester, but it's not the same as a professor grading a student. You and your professor aren't equals. This example shows that the inherent characteristics of a group are determined not just by its size but also by other aspects of its form, including its formal, bureaucratic structures or lack thereof. Whether a group stays small, becomes a party, or evolves into a large group may depend on numbers, but it also depends on the size and configuration of the physical space or technological platform that mediates interactions between and among group members, preexisting social relationships, expectations, and the larger social context surrounding the group itself.

PRIMARY AND SECONDARY GROUPS

In addition to Simmel's theory of basic groups, sociologist Charles Horton Cooley (1909) emphasized a distinction between what he called primary and secondary groups. Primary groups are *limited in the number of members,* allowing for face-to-face interaction. The group is an end unto itself rather than a means to an end. Think about the difference between your family and a sports team or small business: You want the family to function well, but you're not trying to compete with other families or manufacture a product. Meanwhile, primary groups are *key agents of socialization*. Remember the role of family in socialization? Family is a primary group. Your immediate family (parents and siblings) can probably sit down at the same dinner table or at least gather in the same room at the same time (even if some arguing ensues). Members of a primary group are *noninterchangeable*— you can't replace your mother or father. Finally, the relationships within a primary group are *enduring*. Your sister will always be your sister. Another example of a primary group might be your closest friends, especially if you've all known each other since your sandbox years.

The characteristics of secondary groups, such as labor unions, stand in contrast to those of primary groups. The secondary group is *impersonal*; you may or may not know all of the members of your union. It's also *instrumental*, meaning that the group exists as a means to an end; in this case, your union exists in order to organize workers and represent their interests. In a secondary group, affiliation is *contingent*. Your membership in your union relies on holding a certain job and paying your dues. If you change jobs or join another union, your membership in that earlier group ends. Because the members of a secondary group change, the roles are more important than the individuals who fill them. The shop steward (the person chosen to interact with the company's management) may be a different person every year, but that position carries the same responsibilities within the group regardless of who fills it. A sports team is another example of a secondary group, although if you're also close friends with your teammates and socialize with them outside of practice, the line between a primary and secondary group can become blurred.

SECONDARY GROUPS

groups marked by impersonal, instrumental relationships (those existing as a means to an end).

GROUP CONFORMITY

Although we tend to value individuality in American culture, high levels of conformity still define our lives. That is, groups have strong influences over individual behavior. In the late 1940s, the social psychologist Solomon Asch carried out a now-famous series of experiments to demonstrate the power of norms on group conformity. He gathered subjects in a room under the pretense of conducting a vision test, showed them images of two lines, and asked them to identify lines of different length and lines of the same length (Figure 5.3).

FIGURE 5.3 The Asch Test

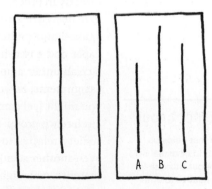

SOURCE: Asch, 1956.

Only one person in each room was a real research subject; the rest of the people were instructed ahead of time to give the same wrong answer. While a majority of subjects answered correctly even after they listened to others give the wrong answer, about one-third expressed serious discomfort and clearly struggled with what they thought was right in light of what everyone else was saying. When the group members gave a range of responses, the research subjects had no trouble answering correctly, but subjects had the hardest time when the entire group offered the same incorrect answer. This experiment demonstrates the power of conformity within a group.

IN-GROUPS AND OUT-GROUPS

In-groups and out-groups also categorize people. The in-group is the powerful group, most often the majority, whereas the out-group is the stigmatized or less powerful group, usually the minority (though the numbers don't always break down this way). For example, in the United States, heterosexuals are the in-group in terms of sexuality (both more powerful and numerically greater), whereas homosexuals, bisexuals, and those identifying with other sexual identities fall into the out-group. Usually, the power of the in-group and the numerical majority coincide; however, in South Africa, despite being a minority group, Whites are the in-group due to their enormous political and economic power (the legacy of colonialism and apartheid), while Blacks make up the out-group despite their greater numbers. The significance of in-groups and out-groups lies in their relative power to define what constitutes normal versus abnormal thoughts and behavior, not their objective numerical measures.

REFERENCE GROUPS

We often compare ourselves to other groups of people we do not know directly in order to make comparisons. For example, your class might compare itself to another introduction to sociology class, which you find out has a take-home midterm and an optional final. If your class has a 20-page term paper and a two-hour comprehensive final exam, you might feel as if you face an unfair amount of work in comparison. If your class has no external assignments, however, and your final grades are based on self-assessment, you might feel comparatively lucky. In either case, the other class serves as a reference group. Reference groups help us make sense of our position in society relative to other groups. The neighboring town's high school and even another socioeconomic class can serve as reference groups. In the first instance, you might compare access to sporting facilities; in the second, you might compare voting patterns.

IN-GROUP

another term for the powerful group, most often the majority.

OUT-GROUP

another term for the stigmatized or less powerful group, the minority.

REFERENCE GROUP

a group that helps us understand or make sense of our position in society relative to other groups.

From Groups to Networks

I Reflect on our most embedded social relationships and the potential
influences of weak ties in our own lives.

Dyads, triads, and groups compose social networks. A social network is a
set of relations—a set of dyads, essentially—held together by *ties* between
individuals. A tie is the content of a particular relationship. Think about "the
ties that bind" as a set of stories we tell each other that explains a particular
relationship. If I ask you how you know a specific person, and you explain
that she was your brother's girlfriend in the eighth grade, and the two of
you remained close even after her relationship with your brother ended, that
story ties you to that person. For every person in your life, you have a story.
Simple stories explain some ties: "That's the guy I buy my coffee from each
morning." This is a uniplex tie. Other ties have many layers, so they are
multiplex: "She's my girlfriend. We have a romantic relationship. We also
are tennis and bridge partners. And now that you mention it, we are classmates at school and also fiercely competitive opponents in Trivial Pursuit."

A narrative is the sum of stories contained in a set of ties. A street gang
has its own narrative, for example, and so does the company that might
employ you someday. And the college or university that probably inspired
you to buy and read this book is also a narrative. Every person with whom
you have a relationship at your university forms part of that network. Your
school plays a significant role in the stories of all of your relationships with
professors, teaching assistants, and classmates. Without the school, in fact,
you probably wouldn't share a tie with these people at all. When you add
up the stories of the many actors involved in the social network of your
school—between you and your classmates, between the professors and their
colleagues, between the school and the vendors on campus—the result is a
narrative of your college. Of course, you may have other friends from high
school or elsewhere who have no relationship to your school, so your college
does not play such a significant part in the narratives of those relationships.

In Chapter 4, we talked about the power of symbols. What would you
have to do if you wanted to change the name of your school? You and your
friends could just start calling it something else, but you'd probably have
to hire a legal team to alter the contracts (a form of tie that is spelled out
explicitly in a written "story") that the school maintains with its vendors.
You would need to alert alumni and advise the departments and staff at
school to change their stationery, their websites, and any marketing materials. You would have to advise faculty to use the new name when citing

SOCIAL NETWORK

a set of relations—
essentially, a set of
dyads—held together by
ties between individuals.

TIE

the connection between
two people in a
relationship that varies
in strength from one
relationship to the next;
a story that explains our
relationship with another
member of our network.

NARRATIVE

the sum of stories
contained in a set of ties.

their professional affiliation. You would need to contact legacy families (let's say a family whose last seven generations have attended this college) and inform them of the name change. Do you now have a sense of how complicated it would be to change this narrative? Making a change that affects a large network illustrates the power of social structures. Ironically, something abstract like a name can be more robust than most of the physical infrastructure around us.

EMBEDDEDNESS: THE STRENGTH OF WEAK TIES

EMBEDDEDNESS

the degree to which indirect ties (i.e., friends of friends) reinforce social relationships.

One important dimension of social networks is the extent to which they are embedded. Embeddedness refers to the degree to which indirect paths (i.e., friends of friends) reinforce a social relationship within a network. The more embedded a tie is, the stronger it is. Compared to a relationship with someone who only you know personally, a tie to someone who also knows your mother, your best friend, and your teacher's daughter typically lasts longer. It may feel less dramatic and intimate than a personal, dyadic relationship to someone who knows nobody else you know (and vice versa), but embedded ties are more robust and more likely to endure simply by virtue of the difficulty you would have escaping them. Your connection to your strong ties will continue even if you don't want them to—if not directly, then through your "mutual" friends.

STRENGTH OF WEAK TIES

the notion that relatively weak ties often hold hidden value because they yield new information.

However, the counterpoint to this dynamic lies in what sociologist Mark Granovetter (1973) calls the strength of weak ties, referring to the fact that relatively weak ties that are not reinforced through indirect paths often have high value because they bring to light novel information and other resources, such as potential new social connections, jobs, sales, and so on. Let's say your college track team is your primary social group. Occasionally, you also see an old high school classmate on campus who you didn't really know (or run in the same circles with) back then, but he's on the university's volleyball team. If the track team has no plans on Friday night but the volleyball team is having a party, you've got an "in" through this relationship. Even though this tie is much weaker than those you have with the other track team members, this new information provides an opportunity for you and your strong social circles. That novelty is the strength of the weak tie you maintain with the classmate from home. If you take your track friends to the volleyball party and they become friends with your old friend, the tie between you and your old classmate is now reinforced by the ties between your old friend and your new track friends regardless of whether you personally interact with him or not. This example explains why the structure of networks matters and why ties between one individual and another can vary based on the entire social network and not only due to factors about that dyadic relationship itself. Even though your own friendships did not change at the volleyball party, the fact that people in one cluster of your social network befriended others on the outskirts of your social network strengthens the ties between you and both sets of the individuals.

The strength of weak ties as compared to strong, multi-reinforced ties has proved especially useful in job searches (Granovetter, 1974). In a highly embedded network of strong ties, all the individuals probably know the same people, hear of the same job openings, maintain the same contacts, and so on. However, your grandparents' neighbor, who you only see every so often, probably has a completely different set of connections. As we saw with your college network, the weak tie paradoxically provides the most opportunities. When Granovetter (1973) interviewed professionals in Boston, he determined that among the 54 respondents who found employment through personal network ties, more than half saw their contact person "occasionally" (less than once a week but more than once a year). Perhaps even more surprising, he discovered that the runners-up in this category were not people whom the respondents saw "often" (once a week or more), but rather those they saw "rarely" (once a year or less), by a factor of almost two to one. Additional research finds that weak ties offer the greatest benefits to job seekers who already have high-status jobs, suggesting that social networks combine with credentials to sort job applicants and that strong ties may be more useful in low-status, low-credential job markets (Wegener, 1991).

As seen in Figure 5.4, by linking two otherwise separate social networks, the weak tie between Natalie and Emily provides new opportunities for dating—not only for them but for their friends as well. Their tie bridges a structural hole between the two cliques, a gap between network clusters, where a possible tie could become an actual tie or where an intermediary could control the communication between the two groups on either side of the hole. In the figure, Jenny serves as the social entrepreneur bridging a structural hole because the people on the left side of the network diagram (Emily and Jason) have no direct ties with the people on the right (Michael, Doug, and Jeff). Their ties are only indirect, through Jenny. Assuming that the two sides have resources (interpersonal, professional, or romantic) that would complement each other's needs, Jenny's position allows her to mediate by acting as a go-between for the groups. When a third party connects two groups or individuals who would be better off in contact with each other, that third party functions as an "entrepreneur," and they profit from the gap. (Sounds like the *tertius gaudens* in the triad? It should.)

Small business owners exchange business cards at a speed networking event. In a limited amount of time, participants hope that making as many weak ties as they can will eventually help them expand and improve their businesses.

STRUCTURAL HOLE

a gap between network clusters, or even two individuals, if those individuals (or clusters) have complementary resources.

FIGURE 5.4 The Strength of Weak Ties

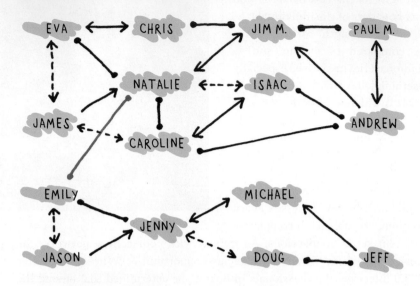

Natalie and Emily are social entrepreneurs; they command information to which the rest of their respective networks do not have access.

When sociologist Ronald Burt (1992) studied managers in a large corporation, he found that those with the most structural holes in their social networks actually rose through the company ranks the fastest and went the farthest. This notion explains profit making in today's economy. At one extreme, the totally free market has no structural holes; no restriction on information exists, and all buyers and sellers can reach one another—think eBay. At the other extreme, in the monopoly, one firm provides necessary information or resources to a multitude of people (i.e., maintains and profits from a gaping structural hole). Everything else occurs somewhere between these extremes: everyone from shipping magnates to spice traders to mortgage brokers to multilevel marketers. Take real estate agents as an example. They earn their money by contractually maintaining (or creating) a structural hole. By signing up sellers, the real estate agents prevent the sellers from directly engaging in a transaction with potential buyers. Recently, the social network possibilities facilitated by the internet (discussed later in this chapter) have done much to erode the power of brokers—for example, by driving once powerful travel agents into near extinction (ditto for stockbrokers).

Sociologist Stacy Torres noticed a third type of tie in her ethnography of a New York City elderly population that was "aging in place" (that is, growing old where they had lived for most of their adult lives rather than moving to a retirement destination or some form of supportive housing). These ties that her subjects cultivated existed somewhere between strong and weak. She called them "elastic ties." Here's Torres:

To see my interview with Stacy Torres about elastic ties, go to digital.wwnorton.com/youmayask8

> I noticed that there were these relationships [that] filled many of the criteria we associate with these [strong] close ties—that these people spent a lot of time with each other. They helped each other when certain crises emerged, they cared about each other. But when I started to interview people about their relationships with each other at the bakery and outside of the neighborhood with family, they often didn't name each other as friends. A lot of times they didn't even know each other's names. They saw each other multiple times a week, multiple times a day, and it took a long time for them to learn each other's names if ever and they didn't know each other's last names. They didn't have a lot of information about each other.
>
> But they would notice if somebody didn't show up to this bakery for a couple of days and they would want to check in on them, or if somebody was in the hospital or had to go to a nursing home, they would visit them. I found that these elastic ties were kind of outside [the framework of] close and weak, and it was a way for these people and this place to meet their needs for connection and closeness and support while maintaining some distance and not having to feel that they were getting overinvolved with people who now were their best friends and they had to visit every day and take care of. (Conley, 2019a)

ELASTIC TIES

social connections that display the repeated interactions characteristic of strong ties while maintaining a degree of protective social distance (i.e., not knowing more than a first name, if that).

SIX DEGREES

The term *six degrees of separation* probably sounds familiar. Is each one of us really connected to every other person by social chains of no more than six people? The evidence supporting the six degree theory came out of research undertaken in the 1960s by Stanley Milgram, whose colleagues posed the question of why the strangers they met at cocktail parties so often turned out to be friends of a friend. Milgram decided to test the reach of social networks

DIGITAL.WWNORTON.COM/YOUMAYASK8

To see my interview with Duncan Watts about six degree theory,
go to digital.wwnorton.com/youmayask8

by asking a stockbroker in Boston to receive chain letters from a bunch of folks living in Lincoln, Nebraska. The Lincolnites could send letters only to friends or relatives whom they believed would be likely to know someone who might know someone who might know the guy in Boston. About 20 percent of the letters eventually reached Boston, and the trip length averaged just over five people, hence the idea that (in the United States, at least) there are no more than five people between any set of strangers, or six degrees of separation.

Duncan Watts (2003) noticed that Milgram's findings applied only to the letters that made it to their final destination. What about the letters that did not complete the journey? Were their chains quite a bit longer than six steps, thus making our six degree theory more like a twelve degree theory? Watts set up a similar—this time worldwide—experiment using e-mail and statistical models to estimate global connectedness and found that Milgram was not quite right. In Watts's words, "It's not true that everyone is connected to everyone else, but at least half the people in the world are connected to each other through six steps, which is actually kind of surprising" (Conley, 2009b). Furthermore, Watts tested the commonsense notion that some people out there just seem to know everyone and these super-connected people allow the rest of us to say we're only six degrees from Kevin Bacon (or whoever). But instead, he found that when it comes to who we know, "the world's remarkably egalitarian," and super-connectors played almost no role in getting the e-mail forwarded all the way to its destination (Conley, 2009b). Social networks don't work like airline networks: There are not just a few hubs—like Kevin Bacon or Atlanta—in a high-density hub-and-spokes system. Rather, most of us have a few weak ties that span long social distances, which help bind all of us.

SOCIAL CAPITAL

SOCIAL CAPITAL

the information, knowledge of people or things, and connections that help individuals enter, gain power in, or otherwise leverage social networks.

When you have many weak ties, you have a lot of what sociologists call social capital. Like human capital, the training and skills that make individuals more productive and valuable to employers, social capital refers to the information, knowledge of people or things, and connections that help individuals

182   **Chapter 5: Groups and Networks**

enter preexisting networks or gain power in them. Consider the importance of networking in endeavors such as preventing neighborhood crime or obtaining a good job. The cliché holds a lot of truth: It's not just what you know but who you know. Weak ties may be the most advantageous for individuals; however, for communities, many dense, embedded ties also signify high levels of social capital.

Neighbors in the Central City section of New Orleans gather for their weekly domino game. Communities with thick webs of connection tend to thrive, usually with lower crime rates and more volunteer involvement.

This trend makes sense when you think about the reasons for it. Dense social capital means that a thick web of connections links people to one another. As a result of these connections, they will feel inclined—perhaps even impelled—to help each other, to return favors, to keep an eye on one another's property. More connections lead to more shared norms of reciprocity, values, and trust. After all, total anonymity doesn't really exist: Even if you don't know someone directly, chances are that you are only one or two degrees removed from that person.

In this way, strong social capital binds people together; it weaves them into a tight social fabric helps communities thrive. "You tell me how many choral societies there are in an Italian region," notes social capital scholar Robert Putnam, "and I will tell you plus or minus three days how long it will take you to get your health bills reimbursed by its regional government" (Edgerton, 1995). After years of research in Italy, Putnam determined that different regions of the country varied widely in their levels of participation in voluntary associations. As it turns out, the strength of participation in a region was a fairly good predictor of the quality and efficiency of its regional government (and, in turn, its economic growth).

The United States and Social Capital If social capital is correlated with economic and political health, some critics would say that the United States may be in trouble, especially when we compare our recent past with what some see as America's golden age of joining.

In the 1830s, Alexis de Tocqueville wrote *Democracy in America* based on his visit to the United States from France. Tocqueville found, to his surprise, that America was, in his words, a "land of joiners." By this, Tocqueville meant that Americans frequently came together to join voluntary associations. "Americans of all ages, all conditions, all minds constantly unite," Tocqueville wrote. "Not only do they have commercial and industrial associations in which all take part, but they also have a thousand other kinds: religious, moral, grave, futile, very general and very particular, immense and very small." Tocqueville observed that in democratic societies such as the United States, citizens enjoyed greater equality than citizens in aristocratic societies. Although Tocqueville praised this equality, he also believed that it made democratic citizens independent and weak, so organizations stepped in to make citizens politically stronger. After all, what good is one vote? He wrote that democratic citizens "can do almost nothing by themselves, and none of them can oblige those like themselves to lend them their cooperation. They therefore all fall into impotence if they do not learn to aid each other freely" (Tocqueville, 1835). Voluntary associations in Tocqueville's land of joiners were a way for independent citizens to join together under the union of a shared cause.

The propensity of Americans to join voluntary groups, such as the Parent Teacher Association (PTA) at the high school, the local softball league, or a knitting club, has puzzled sociologists, historians, and political scientists since Tocqueville first wrote about America as a land of joiners. Why are Americans so likely to join groups? Our participation rates in elections and formal political processes are some of the lowest in the world, which makes the question all the more intriguing. Some, like Tocqueville, suggest that the uniquely egalitarian nature of American democracy has made Americans more likely than Europeans to enlist in voluntary organizations (Doyle, 1977). Other scholars suggest that America's unique pattern of settlement contributes to high levels of voluntary organizations. In particular, the town square culture of early New England, in which people came together in town squares to discuss and debate current civic issues, created a lasting culture of voluntary association (Baker, 1997). Others point to America's long-standing identity as a land of immigrants who formed voluntary organizations to unite with other immigrants who shared similar cultural or political values (Gamm & Putnam, 1999).

In recent years, however, voluntary participation in civic life has declined, and as a result the nation's stock of social capital is at risk. In *Bowling Alone: The Collapse and Revival of American Community* (2000), Putnam traces the decline of civic engagement in the last third of the twentieth century. We are more loosely connected today than ever before, he says, as we experience less family togetherness, take fewer group vacations, and demonstrate little civic engagement.

Indeed, as the title suggests, more and more people have started bowling alone. Actual bowling activity rose at the end of the twentieth century, when Putnam

Bowling alone? Although the overall number of bowlers has increased, the number of people bowling in groups has dropped. Are we seeing a decline in social engagement?

↓

wrote his book. The total number of bowlers in America had increased by 10 percent from 1988 to 1993, but *league* bowling had dropped a whopping 40 percent in the same time frame. Putnam argued that bowling alone reflects a more general trend of civic disengagement and a decline in social capital. This decline shows up in PTAs, the Red Cross, local elections, community cleanups, and labor unions. Even membership in the Boy Scouts has decreased by 26 percent since the 1970s. More people also live alone (Klinenberg, 2013). Some go so far as to say that friendships have become shallower, and the phenomenon of deep, enduring friendships is an increasing rarity (Flora, 2013; Wuthnow, 1998). As civic participation withers, activities once performed by communities have moved toward private markets.

Anthony Fitz poses in front of the historic Malek Theater in Independence, Iowa. Decades after his mother was forced to close the theater in 1996, Fitz created a GoFundMe campaign to raise $150,000 for repairs. Why might crowdfunding— that is, requesting small amounts of money from a large number of people— be more effective than asking face-to-face?

Who's to blame for America's fading civic life: the social entrepreneur with too many structural holes to maintain, helicopter parents, our school systems, the internet, increased diversity, or the gig economy and rising inequality (Gould & Hijzen, 2016)? A combination of these and other factors works in conjunction with broad social trends, creating an increasingly differentiated, specialized, urbanized, and modern world. Social institutions must adjust to the flexibility, sometimes called the liquidity, of modernity by becoming more fragmented, less rigid, and more "porous" (Wuthnow, 1998). It becomes easier to come and go, to pass through multiple social groups such as religious congregations, friends, jobs, and even families. Gone is the rigid fixity of finding and holding on to a lifelong "calling." Similarly, a majority of graduating college students (60 percent) now attend more than one school before receiving a degree (Zernike, 2006).

Mobility and flexibility take a toll on people's lives. More than in previous eras, people report feeling rushed, disconnected, and harried, so it's no surprise that civic responsibilities take a backseat. It's not that Americans don't care; in fact, they join more organizations and donate more money now than ever before. They just don't give their time or engage in face-to-face activities (Skocpol, 2004). The rise of online associations could possibly explain this trend. We may show up less because the internet makes it easy to form new groups whenever we feel the need. It also allows for social connection (of some form) without requiring face-to-face contact. Political activism has moved online as well, with the presidential campaigns of Donald Trump and Joe Biden raising over $1 billion prior to the 2020 election, both of which included significant online contributions (NPR, 2020). The candidates raised a large percentage of their funds online through small donations. The website gofundme.com provides an essential platform for online donations: According to the site's 2021 report, the community raised $15 million in 2021, adding significantly to its $15 billion total donations since 2010 (GoFundMe, 2021).

Lastly, before we blame the internet for a decline in social capital and civic life, we should note that the trend toward giving more but showing up less predates the web. Even if online interactions exacerbate this pattern, increased work hours and other pressures to keep up in an age of rising inequality also play significant roles in this cultural shift.

The social pendulum swinging between loneliness and unity may be starting to turn back toward togetherness, with slightly different characteristics than we are used to seeing. Sociologist Eric Klinenberg (2013) set out to study people who live alone, trying to understand the costs and benefits of leaving some of the ties that bind dangling free. He found that being old and living alone indeed creates a lonely reality and a growing problem for women, who have always tended to outlive their husbands but now age alone in neighborhoods that their children have left to establish jobs and lives elsewhere. But for young and middle-aged people, living alone can still come with a lifestyle frequently filled with friends, dates, coworkers, volunteer work, and plenty of socializing. People who live alone volunteer more often than people the same age who live with partners or families. A decline in civic participation and an increase in independent lifestyles may not go hand in hand, even if these two variables seem similar.

Understandably, Putnam's claims have ignited much controversy. Some researchers noted that even if an increase in participation occurred after the 9/11 attacks, it was short-lived among adults (Sander & Putnam, 2010). Others claim the opposite, insisting that social capital never declined as Putnam declared. Rather, participation simply became more informal. Wuthnow, for example, argues that modernization brings about new forms of "loose connection" but hardly a disappearance of all

Volunteers build an elementary school playground in New Orleans. After Hurricane Katrina devastated the Gulf Coast in 2005, thousands of college volunteers participated in the rebuilding efforts.

connection. Things change, but not always for the worse. Though Putnam laments the loss of face-to-face communal ties, in the past three decades we've witnessed an explosion of non-place-based connections. Think of the rich social life occurring on social media, including Twitter, online blogs, and Facebook.

With the exit of the old (such as the Elks, Rotary, and other fraternal and civic organizations), new kinds of clubs have formed—for example, large national groups, including netroots political groups such as MoveOn.org, which people join by mail or online, informal support groups like WW (formerly Weight Watchers), and hybrids like Meetup.com, where interest groups form online but then meet face-to-face. As methods of interaction change, we define social capital differently; rather than a decline in social capital since the 1970s, civic engagement probably moves more like a pendulum, swinging back and forth between privatism (as in the 1920s) and heightened public consciousness (as in the 1930s). Today's world may feel like the end of social capital in some ways, but perhaps we're just at a low point on a constantly shifting trend line. The calls to save social capital may reflect a form of projected nostalgia, a misplaced romanticizing of the past, rather than signaling any real societal danger.

Sociologist Michael Gaddis uses network structure to look at another challenging aspect of social capital: Even for people with a healthy number of ties to friends, family, and community, not all social capital is equal. As Gaddis points out, "Everyone knows friends, coworkers, family members, but the important part of social capital . . . is the resources that are linked to you through these networks. Do I know someone who knows someone who has a job opening and could refer me? Can I access those resources?" He looked at kids growing up in "low-income families, one-parent families" who applied to the Big Brothers Big Sisters program, where they hoped to connect with an adult mentor. Gaddis compared students who received mentors with those who did not, finding that "mentors with higher education levels, higher income" were "able to make greater changes" among the little brothers and sisters (Conley, 2013b). The number of people you know does not automatically give you great social

DIGITAL.WWNORTON.COM/YOUMAYASK8

To see my interview with Michael Gaddis about the impact of social networks on low-income children, go to digital.wwnorton.com/youmayask8

CASE STUDY:
SURVIVAL OF THE AMISH

Lancaster County attracts more than 5 million visitors per year with its Pennsylvania Dutch country charm. Horse-drawn wagons carry visitors over covered bridges toward historic museums, colonial homes, and restaurants. Lancaster thrives on tourists' curiosity about the Amish, who first settled the land in 1693. Today about 59,350 Amish live in nearby homogenous farm communities. As far as appearances go, they certainly meet tourists' expectations.

Wearing straw hats and black bonnets, riding in horse-drawn buggies, the Amish provide great photo opportunities. Children attend private schoolhouses, typically one room, only until the eighth grade, after which they work full-time on the family farm. The lives of the Amish revolve around going to church, tilling the earth, and working for the collective good. They value simplicity

An Amish barn raising in Tollesboro, Kentucky.

and solidarity. How, visitors wonder, have Amish communities in Pennsylvania and other states survived in our fast-paced society?

The Amish certainly appear to be relics of the past, but looks can be deceiving. Although the Amish place primary importance on agriculture, they do so in anything but a premodern fashion. The Amish, especially those living close to urban areas, have adopted farming innovations like insecticides and chemically enhanced fertilizers. Their homes appear stylishly modern, with sleek kitchens and natural gas–powered appliances.

Because Lancaster County has experienced a certain degree of urban growth and sprawl, the Amish are not immune to the hustle and bustle of commerce. In fact, many Amish are savvy business owners. The number of Amish-owned microenterprises more than quadrupled between 1970 and 1990. By 1993, more than one in four Amish homes had at least one nonfarm business owner (Kraybill & Nolt, 1995). This economic growth results from a curious mix of profit-seeking entrepreneurship with a traditional lifestyle. Imagine finding out that your local rabbi, priest, or imam doubled as a high-rolling stock trader during the week.

How can these seemingly incompatible spheres of religious tradition and commerce coexist? Donald Kraybill (1993) set out to answer this question when he studied 150 Amish business entrepreneurs in Lancaster County (see also Kraybill & Nolt, 1995). Not only do the Amish trade with outsiders, Kraybill documented, but they do so quite successfully. About 15 percent of the businesses he studied had annual sales exceeding half a million dollars. Their success rate is phenomenal with just 4 percent of Amish start-ups failing within a decade compared with the 75 percent of all new American firms that fail within three years of opening. That is, in a time when the majority of new American business ventures flop, virtually all Amish businesses succeed. Are the Amish just naturally better at conducting commerce? Is it something in their faith or their self-discipline? Perhaps the answer lies in the community's hand-pumped water?

The answer is none of the above. The secret to Amish success turns out to be the way they strategically combine their traditions with the rest of the modern world. As the Amish become increasingly entangled in the economic web of contemporary capitalism, they have held on to their cultural traditions by maintaining an ideologically integrated and homogenous community. They are distinctly premodern and un-American in that they believe in the subordination of the individual to the community. They have rejected the prevalent American culture of rugged individualism, the notion of "every man for himself," often said to be the basis for successful entrepreneurship, in favor of "every man for the greater good." Individuals submit not only to God but also to teachers, elders, and community leaders. Their social fabric firmly binds people together. Whereas fashion for many people serves as a means of self-expression, the dark, simple clothing of the Amish signals membership in and subordination to the community. They have no bureaucratic forms of government or business; rather, they operate in a decentralized, loose federation of church districts. They reject mass media and automobiles, and they limit their exposure to diverse ideas and lands. These practices result in homogeneity of belief, unified values, and not surprisingly, dense social capital. Amish businesses, like the people themselves, are tightly enmeshed in the social networks,

Kimberly Hamme works on billing for her online business, Plainly Dressed, in her Paradise Town, Pennsylvania, home office. Hamme sells what most people would call Amish clothing. She does most of her business over the internet.

such as church and kinship systems, that provide economic support. The typical Amish person has more than 75 first cousins, who mostly all shop in the same neighborhood. Add to that the taboo on bankruptcy within the community, and Amish businesses would be a dream come true for investors—that is, if the Amish accepted outside capital (they don't).

Rather than marvel at how this culture maintains its centuries-old traditions while functioning in the business world, we should look at how they succeed in business regardless of their Amish traditions. Kraybill and Nolt found that the cultural restraints of Amish systems do indeed thwart business opportunities to some extent. Amish business owners aren't allowed to accept financial capital from outsiders or prosecute shoplifters (to do so would single out lawbreakers and go against community solidarity). The success of Amish entrepreneurship in spite of value systems that devalue profit-making illustrates the power of positive social capital.

capital; rather, high social capital stems from the resources associated with the people you know and their willingness to share those resources with you.

Through all these examples, we've painted a picture of a complex social world where the decay of some forms of civic life corresponds with new ways of building communities. Americans living in modern, urban, anonymous, and loosely connected communities carve out new social spaces, in turn creating a different kind of social fabric that holds together our republic. People adapt to what's new, retain what they can of the old, and negotiate within global forces and local communities. Just think about how you adapted your social relationships during the pandemic. Many of us went to school online, for example. Some of us conducted a greater amount of our social life virtually. There were, of course, both upsides and downsides to these changes, but either way, in response to extenuating circumstances, we revamped our social lives to adjust to the "new normal."

Network Analysis in Practice

▌ Identify various types of visual models of social networks.

Researchers take these concepts of embeddedness, the iron law of the triad, and network position and apply them to real-world contexts in order to understand how group life shapes individual behavior. Network analysts also map out social relationships to better understand transmission phenomena such as the spread of disease, the rise and fall of particular fads, the genesis of social movements, and even the evolution of language itself.

THE SOCIAL STRUCTURE OF TEENAGE SEX

According to sociologists Lisa Wade (2017) and Kathleen Bogle (2008), "hooking up" has replaced going steady on campus, and college students prefer "friends with benefits" to girlfriends and boyfriends, with all their attendant demands and the corresponding commitment (see Chapter 8). On the other hand, Wade also reports that about one-third of college students do not (or cannot) participate in this romantic culture on campus. In fact, the proportion of teens and young adults who are not having sex at all has risen across the globe in recent years (Institute for Family Studies, 2020).

Let's take a look at some nationally representative numbers for the United States: About 50 percent of American teenagers over the age of 15, when interviewed by researchers, admitted to engaging in sexual intercourse. (Boys probably tend to exaggerate their sexual experience, and girls probably downplay it.) A good number of those who have not yet had intercourse are still sexually active in other ways. Approximately one-third have "had genital contact with a partner resulting in an orgasm in the past year." Bluntly put, these statistics indicate that a good two-thirds of American teens are having sex or participating in some form of sexual activity. Teenagers' romantic relationships tend to be short term compared with those of adults, averaging about 15 months, so a fair amount of partner trading takes place. Survey research among college students, where hook-up culture is prevalent, found that 70 percent use condoms when they engage in vaginal/penile intercourse. That 70 percent is "a lot less than a hundred, but a lot more than zero," notes principal investigator Paula England (Conley, 2009d). To top off that less-than-perfect percentage, most adolescents with a sexually transmitted infection "have no idea that they are infected." All of these factors combine to make American teenagers a breeding ground for sexually transmitted infections (STIs), which have increased dramatically in this age group in the last decade.

Despite sensational media reports about teenage hook-ups, monogamous couples such as the one featured above are more typical. What else does research reveal about high-school sexual relationships?

So, what's a public health officer to do? During the administration of George W. Bush, conservative policy makers suggested the "virginity pledge" and other abstinence policies as a solution. As it turns out, the pledge does delay the onset of sexual activity on average, but when the teenagers who take it eventually do have sex, they are much more likely to practice unsafe sex (Bearman & Brückner, 2001; Brückner & Bearman, 2005). Among many problems in designing safe-sex or other programs to reduce the rate of STIs among teenagers, we also knew very little about the sexual networks of American adolescents until quite recently. It would not be far off to say that, until the turn of the twenty-first century, we knew more about the sexual networks of Aboriginal tribes on Groote Eylandt than we did about those of American teenagers.

One component of the National Longitudinal Survey of Adolescent Health, conducted by J. Richard Udry, Peter Bearman, and others from 1994 to 1996, investigated the complete sexual network at 12 high schools across the nation, including the pseudonymous Jefferson High School, whose 1,000-person student body is depicted in Figure 5.5 (Bearman et al., 2004). They focused their analysis on Jefferson because its demographic makeup (although almost all White) fairly accurately represents most American public high schools. More importantly, the town's isolated geography decreases the chance of the sexual networks spilling over to other schools.

FIGURE 5.5 Analysis of High-School Sexual Relationships

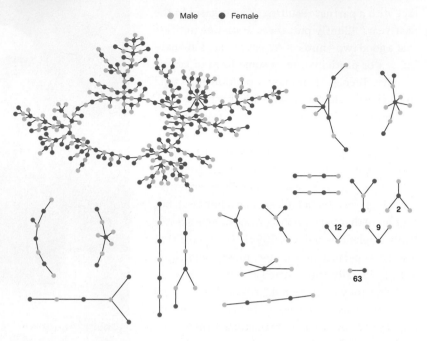

Male   Female

SOURCE: Bearman et al., 2004.

The pink and green dots represent girls and boys respectively. The dyad in the lower right-hand corner tells us that 63 couples have only had sex with each other. There are small, comparatively isolated networks consisting of 10 or fewer people and one large ring encompassing hundreds of students. Preventing the transmission of infection in the small networks is much simpler than preventing the spread in the large ring. One young man in the ring has had nine partners, but even if you persuaded him to use condoms or practice abstinence, you still wouldn't address most of the network. Your action might positively impact the people immediately around him. Lengthening the gap between partners has the potential to slow the spread of STIs: Sleeping with more than one person at a time increases the rate of transmission. The fuzzy ring structure represents a type of network called a circular spanning tree—a spanning tree being one of four ideal types of sexual networks hypothesized by Bearman and other epidemiologists (scientists who study the spread of diseases).

Figure 5.6 illustrates the four possible models of contact and spread for STIs. Panel A shows a core infection model, where the dark, filled-in circles representing infected people all connect to this core group. Therefore, the infection circulates through everyone in the group; however, these individuals also interact with external partners. If you mapped out a sexual network like this, with the objective of stopping the transmission of sexual infections, you

FIGURE 5.6 Models for Spread of Sexually Transmitted Infections

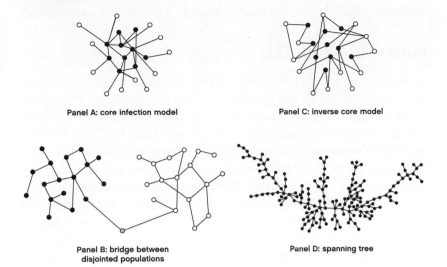

Panel A: core infection model

Panel C: inverse core model

Panel B: bridge between
disjointed populations

Panel D: spanning tree

SOURCE: Bearman et al., 2004.

would try to isolate that core network and either cut them off from sexual relations with others or at least ensure that when they came into contact with uninfected partners, they practiced safe sex. Panel B shows a possible structural hole. Imagine an infected group and an uninfected group, but one person bridges them. Theoretically, addressing such a circumstance should be easy in that simply cutting the tie or persuading that one person to engage in safe sex will protect the uninfected population. Panel C depicts an inverse core model, representing the way much of AIDS transmission occurs in populations where men routinely spend long periods of time away from their families, such as long-haul truckers and some men from African villages. The traveling men visit prostitutes in the city or at truck stops, acquire the virus from one, transmit it to another, and then bring the virus back home. The infected members do not have direct ties to each other (i.e., the prostitutes are not having sex with each other); rather, the individuals at the periphery of the core (the men who solicit the prostitutes) connect the core members to each other and possibly beyond the group to other populations. The last network model, illustrated in panel D, is the spanning tree model, in linear rather than circular form. Like a power grid, this model has a main line, and branches develop off of that line. It is difficult to completely stop transmission along a spanning tree model, which is helpful for electrical grids (if one circuit fails, the power can continue to flow around it, although as anyone who has experienced a blackout knows, specific sections can be left without power if they are severed from the rest of the tree). In terms of STI transmission, this design is less appealing; you could initiate some breaks that would split the tree into two groups, but even those gaps can't completely isolate the infection. If you attack something on a branch, you're not doing anything to the rest of the network. There's no key focal point that allows you to stop the spread.

ROMANTIC LEFTOVERS

When Bearman and his colleagues analyzed the sexual habits of teenagers, they uncovered another rule that governed this social network. They found lots of examples of triads, where internal groups trade partners. The main rule that governed these relationships was "no cycles of four," which means you do not date the ex of your ex's current boyfriend or girlfriend. The most interesting aspect of the rule, sociologically speaking, is that no one was consciously aware of this pattern. The researchers interviewed many students and not one of them directly stated, "Of course not, you don't date the ex of your ex's new flame." Yet this single taboo governs everyone. Figure 5.7 illustrates this rule of thumb graphically.

At time 1, Matt and Jennifer are dating, as are Jareem and Maya. At time 2, Jennifer and Jareem date. The rule suggests that Matt and Maya will never date. Why? Once Jennifer and Jareem start dating, if Matt and Maya decide to date each other, they essentially relegate themselves to the secondary social status of "leftovers." The practical, take-home lesson is that if you want to date the ex of your ex's new crush, act before your ex does. If you're Jennifer and you wish to prevent your old boyfriend Matt from going out with Maya, quickly start dating Jareem because then Maya and Matt will never date. The lack of awareness makes this kind of social norm possible because it's not conscious. This unspoken rule illustrates how social structures govern individual-level behavior and speaks to the limitations of interpretive sociology. If the researchers had taken a more Weberian approach and asked students how they choose partners and, more

FIGURE 5.7 Romantic "Leftovers"

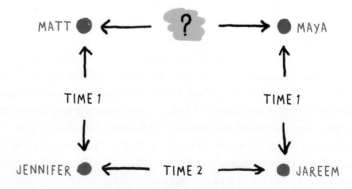

SOURCE: Bearman et al., 2004.

important, why they don't date certain people, they probably wouldn't have discovered this rule. The researchers could see this pattern only by taking a bird's-eye view and analyzing this structure with mathematical tools.

Organizations

> Consider the internal and external factors that affect organizational culture.

I've mentioned several times that sociology—here network analysis—applies not just to individuals but also to all social actors, including school systems, teams, states, and countries. In the contemporary United States, companies and organizations play important roles as social actors. In fact, thanks to the Fourteenth Amendment, they have identities as legal persons: They sponsor charitable causes, they can sue and be sued, and they even have birthdays.

Organization functions as an all-purpose term to describe any social network, from a club to a Little League baseball team to a secret society to your local place of worship to General Motors to the U.S. government, defined by a common purpose with a boundary between its membership and the rest of the social world. *Formal* organizations have a set of governing structures and rules for their internal arrangements (the U.S. Army, with its ranks and rules), whereas *informal* organizations do not (the local Meetup.com group for ambidextrous tennis players [an actual group!]). Of course, a continuum exists, because no organization has absolutely no rules, and no organization has a rule for absolutely everything. Therefore, the study of organizations focuses mainly on the social factors that affect organizational structure and the people in those organizations.

ORGANIZATIONAL STRUCTURE AND CULTURE

Have you ever heard the phrase *the old boys' club*? The term refers to exclusive social groups and derives from fraternities, businesses, and country clubs that allow only men—specifically, certain groups of elite men—to join. These groups have their own customs, traditions, and histories that make it difficult for others to join and feel as if they belong, even when the "boys" aren't being deliberately hostile. The term organizational culture describes the shared beliefs and behaviors within a social group, often used interchangeably with *corporate culture*. The organizational culture at a slaughterhouse, where pay is low, employees must wear protective gear, the environment is dangerous, and animals are killed continuously, probably differs greatly from the organizational culture at a small, not-for-profit community law center. The term organizational structure refers to the distribution of power and authority within an organization. The slaughterhouse probably has a hierarchical structure, with a clear ranking of managers

ORGANIZATION

any social network that is defined by a common purpose and has a boundary between its membership and the rest of the social world.

ORGANIZATIONAL CULTURE

the shared beliefs and behaviors within a social group; often used interchangeably with *corporate culture*.

ORGANIZATIONAL STRUCTURE

the distribution of power and authority within an organization.

and supervisors who oversee the people working the lines. The law center, however, might have a more decentralized and cooperative system, with five partners equally co-owning the business and collaborating on decisions. The structure of an organization often affects the type of culture that results. If a business grants both parents leave when a new child enters the home, allows for flextime or telecommuting, or has an on-site child-care center, those structural arrangements will in turn create a more family-friendly organizational culture than those of a company that doesn't offer such benefits.

The growth of large multinational corporations over the course of the last 100 years has affected organizational structure. One example of this impact is *interlocking directorates*, the phenomenon whereby the members of corporate boards often sit on the board of directors for multiple companies. In 2018, for example, 12 of the 19 biggest pharmaceutical companies had one or more directors who also held leadership positions at health-care nonprofits (BiopharmaDive, 2018). It has been reported that 16 of the 22 directors involved in multiple, potentially conflicting positions did not publicize their director position with a pharmaceutical company in their biographies on their nonprofits' websites (BiopharmaDive, 2018). Does it matter that these people sit together on the same boards? The problem, critics argue, is that doing so allows a select group of people—predominantly rich, White men—to control the decisions made in thousands of companies. Such people also have ties to research institutions and elected officials that may compromise their objectivity and create conflicts of interest. Capitalism, after all, is based on competition, but if board members on interlocking directorates favor the other companies to which they are connected, suppliers may not compete on a level playing field when bidding for contracts. Even worse, take the situation that might develop when a board member of a drug maker asks his friend and fellow board member at a health insurance company to give preferential coverage to his company's drugs over a competitor's drugs. This bias can lead to higher prices for consumers who need to purchase the competitor's drugs. Another situation might arise in which one of these two board members knows a former member of Congress through board service together whom they can use as a lobbyist to see that federal health programs like Medicare and Medicaid also give preferential treatment to a particular drug, costing taxpayers more than they would have paid without the pressure arising from these relationships. This type of situation can lead to what sociologist C. Wright Mills called a "power elite" or aristocracy. (Concern over the consolidation of control in the media industry, for example, is discussed in Chapter 3.)

INSTITUTIONAL ISOMORPHISM: EVERYBODY'S DOING IT

Networks provide information, a sense of security and community, resources, and opportunities, as we saw illustrated by Granovetter's concept of weak ties. However, networks both support and constrain. Paul DiMaggio and

Walter Powell (1983), focusing on businesses, coined the phrase *institutional isomorphism* to explain why so many businesses that evolve in very different ways still end up with such similar organizational structures. Isomorphism, then, is a "constraining process that forces one unit in a population to resemble other units that face the same set of environmental conditions" (Hawley, 1968). In regard to organizations, this concept indicates that those facing the same conditions (say, in industry, the law, or politics) tend to end up like one another.

Let's consider the hypothetical case of a new organization that enters a fairly established industry but wants to approach a topic differently. Perhaps a bank wants to distinguish itself from other banks by being more casual or more community oriented. The theory of isomorphism suggests that such a bank, when all is said and done, will wind up operating as most other banks do. Even this new, innovative organization remains locked into a network of other organizations and therefore receives significant influence from the environment of that network. DiMaggio and Powell represent a part of a school of social theory referred to as the new institutionalism, which essentially tries to develop a sociological view of institutions (as opposed to, say, an economic view). In this vein, networks of connections among institutions help us understand how the institutions look and behave. These theorists would argue that all airlines raise and lower their fares at the same time, for example, not because they are independently reacting to pure market forces but because symmetry, peer pressure, social signaling, and network laws govern their organizational behavior. The collective actions of these Fortune 500 companies are subject to the same forces that affect the sex lives of seniors at Jefferson High School. Pretty scary, huh?

On the other hand, sometimes an organization can achieve a great competitive advantage by breaking the mold of isomorphism, so to speak. The writer Michael Lewis documented such a case of anti-isomorphism in his book *Moneyball*, about how the 2002 Oakland Athletics achieved great success in Major League Baseball despite having a small budget. Under their manager Billy Beane, the team reimagined the traditional structure of a baseball team. They used computer analysis to determine that many of the statistics used by baseball executives, such as RBIs and stolen bases, did not actually predict success while other stats, such as on-base percentage, had more accuracy. Traditional feel-it-in-your-gut approaches to scouting players also turned out to fare poorly. By using cold-eyed computer analysis now known as sabermetrics, the A's made the playoffs in both 2002 and 2003. However, isomorphism usually doesn't last. Once Michael Lewis revealed the "secret" of the A's success, other teams copied the California franchise and became sabermetric as well, thereby diluting the A's competitive advantage. Information tends to spread through networks, even when we try to keep it to ourselves.

ISOMORPHISM

a constraining process that forces one unit in a population to resemble other units that face the same set of environmental conditions.

POLICY

RIGHT TO BE FORGOTTEN

In high school, I thought I would try to up my social status by swiping a bottle of my father's booze and bringing it on a school trip. I had little experience with this sort of activity, so I just grabbed whatever I saw. My plan backfired because it turned out that I had stolen dry vermouth, typically used only in minute amounts for mixing martinis or Manhattans. I had no idea that one did not generally drink vermouth straight. (Though, in an ironic twist, I have since learned that it is actually quite sophisticated to have it alone with an orange peel. My high-school self was cooler than he knew.) However, the moment after I whispered conspiratorially to one of the cool kids that I had booze and showed him the bottle in my possession, laughter spread across the chartered bus. For the rest of my high-school career, I carried the label "vermouth man."

Luckily for me, I went to college 3,000 miles away, where almost no others from my high school attended, so I had the opportunity to reinvent myself. Today, however, social media records almost everything teenagers do for posterity, leaving digital traces. (This is one of the main changes to adolescent social life documented by danah boyd; see my interview with her in Chapter 2.) College counselors tell students to set their privacy settings on the strictest level during application season. Students themselves often use "senior names" on social media to disguise their real identities. These solutions to the privacy problem don't always work. Just ask the 10 students who had their admissions to Harvard revoked after they shared sexually explicit and racially offensive memes in their "Harvard memes for horny bourgeois teens" Facebook group (Natanson, 2017).

But even if these short-term fixes work, what about the rest of your life? A dumb or offensive comment left on a website or an embarrassing party photo that tags you might trail you like a digital ball and chain each time you try to apply for a new job or date someone new. Is there a right to be forgotten just like the right to free speech or the right to a trial by one's peers?

The European Commission, the executive of the European Union (EU), seems to think so. The EU has drafted regulations guaranteeing the right to "obtain from the controller [i.e., the data collector or manager, such as a search engine or online database] the erasure of personal data relating to them and the abstention from further dissemination of such data, especially in relation to personal data which are made available by the data subject while he or she was a child or where the data is no longer necessary for the purpose it was collected for, the subject withdraws consent, the storage period has expired, the data subject objects to the processing of personal data or the processing of data does not comply with other regulation." These regulations—and the results of a lawsuit against Google in Spanish court—essentially mean that search engine firms now provide Europeans with a form they can fill out to request removal of links to information they'd rather not have out there, so to speak. Some jurisdictions now consider the "right to be forgotten" a fundamental human right.

Should there be a universal "right to be forgotten"? What are some arguments for, and some arguments against, data erasure on social networking websites?

interests. Does your right to be forgotten trump my right to know about you as a potential employer, neighbor, or romantic partner? Where does erasure end if we allow whitewashing of historical records? While we might all agree that revenge porn should be banned, what about links to bad reviews? Or even tags by former flames in photos that might upset new partners? The line is hard to draw. Perhaps, like sealed criminal records, the age of maturity should be used to wipe the slate clean. What about material moved to jurisdictions with looser laws (like the United States, which privileges free speech to a greater extent than Europe does)? The global reach of the internet's many-headed hydra makes slicing off one head of information without another popping up elsewhere difficult.

Sounds reasonable, no? Why should this generation enjoy less privacy than prior ones just because technology has changed? Well, not so fast. As with almost any "right," there are competing

While this battle between privacy advocates and free-speech diehards will likely continue for many years on multiple fronts, the fact that remains clear is the changing nature of social media and online networks means you should think more carefully about swiping a bottle of booze than I did back in the dark ages of 1985.

Conclusion

What do we learn from the formal analysis of group characteristics and social networks? Simply knowing the formal characteristics of a group helps us understand many of the social dynamics that take place within it. Is it a dyad or a triad? What is the proper reference group for a particular social process? Is this group a primary or secondary group, and what does that mean for an individual's obligations to it? Likewise, we can use network analysis in micro- and macro-level studies. On a micro level, you could carefully weigh the potential consequences of dating your best friend's ex by mapping out your social network and anticipating shifts in ties that might transpire. On a macro level, you could analyze President Richard Nixon's strategy of "triangulation" of the Soviet Union and Communist China during the early 1970s using the iron law of the triad. Sociologists use network analysis to study everything from migration and global politics to social movements and cultural fads.

PRACTICE

HOW TO DISAPPEAR

In 1995, on a red eye to Poland, I fell asleep and had my passport stolen. For all I know, there is another Dalton Conley with my papers who is still off drinking vodka and eating kielbasa. That happened before RFID chips, computerized global databases, and biometrics. Today, it would be a lot harder for me to mimic what my thief did—that is, either disappear or assume a new identity. Back then, records of documents were more easily falsified and one didn't leave digital traces with every trip to the supermarket. Before 9/11, you could even check into a hotel with no ID. But in today's hyperconnected world, it's much harder to fall off the grid. With surveillance cameras and facial recognition, those persecuted by their governments may find it harder to live on the down low. Conversely, refugees fleeing violence may have a harder time proving their identities and bolstering their claims in an age of smart documents.

TRY IT!

Let's say you wanted to disappear. How would you try to drop off the face of the earth, at least according to the social networks in which you're embedded? Here are the steps I personally would take:

Sell all my worldly possessions for cash on Craig's List

↓

Buy a burner phone

↓

Hitchhike to Mexico (certain border crossings
don't check ID in that direction)

↓

Learn Spanish

↓

Find a job picking fruit

↓

Never contact anyone from my prior life ever again

THINK ABOUT IT

Disappearing doesn't just mean shutting down your social media and saying goodbye to your friends. How would you actually function in society if you had to be completely on the DL—invisible to banks, the government, and every other institution?

6

IT IS THE DEVIANTS AMONG US WHO
HOLD SOCIETY TOGETHER.

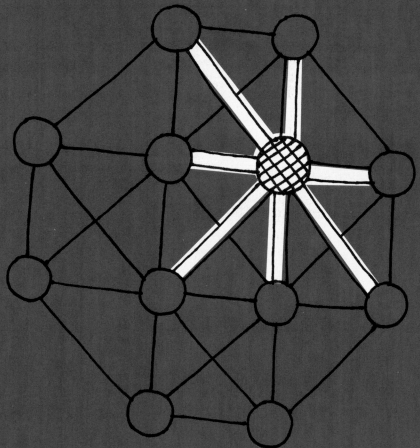

Animation at digital.wwnorton.com/youmayask8

Social Control and Deviance

Smiley got his nickname because he always smiled at the most improbable times. When teachers yelled at him because he had trouble paying attention, he smiled. When his smile upset the teachers and incited more yelling, he kept smiling. When he and a friend broke into a car for a place to sleep after his abusive parents kicked him out, he smiled. He surely smiled at the pretty girls with lipstick-reddened lips and pompadours when he and a couple of homies visited them in the neighborhood of a rival gang. He likely continued smiling when eight rival gang members showed up, bringing guns to what might have been a fistfight. One of those rival gang members shot Smiley in the head. His homie Victor scooped him off the pavement, bits of fresh brain matter clinging to his new sneakers. In lieu of waiting for an ambulance that might never show up to their ghetto address, Victor cradled the dying Smiley in the backseat on the way to the emergency room.

When the police arrived at the hospital, they assigned partial blame to Victor, threatening to charge him as an accessory to murder for being present at the scene. Victor, in anger and disbelief, instead demanded that the police find the real shooter. "What for?" one of the officers replied. "We want you to kill each other off."

Victor now goes by Associate Professor Victor Rios, working at the University of California, Santa Barbara. The other 67 homies from his original gang have not had Victor's success: 4 were murdered; 9 were permanently injured, mostly from handguns; 12 became addicted to drugs, sometimes living on the streets and panhandling to survive. Just two graduated from high school; only Victor went on to college. Why does it surprise us that Victor, a gang-member son of a single mother on welfare in an impoverished neighborhood, achieved status in one of the most heavily credentialed occupations? What does that surprise factor tell us about the relationship between deviance and social mobility?

Because Victor now works as a sociologist himself, I asked him about getting out of the ghetto and into the ivory tower. "A lot of times people say to me, 'Oh, Professor Rios, you're so unique. You have all these qualities, you made it out. You pulled yourself up by the bootstrap. You made it out of the ghetto and now you are here.' And my response is, 'Well, part of it is hard work, but everyone works hard.' For example, my mom, she's washed dishes 30 years of her life, working 10 hours a day, and she still makes 10, 11 dollars an hour. That's hard work. But she never progressed." He argues that hard work rarely pays off without an opportunity trajectory leading out of poverty.

Victor clearly recalls when he started to recognize systemwide shortcomings: "I was fortunate to find a teacher that cared, and she heard what happened [to Smiley], and she reached out to me and got me mentors from the university—students, college students, that wanted to go help the ghetto kids." These students provided enlightenment through the sociological imagination; they helped Victor see a bigger system at work, larger than himself and his entire community: "I was actually living in a world of poverty that wasn't necessarily just produced by the way that people in my community acted, but it was also produced by a larger system of racism, classism, and segregation" (Conley, 2009e).

In his book *Punished: Policing the Lives of Black and Latino Boys* (2011), Rios examines the criminalization of young boys in poor neighborhoods through aggressive policing strategies. The presence of police and parole officers in schools and community centers, the spaces in which education and mentoring traditionally occur, creates a self-fulfilling prophecy that projects criminal behavior on teenagers, treats them with suspicion bordering on aggression, and surveils them closely until catching them in some criminal act. Is flooding crime-ridden neighborhoods with aggressive policing the right thing to do? Or does sending more police to a neighborhood with highly concentrated criminal activity simply increase the number of people who get caught, closing routes out of that neighborhood by saddling its residents with criminal records?

This chapter examines how society coheres and why some people transgress the boundaries

DIGITAL.WWNORTON.COM/YOUMAYASK8

To see my interview with Victor Rios, author of *Punished*, go to digital.wwnorton.com/youmayask8

of normality. For starters, how do people who presumably started life as innocent kids end up in prison as teenagers and adults? How did Rios, an impoverished gang member growing up amid violence and theft, end up getting a PhD and becoming a professor? We can then turn to broader questions: Why doesn't society at large look like the violence-ridden Oakland, California, neighborhood of Victor's youth? Why do most of us choose to sacrifice some of our personal interests for the sake of the social whole? How can we explain how society achieves predictable order, and what role does the criminal justice system play? Theorists of social deviance have produced various answers to these questions.

By the end of this chapter you'll be able to:

- Identify basic concepts and terms related to social deviance.
- Describe Durkheim's understanding of deviance and social cohesion.
- Analyze theories of deviance.
- Identify different types of crime and their social influences.
- Apply sociological theories of social control and deviance to modern systems of justice.

What Is Social Deviance?

❙ Identify basic concepts and terms related to social deviance.

Social deviance, loosely understood, refers to any transgression of socially established norms. Transgressions can be as minor as farting in church or as serious as murder, so long as they break the rules by which most people abide. Minor violations are acts of informal deviance, such as picking your nose. Even if no one will punish you, you sense that the behavior is somehow wrong. At the other end of the continuum, we have formal deviance, or crime, which violates laws enacted by society. When deviant persons get caught in deviant acts, depending on the seriousness of the offense, they are subject to punishment. For instance, farting in church might result in glares from your fellow churchgoers, whereas a crime like theft may result in formal state-sanctioned punishments such as fines, community service, or jail time.

Because social norms and rules are fluid and subject to change, the definitions of deviance vary across contexts. For example, during the COVID-19 pandemic, not wearing a mask while shopping in a supermarket or riding a bus in certain communities became deviant behavior because wearing a mask became the local norm. However, other communities did not accept mask mandates, so the act of wearing a mask was seen as deviant, as if the

SOCIAL DEVIANCE

any transgression of socially established norms.

INFORMAL DEVIANCE

minor violations of social norms that may or may not be punished.

CRIME

the violation of laws enacted by society; formal deviance.

wearer felt "superior" or safer than others around them. Even seemingly obvious cases of deviance, such as killing another person, may not be so clear upon further investigation. When a soldier kills an enemy combatant, that act seems heroic to those on the same side. But if the same soldier kills their spouse, even fellow soldiers would consider the act heinous and punishable by a long prison sentence. Cultural and historical context also affects what is considered deviant. When women engaged in premarital sex in the Puritan colonies, they were subject to social exile; when women do so today in some Islamic countries, they risk public execution by stoning. In contemporary American society, however, sex outside of marriage is common and largely accepted. Similarly, 50 years ago, it was a crime for African Americans to share water fountains and swimming pools with White people; today, such segregation has no place in everyday American society. Just four decades ago, homosexuality was illegal nationwide. Police raids frequently targeted gay bars, and sexual orientation was grounds for excluding immigrants (a rule that held until the Immigration Act of 1990; Foss, 1994). As recently as 2003, before the U.S. Supreme Court struck down Texas's criminalization of homosexual sex in *Lawrence v. Texas*, it was punishable by arrest and a $500 fine. Changes in laws signal shifting social values and changes in social norms, such as increased tolerance of racial and sexual diversity.

In the popular conception, deviance typically takes the form of blatant rule-breaking or lawlessness. But deviance does not necessarily require outlandish activity. Deviance covers everything from answering your cell phone during a lecture to committing murder. It is a label that can be given to people who bike down crowded city streets and to those who sing along with their smartphones on the subway or bus. When reserved, soft-spoken people find themselves in a noisy crowd, their behavior goes against the grain, making them momentary social deviants. Even with strong roots in context, deviance is sticky; it cannot be turned off and on easily. Deviance can be a powerful label, capable of reproducing the entrenched social inequalities that punishment purports to correct. For example, transgender and non-binary people who identify differently than their biological sex at birth or do not have a categorical masculine or feminine identity are often subject to informal and formal punishments for their gender "deviance," although most are perfectly law-abiding citizens.

SOCIAL CONTROL

SOCIAL CONTROL

mechanisms that create normative compliance in individuals.

FORMAL SOCIAL SANCTIONS

mechanisms of social control by which rules or laws prohibit deviant criminal behavior.

The flip side of deviance is social control. Social control describes the set of mechanisms that creates normative compliance, the act of abiding by society's norms or simply following the rules of group life. That is, social control makes us into good law- and norm-abiding citizens.

Sociologists classify mechanisms of social control into two categories. The first are called formal social sanctions. In most modern societies, these formal sanctions would be rules or laws prohibiting deviant criminal behavior such as murder, rape, and theft. These sanctions are formal, overt "expressions of official group sentiment" (Meier, 1982). Informal social sanctions reflect the usually unexpressed but widely known rules of group membership. Have you ever heard someone use the expression "an unwritten rule"? Informal social sanctions are the unwritten rules of social life. So, hypothetically, if you loudly belch in public, you will probably receive a few disgusted looks. These gestures of contempt at your socially unacceptable behavior are examples of informal social sanctions, or the ways we keep each other in check by watching and judging those around us. As discussed in Chapter 4, we acquire a comprehensive understanding of these unspoken collective rules through the process of socialization. Through years of trial and error, we internalize the rules of the social game.

The idea behind informal social sanctions is that we all simultaneously reinforce social rules and have social rules enforced on us by others. How does this structure work? As we observe others' behavior, they observe ours, too; we all occupy the role of spectator and object of spectacle. Beyond watching, all of us have the power to grant rewards for others' good behavior in the form of smiles and encouragement, but we can also sanction with dirty looks, snide comments, and worse. In this way, we all contribute to the daily construction and reconstruction of the social whole.

Think about the neighborhood watch groups that preceded the widespread adoption of electronic home security systems. People in a community banded together and agreed to keep an eye out for trespassers, burglars, and suspicious strangers. Neighborhoods attempted to maintain social order by overtly declaring their intention to visually monitor their turf. Sometimes such groups issued signs or decals for doors and windows to signal to unsavory characters that watchful eyes "protected" the neighborhood. The urban theorist Jane Jacobs (1961) coined the term *the eyes and ears of the street* to describe the fact that, ideally, in mixed-use (i.e., commercial and residential) neighborhoods, formal neighborhood watch groups are unnecessary because the thread of social control already implicitly permeates daily life. Through their windows, grandmothers watch children playing baseball on the street below, on the alert for any trouble. During the course of a busy weekday, a shopkeeper might notice a group of teenagers who should be at school loitering outside his store, and he might report this activity to their parents or to the school.

In any society, many agents of both formal and informal social control exist. Our local neighbors act as the primary agents of informal social control, whereas the state, or the government, often has a hand in the construction of formal social sanctions by making laws. The police are an obvious example of an agent of state social control formed for the protection of the public. The police patrol public parks and neighborhoods after nightfall and contain public protests to ensure social order.

INFORMAL SOCIAL SANCTIONS

the usually unexpressed but widely known rules of group membership; the unspoken rules of social life.

Informal social control forms the bedrock on which formal social control rests, while formal social control serves as the protective surface. If the police go on strike, for example, the amount of chaos that ensues depends on the degree of social cohesion in a given community. Likewise, without strong informal social norms, the police are relatively helpless. Consider the difficulty police officers have in tracking down and arresting those who loot and commit acts of vandalism during an urban riot. Or the difficulty in solving or prosecuting a crime if witnesses are not willing to step forward and testify. If an entire community relaxes its informal social control, formal social control inevitably fails. Lately, the proliferation of surveillance cameras has somewhat blurred the boundary between informal and formal social control, which could potentially affect the balance of this symbiotic relationship. We've been discussing how social control works on a local level, more or less, from attentive grandmas watching the street to the local cop walking a beat. But how do forms of social control vary across history and geography? How do different societies hold together? To answer these questions, we turn to one of the founders of sociology, Émile Durkheim.

Functions of Deviance

❚ Describe Durkheim's understanding of deviance and social cohesion.

Imagine our society as a single, complex organism with many internal organs that perform specific tasks. The state is society's brain, its decision-making center where legislators contemplate the morality of laws and communicate legislative decisions to other social organs charged with implementation.

All of society's organs keep the social organism alive and healthy. Groups of individuals, or cells, compose these organs. A functionalist approach explains the existence of social phenomena by the functions they perform.

In this framework, the state develops because society needs a decision-making center to help organize and direct social life. All of society's various parts, or organs, are defined by their functions and arranged according to the needs of the social organism.

Émile Durkheim, author of *The Division of Labor in Society* (1893/1997), used such a functionalist approach to explain social cohesion—the way people form social bonds, relate to each other, and get along on a day-to-day basis. Durkheim theorized that society coheres in two basic ways: mechanical and organic solidarity. Mechanical or segmental solidarity, which characterized premodern society, is based on the sameness of the individual parts. In this model, the functional units serve as cargo containers; all containers are the same and perform the same functions. Cohesion stems from the reliable similarity of the parts. In a state of organic solidarity, which characterizes modern society, social cohesion is based on interdependence. The individual members in this type of social body perform different, specialized functions, and this mutual dependence among the parts allows for the smooth functioning of the whole. The physical analogy here is a machine in which each part is different, and none would play such a meaningful role outside the context of the machine.

In premodern society, similarity bonded people together. A peasant farmer in feudal times might have eked out a living by tilling a small plot of land, planting seeds, and then harvesting crops. The peasant next door also eked out a living by tilling, planting, and harvesting. Slight variations existed from one farm to the next, but the farmers' life conditions, and particularly their day-to-day experiences in the field, roughly mirrored each other. Social interactions between the two farmers would have flowed smoothly, since their common lifestyles allowed for plenty of shared advice and experiences. Such a situation demonstrates the features of mechanical solidarity.

SOCIAL COHESION

social bonds; how well people relate to each other and get along on a day-to-day basis.

MECHANICAL OR SEGMENTAL SOLIDARITY

social cohesion based on sameness.

ORGANIC SOLIDARITY

social cohesion based on difference and interdependence of the parts.

Social norms and the punishments for violating them change over time and from place to place. From executing women as witches in the seventeenth century to enforcing Jim Crow laws in the segregated South to prosecuting John Geddes Lawrence and Tyron Garner for engaging in a same-sex relationship, our definitions of what constitutes deviance evolve.

Farmers in premodern society would not have struggled to relate to one another; their sense of sameness bred mechanical solidarity. In contrast, most workers in the industrial and postindustrial economy perform such specialized tasks that they relate to one another through organic solidarity.

As Western society became more industrialized in the late eighteenth and nineteenth centuries, however, workers developed specialized skills, allowing them to perform particular tasks more effectively and efficiently. This division of labor resulted in a dramatic increase in productivity, but with the high productivity of specialization come some negative consequences. Specialized workers have less and less in common with one another, and they may be less able to understand each other. For example, if you held a highly specialized position within the economy as, say, a techno-artist punk rocker, you might find yourself thinking that no one understands what it is like to be you. As a techno-artist punk rocker, your highly specialized position—your role within the economy and society more generally—may isolate and alienate you from others around you, making finding common ground difficult. If you sit down on a commuter train next to an investment banker and try to talk with her, an awkward conversation might ensue, in which each of you tries to comprehend the daily activities of the other. You may share your morning commute and nothing more. Labor specialization divides us by increasing the complexity of social bonds. However, specialization of tasks enables everyone to do something best. Maybe you are the best Japanese humane-certified chicken farm sex determiner (actually called a chick sexer, and yes, they make six figures) because, among other reasons, you don't really have much competition. This high degree of labor specialization makes us all interdependent, creating organic cohesion.

Distinguishing between these two types of social solidarity leads us to our first insight into social deviance. When individuals commit acts of deviance, they offend what Durkheim calls the collective conscience, meaning the common faith or set of social norms by which a society and its members abide. Without a collective conscience—a set of shared assumptions about how the world works—there would be no sense of moral unity, and society would quickly dissolve into chaos. So, when individuals rip the agreed-upon moral fabric, societies must repair the tear by realigning the deviant individual through either punishment or rehabilitation.

The ways that societies achieve social realignment, Durkheim concludes, depend on the type of solidarity holding that particular society together. Premodern societies, where sameness unites people, tend to rely on punitive justice: making the offender suffer and thus defining the boundaries of acceptable behavior. Such punishment might involve collective vengeance. If someone in a medieval village committed adultery, stole vegetables, or murdered someone, the villagers would gather together, perhaps in a rowdy, pitchfork-wielding mob, to punish the criminal who had offended the collective conscience. The act of collective group punishment might have culminated in storming the offender's house or hanging the poor sap in public. In either case, the group punishes the criminal in an act of collective vengeance. The collective probably wasn't interested in hearing the criminal's side of the story: the facts of his personal life, his possible motivations for committing the crime, or the details of his regrettable childhood. Mechanical social sanctions both reinforce the boundaries of acceptable behavior and unite collectivity through actions such as hanging, stoning, or publicly chastising a former member of the community. This collective, vengeful action produces, by uniting the group through its perpetration and associated emotions of revenge, a heightened sense of cohesion and unity. (Of course, there are always exceptions, such as the premodern Amish [see Chapter 5] who don't even bother to prosecute shoplifters.)

Along with communal actions, the state administers similar forms of justice through more formal processes. When the infamous Oklahoma City bomber, Timothy McVeigh, received a death sentence, he was, in effect, murdered by the collectivity, by the citizenry of the United States. To opponents of

Two women accused of collaborating with the Nazis are marched through the streets of Paris in the summer of 1944. The mob ripped the women's clothes, then painted swastikas on their shorn heads to punish them. How does this example illustrate a mechanical social sanction?

the death penalty, McVeigh's execution amounted to state-sponsored murder. To others, however, his death signaled a national disapproval of killing innocent people. Although only a small team carried out McVeigh's execution, his death was an act in which—theoretically at least—we all participated. When we collectively and publicly put McVeigh to death, we reinforced our own social norms. Paradoxically, his deviance helped keep our society together.

Organic solidarity, in contrast, by differentiating individuals, produces social sanctions that focus on the individual—that is, they are tailored to the specific conditions and circumstances of the perpetrator. This response to deviance is rehabilitative, meaning that the response attempts to transform the offender into a productive member of society. In the modern mind-set, we supposedly care about the rapist's or murderer's motivations and regrettable childhood. We treat criminals as individuals who can be "fixed" if we root out the causes of, and triggers for, their criminality. For example, what happens if a drug addict steals car radios to support her cocaine habit? The court may order the addict into rehab in hopes of reintegrating her into the productive mainstream.

In the United States, we consider ourselves a modern society, yet both mechanical and organic social sanctions still lurk in the U.S. justice system. While we try to rehabilitate some criminals and reimburse victims, we also employ the death penalty in many states. Does Texas, where approximately one-third of the executions in U.S. history have taken place, have a more premodern division of labor than Wisconsin, which does not punish crimes with the death penalty? Probably not. Did the division of labor suddenly revert to primitive, subsistence levels when the Supreme Court reinstated

Eric Todaro (left) and Richard Grooms, inmates at a state penitentiary in Oregon, work on a General Education Diploma (GED) test. According to Durkheim, why would prisons provide educational programs and other rehabilitative tools?

the legality of the death penalty in 1976? Of course not. Durkheim doesn't argue that these forms of social sanctions are mutually exclusive—that is, that they can't exist together. In fact, he would expect to find both forms of social sanctions in a given society—societies would just vary on their relative frequency and importance. It's important to remember, however, that both types of social sanctions hold us together by reinforcing the boundaries of normal, socially acceptable behavior.

To make his case, Durkheim analyzed different historical penal and moral codes to discern the evolving ratio of premodern sanctions to modern sanctions. He examined the Code of Hammurabi in Babylon dating back to 1750 B.C.E. as well as the Pentateuch, the first five books of the Hebrew Bible. He studied more recent sanctions in the Magna Carta, the Napoleonic Code in France, and the South American Drago Doctrine. He argued that, as history progressed and the division of labor developed, the ratio of premodern to modern sanctions changed to favor modern, less punitive sanctions. So, although some U.S. states still apply the death penalty, Durkheim would hypothesize that modern sanctions will gradually overtake this premodern practice as our labor market changes to favor even more specialization. Approximately a dozen states have repealed the death penalty in recent decades, but we should be cautious in drawing overall conclusions about the relationship between division of labor and forms of punishment by focusing on one particular form of sanction. Maybe you, a budding sociologist, can conduct a more thorough update to Durkheim's hypothesis.

A NORMATIVE THEORY OF SUICIDE

After making his observations on social solidarity and social control in *The Division of Labor in Society*, Durkheim next applied his ideas to the sociological study of suicide, perhaps the most individual act of deviance. Or is it? If you had to explain the cause of suicide, you might say mental illness, depression, drug addiction, or perhaps a catastrophic event. These accounts reflect our perception of suicide as something intensely personal, mediated by individual life circumstances or caused by chemical imbalances and emotional disorders. These explanations contain a piece of the answer, but Durkheim wanted to look past the individual and consider the impact of the all-encompassing social environment.

In his book *Suicide* (1897), Durkheim sought to explain how social forces beyond the individual shaped suicide rates. According to Durkheim, suicide is, at its root, an instance of social deviance. By observing patterns in suicide rates across Europe (just as he had previously discerned patterns in penal codes), Durkheim developed a normative theory of suicide.

Durkheim proposed that by plotting "social integration" on the y-axis and "social regulation" on the x-axis of a Cartesian coordinate system,

FIGURE 6.1 A Normative Theory of Suicide

FIGURE 6.1 A Normative Theory of Suicide

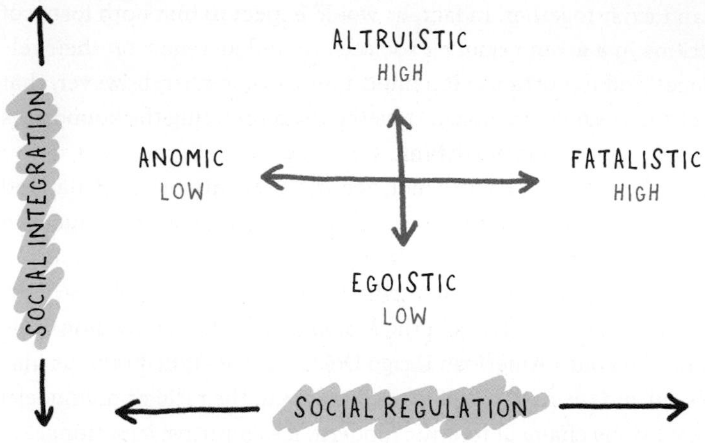

we can better see how social forces influence suicide rates (Figure 6.1). Social integration refers to the degree to which you are one with your social group or community. A tight-knit community in which members interact with each other in a number of different capacities—say, the coach of your child's Little League team is also your dentist and you are the dentist's mechanic—is more socially integrated than one in which people do not interact at all or interact in only one role. Social regulation refers to how many rules guide your daily life and what you can reasonably expect from the world on a day-to-day basis—that is, the degree to which you expect tomorrow will look like today, which looks like yesterday. A low risk for suicide (and other deviant behavior) requires balance: You want to feel integrated into your community with a reasonable (not oppressive) set of guidelines to structure your life. If you go too far in either direction along either axis, you end up with too much or too little of some important facet of "normal" life.

Let's say you drop down the *y*-axis significantly in the direction of egoism. You are not very well integrated into your group. Durkheim argues that, because others give your life meaning, you would feel hopeless. You wouldn't be part of some larger long-term project, would feel insignificant, and would be at risk of committing egoistic suicide. We all need to feel as if we have made a difference in other people's lives or produced something for the greater good that will endure after we are gone.

Durkheim demonstrated the prevalence of egoistic suicide using statistics about suicide rates across different religious groups. Although many Western religions formally prohibit suicide, rates varied substantially across religious affiliations. Durkheim found that throughout Europe, Protestants killed themselves most often, followed by Catholics

---

SOCIAL INTEGRATION

the extent to which you are integrated into your social group or community.

SOCIAL REGULATION

the number of rules guiding your daily life and, more specifically, what you can reasonably expect from the world on a day-to-day basis.

EGOISTIC SUICIDE

suicide that occurs when one is not well integrated into a social group.

and then Jews. Why? Protestantism emphasizes individualism. Unlike the Catholic Church, most Protestant denominations lack an elaborate church hierarchy because Protestants maintain direct personal relationships with God. By changing the individual's relationship to God (and therefore the individual's relationship to the church), Protestantism also stripped away many of the integrative structures of Catholicism, putting its members at greater risk for egoistic suicide. (More recent research shows that today the greater distinction exists between people with religious affiliations and those without, as the latter experience significantly higher levels of suicide.)

But why did Jews have the lowest suicide rate of any major European religious group if these religions all prohibited suicide? Although less institutionally structured than Catholicism, Jews have historically remained a persecuted minority group. Members of an oppressed group rejected by the so-called mainstream often will band together for protection from persecution. For example, in the United States today, African Americans have one of the lowest suicide rates, partially as a result of their bonding as a minority group, united in a common struggle against a history of oppression.

Too little social integration increases the risk of suicide, but too much social integration can also have negative effects. A person who strays too far up the y-axis might commit altruistic suicide, because a group dominates the life of that individual to such a degree that they feel meaningless aside from this social recognition. Think about Japanese ritual suicide, sometimes called seppuku (and sometimes colloquially known as hara-kiri). In this scenario, samurai warriors who had failed their group in battle would disembowel themselves with a sword rather than continue to live with disgrace in the community. Durkheim uses the example of Hindu widows in some castes and regions of India, who were expected to throw themselves on their husbands' funeral pyre to prove their devotion. This practice, called suttee or sati, symbolized that a woman properly recognized that her life was meaningless outside her social role as a wife. Official efforts to ban suttee commenced as early as the sixteenth century, and the practice is now illegal and extremely rare in India.

Altruistic suicide can also come from more personal motivations, as well. For example, do you think that suicide rates in the

ALTRUISTIC SUICIDE

suicide that occurs when one experiences too much social integration.

A Japanese man performs hara-kiri in this staged photograph from the 1880s. What makes this action altruistic suicide?

military are higher among enlisted soldiers or officers? Enlisted soldiers experience a lower standard of living and less social prestige, but statistics show that the suicide rate is, in fact, higher among officers. Why? Too much social integration. The identity of officers—specifically, their sense of honor and self-worth—relies more strongly on their role in the military. Enlisted soldiers, in contrast, have less responsibility for group performance. More likely, these soldiers perceive their military service as a job and still identify strongly with their civilian roles, so they have a lower risk of altruistic suicide.

As we consider the *x*-axis, social regulation, why or how would social regulation influence suicide rates? Imagine you commute to school every day. You rise at approximately 7:00 A.M., leave the house by 8:00, and take the 8:10 bus to school. Maybe some days the bus comes late, some days the bus comes early, and sometimes it never comes at all. You have no way of knowing when or if the bus will come. You get tired of standing on a cold, lonely corner waiting for a bus that may never come, and after a while, you might just stop trying to get to class at all. What's the point of waking up if you won't make it to class on time despite your effort? You have developed a sense of learned helplessness, a depressed outlook in which sufferers lack the will to take action to improve their lives, even when other avenues exist. The lack of social regulation, or a low mark on the *x*-axis, in this example leads to this learned helplessness.

At the heart of learned helplessness is the sense that we cannot stave off the sources of our pain, that we have no control over our own well-being. Durkheim studied a similar condition, which he termed *anomie*. Literally meaning "without norms," anomie refers to feelings of aimlessness or despair that arise when we can no longer reasonably expect life to be more or less meaningful. With too little social regulation, the connections between our actions and values erode. Durkheim labeled suicide that resulted from insufficient social regulation anomic suicide. For example, after the stock market crashed in 1929, many businessmen jumped out of skyscraper windows to their deaths. These stockbrokers and investors may have felt that they did everything right and still ended up destitute. For them, the connection between what they thought was the right thing to do—namely, work hard on Wall Street—and just rewards was severed, and they felt helpless to cope with the changes.

Anomic suicide intuitively refers to negative events rupturing our everyday lives, but the concept also encompasses abrupt change from positive life events. For example, many lottery winners report spells of severe depression after winning millions of dollars, displaying another case of anomie (Nissle & Bshor, 2002). If a very poor, frugal man wins the lottery, all of his money-saving habits instantaneously become irrelevant, unnecessary, or even a bit silly. Maybe he previously structured his Sundays by

ANOMIE

a sense of aimlessness or despair that arises when we can no longer reasonably expect life to be predictable; too little social regulation; normlessness.

ANOMIC SUICIDE

suicide that occurs as a result of insufficient social regulation.

walking down to the corner store just before closing time to pick up a castoff of the Sunday paper, painstakingly cutting coupons from the circulars for hours, and then planning a visit to each of three local grocery stores to find the best deals throughout the week. Maybe he always took lunch to work in reused brown paper bags to save money. Now, with $5 million in his checking account and no behavioral template (something that social processes yield) for life as a wealthy man, the rules of his previous life suddenly seem meaningless.

The final coordinate is fatalistic suicide, which occurs when a person experiences too much social regulation. Instead of floundering in a state of anomie with no guiding rules, you find yourself doing the same thing day after day, with no variation and no surprises. In 10 years, where do you see yourself? Doing the same thing. In 20 years? The same thing. You have nothing to look forward to because you reasonably expect that nothing better than your current life will come to fruition. This type of suicide usually occurs among slaves and prisoners. You might imagine that slaves and prisoners would die by suicide because of their physical hardships, but Durkheim's research suggested that their suicidal deaths more likely result from the suffocating tyranny of monotony.

Early feminists wrote of the "problem that has no name," or the stifling routine of a 1950s suburban stay-at-home mother. Sylvia Plath, a feminist poet and writer, died by suicide in 1963 shortly after the publication of her novel *The Bell Jar*, in which she describes the palpable fatalism of her semiautobiographical character Esther: "I saw the days of the year stretching ahead like a series of bright white boxes, and separating one box from another was sleep, like a black shade. Only for me, the long perspective of shades that set off one box from the next had suddenly snapped up, and I could see day after day after day glaring ahead of me like a white, broad, infinitely desolate avenue" (1971, p. 143). The tight control of women's roles in society thus increased their risk of fatalistic suicide.

According to many theories of deviance, what happens at the group level affects what happens at the individual level. For example, Durkheim hypothesized that members of minority groups were more socially integrated within their group and, therefore, Jews in Europe had lower suicide rates. Perhaps minority solidarity inspires feelings of belonging and love between family and nonfamily alike within the group. Because most people generally want to feel loved and needed, we could say that this solidarity makes group members happy or at least staves off depression. Less depressed, happier people die by suicide less often than those who feel unimportant, worthless, and hopeless. Group dissimilarities start at the macro level (group solidarity) and filter down to the individual level (feelings of depression or happiness), waiting for sociologists to detect them again in the aggregate (differential suicide rates).

FATALISTIC SUICIDE

suicide that occurs as a result of too much social regulation.

Social Forces and Deviance

▌ Analyze theories of deviance.

In keeping with Durkheim's attempt to discover the social roots of suicide and other forms of deviance, sociologist Robert Merton pioneered a complementary theory. Instead of stressing the way sudden social changes lead to feelings of helplessness, Merton argued that anomie really occurs when a society holds out the same goals to all its members but does not give them equal ability to achieve these goals. Merton's strain theory, advanced in 1938, explains how society gives us certain templates for acting appropriately. More specifically, we learn what society considers appropriate goals and appropriate means of achieving them. The *strain* in strain theory arises when the means don't match the ends; hence, Merton's theory is also called the "means-ends theory of deviance." When someone fails to recognize and accept either socially appropriate goals or socially appropriate means (or both), they become a social deviant.

If you have decided to pursue a college education to land a decent job, you are probably what Merton terms a conformist. A conformist accepts both socially acceptable goals and socially acceptable strategies to achieve those goals. Your goal is to earn a good living, maybe start a family, and take exotic vacations where you take photos with a fancy camera and then post them online to impress your friends. You've decided to pursue this lifestyle through a better education, the deliberate cultivation of the right social network, and hard work.

Let's say that you go to class every day, take minimal notes, and read just enough to earn a passing grade. You want to get by and you want others to leave you alone. You don't care how much money you will earn, as long as it's enough to pay for your studio apartment and other small monthly bills. You've accepted society's acceptable means (you're still going to college, after all), but you've rejected society's goals (the big house, the 2.3 kids, and the new car). You've rejected the idea of getting ahead through hard work, the American dream. You are a ritualist, a person who rejects socially defined goals but not the means.

If, however, you yearn to be rich and famous but don't have the scruples, patience, or economic resources to get there by using socially acceptable means, you may be an innovator. Let's say you are particularly interested in buying a mansion to fill with expensive art and furniture. Instead of slaving away on Wall Street for years, you sell drugs, fence stolen goods, and make a few friends in the Mafia.

STRAIN THEORY

Robert Merton's theory that deviance occurs when a society does not give all of its members equal ability to achieve socially acceptable goals.

CONFORMIST

an individual who accepts both the socially acceptable goals and socially acceptable strategies to achieve those goals.

RITUALIST

an individual who rejects socially defined goals but not the means.

INNOVATOR

social deviant who accepts socially acceptable goals but rejects socially acceptable means to achieve them.

Retreatists and rebels reject both means and goals, although the boundaries between the two are not always so clear. Retreatists completely stop participating in society. Adventurer Christopher Johnson McCandless, the subject of Jon Krakauer's best-selling 1996 book *Into the Wild*, exemplifies this type by deciding not to play the game and moving to the Alaskan woods, where he lived without running water or electricity. (I won't tell you what happens to him in case you want to read the book or watch the 2007 film adaptation.) A rebel also rejects both traditional goals and traditional means but wants to change (or destroy) the social institutions from which they are alienated. One example is Ernesto "Che" Guevara, the Argentine Marxist who famously fought for communism in Cuba. His disgust at the impoverished conditions he encountered as a doctor traveling through Latin America led to the formation of a guerrilla group. Che chose to fight the government rather than, say, propose new legislation or raise money for a new hospital like a conformist or abandon society altogether like a retreatist.

RETREATIST

one who rejects both socially acceptable means and goals by completely retreating from, or not participating in, society.

REBEL

an individual who rejects both traditional goals and traditional means and wants to alter or destroy the social institutions from which they are alienated.

Conformist

Ritualist

Innovator

Retreatist

Rebel

Which type are you? Do you follow socially accepted means and goals? According to Robert Merton, you're a conformist. Doing the bare minimum? You're probably a ritualist. If you want to earn big rewards but have few scruples about how you reach them, you're an innovator. You're a retreatist if, like members of a self-supporting commune, you reject all means and goals of society. You're a rebel, like Che Guevara, if you not only reject social means and goals but also want to change society itself.

CONFLICT THEORY

While functionalism provides one societal level model of deviance and social control, conflict theory—an extension of Marxist analysis that places class as the central factor in societal dynamics—also offers an explanation for why society experiences crime and other forms of deviance. Conflict theory stems from the premise that social order results not from solidarity but from domination of the poorer classes by the richer ones. First, the ruling class gets to define deviant and socially acceptable behavior in opposition to each other. For example, laws against vagrancy or loitering literally criminalize being poor or homeless. The sanctity of private property and, thus, the crime of theft are central to the maintenance of power by the elite. The ruling class then enforces its laws and norms on the working class through both informal sanctions, such as social exclusion based on styles of speech, dress, and so on, and formal mechanisms such as policing with the primary intention of exploiting the powerless for profit. In this paradigm, the proletariat (working class) uses deviance as a method for resisting domination.

SYMBOLIC INTERACTIONIST THEORIES

Whereas Durkheim, Merton, and the conflict theorists focused on the ways different parts society articulated together as a whole, another school of sociologists in the 1960s and 1970s took a different approach to the study of deviance. Working in the tradition of symbolic interactionism (see Chapters 1 and 4), a term coined by Herbert Blumer (1969), these sociologists stressed the particular meanings individuals attach to their actions rather than the broader social structures in which they unwittingly take part. To determine why people commit crimes or to seek the root causes of deviance in a given society, a symbolic interactionist looks at the small and subtle particulars of a social context, as well as the beliefs and assumptions people carry into their everyday interactions. Functionalist theories, such as those of Durkheim, are sometimes called macro theories because they seek to paint the social world in wide brushstrokes: generalizable trends, global or national forces, and broad social structures. At the opposite end of the spectrum, micro theories such as symbolic interactionism zoom in on the individual. Symbolic interactionism takes seriously our inner thoughts and everyday interactions on a local scale, including how others see us and how we respond to our immediate surroundings.

Labeling Theory As a child, did you ever shoplift, trespass, or forge a document? If you were slow and tactless enough to get caught, your parents probably gave you a stern lecture and maybe grounded you. Chances are, however, that over time the incident slowly faded into the background and you stopped feeling guilty. You probably never came to think of yourself as a shoplifter or trespasser, as a criminal or social deviant. You simply made a stupid mistake, never to be repeated. Let me give you an example from my own past. When I was in junior high school, one afternoon a friend and I decided to play "fireman, waterman," a game that required one person (the fireman) to flick lit matches into the air, while the waterman tried to extinguish them with a plant mister. To make a long story short, I was the fireman, and I won. As you might expect, the incident ended badly— specifically, one of the stray, airborne matches set my friend's apartment on fire. After extinguishing the blaze, fire department officials questioned me about my role in starting the fire, but they ultimately absolved me from blame and declared the fire an accident. My parents, although obviously shaken and disappointed, never formally punished me. The trauma of the incident, they said, was lesson enough. Now imagine that, instead of being pardoned, the authorities held me accountable for my role in starting the fire and sent me to a juvenile corrections facility. Do you think I still would have followed the same life trajectory, eventually going to college and graduate school? Do you think I would have become a sociology professor? Would I be authoring your textbook right now?

The labeling theory of social deviance offers insight into how people become deviants. According to this theory, individuals subconsciously notice how others see or label them, and their reactions to those labels over time form the basis of their self-identity. The social process of labeling creates deviance by assigning shared meanings to acts. We all know that stealing, trespassing, and vandalizing are wrong, abnormal, and criminal behaviors, but our shared meanings about the sanctity of private property and our own rules about respecting that property ultimately label these acts deviant. Although the fire caused by my unfortunate stint in pyrotechnics was labeled an accident, it might have been termed a crime just as easily. There was and is nothing inherently deviant about setting an apartment on fire, accidentally or otherwise. Howard S. Becker (1963), a proponent of labeling theory, made precisely this point, arguing that individuals don't commit crimes in a vacuum. Rather, social groups create deviance, first by setting the rules for what's right and wrong, and second by labeling wrong-doers as outsiders. Offenders are not born; they are made as a consequence of how other people apply rules and sanctions to them.

Social groups create rules about the correct or standard mode of conduct for social actors. When individuals break these rules, society's reaction to the act determines if the offense counts as deviance. Take, for example, the case of opioid use. When opioid use was dominated by heroin and disproportionately afflicted Black Americans, the addiction was criminalized. However, when such drug addiction soared among Whites, the trend became a health issue rather than one of crime or deviance, referred to in medical

LABELING THEORY
the belief that individuals subconsciously notice how others see or label them, and their reactions to those labels over time form the basis of their self-identity.

↑

How did Howard Becker apply labeling theory to the use of marijuana?

terms such as "epidemic." Becker also argues that not only are deviant acts created by a process of labeling but deviants are also created by a process of labeling. If you break a rule—say, accidentally burn down an apartment—but your violation is not labeled a crime or otherwise recognized as deviant, then you are not recognized as a criminal or deviant. We become (or don't become) deviant only in interaction with other social actors. The social reaction to an act and the subsequent labeling of that act and offender create social deviance.

To illustrate the process of becoming deviant, Becker interviewed 50 marijuana users in "Becoming a Marihuana User" (1953), during a period when marijuana was illegal in all states and socially stigmatized. He began his study with a simple inquiry: Are marijuana users different from nonusers in terms of individual psychology? The answer given by most scientists, politicians, and parents in the 1950s was a hearty *yes*. But Becker argues that chronic marijuana use results from a process of social learning. Before people light up, they must first learn how to smoke marijuana. More important, they must then redefine the sensations of marijuana use as "fun" and desirable. Just as setting an apartment on fire is not inherently a crime, getting high is not "automatically or necessarily pleasurable" (Becker, 1963); in fact, one user he spoke with never could learn to enjoy pot:

> It [marijuana] was offered to me, and I tried it. I'll tell you one thing. I never did enjoy it at all. I mean it was just nothing that I could enjoy. [Becker: Well, did you get high when you turned on?] Oh, yeah, I got definite feelings from it. But I didn't enjoy them. I mean I got plenty of reactions, but they were mostly reactions of fear. [You were frightened?] Yes. I didn't enjoy it. I couldn't seem to relax with it, you know. (p. 240)

A person trying marijuana can usually redefine the experience when smoking with long-term users who assure the novice that the physical effects are normal, even enjoyable. One of Becker's interviewees, a veteran smoker, recalled how a beginner "became frightened and hysterical" after smoking for the first time. An older user told the newbie, "I'd give anything to get that high myself" (Becker, 1963). This comment and similar ones apply new meanings to the sensation of getting high. For some, marijuana smoking becomes pleasant only through a social process. How objects and sensations become meaningful (or pleasant) through social processes is the focus of Becker's study, in contrast to explanations that focus on what objects *are*. Similarly, the taste of alcohol probably didn't appeal to your palate when you first tried it; however, because alcohol had a certain social allure, being associated with either adulthood or rebellion, you may have learned to appreciate its taste (perhaps even before you reached the legal drinking age).

Another example of a social process may help illustrate the power of labeling theory. As part of a psychology experiment, a group of eight adults with steady employment and no history of mental illness presented themselves at different psychiatric inpatient hospitals and complained of hearing voices (Rosenhan, 1973). Each of the pseudo-patients was admitted after describing the alleged voices, which spoke words like "thud," "empty," and "hollow." In all cases, the pseudo-patients received a schizophrenia diagnosis. The researchers instructed the pseudo-patients, once they were hospitalized, to stop "simulating any symptoms of abnormality." Each pseudo-patient "behaved on the ward as he 'normally' behaved." Still, the doctors and staff did not suspect that the pseudo-patients were imposters. Instead, the treating psychiatrists changed their diagnosis of schizophrenia to "schizophrenia in remission." Something even more troubling than the misdiagnosis occurred. Once the pseudo-patients had been labeled insane, all their subsequent behavior was interpreted accordingly. One male pseudo-patient, for example, gave the hospital staff a truthful account of his personal history. During his childhood, he had been close to his mother but not his father. Later in life, he became close with his father and more distant from his mother. His marriage was "characteristically close and warm," with no

In experiments such as those of David L. Rosenhan or films like *Shock Corridor* (left), people with no history of mental illness are admitted to psychiatric hospitals. These examples raise questions about the stickiness of labels. What are some of the consequences of being labeled a deviant?

THE STANFORD PRISON EXPERIMENT AND ABU GHRAIB

The force of labels and roles can affect us very quickly. The Stanford Prison Experiment, conducted by Philip Zimbardo in 1971, provides insight into the power of such social labels and how they might explain the incredibly inhumane acts of torture, most involving violence and humiliation, committed at Abu Ghraib, the American-run prison in Iraq. Zimbardo, a psychology professor at Stanford, rounded up some college undergraduate men to participate in an experiment about "the psychology of prison life." Half the undergraduates were assigned the role of prisoner, and half were assigned the role of prison guard. These roles were randomly assigned, so there was nothing about the inherent personalities of either group that predisposed them to prefer one role over the other.

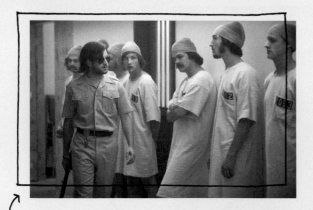

A film still from *The Stanford Prison Experiment*, which reenacted Philip Zimbardo's now infamous study.

To simulate the arrest and incarceration process, the soon-to-be prisoners were taken from their homes, handcuffed, and searched by actual city police. Then all the prisoners went to "prison"—the basement of the Stanford psychology department set up with cells and a special solitary confinement closet. The guards awaited their prisoners in makeshift uniforms and dark sunglasses to render their eyes invisible to inmates. Upon arrival at the prison, the criminals were stripped, searched, and issued inmate uniforms, which were like short hospital gowns. The first day passed without incident, as prisoners and guards settled into their new roles. But on the morning of the second day, prisoners revolted, barricading themselves in their mock cells and sparking a violent confrontation between the fictitious guards and prisoners that would ensue for the next four days. From physical abuse (such as hour-long counts of push-ups) to psychological violence (such as degradation and humiliation), the guards' behavior verged on sadism, although just days before, these two groups of young men were all normal Stanford undergrads. The prisoners quickly began "withdrawing and behaving in pathological ways," while some of the guards seemed to relish their abuse. The planned 14-day experiment ended after just 6 days, spiraling completely out of control.

The lesson, claims Zimbardo, is that good people can do terrible things depending on their social surroundings and on expectations. When thrown into a social context of unchecked authority, anonymity, and high stress, average people

This Iraqi detainee in Abu Ghraib prison was hooked up to wires after American soldiers made him stand on a box. How can Zimbardo's experiments help us understand the torture at Abu Ghraib?

can become exceptional monsters. Zimbardo calls this phenomenon the "Lucifer effect," and this historic experiment offers insights into how the atrocities at Abu Ghraib prison in Iraq became possible (Zimbardo, 2007). In 2005, when the media made public the horrifying images of Iraqi prisoners being degraded and abused—some naked and on their knees inches from barking dogs; some wearing hoods and restrained in painful, grotesque positions; some forced to lie atop a pile of other naked prisoners—with grinning American soldiers looking on, many commentators (and military officials) sought to explain the abuses as a case of "bad apples" among otherwise good soldiers. Bad apples don't just arise out of nowhere, however, nor are people inherently malicious or brutal by nature. Zimbardo's experiment seemed to offer a viable explanation.

In 2018, however, the Stanford Prison Experiment again appeared in the news when journalist Ben Blum published an article calling the experiment a "sham," questioning its ethical and methodological basis. Blum (2018) claimed that Zimbardo engineered the study to encourage the "guards" to humiliate and abuse the "prisoners." In response, Zimbardo forcefully defended his experiment, insisting that its goal was not to faithfully recreate the conditions of a prison, but rather to provide a "cautionary tale of what might happen to any of us if we underestimate the extent to which the power of social roles and external pressures can influence our actions" (Zimbardo, 2018). Sounds pretty sociological to me.

Wherever we stand on this debate, Zimbardo's quote confirms what we already know about socialization: When given limitless power under high stakes and in an environment of extreme uncertainty, as happened to the soldiers at Abu Ghraib, abuse can become the norm, and good people can do bad things.

persistent problems. He reported rarely spanking his children. Sounds like a fairly typical guy, right? This is how the hospital record described the pseudo-patient's personal history:

> This white 39-year-old male . . . manifests a long history of considerable ambivalence in close relationships, which begins in early childhood. A warm relationship with his mother cools during adolescence. A distant relationship to his father is described as becoming very intense. Affective stability is absent. His attempts to control emotionality with his wife and children are punctuated by angry outbursts and, in the case of his children, spankings. And while he says that he has several good friends, one senses considerable ambivalence embedded in those relationships also. (Rosenhan, 1973, p. 253)

Even though the pseudo-patient acted "normally" shortly after his admission, the "abnormal" label stuck and continued to color the staff's perceptions and diagnoses. Just in case you are curious, the pseudo-patients remained in the hospitals for 7 to 52 days, with an average stay of 19 days. Sticky label, indeed.

Labeling theorists believe that these sticky deviant labels have important consequences for behavior. After committing a crime or hearing voices, how would you feel if people treated you and thought about you in the context of a deviant label? Would you feel like the same person but just someone who, say, was arrested for committing a crime? Or would the criminal label become part of the way you thought about yourself? Labeling theorists call the first act of rule breaking (which can include experiences or actions such as hearing voices, breaking windows, or dyeing one's hair neon orange) primary deviance. After you earn your deviant label (e.g., a criminal, a drug addict, a shoplifter, or even a sex worker), others' expectations about how you will act affect how you do act. Secondary deviance refers to deviant acts that occur after primary deviance and as a result of your new deviant label. For example, a deviance researcher interviewed a woman in her sixties who had been under psychiatric care for some 20 years (Glassner, 1999). This is how she recalls the process of becoming mentally ill:

> The first time I was taken to a psychiatrist for help was when I was getting depressed over a miscarriage. I had tried for many years to have that baby, and finally I was pregnant and planning to be a mother and all, and then I lost it. Anyhow, they told me I was "deeply depressed," but it didn't really mean much to me. I figured I'd get over it once I got pregnant again or something. But when I went home, everybody treated me differently. My husband and my mother had met with the social worker, who explained that I had

PRIMARY DEVIANCE

the first act of rule breaking that may lead to a new label of "deviant," thus influencing how people think about and act toward you.

SECONDARY DEVIANCE

subsequent acts of rule breaking that occur after primary deviance and as a result of your new deviant label and people's expectations of you.

this problem, with depression and all. From then on I was a depressive. I mean, that's the way everyone treated me, and I thought of myself in the same way after a while. Maybe I am that way, maybe I was born that way or grew up like that, but anyhow, that's what I am now. (Glassner, 1999, p. 73)

First, the woman sees her experience with depression as a passing phase that she will recover from with time. Then a psychiatrist labels her "deeply depressed." When she arrives home, family members treat her differently, and "from then on" she is "a depressive." You can see how the woman's interactions with the psychiatrist (crucially, the imposed label) redefine her identity, becoming an integral part of her that others around her continuously reinforce. Of course, these labels themselves are socially structured by group stereotypes that often serve as default cognitive categories.

Stigma We've seen how primary deviance can snowball into secondary deviance, whereby a few initial wrong steps or unlucky breaks start to define a person's future actions and reactions. It doesn't end there. Secondary deviance can quickly become social stigma. A stigma is a negative social label that changes others' behavior toward a person and, as a consequence, also alters that person's self-concept and social identity. We frequently call certain behaviors, groups, identities, and even objects "stigmatized." Mental illness still carries a stigma in our society. Pedophilia carries a bigger one.

> STIGMA
>
> a negative social label that changes others' behavior toward a person and therefore alters that person's own self-concept and social identity.

Having a criminal record can also carry a stigma, as can a person's race. In 2001, the late sociologist Devah Pager, then a graduate student in sociology, conducted a study to determine the effects of race and a criminal record on employment opportunities. She dispatched potential job candidates (African American and White male college students who had volunteered for the experiment) with similar résumés to apply for entry-level service positions. Half the participants of each race indicated a prior felony conviction on their job applications. Pager (2003a) found that of those with no criminal record, the White applicants were more likely to get a response (34 percent compared with 14 percent) but also that the White men with a supposed felony conviction were more likely to be called back than the Black men who did not report a criminal record (17 percent compared with 14 percent). The employers in Pager's study were slightly more willing to consider a White applicant with a felony record than a Black applicant with a clean history. In this case, the lasting stigmatization of non-White employees actually holds more weight than a stigma against those with criminal records. One possible explanation, reasoned Pager, is that

> employers are attempting to select the best candidate for the job, but are affected by all kinds of pervasive and largely unconscious

DIGITAL.WWNORTON.COM/YOUMAYASK8

To see my interview with Devah Pager, author of *Marked*, go to
digital.wwnorton.com/youmayask8

stereotypes that result in privileging or preferring a White candidate to a Black candidate. . . . Employers have these negative stereotypes based on really pervasive media imagery, for example, of young Black men involved with the criminal justice system or acting out in some negative way. There's lots of information we get about all of the negative characteristics that we might attribute to the African American population. . . . They talked about Black men as being lazy and dangerous and criminal and dressing poorly; they were very candid about all of these negative characteristics that they attributed to Black men. But then, right after that, when I asked them about their experiences over the past year with Black applicants or Black employees, they had a much harder time coming up with concrete examples of those general attitudes, and for the most part, employers reported having very similar kinds of experiences with their Black and White employees. (Conley, 2009f)

Pager's research reveals the real consequences of stigma, which shape the landscape of opportunities for men with criminal records. The work also illuminates the challenges faced by Black men, whose skin color carries a stigma of deviance into the labor market irrespective of their actual actions and behaviors.

BROKEN WINDOWS THEORY OF DEVIANCE

As labeling theory predicts, others' perceptions of you affect your behavior and overall life chances. So, too, does the way you see your social surroundings, according to the broken windows theory. In 1969, Zimbardo conducted another experiment in which he and his graduate students abandoned two cars, leaving them without license plates and with their hoods propped up, in two different neighborhoods (Wilson & Kelling, 1982). They abandoned the first car in a seemingly safe neighborhood in Palo Alto, California, where

Stanford University is located, then left the second car in the South Bronx in New York City, one of the most dangerous urban ghettos in the country at the time. Unsurprisingly, the abandoned car in Palo Alto remained untouched, whereas the car deposited in the South Bronx lost its hubcaps, battery, and any other usable parts almost immediately. However, it was the next stage in the experiment that offers valuable insight into the relationship between social context and deviance. Zimbardo went back to the untouched car in Palo Alto and smashed it with a sledgehammer. He and his graduate students shattered the windshield, put some dents in the car's sides, and again fled the scene. What do you think happened to the smashed and dented car in the "safe," rich neighborhood? Passersby began stopping their cars and getting out to further smash the wreck or tag it with graffiti. The social cues, or social context, influenced the way people treated the car even in a rich neighborhood.

In the South Bronx, the overall social context crowded with broken windows, graffiti, and dilapidated buildings encouraged deviant acts at the outset because the neighborhood setting of decay and disorder signaled to residents that an abandoned car was fair game for abuse. In Palo Alto, where neighborhood conditions were clean and orderly, people were unlikely to vandalize an abandoned car. However, when the vehicle was already vandalized in Palo Alto, that cue of turmoil signaled to others that it was okay to engage in the otherwise deviant act of vandalism. The broken windows theory of deviance explains how social context and social cues impact individuals' actions—specifically, whether local, informal social norms allow such acts. When signals seem to tell us that it's okay to do the otherwise unacceptable, sometimes we do. The broken windows theory of deviance has inspired some politicians to institute policies that target the catalysts for inappropriate behavior (vandalism, burglary, and so forth). In fact, George Kelling, one of Zimbardo's graduate students who participated in the car experiment, later worked as a consultant for the New York City Transit Authority in 1984, devising a plan to crack down on graffiti. The plan assumed that the continued presence of graffiti-covered cars served as a green light for more graffiti and perhaps even violent crimes. The Transit Authority then launched a massive campaign to clean up graffiti, car by car, to erase the signs of urban disorder in the hope of reducing subway crime. In the mid-1990s, New York City mayor Rudy Giuliani also initiated a campaign of "zero tolerance" for petty crimes such as jumping turnstiles, urinating in public, drinking alcohol in public, and creating graffiti in public spaces. Today, the city's newer subway cars are "graffiti-proof," meaning that spray paint doesn't adhere to the metal exterior of the cars. Indeed, both petty and serious crime rates have dropped dramatically in New York City since the 1990s (Kelling & Sousa, 2001), although some criminologists dispute the causal impact of the Giuliani strategy.

BROKEN WINDOWS THEORY OF DEVIANCE

theory explaining how social cues impact whether individuals act deviantly—specifically, whether local, informal social norms allow deviant acts.

Crime

▌ Identify different types of crime and their social influences.

As noted earlier, crime is a more formal type of deviance, both subject to social sanction and punishable by law. Sometimes an act falls clearly at one end of the spectrum or the other. Situations of self-defense aside, we all generally agree that killing a person is a crime; nose picking, however unpalatable, is not. In other cases, though, the distinction is not so clear. Whereas you might get strange looks for wearing aluminum-foil hot pants to class, if you show up with no clothes on at all, you will likely be sent to a mental health care provider for assessment or arrested and thrown in jail for indecent exposure. But what if your hot pants weren't foil at all but just silver paint? Would this instance be indecent exposure or just a questionable fashion choice?

Crime runs the gamut in type and degree. Most of us think of violence or drugs when we contemplate crime, but there are many other ways of breaking the law.

STREET CRIME

> You don't make up for your sins in church. You do it in the streets.
> —"Johnny Boy" Civello in *Mean Streets*

STREET CRIME

crime committed in public and often associated with violence, gangs, and poverty.

Street crime generally refers to crime committed in public. The term invokes specific images, however, of violent crime, typically perpetrated in an urban landscape. Both historically and today, street crime is often associated with gangs, and currently it is also associated with both disadvantaged minority groups and poverty. Just why people are drawn to a career of street crime has long been a favorite question of social scientists and is still a matter of heated debate. One theory, for example, posits that street crime rises and falls in relation to the availability of opportunity within the legitimate economy. When an environment lacks sufficient opportunity within the bounds of the law, people may turn elsewhere. A wrinkle on this theory is provided by "differential opportunity theory" (Cloward & Ohlin, 1960), which states that in addition to the legitimate economic structure, an illegitimate opportunity structure also exists that is unequally distributed across social classes. That is, some groups have more opportunities than others in the illicit economy, and the ratio of risks and rewards in the formal and black market economies influences participation in crime (rather than just the opportunities in the mainstream economy alone).

One way, then, to reduce crime would be to raise the costs of working in the illegitimate economy, thereby lowering the net returns. Such a strategy lies behind tougher sentencing policies, such as "three strikes" laws (if you are convicted of three felony crimes, you are imprisoned for life), which aim simultaneously to deter criminals and to incarcerate habitual offenders. Increasing the returns to entry-level opportunity in the legitimate economy (e.g., raising the minimum wage) would do the opposite, raising the benefits of the legitimate economy and lowering the returns of the illegitimate economy. Either strategy—decreasing the returns to the illegitimate economy or increasing the returns to the legitimate economy—shortens the distance, or differential, between the two economies.

WHITE-COLLAR CRIME

Bernard L. Madoff rose through the social ranks of wealth on Long Island, then Manhattan, and then London, eventually becoming the chairman of the NASDAQ exchange, which was based on technology his privately held firm had developed. In 2009, he was sentenced to 150 years in prison—a life sentence for the 71-year-old—for taking money from investors and fabricating great rates of return to pump up his reputation and keep money coming in. Madoff lived an opulent lifestyle, using well-connected friends and family to keep a steady stream of new investments coming in. During the economic downturn in 2008, Madoff could not keep up with investors' demands to cash out. An investigation by the Federal Bureau of Investigation (FBI) led to his arrest. Madoff estimated that he had lost $50 billion, making his crime the largest fraud in American history.

Infractions such as fraud are called white-collar crime, a term coined by sociologist Edwin Sutherland in 1939 to refer to crime committed by professionals in their capacity in the professional world against a corporation, agency, or other professional entity. According to the FBI (2003),

> [w]hite-collar crimes are categorized by deceit, concealment, or violation of trust and are not dependent on the application or threat of physical force or violence. Such acts are committed by individuals and organizations to obtain money, property, or services, to avoid the payment or loss of money or services, or to secure a personal or business advantage.

A particular type of white-collar crime is corporate crime, offenses committed by the officers (CEOs and other executives) of a corporation. In the late spring of 2012, JPMorgan Chase trader Bruno Iksil (also known as the London Whale) placed a giant risky trade and ended up losing $6.2 billion for the bank. Losing billions on a trade is deviant but not illegal. Iksil was fired, but he avoided arrest. U.S. federal prosecutors indicted his boss and his assistant for conspiring to cover up the losses by filing false reports. Penalties for their crimes include a $920 million fine for JPMorgan, but no individuals did time (Stewart, 2015). On a broader level, although the 2007–8 meltdown of the

WHITE-COLLAR CRIME

offense committed by a professional (or professionals) against a corporation, agency, or other institution.

CORPORATE CRIME

a particular type of white-collar crime committed by the officers (CEOs and other executives) of a corporation.

Bernie Madoff

banking system was the worst financial crisis since the Great Depression, nobody went to jail for the shady practices that caused it.

INTERPRETING THE CRIME RATE

Although crime rates may seem worse after a glance at the gruesome headlines in today's newspapers, deviance has always been present. Kai Erikson, in *Wayward Puritans* (2005), demonstrates how even America's seemingly most upstanding and God-fearing community, the Puritans, produced some bad apples such as drunkards, adulterers, and thieves. Erikson demonstrated that while definitions of deviance change over time, deviance itself stays with us forever. For example, Erikson found "crimes against the Church," particularly by Quakers in the late 1650s, to be of central concern to the Puritan community. Religious or moral offenses, such as drunkenness and adultery, mattered more than economic or political ones—at least those were the crimes taken most seriously and probably reported most frequently during the Puritan era. Erikson theorizes that a relatively stable amount of deviance may be expected in a given community, but what counts as deviance evolves depending on the type of society or historical period we examine. Think back to our early definition of social deviance: It is, after all, a social construct and subject to change over time and across cultural values.

If the definitions of deviance and crime constantly change, how can we discern if the crime rate is going up or down? In 1960, the total crime rate was around 160.9 per 100,000 people. By 1992, that number had soared to a little over 757, but it has now fallen back to around 398.5. Figure 6.2 shows the violent crime rate in the United States from 1960 to 2020.

FIGURE 6.2 Total U.S. Violent Crime Rate, 1960–2020

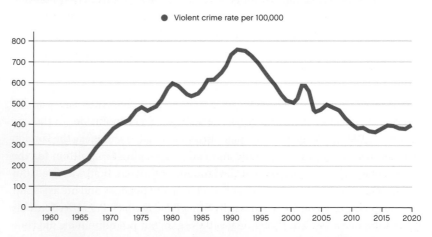

SOURCE: FBI, 2021b.

How can so much change occur in the crime rate in so little time? Is society rapidly degenerating into complete chaos? Probably not. To make a statement about the crime rate going up or down, we have to break down the details of the crime rate. For instance, the definition of assault may change to include more minor offenses. Recently, one local government proposed including brawls at sporting events in the assault category. And with the changing classifications of violent crimes, comparing the crime rates over time becomes more difficult. Levels of crime reporting by victims fluctuate. In times of economic recession, people feel helpless, depressed, or apathetic and, therefore, feel less motivated to report crime. Alternatively, a presidential address on fighting terrorism or injustice might inspire us to be more diligent in defending the social order.

The point is that the crime rate changes in response to fluctuations in how society classifies and reacts to deviance. In fact, reporting bias may work in the opposite direction from the actual crime rate. Imagine a neighborhood where crime is common. After reading about three murders, someone might feel reluctant to report a pickpocketing incident on the same day. Conversely, in a situation where crime rates are perceived to be low, such as at the opera house, you might be more likely to report a missing wallet. In this way, the reporting of petty crimes may vary inversely to the rate of serious crimes. For these reasons, criminologists (experts trained in studying crime) usually reject the overall crime rate as a reliable indicator of trends in crime. Instead, criminologists use the murder rate to make statements about the overall health of society. Why do they use these statistics instead of violent crime rates? For one thing, it's difficult to fake a murder—either there is a body or there isn't. Since murder is almost always reported or discovered, it is generally thought of as the least biased measure of crime. The murder rate is the best indicator we have of crime in general (Figure 6.3), but even it is not immune to broader changes in society.

Murder rates can be subjected to changes not due to actual changes in crime rates. For example, if you were shot today in the United States, you would have a much better chance of surviving the gunshot injury than you would have had in 1960. It could be that many more people arrive at the hospital with bullet wounds in the twenty-first century, but far fewer of those victims die on the operating table thanks to advances in medical technology. The greater survival rate complicates our interpretation of the murder rate (Harris et al., 2002). Has there been a decline in the number of murder attempts, or are doctors just better able to treat bullet wounds? It's difficult to say definitively. We can use the murder rate as a gauge to gain a general sense of crime fluctuations, but precise statistics are practically impossible to gather.

Even if we adjust for better survival rates, the murder rate has indeed declined precipitously since the early 1990s. Scholars like Patrick Sharkey in his book, *Uneasy Peace,* attribute this decrease, at least in part, to the

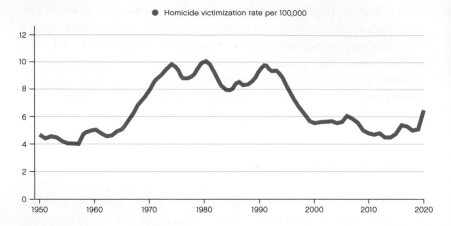

FIGURE 6.3 Homicide Victimization Rate, 1950–2020

● Homicide victimization rate per 100,000

SOURCE: FBI, 2021a.

tough-on-crime policies that led to an era of mass incarceration (see next section; also see Corman & Mocan, 2005; Levitt, 2004). Others point to factors as varied as the elimination of lead in gasoline and the passage of the Clean Air Act (reducing exposure to toxins that can induce behavioral problems and cognitive deficits; Reyes, 2007), the legalization of abortion in the early 1970s (leading to a reduction in unwanted children who might be more likely to commit crimes; Berk et al., 2003), an aging population (retirees are less likely to mug someone; Perkins, 1997), the stabilization of the crack epidemic (which had spurred turf wars when it first arrived on the scene; Johnson et al., 2005), the growing ubiquity of surveillance cameras (which act as a deterrent by making it harder to get away with property or violent crime; Welsh & Farrington, 2004), and even the digitization of the economy (since it's easier to scam people for their Social Security numbers online than it is to break into their houses and steal their TV sets).

Since the COVID-19 pandemic, however, the decline in crime stopped and even turned around with rises in both 2020 and 2021. In fact, in the first half of 2022, although violent crime decreased, street crime increased by around 20 percent (Council on Criminal Justice, 2022). Initially, the global pandemic reduced street crime (as hardly anyone was on the streets) and increased domestic violence. But a few months in, homicides and other crimes began to surge. Explanations for this rise are almost as many in number as the explanations for the great crime decline in the three prior decades. Some attribute the latest rise to the psychological depression and anger that collectively enveloped the nation in response to worry over the virus, social isolation, job losses, and the overall shock to our way of life as downtowns emptied out and our lifestyles changed very abruptly. This general breakdown in social norms due to the disruption of everyday life led to anomie, to use Durkheim's term, which in turn led to more crime. Supporting this interpretation is the fact that not only did violent crime rise during and after the pandemic but so did suicides and drug overdoses—so-called "deaths of despair." Others suggest that the murder of George Floyd by a Minneapolis police officer and the protests in response led police to pull back across cities, which contributed to the rise in homicide and other crimes. We may never nail down an exact explanation; it remains to be seen how long this new, unsettling trend will last.

Crime Reduction

| Apply sociological theories of social control and deviance to modern systems of justice.

Thus far, we have studied some of the functions and social origins of criminal behavior, as well as the prevalent methods of measuring crime. Now, how do crime fighters fight crime?

DETERRENCE THEORY OF CRIME CONTROL

In 1971, President Richard M. Nixon ushered in America's first War on Drugs. Linking drug use to violent crimes and the decay of social order, federal and state governments instituted an array of harsher penalties for the possession or sale of illegal substances. The philosophy of deterrence, or deterrence theory, suggests that "crime results from a rational calculation of the costs and benefits of criminal activity" (Spohn & Holleran, 2002). If you know you can make a quick buck by selling cocaine (maybe enough to pay your rent, say, or put food on the table), you might find such illicit activities tempting. But what if, instead of getting a slap on the wrist, a person caught with small quantities of cocaine receives a minimum sentence of 15 years in prison? If the cost of getting caught is higher than the potential benefits of selling drugs, the temptation decreases. Let's say you are arrested and wind up in prison for 15 years. Would you choose to sell cocaine again? How might the criminal justice system prevent you from doing so?

There are two types of deterrence. When the system attempts to monitor and prevent known criminals from committing more crimes, they engage in specific deterrence. An example would be the prison parole system, because the criminal remains under supervision and is being specifically deterred from committing another crime. An example of general deterrence would be if, from word on the street, you learn that dealing cocaine carries a prison sentence of 15 years and decide not to risk it. Deterrence theory suggests that general deterrence reduces overall crime, and specific

DETERRENCE THEORY

philosophy of criminal justice arising from the notion that crime results from a rational calculation of its costs and benefits.

RECIDIVISM

when an individual who
has been involved with
the criminal justice
system reverts to criminal
behavior.

deterrence reduces recidivism in particular. Recidivism is the "reversion of an individual to criminal behavior" after involvement with the criminal justice system (Maltz, 2001).

However, deterrence theory in practice has other, unintended consequences that may lead to more crime. For one thing, additional supervision and stricter parole codes have increased the likelihood that offenders will commit technical violations against their parole terms. The surveillance of former prisoners (who meet with parole officers in time-consuming meetings) creates better odds for technical slipups and methods for catching and punishing them. Studies show that rates of new criminal offenses (as opposed to technical violations) for parolees tend to resemble those of people with comparable sociodemographic characteristics who have never been incarcerated. In addition, the prison experience might not have the intended rehabilitative effect, disrupting individuals' normal lives and embedding them more deeply in a social network of others with deviant identities. Could prisons make it more difficult for offenders to return to the straight and narrow?

Let's first think back to Durkheim and his theory of anomie, which affirms that a disruption of normal life and a lack of stability make suicide or other deviant acts more likely. Going to prison for 10 or 15 years might have just this effect; it would be very difficult to "find stable employment, secure suitable housing, or reconcile with . . . family" afterward. Also, reintegration into a community after release from prison is extremely difficult because of "the absence of . . . informal social controls and strong social bonds" (Spohn & Holleran, 2002). Furthermore, while in prison in the United States, drug offenders rarely receive the kind of substance abuse treatment that addicts need. They are thus more likely to revert to drug use upon release. Therefore, imprisonment may be particularly counterproductive for drug offenders and getting tough on crime may inadvertently breed criminals. In addition, as low-level offenders interact daily with serious criminals in prison, they may become socialized by these new peers, adopting their attitudes and behaviors.

Ex-convict turned prison reentry social worker (and later lawyer) Marc Ramirez has an insider's perspective on the system, arguing that the violent, punitive culture of incarceration is counterproductive to rehabilitating prisoners, socializing them productively, and preparing them to give back to society.

> We're paying top dollar to incarcerate people when there are cheaper alternatives. There's been study after study on the [rehabilitative] effects of education, but yet we take Pell Grants and education programs out of prison. Family, having a family base [is critically important for successful reentry], but then these people in prisons

are so far away from their families, that they lose ties. We make visiting so difficult for families, you know, it's hard to maintain the family. The cost of making a phone call from a lot of prisons is prohibitive. (Conley, 2014c)

Ramirez finds the limited options for newly released prisoners disappointing. He remembers seeing prisoners "terrified to leave prison because they have not prepared, they have no support system. They don't know what they're going to do . . . there were so many people who would come back. And my thing was always like wow, so many of you guys have had breaks your way and I can't get a break. You gotta do better. You gotta want better. But you're not really given the tools to do better . . . the system is kind of designed to fail." Ramirez's story suggests that providing more housing, employment, and counseling to former convicts as they reenter society may help reduce the number of former prisoners who commit more crime upon release.

Sociologists and geographers have also examined the impact of incarceration on the communities prison inmates call home (Fagan et al., 2003; Williams, 2005). In New York City the incarcerated population disproportionately comes from a small handful of neighborhoods, a pattern that continues even as crime rates drop dramatically. In prison, inmates cannot make positive contributions to the community in terms of providing steady incomes, starting families, or building up social networks that lead to employment in legitimate industries. At the community level, high rates of incarceration among community members create conditions for continued poverty, as those left behind must support families on fewer salaries both during and after incarceration. From Pager's research earlier in this chapter, we know that former felons have a difficult time finding employment. Blocked access to legitimate employment creates conditions for sustained poverty. At the same time, historical crime rates still determine current police involvement, which means that once-crime-ridden neighborhoods continue to receive disproportionate formal surveillance and their residents are arrested at higher rates.

DIGITAL.WWNORTON.COM/YOUMAYASK8

To see my interview with Marc Ramirez, go to
digital.wwnorton.com/youmayask8

GOFFMAN'S TOTAL INSTITUTION

The high rates of recidivism in the United States bring us back to labeling theory, which suggests that the process of becoming a deviant often involves contact with, even absorption into, a special institution such as a prison or mental health institution. As labeling theorists have shown, our interaction with others very significantly impacts the formation of our personal identity. Erving Goffman (1961), writing in the symbolic interactionist tradition, theorized that institutions such as prisons and mental health hospitals often become breeding grounds for secondary deviance, providing an important link in the reproduction of deviance through their effects on inmates and patients.

Presumably, most of us sleep, play, and work in different places, with different people and rules structuring our interactions at each location. For example, you probably spend the evening in your home or dorm, relatively undisturbed in your pajamas, and leave in the morning for class, where you dress appropriately and respect your professors. Total institutions are distinguished by "a breakdown of the barriers separating" these "three spheres of life" (sleep, work, play). In total institutions, "all aspects of life are conducted in the same place and under the same single authority" (Goffman, 1961). In total institutions such as prisons and mental hospitals, the inmates take part in scheduled, highly regimented activities together. The inmates have no control over the form or flow of activities, which the institutional authorities choose to "fulfill the official aims of the institution." Thus, if the official aim of prisons is rehabilitation, prisoners might attend at least one self-improvement class a day or engage in some sort of productive labor. All of these activities occur in the same place with the same group of people every day.

TOTAL INSTITUTION

an institution in which one is totally immersed and that controls all the basics of day-to-day life; no barriers exist between the usual spheres of daily life, and all activity occurs in the same place and under the same single authority.

Inmates in an Arizona jail. The local sheriff requires all of the county's inmates to work seven days a week. They eat only twice a day, are denied recreation, and receive no coffee, cigarettes, salt, pepper, or ketchup.

In Chapter 4, we examined the various theories of socialization and the development of the self through our interactions with other social actors. All your life you slowly accumulated knowledge about your place in the world. Once you enter a total institution such as a prison, a process that strips away your sense of self begins. As Goffman puts it, "a series of abasements, degradations, humiliations, and profanations" quickly commences. Once people enter a prison or a mental institution, they are closed off from their normal routines and cease to fulfill their usual social roles. Because the roles people play reinforce the way they perceive themselves, this separation from the world erodes that sense of identity. In the Stanford Prison Experiment, what first occurred when the "inmates" arrived at the "prison" in the basement of the psychology department? They received issued uniforms and numbers in place of names. The mandated homogeneity of prisoners (and patients) results in an erasure of self. The total institution simultaneously strips away clothes, personal belongings, nicknames, hairstyles, cosmetics, and toiletries—all the tools that people use to identify themselves. The inmates no longer have control over their environment, peer group, daily activities, or personal possessions. It's not hard to imagine how this process would lead to a sense of helplessness. The total institution rapidly destroys a prisoner's sense of self-determination, self-control, and freedom.

FOUCAULT ON PUNISHMENT

> On March 2, 1757, Damiens the regicide was condemned "to make the amende honorable [a kind of ritual abasement] before the main door of the Church of Paris," where he was to be "taken and conveyed in a cart, wearing nothing but a shirt, holding a torch of burning wax weighing two pounds"; then, "in the said cart, to the Place de Greve, where, on a scaffold that will be erected there, the flesh will be torn from his breasts, arms, thighs, and calves with red-hot pincers, his right hand, holding the knife with which he committed the said parricide, burnt with sulfur, and, on those places where the flesh will be torn away, poured molten lead, burning oil, burning resin, wax and sulfur melted together and then his body drawn and quartered by four horses and his limbs and body consumed by fire, reduced to ashes and his ashes thrown to the winds." (Foucault, 1977, p. 1)

Besides possibly turning your stomach, the above passage vividly illustrates the dramatic shift in penal practices from the eighteenth century to the present day. How do we conceive of punishment nowadays? We usually think of prisons, juvenile detention centers, and probation. In *Discipline and Punish* (1977), the French theorist Michel Foucault examines the emergence of the modern penal system and how this system represents a transformation in social control. How did the modern prison system emerge, and what functions does it serve in the disciplining of modern life?

The execution of Robert-François Damiens, a French servant who attempted to assassinate King Louis XV at Versailles in 1757.

When Robert-François Damiens was publicly tortured and then eventually drawn and quartered for trying to kill King Louis XV, the punishment itself targeted Damiens's body. The entire public spectacle revolved around Damiens suffering for his wrongdoing, culminating in his death. Damiens was even put to death holding the same knife he used to attack the king. According to Foucault (1977), this gruesome "violence against the body" exemplifies a premodern form of punishment, which is concentrated on the body and associated with the crime committed. So, for example, if you kill someone, you are publicly executed. If you steal something, perhaps your fingers or hand will be cut off. This "eye for an eye" mentality parallels Durkheim's mechanical social sanctions.

We might like to believe that modern punishment came about because prison reformers lobbied for more humane penal tactics that aimed to reform the criminal through rehabilitation. We no longer (with the exception of the death penalty) publicly violate the criminal's flesh by, for example, pouring molten lead on his excoriated body. Punishment takes place in private, away from the public eye, and it leaves the criminal's body intact. (Although much violence, including rape, does occur inside prison walls, the state attempts to protect prisoners from such attacks.) Foucault claims that modern punishment has as its target what he calls "the soul" of the prisoner. The soul, for Foucault, is the sum of an individual's unique habits and peculiarities: what makes me *me* and you *you*. Such a penal system tries to understand the individual and their abnormalities to correct or reform bad habits. (Again, this is a highly stylized view of the history of criminal justice, given that in the United States, some jurisdictions still impose the death penalty and our government has even tortured political detainees. At the very least, we have witnessed an incomplete Foucaultian transformation.)

By "reforming the soul," Foucault means the use of experts such as social workers, psychologists, and criminologists to analyze and correct individual behavior. How does a prisoner become eligible for parole? The *New York State Parole Handbook* (New York State Division of Parole, 2007) indicates that "parole 'readiness'" depends on the inmate's "good prison behavior," involvement in "prison programming" for education and skills acquisition, and substance abuse counseling, all to "make important strides in self-improvement." After a criminal leaves prison on parole, the newly released prisoner meets with a field parole officer who monitors the whereabouts of the parolee and guides their reentry into community life. The handbook also indicates that a parole officer must help parolees "develop positive attitudes and behavior" and "encourage participation in programs for self-improvement." In principle, parole officers scrupulously supervise parolees, sometimes showing up at their workplaces or homes unannounced. Foucault would consider this rehabilitation system the modern face of penal practices.

How did the transformation in penal practice, from punishment targeted at the body to reform of the soul, take place? Foucault believes that this transformation stemmed from changes in how social control operates more generally, which in turn led to innovations in penal practices. Foucault (1977) uses the following example to illustrate the way modern punishment is organized and its implications for modern social control:

> The prisoners' day will begin at six in the morning in winter and at five in the summer. They will work for nine hours a day throughout the year. Two hours a day will be devoted to instruction. Work and the day will end at nine o'clock in winter and at eight in summer. . . . At the first drum-roll, the prisoners must rise and dress in silence, as the supervisor opens the cell doors. At the second drum-roll, they must be dressed and make their beds. (p. 6)

Foucault's example, extracted from a contemporary prisoners' timetable in France, contrasts strikingly with the way poor Damiens was punished several centuries earlier. Foucault points out that this sort of regimentation happens not only in prisons but also in society at large. Penal practices reflect the exercise of social control outside prison walls. Disciplinary techniques are modes of monitoring, examining, and regimenting individuals diffused throughout society. Foucault gives many examples of where and how this discipline takes place both in and out of prisons—in the military, in schools, in medical institutions, and so forth.

Foucault used the imagined architectural design of the panopticon as a metaphor for this march toward total surveillance and control. Jeremy Bentham, an English philosopher, devised the panopticon as a prison design. The panopticon is a circular building composed of an inner ring and an outer ring. Prisoners' cells are located in the outer ring, and large windows

PANOPTICON

a circular building composed of an inner ring and an outer ring designed to serve as a prison in which the guards, housed in the inner ring, can observe the prisoners without the detainees knowing whether they are being watched.

compose the front and back of each cell, allowing ample natural light to flood the rooms. The inner ring is a guards' tower, which also has large windows that open onto the windows of prisoners' cells. The guards can always see the prisoners, regardless of where they are in their cells, but the prisoners do not know when they are being watched (although the visibility of the central tower serves as a reminder that they are always under scrutiny). Foucault (1977) asserts that the "power" of the guards under this design is both "visible and unverifiable."

Foucault uses the panopticon as a metaphor for the general functioning of disciplinary techniques in society. Therefore, when the modern prison system emerged, based on monitoring, examining, and regimenting individual prisoners, there was a "gradual extension of the mechanisms of discipline," and they "spread throughout the whole social body," which led to "the formation of what might be called in general the disciplinary society." When you started kindergarten, you had to take tests and get medical checkups to gain entrance; then, once you started school, you entered the world of report cards, the parent–teacher conferences, and the tidy rows of desks. These are the sorts of panoptic (literally, "all-seeing") disciplinary techniques diffused throughout the social body. In Foucault's words, "our society is one not of spectacle, but of surveillance."

The Stateville Penitentiary in Illinois was built along the principles of Bentham's panopticon, a model for a prison in which inmates would always be visible.

THE U.S. CRIMINAL JUSTICE SYSTEM

At various points in history, the U.S. criminal justice system has fluctuated between two approaches to handling criminals: rehabilitation and punishment. Since the 1890s, argues Frank Allen (1981), the rehabilitative ideal has lost most of its significance and appeal because of shifting cultural values among Americans. Despite Durkheim's predictions, the concept of punishment ("lock 'em up and throw away the key") has largely replaced rehabilitation, winning political and popular favor and influencing criminal justice policy. The result? Up to 2020, about 5.5 million people were on probation, on parole, or in state/federal prison (Figure 6.4). In 2022, about 2 million people in the nation were incarcerated, with the U.S. system putting 573 people per 100,000 residents behind bars (Sawyer & Wagner, 2022). We are in an era of what sociologists call "mass incarceration."

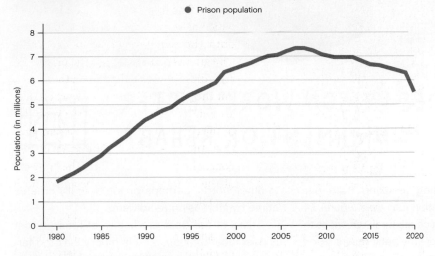

FIGURE 6.4 Size of U.S. Prison Population, 1980–2020

● Prison population

SOURCE: Bureau of Justice Statistics, 2020.

Not all Americans have been affected equally by the policy of mass incarceration, however. While Black adults have experienced the largest declines in incarceration over the past decade among any racial category, in 2017 Black Americans represented just 12 percent of the overall U.S. population but 38 percent of the incarcerated population (Sawyer & Wagner, 2022). If current incarceration rates were not to change (but see below on prison reform), a whopping 32 percent of Black males would be predicted to serve time in a state or federal prison during their lifetime, compared with 17 percent of Hispanic men and 5.9 percent of White men. The numbers of prisoners are strikingly high for an industrialized democracy. In addition, the United States is the only industrialized nation in the world to use capital punishment (U.S. Department of Justice, 2007).

However, the pendulum in U.S. policy might finally swing back to a more rehabilitative stance. One of the major pieces of legislation enacted by President Donald Trump was federal prison reform, the First Step Act of 2018, which intended to reduce the number of prisoners under lock and key but ultimately created logistical confusion that held more prisoners beyond their release dates. Many states are passing similar attempts at sentencing reforms, reducing terms for nonviolent crimes. Such state-level changes are more critical to the size of the incarcerated population, since the vast majority of detainees are held by the states (about 1.3 million) and not by the national government (about 220,000; Sawyer & Wagner, 2019).

One area where the federal government detains a lot of people is in the immigration domain. While those migrants (or suspected migrants) detained by U.S. Immigration and Customs Enforcement (ICE) are officially civil and not criminal detainees, they have been treated in many cases worse

DOES PRISON WORK BETTER AS PUNISHMENT OR REHAB?

With prison overcrowding resulting from our extremely high incarceration rate (see Figure 6.4 on page 243), criminal justice research continues to question the proper role of time behind bars. Does going to prison give inmates access to services and treatment that better equip them to be productive members of society, thereby reducing the number of crimes they might commit in the future? Is it plausible to think that incarcerated individuals may spend their time kicking drug habits, gaining religion, avoiding negative influences in their community, and obtaining an education and emerge less likely to commit crime when they are released?

Prison could end up being like "college for criminals"—a chance to network with other convicts, learn new illicit skills, and harden oneself to mainstream social norms, all while missing out on work experience and educational opportunities and acquiring the stigma of having done time.

In other words, perhaps prison actually creates crime by increasing recidivism.

One of the best predictors of future arrest is past incarceration, so this theory isn't too far-fetched. A solution to this problem comes from the fact that some states and localities randomly assign judges to cases. Like anyone else, judges are human beings with certain tendencies. Specifically, some judges give harsher sentences than others, which means that some convicts get the "treatment" (the harsh judge who sends them to prison) and some get the "placebo" (the more lenient judge who gives them probation). By examining variability in outcomes among convicted criminals based on the type of judge (not on the prisoners' own characteristics), we can identify the effects of incarceration and, by extension, the effects of the massive investment we've made in the prison system.

Inmates at San Quentin State Prison in an adult education class. Why do prisons spend taxpayer money to fund educational opportunities for inmates?

As it turns out, for adults, going to prison does not affect the probability of committing a future crime (and getting caught). (This lack of a difference suggests that taxpayers could get roughly the same crime rate but save a bunch of money on prison overhead by sentencing most criminals to house arrest. Of course, for this tactic to work, we have to assume that the deterrent effect against first-time offenses is minimal as well.)

For youth, the story is even starker: Across the United States, more than 130,000 juveniles are detained each year, and on any given day 70,000 minors are in formal detention. But as it turns out, locking these kids up makes them less likely to complete high school and more likely to commit crimes as adults (as evidenced from the random assignment to judges). In other words, far from being "scared straight," kids sent to detention simply get prepped for criminal life. Of course, locking kids up is both expensive and generates future costs in the form of more crime to deal with when they grow up.

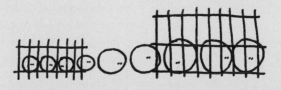

DIGITAL.WWNORTON.COM/YOUMAYASK8

To see my interview with Jacqueline Stevens about the conditions of ICE detention, go to **digital.wwnorton.com/youmayask8**

than some criminal offenders. The separation of children from their parents at the border received much press attention, as did the terrible conditions of some detention centers; however, other important aspects of ICE detention practices garnered less attention. For instance, since these immigrants are not criminal detainees, they should be paid minimum wage when doing work. But instead, they receive only a dollar per day, as if they were criminally incarcerated. The lack of proper due process has also led to a large number of U.S. citizens being deported! The private prison industry drives many of these practices, profiting off the detention of migrants and receiving a "promised" number of filled beds per federal law. Political scientist Jacqueline Stevens has spent much time writing about the conditions of ICE detention and has initiated a number of lawsuits to change them (Conley, 2019b).

Similar to both criminal and civil imprisonment rates and conditions, justice on death row is not color-blind (see Figure 6.5; Death Penalty Information, 2022a). In 1998, a study of Philadelphia death penalty cases revealed ample evidence of racial discrimination: Either the race of the defendant or the race of the victim came to bear on the outcome of the case (Baldus et al., 1998). First, the race of the murder victim matters. For example, in a study of the North Carolina criminal justice system, researchers found that the odds of a murderer receiving a death sentence rose 3.5 times if the victim was White, holding constant other relevant factors (Unah & Boger, 2001). Second and more obviously, the race of the accused matters. Contrary to popular belief about Black-on-White violence, interracial murders are fairly rare. As of 2019, out of 1,512 executions carried out in the United States since 1976 (when the Supreme Court reinstated the death penalty), 294 involved cases of Black-on-White homicide, but only 21 involved executions arising from cases of White-on-Black murder (Death Penalty Information Center, 2020a). One hypothesis would assert that these statistics result from African Americans committing disproportionately more crime than Whites while receiving, on average, appropriate penalties for their criminal behaviors. To make this sort of claim, we would need to have faith in the criminal justice system as a sound entity that generally delivers fair and accurate punishment. However, more than enough data to the contrary exist. Between 1973 and 2022, at least 190 people were

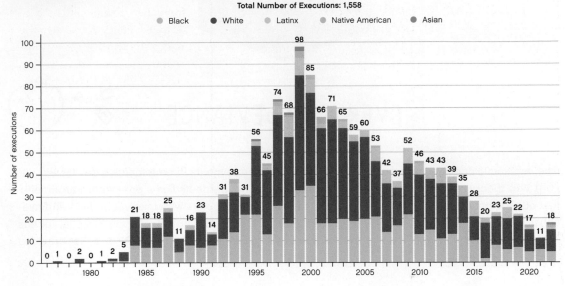

FIGURE 6.5 Number of Executions by Race, 1976–2022

Total Number of Executions: 1,558

● Black ● White ● Latinx ● Native American ● Asian

Number of executions

SOURCE: Death Penalty Information Center, 2022a.

exonerated from death row: Of these, 103 were Black, 67 White, and 17 Latinx (Death Penalty Information Center, 2022b). In 2020 and 2021, nine persons were released from death sentences (Death Penalty Information Center, 2020b; 2021). Some of these exonerations resulted from new DNA evidence, but these individuals' lives were forever changed, their careers and families having been permanently altered. In a sense, the new technology has shed light on the flaws in the system, raising the question of how many cases were wrongly judged before the deployment of DNA testing. This evidence of injustice has led to the abolition of the death penalty in Illinois, Connecticut, New Jersey, New York, New Mexico, Maryland, Delaware, New Hampshire, and Nebraska since 2007.

Conclusion

Training a sociological lens on deviance requires a careful and thorough review of not only the immediate causes and effects of deviance but also the broader social forces that undergird and define it. Sometimes, doing so takes us to paradoxical places, such as Émile Durkheim's finding that some degree of crime helps maintain social structure, allowing us to rally together against a common enemy. Sometimes, doing so reveals the unintended consequences of labels such as "deviant." And quite often, sociologists study tragedies in order to seek the social answers to violence and death. Sociology does not hope to provide comprehensive accounts of criminal acts or injustice, but it does dig deeper for concrete answers about our social world.

EVERYDAY DEVIANCE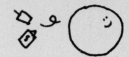

One legal scholar claims that the average American citizen commits three felonies a day (Silverglate, 2011). This theory may sound like a gross overestimate, but underneath lies a provocative argument: that our society has become overcriminalized by federal prosecutors who take vague laws and misconstrue seemingly ordinary activity as criminal. Regardless of your opinion, I hope this chapter has helped convince you that crime and deviance are part of the fabric of our society and that breaking the rules is more common than some care to admit.

TRY IT!

Write a list of the petty crimes you commit on a regular basis. I'll start us off.

ON A TYPICAL DAY, I MAY (OR MAY NOT) HAVE:

JAYWALKED
_____

SPED WHILE DRIVING (AND BROKEN OTHER MOTOR VEHICLE RULES)
_____

STREAMED A TV SHOW ON A SKETCHY WEBSITE
_____

LOITERED
_____

ROBBED A BANK (JUST KIDDING)
_____

_____

_____

_____

_____

THINK ABOUT IT

Have you ever been cited or arrested for any of your activities? If not, why not? If so, did it affect your future behavior?

Do you think everyone (i.e., people in different demographic groups) could get away with the same things you do? Why or why not? How do informal social norms and formal laws mesh or clash?

INEQUALITY IS THE RESULT
OF ABUNDANCE.

Stratification

Sarah Katz, meet Jeff Rutgers. While first names probably don't predict success with much accuracy, last names not only tell us more about our chances for success today, but also link us to the successes (or lack thereof) of our distant ancestors. By analyzing the distribution of last names in the professional directories of lawyers and doctors, economic historian Gregory Clark (2014) assessed the degree to which societies demonstrate social mobility or its opposite, social reproduction.

For example, as an Ashkenazi Jew (those who populated Europe), Sarah Katz enjoys about an eightfold greater chance of being a medical doctor today than does Jessica Smith (Smith being the most common surname in the United States). Jeff Rutgers, meanwhile, by virtue of a male ancestor who attended an Ivy League or similarly old university sometime between 1650 and 1850, enjoys an approximate threefold advantage. Also of advantaged pedigree are Hiro Suzuki, by virtue of having a Japanese surname, and Patricia Winthrop, who shares a name with a rich family of the 1920s.

The actor Denzel Washington does not hail from a family of doctors and lawyers. Washington is among the most common African American surnames and displays the marks of racial inequality: Black Washingtons are two-thirds less likely to be represented among the directory of physicians than they should be based on overall numbers in the population. Ditto for Annie Begay and John Yazzie, who have the two most common Native American names and are 94 percent less likely to be doctors compared with the U.S. average! Racial inequality presents a serious challenge for a huge number of people in the United States and the world as a whole, but we sociologists look at a number of other types of inequality too. Now, I'd like to introduce you to Ralph Gagnon, a White person who faces a number of non-race-related disadvantages.

According to Clark, the descendants of New France settlers—that is, the mostly French people who came through Québec, Canada, and other northern areas—have 40 percent lower odds of becoming a doctor. Unlike Black, Latinx, or Native American people, who have faced systemic discrimination for centuries, we tend to think of French people as not only White but also of relatively high status (people of French origin have been associated with an elite status since the time of the Norman conquest of England in 1066). Indeed, some of our most snooty words today come from French origins (hors d'oeuvres, anyone?).

More than figuring out what your name says about your postgraduation chances for a given job, Clark's analysis challenges some of our most cherished assumptions about social mobility. Through his analyses of names in Sweden, India, medieval Europe, the modern United Kingdom, the United States, Chile, and other societies, Clark finds that social status is transmitted across generations to a much greater degree than we previously thought. Typically, sociologists and economists examine the extent to which parent-and-child measures of social class, such as income, are the same. Zero would mean that your parents' earnings make no difference whatsoever to your income. One would mean that some sort of absolutely rigid caste system ensured that each generation's members perfectly reflected the success level of their progenitors. Most societies obviously fall in the middle somewhere. The latest research on income, for example, has busted the myth that the United States, despite being more unequal than most European societies, has higher rates of economic mobility. Indeed, the United States consistently ranks as the least mobile rich country in the world in terms of income.

But Clark's analysis tells us that the U.S. parent–child correlation in "social class" overall is about .84, compared to .5 to .6 in income depending on the study. To explain the discrepancy, he suggests that earlier work focused on one measure of social class—such as education, occupation, income, or wealth—making social mobility seem more common than it actually is. Take Microsoft founder Bill Gates Jr., for example. He dropped out of college even though his father graduated from law school, so by education measures Gates Jr. would seem downwardly mobile. By any measure of income or wealth, however, he is massively upwardly mobile. However, Clark contends that in some underlying, summary measure of class or status, most of us reflect our parents' social position a lot more than we may care to believe. This pattern of inheritance goes way back through 15 or more generations, according to Clark, which explains the influence of family names on what you might do for a living.

Not only are rates of social mobility lower than previously thought, according to Clark's findings, but also they don't vary all that much across time and place. Medieval Europe with its feudal system had more or less the same degree of social exchange between classes as in modern Britain today. The unequal, deregulated United States enjoys more or less the same fluidity as social democratic Sweden, on the one hand, and about the same social mobility as India, with its rigid social caste system, on the other (even though discrimination based on castes has been outlawed in India since 1950, enormous inequalities by caste membership persist). Even conscious efforts to totally remodel society, including the slaughtering of elites, can only slightly temper the degree of social inheritance. Despite the murderous purges during the Cultural Revolution, massive land redistribution, and a complete political transformation, Communist China under Mao Zedong reduced its intergenerational persistence to only about .7, down from .8.

So if we value social mobility, what's a poor old sociologist to do in light of Clark's hypothesis? Maybe we should all give up and change our last names to Potros, a Coptic Christian name from Egypt. In the United States at least, Copts are the most successful group of all. One version of Coptic lore claims that they are the true descendants of the pharaohs. If that's right, maybe the long arm of social history reaches back further than even Clark imagined.

By the end of this chapter you'll be able to:

- Understand the different characteristics of lay class groupings in U.S. society.

- Describe social equality based on evolving historical contexts.

- Analyze opportunity, condition, and outcome in determining social equality and inequality.

- Identify real-world examples of social hierarchy types.

- Design sociological studies that investigate the reproduction of social stratification.

- Describe the effects of European colonialism and modern globalization on international inequality.

How Is America Stratified Today?

Understand the different characteristics of lay class groupings in U.S. society.

Sociologists often use the phrase socioeconomic status to describe an individual's position in a social system based in stratification, or a hierarchical organization of a society into groups with differing levels of power, social prestige, or status and economic resources. When sociologists talk about socioeconomic status, they are referring to any measure that attempts to classify groups, individuals, families, or households in terms of indicators such as occupation, income, wealth, and education. Despite the somewhat

SOCIOECONOMIC STATUS

an individual's position in a stratified social order.

STRATIFICATION

the hierarchical organization of a society into groups with differing levels of power, social prestige, or status and economic resources.

INCOME

money received by a person for work, from transfers (gifts, inheritances, or government assistance), or from returns on investments.

WEALTH

a family's or individual's net worth (i.e., total assets minus total debts).

blurred boundaries between socioeconomic categories, the lay public generally divides society into the upper class, the middle class, the working class, and the poor. Although these terms lack sufficient specificity, they have useful applications nonetheless.

INCOME VERSUS WEALTH

Most people, when they consider economic status, think of income: money received by a person for work, from transfers (gifts, inheritances, or government assistance), or from returns on investments. Recent trends in earnings in the United States suggest an increasing divergence or inequality between the bulk of the people and the rich, but especially between the super-rich and the merely rich. For instance, from 1950 to 1970, for every dollar earned by the bottom 90 percent of the American population, those in the top .01 percent earned an additional $162. If that sounds like a big distinction, it's nothing compared with more recent data. Between 1990 and 2002, for every dollar earned by those in the bottom 90 percent, each taxpayer at the top (and this would include Bill Gates) took home $18,000 (Johnston, 2005). And between 1979 and 2019, annual wages grew by 160.3 percent for the top 1 percent, while the rest of the population experienced an expansion of a mere 26 percent (Economic Policy Institute, 2020).

A recent trend in sociological analysis, however, analyzes stratification in terms of wealth ownership. What is wealth in relation to income? Wealth is a family's or an individual's net worth (total assets minus total debts). For the majority of American families, assets include a home, cars, other real estate, and business assets, along with financial forms of wealth such as stocks, bonds, and mutual funds. Put simply, wealth is everything you own minus debts such as mortgages on a home, credit card debt, and, as most of you will probably have, debt from student loans. Think about the difference between income and wealth by imagining income as a stream or river of money flowing through a family's hands. Wealth, by contrast, is a pool of collected resources that can be drawn on at specific times, a financial reservoir. In 2022, the top 10 percent held about three-quarters of the world's wealth (World Inequality Lab, 2022).

THE UPPER CLASS

Generally, the upper class refers to the group of individuals at the top of the socioeconomic food chain. In practice, however, the term describes diverse and complex concepts. Historically, the upper class was often distinguished by not having to work. (The economist and social critic Thorstein Veblen dubbed this group "the leisure class.") Its members maintained their lifestyle by collecting rent and/or other investment returns. They were the aristocracy, the wealthy, the elite, the landowners. The only way to join this sphere was by birth or (occasionally) marriage. Today, however, the upper class also includes folks who "struck it rich," so to speak, through work, entrepreneurship, or other means. Think the founders of the big tech companies, for example, or titans of Wall Street who may have come from middle-class backgrounds.

In the United States, "upper class" is associated with income, wealth, power, and prestige. Sources of income primarily distinguish upper-class individuals from members of other classes, as they receive more from returns on investments than wages. Although estimates vary, approximately 1 percent of the U.S. population falls into this stratum (Figure 7.1). The COVID-19 pandemic came with significant disadvantages for all, particularly for lower- and middle-class Americans; at the peak of the COVID-19 pandemic in 2020, at least 3 in 10 lower-income adults struggled with unemployment, with the median income of lower-income households falling by 3 percent (Pew Research Center, 2022a). In contrast, the wealth held by U.S. billionaires rose

UPPER CLASS

a term for the economic elite.

FIGURE 7.1 Top 1% Versus Bottom 50% Wealth Shares in Western Europe and the United States, 1910–2020

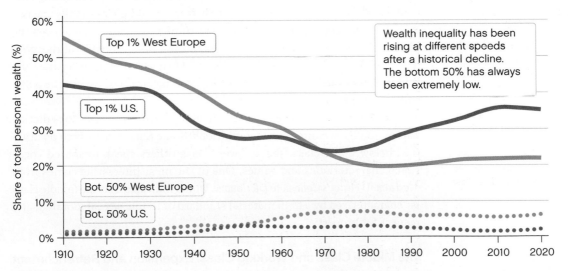

SOURCE: Bauluz et al., 2021.

from \$2.947 trillion to \$5.019 trillion, an increase of 70 percent compared to pre-pandemic assets (Inequality.org, 2022). Over and above income levels, levels of prestige and power also characterize the upper class. This social influence allows the upper class to promote personal agendas and influence everything from political decisions to consumer trends, which matters because members of the upper class often wear many hats. As Dennis Gilbert states in *The American Class Structure in an Age of Growing Inequality* (1998):

> The members of the tiny capitalist class at the top of the hierarchy have an influence on economy and society far beyond their numbers. They make investment decisions that open or close employment opportunities for millions of others. They contribute money to political parties, and they often own media enterprises that allow them influence over the thinking of other classes. (p. 286)

THE MIDDLE CLASS

Although those in the upper class have very real influence and control, public perception can limit the effects of this power. In the 2007 article "The American People: Social Classes," published in the online magazine *Life in the USA* (a "complete web guide to American life for immigrants and Americans"), Elliot Essman speaks for much of the mainstream media. "The very rich control corporations and have some political power, but the lifestyle and values of the very wealthy do not have much impact on the country in general," he states. "America is a middle-class nation."

The middle class often characterizes the United States—so much so that almost 90 percent of Americans self-identify with this stratum. That said, there is no consensus on what the term middle class really means. Sociologists, economists, policy makers, think tank analysts, and even the public at large all work with different operating assumptions about the term. The categories become particularly blurry when we attempt to separate the middle class from the working class (or "working families," to use the political campaign euphemism).

So, what is the middle class? If you look up the term in various dictionaries, you'll encounter lots of definitions. Some refer explicitly to position (i.e., below upper class, above lower class); others speak to shared vocational characteristics and values. One of the most interesting comes from *Merriam-Webster's Collegiate Dictionary,* which indicates that the middle class is "characterized by a high material standard of living, sexual morality, and respect for property."

The Middle Class and Working Class: Expansion and Retrenchment

In the United States, the middle class has historically been composed of white-collar workers (office workers) and the working class composed of

MIDDLE CLASS

a term commonly used to describe those individuals with nonmanual jobs that pay significantly more than the poverty line—though this is a highly debated and expansive category, particularly in the United States, where broad swaths of the population consider themselves middle class.

those individuals who work manually (using their hands or bodies). However, this distinction eroded with two trends. First, the post–World War II boom led to the enrichment of many manual workers. In those days, most working-class Whites, ranging from factory workers to firemen to plumbers, could buy their own homes, afford college for their children, and retire comfortably. The working class became the newly expanded middle class.

From the post–World War II era of the late 1940s through the oil crisis of 1973, this middle class remained a large and fairly stable group, maintained by corporate social norms emphasizing equality in pay and salary increases (Krugman, 2005). From 1947 through 1979, the average salary increased consistently across all household income levels—in fact, the lowest-earning 20 percent of households showed the highest average earnings increase at 116 percent.

A second, countervailing trend has also eroded the traditional manual–nonmanual distinction between the working and middle classes: the rise of the low-wage service sector. Since 1973, manufacturing has steadily declined in the United States, and the service jobs replacing factory work have generally been either very high skilled (and well rewarded) or relatively low skilled (and not very well paid). This new and expanding group of low-wage service workers challenges the notion that working-class status arises from physical labor. Data-entry clerks, cashiers, paralegals, and similar occupations are technically white-collar jobs, yet they pull in working-class wages.

Over the past three decades, the income gap between a corporate CEO and a single-mother waitress has grown exponentially, and the relatively stable middle class of previous decades has become increasingly stratified (Figure 7.2). For example, a CEO who makes at least $200,000 is in the top

FIGURE 7.2 Ratio of U.S. CEO Pay to Average Worker Pay, 1965–2021

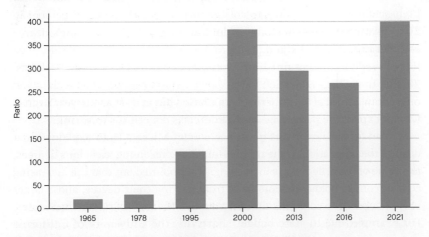

SOURCES: Davis & Mishel, 2014; Bivens & Kandra, 2022; Mishel & Schieder, 2017.

5 percent of households, and their average expected salary increase since 1979 (adjusted for inflation) is about 50 percent. On the other end of the scale, a waitress who makes only $22,000 is in the bottom 20 percent of households, and her average expected salary increase over the same period is about 27 percent. And an average family, such as a two-parent household with two kids and a middle-range annual income of $52,000, probably has experienced an income increase of only 14 percent since 1979, a sign of what some call the shrinking middle class (Gould, 2014). Since the mid-twentieth century, the income gap between CEOs and typical workers has increased significantly. The average CEO outearned the average worker at a rate of 20 to 1 in 1965 and 59 to 1 in 1989 (Economic Policy Institute, 2022). Inequality in pay has only increased since the turn of the twenty-first century. The average salary for top CEOs in the United States was $15.6 million in 2021, with CEOs now outearning the average worker at a rate of 399 to 1 (Economic Policy Institute, 2022). CEOs even earn higher pay than other high-earning workers, making almost seven times more than other workers in the top .1 percent (Economic Policy Institute, 2022).

How can we explain this differential income growth? One factor may be the changing nature of available employment. As the technological sector expands, the majority of jobs either require very high skill levels with correspondingly high salaries (engineers and hedge fund managers) or very low levels with little room for upward mobility (baristas at Starbucks who serve lattes to those hedge fund managers). And the fastest-growing job category for those with no more than a high-school education is food preparation and service.

Changes in educational expectations of potential employers further reflect this bifurcated job growth. Whereas for much of the post–World War II period, a high-school diploma could earn a person (a White man, specifically) enough to support a family, decent employment now often requires a college degree in the twenty-first century. But although the number of high-school graduates going to college increased to roughly 68 percent in 2020 (National Center for Education Statistics, 2022a), bachelor's degree completion rates still stand at approximately 64 percent nationally (i.e., lots of students are not finishing; National Center for Education Statistics, 2022b). If a college education is the gateway to becoming middle class and only about a third of the American population has at least a four-year degree, we can expect the percentage of middle-class Americans to shrink.

In an interview for this book, sociologist Michael Hout explained that despite the stagnation in the number of people receiving bachelor's degrees, the value of those degrees is increasing. Hout pointed out that the increasing cost of college holds students back from getting their degree, and a larger proportion of the cost falls on individuals and families rather than states. For example, due to state budget shortfalls, the University of California

(UC) system—one of the biggest and best—announced a tuition hike of 32 percent for the academic year starting in 2010 that was swiftly followed by another 9.6 percent rise in 2011. The UC system planned another increase in 2019 but put those plans on hold during the peak of the COVID-19 pandemic; however, in 2021, the board announced another 4.2 percent increase, the first actualized tuition increase since 2017 (McMillan, 2011; New University, 2021; Pickert, 2014). Hout goes on to describe the way that sacrificing to pay for college plays out differently across social classes.

DIGITAL.WWNORTON.COM/YOUMAYASK8

To see sociologist Michael Hout discuss the benefits of a college education, see **digital.wwnorton.com/youmayask8**

> There is a class-specific preference for these kinds of risks. The sons and daughters of college graduates see the benefit of a college education more clearly. They have had it drummed into them since they could talk. . . . Sons and daughters of people who haven't been to college can exercise a certain skepticism about it, and they see in their neighborhoods evidence that it might not pay off. Who leaves the neighborhood? Somebody who has reaped the full benefit of the college education. They're out of sight and out of mind. Who's back in the neighborhood? That kid who maybe dropped out after three years, with a three-figure loan debt, [or] six-figure loan debt. And the presence of those people makes it look like college doesn't pay off. (Conley, 2009h)

Some argue that along with income inequality, income insecurity (or volatility) has also increased for the middle classes. In *The Great Risk Shift* (2006), Jacob Hacker asserts that the chances of an American family experiencing a 50 percent drop in their annual income from one year to the next were 17 percent in 2002, up from around 7 percent in 1970. A 50 percent salary cut would still leave the CEO mentioned earlier in the top 40 percent of household incomes, but how about our waitress and our middle-income family? Cutting their salary by half would send either into a major financial crisis, maybe even bankruptcy. However, other researchers argue that income instability stems from two significant changes in family dynamics rather than fluctuating earnings or job insecurity. First, there are more changes to household structure today because of divorce and remarriage; second, women now play a greater role in breadwinning (even exceeding men as a proportion of the workforce at one point during the recent recession), but they also enter and exit the workforce with greater frequency than men. (See Chapter 8 for more about women in the workforce.)

THE POOR

Unlike the fuzzy definitions of other classes, poverty has an official, government definition. In 2023, the poverty line for a family of four was $30,000 (U.S. Department of Health and Human Services, 2023). The poor, ironically, often resemble the rich in being more oriented toward the present and therefore less worried about the future than their middle-class and working-class counterparts (although this characteristic is highly debated). Day-to-day survival keeps the poor clearly planted in the present. Of course, like any class, the poor are not a unified group. In fact, political speeches often distinguish between the "working poor" (those who deserve our assistance) and the "nonworking poor" (those who can work but don't and therefore have a weaker moral claim on assistance). This latter group is sometimes called the "underclass." Of course, even these two categories obscure huge distinctions within either group; in fact, families usually shift in and out of poverty throughout their history, and often a clear distinction does not exist between the working class and the poor.

Views of Inequality

❚ Describe social equality based on evolving historical contexts.

While shorthand terms like upper class, middle class, and working class are useful for conversing in everyday life, in order to answer important questions about stratification in society, we need more precise definitions of unequal groups in society as well as a conceptual framework through which to view inequality. In the following section, I present three possible frameworks to explain the intersection of various dimensions of stratification. We start with the Enlightenment in the eighteenth century and move forward from there.

ROUSSEAU: HUMANS GOOD, PROPERTY BAD

Writing prolifically from 1750 to 1782, Jean-Jacques Rousseau greatly influenced the political ideas of the French Revolution and the development of socialist thought. Seeing humankind as naturally pure and good, Rousseau appealed to biology and human instincts to explain social outcomes. For Rousseau, the process of building society and repressing natural human character creates social problems. Specifically, Rousseau sees the emergence of private property, the idea that a person has the right to own something, as the primary source of social ills. If we stripped away the elements of society that result from the institution of private property—the competition, isolation, aggression, and hierarchical organization—only social equality, a condition in which no differences in wealth, power, prestige, or status based on nonnatural bases exist, would remain. According to Rousseau (1754/2004), two forms of inequality exist: physical (or natural), which "consists in a difference of age, health, bodily strength, and the qualities of the mind or of the soul," and social (or political), which

> depends on a kind of conventional inequality and is established or at least authorized by the consent of men. This latter consists of the different privileges which some men enjoy to the prejudice of others, such as that of being more rich, more honored, more powerful, or even in a position to exact obedience. (p. 15)

Rousseau acknowledges that a certain amount of natural inequality will always exist among people: Some are always going to be better than others at kicking a ball, hunting large game, doing math, or seeing over long distances. Some of these inequalities result from aging, as basketball players in their twenties will almost certainly have greater physical abilities than basketball players in their eighties. In contrast with natural inequality, social inequality results from privileges and unequal access to resources (i.e., private property) and eventually leads to social ills. There are only so many resources available in any society (and, more broadly, in the world as a whole), and when certain people "arbitrarily" hold those resources (i.e., when inequality emerges thanks to private property), conflict can emerge.

SCOTTISH ENLIGHTENMENT: INEQUALITY IS GOOD

In the eighteenth century, Rousseau saw the move away from the pure state of nature as a negative historical development, complaining that "man was born free, and he is everywhere in chains." But thinkers of the later Enlightenment, including Adam Ferguson and John Millar of Scotland and Thomas Malthus of England, saw inequality as good—or at least necessary. These three agreed that inequality arises when private property emerges and that, in turn, private property emerges when resources can be preserved, because it is only through surpluses that some people are able to conserve and increase their bounty. This concept leads to the paradox of this chapter: Inequality results from surplus.

SOCIAL EQUALITY

a condition in which no differences in wealth, power, prestige, or status based on nonnatural conventions exist.

Jean-Jacques Rousseau.

When individuals or groups in society become more efficient and productive, they can gather, hunt, or grow more than they themselves can consume at a given time. They can then conserve such a surplus, whether that means turning milk into cheese, making berries into preserves, or putting their money into a hedge fund. In whatever way they choose, they transform their current resources into assets, a form of wealth stored for the future. (In fact, the word *asset* comes from the French legal expression *aver assetz*, meaning "to have enough.") The ability to preserve resources may lead to a decrease in collective effort and trust. Whereas previously the incentive might have been to share the wealth when you couldn't store it—to generate reciprocal goodwill for the rainy day when you don't have enough to eat and your neighbor does—now, the incentive is for individuals to hoard as much as possible, so that when a rainy day comes along, personal savings are available. Alternatively, if a resource-rich individual decides to distribute surplus wealth, then that individual might decide to extract power, promises, and rewards in return for what they provide rather than rainy-day goodwill.

For Ferguson and Millar, such social developments resulting from the establishment of private property represent a huge improvement in society because private property leads to higher degrees of social organization and efficiency: If an individual can preserve and accumulate resources and become more powerful by storing up assets (private property), they will have much more incentive to work. Personal incentives inspire people to continue working even after accumulating what they need for today, and that extra work will build up society and improve civilization as a whole. For the Scottish Enlightenment thinkers, inequality was a prerequisite for social progress, and social progress was a prerequisite for the development of civilization—the greatest goal toward which humankind could strive.

MALTHUS: MAN IS DESTINED TO STARVE

Malthus also had a positive view of inequality but for a different reason. In 1798, Malthus published an anonymous treatise titled "An Essay on the Principle of Population as It Affects the Future Improvement of Society," arguing that human populations grow geometrically (multiplicatively, like rabbits), while our ability to produce food increases only arithmetically (much more slowly). Simply put, his theory suggests that a rising number of people on the planet will eventually use up all the available resources and bring about mass starvation and conflict. Humankind, Malthus believed, was destined to live in a state of constant near-death misery, as population growth always pushed society to the limits of food availability.

Because of these dire trends, Malthus believed inequality played a beneficial, or at least necessary, role in avoiding the problem of massive overpopulation and hence starvation. Inequality, from his perspective, kept the population in check. After all, for Malthus, the main problem with the world—especially with England—was the number of people in it, and anything that restrained population growth was supremely good. In this vein, he denounced soup kitchens and early marriages while defending the effects of smallpox, slavery, and child murder (Heilbroner, 1999). Malthus believed that overpopulation would create more and more human misery and, therefore, reducing the levels of inequality by a measure that would "temporarily" ease the condition of the "masses" and thereby cause their numbers to swell even more would only exacerbate the problem in the long run. Such a condition is today called a Malthusian population trap—a situation in which population growth leads not to abundance but to increased poverty.

Farmworker Stella Machara with her sons Kudakwachi and Simbaracha in front of their home in Zimbabwe. According to Jeffrey Sachs, why is sub-Saharan Africa stuck in a Malthusian population trap? To see more of the conversation with Sachs, visit **digital.wwnorton .com/youmayask8.**

Recent history and scholarship show that Malthus's predictions were too dire. Paradoxically, helping children survive reduces population pressure by causing parents to reduce their fertility. In an interview for this book, I asked Jeffrey Sachs of the Earth Institute at Columbia University if he thought that sub-Saharan Africa might face a Malthusian trap as the per capita land available for farming dwindles. Sachs captured the paradox of helping more children survive in order to escape the Malthusian trap: "Save the children. It seems paradoxical. But when the children are staying alive, the families say, 'Ah! It's safe to have fewer children. I don't need to have six for insurance. My children will survive'" (Conley, 2009g).

HEGEL: THINGS ARE GETTING BETTER

A third view of inequality comes from the German philosopher Georg Wilhelm Friedrich Hegel, who conceptualized a master–slave dialectic (sometimes called a master–servant dialectic). The word dialectic means a two-directional relationship—that is, one that goes both ways, like a conversation between two people. First, one person talks, putting out an idea or thesis; then the other responds, pointing out some problems with the thesis or posing a counterposition, an antithesis. Then the original speaker responds, and ideally, the two arrive at a synthetic arrangement constructed from elements of the original position and the strongest counterpoints.

In Hegel's master–slave dialectic, the slave depends on the master because the master provides food, shelter, and protection. In this way, the slave is akin to a child raised by the master. However, as Hegel observed, the master also depends on the slave, who performs the basic duties of survival until the master can no longer function on his own. He doesn't remember how to grow his own food, prepare meals, or even get dressed without help.

DIALECTIC

a two-directional relationship, following a pattern in which an original statement or thesis is countered with an antithesis, leading to a conclusion that unites the strengths of the original position and the counterarguments.

Basically, the master would not be able to function if left to fend for himself. Thus, the master—slave nexus becomes a relationship of mutual dependency.

Hegel views history as marching steadily forward from a situation of few masters and many servants or slaves—such as monarchies and empires, not to mention the entire feudal system—to a society with more and more free men and women, a situation of democracy and equality. His was an optimistic view of history, to say the least. According to Hegel, notions of inequality are constantly evolving in a larger historical arc. He saw this as a trajectory that would eventually lead to equality for all (or very nearly all). We will see that many sociologists have had a bone or two to pick with this position, as well as with those laid out by Rousseau, Ferguson, Millar, and Malthus.

MODERN THEORIES OF INEQUALITY

Karl Marx challenged Hegel's notion of an automatic march to greater freedom (and equality). Marx's theory of history emphasized class conflict and struggle that would only end with a Communist revolution that eliminated private property (what the Enlightenment thinkers praised as the seed of innovation). Marx's theory of history—dialectic materialism—put group struggles for control of economic resources at the center of social change. Hegel, according to Marx, had focused too much on cognitive states (i.e., the mind) and not enough on real-world material struggles for survival.

If Marx stood Hegel on his head, then Max Weber can be said to have stood Marx on his. Weber's theory of inequality reasserted the Hegelian notion that ideas—and not just material interests—play an important causal role in determining who gets what, which societies are rich and which are poor, and how history evolves. For example, in *The Protestant Ethic and the Spirit of Capitalism* (1904/2003), Weber points to the role of religion in determining economic success. (Marx would have seen religion as a means to justify the mode of production and exploitation of the working class and not as a cause of economic conditions.) Specifically, he argued that medieval Catholicism touted the virtues of poverty and also ensured that its followers would go to heaven after death as long as they followed the rituals of the church. But, among other changes, the Protestant Reformation induced a spiritual insecurity as to whether believers would go to heaven. Material riches were a sign that one was blessed and among those chosen to ascend to heaven. This view flipped the script on the relative virtue of wealth versus poverty and provided an incentive for individuals to work hard, save, and accumulate wealth.

In the twentieth century, in most Western societies, history did not play out as Marx's theory of conflict and violent revolution had predicted. Capitalism did not collapse under its own contradictions. Indeed, moderating forces like the welfare state (social insurance) and labor unions

DIALECTIC MATERIALISM

a notion of history that privileges conflict over economic, material resources as the central struggle and driver of change in society.

emerged, and a tacit peace between capital and labor—Marx's two great oppositional forces in the capitalist phase—developed. The proletariat did not get poorer and poorer and rise up in revolt. To explain this turn of events, a new group of theories emerged to explain this economic and social cohesion. Stemming from Durkheim's notions of organic solidarity (Durkheim, 1893/1997; see Chapter 6) and Herbert Spencer's metaphor of society as an organism (Spencer, 1898/1967), the school of thought called structural functionalism emphasized the economy and society as an organized system that—though it occasionally faced strains—for the most part efficiently allocated individuals to their most suitable occupations. Most famously described in a 1945 article by Kingsley Davis and Wilbur Moore (1945), a necessary inequality in this rendering induced the most talented people to fill the most demanding positions that require the highest skills and dedication. That is, medical doctors make more money because of the necessary role that they fill within society, while also being members of a profession that demands great talent and sacrifice. This theory was critiqued on many grounds—notably the fact that there is no reason to assume that high rewards go to people or positions that are "needed" by society (whatever that means).

Conflict theory emerged to reconcile the views of Marx and the functionalists. As embodied by the work of Ralf Dahrendorf (1958), this paradigm suggested that while the world did not turn out as Marx had predicted, different interest groups did constantly struggle for authority, and these conflicts drove societal change. Another strand of the theory, as offered by Lewis Coser (1957), suggested that conflict itself could serve a cohesive role in society. For example, conflict against an external enemy (or out-group) unified individuals in the in-group. Conflict also served a communication function by making various interests and points of view known to the various parties. The bottom line was that conflict among groups for limited resources was a perennial feature of human societies and this conflict, in turn, drove historical change. To the extent there appeared to be consensus in a given moment, it was a veneer that was maintained by top-down coercive authority that sought to tamp down claims for resources on the part of less powerful groups.

STRUCTURAL FUNCTIONALISM

a theory in which society's many parts—institutions, norms, traditions, and so on—mesh to produce a stable, working whole that evolved over time; best embodied by Talcott Parsons.

CONFLICT THEORY

the idea that conflict between competing interests is the basic, animating force of social change and society in general.

Standards of Equality

Analyze opportunity, condition, and outcome in determining social equality and inequality.

Assuming that we do value equality in society, what kind of equality do we want? There are different ideologies or belief systems regarding equality, so it's important to recognize that when various groups use the rhetoric of

Civil rights activists in San
Francisco demonstrate
against Jim Crow laws in
1964. Why did the demand
for equal opportunity
resonate with most
Americans?

equality, particularly in the political sphere, they may be talking past each other or jostling for advantage. What did Thomas Jefferson mean when he proclaimed in the Declaration of Independence that "all men are created equal"? How have our definitions of equality changed in the twenty-first century?

EQUALITY OF OPPORTUNITY

One standard of equality is termed equality of opportunity. Let's think of society as a game of Monopoly, in which all of the players try to maximize their holdings of wealth (the game's houses and hotels) and their income (the rent collected from other players who land on built-up properties after an unfortunate roll of the dice). In this game, the person with the most money in the end is the winner. Monopoly follows the rules of equality of opportunity. Sure, one player may wind up flat broke and another player may control 95 percent of the wealth, but the rules were fair, right? Everyone had an equal chance at the start. Assuming nobody cheated, any differences resulted from luck (the dice) and skill (the players' choices). The same goes for society under the equality of opportunity model. The mere existence of inequality is not at issue here. Some people have more wealth and income than others, and some people enjoy greater social prestige or power than others, but the rules of the game are presumed fair. We all go into the game of society, as we do into a game of Monopoly, knowing the rules, and therefore any existing inequality is fair as long as everyone plays by the rules.

This theory models equality in a bourgeois society, such as modern capitalist society. Although the word *bourgeois* is often used pejoratively, here I mean it as a neutral description—a society of commerce in which the maximization of profit is the primary business incentive. Almost all modern capitalist societies purport to follow an ideology of equal opportunity. However, civil rights activists in the 1960s argued that the rules were unfair; for instance, the segregation of public spaces and other Jim Crow laws (a rigid set of anti-Black statutes that relegated African Americans to the status of second-class citizens through educational, economic, and political exclusion) did not reflect a bourgeois notion of fairness or equality of opportunity.

The rallying cry for equality of opportunity resonates with our overall capitalist ideology. Unequal opportunity clearly stifles meritocracy, a system in which individuals advance through achievement or ability. For example, if you had a heart transplant, would you not want the most knowledgeable heart surgeon with the most dexterous hands? Or would you settle for the one born to rich parents who finagled their child's way into medical school? Under a system of equal opportunity, everyone can compete to become a heart surgeon if they choose, and eventually the most talented will rise to fill the most demanding, important positions.

EQUALITY OF CONDITION

A second more progressive standard of equality is equality of condition. Going back to our Monopoly analogy, imagine if at the beginning of the game, two players started out with an extra $5,000 and already owned hotels on Boardwalk and Park Place, and Pennsylvania and North Carolina Avenues, respectively, while the other two players started out with a $5,000 deficit and owned no property. The ideology behind equality of condition argues that the rules of the game should compensate for inequalities in the relative starting positions. An example of this ideology is affirmative action, which involves preferential selection to increase the representation of women, racial and ethnic minorities, and people from less privileged social classes in areas of employment, education, and business from which they have historically been excluded (see the policy discussion at the end of this chapter). Affirmative action occurs when a person or group in a gatekeeper position, such as a college admissions office or the human resources department in charge of hiring new workers, actively selects some applicants who have faced the steep slope of an uneven playing field, often due to racism or sexism in society. Sometimes these policies can enhance efficiency if they result in fairer competition; other times they may result in a trade-off between efficiency and equality in favor of the latter. We want to accept that certain colleges admit applicants with slightly lower SAT scores who faced much greater obstacles to attain those SAT scores than other groups of test takers who enjoyed more advantages. Such "social engineering" may be based on race, class,

EQUALITY OF CONDITION

the idea that everyone should have an equal starting point.

Middlebury College student Laura Blackman received help from the Posse Foundation, which recruits inner-city kids for elite colleges. How were affirmative action policies an example of equality of condition?

gender, or any other social sorting category, attempting to rectify a playing field tilted against individuals because of their backgrounds or identities.

EQUALITY OF OUTCOME

EQUALITY OF OUTCOME

the idea that each player must end up with the same amount regardless of the fairness of the "game."

The final and most radical (or rather most antibourgeois and anticapitalist) form of equality is equality of outcome, the position that each Monopoly player should end up with the same amount regardless of the fairness of the "game." This model admittedly would make for a dull round of Monopoly: In this scenario, the players on Baltic Avenue would make just as much as those on Boardwalk, and some mechanism in the game—say, a central banker or all the players pooling their resources—would ensure game play that lived up to Karl Marx's maxim in the *Critique of the Gotha Programme* (1890–91/1999), "From each according to his ability, to each according to his needs." This standard focuses less on the rules of the game and more on the distribution of resources; it essentially employs a Marxist (or Communist) ideology. Like Rousseau's idea that there will always be physical inequalities—some will be better at math, others will be better at physical work, and so on—equality of outcome is the idea that everyone contributes to society and to the economy according to what they do best. For instance, someone who is naturally gifted at math might become an engineer or a mathematician, whereas someone better at physical work might build infrastructure such as roads and bridges. A centrally organized society calls on its citizens to contribute to the best of their ability, yet everyone receives the same rewards. The median income is everyone's income regardless of occupation or position.

Equality of outcome, or equality of result, eliminates the individual incentives touted by the Scottish Enlightenment thinkers. Nobody earns more power, prestige, and wealth by working harder. In this system, the only incentive is altruistic; you devote your labor to society for the sake of its progress and not merely for your own betterment (although, arguably, it may be in the self-interest of the individual to see society progress as a whole). Facebook founder Mark Zuckerberg and his wife, Priscilla Chan, would probably have to give up 99.99 percent of their wealth rather than the "mere" 99 percent they have pledged to charity to help equalize outcomes (Brandon, 2015), whereas a single mother working two jobs in order to provide food, shelter, and day care for her children would receive a helpful step up. Critics worry that without the selfish incentives of capitalism, all progress would halt, and sloth might take over. Unless an oppressive rule emanated from some central agency, collective endeavors would fail on account of the free rider problem, the notion that when more than one person is responsible for getting something done, each individual shirks responsibility and hopes

FREE RIDER PROBLEM

the notion that when more than one person is responsible for getting something done, the incentive is for each individual to shirk responsibility and hope others will pull the extra weight.

others will pull the extra weight. (You might have encountered this sort of situation while collaborating on group projects for school.) Critics of this system argue that even with a relatively strong central planning agency to assign each worker a task and enforce productivity, such an administrative mechanism cannot make decisions and allocate resources as efficiently as a more free-market approach does.

Forms of Stratification

▌ Identify real-world examples of social hierarchy types.

Thus far we have discussed standards of equality and inequality only in general terms, but these models emerge in several forms in society. For example, a society can be stratified based on age. In many tribes, for instance, age determines the social prestige and honor that the group accords an individual. (By contrast, some argue that in the youth-obsessed culture of the United States, age is a source of dishonor.) Those younger than you would place great weight on your words and in some cases treat them as commands. Similarly, birth order within a particular family can form a foundation of inequality. In nineteenth-century European society, the firstborn male typically inherited the family estate; in certain parts of the world, birth order still plays a role in resource distribution. Gender or race and ethnicity also can be the predominant form social stratification takes. Ultimately, many dimensions exist within which inequality can emerge, and often these dimensions overlap significantly.

Stratified societies are those that rank human groups within them into strata, creating divisions along one or more social dimensions. Many sociologists and philosophers believe that there are four ideal types of social stratification—namely, estate system, caste system, class system, and status hierarchy system—although all societies have some combinations of these forms, and no type ever occurs in its pure form. Some sociologists propose a fifth ideal type, an elite—mass dichotomy (also known as an oligarchy). Each system has its own ideology that attempts to legitimate the inequality within it.

In Western Australia, Aboriginal elder Brandy Tjungurrayi wears a pencil through his nose as a sign of his senior status.

ESTATE SYSTEM

ESTATE SYSTEM

a politically based system of stratification characterized by limited social mobility.

The first ideal type of social stratification is the estate system. Primarily found in feudal Europe from the medieval era through the eighteenth century, and in the American South before the Civil War, social stratification in estate systems has a political basis. That is, laws distribute rights and duties (and, therefore, power) unequally. For example, in the antebellum American South, many states required land ownership for voting privileges. Europe also historically restricted voting rights to landowners. Before reforms, political participation depended on the social group (the estate) to which you belonged. These practices limited mobility among the three general estates—the clergy, the nobility, and the commoners (the commoners were typically further divided into peasants and city dwellers)—and each group enjoyed certain rights, privileges, and duties. In certain eras, a rich commoner could buy a title and become a member of the nobility. And often, one son or daughter of a noble family would join the clergy and become part of that estate. Therefore, there was some mobility, but social reproduction—you are what your parents were and what your children will be—generally prevailed. (We examine the concept of social mobility more closely below.)

CASTE SYSTEM

CASTE SYSTEM

a religion-based system of stratification characterized by no social mobility.

A second type of stratification is a caste system. As opposed to a political basis, the caste system has religious foundations. That is, caste societies are stratified on the basis of hereditary notions of religious purity. Although contradictory opinions exist, origins of the caste system are rooted in Hinduism and a division of labor predetermined by birth. The preferential treatment of upper-caste members during British colonialism further entrenched the social hierarchy. The caste system consisted of the rigid social stratification of four main castes or *varnas*: Brahman (priests and scholars), Kshatriya (soldiers), Vaishya (merchants and farmers), and Shudra (servants). Excluded completely from the caste system are both Adivasi (India's indigenous people) and Dalit or "Untouchables," the least pure of all caste distinctions. Over time, the caste system in India has evolved into a complex matrix of thousands of subcastes. Each of the major castes engages in certain ritual practices from which the others are excluded. For instance, the Shudra caste is not permitted to study ancient Hindu texts, while Dalits are prohibited from entering temples or performing any rituals that confer purity. These restrictions place them at the bottom of the social hierarchy and typically leave them with occupations seen as impure, such as the cremation of corpses or disposal of sewage, reinforcing their "untouchable" social status.

The historical legacy of the caste system still dominates rural India despite its constitutional abolition more than 70 years ago and despite affirmative action policies to help those of lower caste origins. Even if castes don't retain a formal role in the social stratification system there, they still exert a strong informal power over inequality in India. Moreover, castes are largely endogamous, meaning members generally marry within their group, thereby preserving divisions. Practicing endogamy is an example of *social closure,* a powerful method of maintaining hierarchy. For example, if you are born into the Dalit or "Untouchable" caste, you will likely marry a Dalit and your children will be Dalits. An increase in exogamy (cross-caste marriage) is creeping in, but social mobility remains low, especially for Dalits.

Islamic law prohibits Muslims from serving or imbibing alcohol, so the Christian Vaishya handle beer distribution in Pakistan. This employee inspects a bottle of vodka at the Murree Brewery Company, Pakistan's oldest public company and only brewery.

Although there is little to no individual mobility in caste systems, one unique fact of the system is that an entire caste could obtain a higher position in the hierarchy by adopting practices and behaviors of the upper castes. This process is called sanskritization. Typically practices that are adopted are those that pertain to a higher degree of religious purity (vegetarianism or fasting, for example). At the same time, a caste will eschew aspects of its own traditions that are considered impure (animal sacrifice or the consumption of alcohol). In this way, an entire group of people can rise in social status in one to two generations. Sometimes such an attempt works, and sometimes it doesn't. During the colonial period, when the British governed South Asia, the Vaishya, the second-lowest caste in Pakistan, adopted Christianity, the religion of the British, in an attempt to jump ahead in the hierarchy. Their attempt was not successful. However, by becoming Christian, the Vaishya caste did enjoy a unique fate after the partition of Pakistan from India when Pakistan became a Muslim state in which Islamic law (the shar'ia) was enforced. One of the rules of the shar'ia is that Muslims are forbidden from imbibing or serving alcohol (or any mind-altering substances). So who got the jobs serving foreigners in the hotel bars? The Vaishya, who were now Christian. Their efforts to jump ahead in the caste system may have failed, but they ended up with fairly decent jobs in a relatively impoverished country by capitalizing on westernization.

Some scholars have argued that U.S. racial inequality between Blacks and non-Blacks also has a caste-like quality. Isabel Wilkerson (2020), for example, suggests that given the various ways African Americans have been

CLASS SYSTEM

an economically based hierarchical system characterized by cohesive oppositional groups and somewhat loose social mobility.

Why is the concept of class problematic? For example, Oseola McCarty of Hattiesburg, Mississippi, worked as a washerwoman and had only a sixth-grade education. However, she donated $150,000 to the University of Southern Mississippi from her savings.

excluded from the fruits of mainstream society, starting with slavery up through the era of Jim Crow and onto the period of mass incarceration, it is accurate to call the racial system in the United States a caste system. However, by our more precise sociological definition, racial inequality in the United States (however extreme) does not meet the criteria of being caste-based given the absence of a religious or purity-ritual basis to the inequality. In addition, while Black–nonblack intermarriage is the rarest form of intermarriage, it does indeed exist, so endogamy is not as complete as it is in other caste systems such as that of India.

CLASS SYSTEM

A third type of stratification is a class system, an economically based hierarchical system characterized by cohesive oppositional groups and somewhat loose social mobility. Class means different things to different people, and there is no consensus among sociologists as to the term's precise definition. For instance, some might define class primarily in terms of money, whereas others see it as a function of culture or taste. Some people barely even notice it (consciously at least), whereas others feel its powerful effects in their daily lives. So, what is class? Is it related to lifestyle, consumption patterns, interests, or attitudes? Or is it just another pecking order similar to the caste system? As in the caste and estate systems, the distinctions between separate class categories in theory should appear clear, but drawing boundaries around class categories—for instance, upper class, middle class, and so on—has proven difficult. Some scholars have even argued that class should be abandoned as a sociological concept altogether. So, let's try to clear up some of the misconceptions.

Unlike other systems, a class system implies an economic basis for the fundamental cleavages in society. That is, class reflects a particular position in the economic market. Two theorists, Karl Marx and Max Weber, primarily influenced notions of class in sociological analysis. In Marxist sociological analyses, every mode of production—from subsistence farming to small-scale cottage industries to modern factory production to the open-source information economy—has its own unique social relations of production, which are basically the rules of the game for various players in the process.

Who controls the use of capital and natural resources? How are the tasks of making and distributing products divided up and allocated? And how are participants compensated for their roles? Do they receive tips, hourly wages, in-kind goods, profits, or rents? Thus, talking about class in this Marxist language places an individual in a particular group that has a particular set of interests that often stand opposite to those of another group. For example, workers want higher wages; employers (specifically, capitalists) wish to depress wages, which come largely out of profits.

In this sense, class is a relational concept. That is, one can't gain information about a person's class by simply looking at their income (as in, "That person made only $13,000 last year; therefore, she is working-class"). Class identity, in fact, does not correspond to an individual at all but rather corresponds to a role. A person may pull in a six-figure salary, but as long as she owns no capital (i.e., stock or other forms of firm ownership) and earns her salary by selling her labor to someone else, she finds herself in the same category as the lowest-paid wage laborer and antagonistic to "owners," who may net a lot less income than she does. And an individual may, over the course of her career, change class positions as she changes jobs. Class positions of jobs themselves—that is, their roles with respect to the production process—do not change, however.

Indeed, for Marx, the entire system boils down to two antagonistic classes in a fully mature capitalist society: the employing class (the bourgeoisie or capitalist class) and the working class (the proletariat). The proletariat sells its labor to the bourgeoisie for wages to survive. But, according to Marx, the bourgeoisie extracts surplus value from the proletariat, even when some of the proletarians make high incomes. This fixed-pie or zero-sum view of economic production means that an exploitative and hence inherently conflict-ridden relationship exists between the two classes. Exploitation plays a central role in Marxist class analysis with capitalists taking more of the value of the work of laborers than they repay in wages.

Because the two-class model does not appear to adequately describe the social world in most modern capitalist economies, more recent Marxist theorists such as Erik Olin Wright have elaborated this basic model with the concept of contradictory class locations. Wright suggests that people can occupy locations in the class structure that fall between the two "pure" classes. For instance, managers might be part of both the working class and capitalist class: They are part of the working class insofar as they sell their labor to capitalists in order to live (and don't own the means of production), yet they are in the capitalist class insofar as they control (or dominate) workers within the production process. Conversely, the petit bourgeoisie, a group including professionals, craftspeople, and other self-employed individuals or small-business owners, according to Wright, occupy a capitalist position in that they own capital in the form of

PROLETARIAT

the working class.

BOURGEOISIE

the capitalist class.

CONTRADICTORY CLASS LOCATIONS

the idea that people can occupy locations in the class structure that fall between the two "pure" classes.

businesses, but they aren't fully capitalist because they don't control other people's labor. The issue of class definition could also be further complicated by multiple class locations (multiple jobs), mediated class locations (the impact of relationships with family members, such as spouses, who are in different class locations), and temporally distinct class locations (for instance, many corporations require that all their managers spend a couple of years as a shop floor worker before becoming a manager). Marxists use these distinctions to analyze how various classes rise and fall under the capitalist system.

Max Weber takes an alternative view of class. He conceptualizes class as a group that has as its basis the common life chances or opportunities available to it in the marketplace. In other words, members of the same class have similar value in the commercial marketplace in terms of selling their own property and labor. Thus, for Weber, property and skills are the basic ingredients for all class situations. If you have just graduated from law school, you may have no current income or wealth, but you enjoy a great deal of "human capital" (skills and certification) to sell in the labor market, so you would clearly be in a different class from someone with little education but a similar current economic profile. But if you owned a company that you inherited, for instance, you would belong to yet another (higher) class. Weber's paradigm is distinct from the Marxist class framework, where the basic framework is antagonistic and exploitative; rather, for Weber, class is like a ladder: hierarchical but not relational. Put another way, your class as a newly minted attorney does not affect or determine my class as an accountant, computer programmer, or day laborer. We are not enmeshed in a never-ending conflict due to fundamentally opposed economic interests.

STATUS HIERARCHY SYSTEM

The fourth type of stratification system, a status hierarchy system, has its basis in social prestige, not in political, religious, or economic factors. In classical sociology, Weber contributed most heavily to the modern-day sociologist's understanding of status. For Weber, status groups are communities united by either a positive or negative social estimation of their honor. Put more simply, society's conception of the particular lifestyle of the community to which you belong determines your status. In this sense, those with and without property can belong to the same status group if they live the same lifestyle. Let's use the example of professors. Many professors probably have common behaviors: They attend conferences to discuss scholarly issues, they teach college courses, and they read a lot. These shared habits lead society to confer a certain status on professors, without placing the sole focus on income, which can vary widely among professors.

But even this lumping of professors (or other occupational categories) into one group can obscure huge status distinctions within that group. Some faculty enjoy the stability of the tenure track, a system designed to protect academic freedom. Once tenure-track faculty achieve tenure, they obtain a level of job security similar to that of civil servants and others who cannot easily be fired. Unless an entire school goes bankrupt, they can lose their jobs only if they grossly violate the terms of their employment by, say, not showing up to teach or

Can you tell which professors are tenured and which aren't? (Spoiler alert: You probably can't based simply on their appearance.)

falsifying their research. Compare that level of security to that of the growing ranks of adjunct professors, who these days are the workhorses of academia. They get paid by course taught, typically without benefits, usually must teach many more courses than full-time or tenured professors, and often do not know whether they will have enough work until right before a semester starts. Though they are also professors, usually with the same credentials as their tenured peers, their lifestyle shares some similarities with that of itinerant laborers, salespeople who work on commission, or others who enjoy only a minimal level of predictability in their income flows. Of course, the converse can also hold true. That is, various individuals in a society who earn similar incomes may not have much in common in terms of lifestyles (and therefore status). Think again of a professor and, say, a plumber, who may earn the same annual incomes but have very different day-to-day experiences of work and orientations to the world.

Although a status group can be defined by something other than occupation, such as a claim to a specific lifestyle of leisure (skate punks) or membership in an exclusive organization that defines one's identity (Daughters of the American Revolution), much work by sociologists has been related to occupational status. After all, work is one of the most centrally defining aspects of our lifestyle. In the 1960s, for example, Peter M. Blau and Otis Dudley Duncan (1967) created the Index of Occupational Status by polling the general public about the prestige of certain occupations (an abbreviated version based on more recent data appears in Table 7.1). Many folks have since refined this rank ordering, but the story stays much the same. The hierarchy remains largely stable over time and place; occasionally, new jobs get slotted in (there were no web designers in the 1960s), but they generally occupy fairly predictable rankings based on the status of similar occupations

TABLE 7.1 The Relative Social Prestige of Selected U.S. Occupations

Occupation	Prestige Score	White-Collar Occupation	Blue-Collar Occupation
Surgeon	88.1	X	
Neurologist	87.9	X	
Aerospace engineer and operations technician	84.1	X	
Biochemist	83.9	X	
Aerospace engineer	83.8	X	
Neuropsychologist	82.8	X	
Physicist	82.7	X	
Nuclear medicine physician	82.7	X	
Pediatrician	81.8	X	
Nuclear engineer	81.5	X	
Obstetrician/gynecologist	81.4	X	
Medical scientist	81.2	X	
Judge/magistrate	80.9	X	
Administrative services manager	54.3	X	
Electrician	54.2		X
Physical therapist assistant	54.2	X	
Property, real state, and/or community association manager	54.1	X	
Human resources manager	54.1	X	
Compensation, benefits, and/or job analysis specialist	54.0	X	
Education administrator	53.9	X	
Manager of personal service workers	53.7	X	
Wind turbine service technician	53.7	X	
Precious metal worker	53.7		X
Septic tank servicer	23.0		X
Food service attendant	23.0		X
Housekeeping cleaner	22.7		X
Food preparation worker	22.6		X
Dry-cleaning worker	22.2		X
Door-to-door sales worker	22.2	X	
Food server	22.0		X
Street vendor	22.0		X
Meat-packer	21.6		X
Building cleaning worker	21.3		X
Fast-food cook	20.5		X
Locker room attendant	20.0		X
Parking lot attendant	19.5		X
Telemarketer	15.0	X	
Dishwasher	14.5		X

SOURCE: Hughes et al., 2022.

and do not create much upheaval within the overall ordering. The scores on the Duncan scale (as it is known) range from 0 to 96, with 0 being the least prestigious and 96 the most prestigious.

Table 7.1 shows that occupations with very different characteristics may have similar prestige scores. For instance, actors and firefighters enjoy roughly the same amount of prestige despite being very different in both their daily labor and their job security (firefighters are usually civil servants with job protection, while actors often piece together a living through gig work). Blau and Duncan observed that five-sixths (just over 83 percent) of the explanation for people's status ratings of occupations was attributed to the education necessary for the position and not the income corresponding to that position.

Although status may have its basis in occupation, it can also form through consumption and lifestyle, though these factors often correlate closely with occupation. In other words, rather than existing in fundamentally antagonistic status groups such as capitalists and laborers or owners and renters, people exist along a status ladder with a lot of social mobility. Often individuals seek to assert their status or increase their status not just through their occupation but also through their consumption, memberships, and other aspects of how they live. They might try to generate social prestige by driving a fancy car, living in a gated community, wearing stylish clothes, or using a certain kind of language.

ELITE-MASS DICHOTOMY SYSTEM

The fifth and final stratification system is the elite–mass dichotomy system, with a governing elite, a few leaders who broadly hold the power in society. This system can also be termed an "oligarchy," meaning rule by the few, though that term generally has more political connotations. Vilfredo Pareto, in *The Mind and Society* (1983), took a positive view of elite–mass dichotomies, whereas C. Wright Mills saw much to dislike in such systems. For Pareto, when a select few elite leaders hold power the masses are all the better for it—as long as the elites are the most able individuals and know what they are doing. This imbalance, where a small number of people (say 20 percent) cause a disproportionately large effect (more like 80 percent), is known as the Pareto Principle or the 80/20 rule. Pareto argues that individuals are inherently unequal physically, intellectually, and morally. He suggests that the most capable members of organizations and societies should lead. In this way, Pareto believes in a true meritocracy, a society where status exists and mobility occurs based on individual attributes, ability, and achievement. Pareto opposed caste systems of stratification that create systematic inequality on the basis of birth into a specific group. He criticized societies based on strict military,

ELITE-MASS DICHOTOMY SYSTEM

a system of stratification that has a governing elite, a few leaders who broadly hold power in society.

MERITOCRACY

a society where status and mobility are based on individual ability and achievement.

religious, and aristocratic stratification, arguing that these systems naturally tend to collapse. Concerning such systems, he argued that aristocracies do not last and that, in fact, history is a "graveyard of aristocracies" (Pareto & Finer, 1966).

Along these lines, the ideal governing elite for Pareto combines foxes and lions—that is, individuals who are cunning, unscrupulous, and innovative along with individuals who are purposeful and decisive, using action and force. This balance applies not only to the political realm but also to the economic realm and benefits not only the leaders but also the masses. The whole system works over time, in Pareto's view, with enough opportunity and social mobility to ensure that the most talented individuals end up in the elite and the system does not stagnate into a rusty aristocracy.

Mills takes a much more negative view of the elite—mass dichotomy, arguing that it is neither natural nor beneficial for society. In Mills's view, the elite do not govern the way Pareto claims they do. Mills argues in *The Power Elite* (2000) that there are three major institutional forces in modern American society where the power of decision making has become centralized: *economic institutions* (with a few hundred giant corporations holding the keys to economic decisions), the *political order* (the increasing concentration of power in the federal government and away from the states and localities, leading to a centralized executive establishment that affects every cranny of society), and the *military order* (the largest and most expensive feature of government). According to Mills, "families and churches and schools adapt to modern life; governments and armies and corporations shape it; and, as they do so, they turn these lesser institutions into means for their ends." For Mills, the elite simply have the most of the resources that can be possessed: money, power, and prestige. But, without the support of society's great institutions, they would not enjoy this lion's share. Whereas Pareto views elite status as the reward for the talent

Who are the modern power elites? Before serving as U.S. treasury secretary in the Trump administration, Steven Mnuchin worked at Goldman Sachs for 17 years (where his father was also a general partner), founded several hedge funds, and launched a film production company.

that helped certain individuals rise through the ranks of society, Mills sees the unequal power and rewards as determining the positions. And whereas Pareto sees a benefit in having power centralized in a large, otherwise ungovernable society, Mills warns of the dangers. For Mills, such a system hurts democracy by consolidating the power to make major decisions into the hands (and interests) of the few. As these few decision makers solidify their commanding roles at the top of one institutional order, they communicate with those powering other institutions, creating a highly centralized, highly stratified core of power elite. This inner core includes politicians, corporate lawyers, and investment bankers, who all receive support from an outer fringe who inform but do not make critical societal decisions.

Let's take, for example, the business sector in America. More than 80 percent of the 1,000 largest corporations share at least one director with another large company, and on average any two of the corporations are connected by fewer than four degrees of separation (Davis, 2003). Wall Street has particularly dense connections. Many U.S. Treasury secretaries have worked at a single firm: the investment bank Goldman Sachs. As a result of these networks, which Mills both saw and predicted, decisions by various companies become increasingly similar. Many studies suggest that these elite networks share practices, principles, and information that account for some of the surprising conformity in approaches to corporate governance and ethics. For example, the response to the 2008 financial crisis evidently occurred in a room with a dozen or so top bankers and the president of the New York Federal Reserve, Tim Geithner, who later became Treasury secretary in the Obama administration.

Social Reproduction versus Social Mobility

┃ Design sociological studies that investigate the reproduction of social stratification.

Once we begin to understand the basics of stratification—that is, how members of a society are hierarchically organized along different lines—the next issue is the possibility of those members changing their social position in the hierarchy. This concept is generally called social mobility, the movement between different positions within a system of social stratification in any given society. Pitirim A. Sorokin (1959) emphasized the importance of not just looking at the mobility of individuals but also examining group mobility.

SOCIAL MOBILITY

the movement between different positions within a system of social stratification in any given society.

For example, rather than just asking why Ugo, a cashier at Sears, earned a promotion to regional manager, thereby increasing his income and status, Sorokin suggests we also look at why the group Ugo belongs to—Black males of Nigerian descent in their mid-twenties—does or does not appear to be generally mobile.

Sorokin noted that social mobility can be either horizontal or vertical. *Horizontal social mobility* means a group or individual transitioning from one social status to another situated more or less on the same rung of the ladder. Examples of this might be a secretary who changes firms but retains her occupational status, a Methodist person who converts to Lutheranism, a family that migrates to one city from another, or an ethnic group that shifts its typical job category from one form of unskilled labor to another. *Vertical social mobility*, in contrast, refers to the rise or fall of an individual or group from one social stratum to another. We can further distinguish two types of vertical mobility: *ascending* and *descending* (more commonly termed *upward* and *downward*). An individual who experiences ascending vertical mobility either rises from a lower stratum into a higher one or creates an entirely new group that exists at a higher stratum. Ugo's promotion to regional manager at Sears is an example of rising from a lower stratum to a higher one. By becoming a manager, he has changed his class position, a change that confers both a higher salary and more prestige. Conversely, imagine that for some reason there was an immediate need for translators of Igbo (or Ibo, the language spoken by the Igbo people based in southeastern Nigeria) in the United States. Ugo, who speaks Igbo, along with many other Nigerians who speak the language, would then find better jobs and thereby enjoy higher social status. This would be an example of a new group, Igbo translators, existing in a higher stratum.

Descending vertical mobility can similarly take either of two forms: individual or group. These two forms distinguish between a particular person falling overboard from a ship and the whole ship sinking. Sorokin (1959) asserted that "channels of vertical circulation necessarily exist in any stratified society and are as necessary as channels for blood circulation in the body."

Most sociologists concerned with studying mobility focus on the process of individual mobility. These studies generally fall into two types: mobility tables (or matrices) and status-attainment models. Constructing a mobility table is easy, although making sense of it is much more difficult (see Table 7.2 for an example). Along the leftmost column of a grid, list a number of occupations for people's fathers (it was traditionally done for males only). Across the top, list the same occupational categories for the sons (the respondents). There can be as many or as few categories as you see fit, so long as they are consistent for the parental and child generations. For example, a five-category analysis might include upper nonmanual occupations (managers and professionals), lower nonmanual occupations

TABLE 7.2 Mobility Table: Father's Occupation by Son's First Occupation

FATHER'S OCCUPATION	SON'S OCCUPATION					
	UPPER NONMANUAL	LOWER NONMANUAL	UPPER MANUAL	LOWER MANUAL	FARM	TOTAL
Upper nonmanual	1,414	521	302	643	40	2,920
Lower nonmanual	724	524	254	703	48	2,253
Upper manual	798	648	856	1,676	108	4,086
Lower manual	756	914	771	3,325	237	6,003
Farm	409	357	441	1,611	1,832	4,650
TOTAL	4,101	2,964	2,624	7,958	2,265	19,912

SOURCE: Hout, 1983.

(administrative and clerical workers, low-level entrepreneurs, and retail salespeople), upper manual occupations (skilled workers who primarily use physical labor, such as plumbers and electricians), lower manual occupations (unskilled physical laborers), and farmworkers. The number of categories can be expanded, and it is not uncommon to see seven-, nine-, or even fourteen-category tables. The key is filling in the boxes. Probably not many people fall into the cell where the father is upper nonmanual and the son is a farmer. However, because of the decline in the agricultural workforce over the course of the twentieth century, you are likely to observe (at least in the United States) a fair bit of movement from farmwork in the parental generation to other occupations in the children's generation. Changes in the distribution of jobs lead to what sociologists call structural mobility, mobility that is inevitable given changes in the economy. With the decline of farmwork because of technology, the sons and daughters of farmers must find other kinds of work. This type of mobility stands in contrast to exchange mobility, in which, if we hold fixed the changing distribution of jobs, individuals trade jobs such that if one person is upwardly mobile it necessarily entails someone else being downwardly mobile.

STRUCTURAL MOBILITY

mobility that is inevitable from changes in the economy.

EXCHANGE MOBILITY

mobility resulting from the swapping of jobs.

As most measures of economic inequality have risen each year since the 1960s, Americans have comforted themselves with the thought that they still live in the land of opportunity. Rates of occupational (and income) mobility in the United States supposedly dwarf those of European societies with their royalty, aristocracies, and long histories. However, recent research suggests that this dream may be cold comfort: Some economists argue that U.S. mobility rates have declined significantly since the 1960s. Others go so far as to say that Americans now enjoy less mobility than their European counterparts. A fierce debate has ensued, because many of these studies compare apples and oranges—different measures, different data, different years. However, an emerging consensus posits that mobility rates should be broken down into the two components discussed above, structural and exchange mobility. When we do this, rates of "trading places" remain fairly fixed across developed societies. By contrast, historically, the United States has enjoyed an advantage in growth-induced upward mobility; as the farm and blue-collar sectors withered and white-collar jobs expanded, sons and daughters of manual workers experienced, by necessity, a degree of upward occupational mobility. However, sociologists and economists debate whether economic growth still drives upward mobility or bifurcated job growth means intergenerational stagnation.

STATUS–ATTAINMENT MODEL

approach that ranks individuals by socioeconomic status, including income and educational attainment, and seeks to specify the attributes characteristic of people who end up in more desirable occupations.

Another common methodology for studying social mobility is the status-attainment model. This approach ranks individuals by socioeconomic status, including income and educational attainment, and seeks to specify the attributes characteristic of people who end up in more desirable occupations. The occupational status research of Peter M. Blau and Otis Dudley Duncan (1967), who ranked occupations into a status hierarchy to study social attainment processes, generally establishes the paradigm for this type of work. Unlike mobility tables, the status-attainment model allows sociologists to study some of the intervening processes. For example, how important is education in facilitating upward occupational shifts in status? How critical is the prestige of a person's first job out of school? How does IQ relate to the chances for upward or downward mobility? The status-attainment model is an elastic one that allows researchers to throw in new factors as they arise and see how they affect the relationships between existing ones, generally ordered chronologically over a typical life course. For the most part, education serves as the primary mediating variable between parents' and children's occupational prestige. That said, research shows that parental education and net worth, not occupation or income, best predict children's educational and other outcomes (Conley, 1999). Blau and Duncan didn't measure net worth, but by now it has become a fairly standard factor in many socioeconomic surveys.

Although there is increasing consensus on what aspects of class background matter (and how much they do), there is relatively little understanding of the multiple mechanisms by which class is reproduced (or how mobility happens). For instance, families with a higher socioeconomic status are likely to have more success in preparing their children for school, entry exams, and ultimately the job market because they have greater access to resources that promote and support their children's development. These might include educational toys when the children are very young, tutors in grade school, and expensive test-preparation courses for exams such as the SAT, GRE, LSAT, and MCAT. Once again, let us compare the CEO of a large, profitable U.S. corporation with a single mother working as a waitress at the local diner. The status of the CEO's occupation and his disproportionate income and wealth in relation to the waitress's easily put his socioeconomic status leaps and bounds ahead of hers. Because of this disparity, the CEO can send his children to the top private schools, where they can work toward highly paid positions after graduation. In contrast, assuming that the single mother has no other source of income, her children are likely to get a public education without the extras. This disparity by no means mandates her children's futures, but it certainly illustrates the advantages that the CEO's children enjoy.

Global Inequality

Describe the effects of European colonialism and modern globalization on international inequality.

One of the main reasons cited for rising income and wealth inequality in the United States is globalization—the rise in the trade of goods and services across national boundaries, as well as the increased mobility of multinational businesses and migrant labor. If the effect of globalization in the United States has been to bifurcate labor into high-skilled and low-skilled jobs, how has this trend affected worldwide inequality? The answer to that question depends on how you frame the analysis. In the long view, global income inequality has undoubtedly rose steadily over the last few centuries. At the start of the agricultural and industrial revolutions, almost the entire population of the world lived in poverty and misery (see the discussion of Malthus earlier in the chapter). Birthrates were high, but so was mortality. Most people barely survived, no matter where they lived.

But then, thanks to technological innovations, food production started to increase dramatically in some areas of Europe. Simultaneously, European powers began to explore, conquer, and extract resources from other areas of the globe. Fast-forward a few hundred years to the mid-twentieth century,

Watch an interview with economist Jeffrey Sachs about overcoming poverty in Africa at **digital.wwnorton.com/youmayask8**

when the world and most of its wealth were carved up and ruled by major Western powers. Enormous global inequalities had emerged through the combination of colonialism and unequal development. Since around 1950, many of these former colonies have gained political independence, but they have lagged well behind the West in terms of income per capita.

Scholars have long been trying to figure out why Europe developed first. Early explanations, dating back to the French essayist Montesquieu (1748/1750/1899), focused on geographic differences between the peoples of Europe and the global South (as the less developed regions of the world are sometimes called). More recent versions of the geographical explanation focus on differences in the length of growing seasons, the higher variability of water supply (because of more frequent droughts), the types of cereal crops that can grow in temperate zones compared with tropical and subtropical regions, the lack of coal deposits (the first fuel that drove industrialization, long before oil), and perhaps most important, the disease burden in warmer climates (Sachs, 2001).

Economist Jeffrey Sachs explains that Africa's geography made an agricultural revolution much more difficult. He prods us to understand the complexity of the constraints on Africa's development before pointing fingers:

> Africa is a continent largely of that rain-fed agriculture, whereas the Green Revolution was based first and foremost on irrigation agriculture. Now is that bad governance that Africa does not have vast river systems? Or is that a matter of the Himalayan Tibetan plateau, which creates the Indus, the Punjab (meaning five rivers, after all), the Ganges, the Yangtze, and so forth? These are functions of physical geography. Africa has a savannah region, which means a long dry season together with a single wet season typically. (Conley, 2009g)

Others argue that geography doesn't matter as much as social institutions. In one version of this line of reasoning, a strong foundation of property rights, incorruptible judiciaries, and the rule of law in general predict economic development (Easterly & Levine, 2002). These, in turn, were institutions "native" to Europe and were transferred to the areas where European colonists settled and lived in significant numbers (Acemoglu et al., 2001), spurring later development in areas such as India and Latin America (compared with much of Africa where Europeans did not settle, which has lagged in development). Other scholars argue that the types of relationships different colonized regions had with the European powers largely determined their fate today: For example, under the rule of the British Raj, India was endowed with a huge network of railways to move cotton, tea, and other products to market. This network, in turn, helped spur economic growth once India got over the rocky transition to self-government after gaining its independence. By contrast, because of the disease burden in most sub-Saharan African countries, Europeans didn't stay and invest but rather focused on extractive industries, building railways that ran just to and from mines instead of extensive networks of roads and train tracks.

Today, that legacy of unequal starting places and economic potentials means that the latest spurt of globalization has engendered an even greater level of income inequality across the North–South divide while creating huge differences within developing countries (see Figure 7.3). Indeed, some regions, such as sub-Saharan Africa and eastern Europe, have become poorer over the last 25 years, whereas in some previously poor regions, such as South and East Asia, income levels have risen. In 1990, about 2 billion people or approximately 35 percent of the world population lived

Tremendous global inequalities have emerged through the combination of colonialism and unequal development. How do social scientists explain the gap between rich and poor regions of the world?

FIGURE 7.3 Gross Domestic Product (GDP) per Capita, 2023

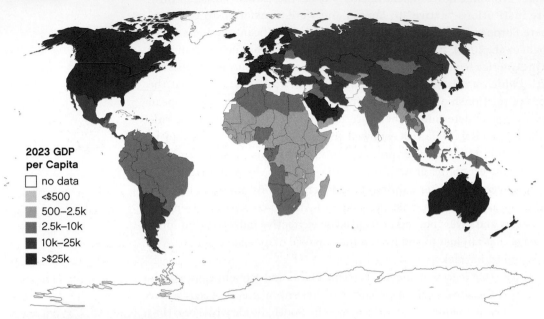

2023 GDP per Capita
- no data
- <$500
- 500–2.5k
- 2.5k–10k
- 10k–25k
- >$25k

SOURCE: IMF, 2023.

in poverty; by 2015, that number decreased to 730 million or around 10 percent of the global population (Roser & Ortiz-Ospina, 2019). Current estimates predict that by 2030 the number of poor people in the world will have dropped to under 500 million (Roser & Ortiz-Ospina, 2019). There have indeed been global reductions in population-weighted, between-country differences, which can largely be attributed to the rapid growth of the Chinese and Indian economies over this period. Within individual countries, however, inequality has generally risen over the same time frame. The story of globalization and inequality is thus a complex and constantly changing one.

CLASS-BASED AFFIRMATIVE ACTION

The push for class-based affirmative action (for lack of a better term) has rapidly accelerated in the wake of the Supreme Court's ruling in *Students for Fair Admissions, Inc. v. President and Fellows of Harvard College* that banned the use of race in admissions. In addition to possibly being a way to increase racial diversity in a color-blind way, the call for economic considerations in the college admissions process arises from mounting evidence that class has become an increasingly salient driver of academic opportunity (and success).

The statistics about increasing class stratification on American campuses are alarming: "The college-completion rate among children from high-income families has grown sharply in the last few decades, whereas the completion rate for students from low-income families has barely moved" (Bailey & Dynarski, 2011). Moreover, high-income students make up an increasing share of the enrollment at the most selective colleges and universities (Reardon et al., 2012), even when compared with low-income students with similar test scores and academic records (Bailey & Dynarski, 2011; Belley & Lochner, 2007; Karen, 2002).

Class-based admissions policies, then, offer a way to redress unequal access to selective institutions of higher education while also indirectly tackling racial disparities. In addition, class-based policies, if well designed, can address some of the criticisms of traditional, race-based affirmative action. One of the most common criticisms of race-based affirmative action is its focus on helping those minorities who least need it. Today, we view race and class as ultimately working together to create disadvantage, forming a complex, intersectional system of inequality; however, historically, race seemed to overpower class. Back in 1967, Peter M. Blau and Otis Dudley Duncan described the process of stratification in the United States in their landmark book, *The American Occupational Structure*. In this study, they found that class background mattered little for African Americans compared with Whites. Instead, they described a dynamic called "perverse equality": No matter what the occupation of the father of a Black man (this was a period of low labor-force participation for women overall, even if Black women did work at significant rates), the son himself was most likely to end up in the lower manual sector of the labor market. Meanwhile, in each generation a small, new cadre of professional Blacks would emerge seemingly randomly through a dynamic they described as "tokenism"—that is, family background mattered little in predicting who emerged into the small Black professional class.

By the mid-1970s, however, this dynamic had changed. In 1978, sociologist William Julius Wilson described a Black community where class stratification increasingly reared its head. Later work confirmed intergenerationally what Wilson observed cross-sectionally: There were increasing class divisions within the Black (and Latinx)

What challenges do colleges face in promoting diversity through admissions policies?

communities, and class background was an increasingly salient predictor of economic success, not just for Whites but for minorities as well (Conley, 1999; Killewald, 2013).

Sean Reardon (2013) goes so far as to argue that class disparities have eclipsed racial ones, at least in terms of achievement: "The Black-White achievement gap was considerably larger than the income achievement gap among cohorts born in the 1950s and 1960s, but now it is considerably smaller than the income achievement gap. This change is the result of both the substantial progress made in reducing racial inequality in the 1960s and 1970s and the sharp increase in economic inequality in education outcomes in more recent decades." Economist Roland Fryer Jr. (2010) sums this trend up nicely: "Relative to the 20th century, the significance of discrimination as an explanation for racial inequality across economic and social indicators has declined."

In short, although class divisions within historically underrepresented minority groups are increasing, 1960s identity-group policies treat disadvantaged groups uniformly. Such a homogenizing admissions policy results in a lack of support for the most disadvantaged minorities today and the enhancement of intraracial stratification. Thus, in lieu of race-based policies, class-based affirmative action could address these inequalities within minority (and majority) communities.

If you designed a class-based admissions policy, how would you implement such a scheme? Can we just ask students' parents to self-report their "class" or socioeconomic status by disclosing their income, education, and wealth? Here's where the devil lies in the details. Colleges can easily verify parental income by asking for tax returns, but parental income matters the least in predicting college enrollment and completion. In other words, by designing admissions policies around income, we won't consistently help those who need it. Parental education is actually the strongest predictor but the least verifiable. (How can you check that someone has more education than they report on a form?) Parental wealth, meanwhile, is the most unequal by race—getting us the most racial bang for the buck, so to speak. The typical African American family has about 10 percent of the net worth of the typical White family. Wealth also predicts college outcomes (though not as strongly as parental education).

Unlike the case of education, however, where self-reporting is the only metric to go by for parental wealth, we can infer a lot based on a few factors that are less apt to be gamed. First, we can measure the median housing value of a community in which a student lived. This measure serves as a very good proxy for individual wealth level. Second, other forms of wealth can be ascertained or imputed through property tax records, estate tax records, and Schedules A–D of federal income tax returns.

Or, when all is said and done, if we want to maintain or increase diversity on campus, we can do what we are already doing: just asking applicants to check a box on the race question on their application (never asking for verification), while hoping that people are honest and the courts are sympathetic.

Conclusion

Horatio Alger Jr. (1832–1899) was an American author of dime novels that told rags-to-riches stories. The narratives typically depicted a plucky young downtrodden boy who eventually achieved the American dream of success and fortune through tenacious hard work while maintaining a genuine concern for the well-being of others. Alger wrote more than 130 novels with titles such as *Sink or Swim* (1870), *Up the Ladder* (1873), *From Boy to President* (1881), *Making His Way* (1901), *A New Path to Fortune* (1903), and *Finding a Fortune* (1904). Works like these contributed to the national ideology that all Americans could achieve financial success if they only pulled themselves up by their own bootstraps.

Although more than 100 years old, Alger's novels still resonate with a faith in mobility that is woven into the national fabric and self-image of Americans. Today, though, the majority of Americans feel less optimistic about the possibility of upward mobility. A 2013 poll by the Pew Charitable Trusts found that only 37 percent of Americans thought that their children would be better off than they were (Stokes, 2017), and in 2017 only 36 percent of Americans believed that they themselves had achieved the American dream (Pew Research Center, 2017b). What is so striking is that more and more Americans are buying into the Alger myth—that is, more Americans now than 20 years ago believe it is possible to start at the bottom and work your way to the top. People generally believe that hard work and education are more important than social connections or a wealthy background. Are Americans overly optimistic or are sociologists just being naysayers? Only more research will tell us for sure.

This Horatio Alger Jr. novel features a newsboy who rises to newspaper editor. Are most Americans today likely to achieve upward mobility?

THE $5,000 TOOTHBRUSH

Scholars from Weber to Bourdieu have talked about lifestyle and consumption choices as an important part of the stratification system. The most extreme examples tend to remind us of so-called conspicuous consumption, a term first coined in 1899 by sociologist Thorstein Veblen in his book *The Theory of the Leisure Class.* For example, in a video for *GQ*'s series "Most Expensivest Shit," rapper 2 Chainz tries out a $5,000 luxury toothbrush, one of the most costly toothbrushes in the world. (His reaction? "Tastes like titanium" [*GQ*, 2014].)

TRY IT!

Pick an object you frequently use, such as an article of clothing, a toothbrush, or your phone. Then choose a service you often buy, such as getting your hair cut, getting around town, or eating out. Research the most and least expensive of each of these goods and services and provide specific examples.

Where do your consumption practices fall in relation to these extremes? Where do your practices fall compared to those of your friends?

FREQUENTLY USED OBJECT

_____

MOST EXPENSIVE

$ _____

LEAST EXPENSIVE

$ _____

FREQUENTLY USED SERVICE

_____

MOST EXPENSIVE	LEAST EXPENSIVE
_____	_____
$	$

THINK ABOUT IT

What geographic areas tend to have more narrow ranges of inequality, with most products priced similarly, and what areas tend to have wider ranges, with extremes on both ends? What do these differences imply about income inequality in the United States?

 If rich people spend their money on titanium toothbrushes, does that mean inequality is harmless or even beneficial because it stimulates the economy? Along these lines, is it better or worse for society as a whole if one rich person buys a $5,000 toothbrush meant to last a lifetime, or buys a 10-cent toothbrush for every day of the year, keeping the difference in the bank?

8

HOW DO WE INVESTIGATE INEQUALITY
BETWEEN MEN AND WOMEN
WITHOUT REINFORCING BINARY
THINKING ABOUT GENDER?

Animation at digital.wwnorton.com/youmayask8

Gender

When most people go to the bathroom, they need to pee. But for one student in Bentonville, Arkansas, nature calling wasn't such a simple affair:

> I got followed into a women's bathroom today at school.
>
> The man who followed me, a teacher, called, "Young man!" in a shocked voice.
>
> I turned, and immediately realized what had happened. Several people, men and women alike, have confronted me in bathrooms at this point. Most apologize after they hear my voice; I look fairly androgynous, but I sound like a Disney princess.
>
> I am a trans man, but in situations like this, people assume that I am a trans woman.
>
> In most cases, I back down quickly when someone confronts me, for my own safety. Today, though, I saw an opportunity to fight back a little. I'm on my period, and I had a new, unopened pad in my pocket.
>
> "Sorry," I said to the teacher in my highest pitched voice. I pulled out the pad and held it up. "I was just going to change my pad."
>
> He muttered something about me looking like a boy and backed up a little.
>
> I was secretly flattered, because I *want* to look like a boy, but obviously that isn't a good reason to chase someone into a bathroom. "No worries," I said in my sugarplum fairy voice. "Sometimes it's easy to forget that there are a lot of ways to look like a girl." Then I marched into a stall and shut the door.

The boy's name is Elliot Jackson. In this story, the teacher makes a key assumption: that because Elliot looks like a boy, he shouldn't go into a girl's bathroom. But when Elliot turns up the volume on his self-described "sugarplum fairy" voice and brandishes a feminine hygiene product, the

Demonstrators in Oklahoma protest a series of bills that would place restrictions on trans rights in the state.

teacher becomes confused—Elliot blurs lines that many often take for granted.

The teacher isn't unlike many Americans, who in recent years have reacted to the increased visibility of transgender people in our society. Television and film include more transgender characters; two notable TV shows are *Pose* and *Orange Is the New Black*. Transgender rights issues also appear in the news, for the very reason Elliot experienced so much discomfort: A series of "bathroom bills," passed in states like Oklahoma and considered in others, have made the bathroom the site of gender policing (Rose & LeBlanc, 2022). Such laws require individuals to use the public restroom that corresponds to the sex on their birth certificate rather than their current sex or gender identity. Other states have legally enshrined the right for individuals to use whichever facility corresponds to their current identity.

Of course, gender plays a powerful role outside of the bathroom as well, affecting everything from the toys we play with to our opportunities in school and at work. A key idea we'll encounter throughout this chapter is that gender is composed of a set of traditions, assumptions, and expectations—and that together, these norms are a key building block of society. As Elliot opened the door to the girls' restroom, he violated one of these unspoken rules.

We'll hear more from Elliot later in this chapter, but first we have an important sociological question to answer: What are the differences between gender, sex, and sexuality?

By the end of this chapter you'll be able to:

- Define the biological aspects of "sex" and the socially constructed connotations of "gender."

- Describe different conceptions of gender across modern culture and historical periods.

- Identify the systemic and persistent challenges faced by women in the workplace.

- Explain gender inequalities in terms of various functionalist, conflict, and interactionist theories.

- Analyze historical and contextual interpretations of sexuality.

Let's Talk about Sex and Gender

| Define the biological aspects of "sex" and the socially constructed connotations of "gender."

Sex typically describes socially accepted, perceived biological differences that distinguish males from females. There are many biological differences between humans; society gives some of those biological differences gendered labels that, in turn, define sex categories such as "male" and "female." The categories have foundations in scientific reality, since these biological differences tend to cluster into two groups according to sex chromosomes a person has. Gender denotes a social position—namely, the set of social arrangements built around normative sex categories. Sexuality, meanwhile, refers to desire, sexual preference, and intimate behavior.

As sociologists, we care less about the biological differences of sex—specifically, the difference between having two copies of the X chromosome (XX, female) versus one X and one Y (XY, male)—and more about how people enact and perceive those differences (that is, gender). Like many social categories, gender is one set of stories we tell each other to get by in the world. It's a collectively defined guidebook that humans use to make distinctions among themselves to comprehend an otherwise fuzzy mass of individuals. But the gender story can change, and we'll trace its evolution throughout history and across cultures.

As a human invention, gender structures our lives just as much as other social institutions. In *Paradoxes of Gender* (1994), Judith Lorber claims that gender "establishes patterns of expectations for individuals, orders the social processes of everyday life, is built into the major social organizations of society, such as the economy, ideology, the family, and politics, and is also an entity in and of itself." Although gender is a social construction, it matters in the real world, organizing our day-to-day experiences and having profound and unequal consequences for the life chances of people—effects that themselves vary by the other social categories to which an individual belongs. Gender does not only categorize people—institutions, occupations, and even nouns (in some languages) also can have gendered connotations. In this way, gender ultimately embodies power struggles and how they organize daily life, from household economies and wage labor to birth control and babies' names.

We make sense of much variation between men and women by referring to their assumed biological differences. Such differences include the behavioral consequences of hormones (such as premenstrual syndrome), relative

SEX

the perceived biological differences that society typically uses to distinguish males from females.

GENDER

a social position; behaviors and a set of attributes that are associated with sex identities.

SEXUALITY

desire, sexual preference, and intimate behavior.

physical strength of bodies (for example, women's gymnastics emphasizes balance, while men's gymnastics focuses on upper-body strength), brain architecture (for example, men are supposedly more left-brain dominant), and chromosomes (XX or XY). But in so doing, we tend to miss a crucial link between nature and nurture. The study of gender essentially involves seeing how the spheres of nature and nurture overlap, penetrate, and shape each other. The biological world of sex and bodies does not exist outside of a social world, and the social world of human beings is always made up of human bodies. Studying the links between the two allows us to see the social construction of both gender and sex.

SEXED BODIES IN THE PREMODERN WORLD

Whereas today many of us operate on a mutually exclusive two-sex model of human body types, a lesser known "one-sex" model dominated Western biological thought from the ancient Greeks until the mid-eighteenth century (Laqueur, 1990). In the old one-sex way of thinking, there was only one body (a male body) and the female body was regarded as its inversion—that is, as a male body whose parts were flipped inside rather than hanging on the outside. People believed that women were a lesser but not so radically different version of men—an illustration of how social power relationships can shape scientific belief.

Not until the two-sex model of human bodies gained ground did women and men become such radically different creatures in the popular conception. Incidentally, historian Thomas Laqueur shows us that this differentiation of bodies prompted changes in ideas about the female orgasm. In the one-sex model, people believed that conception required both a man's orgasm and a woman's. (There is new medical evidence, in fact, that dual orgasms do increase the chance of conception.) But in the mid-1800s, around the time the two-sex model was gaining ground, female orgasm became unnecessary. Whereas seventeenth-century (female) midwives advised would-be mothers that the trick to conceiving lay in an orgasm, nineteenth-century (male) doctors debated whether female orgasm was even possible.

CONTEMPORARY CONCEPTS OF SEX AND THE PARADOXES OF GENDER

ESSENTIALIST

arguments explaining social phenomena in terms of natural, biological, or evolutionary inevitabilities.

The point of all this sex talk is to challenge our tendency to think of bodies as wholly deterministic, that is, to acknowledge that our understandings of, categorizations of, and behavior toward bodies are not set in stone. We're pushing back against essentialist arguments, which explain social phenomena wholly in terms of natural ones. Essentialist thought relies on biological determinism, which assumes that what you do in the social world directly results from who you are in the natural world. If you are born with male parts, essentialists believe, you are essentially and absolutely a man, and as preordained by nature, you will be sexually attracted to women only. As we've seen, medical experts have maintained the ideal of a dimorphic or binary (either male or female)

A Möbius strip.

model of sex by tweaking babies who blur the boundaries. The trick is to recognize that the very boundaries separating male and female bodies are themselves contested.

This is not to say that there is no reality to biology. Simply put, rather than believing biology comes before or dictates behavior, sociologists now think of the nature—behavior relationship as a two-way street. Feminist philosopher Elizabeth Grosz (1994) proposes that we view the relationship between the natural and the social (in this case, sex and gender) as akin to a Möbius strip. The Möbius strip is an old math puzzle that looks like a twisted ribbon loop, yet it has just one side and one boundary. Biological sex makes up the inside of the strip, whereas the social world—culture, experience, and gender—makes up the outside. But as happens in the contours of gender, the inside and outside surfaces are inseparable. In thinking or talking about sex and gender, we often switch from one to the other without even noticing that we've changed our focus (Fausto-Sterling, 2000).

Take, for example, people who are born with both male and female genitalia, with neither one, or with ambiguous ones that do not conform to the gender binary (also included in this category are those whose sex chromosomes do not match up in the normative way to outward sexual appearance). The medical industry used to refer to such children as "intersex" but these days refer to a "disorder of sex development." Most doctors today still typically recommend secretive surgery during infancy to make nonbinary children conform to a preconceived notion of what "unambiguous" genitalia should look like. About 90 percent of these surgeries reassign an ambiguous male anatomy into a female one since it's an easier operation (Hendricks, 1993).

If they think about it at all, most people think that the socio-medical assignment of sex applies only to a handful of individuals. However, Brown University biology researcher Anne Fausto-Sterling (2000) estimates that the number of deviations from the binary of male or female bodies may be as high as 2 percent of live births, and the number of people receiving "corrective" genital surgery runs between 1 and 2 in every 1,000 births. Just to give you an idea of what 2 in 1,000 looks like, there are now about 2 in

1,000 children born with trisomy 21 (also known as Down syndrome), a biological condition that is more visible than nonbinary sexual identity. Activists argue that social discomfort and fear of difference, rather than medical necessity, may be what pushes parents and surgeons to the operating table.

The important lesson here is that gender ideas affect sex just as sex affects gender. That lesson impacts not just individuals born with ambiguous genitalia or those who identify as a gender or sex that does not match what they were assigned at birth but also all of us living in a sex-gender social system.

Gender: What Does It Take to Be Feminine or Masculine?

| Describe different conceptions of gender across modern culture and historical periods.

I hope you can now see that biological sex exists neither medically nor historically in the world in some fixed, natural state. Our next step is to trace the different social meanings that humans have taken from sex. There are many historical and cross-cultural meanings, roles, and scripts for behavior that we like to think correspond to more or less fixed biological categories. Sociologists refer to this complete set of scripts as gender, which, broadly speaking, has divided people, behaviors, and institutions into two categories: masculine and feminine.

Much like sex differences, people tend to think of gender differences as a natural cleavage between two static groups. Why do men tend to fight one another in wars, dominate the natural sciences, and outnumber women in the top political and executive offices? Why do women tend to stay more connected with their families and outnumber men in occupations that involve caring for others? The short (essentialist) answer is that men and women are naturally (that is, biologically) different, so they behave differently.

The longer, sociological answer is that gender differences are much more fluid and ambiguous than we may care to admit. Take Elliot, for example. He called himself androgynous—that is, his gender presentation didn't seem obviously masculine or feminine to others. Natural differences between the sexes cannot easily explain Elliot's gender because it doesn't neatly sync up to a clearly male or clearly female outward appearance or biology (remember the pad he was waving?). And it's not just Elliot who challenges

---

ANDROGYNOUS

neither masculine nor feminine.

the essentialist argument: Plenty of people also have behaviors, occupations, and roles that don't correspond neatly to essentialist expectations.

But just because gender isn't tied to some fixed biological reality doesn't mean it doesn't have real consequences. Gender establishes patterns of expectations for people, orders our daily lives, and is one of the fundamental building blocks of society—law, family, education, the economy, everything. The process of forming a gendered identity starts before a person is even born (see the increasingly popular gender reveal parties). Through socialization and personality development, including certain children's games, ways of dressing, and even how parents name their babies, many children acquire a gendered identity that, in most cases, reproduces the attitudes and values of their society. We impose rigid boundaries to maintain a gender order, but if we look at how gender systems vary, we can expose those boundaries as social constructions.

MAKING GENDER

While many Western cultures divide the world neatly between men and women with correspondingly clear male and female bodies, the Navajo society of Native Americans has not two but three genders: masculine men, feminine women, and the *nadle*. The *nadle* might be born with ambiguous genitalia or they may declare a *nadle* identity later on regardless of genitalia. The *nadle* perform both masculine and feminine tasks and dress for the moment, according to whatever activity they're doing. Although they are often treated like women, they have the freedom to marry people of any gender "with no loss of status" (Kimmel, 2000).

Would members of the *hijra* community define their identity in terms of gender or something else?

Nadles are not the only examples of nonbinary gender configurations. Serena Nanda (1999) and Gayatri Reddy (2005) studied *hijras* in India, a group often included in textbooks like this one to disprove the naturalness of a binary either/or gender system. From Reddy, we know that "hijras are phenotypic men who wear female clothing and ideally renounce sexual desire and practice by undergoing a sacrificial emasculation—that is, an excision of the penis and testicles." To our Western ears, then, these men who renounce manhood but who are not women are actively staking a claim for a third gender. But Reddy goes on to develop the definition of what it means to be a *hijra*, which includes behaviors that may have little to do with gender: dedication to the goddess Bedhraj Mata, conferring fertility to newlyweds and newborns; a sometimes reluctant, sometimes dedicated entry into prostitution; communal living; self-sacrifice; and poverty. Thus, *hijra* identity reflects a specific social status rather than a fight for turf between gender categories. Like the Brazilian *travesti* described by Don Kulick (see page 328), the *hijras* may have fewer qualms about the balance they've struck between gender and sexuality than fears about the way their poverty and stigmatization will shape their chances in life.

And as the chapter-opening story about Elliot shows, the growing prominence and social awareness of transgender people in Western society helps us break out of binary thinking about gender, since we tend to assume everyone is cisgender. Amos Mac, a man raised as a girl, came to talk to my class about his experience and the magazine *Original Plumbing* he publishes for a transgender audience. When I asked Mac whether he felt more like a man now than he had before he transitioned, he politely corrected my assumptions about a before–after binary gender narrative: "I actually don't even know what a man is supposed to feel like. You know, I don't really know what a woman is supposed to feel like. . . . I feel comfortable in my skin right now, and I feel comfortable the way people are perceiving me, like strangers on the street. I don't care if people know my history" (Conley, 2014d). He allows that some of his friends may have been "born knowing something [was] terribly wrong . . . or that they [didn't] feel comfortable in their body," but no common narrative encompasses the experience of being transgender. Mac

TRANSGENDER

describes people whose gender does not correspond to their birth sex.

CISGENDER

describes people whose gender corresponds to their birth sex.

DIGITAL.WWNORTON.COM/YOUMAYASK8

To see my interview with Amos Mac, go to
digital.wwnorton.com/youmayask8

explained, "I don't think there's a right or wrong way to have this experience, and I don't think it's necessarily a fun one that you would want to go out of your way to have." Rather than identifying some specific third category, gender is a spectrum that constantly changes along which individuals may change positions over their lifetimes.

GENDER DIFFERENCES OVER TIME

Within a two-gender system, there is enormous variation in what counts as a "good" or "bad" man or woman. For example, how the ideal man or woman looks is itself historically contingent. Specifically, ideal feminine beauty has been a continuous site of change and contestation. Look at the seventeenth-century Rubenesque women, the voluptuous beauties who by today's high-fashion standards are simply overweight. In traditional economies where food was scarce, a plump woman was a sign of good health, wealth, and attractiveness. The long-standing preference for a robust female body has changed as industrialized societies moved from relative scarcity of food to plenitude. Today the cheaper foods are the fattening ones, and only people with enough disposable income can afford gym memberships and healthy diets. So, we can see that dominant or "emphasized" definitions of femininity—as embodied by looks—are always undergoing change, from the hysterical Victorian housewife to the sporty working girl of the 1980s to today's heroically perfect-in-all-ways supermom.

This might be an easy point to grasp about femininity, but most people think that masculinity is less subject to such trends and fashions. It is always harder to denaturalize the dominant category; being the norm, it often is invisible. Among social categories, those who go unquestioned tend to have the most privilege. In *Manhood in America* (1996), Michael Kimmel traces the development of hegemonic masculinity in the West and finds that in the eighteenth century, the ideal man was not associated with physical fitness, money-making endeavors, or sports. Business endeavors were the boorish concerns of the rude trade classes, and physical strength undermined one's gentlemanly dispositions. Ideal masculinity in the 1700s went hand in hand with kindness and intellect, and preferably a little poetry, a very different image from the modern-day ideal of the "man's man."

Erving Goffman (1963) describes the masculine ideal of mid-twentieth-century America as a young man who is "married, white, urban, northern, heterosexual, Protestant, father, of college education, fully employed, of good complexion, weight and height, and [with] a decent record in sports." Today, that definition has blossomed to include more forms of dominant masculine identity, including, for example, the metrosexual male, who, as described by sociologist Kristen Barber (2016), is typically White and wealthy and spends a large amount on grooming activities, such as manicures, that would have been considered feminine in the days Goffman was writing. Likewise,

HEGEMONIC MASCULINITY

the condition in which men are dominant and privileged, and this dominance and privilege is invisible.

THEY GOES TO COLLEGE

In recent years, colleges have been at the forefront of a startling reconfiguration in our society: to acknowledge nonbinary sex/gender identities. For example, the State University of New York, one of the nation's largest state university systems, now allows students to choose among seven gender identities, including "trans man," "questioning," and "genderqueer." Students at Harvard University and other colleges can now choose gender-neutral pronouns such as "they" or "ze." Other schools are sure to follow.

Some activists and scholars advocate a brand-new pronoun like "ze" or "hir," noting that "Ms." seemed strange when first proposed but now is commonly accepted. Others suggest "they" as a non-gender-binary pronoun since it is already readily used informally when English speakers want to avoid gendering the person to whom they are referring. It seems like "they" is winning the linguistic race at the moment. It seems pretty straightforward to allow individuals to select their own pronouns. Elliot Jackson, for example, whose story opened this chapter, asked that I use "he" and "him" pronouns. Easy enough!

But implementing a fluid notion of sex/gender identity for all aspects of life in the institution we call campus gets trickier. Take campus sports. In 2022, the NCAA, the governing body for most varsity college sports, adopted the policy of the International Olympic Committee (National Collegiate Athletic Association, 2022). Namely, it opted to not have a one-size-fits-all policy but instead allow each sport's governing body to set its own rules. The rules on who can compete as a man or a woman in soccer would be different from swimming, which would be different from basketball. So, one could imagine a two-sport college athlete

many men take on what Tristan Bridges and C. J. Pascoe (2014) call "hybrid masculinities," in which, for example, young White men may try to distance themselves from hegemonic masculinity and instead adopt aspects of, say, African American masculinity. They argue, however, that this cultural practice can often serve to conceal inequalities. That is, when White adolescent males emulate the masculine practices of marginalized groups, this dynamic mitigates the real power differences and inequalities between the

competing in the men's division in the fall and the women's division in the spring, depending on the particular sports and their rules.

The final frontier on college campuses and beyond has been locker room and bathroom policy (as illustrated by Elliot's story at the start of the chapter). Under the Obama administration, federal agencies ruled that Title VII of the Civil Rights Act bars discrimination based on gender identity (that is, not just sex), which includes locker room segregation. The Office of Civil Rights of the U.S. Department of Education rejected the argument that female students needed to be protected from being seen naked by an individual who was biologically still male. Separate facilities for transgender individuals were deemed similar to the now unacceptable "separate but equal" racial policy of the Jim Crow era (Phillips et al., 2015).

Harvard University student Schuyler Bailar became the first openly transgender swimmer to compete in the NCAA.

However, as political winds shift so do the policies. For example, the Obama administration interpreted Title IX of the Education Amendments of 1972 as applicable to discrimination based on gender identity, not just gender. This ruling meant that schools that received federal funding (that is, almost all) were required to make nonseparate restrooms accessible to transgender individuals based on their self-identified gender. However, the Trump administration withdrew that guideline in its first year in office, and the Biden administration's attempts to extend protections for transgender students have been blocked by a federal judge (CNN, 2022). (To be continued . . .)

groups, treating race and class as styles one can adopt or shed as one likes (Aboim, 2016, p. 56; Bridges & Pascoe, 2014).

Meanwhile, among African American men, the cultural script of hegemonic masculinity is necessarily refracted through a racial lens. In her book, *Respectable: Politics and Paradox in Making the Morehouse Man* (2022), Saida Grundy shows how the only men's historically black college or university (HBCU), Morehouse College in Atlanta, Georgia, cultivates

↑

Kristen Barber would probably call the man in the photo on the left "metrosexual." He's getting his eyebrows trimmed in a new men-only section of a beauty salon. The White men on the right exemplify what Tristan Bridges and C. J. Pascoe call "hybrid masculinities." By emulating Black hip-hop culture, they attempt to distance themselves from hegemonic masculinity.

(and enforces) a certain formula of Black masculinity. To counteract racist stereotypes surrounding Black men (as criminal, addicted, and so on), Morehouse men are trained to be ambassadors to the (White) world of business. But the cost of this regimented cultural indoctrination is a very narrow vision of what it means to be a Black man. Any form of queerness is squelched on campus. Deviant acts—even sexual assault—are often downplayed for fear of tarnishing the Morehouse brand. In this way, Grundy shows how we cannot think about gender socialization processes as distinct from racial ones—an example of intersectionality (a concept we examine more fully in the next section).

For now, the take-home message is that over time and from place to place, our ideas about gender are fluid, changing, and context specific. Indeed, many of the differences we observe between men and women do not have much to do with sex differences at all; instead, the behaviors arise as a result of the different positions men and women occupy. Sociologist Cynthia Fuchs Epstein (1988) calls these "deceptive distinctions" that grossly exaggerate the actual differences between men and women. To illustrate her idea, here's a quick thought experiment: Imagine a doctor and a nurse. Did you imagine the doctor as a man and the nurse as a woman? Tied up in these expectations are other ideas, such as the stereotypes that women are nurturing and men are analytical. The main difference between the doctor and nurse isn't gender, but power and social status.

Baby names provide another striking example of the power of gender. Analysis by Stanley Lieberson, Susan Dumais, and Shyon Baumann (2000) shows that names flow from male to androgynous to female but never in reverse. If you know, for example, a male named Kim, chances are he was born before 1958, the year that Hitchcock's movie *Vertigo* was released, making the actress Kim Novak a household name. The number of boys named Kim dropped to almost zero the next year. Carol, Aubrey, and Lindsay (and many others) started as male names and became feminized. The one-way flow from male to female in terms of child naming tells us something about gender norms and inequality—that is, masculinity dictates culture more than femininity does, or that femininity seeks to emulate masculinity while the patriarchy sees the feminine as corrupting.

While gender norms can be fluid, one constant across time and culture is that men have held more power than women—a question that has preoccupied feminist social thinkers for a long time. Feminism was at first embraced as a social movement to advocate for women's right to vote; it later became a consciousness-raising movement to get people to understand gender as an organizing principle of life. This "second-wave" feminism argues that gender is important because it structures relations between people. Further, as gender shapes social relations, it does so on unequal ground; more than an identifying characteristic (I'm a guy, you're a girl), gender embodies real powers and privileges. Regardless of which historical "wave" we discuss, the basic idea behind feminism is that women and men (and other-gendered people) should receive equal opportunities and respect.

At the start of the second wave of the feminist movement in the 1960s, theorists scrambled to find an answer to the "woman question": What explains the nearly universal dominance of men over women? That is, what is the root of patriarchy, a system involving the subordination of femininity to masculinity? Before we tackle such a big question (in the Theories of Gender Inequality section on page 315), let's look at how gender inequality manifests in contemporary society.

FEMINISM

a social movement to get people to understand that gender is an organizing principle in society and to address gender-based inequalities that intersect with other forms of social identity.

PATRIARCHY

a nearly universal system involving the subordination of femininity to masculinity.

Growing Up, Getting Ahead, and Falling Behind: Gender Inequality

Identify the systemic and persistent challenges faced by women in the workplace.

In summer 2017, a Google employee named James Damore circulated a memo to his colleagues questioning the pursuit of gender diversity at the company, in which he claimed the real reason that women were underrepresented among coders and in management was due to "biological causes." Perhaps understandably, the memo caused an uproar within the firm, and once it

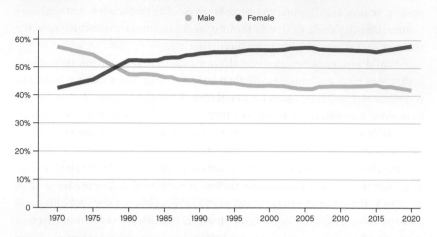

FIGURE 8.1 College Enrollment by Gender, 1970–2020

SOURCE: National Center for Education Statistics, 2021b.

SEXISM

a form of prejudice that occurs when a person's sex or gender is the basis for judgment, discrimination, or other differential treatment against that person.

was leaked to the press, it went viral. Upper-level management at Google disavowed the statement, Damore was forced out of the company, and critics referred to the memo as a blatant example of workplace sexism, while others defended his right to air "un-PC" views on free speech grounds.

Damore's memo shone a light on the underrepresentation of women at Google and companies like it, but the tech industry is just the tip of the iceberg when it comes to gender inequality. Women made up about 58 percent of college students in 2020 (National Center for Education Statistics, 2021b; Figure 8.1). However, despite their increased enrollment, women remain overrepresented in traditionally feminine fields of study: the arts and the humanities. Men also outnumber women at elite colleges, which prepare students for high-power professions in finance, law, or politics.

Do men disproportionately become computer scientists and financiers and women kindergarten teachers and dental hygienists because they are hardwired to do so? Putting aside Damore's controversial argument, we do know that cis-men and cis-women vary in thousands of major and minor measures. Let's start at the beginning.

GROWING UP WITH GENDER

Gender socialization begins at birth (see Chapter 4) when parents dress their children differently by sex. It continues through the school years where teachers call on boys more often than girls (Sadker & Sadker, 1994; Sadker et al., 2009). And it is apparent in family life, where even though women's roles have expanded in the formal labor force, men's have only slightly budged toward more involvement in the domestic sphere.

The average male newborn weighs two ounces more than the average female newborn. For infant death rates, however, the disadvantage is tilted against males, who are at higher risk of death than females. Psychologist Carol Gilligan (1982) contends that by adolescence, the disadvantages are stacked against girls, who "lose their voices" as they suffer blows to their self-confidence. Depending on the study, eating disorders may be up to twice as likely to affect adolescent and teen girls compared with their male peers (Pisetsky et al., 2008). More than half of teenage girls are on diets or think they should be. What's more, girls more frequently report low self-esteem, more girls attempt suicide, and more girls report experiencing some form of sexual harassment in school (Johnson et al., 2016).

Psychologist Christina Hoff Sommers challenges this "girl crisis" in *The War against Boys: How Misguided Feminism Is Harming Our Young Men* (2000). She finds that because they are inadvertently penalized for the shortchanging of girls, boys are the ones suffering in education and adolescent health. For example, although females in general attempt suicide twice as frequently as males, boys ages 15 to 19 succeed in killing themselves four times more often than girls. (That's not to mention transgender people, who unfortunately suffer from extraordinarily high rates of suicide. Researchers estimate that between one-third and one-half of trans people attempt suicide at some point in their lives [Virupaksha et al., 2016].) Teenage girls may sneak more cigarettes than boys, but boys are more likely to be involved in crime, alcohol, and drugs and to be suspended from school or drop out. High-school-aged male teens are also 28 percent more likely to be victimized by violent crime, and that's even taking rape into account (Child Trends Data Bank, 2018).

What accounts for the wide range of statistical differences that exist between men and women? Essentialists might refer to natural sex differences, but as we saw earlier, sociologists call these same differences "deceptive distinctions," which arise because of the particular roles individuals occupy (Epstein, 1988). Why might some people believe men to be more capable of logic, abstraction, and rationality? Perhaps because their employment possibilities more often include jobs with these demands—a circular argument. Why do women seem to be so good at parenting? It may be because their weaker employment prospects encourage them to accept domestic roles and rely on a man's salary. Who is more relational and who is more rational? Anthropologists Jean O'Barr and William O'Barr find that the true test of what type of language an individual uses during testimony in court is the witness's occupation, not gender (O'Barr, 1995). Physicists tend to speak in more abstract terms, teachers in more relational ones, regardless of gender. Deceptive distinctions, like the abstract terminology used by physicists and the relational vocabulary employed by teachers, flip essentialist rhetoric and pin gender differences as products of gender expectations (rather than the cause of them). The question then shifts to how and why gender inequality exists. We need to peel back another layer of the gender onion.

INEQUALITY AT WORK

The past few decades have brought about arguably the biggest change in American gender relations in the world of paid work. Compared to the 1970s, about 44 million more women are in the labor force, an increase from 31.5 million in 1970 to 75.5 million in 2020 (Figure 8.2; Bureau of Labor Statistics, 2020e). Of course, the overall population has increased by 50 percent in that period as well, accounting for part of the rise, but the percentage of women ages 16 to 64 who are in the workforce has risen from approximately 43 percent in 1970 to 56 percent in 2020. Because the Great Recession of 2008–9 hit male-dominated industries the hardest (such as construction), it helped accelerate the trend toward gender equality in labor force participation; in fact, there was a brief period at the depth of the economic crisis during which women's totals exceeded those of men in the workforce. However, men have since caught up and reclaimed their majority position with men's labor force participation at 67.7 percent compared to women's at 56.2 percent. Because women are disproportionately employed in the public sector, and state governments have yet to recover from the twin challenges of economic woes and ballooning budgets, it may be some time before women once again approach parity (Covert, 2011).

The greater number of women entering the labor force has not catapulted them to equality with their male peers in the workplace. Despite the passage of Title VII of the 1964 Civil Rights Act, which declared it unlawful for employers to discriminate on the basis of a person's race, nationality, creed, or sex, women have continued to fare much worse than their male counterparts in the workforce. Although legally entitled to enter all lines

FIGURE 8.2 Increase of Women in the Workforce, 1970–2020

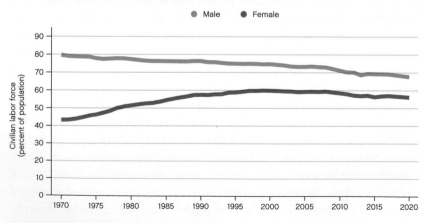

SOURCE: Bureau of Labor Statistics, 2020e.

of work, women sometimes face sexual harassment, an illegal form of discrimination that runs the gamut from inappropriate jokes on the job to outright sexual assault to sexual "barter," in which sexual favors are extracted from victims under the threat of punishment. Intended to make people feel uncomfortable and unwelcome, sexual harassment occurs across many settings and in all kinds of relationships. In the workplace, some argue, sexual harassment is one of the chief ways in which men resist gender equality. In 1982, the U.S. Court of Appeals deemed sexual harassment a violation of the Civil Rights Act, calling it a form of discrimination against an individual on the basis of sex. But even though sexual harassment is illegal, it often takes insidious forms not easily detected by everyone or verifiable in court. Most commonly, sexual harassment takes the form of "hostile environments" in which individuals feel unsafe, excluded, singled out, and mocked.

In addition to sometimes having to work in hostile environments, women consistently receive lower pay than their male peers, earning about 82 cents to every $1 of a man's wage (Bureau of Labor Statistics, 2022i; Figure 8.3). This overall gap obscures stark racial differences, however. Black women earn 88 cents to the Black male dollar (but only 74 cents to the White male dollar). Meanwhile, White women have similar earnings to those of Black men, who also earn 82 cents to the dollar of White men (Bureau of Labor Statistics, 2022i). (In some large, economically successful cities, however, the gender gap may be shrinking or even reversing among young adults [Bacolod, 2017]).

The media touted women's gains in the 1970s and 1980s, when masses of women entered the U.S. labor force. Yet women disproportionately entered

FIGURE 8.3 Pay Discrepancy Based on Gender

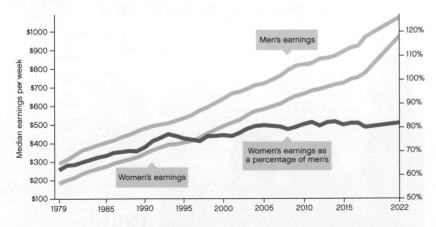

SOURCE: Bureau of Labor Statistics, 2019a; 2022i.

the lower rungs of the occupational hierarchy. These feminized jobs, what Louise Howe (1977) calls "pink-collar" jobs, are low-paid service industry jobs. Cleaning buildings, filing papers, and making coffee are hardly what women imagine when they dream of independence. Caring work tends to be feminized as well, for example, home health aides, nurses, or child-care workers. Meanwhile, "purple-collar" labor—a name given to occupational niches typically filled by transgender individuals—often involves trans women performing emotional work to reduce tensions in high-stress environments, such as one Philippine call center that was studied by Emmanuel David (2015).

In her book, *The Managed Heart* (1983), Arlie Hochschild described the process by which jobs require a person to display certain emotions and not others in the service of the firm's goals (for example, to keep customers happy). She called this work emotional labor. Since Hochschild coined the term over four decades ago, the service economy has grown immensely, and the amount of emotional labor required has increased in tandem. It may not come as a surprise that women disproportionately occupy jobs that require high amounts of emotional labor. This exacts a cost to their physical and mental health that is comparable to the toll of manual labor on men's bodies, but which is more difficult to document and quantify. When someone has a back injury in a warehouse or loses a fingertip working in a sawmill, it's easy to see the cause and effect. But when someone suffers from high blood pressure or depression, it's not so easy to pinpoint the emotional toll of work on the job as the direct cause.

We expect that our flight attendants will serve coffee with a smile, but this is a form of what Hochschild calls "emotional labor."

EMOTIONAL LABOR

managing emotions and their outward expression to meet the expectations of a job, especially in service sector work and female-dominated occupations.

It takes a special kind of girl to inspire this kind of trust

As a Stewardess with British Airways, European Division, you'll be in a very responsible position. Our passengers—some very young, some a little apprehensive—will look to you for the attention and reassurance that is such a vital part of your job. A great deal of trust will be placed in you, as the member of the aircrew most in the public eye.

It takes a special kind of girl—perhaps you? You must be aged 19 to 30 and be 5′ 3″ to 5′ 9″ tall. Looks are important and you must be physically fit. Adaptability and friendliness are called for as is patience and the ability to work happily with the rest of the crew of a modern airliner.

If you feel you can match these requirements we would like to hear from you—training for these **London** based vacancies starts in early 1975. You'll enjoy an initial salary of £1517 rising to £1732 after 3 months, but with generous allowances whilst flying, average earnings are in excess of £2200. (Threshold payments are additional to salaries quoted.) The job may be more demanding than most, but offers travel and the freedom from a 9 to 5 rut.

Send us a postcard for an application form to: Assistant Personnel Officer (NV 1) (Cabin Services), British Airways European Division PO Box 6, Heathrow Airport London, Hounslow, Middlesex.

(Local interviews will be held at selected centres throughout the UK).

British airways

This British Airways recruiting ad from the 1970s seeks a "very special kind of girl" for a stewardess position: "You must be aged 19 to 30 and be 5′ 3″ to 5′ 9″ tall. Looks are important and you must be physically fit. Adaptability and friendliness are called for as is patience and the ability to work happily with the rest of the crew of a modern airliner."

OCCUPATIONAL SEGREGATION

How does this occupational segregation happen? Many new women workers find themselves shuffled into occupations dominated by other women, and women who go into a male-dominated field often find that, soon enough, they are surrounded by women. Like names, jobs become feminized when many more women hit the scene. This trend has occurred in fields such as real estate sales, clerical work, pharmaceuticals, public relations, bartending, bank telling, and more recently, the academic disciplines of sociology and biology. In *Job Queues, Gender Queues* (1990), sociologists Barbara Reskin and Patricia Roos argue that women end up in lower-paid jobs because these occupations lose (or have lost) their attractiveness for White men. When a job becomes deskilled and less autonomous—such as secretarial work, which way back when was men's work—earnings decline, routes of upward mobility close off, work conditions in general deteriorate, and men flee to better positions, leaving (typically White) women next in line to shuffle into the ranks of men's cast-off work.

For example, book editing was a "gentleman's profession" for most of its history but became a virtual female ghetto by the end of the twentieth century (Reskin & Roos, 1990). Formerly the high-cultural mission of men with elite academic records, book editing evolved into a more commercial enterprise in the 1960s and 1970s. As a result, editorial work took a down-turn in autonomy, job security, and importance. As the job lost its attractiveness to male candidates, the female labor supply increased on the crest of second-wave feminism. Thus book-editing jobs, like the other fields that optimists point to as women's inroads into traditionally male-dominated work, became resegregated and ghettoized as women's work. And anything categorized as women's work tends to yield lower pay, prestige, and benefits such as health coverage than men's work.

That's not to say that gender norms do not exact a cost on workers in male-dominated jobs as well. Take, for example, the construction industry. In an era of weak worker protections and declining male job prospects, one study has found that men who work in construction feel a need to demonstrate their masculinity through sexist, homophobic, and racist comments and through displays of physical strength. Such displays of masculinity often involve bodily risk-taking with respect to occupational safety that serves to prove workers are "man enough" to perform and keep their jobs in this era of stiff worker competition, which results in higher rates of worker accidents and disability, acceleration of the decline of union power, and an overall loss of social status for the workers themselves (Landsbergis et al., 2014).

Glass Ceilings When women do enter more prestigious corporate worlds, they often encounter gendered barriers to reaching the very top: the so-called glass ceiling, an invisible limit on women's climb up the occupational

GLASS CEILING

an invisible limit on women's climb up the occupational ladder.

↑

Betty Dukes (right) was a longtime greeter for Walmart and became the lead plaintiff in a class-action gender discrimination lawsuit against the discount retailer. She and her counterparts claimed that they were passed over for promotions and paid less than men for the same work. In 2011, the Supreme Court dismissed the case in a controversial 5–4 decision.

ladder. Sociologist Rosabeth Moss Kanter argues in her classic study *Men and Women of the Corporation* (1977) that the dearth of women in top corporate positions results from a cultural conflation of authority with masculinity. In Indesco, the fictitious name of the corporation Kanter studied, she found that most people believed that men and women come to occupy the kinds of jobs for which they are naturally best suited. To the contrary, as Kanter showed, the job often makes the person; the person doesn't make the job.

Job requirements and the constraints of the organizational structure of the company tend to determine employee behavior. At Indesco, secretarial positions (98.6 percent female) were based on "principled arbitrariness," meaning there were no limits to the (male) boss's discretion as to what his secretary should do (type, fax, pick up his dry cleaning, look after his dog when he's away). Furthermore, secretarial work was characterized by fealty, the demand of personal loyalty and devotion of secretary to boss. Under these conditions, secretaries adopted certain behaviors to get through a day's work, including timidity and self-effacement, addiction to praise, and displays of emotion—all qualities that Indesco bosses tended to think of as just the way women are.

But what happens when a woman breaks into a top managerial position at Indesco? She becomes a numerical minority, which Kanter calls a token, serving as a stand-in for all women. Because tokens have heightened visibility, they experience greater surveillance and thus performance pressures. Male peers tend to rely on gender stereotypes when interpreting a token's behavior, seeing female managers as "seductresses, mothers, pets," or tough "iron maidens." When a token female manager botches the job, it just goes to show that women can't handle the corporate world.

Similarly, Jennifer L. Pierce's (1995) study of law firms showed that sexual stereotypes, as much as organizational structure, are underlying causes of job segregation. Paralegals—who are 86 percent female—are expected to be deferential (that is, they should not stick up for themselves), caring, and even motherly toward the trial lawyers for whom they work. Given the adversarial model of the U.S. legal system, trial lawyers, in contrast, perform what Pierce calls masculine emotional labor. To excel in the job takes aggression, intimidation, and manipulation. Even though almost half of law school graduates are female, women make up only 16 percent of partners at law firms (Scharf & Flom, 2010). When a woman joins the higher ranks of trial lawyering, she's likely to face exclusion from informal socializing with her colleagues (no drinks after work), deflation of her job status (frequently being mistaken for a secretary), and difficulty bringing clients into the firm.

Thus, female litigators find themselves in a double bind not experienced by their male counterparts. When deploying courtroom tactics of aggression and intimidation—the very qualities that make a male lawyer successful and respected—women litigators find themselves being called "bitches," "obnoxious," and "shrill." But when they fail to act like proper "Rambo litigators" in the courtroom, women are equally chided for being "too nice" and "too bashful." The trade-off between being a good woman and being a successful lawyer adds yet another obstacle for women to make it to the top in male-dominated jobs—and that's not even taking into account the added burden of bearing the brunt of sexual harassment in the workplace (see the #Me_Also Policy feature on page 335).

Glass Escalators Just as the odds are stacked against female tokens, they tilt in favor of men in female-dominated jobs. In *Still a Man's World* (1995), Christine Williams found that male nurses, elementary school teachers, librarians, and social workers inadvertently maintain masculine power and privilege. Specifically, when token men enter feminized jobs, they enjoy a quicker rise to leadership positions on the aptly named glass escalator. These escalators also operate in law firms, where male paralegals, themselves tokens in the overwhelmingly female semi-profession, reap benefits from their heightened visibility (Pierce, 1995). Male paralegals enjoy preferential treatment over their female peers, such as promotions and even the simple but substantial benefit of being invited to happy hour with the litigators. Recent research finds, however, that the glass escalator is racialized in that men of color do not ascend within their occupations at the same rates as their White counterparts (Dill et al., 2016; Wingfield, 2009).

Williams's (2013) research suggests that women hold a more equitable share of the top spots in nursing, elementary schools, and libraries, but that an emerging problem hits both men and women and their families' over-all well-being: Wages in these careers have not kept pace with the cost of living. Careers traditionally associated with women are not the only ones that have seen declining wages. Manufacturing, trucking, and warehouse jobs, traditionally dominated by male workers, are also paying less (Mishel & Shierholz, 2013).

In the fashion industry, the escalator reverses the gender filter Williams originally found for women-dominated fields. I talked with sociologists and former model Ashley Mears about the wage structure in the modeling industry. She confirmed that "you see a complete inverse" where "women outearn men by two to one, sometimes much more" and that "there are just more jobs and opportunities for women models." She explained that

GLASS ESCALATOR

the accelerated promotion of men to the top of a work organization, especially in feminized jobs.

Go to digital.wwnorton.com/youmayask8 to see more of my interview with Ashley Mears.

there are two reasons for this, one cultural and one structural. From a cultural perspective, "for a man to do the work of showing his body, displaying his body, it's read as being less than what we fully expect in a hegemonically masculine way. It's read as being effeminate work." From a structural perspective there simply are no stepping-stones to managerial positions or other promotions for models. According to Mears, on the models' job escalator, "there's no place to go" because career positions in the fashion industry go to experienced businesspeople and designers who, surprise, tend to be men (Conley, 2013c; Reimer, 2016). So even though male *models* don't enjoy a glass escalator, the wider industry ends up dominated by men all the same.

THE MOTHERHOOD PENALTY

We might like to think that what happens at home stays at home and what happens at work stays at work. But even before the remote working revolution of the early 2020s, the two were linked. Much research shows that gender inequality in promotions, wages, and so on really emerges when women become mothers. Women suffer from what sociologists and economists call the motherhood wage penalty. Mothers are offered 7.9 percent lower salaries than women who are not mothers. Mothers are considered less competent and committed to their jobs than are women who are not mothers. In one study that experimentally matched résumés to factor out all other possible explanations, childless women received 2.1 times more callbacks for interviews when applying for (real) jobs as compared to applicants who were mothers (Correll et al., 2007). If anything, these differences probably underestimate the impact of motherhood, because women also pull themselves out of more competitive occupational tracts when they become mothers (or even in anticipation of raising children). Meanwhile, fathers actually enjoy a wage premium as compared to men who are not fathers because they are typically seen as more deserving (that is, needing a higher income to support a family), more responsible, and more competent.

Some have argued that employers are reacting to actual productivity differences between women who have children and women who do not have children. They say that mothers cannot commit as many hours or as much effort to their jobs because of their responsibilities at home. In addition to the actual work of feeding children, cleaning homes, and so on, these responsibilities include what sociologist Allison Daminger (2019) calls "cognitive labor," meaning all the planning and organizational tasks entailed in managing a household and family. Think of managing a schedule of playdates, making sure the cupboards are stocked with food and supplies, and making sure homework and other tasks are completed. It's much like managing a small organization such as a startup. In fact, Emily Oster (2022) calls a household with children "the family firm" in her book of the same name. We examine this "second shift" in detail in Chapter 10 on the family. The important take-home point here is that though we might tend to analyze work and the family as two separate domains, the less visible connections between them play a huge role in shaping gender inequality.

Theories of Gender Inequality

| Explain gender inequalities in terms of various functionalist, conflict, and interactionist theories.

Although the contemporary United States has less gender inequality than some other societies on a number of measures, it has more gender inequality compared to other countries on the same measures. Policies like paid family leave, subsidized child care, equal pay laws, and so on all make a difference in the degree of gender equality. However, there is no society we know of where there is total gender equality. Whereas men may suffer a disadvantage on some measure with regard to women, such as life expectancy or total years of schooling, when it comes to power, status, and economic resources, men dominate to some degree in every society. What explains the pervasiveness of the male advantage? When a social phenomenon is so universal, it is tempting to resort to biological explanations. That's just what early thinkers did until feminist scholars came along.

PARSONS'S SEX ROLE THEORY

In the field of anthropology, most scholars studying communities around the world had previously assumed that, since women's subordination occurred everywhere, it must be fulfilling some societal function and, therefore, was less interesting than other possible research questions. What underlies this idea is structural functionalism. This theoretical tradition dominated early anthropological thought, and it assumed that every society

STRUCTURAL FUNCTIONALISM

a theory in which society's many parts—institutions, norms, traditions, and so on—mesh to produce a stable, working whole that evolves over time; best embodied by Talcott Parsons.

In the 1950s, Talcott Parsons advanced the idea that the nuclear family effectively reared children to meet the labor demands of a capitalist system.

SEX ROLE THEORY

Talcott Parsons's theory that men and women perform their sex roles as breadwinners and wives/mothers, respectively, because the nuclear family is the ideal arrangement in modern societies, fulfilling the function of reproducing workers.

had certain structures (such as the family, the division of labor, or gender) that existed to fulfill some set of necessary functions. Talcott Parsons, an influential American sociologist of the 1950s, offered a widely accepted functionalist account of gender relations. According to Parsons's (1951) sex role theory, the heterosexual nuclear family is the ideal arrangement in modern societies because it fulfills the function of reproducing workers. With a work-oriented father in the public sphere and a domestic-oriented mother in the private sphere, children are most effectively reared to be people who can meet the labor demands of a capitalist system. Sex, sexuality, and gender are taken to be stable and dichotomous, meaning that each has two categories. Each category is assigned a role and a given script that actors carry out according to the expectations of those roles, which are enforced by social sanctions to ensure that the actors do not forget their lines. Women and men play distinctive roles that are functional for the whole of society; a healthy, harmonious society exists when actors stick to their normal roles. Generally speaking, according to Parsons, social structures such as gender and the division of labor are held in place because they work to ensure a stable society.

Functionalism was a hit in the 1950s; after all, it makes intuitive sense (and feels very satisfying) that there must be a good reason for the way things happen to be, some internal logic—at least to those who benefit from those arrangements. But Parsons's sex role theory falls short on several points. For starters, the argument is tautological—that is, it explains the existence of a structure in terms of its function, essentially claiming that things work the way they do because they work. In explaining a phenomenon in terms of its function, functionalists relied on the presumption in a tricky leap of logical faith that the need for the function exists before the phenomenon. Furthermore, they glossed over the possibility that ways of organizing society other than the structures of gender, race, and so on that we currently have could fulfill the same functions. There is also the question of whether those functions are indeed legitimate or ultimately desirable. The end result is a theory that tends to justify or naturalize existing forms of social relationships, such as gender wage gaps and the unequal division of labor in housework.

The functionalist sex role story also does not explain how and why structures change throughout history. If traditional husband-and-wife sex roles were so functional, why did they change drastically in the 1970s? In Parsons's account, gender roles appear to be a matter of voluntarism, as if women and men choose independently of external power constraints to be housewives and breadwinners, respectively. Of course, this is a myopic view of roles since women of color and immigrant women have always worked outside the home at high rates. Finally—and this is a problem with much early feminist thinking as well—sex and gender are regarded as being composed of dichotomous roles when these categories are, in fact, fuzzy, flexible, and variable in combination with other social positions, such as race and class.

PSYCHOANALYTIC THEORIES

Where functionalism focuses too much, perhaps, on society as a whole, Freudian theorists have provided an overly individualistic, psychoanalytic account of sex roles. The father of psychoanalysis, Sigmund Freud (1856–1939), famously quipped, "Anatomy is destiny." Although biological determinism plays a major role in Freudian theory, so does the idea that gender develops through family socialization.

According to Freud's developmental psychology, girls and boys develop masculine and feminine personality structures through early interactions with their parents. Boys, so the story goes, have a tormented time achieving masculinity because they must resolve the Oedipal complex. In this stage of development, around age three, every normal boy experiences heterosexual love for his maternal figure. But he soon realizes that he will be castrated (psychologically, not literally) by his father if he continues to fancy his mother. To resolve this Oedipal conflict, the boy rejects his mother, in turn emulating his emotionally distant father and developing rigid ego boundaries.

In Freud's view, girls do not experience quite the same resolution to their analogous "penis envy." When a little girl realizes that she lacks the plumbing to have sexual relations with her mother, she experiences penis envy toward her father, according to Freud. However, she ultimately realizes that one day she too can have a baby, thus providing feminine gratification. Girls end up identifying with their mothers, growing up with less rigid ego boundaries and more easily connecting with others than boys do.

Many thinkers have picked up and used Freudian ideas to theorize differences between men and women. For example, feminist psychoanalyst Nancy Chodorow (1978) modified Freud's theory to answer a particular version of the woman question: Why are women predominantly the caregivers? She reasoned that parents' unequal involvement in child rearing was a partial cause of the universal oppression of women. Her answer was that mothering by women is reproduced in a cycle of role socialization, in which little girls learn to identify as mothers and little boys as fathers (and workers outside the home). Chodorow concluded that egalitarian relations between the sexes would be possible if men shared the mothering.

But before you see a psychoanalyst to discuss your own penis envy, consider the assumptions underlying these psychological accounts. For starters, Freud's theories lacked empirical evidence and assumed a hetero-sexual, two-parent nuclear family. Since only about 64 percent of American children live in households headed by two married parents (National Center for Education Statistics, 2019), many of you reading this probably did not grow up in the nuclear family setting that Freud and Chodorow describe. Sociologist Carol Stack underscored this point in her ethnography of a poor Black community. In *All Our Kin* (1974), she finds that the division between male and female roles and attitudes is not as clear-cut as Freud or Chodorow would have us think. In the community Stack studied, caregiving was a valued responsibility for both men and women. Moreover, these early psy-choanalytic theorists took for granted a binary sex/gender system, whereas we now know that those categories are much more fluid in real life.

Finally, the fact that those who "mother" are typically women is not just a result of socialization. While the invention of bottle feeding can eliminate the need for women to be the sole givers of nutrition early in life, so far we don't have an artificial womb to equalize pregnancy, and we don't give dads shots of oxytocin and other hormones to promote bonding with their children. This is all to say that the biological and the social influences are much like that Möbius strip we discussed earlier: It's hard to separate out sex and gender.

RUBIN'S SEX/GENDER SYSTEM

Anthropologist Gayle Rubin (1975) both borrowed from and challenged structuralist and psychoanalytic explanations of gender roles by proposing a "sex/gender system." In this system, the raw materials of biological sex are transformed through kinship relations into asymmetrical gender statuses. She used the structural perspective of Claude Lévi-Strauss, a French anthro-pologist, to suggest that because of the universal taboo against incest—that is, fathers and brothers cannot sleep with their daughters and sisters—women who start out belonging to one man (their father, or their brother if their father dies) must leave their families of origin and belong to another man (their husband). Women are treated like valuable property whose trade patterns strengthen relations between families headed by men. Indeed, tra-ditional wedding vows in the West involve a commitment to "obey" only on the part of the wife. This "traffic in women" gives men certain rights over their female kin. The resulting sex/gender system, Rubin argued, was not a given; it was the result of human interaction.

Rubin's theories made waves. Feminist thinkers widely agreed that the task at hand was to explain universal male dominance. Why were women—despite a few token examples of matrifocal or women-led tribes in the anthropology books—typically on the bottom of stratification systems? That is, why did women in almost every society seem to get short shrift? Anthropologist Michelle Rosaldo (1974) answered that it must be women's

A "new feminist bookstore" in 1970. Feminist theorists since the 1960s have attempted to explain the "woman question"—why, in nearly every society across history, do men hold power over women?

universal association with the private sphere. Because women give birth and then rear children, they become identified with domestic life, which universally is accorded less prestige, value, and rewards than men's public sphere of work and politics. Meanwhile, anthropologist Sherry Ortner (1974) claimed that women are identified with something that every culture defines as lower than itself—namely, nature. A woman, she reasoned, comes to be identified with the chaos and danger of nature because of bodily functions like lactation and menstruation (what feminist philosopher Simone de Beauvoir [1952] poetically described as "woman's enslavement to the species"). Ortner's answer to the woman question sounds like a plausible one. But note the binary logic at work in these anthropological accounts: culture versus nature, private versus public, man versus woman. The world is less rigid, more nuanced, and certainly less easily molded into binary categories than these theories suggest.

CONFLICT THEORIES

By the 1980s, another wave of thinkers began to tackle an issue missing from earlier discussions of the woman question: power. Conflict theorists mixed old-school Marxism with feminism to claim that gender, not class, was the driving force of history. Socialist feminists, also known as radical feminists, claimed that the root of all social relations, including relations of production, stemmed from unequal gender relations.

Economist Heidi Hartmann (1981) and legal theorist Catharine MacKinnon (1983), for example, both analyzed how capitalism combines with patriarchy to make women economically dependent on a man's income.

Many conflict theorists argue that patriarchal capitalists benefit through systems that subordinate women. For instance, many cotton mills in the nineteenth and early twentieth centuries hired young, unmarried women and required them to live in company boardinghouses in order to regulate their behavior.

In a capitalist society, women occupy a disadvantaged position in the job market and within the family. Capitalists (predominantly men), in turn, reap the benefits of women's subordination. When women are subordinate, men benefit. To radical feminists, gender inequality relies first and foremost on power inequalities, and gender differences (as in personality development) emerge from there. Marilyn Frye (1983) offers a useful metaphor for the pervasiveness of gender oppression: the birdcage. Women, she argued, find themselves like birds trapped in a cage. We can focus on one of the strands of sexism up close, but then we cannot see the other strands or bars that complete the cage. It is the combination of the many strands of sexism that oppresses women, not any single strand in isolation. Bars of the cage may be workplace discrimination, the burdens of unequal housework, and so on.

"DOING GENDER": INTERACTIONIST THEORIES

A useful social theory helps you understand the social world in which you live. For example, Candace West and Don H. Zimmerman argue in their influential article "Doing Gender" (1987) that gender is not a fixed identity or role that we take with us into our interactions. Rather, it is the product of those interactions. In this framework, gender is a matter of active doing, not simply a matter of natural being. To be a man or a woman, they argue, is to perform masculinity or femininity constantly. In this social constructionist theory, gender is a process, not a static category.

The "doing gender" perspective stems from Erving Goffman's dramaturgical theory, symbolic interactionism, and ethnomethodology. (See discussion of these terms in Chapter 4.) That is, West and Zimmerman argue that people create their social realities and identities through interactions with one another. Unlike the structural functionalists, psychoanalysts, and conflict theorists, however, social constructionists view gender roles as having open-ended scripts. Perhaps individuals come to the stage situated differently according to their place in power hierarchies or personality development, but their lines and gestures are far from being predetermined. Regardless of social location, individuals are always free to act, sometimes in unexpected ways that change the course of the play. For example, the presence of openly transgender people has been said to "undo" or "redo" gender by subverting the binary norms (Connell, 2010; Sawyer et al., 2016).

This may sound like a pretty optimistic view of gender: We can perform whatever gender identity we want, and it will come to be! But by and large, as a result of doing gender, people contribute to, reaffirm, and reproduce masculine dominance and feminine submissiveness in the bedroom, kitchen, workplace, and so on. Queer theorist Judith Butler (2002) emphasized this point through her theory of performativity, noting that though we do perform, we don't constitute ourselves from whole cloth when we do it. Rather, what we say and do is largely predetermined by both convention and even language itself. Indeed, Butler avoids the terms "individual" or "person" in favor of "subject" (a linguistic term) to emphasize how our very thoughts and speech acts are necessarily embedded in the social constraints of language. And when we speak, we reinforce those same constraints. Thus, the most mundane acts constitute gender performances—that is, how we talk, walk, and even hold ourselves—and while those gender performances typically reify existing power structures, they can also serve to challenge them. In this way, she asserts, there is no line between the personal and the political. Through the lens of performativity, the personal is political. In other words, be careful what you say!

BLACK FEMINISM AND INTERSECTIONALITY

If gender is a performance, it is much more than a set of neutral scripts that we "voluntarily" follow. Structural forces influence our actions in ways that we might not even realize, such as class or race privilege. As Patricia Hill Collins (1990) claims, we "do" a lot more than gender; gender intersects with race, class, nationality, religion, and so forth. Black feminists have made the case that early liberal feminism was largely by, about, and for White middle-class women. In trying to answer the woman question and explain women's oppression, early feminists assumed that all women occupied the same oppressed boat. In so doing, they effaced multiple lines of fragmentation and difference into one simple category: woman. For example, by championing women's rights to work outside the home in *The Feminine Mystique* (1997), leading second-wave feminist Betty Friedan ignored the experiences of thousands of working-class women and women of color who were already working, sometimes holding down two jobs to support their families. Indeed, a third wave of feminism focuses on how the identities surrounding gender, sex, and sexuality intersect with other meaningful

INTERSECTIONALITY

the idea that it is critical to understand the interplay between social identities such as race, class, gender, ability status, and sexual orientation, even though many social systems and institutions (such as the law) try to treat each category on its own.

MATRIX OF DOMINATION

intersecting domains of oppression that create a social space of domination and, by extension, a unique position within that space based on someone's intersectional identity along the multiple dimensions of gender, age, race, class, sexuality, location, and so on.

social categories like race or class in a process called intersectionality, as articulated by critical race theorist Kimberlé Williams Crenshaw (1989) and sociologist Beatrice Potter Webb back in 1913.

As illustrated by the concept of intersectionality, "woman" is not a stable or obvious category of identity. Rather, women occupy different positions in what Collins calls a matrix of domination. A 40-year-old poor, Black, straight, single mother living in rural Georgia will not have the same conception of womanhood as a 25-year-old professional, White, single, lesbian in Chicago. More fundamentally, Collins (1990) argues, Black women face unique oppressions that White women don't. For instance, Black women experience motherhood in ways that differ from the White masculinist ideal of the family, as "bloodmothers," "othermothers," and "community othermothers," thus revealing that White masculine notions of the world do not capture the daily lived experiences of many Black women.

Gender, sexual orientation, race, class, nationality, ability, and other factors all intersect. Just as some women enjoy privilege by virtue of their wealth, class, education, and skin color, some men are disadvantaged by their lack of these same assets. As bell hooks (1984) noted, if women's liberation is aimed at making women the social equals of men, women should first stop and consider which men they would like to equal. Certainly, not all men are privileged over all women. Making universal comparisons of men to women misses these nuances and implicitly excludes marginally positioned people from the discussion. For example, men of color certainly experience oppression that intersects with their gender identities (for example, Black men bearing the brunt of police harassment). Even going beyond demographic groups, men who do not embody or perform the dominant form of masculine

Patricia Hill Collins criticized feminist leaders such as Betty Friedan (pictured in the red dress), Billie Jean King (in tan pants and a blue shirt on the left), and Bella Abzug (in the gray dress, with the hat) for ignoring the experiences of thousands of working-class women and women of color.

behavior often suffer for it, occupying a subordinate status (Connell, 1987). Power comes from many different angles; it doesn't sit evenly on a plane for all women. When the Black activist Sojourner Truth (1797–1883) asked, "Ain't I a woman?" (Truth, 1851), she summed up some elusive philosophical questions: What is a woman? Who counts as a woman and why?

POSTMODERN AND GLOBAL PERSPECTIVES

As perspectives have expanded and previously rigid categories have begun to crumble, the validity of the woman question is itself now in question. For instance, anthropologist Oyèrónké Oyěwùmí argues that the woman question stems from uniquely Western thought and cannot be applied to African societies. In *The Invention of Women* (1997), she presents ethnographic research on Yoruban society in West Africa, which she claims was once a genderless society. Among the Yoruba, before the arrival of anthropologists, villagers did not group themselves as men or women or use body markers at all. Rather, they ranked themselves into strata by seniority. When Western feminist scholars arrived on the scene, presuming the preexistence of gender relations, they, of course, found a system of gender. But this system of categories with distinct males and females indicates a Western cultural logic, what Oyěwùmí has termed *bio-logic*.

Bio-logic runs deep in our cultural experiences and understandings of gender. It acts as a sort of filter through which all knowledge of the world runs, though there may be different ways of knowing outside such a paradigm. But if "woman" is such an unstable, fragmented category—that is, one that is merely "performed" through discourse, as Judith Butler (2006) suggests—how do we study it? Feminists must have some sturdy ground on which to unite, build coalitions, and tackle injustice. Philosopher Susan Bordo (1990) provides a pragmatic buoy by arguing that hierarchical and binary power structures out there do still oppress women and help address issues such as the wage gap, eating disorders, or rape.

Sociology in the Bedroom

❚ Analyze historical and contextual interpretations of sexuality

Sex. You think it's the most personal, intimate act. The bedroom is surely the one place where the sociological imagination is the last thing you'll need. But just as we've untangled the terms *sex* and *gender*, we'll take a sociological look at sex, which can reveal some startling insights. Connections may be found between the sheets and history, desire and science, how we do it and how it in turn organizes what we do, as well as with whom and with what meanings. As expected, an excavation into the social construction of sexuality divulges a surprising amount of variation in what is considered normal bedroom behavior. By exposing different social patterns of sexuality, throughout history and across cultures, the sociologist can trace unequal gender relations and show how sexuality expresses, represses, and elucidates those relations.

SEX: FROM PLATO TO NATO

BISEXUAL

an individual who is sexually attracted to both genders/sexes.

An ancient Greek image of two male lovers. How can comparing social patterns of sexuality across cultures and throughout history help sociologists understand modern sexuality?

The ancient Greeks accepted relationships between two men as normal. Engaging in same-sex acts did not confer a particular identity, because the practice varied in frequency across the population among those who did and those who did not also participate in opposite-sex sexual relations. Rather, the socially important distinction revolved around an active/passive dichotomy (although historians have shown that many exceptions existed). The active partner was supposed to be older or higher in status than the passive partner. To flip the rules was a violation, and it was considered shameful for a master or noble to be penetrated by a younger man.

Or consider sexual normality among the Sambia, a mountain people in Papua New Guinea. Anthropologist Gilbert Herdt (1981) reported that fellatio played a significant role in a boy's transition into manhood. Young boys are initiated into manhood by a daily ritual of fellatio on older boys and men. By taking in the vital life liquid (semen) of older men, boys prepare themselves to be warriors and sexual partners with women. Fellatio, for Sambia boys, then, is the only way to become "real" men.

Both the Siwans of North Africa and the Keraki, also in New Guinea, prefer homosexuality to heterosexuality, for fairly straightforward, practical reasons (Kimmel, 2000). Because every male is homosexual during his adolescence and then bisexual after heterosexual marriage, limiting straight sex keeps down the birthrate. In these cultures with scant resources, homosexuality makes practical sense to limit the chances of teen pregnancy and overpopulation.

There is enormous variation in how humans have sex and what it means to them. Mouth-to-mouth kissing, common in Western cultures, is unthinkable among the Thonga and Sirono cultures: "But that's where you put food!" (Kimmel, 2000). American, heterosexual middle-class couples have sex a few nights a week for about

15 minutes a pop; the people of Yapese cultures near Guam engage in sex once a month. Marquesan men of French Polynesia are said to have anywhere from 10 to 30 orgasms a night! Which of these is "normal"?

THE SOCIAL CONSTRUCTION OF SEXUALITY

By treating sexuality as a social construction—that is, as always shaped by social factors—the sociologist would argue that the notion of normal, especially pertaining to what happens behind closed bedroom (or bathroom or car) doors, is always contested. In other words, there is no natural way of doing it. If an essentially right way existed, we wouldn't be able to find such wild and woolly variation throughout history and across cultures. Starting from the view that sex itself is a social creation, sociologists tend to argue that humans have sexual plumbing but no sexuality until they are located in a social environment. The range of normal and abnormal is itself a construction, a production of society. The study of this range can lead the willing sociologist into an exploration of the social relations on which sex is built.

Sexuality and Power Marxist feminists argue that sexuality in America expresses the unequal power balance between men and women. Catharine MacKinnon (1983) argued that in male-dominated societies, sexuality is constructed as a gender binary, with men on top and women on the bottom (literally and figuratively). To MacKinnon, sexuality is the linchpin of gender inequality, an expression of male control. Some feminists also argue that our experiences of what is titillating are shaped by the fetishization of male power. So being "taken" is exciting and pleasurable to women, revealing that even those things we think of as the most personal of experiences are shaped by social power arrangements.

Adrienne Rich (1980) called sexuality in America a "compulsory heterosexuality." This "political institution," at least for some, is not a preference but something that has been imposed, managed, organized, and enforced to serve a male-dominated capitalist system in which women's unpaid domestic work is required to support men's paid work outside of the home. Because her work is unpaid, the woman in this situation is unable to leave a bad husband. According to Rich, people see heterosexuality as the norm rather than a mechanism integral to sustaining women's social subordination.

Same-Sex Sexuality The connections between sex and power are best exemplified in the social construction of the homosexual in the current West, the social identity of a person who has sexual attraction to and/or relations with people of the same sex. For most of the past century, the dominant view has been that individuals are born either homosexual or heterosexual, gay or straight, queer or cis. Sexual orientation was thought of as a kind of personhood automatically acquired at birth or something carried

HOMOSEXUAL

the social identity of a person who has sexual attraction to and/or relations with people of the same sex.

in our genes (despite documented cases of identical twins in which one is straight and the other gay). But recall the ancient Greeks' homosexual love or the Sambian rites of manhood. Jane Ward (2015), for example, studied self-defined straight men who have sex with other men in the contemporary United States, including fraternity members, or military personnel who engage in sex acts with their compatriots as part of hazing, or men who answer ads to find other men to masturbate with. Men in these examples engage in homosexual acts without adopting a homosexual identity (Silva, 2017). When do acts, behaviors, or desires crystallize into identities?

Before 1850, there was no such thing as a homosexual. Sure, people engaged in same-sex sexual behaviors, but it was not yet an identity in the way we now know it. French philosopher Michel Foucault (1926–1984) led the way to poststructuralist notions of the body and sexuality as historical productions. In *The History of Sexuality* (1978), Foucault made the case that the body is "in the grip" of cultural practices. That is, there is no pre-social or natural body; instead, culture is always already inscribed on our bodies. Foucault further argued that the way in which we know our bodies is linked to power, and knowledge and power go hand in hand. As the population expanded in nineteenth-century Europe, newly formed states and their administrators developed a concern for population management. The rise of scientific ways of thinking at the time led to the creation of what Foucault calls "bio-power," the control of populations by influencing patterns in births, deaths, and illnesses.

Homosexuality was considered a mental disorder by the American Psychological Association until 1973. Here, in 1967, Dr. Joseph Wolpe treats a homosexual patient by showing a series of risqué images intended to elicit arousal.

Discourses on sexuality had by then surfaced. People talked about sex, scientists studied it, and government officials tried to regulate it, whereas a century before, all this sex talk did not exist. With the development of the biological and human sciences in the nineteenth century, doctors wanted to know which kinds of sex were normal and which were deviant, and new attention was paid to policing those differences. By the late 1800s, "Homosexuality appeared as one of the forms of sexuality when it was transposed from the practice of sodomy onto a kind of interior [identity]" (Foucault, 1978). In Foucault's account, the category of homosexuality arises from the efforts of government bureaucrats trying to assert their power (that of the state) over human populations.

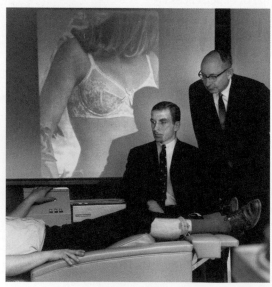

Meanwhile, the American Psychiatric Association and the American Psychological Association listed homosexuality on their list of mental disorders until 1973. Homosexuals needed regulation, observation, studying, and, most importantly, restrictions. Because everyone was capable of, or in danger of, sexual deviance, the urgency to confess one's sexuality grew, as did the scientific need for public surveillance. Who was gay? How could a homosexual be detected? Anyone could be a pervert—your professor, your roommate, even you!

Sexual acts became synonymous with the person who performed them. Even our language reflects the way sexual behavior becomes more than a single event among the many other behaviors that make up an individual's life—it often becomes a master status. Here's what I mean. If a man roasts a whole pig—a serious, time-consuming undertaking that requires research, dedication, and planning—he is not known ever after as a "pig roaster" or even as a gourmand. He's still just Bob from down the block who hosted one heck of a barbecue. But if a man has anal sex with another man—something that takes less time and probably less dedication and research than roasting a pig—he becomes a sodomite, a homosexual, gay, or whatever terminology might fit the context.

At one point, what happened in the bedroom (or car or motel or . . .) stayed there. But over the last century what happened behind closed doors was outed, and a whole new person was produced. Today, our society places a huge emphasis—our entire selfhood, according to Foucault—on sexuality. Sexuality, in other words, is a prime factor that goes into the construction of gender—a dynamic that may not have been as important in days gone by. Now, what you do (and with whom) defines who you are: not just how others see you, but how you experience yourself.

Thousands participate in a pride parade in 2018. How does Foucault show that the rise of the "homosexual" as an identity was a historical process? How might he respond to pride parades and other contemporary assertions of gay identity?

Consider a widely used argument against lesbian and gay couplings: "It's unnatural," meaning that sex should lead to reproduction. This is a popular argument against same-sex marriages, but it also stigmatizes straight couples who can't or don't have children. Besides, homosexuality occurs widely in nature; one of our closest primate cousins, the bonobo, practices homosexuality (Parker, 2007). Though based on questionable data, Alfred Kinsey's 1948 study *Sexual Behavior in the Human Male* suggested that at least 10 percent of men were homosexual. He challenged the psychiatric model of homosexuals as perverse and abnormal and instead viewed sexuality as a continuum. Most people, he claimed, experience both heterosexual and homosexual desires and behaviors. Kinsey's figures have since been disputed because his sample was not representative of the U.S. population as a whole, but the basic idea holds. Across the globe and throughout history, there has been more or less the same degree of homosexual behavior.

What is different across time and place, however, is the perception of sexuality. Gender often plays a large role. For example, Yale historian George Chauncey makes the case in *Gay New York* (1994) that in early twentieth-century New York, an emerging working-class gay world was split between masculine men (tops) and the effeminate men who solicited them (bottoms). As long as men stuck to their masculine gender scripts, no matter how often they engaged in gay sex, they were not considered abnormal like the more feminine men who were derided for their effeminacy.

How do *travesti* challenge common binary models of understanding gender and sexuality?

The reverse is true among the *travesti*, transgender prostitutes in Brazil. Anthropologist Don Kulick (1998) conducted an ethnography of the *travesti*, males who adopt female names, clothing styles, hairstyles, cosmetic practices, and linguistic pronouns; ingest female hormones; and inject industrial silicone directly into their bodies to give themselves breasts and round buttocks or *bunda*. They display stereotypically feminine traits, yet they do not self-identify as women. In fact, they think it is both repugnant and impossible for men to try to become women. Kulick argues that in Brazil, sexual practice determines gender: "What one does in bed has immediate and lasting consequences for the way one is perceived (and the way one can perceive oneself) as a gendered being. If one penetrates, in this particular configuration of sexuality and gender, one is a 'man.' If one expresses interest in the penis of a male, and especially if one 'gives'—allows oneself to be penetrated by a male—then one is no longer a man." However, the *travesti* do not think they are women; they think of themselves as *travesti*, men who emulate women but are not women. The primacy of penetration as a determinant of gender appears commonly across cultures and challenges Americans to look beyond chromosomes and hormones to practices and cultural context.

CONTEMPORARY SEXUALITIES: THE Q WORD

The term LGBTQIA has seemed to add letters lately—there's a growing recognition that if we look closely and without judgment, we see many forms of gender/sexuality identity that do not conform to categories that dominated discussion since, roughly, the 1850s that Foucault marked as the start of the era of the "homosexual."

We have already discussed L (lesbian), G (gay [male]), B (bisexual), and T (trans). We have also discussed I (intersex). So, let's skip to the last letter in the acronym, "A." Asexuality has, of late, become a more visible sexual identity. Many individuals do not feel sexual attraction; these individuals may identify as asexual (often "ace" for short). They may not experience sexuality-related bodily feelings or actions, but others who identify as asexual may, for example, masturbate to fantasies of fictional characters. The American Psychiatric Association has defined asexuality as a paraphilia, which is an atypical sexual attraction. This label lumps the identity in with medical disorders, whether or not asexuality results in significant distress for the individual or others, such as a partner. Sociologists challenge this definition, pointing out that many ace individuals enjoy sexual fantasies that involve others or involve themselves in a completely fictional way (that is, younger, kinkier, or even a superhero; Scherrer & Pfeffer, 2017). A better way to think about asexuality is as an identity based on membership in a shared sexual community. Hence, the "A" was added to the LGBT alphabet as asexual activists have sought to be included in nondominant gender/ sexuality social movements, protests, and so on.

What about the Q word? *Queer* is a derogatory term, reclaimed by those it was originally intended to wound, to become a broader, encompassing term for nonheteronormative sexual behaviors/identities. That is, when individuals self-identify as queers, they may be lesbians looking for a broader, more inclusive umbrella that is not already overly associated with, say, White middle-class people. Or they may participate in what might be called "kinky" sexual practices, such as BDSM (a term meant to capture bondage/discipline/submission/sadomasochism and related practices). Or they may simply not feel comfortable with and wish to reject other aspects of heteronormativity. For instance, some queer people reject the notion of same-sex marriage. They reject what they see as assimilation into heteronormative culture and instead prefer to organize their lives differently in terms of kinship, sexuality, and so on.

HETERO-NORMATIVITY

the idea that heterosexuality is the default or normal sexual orientation from which other sexualities deviate.

One form of nonheteronormativity that has garnered a lot of attention of late is non-monogamy. Non-monogamy is not just having sex with multiple people (because, for example, people can be in monogamous relationships and cheat on their partners). Rather, it is the practice of having multiple sexual (or intimate) relationships (or merely the desire to) with the full knowledge and consent of all the people involved. Polyamory is a particular form of non-monogamy (Sheff, 2014). While there is no agreed on, universal definition of polyamory, it usually involves *intimate* relationships with more than one partner (again, with the knowledge and consent of all involved). So a couple that agrees they can have one-night stands with other people are non-monogamous but not polyamorous. Mimi Schippers (2016) finds that some forms of polyamory subvert gender/sexuality norms more than others. For example, a relationship including a woman and two men challenges heterosexual norms and gender power relations more than a relationship among one man and two women, since the latter more easily allows for male dominance and because female bisexuality is more socially acceptable than male bisexuality.

Fluid notions of acceptable sexual relationships aren't only limited to those under the LGBTQIA umbrella: Indeed, how we think about sex among teen and college-aged people is rapidly changing.

"HEY": TEEN SEX, FROM HOOKING UP TO VIRGINITY PLEDGES

Sometimes the policies meant to achieve one goal backfire and cause the opposite outcome, despite the best intentions. Government efforts to influence healthy teen sexuality provide one example. Recent studies have described the blasé attitude that contemporary American teenagers supposedly bring to their love lives. When sociologist Paula England surveyed students at one midwestern university about their sex lives, half reported that their previous sexual partner was someone they had slept with only once. Here's how she explained hook-up culture, which has replaced dating as the route to romance on college campuses around the country. She did her first surveys at Northwestern, where "before people ever go on a date, they hook up." Lest there be any confusion: A hook-up is not sex . . . unless it is. (According to sociologist Lisa Wade, 40 percent of hook-ups involve intercourse.) A hook-up means "something sexual happens, that 'something sexual' is not always intercourse, often in fact [in] the majority of cases it isn't, and there is no necessary implication that anybody's interested in a relationship, but they *might* be interested." Why so many short-lived hook-ups instead of longer-term relationships? For one thing, "so many" hook-ups, according to the average in Lisa Wade's study, means about eight over four years. Moreover, a third of students never hooked up. Meanwhile, dating is infrequent but not completely dead. It is "charged with more meaning now, and it's more likely to be leading to a relationship." Furthermore, "there's a strong norm that relationships should be monogamous and marriages should be monogamous and that people eventually want to get to monogamy and a marriage. They're just putting it off a lot longer. That's really what's changed, I think" (Conley, 2009d).

That is, most students do not plan to begin families anytime soon. For another, relationships just seem like more work—for the men, at least. England found that heterosexual males are not necessarily expected to sexually satisfy the women they hook up with, but the opposite is true in relationships (Armstrong et al., 2012). This trend has led to what they call "the orgasm gap." England and coauthors' analysis shows "that specific sexual practices [such as oral sex or genital stimulation], experience with a particular partner, and commitment all predict women's orgasm and sexual enjoyment"—all conditions less present in hook-ups than in relationships. For example, with respect to oral sex, England explains that in a hook-up "it's much more likely that the woman is servicing the guy than vice versa. So it seems like the hook-ups are prioritizing male pleasure" (Conley, 2009d).

In a hook-up culture, what might determine whether a pair continues to hook up or moves on to new partners? England has a theory that goes like this:

> Partner-specific investment may well be important. In other words, . . . our ability to please partners may not just be generally what have we learned from a lifetime of experience but what have we actually learned about this particular partner and what works for them and what they like and what they need. . . . If it's hook-up number two, she's more likely to have an orgasm than if it's one, and if it's three more likely, and if it's four even more likely. (Conley, 2009d)

She also noted that these hook-ups rarely produce babies, but nearly 14 percent of students still did not use any method to prevent pregnancy the last time they had sex.

To see an interview with Paula England about hook-up culture, go to digital.wwnorton.com/youmayask8

Let's look at a few more numbers: Fewer than 40 percent of American high-school students tell surveyors that they have had sexual intercourse (Figure 8.4), but this rate is not growing; it has remained more or less steady since 2003 (Centers for Disease Control and Prevention, 2019). Boys probably lie more often about the extent of their sexual experience (citing the proverbial girlfriend in a different state), and girls possibly downplay their sexual activity. Many of those who have not had intercourse are still sexually active in other ways. With teenagers' romantic interludes lasting about 15 months on average, they have plenty of time left before marriage to have many partners (in 2021 the median age at first marriage for women was 28.6 and for men 30.4; U.S. Census Bureau, 2021a). To top it off, most adolescents with a sexually transmitted disease (STD) don't know that they are infected. All of these factors combine to put American teenagers at high risk for STDs, which have been increasing dramatically since the 1970s.

So, what's a public health officer to do? During the early 2000s, the Bush administration (2001–9) advocated a "virginity pledge" and other abstinence policies, and the abstinence advocacy group True Love Waits says that 2.5 million young people have made the virginity pledge since 1993 (Herbert, 2011). As it turns out, the pledge does, on average, delay the onset of sexual activity as well as reduce a teenager's number of sexual partners, according to the National Longitudinal Study of Adolescent Health (Brückner & Bearman, 2005), particularly when it occurs in a school context where a sizable number of students take the pledge, creating a meaningful identity of sorts through collective abstinence (Bearman & Brückner, 2001). That said, most pledgers (about 60 percent) break their pledge. And when sex happens, it's much more likely to come in a rush of surprisingly strong,

FIGURE 8.4 Percentage of High-School Students Who Have Had Sex, 1991–2019

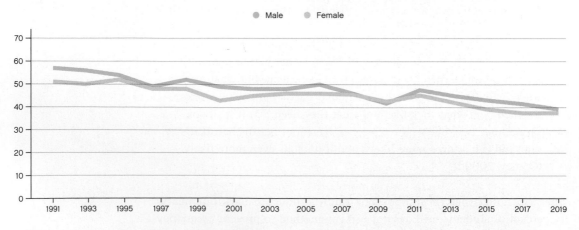

SOURCE: Centers for Disease Control and Prevention, 2018a; 2021b.

unfettered desire. Among the pledgers, only 40 percent ended up using a condom during sex—why would they have a condom if they were planning to be virgins until marriage?—compared with 60 percent of teens who had not pledged. The end result was a net higher rate of HPV infection and pregnancy among the pledgers (Paik et al., 2016).

Like their adult counterparts, teens are certainly navigating new terrain in terms of romantic and sexual relations thanks to technology. One way we can see this is in the debate over opening lines in online dating apps. Three million messages per day on the Tinder app begin with "Hey." Does such a generic approach represent laziness (that is, not having read someone's profile in order to say something specific)? Or is it just a universal human way to say "hi" without concocting some phony pickup line (even if it is not as vulnerable online as it would be in person at a party or a bar)? One thing is for sure—it probably beats the most searched GIF on Tinder: Joey from the show *Friends*, asking "How you doing?" (Verdier, 2016).

Figuring out the right way to approach someone online is not the only challenge that teens and adults have in the evolving world of Tinder, Grindr, and OkCupid. A new phenomenon of the "define-the-relationship" (DTR) conversation is emerging. In a world where a new potential partner is only a swipe away and people are inventing new ways of being romantic or sexual and where one cannot assume a single narrative arc of how such relationships are meant to progress, the DTR talk can clarify expectations, hopes, fears, and so on after getting to know each other. Will we be monogamous or friends with benefits? If monogamous, do we delete our dating apps? Will we be public on Facebook as a couple? Is this just something fun for now, or do we mutually envision a longer-term relationship between us? These are just some of the questions the DTR conversation may address. As to when to have (or avoid) that conversation, just as there are myriad relationship types nowadays, there is no clear norm on what's too soon (or too late) to discuss or define one's relationship. Stay tuned: Norms can evolve fast in the face of technological innovation.

SEX AND AGING

Sex, as it turns out, isn't just for teenagers. It may come as a surprise to many college students that sex continues to play an important role well after retirement age. Moreover, like most important aspects of life, sex at older ages displays inequalities that match patterns in other domains like work and family.

Specifically, the discrepancy in life expectancy between men and women colors many aspects of social life at older ages, but perhaps no domain as much as sexuality. In fact, the life expectancy difference comes on top of the typical age difference in married, heterosexual couples—the man is typically almost three years older than the woman in such unions. The result is the starkly different sociosexual positions in which older adults find themselves. For example, among men age 65 or older, over 71 percent are currently married, whereas the corresponding figure for women is a mere 43 percent. Indeed, there are as many widowed women over 65 as there are married women. (Meanwhile, a mere 14 percent of men in this age bracket are widowed.)

Such a disparity translates into a gender gap in sexual activity as well since most sex takes place within an ongoing relationship. So, along with the so-called sex recession among youth and the orgasm gap on college campuses, we can more frequently see social patterning of sexual behavior at older ages. For instance, among those 70 or older, men were about twice as likely to have had sexual intercourse as compared to women in the past year (43 percent to 22 percent). That disparity carries over to other forms of sexual activity such as oral sex, mutual masturbation, and anal sex. Curiously, when asked about masturbating alone, despite their greater access to sexual partners, men also reported having engaged in that activity more frequently than women did (46 percent to 33 percent). All else equal, we might expect older women to masturbate more often than men given their relative lack of other options. However, many older individuals surveyed today came of age before the sexual revolution of the 1960s and maintain social norms about sexuality formed early in life. It will be interesting to see if that gap closes among later cohorts where female masturbation was more socially accepted. It may even be the case that part of the current difference is due to social desirability bias. That is, given discomfort around discussing female masturbation, perhaps more older women are doing it than admit to doing it to the interviewers of the National Survey of Sexual Health and Behavior.

As paradoxical as the masturbation figures are by gender, so too are those regarding chronic diseases that affect sexual activity. Among those 75 and older, only 13 percent of women report experiencing a health condition that restricts sexual activity—the single largest cause being arthritis. But a full 45 percent of men report such biological impediments—most frequently due to prostate cancer or high blood pressure. But of course, older men are still having more sex! Why? Because there is a pill for men—developed by big pharma—and there isn't one for women.

By age 70, only 10 percent of men report "always or almost always" maintaining an erection adequate for satisfactory intercourse, while 38 percent report never being able to. Into this epidemic of erectile dysfunction (or ED) has stepped big pharma with drugs such as Viagra, Cialas, and Levitra, all of which treat ED to great success.

Meanwhile, while Viagra was approved by the FDA in 1998, it wasn't until 17 years later that Addyi, a drug for women with hypoactive sexual desire disorder (HSSD), was approved. The drugs work completely differently. Whereas the male drugs work on the blood vessels of the penis and

#ME _ ALSO

The #MeToo moment that began in 2017 unleashed a tsunami of sexual harassment and assault allegations that had built up over decades while predatory behavior went on unabated. It has prompted many policy makers to ask what can be done to prevent such a buildup of allegations in the future. That is, how do we get harassment or assault victims to step forward in real time? Or better still, get perpetrators fearful enough of being called out with consequences for bad behavior so that they don't perpetrate it in the first place! One thing is for sure: What organizations from colleges to corporations to Congress are doing presently does not work. Namely, watching videos or even engaging in live training with HR professionals does not seem to have the intended effects on actual workplace or school harassment and assault. It can even backfire by reinforcing gendered roles, according to sociologist Justine Tinkler (2013), by depicting men exclusively as harassers and women only as victims. This criticism doesn't mean nothing works and we should give up hope of a civil public space where individuals can feel safe and respected.

The ideas that have been offered include rewarding managers when reports of harassment increase, focusing training on getting bystanders (as opposed to the victims themselves) to intervene in some way, and promoting more women into leadership roles (which often changes the norms of what is acceptable behavior). One particularly novel notion is the formation of "information escrows," secret repositories where complaints can be reported anonymously. The idea is that many people may want to give others the benefit of the doubt. They don't want to start a huge stir and possibly ruin someone's career if it is truly a case of a one-off mistake or a misunderstanding. They also don't want to risk the cost to their own reputation (or career) in coming forward in what may end up being a he said–she said (or he said–he said, or . . .) situation that ends up being inconclusive and uncomfortable for all involved. But if the action—say, a misplaced hand or inappropriate humor or a refusal to take no for an answer when asking out a coworker— is part of a larger pattern of behavior, then as most would agree, it should have consequences. That's where the information escrow comes into the picture.

If I experience something that may qualify as harassment, I can lodge a complaint confidentially to someone in human resources or via a computer system, detailing the alleged infraction. I can then specify the conditions under which I want my grievance to trigger action. For example, I might say, as long as nobody else has complained about our shift manager pinching them, my allegation should remain secret and dormant. But the moment someone else also files a report to the information escrow of inappropriate touching (or perhaps other infractions), my testimony becomes an official complaint, too. That way, it is no longer one person's word against another's but an established pattern of behavior documented independently—in other words, a much more powerful case. Likewise, if the behavior was a one-off and never occurred again, I might choose to let it go. Of course, the presence of the information escrow option doesn't (and isn't meant to) preclude someone from reporting someone else's misbehavior straightaway through formal channels, but it provides alternative options for victims to consider.

As proposed by Ian Ayres and Cait Unkovic (2012), such harassment escrows are a particular case of a broader class of possible information escrows that can cover everything from bids in a trade (where the trade occurs and bids are revealed only if the seller and buyer overlap in price) to a revelation of mutual romantic crushes. In fact, some modern dating apps like Tinder and Bumble essentially act as escrows: Only if we both swipe right does our mutual interest get revealed. Imagine a similar app for deterring harassers. In an era where one camp worries about the potential for false accusations to ruin someone's life without due process while the other side focuses on victims who fear going public alone, it may be worth a try.

surrounding area to promote flow, the female-targeted drugs work on the brain, altering the balance between the neurotransmitters serotonin, on the one hand, and dopamine and norepinephrine, on the other hand, in order to increase sex drive. During clinical trials, Addyi generated a 10 percent positive response in the treatment group when adjusted for the placebo effect and also had much more frequent adverse side effects, including dizziness, fainting, nausea, and insomnia. So, all in all, not a great deal for women. Until the pharmaceutical industry invents a female sex pill that generates the kind of global response that Viagra and its kin have, some women have decided to take the men's drugs themselves. Evidence is mixed on how well they work; so, the search continues for the blockbuster female sex pill.

Conclusion

Starting with our friend Elliot, we've learned that what seems normal or natural to us often turns out to be fluid and contingent. The stuff we build up around biological plumbing, including roles, expectations, psyches, and institutions, is not essential. These socially constructed facts are built less on the biological and more on the existing social structures of power.

We've learned a lot about how these norms of gender create inequality, but what happens when gender can become something empowering? Elliot concludes his story on an uplifting note:

> Today, I felt gender euphoria.
>
> Euphoria is the opposite of dysphoria. I see my reflection, and I love the guy I see. No matter what I'm wearing, I feel nothing but confidence in how I look and who I am. I am brave enough to confront rude people who follow me into bathrooms, to wave menstrual hygiene products at them. I feel like myself. I feel like an Elliot.
>
> Days like today were almost nonexistent before I realized I was trans and began socially transitioning. When I was pretending to be a girl, even the highest joys and deepest sadnesses in my life were missing something, a certain depth, a certain extra grounding in reality. I'm not a girl. No matter how I try, dressing like a girl, acting like one, will always ring hollow, always feel wrong. That isn't who I am.
>
> I'm a boy. Maybe nobody but me sees or feels a difference when I present male, but I feel better. I feel real, alive. I feel every bit of emotion the world has to offer me.
>
> That, no matter how many self-appointed bathroom guardians I have to face, will always be worth it.

We've traced how our intricate system of sexes, genders, and sexualities has evolved. Can we "undo gender," or are we stuck in the paradox of reproducing the binaries we started with, even if we recognize their inequalities? If humans constructed gender as a way to organize, simplify, and control a messy social world, then indeed we can deconstruct it. As Judith Lorber (1994) argued, only when we stop using gender as a basis for dividing up the world—in terms of which jobs people hold, what rights they exercise, how much money they earn, how much control they have over their bodies, with whom they can have sex, and, yes, what bathroom they use—will we find true equality.

MEASURING MANSPLAINING

Sites like **arementalkingtoomuch.com**, the "Time to Talk" app, and others have sprung up recently after it became widely reported that men tend to dominate conversations and talk over women. Sociologists have noted this trend since Carol Stack and Don Zimmerman (1975) famously found that men overwhelmingly interrupt women in everyday conversations. More recent research has continued to support this finding. For example, a recent study by the *Harvard Business Review* used 15 years of oral argument transcripts to show that male Supreme Court justices interrupt each other three times less often than they interrupt their female peers (Jacobi & Schweers, 2017). And it's not just a matter of interruptions: Compared to women, men also tend to take up more conversational airtime in social settings from the classroom to the boardroom.

TRY IT!

Observe a class discussion and measure how much time men speak versus how much time women speak. You can try any of the apps or websites mentioned above, or simply use a stopwatch. It would be ideal to sit in on a class you're not taking (but be sure to check with the instructor first). And don't spill the beans about your project—if your research subjects know what you're measuring, you'll probably get lousy results.

　　While you're measuring female versus male airtime, also note how many times a male student interrupts a female student and vice versa.

THINK ABOUT IT

Once you have your results, compare the amount of airtime to the proportion of men and women in the class. Did men disproportionately dominate the conversation? Did men interrupt women more often than women interrupted men? Did these gender dynamics vary intersectionally—that is, for example, by the race of the would-be speakers?

   Whether or not the results of your study support the finding that men are socialized to talk over women, reflect on the assumptions you made in performing the experiment. Did a two-category scorecard force you to make any assumptions about the gender of individuals—assumptions that you might not have made without discrete categories?

9

RACE AS WE KNOW IT HAS NO
DETERMINISTIC BIOLOGICAL BASIS:
ALL THE SAME, RACE IS SO
POWERFUL THAT IT CAN HAVE
LIFE-OR-DEATH CONSEQUENCES.

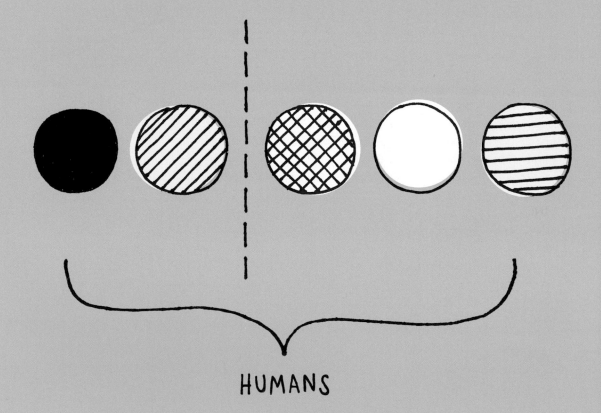

HUMANS

Race

"I found my baby sister!" I declared to my mother, wheeling a carriage around for her to see the newest member of our family, whom I had just kidnapped. I was not quite three years old, and the toddler was only a few months younger than that, with cornrows braided so tightly on her little head that they pulled the brown skin of her face tautly upward. I remember that she was smiling up at me, and I must have taken her smile as permission to swipe the unattended stroller from the courtyard of our housing complex. Given the history of forceable removal of children from Black families during slavery (and from Native American families), my action had a nefarious resonance with racism in the United States that my own White privilege blinded me from seeing at the time.

"No, you haven't!" my mother gasped, putting a hand over her open mouth. The child was quickly returned to her frantically searching mother, despite my tearful protests.

This story fascinates me today: I wanted a baby sister so badly that I kidnapped a Black child, not realizing that race is a primary way we divide families. How could I be so oblivious to the meaning of race—something that years later feels so natural, so innate? To my childhood self, race was neither a meaningful category nor an obvious one. In the largely minority housing project where I grew up in the 1970s, race was not something mutable, like a freckle or hairstyle; it defined who looked like whom, who was allowed to be in the group and who wasn't. But for my sister and me, as Whites in a predominantly minority community, race was turned inside out. We had no idea that we belonged to the majority group, the privileged one. We just thought we didn't belong.

Is race real? You might consider this question paradoxical. After all, how is a huge part of your identity *not* real? The sociological study of race treats it as yet another social phenomenon that seems natural but isn't. That is, race is a real social distinction, and people around the world and throughout history have drawn sharp lines between "us" and "them" on the basis of race. But as a biological, genetic, geographic, or cultural category, race has fluid and changeable boundaries. In this sense, race caters to the interests of groups that wish to maintain power and social exclusion. To the sociologist, understanding racial differences—including by income, educational attainment, crime rates, and teen pregnancy—means treating differences not just as personal matters but also as pieces of a larger social picture.

Having grown up as a fish out of water, a "honky" in an area of housing projects on New York City's Lower East Side, I've been looking at race with the sociological imagination ever since my failed kidnapping. Now, it's your turn.

By the end of this chapter you'll be able to:

- Define "race" and "ethnicity," and explain how and why these terms are socially constructed.
- Trace changing conceptions of race across historical place and time.
- Explain how race functions in the real world with varied social and institutional effects.
- Identify the four primary types of inter-group relations and how they impact different racial and ethnic groups.
- Describe the demographics of racial classification in the United States.
- Discuss the societal implications of the changing racial makeup in the United States.

The Myth of Race

Define "race" and "ethnicity," and explain how and why these terms are socially constructed.

RACE

a group of people who share a set of characteristics—typically, but not always, physical ones—and are said to share a common bloodline.

Perhaps you have heard claims that race is fake, that it's "just a myth." Race refers to a group of people who share a set of characteristics—typically, but not always, physical ones—and, therefore, supposedly share also a common bloodline. People obviously have different physical appearances, including eye color, hair texture, and skin color, so it's perhaps puzzling to hear that (biological) racial differences somehow do not exist. To speak of the myth of race is to say that it is largely a social construction, a set of stories we tell ourselves to organize reality and make sense of the world, rather than a fixed biological or natural reality. In this sense, it resembles the socially constructed notions of childhood and adolescence that we discussed in Chapter 4. We tell the set of stories over and over and, collectively, believe in it and act on it, therefore making it real through practices such as largely separate marriage and reproductive communities. But we could organize our social distinctions a different way (for example, based on foot size or hair color), and indeed, throughout history, we have told this set of stories in myriad ways.

Take, for example, the following passage from an 1851 issue of *Harper's Weekly Magazine*, in which the author attempts to assess the character of a certain racial group based on facial features or expressions—a pseudoscience known as physiognomy. Try to guess which race the author is describing:

> [They are] distinctly marked—the small and somewhat upturned nose, the Black tint of the skin. . . . [They] are ignorant, and as a consequence thereof, are idle, thriftless, poor, intemperate, and barbarian. . . . Of course they will violate our laws, these wild bisons leaping over the fences which easily restrain the civilized domestic cattle, will commit great crimes of violence, even capital offences, which certainly have increased as of late.

Many people, knowledgeable about the history of racism in the United States, might guess that the minority group in question here is African Americans. This passage was written, in fact, about Irish immigrants, who in late-nineteenth-century America struggled to assimilate amid fierce and widespread racism (Knobel, 1986). It was believed that the Irish were a distinct category of people who carried innate differences in their blood, differences that made them permanently inferior to their White American neighbors.

When the term *race* comes up in the United States today, we typically think of five or so categories: Black, White, Latino, Asian, and other. (These are not the official categories of the U.S. Census, but they are close.) However, at the turn of the twentieth century, Americans categorized themselves into anywhere from 36 to 75 different races that they organized into hierarchies, with Anglo-Saxon at the top followed by Slav, Mediterranean, Hebrew, and so on down the list (Jacobson, 1998). Even though the United States was a nation of immigrants, many Americans doubted whether "ethnic stock," such as the Irish, could be fit for self-governance in the new democracy.

In 1790, Congress passed the first naturalization law, limiting the rights of citizenship to "free White persons." This law strikes us today as obviously restrictive because it granted naturalization only to free Whites, thereby coloring American citizenship. In doing so, it also set up an initially broad understanding of "Whiteness," an umbrella term that in common parlance included not just Anglo but also Slavic, Celtic, and Teutonic (German) Europeans. However, as millions of immigrants surged to the shores of

EVERYTHING OBNOXIOUS TO US, SHALL BE ABOLISHED.

SLAUGHTER OF PEACEFUL LAW-ABIDING IRISH CITIZENS MASSACRED BY RIOTOUS MILITIA.

SEE THE IRISH PAPERS.

FENIAN COUNCILS

HANG THE DUTCH GOVERNOR

ENGLISH GOLD

IT IS DOUBTFUL IF THE AMERICAN REPUBLIC CAN STAND THE TABLET

OUR LIBERTY HAS BEEN TAKEN AWAY. KILLING ORANGEMEN

DOWN WITH THE BASE HIRELING POLICE.

PEACEFUL CITIZENS MUST AVENGE THE MASSACRE OF THE 12TH INSTANT.

THE WRETCH THE BUTCHER OF DUTCH DESCENT.

MASS MEETING WE MUST RULE.

GUN POWDER

UNCLE SAM'S

Th. Nast.

THE USUAL IRISH WAY OF DOING THINGS.

An anti-immigration cartoon from an 1871 issue of *Harper's Weekly*. How have attitudes about race changed over the course of American history?

RACISM

the belief that members of separate races possess different and unequal traits.

America—25 million European immigrants arrived between 1880 and World War I—the notion of "free White persons" was reconsidered. With an Irish-born population of more than 1 million in 1860, Americans began to theorize racial differences within the White populace. Questions arose in the popular press and imagination, such as "Who should count as White?" "Whom do we want to be future generations of Americans?" "Who is fit for self-governance?" The inclusiveness of "White persons" splintered into a range of Anglos and "barbarous" others, and Americans began to distinguish among Teutons, Slavs, Celtics, and even the "swarthy" Swedes. The Immigration Act of 1924 formalized the exclusive definition of Whiteness by imposing immigration restrictions based on a quota system that limited the yearly number of immigrants from each country. The law set an annual ceiling of 18,439 immigrants from eastern and southern Europe, following the recommendation of a report stating that northern and western Europeans were of "higher intelligence" and thus ideal "material for American citizenship" (Jacobson, 1998).

This early line of thinking about Whiteness reflects a racist ideology. Racism describes the belief that members of separate races possess different and unequal traits coupled with the power to restrict freedoms based on those differences. Three key beliefs characterize racist thinking: that humans are divided into distinct bloodlines and/or physical types; that these bloodlines or physical traits are linked to distinct cultures, behaviors, personalities, and intellectual abilities; and that certain groups are superior to others.

European immigration slowed during World War I and essentially came to a halt as a result of the 1924 National Origins Act, while internal African American migration from the rural South to the industrial North skyrocketed. These shifts, along with the solidification of the one-drop rule (see later in the chapter), shifted national attention away from White–nonwhite relations toward White–Black relations. Whites of "ethnic stock" were drawn back into the earlier, broad category of White, thereby reuniting Anglos and other Europeans. Public horror at Nazi crimes following the conclusion of World War II further strengthened the idea of Whiteness as an inclusive racial category.

Today, we view Irish descent as a matter of ethnic—not racial—identification, a reason to celebrate on St. Patrick's Day. I know this first-hand: being one-eighth Irish and having an Irish-WASP (White Anglo-Saxon

Protestant) name like Dalton Conley entitles me to free drinks on the Irish holiday. Irish American is no longer considered a restrictive racial category, as once was the case. We take whiteness for granted today, as a natural part of the landscape. But dig back just a hundred years into the unnatural history of race, and you might not even recognize it. Not only have groups of people been categorized differently over time, showing that there is nothing natural about how we classify groups into races today, but the very concept of race itself has changed over time as well.

RACE VERSUS ETHNICITY

If race and ethnicity are both social constructions, what's the difference between them anyway? Some books use the terms interchangeably; most subsume *race* under the umbrella label of "ethnicity." Today's understanding of race describes it as:

- *Externally imposed:* Someone *else* defines you as Black, White, or other.

- *Involuntary:* It's not up to you to decide to which category you belong; someone else puts you there.

- *Usually based on physical differences:* Those unreliable bumps on your head.

- *Hierarchical:* Not White? Take a number down the ranks.

- *Exclusive:* You don't get to check more than one box.

- *Unequal:* It's about power conflicts and struggles.

This last point allows us to make sense of groups like the Burakumin and Muslim Americans. Racial groupings are about domination and struggles for power, serving as organizing principles for social inequality and a means of legitimating exclusion and harassment.

Ethnicity, one's ethnic affiliation, is by contrast

- *Voluntary:* I choose to identify with my one-eighth Irish background (it makes me feel special, so why not?).

- *Self-defined:* It is embraced by group members from within.

- *Nonhierarchical:* Hey, I'm Irish, you're German. *Great!*

- *Fluid and multiple:* I'm Irish *and* German. *Even better!*

- *Cultural:* It is based on differences in practices such as language, food, music, and so on.

- *Planar:* It is much less about unequal power than race is.

ETHNICITY

one's ethnic quality or affiliation. It is voluntary, self-defined, nonhierarchical, fluid and multiple, and based on cultural differences, not physical ones per se.

Ethnicity is like a nationality, not in the sense of carrying the rights and duties of citizenship but in the sense of identifying with a past or future nationality. (There is, for example, a Kurdish ethnicity even though there has yet to be a Kurdistan.) The story of a friend of mine might help clarify the distinction between race and ethnicity: She was born in Korea to Korean parents, but she was adopted shortly after birth by an Italian couple who brought her back to Italy and raised her there. She never learned to speak Korean and does not enjoy Korean cuisine. She is, in fact, an excellent cook of Italian food and an Italian film maven. She is an Italian citizen with an Italian last name who self-identifies as Italian. At one point in her life, she came to the United States to study. By living in the country of her citizenship, she had developed an Italian identity that became her ethnic identity. She bonded with fellow Italian speakers in the United States, for example, and went to Italian restaurants to watch when big soccer games were broadcast. However, the U.S. racial system perceived her differently than she presented herself: Whites and Blacks and Asians treated her as Asian based on how she looked. She had no control over this externally imposed identity. Her racial "Asian-ness" overpowered her ethnic "Italian-ness" based on appearances alone.

For Americans, Herbert Gans (1979b) called the voluntary, chosen form of ethnic identification "symbolic ethnicity." While asserting symbolic ethnic identity was particularly difficult for my Italian friend, for most White middle-class Americans today, symbolic ethnicity is largely a matter of choice. It has no risk of stigma and confers the pleasures of feeling like an individual.

In this way, the differences between race and ethnicity underscore the privileged position of Whites in America, who have the freedom to pick and choose their identities, to wave a flag in a parade, or to whip up Grandma's traditional recipe and freely show their ethnic backgrounds. The surge of ethnic pride among White Americans today implies a false conception of ethnicity as voluntary for everyone; however, nonwhite Americans such as African Americans, Latinxs, and Asians (like my friend) lack the freedom to express symbolic ethnicity. As soon as someone classifies you as racially different on the basis of your physical features, you lose the ability to choose your ethnic identity. It becomes racialized—subsumed under a forced identifier, label, or racial marker of "otherness" that you cannot escape. Thus, although the term *ethnicity* commonly refers to Latinx, Black, Asian, and Irish backgrounds, being Irish in America is an affiliation that a person can turn on or off at will. You can never *not* be Asian or Black: Your body gives away your otherness, no matter how much you want to blend in.

To be Black in America is to be just that—Black. Some scholars argue that this is the fundamental issue about race in America. Until recently, Blacks were considered a monolithic group. They were unique among racial groups in that their ethnic (tribal, language group, and national) distinctions were deliberately wiped out during the slave trade in order to prevent

SYMBOLIC ETHNICITY

a nationality, not in the sense of carrying the rights and duties of citizenship but in the sense of identifying with a past or future nationality. For later generations of White ethnics, it is something not constraining but easily expressed, with no risks of stigma and all the pleasures of feeling like an individual.

social organization and revolt (Eyerman, 2001), resulting in the stripping of "ethnic honor." Alex Haley's landmark novel *Roots* (1976) raised an awareness among African Americans about tracing their ethnic rather than racial identity. This is changing now as more African Americans trace their roots to specific places in Africa through genealogical research or DNA testing. Likewise, immigration from Africa and the Caribbean has created distinctly recognizable national groups of origin among the U.S. Black pop-

Crowds line the street at the St. Patrick's Day Parade in New York City. How is this an example of symbolic ethnicity?

ulation. Finally, the presidential campaign of Barack Obama led, perhaps, to a symbolic expansion of who counts as Black within the African American community: even the son of a White, Kansan mother and a Kenyan father who has half-Asian and fully African half-siblings. Though some African Americans initially struggled to embrace Obama and his mixed racial heritage as "Black like us," their attitudes would have had little impact on the wider perception of Obama as a Black man because of the continuing significance of the one-drop rule in America. Indeed, the White nationalist backlash that followed Obama's inauguration, which continued through the campaign and election of Donald Trump, suggests that the one-drop rule is alive and well. That is, the fact that Obama was biracial and not a descendant of enslaved U.S. ancestors did not seem to matter to Americans who cheered his ascent or those who wished for his downfall.

The Concept of Race from the Ancients to Alleles

▌ Trace changing conceptions of race across historical place and time.

How did we get to the current conceptions of race and ethnicity? Since they are social constructions, they have evolved much over the course of global history. Indeed, some scholars have claimed that the idea of race did not exist in the ancient world (Fredrickson, 2002; Hannaford, 1996; Smedley, 1999; Snowden, 1983). Well, it did, and it didn't. It existed in the sense that the ancients recognized physical differences and grouped people accordingly. In ancient Egypt, for example, physical markers were linked to geography. Believing that people who looked a certain way came from a certain part of the world, the Egyptians spoke, for instance, of the "pale, degraded race of Arvad" and designated their darker-skinned neighbors the "evil race of Ish." The Chinese also linked physical variation to geography, as laid out in a Chinese creation myth. As the ancient tale goes, a goddess cooked human beings in an oven. Some humans were burned Black and sent to live in Africa. The underdone ones turned out White and were sent to Europe. Those humans cooked just right, a perfect golden brown, were the Chinese.

However, in the ancient worlds of Greece, Rome, and early Christendom, the idea of race did not exist as we know it today, as a biological package of traits carried in the bloodlines of distinct groups, each with a separate way of being (culture), acting (behavior), thinking (intelligence), and looking (appearance). The Greek philosopher Hippocrates, for instance, believed that physical markers such as skin color were the result of different environmental factors, much as the surface of a plant reflects the constitution of its soil and the amount of sunlight and water it receives. To be sure, the Greeks liked the looks of their fellow Greeks the best, but the very notion of race goes against Aristotle's principle of civic association on which Greek society was based. The true test of a person was to be found in his (women were excluded) civic actions. Similarly, the Romans maintained a brutal system of slavery, but those they enslaved, as well as their citizens, represented various skin colors and geographic origins. The ancients may have used skin color to tell one person from the next—they weren't color-blind—but they didn't discriminate in the sense of making judgments about people on the basis of their racial category without regard to their individual merit (Hannaford, 1996). The notion has been so thoroughly displaced by racialized thinking that to us modern Americans, imagining a society without racial distinctions feels almost impossibly idealistic.

RACE IN THE EARLY MODERN WORLD

Modern racial thinking developed in the mid-seventeenth century in parallel with global changes, such as the Protestant Reformation in Europe, the Age of Exploration, and the rise of capitalism. For example, European colonizers, confronted with people living in newly discovered lands, interpreted human physical differences first with biblical and later with scientific explanations, and race proved a rather handy organizing principle to legitimate the imperial adventure of conquest, exploitation, and colonialism. To make sense of what they considered the "primitive" and "degraded" races of Africa, Europeans turned to a biblical story in the book of Genesis, the curse of Ham. According to this obscure passage, when Noah had safely navigated his ark over the flood, he got drunk and passed out naked in his tent. When he woke from his stupor, Noah learned that his youngest son, Ham, had seen him naked, whereas his other sons had respectfully refused to behold the spectacle. Noah decided to curse Ham's descendants, saying, "A slave of slaves shall he be to his brothers" (Gourevitch, 1998). European Christians and scientists interpreted this tale to mean that Ham was the original Black man, and all Black people were his unfortunate, degraded descendants. For an expanding Europe and America, the Hamitic myth justified colonialism and slavery.

When the divine right of conquest lost its sway, science led the way as an authority behind racial thinking, legitimating race by scientific mandate. Scientific racism, what today we call the nineteenth-century theories of race, brought a period of feverish investigation into the origins, explanations, and classifications of race. In 1684, François Bernier (1625–1688) proposed a new geography based not on topography or even political borders but on the body, from facial lineaments to bodily configurations. Bernier devised a scheme of four or five races based on the following geographic regions:

- *Europe* (excluding Lapland), *South Asia, North Africa,* and *America:* people who shared climates and complexions

- *Africa proper:* people who had thick lips, flat noses, Black skin, and a scanty beard

- *Asia proper:* people who had White skin, broad shoulders, flat faces, little eyes, and no beard

- *Lapps* (small traditional communities living around the northern regions of Finland and Russia): people who were ugly, squat, small, and animal-like

Scientific racism sought to explain the differences between White Europeans—who constituted the norm, according to the French scientist Comte de Buffon (1707–1788)—and other groups that they encountered. This way of thinking, called ethnocentrism, the judgment of other groups by one's own standards and values, has plagued scientific studies of "otherness." In Buffon's classification schemes, anyone different from Europeans was a deviation from the norm. His pseudoscientific research, like all racial thinking of the time, justified imperial exploits by automatically classifying nonwhites as abnormal, improper, and inferior.

With the publication of *On the Natural Varieties of Mankind* in 1775, Johann Friedrich Blumenbach (1752–1840), widely considered the founder of anthropology, cataloged variation by race in part using differences in head formation, a pseudoscience called phrenology. Blumenbach's aim was to classify the world based on the different types of bumps he could measure on people's skulls. Based on these skull measurements, he came up with five principal

Charts like this one helped phrenologists interpret the shapes of human skulls. How did nineteenth-century theorists use this sort of pseudoscience to justify racism?

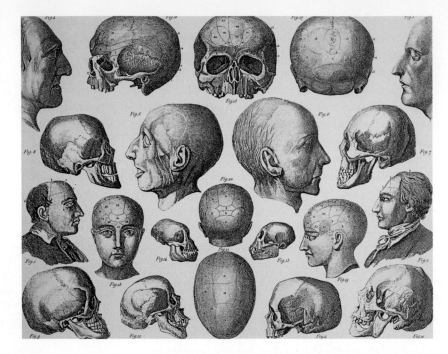

varieties of humans: Caucasian, Mongoloid, Ethiopian, American, and Malay. Caucasians (named after the people who live on the southern slopes of the Georgian region of eastern Europe), he decided, were the superlatives of the races based on their excellent skull qualities. Scholars like Blumenbach and Immanuel Kant (1724–1804), who argued for a link between inner character and outer physiognomy and further claimed that these individual markers were also imprinted on an entire nation's moral life, reinforced conceptions of race as a set of physical traits with powerful social implications.

However, many people still believe that racial differences resulted from variations in climate (therefore, race could not be immutable or innate to the soul). In fact, in 1787, the Reverend Minister Samuel Stanhope Smith (president of what is now Princeton University), wrote an essay in which he proposed that dark skin should be thought of as a "universal freckle." Differences in skin shade, he maintained, were really just like different levels of suntans. He believed that if an African from the sub-Sahara were transplanted to Scandinavia, his dark-brown skin would turn lighter over the course of generations (and perhaps the underlying social and cognitive characteristics associated with race would change as well). Notice how Smith's pliable view of race captures a spirit of ontological equality: We all have at least the potential to be the same, that is, if we were just exposed to the same environments—sun and all. Ontological equality is the philosophical and religious notion that all people are created equal.

The Reverend Smith's line of thinking also demonstrates the scientific influence of Lamarckism, now a largely discredited footnote in the history of

ONTOLOGICAL EQUALITY

the philosophical and religious notion that all people are created equal.

scientific thought. Lamarckism theorizes that acquired traits can be passed down across generations. For example, an acquired attribute such as flexibility, language skill, or sun exposure can be passed down to a person's offspring, affecting generations to come.

Charles Darwin, who in 1859 published his theory of natural selection, debunked Lamarckism. Darwin argued that acquired attributes could not be transmitted; instead, change can occur only through the positive selection of mutations. Darwin's theory had an enormous impact on how people thought of race. In effect, it called into question the popular belief that climate influenced racial difference and instead offered an account of deeply rooted and long-standing racial lineages. What's more, humankind had a new trajectory in which some groups were seen to have advanced (or evolved) more than others. The popular nineteenth-century notion of social Darwinism was the application of Darwinian ideas to society—namely, the evolutionary "survival of the fittest." Social theorist Herbert Spencer (1820–1903) promulgated the idea that some people, defined by their race, are better fit for survival than others and therefore intended by nature to dominate inferior races. A new puzzle arose with Darwinian ideas: What, if not inherited climate change, could explain the development of humans along such radically different lines?

Scientists now had to arrive at a new explanation of physical difference among humans, and the scientific community confronted a growing debate: monogenism versus polygenism. The debate turned on the origins of the various races of humans. Were humans a united species, or did we come from separate origins? Monogenists, including religious traditionalists, believed that humans were one species, united under God. Polygenists believed that different races were, in fact, distinct species. Darwin sided with the monogenists, calling the notion of different species absurd. (Politics, it is said, makes for strange bedfellows. It certainly did in this case, as Darwinists and religious traditionalists, usually opposed, became allies in arguing that all humans were one species.)

Even though the monogenists won the debate, the notion of separate roots and distinct reproductive genetic histories has had a lasting impact on how we think of human difference. Under the model of natural selection, human difference must have evolved over tens or hundreds of thousands of years (if not millions), not just over a few generations in relative sun or shade. Such a vast time frame only reinforced the perceived differences among races (and not just on a superficial basis).

TWENTIETH-CENTURY CONCEPTS OF RACE

The problem with race for those who want to reify the concept has always been that if race is such an obvious, natural means of dividing the world, why does no foolproof way of determining racial boundaries exist? According to

Herbert Spencer coined the term "survival of the fittest." How did Spencer draw from the work of Darwin to justify racism?

SOCIAL DARWINISM

the application of Darwinian ideas to society—namely, the evolutionary "survival of the fittest."

Bhagat Singh Thind.

the social historian Ian Haney López (1995), the U.S. Supreme Court grappled with this question in the late nineteenth and early twentieth centuries. In a landmark case in 1923, for example, Dr. Bhagat Singh Thind, a Sikh from India, was denied American citizenship. The Supreme Court ruled that he did not qualify as a "free White person," despite being the first Indian Sikh inducted into the U.S. Army in World War I. In previous cases, the Court relied on a combination of scientific evidence and "common knowledge" to decide who counted as White. But the Thind case posed a particular challenge because leading anthropologists at the time uniformly classified Asian Indians as members of the "Caucasian" race. The very notion of Whiteness was at stake: If the anthropologists were right, then the commonly accepted conception of Whiteness would have to radically change to include dark-skinned immigrants like Thind. The Court therefore decried science as failing to distinguish human difference sufficiently, relying on common knowledge alone to deny Thind's claims to Whiteness. As the Court put it, "The words 'free White persons' are words of common speech, to be interpreted in accordance with the understandings of the common man" (Haney López, 1995).

The judges in the Thind case were not the only people who attempted to define Whiteness and nonwhiteness in the absence of a stable scientific taxonomy of race. In Nazi Germany, for example, race posed certain key questions: How can Jewishness be detected? Are Jews a race or a religious group? Both, actually: They are a religious group that has been racialized. Scholars have pointed out that the seeds of racism may be traced to anti-Judaism among early Christians, who forced Jews to convert. Anti-Semitism grew in the eleventh century and was based on the belief that getting rid of Jews was preferable to converting them. But Jewishness was still a social identity at this point—a matter of having religious beliefs that differed from the norm. Anti-Semitism did not turn into racism until the idea took hold that Jews were intrinsically inferior, having innate differences separating them from their Christian neighbors (Fredrickson, 2002; Smedley, 1999). In Nazi Germany, where Jews were believed to have such innate and inherited differences, the problem remained: How can a person be identified as Jewish? Categorization became an obsession during the Nazis' program of racial purification. They devised a "scientific" way to detect Jewishness by measuring ratios of forehead to nose size to face length, but they had little luck in nailing down a reliable method for making such a determination (hence, Jews in Nazi-occupied countries wore a yellow Star of David as a marker of their identity by law). A similar practice appeared in rural America in the 1960s, where many Whites similarly failed in trying to distinguish themselves from their neighbors who had a mix of European, Indigenous, and African ancestry (known as "tri-racial isolates") by searching for signs on the body, such as differences in fingernails, feet, gums, and lines on the palm of a hand. In exasperation, some Whites reported having to rely on good, old-fashioned "instinct" to distinguish themselves from nonwhites (Berry, 1963).

One means of drawing sharp racial boundaries in America was the one-drop rule, asserting that just "one drop" of Black blood makes a person Black. The rule developed out of the laws passed in many U.S. states forbidding miscegenation, or interracial marriage. By 1910, most Whites in the United States had accepted this doctrine. The one-drop rule played an integral role in maintaining the Jim Crow system of segregation upheld in the 1896 Supreme Court decision in *Plessy v. Ferguson*. In the American South, anyone of Black lineage fell on the unfortunate side of the racial divide, and the rule essentially cleaved America into two societies: one Black, one White. This division meant again clumping together all "White ethnics" into one united category. As F. James Davis notes (1991), much in the same way that the rule united Whites, it also erased stratification *within* the Black community that had previously been based on skin tone.

Scientific racial thought slowly passed out of vogue as theories of cultural difference gained momentum among American intellectuals from the 1920s to the 1940s. Anthropologist Franz Boas dismissed the claims of the biological basis of discrete races, and sociologists such as Robert Park advanced new ideas about culture's importance in determining human behavior. Race, these thinkers argued, was less about fixed inherited traits than about particular social circumstances. Furthermore, when World War II exposed the kind of atrocities to which scientific racism could lead, it became socially and scientifically inappropriate to discuss race in biological terms. With the decline of scientific racism and the shift toward cultural theories of race and ethnicity, the government gradually chipped away at the Immigration Act of 1924 and then completely repealed it in 1965. Don't let the formal denunciation of racial thinking fool you, however. Cultural explanations of race often reflect a disguised racist ideology just as much as biological ones do.

Despite the ideas of scholars such as Boas and Park, the old idea of fixed, biological racial differences remains alive and well today, although in modified form. The search for racial boundaries continues in the twenty-first century with the rise of molecular

ONE-DROP RULE

the belief that "one drop" of Black blood makes a person Black, a concept that evolved from U.S. laws forbidding miscegenation.

MISCEGENATION

the technical term for interracial marriage, literally meaning "a mixing of kinds"; it is politically and historically charged— sociologists generally prefer the term *exogamy* or *outmarriage*.

Marion West (center) embraces Vy Higgensen (right). The distant cousins discovered their relationship after the results of separate DNA tests were entered into a database.

CRITICAL RACE THEORY: WHAT'S ALL THE FUSS ABOUT?

You may have heard about politicians and school boards banning or trying to ban books they consider teaching "critical race theory" (CRT). Most books that have suffered this fate have nothing actually to do with critical race theory but, rather, simply touch on the theme of racial inequality in U.S. history. Critical race theory, in fact, is almost never discussed in K–12 education. Indeed, until very recently, it was not even talked about much in colleges but did make the curricula of many law schools. So, what's all the fuss about? What exactly is critical race theory?

While critical race theory encompasses a large movement in which there is no dogmatic consensus, there are some basic principles that are largely shared. Some of these tenets of critical race theory we have actually already covered. Some we have not yet touched upon.

- Race is a social construction.
- Race is constructed to oppress nonwhite people, especially Blacks.
- Racism is central to the organization of society—that is, it is the rule, not the exception.
- The nature of stereotypes changes, but they always serve to oppress the out-group (namely, Blacks in the U.S. context).

CRITICAL RACE THEORY

a legal theory that asserts that race is not natural but rather is socially constructed in order to oppress nonwhites and that racism is inherent in U.S. legal institutions.

genetics. DNA research now allows us to look deeper than the bumps on our heads, deeper than skin tone or palm lines. Today, you can find a number of DNA testing companies offering you an inside look at your heritage. For as little as $70 or so, a testing kit arrives in the mail, you swab your mouth according to the directions, and then send the swab to the company. Your "real" identity comes back from the lab in about seven weeks.

Wayne Joseph, a 53-year-old Louisiana high-school principal with Creole roots, did just that. Born and raised Black, but having light skin,

- Racism manifests in the forms of institutional bias, microaggressions, and other interpersonal discrimination.

- When racial progress is made, it is made because it serves the interests of Whites.

- People of color themselves are uniquely qualified to speak about racism.

- Racial identity is intersectional. That is, the experience of racism is different for people within the same race based on their other identities (such as being queer, religious, male, and so on).

What makes critical race theory such a hot button topic for politicians like Ted Cruz?

This is, of course, a partial list and some of these claims are more controversial than others. For example, there are many scholars who would question the argument that when the Supreme Court decided *Brown v. Board of Education* in 1954, it was driven by White interests, as law professor Derek Bell has argued. There are other scholars who agree that racism is pervasive but stop short of claiming that race—and White supremacy specifically—is the centrally organizing principle of U.S. society. Other ideas from critical race theory are more widely accepted: specifically, that race is a social construct, that race is experienced intersectionally, and that racism manifests in a number of ways.

Joseph received some unexpected results about his ancestry: His genetic makeup is 57 percent Indo-European, 39 percent Native American, 4 percent East Asian, and 0 percent African (Kaplan, 2003). Despite the findings, Joseph continues to embrace his identity as Black. As he put it to reporters, "The question ultimately is, are you who you say you are, or are you who you are genetically?"

Cells, alleles, and gene sequences have become the new tools of science that promise to reveal our racial truths, but the old idea hasn't much changed—that we can trace a biological and social package of traits inside our bodies to determine our lineage—despite our knowledge that humans are biologically one species. The belief that we can draw fine distinctions between ourselves and others based on these genetic traces continues to inform contemporary social stereotypes, labeling individuals with misconceptions about appearance, genetic makeup, and capability.

Racial Realities

Explain how race functions in the real world with varied social and institutional effects.

The biological validity of discrete racial categories—be it the bumps on your skull or the DNA in your blood—may be debunked, but in social life, race is real, with real consequences. Just ask someone of the Burakumin race in Japan. Today making up anywhere from 1 to 3 percent of the Japanese population, depending on the estimate, the Burakumin originated as a group of displaced people during fourteenth-century feudal wars (Hankins, 2014). With no connection other than being Japanese, the Burakumin suddenly shared something undesirable—they were homeless, destitute, and forced to wander the countryside together. Imagine all the homeless people today in Miami or Los Angeles suddenly uniting. The Burakumin formed a distinct social category, with complete social closure, their own reproductive pool, their own occupational pool, and so on, although they were not a distinct group genetically. Today, however, outsiders often argue that the Burakumin "are descendants of a less human 'race' than the stock that fathered the Japanese nation as a whole" (De Vos & Wagatsuma, 1966). Six hundred years later, the Burakumin still display no physical distinctions from their fellow Japanese citizens. For those people in Japan wishing to avoid interrelations with the Burakumin, this lack of distinctiveness poses a dilemma. So for a hefty price, private investigators for hire will confirm the pedigree of your prospective employee, tenant, or future son-in-law.

In Japan, the Burakumin live in ghettos, called *burakus*, and score lower on health, educational achievement, and income compared with their fellow Japanese citizens. Yet when Japanese and Burakumin emigrate to America, the scoring gap narrows dramatically. The gap

The Burakumin are a minority who can be distinguished from the rest of the Japanese population only by genealogical detectives. Prejudice against this group often leads to homelessness.

distinguishing the Burakumin from other Japanese is meaningless outside of their home country. Again, we see that shared social and cultural meanings give race meaning, extending far past physical or biological differences.

To take an example of racial realities closer to home, consider the consequences of being Arab—or perhaps I should say being perceived as Muslim—in post-9/11 America. In an interview for this book, Jen'nan Read used the image of a Venn diagram to explain that "Arab is an ethnicity; being a Muslim is a religious categorization. In the U.S. context a lot of Muslims and Arabs seem to be the same group. In fact, most Arabs in the United States are Christians who immigrated prior to World War One. And most Muslims are actually not Arab . . . one-third are South Asian, one-third are Arab, and about a quarter are African Americans who have converted to the religion" (Conley, 2009i). In the United States, Muslims are often identified with Islamic terrorists and lumped into a fixed racial category as a dangerous and undemocratic "other," seen as separate from, and inferior and hostile to, Christians.

DIGITAL.WWNORTON.COM/YOUMAYASK8

To see my interview with Jen'nan Read, go to
digital.wwnorton.com/youmayask8

In the first year after the events of 9/11, the number of anti-Muslim hate crimes shot up 1,600 percent (Read, 2008). And though reported crimes dropped over the following decade and a half, such backlash resurged after the 2016 presidential campaign of Donald Trump, which some see as linked to his tendency to retweet incendiary remarks or memes. In the first year of his administration, anti-Islamic hate crimes rose by 17 percent from the prior year (marking the third year of rise, which suggests that Trump's behavior was perhaps more of a reflection than a cause) (Birnbaum, 2018). Most notable were mosque torchings, cemetery vandalism, and an incident in Bloomington, Minnesota, when a bomb exploded in a mosque in an act Governor Mark Dayton called terrorism (Bromwich, 2017). The following year, total hate crimes decreased slightly, but the number of violent incidents rose (Treisman, 2019).

In the wake of anxiety about terrorists, and several years into the war on terror, Muslims in America have undergone what scholars call racialization, the formation of a new racial identity by drawing ideological boundaries of difference around a formerly unnoticed group of people. These days, any brown-skinned man with a beard or woman with a headscarf is subject to

RACIALIZATION

the formation of a new racial identity by drawing ideological boundaries of difference around a formerly unnoticed group of people.

A group of Sikhs protest after the murder of Balbir Singh Sodhi.

threats, violence, and harassment. And men with turbans bear some of the worst discrimination, although nearly all men who wear turbans in the United States are Sikh, members of one of the world's largest religious groups, which originated in India. Four days after 9/11, Balbir Singh Sodhi, a Sikh living in Mesa, Arizona, was shot five times and killed in the gas station he owned. He was the first victim of an anti-Muslim epidemic, and he wasn't even Muslim. In one Harvard study, 83 percent of Sikhs interviewed said that they or someone they knew personally had experienced a hate crime or incident, and another 64 percent felt fear or danger for their family and themselves (Han, 2006). The experiences of White Americans who convert to Islam demonstrate the dangerous effects of appearances. One woman, despite having fair skin and green eyes, has been categorized by people as Palestinian when she wears the Muslim headscarf, called the *hijab*. She's even heard, "Go back to your own country," although she was born and raised in California (Kuruvil, 2006; Spurlock, 2005).

People make stereotyped assumptions, especially ones that link race to religion, based on appearance. In fact, two-thirds of Arabs in the United States are not Muslim but Christian (Pew Research Center, 2011a). American Muslims are both a highly diverse population and a very mainstream one. Muslims have lived in North America since the seventeenth century, when they were transported from Africa as enslaved people, and about 42 percent of Muslims were born in America (Pew Research Center, 2017a). As a group, they are assimilated with the mainstream, having income and education levels similar to those of the rest of the population. By and large, they hold fast to the ideas that education is important and that hard work pays off in a successful career. Doesn't sound too radical, does it? That's because the overwhelming majority of Muslims in America and throughout the world strongly disagree with Islamic extremism (Pew Research Center, 2011a). Of course, no racial boundaries are drawn along accurate lines or real differences, but once racialized, a group faces real social consequences.

PREJUDICE, DISCRIMINATION, AND THE NEW RACISM

The social fallout of race occurs both at an individual or interpersonal level and at a structural or societal level. Of course, the micro and macro levels of race mutually reinforce each other (as we learned about with respect to culture more generally in Chapter 3). On the individual level, racism can manifest itself as prejudice or discrimination. Prejudice refers to thoughts and feelings about an ethnic or racial group, whereas discrimination is an act of prejudice. Robert Merton (1949) developed a diagram for thinking about the intersections of prejudice and discrimination (Figure 9.1). One who holds prejudice and discriminates is an "active bigot," the prototypical racist who puts his money (or burning cross) where his (or her) mouth is. Those who are neither prejudiced nor discriminatory are "all-weather liberals," not only espousing ideologies of racial equality or talking the talk, but also walking the walk when faced with real choices.

Many people fall between these two stances. A "timid bigot" is prejudiced but does not discriminate—a closet racist perhaps, who backs down when confronted with an opportunity for racist action. Conversely, one who is not prejudiced but does discriminate is termed a "fair-weather liberal." Despite the fair-weather liberal's inner ideological stance in favor of racial equality, they still discriminate, perhaps without knowing it. For instance, a couple who consider themselves open-minded about race relations may feel compelled to sell their home as soon as they are confronted with new Black neighbors (White flight, as discussed later). Of course, they do not cite residential integration as their motivation for leaving, but instead offer an excuse that has embedded racist reasons, such as the differences in school districts. In fact, the prime time for families to move out of integrated neighborhoods happens to be around the time when the eldest child of the family turns five and begins school.

Active bigots are rarer to come by, because prejudicial viewpoints are largely unacceptable in most of the ostensibly antiracist West. But don't be fooled into thinking that race doesn't matter anymore. It does, and racism is still alive and going strong, although it's veiled in different terms. You just have to know how to look for it. Old-fashioned, overt racism tended to

PREJUDICE

thoughts and feelings about an ethnic or racial group, which lead to preconceived notions and judgments (often negative) about the group.

DISCRIMINATION

harmful or negative acts (not mere thoughts) against people deemed inferior on the basis of their racial category, without regard to their individual merit.

FIGURE 9.1 Merton's Chart of Prejudice and Discrimination

ACTIVE BIGOT (PREJUDICED-DISCRIMINATES)

TIMID BIGOT (PREJUDICED)

FAIR-WEATHER LIBERAL (DISCRIMINATES)

ALL-WEATHER LIBERAL

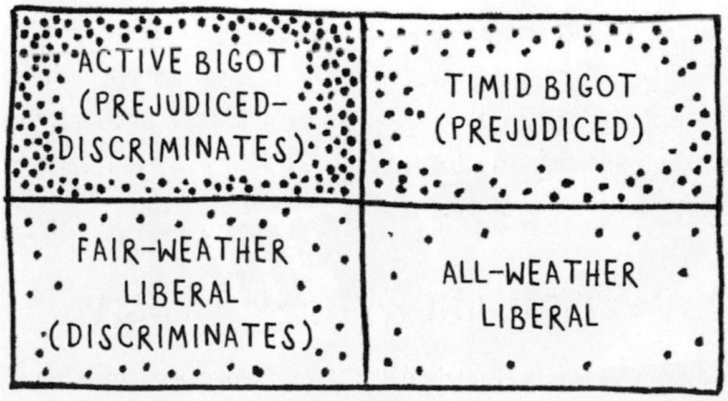

SOURCE: Merton, 1949.

convey three basic ideas: Humans are separable into distinct types; they have essential traits that cannot be changed; and some types of people are just better than others.

Not many people openly make such claims in America today, but scholars still find traces of new strains of racism. Eduardo Bonilla-Silva calls this "color-blind racism." According to Howard Winant (2001), such new racial hegemony comes with "race-neutral" rhetoric and relies more on culture and nationality to explain differences between nonwhites and Whites than immutable physical traits. The new line of thinking replaces biology with culture and presumes that there is something fixed, innate, and inferior about nonwhite cultural values. In America, this kinder, gentler anti-Black ideology is characterized by the persistence of negative stereotyping, the tendency to blame nonwhites for their own problems, and resistance to affirmative action policy (Bobo et al., 1997). Ironically, since the civil rights triumphs of the 1960s, the official stance of formal equality has brought about subtler forms of prejudice and discrimination, making it harder to tackle racism and inequality. When a state proclaims racial equality, White privilege is let off the hook and goes unnoticed.

How do we know that prejudice is still fairly pervasive if people don't express racist attitudes as often? For one, we can test people's implicit attitudes with the Implicit Association Test. This test asks participants to play a game in which they sort words, such as "happiness" or "suffering," into categories labeled, for example, as "pleasant" or "unpleasant." They also sort words, like racially coded names, into racial buckets (like Black or White). The two tasks are then combined so that categories are labeled "Black-Pleasant" and "White-Unpleasant" (and then switched). When the

---

COLOR-BLIND RACISM

the view that racial inequality is perpetuated by a supposedly color-blind stance that ends up reinforcing historical and contemporary inequities, disparate impact, and institutional bias by "ignoring" them in favor of a technically neutral approach.

Right-wing National Democratic Party members protest immigration and refugee policies in Germany. How is this an example of cultural racism?

racial and subjective categories line up with stereotypes held by the participant, the participant is able to do the sorting task more quickly, presumably because it feels more natural and intuitive and requires less conscious effort. These tests are not without their detractors, but they seem to suggest that many people harbor unconscious stereotypes even when they claim to be unprejudiced.

A second important way we know that discrimination occurs even when people say they are not racist is by conducting audit or correspondence studies. An audit study is conducted in person by sending trained actors into a social situation. The actors vary only on their race, and the researchers record the outcome of the interaction. The situation may be applying for a job or a loan, looking for a roommate, or even getting a quote for an auto repair. A correspondence study uses the same approach by sending in applications for jobs, housing, and so on, that are identical, varying only the name (for instance) to signal racial identity. Studies such as these have found, for example, that fictitious Black job applicants get 50 percent fewer callbacks for interviews than made-up White applicants with the exact same résumés (Bertrand & Mullainathan, 2004). Devah Pager conducted an audit study that even showed that a Black applicant with no criminal record for an entry-level job got fewer callbacks than a White applicant with a criminal conviction (Pager, 2003b).

Racial discrimination is not limited to the U.S. context, or even to countries where race is recognized by the government as an official category. In France, for example, the government does not collect information about race, but social scientists have conducted correspondence studies by sending in job applications with identical résumés other than the names being changed. They show that, with all else equal, those with names sounding Arab (Adida et al., 2010) or North African (Pierné, 2013) get fewer callbacks. Racism can exist even when race does not officially exist.

INSTITUTIONAL OR STRUCTURAL RACISM

The abovementioned experiments show that racism can be alive and well even when people say that they are not racist. Racism can even play a substantial role in society even when nobody is racist on an individual level. That is, racism can be baked into the institutions and social structures of a society. Let's take housing as an example.

Homes in Black neighborhoods don't accrue value at the same rate as those in mostly White areas. Property reflects only the value accorded to it in the marketplace. In this vein, when a neighborhood's housing values decline as the proportion of Black residents rises, the price changes provide a record of the economic value of "Blackness." No "active bigots" or otherwise racist individuals are needed to generate this phenomenon. Namely, aside from any personal ideology, Whites have an economic incentive to sell when they sense a neighborhood starting to integrate, as evidence shows that once a neighborhood reaches somewhere between 5 and 20 percent Black, it quickly becomes predominantly Black due to a rash of selling with an accompanying drop in values (Card et al., 2008). And why do Black neighborhoods lose value, all else equal? Because of the flight of Whites (the larger group in the marketplace) due to fear of property price drops. In other words, it's a vicious circle that creates institutional racism in home values. (Meanwhile, property value does not follow the same clear-cut, self-fulling prophecy for other ethnic minorities, although minority enclaves generally have lower real estate values than exclusively White neighborhoods.)

INSTITUTIONAL RACISM

institutions and social dynamics that may seem race-neutral but actually disadvantage minority groups.

The case of race and property values is an example of institutional racism—institutions and social dynamics that may seem race-neutral but actually end up disadvantaging minority groups. Another example is sentencing laws for dealing or consuming cocaine. At the height of a period of panic over crack cocaine infiltrating neighborhoods, the United States passed the Anti–Drug Abuse Act of 1986. This law declared that for sentencing purposes, 1 gram of crack cocaine was equivalent to 100 grams of powdered cocaine. The result was a mandatory minimum sentence of five years for a first-time possession charge for a typical crack user. Because crack was cheaper and more prevalent in low-income, predominantly Black communities, this policy resulted in a huge racial disparity in drug sentences by race. President Obama addressed this issue in 2010 by signing the Fair Sentencing Act, which reduced the sentencing ratio between powder cocaine and crack from 100 to 1 to 18 to 1. This ratio, while an improvement, still leaves a significantly disparate impact by race (Davis, 2011).

Policing can also be a domain where we see institutional racism. The murder of George Floyd and other high-profile cases of police violence against minorities are both a product of direct racism as well as institutional racism. The old-fashioned racism is evident if we ask this counterfactual question: Would Derek Chauvin have knelt on Floyd's neck for nine minutes had Floyd been White? Most people would conclude no. But Floyd's death also reflects institutional racism within the Minneapolis Police Department. For example, there had been 18 complaints against Chauvin, most of which involved interactions with minority residents, and only two resulted in any consequences (letters of reprimand). Moreover, a U.S. Department of Justice investigation found that the majority of shootings by Minneapolis police, mostly against minorities, were unlawful uses of deadly force. Decisions about where and how to deploy police resources, like stop and frisk in New York City, can also reflect institutional racism if not applied equally across White and minority neighborhoods. These examples don't require individual officers to be prejudiced in order to reflect institutional racism if those officers are simply going along with official policy or the collective social norms of the organization.

Hiring patterns by employers show another aspect of institutional racism. With limited information about job applicants, employers may rationally use social networks to recruit employees since informal ties (i.e., references) can provide more reliable information about individuals than paper job applications. Because Whites tend to hold more managerial positions and social networks tend to be segregated by race, this need for additional information on the part of employers also perpetuates racial disparities with no racially explicit motivation.

A related dynamic is called statistical discrimination, where firms use race as a shorthand proxy for having attended poorer schools and having experienced other disadvantages that would lead to less productive performance. Although this dynamic is not completely color-blind, it is different from overt racism in that the motivation is not about race per se but about underlying characteristics that tend to be associated with race. (The audit and correspondence studies mentioned in the previous section try to but cannot always distinguish between statistical discrimination and "taste-based" or overt discrimination.)

Institutional racism can even be encoded into the educational system through test construction. There has been much debate about cultural bias in testing. Beyond this issue, however, is the effect of stereotypes on performance. The psychologists Claude Steele and Joshua Aronson, for example, have shown that they can drive Black students' test scores down just by priming them with negative stereotypes before they sit for the exam (Steele & Aronson, 1998). These are just a few of the ways race can continue to disadvantage certain groups even in an age when overt racial animus may have waned in significance.

HOW STRUCTURAL RACISM MATTERS: THE CASE OF WEALTH

Nonwhites, especially African Americans, Latinxs, and Native Americans, lag behind Whites on a number of social outcomes, from income and educational attainment to crime rates and infant mortality rates. For example, Blacks are half as likely as Whites to graduate from college or hold a professional or managerial job and are twice as likely to be unemployed and to die before their first year of life. As striking as the figures are, net worth most effectively captures the persistence of racial inequality in the United States. If you want to determine your net worth, all you have to do is add up everything you own and subtract from this figure the total amount of your outstanding debt. When you calculate this figure for nonwhite and White families, the differences are glaring. While most of America felt the impact of the housing market crash and 2008–09 recession, African Americans and Latinxs felt the blow far more sharply than Whites. Median wealth for

Whites fell 16 percent, yet African Americans and Latinxs experienced 53 and 66 percent losses, respectively (Pew Research Center, 2011b).

Latinxs are a varied group, but their wealth measures are largely similar to those of African Americans, who have an average household net worth of $14,100 (U.S. Census Bureau, 2022a). The median Latinx family in 2016 had about $31,700 in net assets (U.S. Census Bureau, 2022a). Compare those figures to the $187,300 in household wealth of the average White family (U.S. Census Bureau, 2022a). We know considerably less about Native Americans because reliable data are lacking, but given that they have a poverty rate of 24.3 percent (compared with just 10 percent for Whites), their wealth is not likely to be high (U.S. Census Bureau, 2022e). Asian Americans, however, have low rates of poverty at 10.8 percent (U.S. Census Bureau, 2017b) and high rates of home ownership at about 59 percent (U.S. Census Bureau, 2020a).

This "equity inequality" has grown in the decades since the civil rights progress of the 1960s. What's more, income difference alone cannot explain the wealth gap. That is, the asset gap remains large even when we compare Black and White families at the same income levels. For many among the growing Black and Latinx middle classes, the lack of assets may mean living from paycheck to paycheck, being trapped in a job or neighborhood that is less beneficial in the long run, and not being able to send kids to college. Parents' wealth also predicts children's teenage and young adult outcomes— everything from teenage premarital childbearing to educational attainment to welfare dependency (Conley, 1999).

Equity inequality captures the historical disadvantage of minority groups and the way those disadvantages accrue over time. Institutional barriers to Blacks acquiring property were only one such mechanism. These barriers included redlining by banks (whereby loans, especially mortgages, were not given in predominantly Black neighborhoods seen as higher risk), racially restrictive covenants (whereby owners had to agree to sell their homes to only Whites), and Blacks' disproportionate exclusion from government benefits such as FHA and VA mortgages and Social Security retirement pensions (agricultural and domestic workers, who were largely Black, were initially excluded from these programs; Truman corrected this). Even if those policies have been lifted, their legacy can still be felt today, since wealth is accrued and directly passed on unlike, say, earnings.

Similar processes and policies have decimated the wealth of Native Americans, who went from living off the land (the entire U.S. territory) to being disproportionately impoverished and dispossessed over the course of a century by exploitative U.S. policies. One of the most telling examples of this sort of institutionalized dispossession happened to Japanese Americans. As skilled farmers, Japanese immigrants accrued enough wealth in the early twentieth century to attract resentment, culminating in the 1924 Alien Land Act, which prohibited noncitizens from owning land. Japanese immigrants then found success in business, running nurseries and selling cut flowers, and amassed considerable wealth by 1941, about $140 million cumulatively (Lui, 2004). When World War II broke out and panic spread over the possibility of a treacherous Japanese population in America, the Roosevelt administration mandated a program of internment by Executive Order 9066. Japanese American citizens were placed into camps in the western part of the United States and given only a week to dispose of all their assets, forcing them to sell their homes and businesses to Whites at scandalously low prices (Lui, 2004). The result was a huge, forced transfer of wealth from Japanese to Whites under discriminatory government policy.

Japanese Americans still alive at the time were paid reparations in 1988. Some have argued for a similar policy to compensate African Americans for the institution of slavery (and racially unequal asset policies since Emancipation). Each year, until his retirement in 2017, Congressman John Conyers introduced a bill to study the issue; so far, even the creation of a commission to assess the issue has been blocked. Meanwhile, the tax reform bill known as the Tax Cuts and Jobs Act of 2017 raised the amount of an estate not subject to taxes to $11.2 million. Because the number of African Americans and Hispanics who benefit is extremely small, it will serve to widen the already large racial wealth gap.

What were the consequences of the Japanese internment camps? How are they an example of equity inequality?

In summary, policies intending to address disparities between non-whites and Whites must take into account the extreme wealth gap and its historical trajectory. Policies that aim to improve wages and increase job openings for Blacks, Hispanics, and Native Americans can address only a piece of a larger cycle of wealth inequity and structural inequality. Income from work provides for the day-to-day, week-to-week expenses; wealth is the stuff long-term upward mobility is made of. In other words, wealth gaps not only capture the historical (and contemporary) legacy of racial inequity, but they are also a linchpin in reproducing that same inequality.

Inter-Group Relations

Identify the four primary types of inter-group relations and how they impact different racial and ethnic groups.

What are the social consequences of race in general? Scholars have defined four broad forms that inter-group relations can take: assimilation, pluralism, segregation, and conflict.

In the 1920s, sociologist Robert Park began to wonder what, on the one hand, held together the diverse populations in major American cities and, on the other hand, sustained their cultural differences. He came up with a race relations cycle of stages: contact, competition, accommodation, and assimilation. His model, called straight-line assimilation, was at first accepted as the universally progressive pattern in which immigrants arrive, settle in, mimic the practices and behaviors of the people who are already there, and achieve full assimilation in a newly homogenous country.

Milton Gordon (1964) tweaked Park's model by suggesting multiple kinds of assimilation outcomes. For Gordon, an immigrant population can pass through (or stall in) seven stages of assimilation: cultural, structural, marital, identification, attitude reception, behavior reception, and civic assimilation (Table 9.1).

With Park and Gordon in mind, let's do a thought experiment. Imagine yourself as a Polish immigrant arriving at Ellis Island in 1900. You don't have much money, and you've come to America in search of opportunity; this is the land of plenty, so you've been told. You settle into a Polish enclave of Manhattan, where you connect with friends and maybe some family. You do your best to learn English. You buy a pair of riveted denim pants, popular among American workmen. You secure work in a factory thanks to your connections in the Polish community. After an initial period of tension and conflict stemming from job competition and housing constraints, your Anglo-American neighbors eventually accept you, first by allowing you to join the workers' union and then—and this probably only happens to your children—by allowing you to marry into an Anglo family. By this time, you

STRAIGHT-LINE ASSIMILATION

Robert Park's 1920s universal and linear model for how immigrants assimilate: They first arrive, then settle in, and achieve full assimilation in a newly homogenous country.

TABLE 9.1 Gordon's Stages of Assimilation

STAGES OF ASSIMILATION	CHARACTERISTIC
Cultural assimilation	Change of cultural patterns to those of host society
Structural assimilation	Large-scale entrance into cliques
Marital assimilation	Large-scale intermarriage
Identification assimilation	Development of sense of collective identity based exclusively on host society
Attitude reception assimilation	Absence of prejudice
Behavior reception assimilation	Absence of discrimination
Civic assimilation	Absence of value and power conflict

think of yourself as an American. Congratulations, you have reached Milton Gordon's final stage of civic assimilation.

Harold Isaacs (1975) noticed something that these theories of assimilation could not explain: People did not so easily shed their ethnic ties. Ethnic identification, among White ethnics and everyone else, persisted even after a group attained certain levels of structural assimilation. Clifford Geertz (1973) explained this persistence as a matter of primordialism—that is, the strength of ethnic ties resides in deeply felt or primordial ties to one's culture. Ethnicity is, in a word, *fixed*. If not biologically rooted, it's rooted in some other intractable source that Geertz reasoned must be culture.

The flip side of this argument came from Nathan Glazer and Daniel P. Moynihan in *Beyond the Melting Pot* (1963). Far from being a deeply rooted structure that kept people bonded to their culture, ethnic identification, they reasoned, persisted because maintaining those connections was in an individual's best interest. They saw ethnic groups as miniature interest groups—individuals uniting for instrumental purposes, such as fending off job competition. Glazer and Moynihan viewed ethnicity as fluid and circumstantial. More recently, scholars have posited that ethnic identification is both a deeply felt attachment and an instrumental position that can change according to circumstance (Cornell & Hartmann, 1998).

PLURALISM

Most people find assimilation into American society more difficult. Acceptance varies systematically. At times, a pressure cooker has been invoked as a more appropriate metaphor than a melting pot. Park's model shifted attention away from essentialist explanations of the so-called innate differences among immigrants, but it suffers from several shortcomings. Most obviously, it does not apply to nonwhite immigrants, many of whom are not fully accepted into all areas of American society. Park's model also does not apply to involuntary immigrants, notably African Americans and some refugees. Ernest Barth and Donald Noel (1972) noted that assimilation may not necessarily reflect the end result for immigrants, as other outcomes such as exclusion, pluralism, and stratification exist. As others point out (Lieberson, 1961; Massey, 1995; Portes & Zhou, 1993), some immigrants assimilate more easily than others, depending on a variety of structural factors, like migration patterns; differences in contact with the dominant or majority groups; demographics including fertility, mortality rates, and age structure; and ultimately, power differentials among groups. This is the case for the "new immigration," which, in comparison with the earlier era of European immigration (1901–30), is a large-scale influx of non-European immigration that began in the late 1960s and continues to the present (Figure 9.2).

PRIMORDIALISM

Clifford Geertz's term to explain the strength of ethnic ties because they are fixed and deeply felt or primordial ties to one's homeland culture.

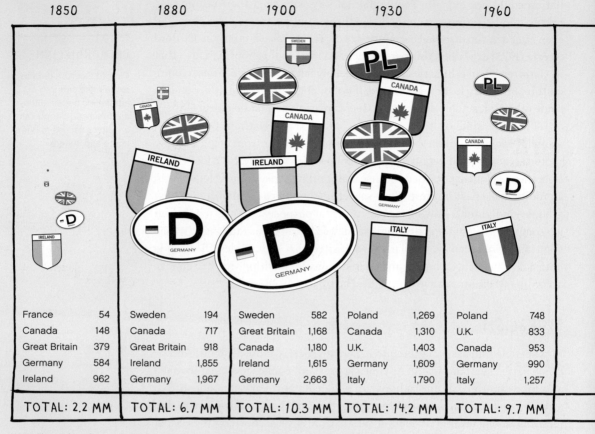

FIGURE 9.2 Five Largest Foreign-Born Populations in the United States, 1850–2021 (in thousands)

1850		1880		1900		1930		1960	
France	54	Sweden	194	Sweden	582	Poland	1,269	Poland	748
Canada	148	Canada	717	Great Britain	1,168	Canada	1,310	U.K.	833
Great Britain	379	Great Britain	918	Canada	1,180	U.K.	1,403	Canada	953
Germany	584	Ireland	1,855	Ireland	1,615	Germany	1,609	Germany	990
Ireland	962	Germany	1,967	Germany	2,663	Italy	1,790	Italy	1,257
TOTAL: 2.2 MM		**TOTAL: 6.7 MM**		**TOTAL: 10.3 MM**		**TOTAL: 14.2 MM**		**TOTAL: 9.7 MM**	

NOTE: The total numbers include all foreign-born populations, not just those in the top five.
SOURCES: Gibson & Jung, 2006; U.S. Census Bureau, 2021h.

PLURALISM

the presence and engaged coexistence of numerous distinct groups in one society.

A society with several distinct ethnic or racial groups exhibits pluralism, meaning that a low degree of assimilation exists. A culturally pluralistic society has one large sociocultural framework with a diversity of cultures functioning within it. This is the premise of multiculturalism in America. Statistically speaking, in a pluralist country, no single group commands numerical majority status. Switzerland, with its three linguistic groups—German, French, and Italian—is a striking example of ethnic autonomy and balance. Demographic projections suggest that non-Hispanic Whites will make up about 44.3 percent of the U.S. population by 2060 (U.S. Census Bureau, 2017a). A broader definition of pluralism, however, is a society in which minority groups live separately but equally. Imagine America with no

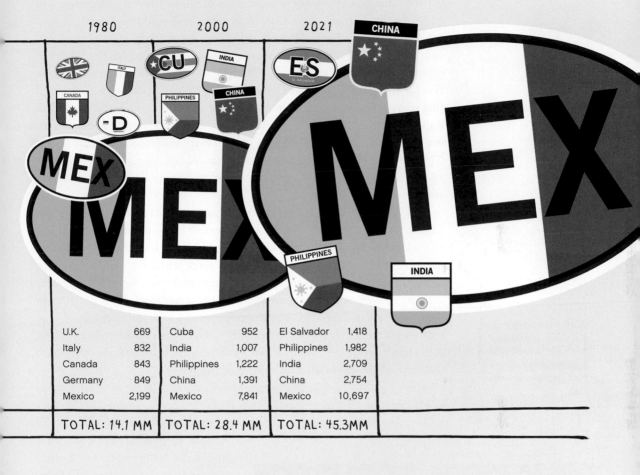

		1980			2000			2021	
U.K.		669	Cuba		952	El Salvador		1,418
Italy		832	India		1,007	Philippines		1,982
Canada		843	Philippines		1,222	India		2,709
Germany		849	China		1,391	China		2,754
Mexico		2,199	Mexico		7,841	Mexico		10,697
TOTAL: 14.1 MM			**TOTAL: 28.4 MM**			**TOTAL: 45.3MM**		

substantial stratification, no oppression, and no domination. In Switzerland, despite slight income differences among ethnic groups (with the exception of recent immigrant groups like the Turkish), no one group dominates politically, but the same cannot be said for America.

SEGREGATION AND DISCRIMINATION

A third paradigm for inter-group relations is segregation, the legal or social practice of separating people on the basis of their race or ethnicity. The southern United States provided an extreme case of segregation before the civil rights movement. Under the Jim Crow system of segregation, reinforced by the Supreme Court's 1896 ruling in *Plessy v. Ferguson*, a "separate but equal" doctrine ruled the South. Strictly enforced separation existed between Blacks and Whites in most areas of public life—from residence to health facilities to bus seats, classroom seats, and even toilet seats.

Although the *Plessy* decision ruled that separate facilities for Blacks and Whites were constitutional as long as they were equal, the doctrine essentially legalized unequal facilities for Blacks. The National Association for the Advancement of Colored People (NAACP) has long recognized that segregation and discrimination are inescapably linked, and education illustrates this point clearly. Social science data consistently show that an integrated educational experience for minority children produces advantages over a nonintegrated school experience. School segregation almost always entails fewer educational resources and lower quality for minority students.

As Anthony Marx (1998) has noted, concern over segregation grew during World War II as America attempted to espouse antiracist rhetoric against its Nazi foes while upholding an egregiously racist doctrine at home. America emerged from the war as a global force with heightened stakes for its world reputation; this new status, along with growing public dissent, perhaps helped motivate the Supreme Court's landmark 1954 decision in *Brown v. Board of Education*. The Court's majority opinion that legally segregated public schools were "inherently unequal" is considered the ruling that struck down the "separate but equal" doctrine. It was also the spark that ignited the civil rights movement of the 1960s.

However, school desegregation has been under fire since several Supreme Court decisions in the 1990s (*Dowell*, 1991; *Pitts*, 1992; *Jenkins*, 1995). Two 2007 cases in Louisville, Kentucky, and Seattle, Washington, came the closest to overturning the spirit (if not the letter) of *Brown*. Earlier, former presidents Richard Nixon and Ronald Reagan had both openly attacked desegregation initiatives, especially busing. In 1981, President Reagan's attorney general, William Bradford Reynolds, flatly proclaimed that the "compulsory busing of students in order to achieve racial balance in the public schools is not an acceptable remedy" (Orfield, 1996). Today, most U.S. schools are only marginally less segregated than they were in the mid-1960s. It seems that 1988 was the least segregated

Black actor, singer, and civil rights leader Paul Robeson leads Oakland dockworkers in singing the national anthem in 1942.

Elementary school students in Ft. Myer, Virginia, face each other on the first day of desegregation.

year in U.S. schools. Namely, researchers at the University of California, Los Angeles, found the number of "hyper-segregated schools, in which 90% or more of students are minorities, grew since 1988 from 5.7% to 18.4%" (Orfield et al., 2016). School segregation is invariably linked to poverty, which is perpetuated by residential segregation, and mitigating racial disparities relies on unraveling the complex systems that still maintain remnants of the "separate but equal" institutions.

In 1968, under President Lyndon B. Johnson's initiative, the Kerner Commission reported that despite the civil rights movement sweeping the nation, America was split into two societies: "one Black, one White—separate and unequal." The main reason for the fissure was residential segregation, what sociologist Lawrence Bobo (1989) has termed the "structural linchpin of American racial inequality." Residential segregation, scholars argue, maintains an urban underclass in perpetual poverty by limiting its ties to upwardly mobile social networks, which connect people to jobs and other opportunities. When you live in the ghetto, your chances of landing a good job through your social network are indeed slim (Wilson, 1987).

It has also been suggested that residential segregation inflicts poverty through a "culture of segregation" (Massey & Denton, 1993). According to this argument, you live in a ghetto that's extremely isolated from the outside world—no family restaurants like the Olive Garden, no mainstream bank branches, and not even a chain grocery store that sells fresh vegetables. You're surrounded daily by the ills that accompany poverty: poor health, joblessness, out-of-wedlock children, welfare, educational failure, a drug economy, crime and violence, and in general, social and physical deterioration. In the ghetto, the most extreme form of residential segregation, social ills become normative. It's no big deal to sell drugs, drop

In 1942, a race riot broke out in Detroit, Michigan, during an attempt by White residents to force African Americans out of the neighborhood.

out of school, depend on welfare, or run with a gang. You slide into the very behaviors that, in turn, reproduce the spiral of decline of your neighborhood.

Whether you buy this line of thought or not (and this viewpoint has been criticized as being overly deterministic), consider how a segregated neighborhood got that way in the first place. It didn't just pop up out of nowhere, nor was it always there. As Douglas Massey and Nancy Denton (1993) have argued, Whites deliberately and systematically constructed ghettos to keep Blacks locked into their (unequal) place. Before 1900, Blacks faced job discrimination but relatively little residential segregation. Blacks and Whites lived side by side in urban centers, as the index of dissimilarity numbers in Figure 9.3 show. The index of dissimilarity, the standard measure of segregation, captures the degree to which Blacks and Whites are evenly spread among neighborhoods in a given city. The index tells you the percentage of nonwhites who would have to move in order to achieve residential integration.

Various structural changes—industrialization, urbanization, and the influx to the North of southern Blacks who competed with huge waves of European immigrants—led to increased hostility and violence toward Blacks, who found themselves shut out of both White jobs and White neighborhoods. The color line, previously more flexible and fuzzy, hardened into a rigid boundary between Black and White.

Whites manufactured the Black ghetto through a set of deliberate, conscious practices. They policed boundaries separating Black neighborhoods, first with the threat of violence and periphery bombings in the 1920s and then with "neighborhood associations" that institutionalized housing discrimination. Property owners signed secret agreements promising not to allow Blacks into their domain. When a Black family did move to a neighboring block, Whites often adopted the strategy of flight instead of fight, and this process of racial turnover yielded the same result: Black isolation. Even today, when a Black family moves into a White neighborhood, the property value declines slightly, in subtle anticipation of the process of White flight, which leaves behind a run-down, undesirable Black neighborhood—a veritable vicious circle.

FIGURE 9.3 Index of Racial Dissimilarity

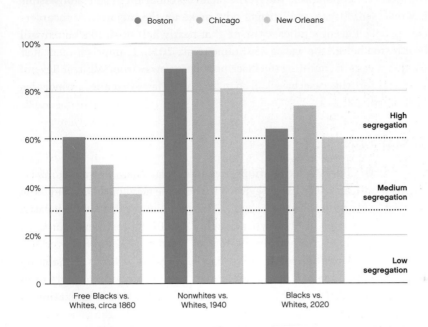

NOTE: The index of dissimilarity measures the degree of segregation in a given city. A value under 30 is low, one between 30 and 60 is medium, and one over 60 is high.
SOURCES: Massey & Denton, 1993; City Observatory, 2020.

Specific government policies also helped create the Black ghetto, including the Home Owners' Loan Corporation (HOLC), which in the early 1930s granted loans to homeowners who were in financial trouble. The HOLC also instituted the practice of "redlining," which declared inner-city, Black neighborhoods too much of a liability and ineligible for aid. Following the HOLC's lead, the Federal Housing Administration (FHA) and the Veterans Administration (VA), both designed to make home ownership a reality for struggling Americans, funneled funds away from Black areas and predominantly into White suburbs. Finally, by the 1950s, urban slums were razed in the name of "urban renewal," which essentially became a program of removal, as African Americans were relocated to concentrated public housing projects (Massey & Denton, 1993). These deliberately discriminatory policies are perpetuated today by de facto segregation in the form of continued suburban White flight and the splintering of school districts along racial lines.

Some scholars argue that a new form of segregation has emerged in America: the criminal justice system. During the 1960s, Blacks were slightly overrepresented in the nation's prisons, but in absolute numbers there were many more White felons, because Whites made up a larger percentage of the total U.S. population. Today, the racial distribution in jails and prisons has reversed. Blacks and Latinxs now make up the majority of incarcerated people. Recent studies estimate that nearly half of all Black men will be arrested before the age of 23 (Brame et al., 2014). Is imprisonment just another means of confining the Black population away from Whites? Several scholars make this case, based on changes in drug laws that affect minorities disproportionately.

RACIAL CONFLICT

GENOCIDE

the mass killing of a group of people based on racial, ethnic, or religious traits.

Tutsi troops overlook a pile of skulls that will be reburied in a memorial to approximately 12,000 Tutsi massacred by Hutu militias.

The final paradigm of race relations is conflict relations, when antagonistic groups within a society live integrated in the same neighborhoods, hold the same jobs, and go to the same schools. This paradigm describes the volatile scenario in Rwanda in 1994, when roughly 800,000 Tutsi were murdered by Hutu, mostly by machete, in the span of 100 days. That's well over 300 killings per hour (Gourevitch, 1998). The killings, as well as the maiming and systematic rape of Tutsi women, were the culmination of more than a century of racial hostility that began with the Belgian colonization of Rwanda.

Belgian explorers, immersed in discourses of scientific racism, confronted two Rwandan tribes, the Hutu and the Tutsi, who for ages had been living together, working together, and intermarrying. Because of their shared social, cultural, and genetic heritages, scientists today cannot distinguish Hutu and Tutsi into separate biological populations. But in the late nineteenth century, the Belgians gave preferential treatment to the Tutsi, whom they believed to be superior to the Hutu. A brutal system of oppression followed, in which the Tutsi dominated the Hutu. In other words, the Belgian imperialists racialized an ethnic distinction by creating inequality and thus hardening the inter-group boundaries.

When Rwanda won its independence in 1962, after a century of hatred brewing between the two groups, the Hutu took power under a dictatorship masked as a democracy, and their long-standing animosity simmered into an explosion in April 1994 after three years of failed crops. The result was genocide, the mass killing of a particular population based on racial, ethnic, or religious traits. The genocide, backed by the government and media, turned neighbors into murderers overnight: Friends killed friends, teachers killed students, and professionals killed coworkers. The Rwandan genocide served as a stark reminder that when we speak of the myth or fiction of race, we cannot deny its reality in social life.

GROUP RESPONSES TO DOMINATION

There are several forms of response to oppression, four of which this section briefly outlines: withdrawal, passing, acceptance, and resistance. Although we tend to think of minority groups as being oppressed by majority groups, keep in mind that sometimes the majority are the oppressed group, as in South African apartheid, where 4.5 million White Afrikaners and British dominated 19 million Indigenous people.

WITHDRAWAL An oppressed group may withdraw, as the Jewish population did after Nazi persecution in Poland. Before World War II, Jews in Poland numbered 3.3 million, the second-largest Jewish population in the world. Eighty-five percent of Polish Jews died in the Holocaust, leaving roughly 500,000. After World War II, violence against Jews continued, and many moved. These conditions, plus the bitter taste of Polish complicity in the Holocaust itself, caused many Jews to leave for good. By 1947, Poland was home to just 100,000 Jews.

Another case of withdrawal was the Great Migration of the mid-twentieth century in the United States. Blacks streamed from the Jim Crow rural South in search of jobs and equality in the industrialized urban North and West; an estimated 1.5 million African Americans left per decade between 1940 and 1970. The North opened opportunities to Blacks that previously had been violently denied them in the South, including economic and educational gains as well as the cultural freedom manifested in the Harlem Renaissance. But leaving the South did not always lead to immediate improvements. In their search for a better life, many African Americans found cramped shantytowns on the edge of urban centers, exploitation by factory owners looking for cheap Black labor, and increasing hostility from White workers. Racialized competition for housing and employment sometimes led to violent clashes, such as the East St. Louis riots in the summer of 1917. The riots, principally involving White violence against Blacks, raged for nearly a week, leaving nine Whites and hundreds of African Americans dead. An estimated 6,000 Black citizens, fearing for their lives, fled the city, another stark example of withdrawal.

PASSING Another response to racial oppression is passing, or blending in with the dominant group. In 1848, Ellen Craft successfully escaped from slavery in Macon, Georgia, by asserting a White (male) identity, bringing her darker-skinned husband along as her "servant." And an even more recent, interesting case is that of Rachel Dolezal, who was of White, European ancestry but tried to (and did for a while) pass as African American by altering her hair and skin tone, even becoming president of the Spokane, Washington, chapter of the NAACP. Once it was revealed that she did not have any African ancestry, she was dubbed the "undisputed heavyweight champion of racial appropriation" (Vestal, 2017). She then lost her leadership position in the Spokane chapter of the NAACP as well as her job teaching in the Africana Studies department at Eastern Washington University (Samuels, 2015).

Passing is not necessarily about physical changes, though. One of the most common ways people have tried to pass has been to change their surnames. The single largest ethnic group in the United States today is German Americans. Not English, but German. Where, do you ask, are all the Schmidts and Muellers? They now go by Smith and Miller, after a huge wave of name changing among German Americans during the world wars—if not during the first one, then often by the time of the second. Since there is no true, innate, fixed nature to racial identity, the whole idea of passing, of course, is a bit paradoxical, as the historian Allyson Hobbs (2014) points out.

ACCEPTANCE VERSUS RESISTANCE Another response is acceptance, whereby the oppressed group feigns compliance and hides its true feelings of resentment. In Erving Goffman's (1959) terms, members of this group construct a front stage of acceptance, often using stereotypes to their own advantage to "play the part" in the presence of the dominant group (see Chapter 4). Backstage, however, privately among their subaltern or oppressed group, they present a very different self. Sociologist Elijah Anderson refers to this practice as "code-switching," a strategy used by African Americans in the presence of dominant White society. In Anderson's ethnography of a Black neighborhood in Philadelphia, Blacks learn two languages, one of their neighbors and one of mainstream society, and daily survival becomes a matter of knowing which one to speak at the right time. For an inner-city youth, an act of code-switching could be as simple as putting on a leather jacket and concealing his textbook beneath it for the walk home from school (Anderson, 1999). (Code-switching is akin to the double consciousness that W. E. B. Du Bois ascribed to African Americans who maintain two behavioral scripts; see Chapter 1.)

A more overt form of resistance, the fourth paradigm of group responses to domination, would be collective resistance through a movement such as revolution or genocide or through nonviolent protest as in the U.S. civil rights movement.

SUBALTERN

a subordinate, oppressed group of people.

COLLECTIVE RESISTANCE

an organized effort to change a power hierarchy on the part of a less powerful group in a society.

Racial Groups in the United States

| Describe the demographics of racial classification in the United States.

The United States houses numerous racial groups today, and many of the forms of group relations discussed above are at play here—assimilation, segregation, discrimination, collective resistance, even withdrawal—depending on which groups we are talking about. The United States has such a heterogeneous population, in fact, that it is on its way to having no single numerically dominant group. Until the mid-nineteenth century, low immigration rates limited racial diversity. Early in the country's formation, White Anglo-Saxon Protestants dominated over Native Americans as well as enslaved Black people. From that point forward, Anglos secured their place at the top of the cultural, political, and economic hierarchy, prevailing over other immigrant populations. As exemplified in the following snapshot of racial groups in America today, these historical hierarchies have remained relatively stable and intact despite drastically changing demographics.

NATIVE AMERICANS

According to archaeological findings, the original settlers of the North American continent arrived between 12,000 and 50,000 years ago from northeastern Asia, traveling by foot on glaciers. Some tribes, such as the Ojibwe, believe that their ancestors came from the east, not the west. Before European explorers arrived in significant numbers for extended periods in the fifteenth century (evidence shows that the Vikings had reached North America before then), the Indigenous population was anywhere between 10 and 100 million. The tribes living here when Europeans showed up were geographically, culturally, and physically diverse, but they were categorically viewed as a single uncivilized group by arriving Spanish, French, and British explorers. Even today, "Indians" in America are part of 280 distinct cultural groups (Gray & Nye, 2001). Foreshadowing the lack of respect to come, Columbus called all of the people he met Indians, despite their clear cultural differences, because he thought he was in India. Confronted with foreign diseases and unfamiliar military technology, White invaders quickly dominated the supposed Indians. In Central and South America, the Spanish brutally enslaved them as labor for the mining industry. In the northern parts of North America, French colonialists nurtured their relationships with the Indians in order to cultivate a profitable fur trade. The British, chiefly concerned with

The Oglala Nation Powwow and Rodeo parade is a bright spot for the Pine Ridge Indian Reservation, which, like many federal reservations, faces many problems linked to low socioeconomic status.

acquiring land, settled colonies with the long-term goal of expanding the British state, dispossessing and "civilizing" America's Indigenous population in the process (Cornell, 1988).

European settlements completely obliterated American Indians' way of life by taking vital land from them and disrupting their communal infrastructure. Most devastating were the newly imported diseases, such as smallpox and cholera, against which the Indians, having no native immunity, were virtually defenseless. There were also grueling forced marches from native lands to dedicated reservations. By the end of the 1800s, the Native American population had dwindled to approximately 250,000 (U.S. Census Bureau, 1993). The Indian Bureau (later called the Bureau of Indian Affairs) was established as part of the War Department in 1824 to deal with the remaining "Indian problem," and its chief means was "forced assimilation." This method involved removing Indian children from their families and putting them in government-run boarding schools that taught the superiority of Anglo culture over "primitive" Native culture and religion. Children who refused to adopt Western dress, language, and religion met with harsh physical and emotional punishment (Cornell, 1988). (A similar project was undertaken in British-ruled Australia with the native Aboriginal tribes.) Despite this poor treatment, Navajo men served the United States in World War II, in which 29 "code talkers" used the Navajo language in lieu of cryptography to protect the secrecy of American communications. The code talkers played an instrumental role in the American victory at Iwo Jima and many other battles throughout the war (Bixler, 1992).

In 2020, the number of people claiming at least some Native American ancestry was about 9.7 million (Jones et al., 2021). Only about one-fifth of Native Americans live in a designated American Indian area. The largest reservation, Navajoland or Diné Bikéyah, covers approximately 16 million acres of Arizona, New Mexico, and Utah. Reservations are generally impoverished areas rife with health problems, domestic abuse, substance abuse, poor infrastructure, and crime. In fact, Native Americans as a whole are plagued by the lowest average socioeconomic status in the United States. They rank among the worst in terms of high-school dropout rates and unemployment, which go hand in hand with poor health outcomes such as alcoholism, suicide, and premature death. Around 33 percent of Native Americans die before age 45, compared with 11 percent of the U.S. population as a whole (Garrett, 1994).

Though facing many social problems, Native Americans are becoming more politically organized and active as a bloc. For example, sustained protests against the Dakota Access Pipeline crossing sacred ground—and the reservation's water source—in North Dakota led to a delay and rerouting of the oil conduit (McKenna, 2016). And recent lawsuits brought by Native Americans in Colorado have successfully challenged the gerrymandering that had concentrated their numbers into a single state district, thereby diluting their power (Turkewitz, 2018).

AFRICAN AMERICANS

The first Black people in North America arrived not as enslaved people but as indentured servants contracted by White colonialists for set periods, much like poor, unfree Whites from Ireland or Scotland (Franklin, 1980). Colonialists developed the system of slavery to meet labor needs, though, establishing the slave trade as a fixed institution by the end of the seventeenth century. Even today, the remnants of this only partially dismantled system have exacerbated challenges for African Americans in the United States.

Just before the American Revolution, enslaved people made up more than 20 percent of the colonial population (Dinnerstein et al., 1996). As of 2021, about 13.8 percent of the American population is Black (U.S. Census Bureau, 2021i). Like the Japanese Burakumin, this minority group has high rates of poverty, health problems, unemployment, and crime. According to the U.S. Census Bureau, African Americans have the highest poverty rate of any minority group in the nation at 19.5 percent compared to 8.2 percent for non-Hispanic Whites (U.S. Census Bureau, 2021f). African Americans also have higher rates of imprisonment than Whites and other minority groups;

Wiley College student body president Kabamba Kiboko dances at a pep rally. Her family came to the United States from the Congo. For the first time, more Africans are entering the country than during the slave trade.

according to the NAACP, 1 in 3 Black boys will go to prison in their lives compared to 1 in 6 Latinx and 1 in 17 White boys (NAACP, 2019).

Sociologists and demographers today study how new Black immigrants might fracture the holistic conception of "African American." For the first time, more Africans are entering the country than during the slave trade. About 10.2 percent of the Black population is foreign-born (U.S. Census Bureau, 2020g). Afro-Caribbeans such as Cubans, Haitians, and Jamaicans resent being unilaterally categorized as African American, because each of these immigrant groups enjoys a unique history, culture, and language that do not correspond to the American stereotypes of people with Black skin. For this reason, new Black immigrant groups would rather not assimilate, but instead retain their distinctive immigrant status, setting themselves apart from the lowest status group in America, the Blacks (Greer, 2006).

LATINXS

Latinx (the gender-neutral construction of Latino) means individuals who trace their ancestry back to Latin America. So in theory, this group includes Brazilians who speak Portuguese and Belizeans who speak English. *Hispanic* means descended from (or identifying with) Spanish-speaking populations (including from Spain itself). Although two distinct groups, the terms are often used interchangeably in practice. In 2018, the majority of Latinxs in the United States were from Mexico (about 61.9 percent), Puerto Rico (about 9.7 percent), Cuba (4 percent), and the Dominican Republic (3.5 percent) (U.S. Census Bureau, 2020b). They are a huge and rapidly expanding segment of the American population (Figure 9.4 provides a breakdown of the U.S. Hispanic population by region of origin); in 2018, they made up approximately 18 percent of the population, surpassing African Americans (U.S. Census Bureau, 2020b). Latinxs also live in a wide array of locations,

FIGURE 9.4 U.S. Hispanic Population by Region of Origin, 2021

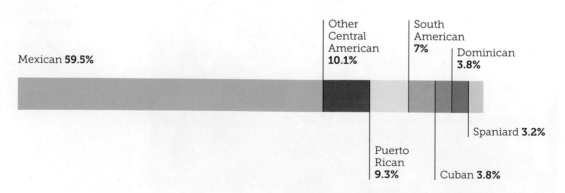

SOURCE: U.S. Census Bureau, 2021e.

although they have clustered in the West Coast and Southwest regions (U.S. Census Bureau, 2020c).

Hispanics are often called an "in between" racial group because of their intermediate status, sandwiched between Whites and African Americans. Unlike African Americans, the majority of Latinxs in America today have come by way of voluntary immigration, particularly during the last four decades of heavy, second-wave immigration. Puerto Ricans are the exception because they have been able to travel freely to the United States since 1917, when Puerto Rico became an American territory and its inhabitants U.S. citizens. The chief motivation for Latinx immigration is economic because of America's high demand for labor in the service, agriculture, and construction industries.

So ambiguous is the Latinx label that at various times the U.S. Census has classified them as part of the White race and as a separate race. At the moment, being Hispanic or Latinx is considered by the U.S. government to be an ethnic identity, not a racial identity, although, as I mentioned above, many researchers consider Latinxs a racialized group. This is, of course, complicated. Take Cubans. Most Cubans consider themselves Hispanic Whites, although their immigration status has changed drastically in recent years. Following the Communist revolution led by Fidel Castro, the first large wave of Cuban immigrants arrived in southern Florida in the 1960s. These immigrants were of the upper or middle class, educated, and perceived as the victims of a Communist regime that came to power during the Cold War. As such, they were welcomed enthusiastically to this country, and their assimilation started smoothly (Portes, 1969). By 1995, however, that warm welcome had faded. The U.S. federal government terminated its 35-year open-door policy toward Cuban refugees, and the heavy media coverage of Cubans arriving since then in small boats has led to stereotypes of a desperate "wetback" invasion. Arrivals since the 1970s, generally from lower socioeconomic backgrounds in Cuban society, have met more resistance from their host society, consequently experiencing higher rates of unemployment, low-wage work, and dependence on welfare and charity than native Whites and previous Cuban émigrés (Portes et al., 1985). More recently, with the normalization of relations between the United States and Cuba, the special status that Cubans had with respect to immigration (essentially a fast track to American citizenship) has been terminated, and as a result,

A crowd gathers for a Cinco de Mayo parade in southwest Detroit. How do the boundaries between race and ethnicity overlap in the Latinx community?

deportations have increased. Some 37,000 Cubans face deportation orders as of 2018 (Torres, 2017). The Trump administration revised the Obama administration's policies, so limbo and uncertainty may continue for a while.

ASIAN AMERICANS

Like *Latinx*, the broad term *Asian American* encompasses diverse and sometimes clashing peoples from China, Korea, Japan, and Southeast Asia. The first wave of Asians to arrive in the United States in the mid-nineteenth century were predominantly laborers of Chinese, then Japanese, then Korean and Filipino origin. A second large wave of immigration is currently under way, mostly made up of well-educated and highly skilled people from Asia.

Early Asian immigrants were perceived as a labor threat and therefore met with extreme hostility. The Chinese Exclusion Act of 1882, which led to a ban against the Chinese in 1902, marked the first time in American history in which a group was singled out and barred entry. Urban "Chinatowns" developed out of ghettos in which marginalized Chinese workers, mostly men, were forced to live. Japanese immigrants faced similar hostilities and were formally barred entry by the Oriental Exclusion Act of 1924. By 2018, Asian and mixed-Asian U.S. residents amounted to 6.7 percent of the population. This was a 28 percent increase since 2010, making Asian Americans the fastest-growing racial group (U.S. Census Bureau, 2020h). They are most heavily concentrated in California, Hawaii, New York, Illinois, and Washington.

Asian Americans' high average socioeconomic status makes them unique, surpassing the financial security of most other minority groups as well as most Whites in terms of educational attainment. For example, the median household income for the U.S. population as a whole in 2018 was $61,937, whereas for Asian Americans it was $87,243 (U.S. Census Bureau, 2020e). That said, despite the overall success of Asian Americans, certain groups—notably Cambodians and Hmong (from Laos and Vietnam)—experience very high poverty rates.

Furthermore, Asian Americans overall find it a bit more difficult to be reemployed once they lose a job. In the first quarter of 2020, the Asian American unemployment rate for those with bachelor's degrees or higher was 0.9 percentage point higher than the rate for Whites (Bureau of Labor Statistics, 2020c), and Asian Americans and Blacks suffer from the longest average duration of unemployment spells. In March 2020, unemployed Asian Americans experienced a median 6.6 weeks before they found work again. For Blacks that year, the figure was 8.8 weeks. Whites and Latinxs had 6.5- and 5-week median durations between jobs, respectively, in 2020 (Bureau of Labor Statistics, 2020d). However, these Black–Asian and White–Latinx similarities obscure different reasons for the long duration of unemployment for the various groups. Whereas Blacks typically face barriers to employment, Asians have more family support and savings and thus are able to wait out a bad labor market for the best possible job.

In recent years, Asians have been applauded for their smooth assimilation as the "model minority," implying that if only other racial groups could assimilate so well, America would have fewer social problems. Such a view, however, effaces the rather unsmooth history Asian immigrants have faced in this country as well as the continuing poverty and discrimination faced by some Asians. Furthermore, "positive" stereotypes of high achievement place enormous pressure on Asian youths to measure up to an impossibly high ideal.

MIDDLE EASTERN AMERICANS

Middle Easterners come from places as diverse as the Arabian Peninsula, North Africa, Iran, Iraq, and the Palestinian territories. The group established communities in the United States as far back as the late 1800s, but their numbers have swelled since the 1970s as part of the rising tide of non-European immigration. Middle Easterners in this second wave of immigration often arrive from politically tumultuous areas to seek refuge in the United States, such as the many refugees who have recently fled from war-torn Syria.

Today, about 2.1 million Americans report Arab ancestry, and even more Americans have a Middle Eastern heritage, because not all Middle Easterners are Arab (U.S. Census Bureau, 2020f) despite the fact that most Americans regard anyone from the Middle East as Arab and Muslim. In fact, the largest Middle Eastern population in the United States today comes from Iran, and they are Persians, not ethnic Arabs, who do not generally speak Arabic. Similarly, although the majority of new Middle Eastern Americans are Muslim, many of them are Christian, and a small number are Jewish (Bozorgmehr et al., 1996).

Widespread misunderstandings about Middle Easterners derive, in part, from their negative stereotyping in the mainstream media. In one study of television portrayals of Arabs, researchers found four basic myths that continue to surround this group. First, they are often depicted as fabulously wealthy—as sultans and oil tycoons. Second, they are shown as uncivilized and barbaric. Third, they are portrayed as sex-crazed, especially for underage White sex slaves. Fourth, they are said to revel in acts of terrorism, desiring to destroy all things American (Shaheen, 1984). Little has changed since this study came out over 30 years ago, although after 9/11, the emphasis shifted away from stereotypes of Arabs as extremely rich and toward one of Middle Easterners as terrorists.

WHITES

We've seen some of the trajectories of various ethnic and racial groups in America, but what about the largest racial population, Whites? Scholars have begun to pay more attention to what it means to be a White person.

Every year on the first day of my Introduction to Sociology class, I ask my 200 or so students to write down the five social categories that best describe who they are. Black students almost always put their race at or near the top of the list. Latinx and Asian American students usually list their ethnicity as well. Until recently, I could be fairly confident that Whites would not list their race. Some might identify Polish, German, or another ethnic or national origin, but not one White student would write down Caucasian, White, or even Euro-American, which served as the point of my experiment.

We have already seen how the category of Whiteness is socially constructed—first inclusively defined as all "free White persons" in 1790, then restrictively defined as only northern and western European Whites in the early twentieth century, and reformulated back to an umbrella category by the mid-twentieth century. We know now that this category, which seems so natural and innate, is actually a flexible label that has expanded over time to include many formerly nonwhite groups such as Jews, Irish, and Italians. Today, most White people have little awareness of the meaning of Whiteness as a category. As Nell Irvin Painter, the author of *The History of White People*, says, "The foundation of White identity is that there isn't any. You're just an individual" (Schackner, 2002).

Whiteness, argues Peggy McIntosh (1988), is an "invisible knapsack of privileges" that puts White people at an advantage, just as racism places nonwhites at a disadvantage. In her now classic essay "White Privilege: Unpacking the Invisible Knapsack" (1989), McIntosh catalogs more than 50 "Daily Effects of White Privilege," ranging from the mundane to the major. She notices:

- I can count on finding movies and TV featuring people of my race represented, go into a supermarket and find the staple foods which fit with my cultural traditions, and walk into a hairdresser's shop and find someone who can cut my hair.

- I can take a job with an affirmative action employer without having my co-workers on the job suspect that I got it because of my race.

- I do not have to educate my children to be aware of systemic racism for their own daily physical protection.

- I am never asked to speak for all the people of my racial group.

- I am not made acutely aware that my shape, bearing, or body odor will be taken as a reflection on my race.

- I can choose blemish cover or bandages in "flesh" color and have them more or less match my skin. (pp. 3–5)

According to McIntosh, Whiteness is largely about not feeling the weight of representing an entire population with one's successes or failures. It's about not having to think about race much at all. In recent years, however, awareness of Whiteness has been on the rise, as evidenced by the profusion of scholarship on Whiteness, which aims to call attention to the social construction and ensuing privilege of the category. Calling attention to Whiteness helps Whites understand the slanted playing field. It also helps rectify something wrong with the way we study race in America: By traditionally focusing on minority groups, studies implicitly situate nonwhites as "deviant," to borrow from the Comte de Buffon, and that's why we study them. Even popular culture has caught on with memes like "stuff White people like," "columbusing," and "if Black people said the stuff White people say," which offer humorous yet pointed critiques of privileges that affluent White people tend to have in America.

Indeed, since the time McIntosh was writing, critical race theorists have worked to show how Whiteness is connected to the same structural forces that Blackness is, engendering advantages that represent the flip side of the disadvantages nonwhites face. For example, structural White privileges that McIntosh did not list include being less likely to be stopped, searched, or harmed by the police; getting a lighter sentence if convicted of a crime; being likely to earn higher wages in the same position; having, on average, greater intergenerational wealth to rely on; and so on.

Some scholars argue that in order for progress toward racial equality to be made, Whites need to recognize and work to undo these structural advantages. However, many Whites react defensively when confronted with the meaning of White privilege. To explain this, Robin DiAngelo (2018) coined the term "white fragility." White fragility is the defensiveness that often arises in White people when they are called out for their role in structural racism—that is, when their White privileges are put to them and linked to the system that produces racial inequality, a system some scholars call "White supremacy."

Former Klansman David Duke stands under a Confederate battle flag. How was Duke able to cast the NAAWP as a pro-White movement instead of a racist organization?

Are Whites becoming more aware of themselves as a race and of their role in White supremacy? Hard to know. But rising White consciousness may have another, more troubling side. In 1980, before White studies got underway in universities, the White supremacist David Duke left his position as the grand wizard of

the Knights of the Ku Klux Klan and founded the National Association for the Advancement of White People (NAAWP), attempting to sugarcoat his racist movement with a seemingly more politically correct approach. In this new framework, Duke presented Whites as a besieged minority, writes sociologist Mitch Berbrier (2000), defining the NAAWP's mission as a pro-White heritage movement as opposed to an anti-Black one. Sociologist Abby Ferber has analyzed the clever appropriation of civil rights language in Duke's White supremacist discourse. For example, in an article by Duke in the *White Patriot,* Ferber finds the rhetoric of reverse discrimination, victimhood, and the right to cultural difference:

> [O]ur race and all others should have the right to determine their own destiny through self-determination and rule. . . . [E]very people on this planet must have the right to life: the continued existence of its unique racial fabric and resulting culture. (*White Patriot,* no. 56, p. 6, quoted in Ferber, 1999)

Sounds reasonable, right? That's because the new language of White supremacy allows racists to move away from explicitly racist language (of biological inferiority, for example). Duke's NAAWP also co-opts civil rights discourse, as in the organization's original mission statement: "The NAAWP is a not for profit, nonviolent, civil rights educational organization, demanding equal rights for Whites and special privileges for none."

Such examples demonstrate one possible outcome of the emergence of White consciousness: to politically empower extremists by giving them a legitimate language for their racist ends. Note, however, that this rhetoric

FIGURE 9.5 An Ethnic Snapshot of America in 2021

White, not Hispanic
59.3%

SOURCE: U.S. Census Bureau, 2021i.

does not acknowledge the advantages Whites typically enjoy. Whiteness studies expose the social construction of a seemingly natural (and neutral) category, giving a sense of the unequal footing beneath the labels "White" and "Black."

The Future of Race

Discuss the societal implications of the changing racial makeup in the United States.

This brief overview of the history of race and its present-day ramifications allows us to make some guesses about the future of race. For starters, racial and ethnic diversity in America will increase. The 2010 Census data show a 134 percent increase in Americans who identify as multiracial—that is, 9 million people (Pew Research Center, 2011c). Compared to 1 in 20 people in 1960, the ratio of foreign-born people in the United States has increased to 1 in 8 residents (U.S. Census Bureau, 2019). And according to National Research Council projections, by the year 2060, largely thanks to the most recent wave of immigration (along with differential fertility rates), America's Latinx and Asian populations will triple, making up about 28.6 percent and 11.7 percent of the U.S. population, respectively (Colby & Ortman, 2015). No longer Black and White, America is now a society composed of multiple ethnic and racial groups with an ever-shifting color line marking fuzzy boundaries (Figure 9.5).

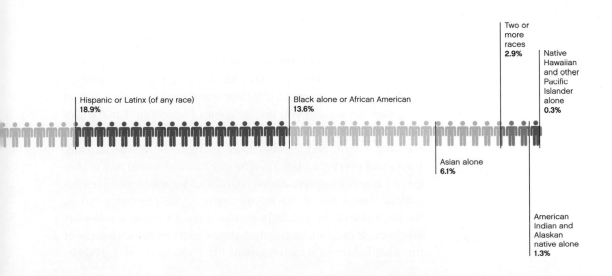

FIGURE 9.6 Race Questions from the 2020 U.S. Census

→ **NOTE: Please answer BOTH Question 6 about Hispanic origin and Question 7 about race. For this census, Hispanic origins are not races.**

6. Is this person of Hispanic, Latino, or Spanish origin?

☐ **No**, not of Hispanic, Latino, or Spanish origin

☐ Yes, Mexican, Mexican Am., Chicano

☐ Yes, Puerto Rican

☐ Yes, Cuban

☐ Yes, another Hispanic, Latino, or Spanish origin – *Print, for example, Salvadoran, Dominican, Colombian, Guatemalan, Spaniard, Ecuadorian, etc.* ↘

[| | | | | | | | | | | | | | | | | | |]

7. What is this person's race?
Mark ☒ *one or more boxes* **AND** *print origins.*

☐ White – *Print, for example, German, Irish, English, Italian, Lebanese, Egyptian, etc.* ↘

[| | | | | | | | | | | | | | | | | | |]

☐ Black or African Am. – *Print, for example, African American, Jamaican, Haitian, Nigerian, Ethiopian, Somali, etc.* ↘

[| | | | | | | | | | | | | | | | | | |]

☐ American Indian or Alaska Native – *Print, name of enrolled or principal tribe(s), for example, Navajo Nation, Blackfeet Tribe, Mayan, Aztec, Native Village of Barrow Inupiat Traditional Government, Nome Eskimo Community, etc.* ↘

[| | | | | | | | | | | | | | | | | | |]

☐ Chinese   ☐ Vietnamese   ☐ Native Hawaiian

☐ Filipino   ☐ Korean   ☐ Samoan

☐ Asian Indian   ☐ Japanese   ☐ Chamorro

☐ Other Asian –   ☐ Other Pacific Islander –
Print, for example,   *Print, for example,*
Pakistani, Cambodian,   *Tongan, Fijian,*
Hmong, etc. ↘   *Marshallese, etc.* ↘

[| | | | | | | | | | | | | | | | | | |]

☐ Some other race – *Print race or origin.* ↘

[| | | | | | | | | | | | | | | | | | |]

In 1996, there was a Multiracial March on Washington in which multiracial activists demanded a separate census category to bolster their political claims and recognition. Although the movement did not result in a multiracial identity category, for the first time ever, the 2000 Census allowed respondents to check off more than one box for racial identity. The resulting multiracial population is currently estimated to be 33.8 million (Jones et al., 2021). Starting in 2020, the census also asked separate questions about race and ethnicity, which means that census data can now be used to examine some of the racial diversity within the Hispanic population, as well as some ethnic diversity among African American and White populations (Figure 9.6).

This so-called browning of America brings us to a new crossroads. The White–Black divide may become the White–nonwhite divide or the Black–nonblack divide. Sociologist Jennifer Lee has looked at just this question, and her research shows that the experience of first- and especially second-generation Asians and Latinxs indicates the new color line is Black–nonblack. What does this mean? In the simplest terms, it means that the biggest differences in demographic characteristics like income, educational attainment, and interracial marriage will be between Blacks and all other groups, while the distinctions between these other groups continue to narrow. Lee notes,

If you look at rates of educational attainment or interracial marriage or multiracial reporting among Asians and Latinos, their disadvantage stems from their immigrant histories, and so with each generation you see outcomes improving. For African Americans, you see there's some progress, but it's not nearly at the same speed, and so what I see is [that] the divide is really Blacks and everyone else. . . . The one caveat I would add is that those Latinos who have darker skin, who are more mistaken for African Americans or Black Americans . . . will probably fall on the Black side of the divide. In part because of their skin color, but also because their socioeconomic status is not on par with some of the other lighter skin Latino groups like Cubans. (Conley, 2009j)

Lee points out that the group with the least advantages and opportunities in this new configuration of race in America are likely to be—no surprise—Blacks, who may be blamed for their own poverty when compared with successful Latinx and Asian immigrants. Lee cautions, "Someone will look at African Americans who have been here longer and who aren't attaining certain levels of mobility and say, why can't they make it? If race isn't an issue for Asians and Latinos, it shouldn't matter for Blacks. What I argue is that the stigma attached to Blackness because of the history of Black-

DIGITAL.WWNORTON.COM/YOUMAYASK8

To see my interview with Jennifer Lee, go to
digital.wwnorton.com/youmayask8

ness is so different; they are not immigrants. To compare African Americans to immigrants is never fair."

How close are we to this new Black–nonblack color line? At least four states (California, Texas, Hawaii, and New Mexico) are deemed "majority minority" states, where Whites do not make up the majority of the population within major metropolitan areas (U.S. Census Bureau, 2010a). However, racial categories are social constructions, not static entities. To claim a multiracial identity presupposes the existence of a monoracial identity, when we know no scientifically pure or distinct race of people exists. Similarly, the notion of a White minority presumes that Whiteness is a fixed racial category, whereas Whiteness has expanded to include groups that were considered nonwhite in the past and may continue to fold Asians and Latinxs into a kind of Whiteness that emphasizes symbolic ethnicity. Indeed, as Warren and Twine (1997) point out, as long as Blacks are present, a back door is open for nonblacks to slip under the White umbrella. For example, the Asian success story as the "model minority" is made possible by Asians' ability to blend in with Whites, because they are unequivocally not Black. We are at a point in American history when Whiteness may be expanding again, with Blacks, as always, serving as the counterweight.

Another consequence of the "browning of America" is the adoption by White nationalists of the rhetoric of minority status. Though it will not be until 2044 that Whites are no longer a majority—at which time they will still be the single biggest racial group at 49.9 percent of the population

DIGITAL.WWNORTON.COM/YOUMAYASK8

To see my interview with Maria Abascal, go to
digital.wwnorton.com/youmayask8

(Colby & Ortman, 2015)—that has not stopped many alt-right politicos from using the fears of being lost in the melting pot to effectively bolster their political power. Once we actually do arrive at a population distribution in which Whites are a minority—though if history holds, likely a wealthy and politically powerful one—new and interesting dynamics will emerge. When the minority group is the economically and socially dominant group (i.e., Whites in South Africa, Chinese in Indonesia, and Indians in some Caribbean nations), blame and backlash can flare up when that country's economic prospects falter. For the time being, however, (some) Whites themselves still play the part of aggrieved, oppressed minority group—at least at the ballot box.

Professor Maria Abascal and I discussed how inter-group relations are changing and how racial groups are even being redefined in the context of the anticipated decline of the White majority over the next few decades. In our discussion, she points out that Latinx individuals are fluid in terms of their racial identification (and with whom they intermarry), making it tough to predict just how big the "White" and "nonwhite" populations will be in the coming years.

Moreover, in her research, Abascal found that when faced with a growing Latinx population, Whites and Blacks reacted very differently in a game of altruism. She experimentally primed some respondents to hear about the growing numbers of Latinx Americans while a control group did not get this "reminder." She then administered a "dictator game" to each subject. Abascal explains what this game entails:

> In a dictator game, it's a very simple experiment in which you give somebody some amount of money. I gave people $10, and I said, "You can split this money however you want with a stranger." And that stranger was either someone who had a distinctively White name or someone who had a distinctively Black name. They could give zero of those $10, they could give all $10 to the other person. (Conley, 2020c)

Among Whites, those who were informed about the growing Latinx population became less charitable to African Americans, while Blacks actually became more equal in their treatment of African Americans and Whites. When perceiving a demographic threat, Whites circled the wagons, so to speak, treating all minority groups less charitably—that is, not just the group that was growing. By contrast, when African Americans were confronted with a trend toward a more multiracial society, their own in-group preferences declined—that is, they become more charitable to Whites. In this way, Abascal's results suggest that the social categories of race will change and that interracial relations will evolve in a complex way in the decades ahead.

DIGITAL.WWNORTON.COM/YOUMAYASK8

To see my interview with Kevin Lewis, go to
digital.wwnorton.com/youmayask8

Another factor affecting the future of race relations is technology. Specifically, the changing nature of how we interact (i.e., online)—or in this case, date—is also affecting race relations. Back in the day, so to speak, we were limited in our dating pool to those in our local neighborhood or our social networks, to those in our workplace, and so on. That is, we had to meet in person to be able to date someone. Today, dating apps have, essentially, lifted those structural constraints on whom we can meet and date. As a result, interracial romantic contact has risen (though there is still segregation online). Sociologist Kevin Lewis found this to be the case when analyzing data from a major online dating site: "The punchline of that particular paper is essentially that people are a lot more open to interracial interaction than we might think—so long as the other person goes first. If someone from a different racial background reaches out to me, not only am I more likely to reply to them than you would guess based on my initiation behavior, I'm actually more likely, in the short term future, to reach out to other people from a different background." While Lewis notes that people reproduce the same fences in a digital space as they put up offline, his findings provide justification for the optimistic take that those structures need not be permanent (Conley, 2019c).

DNA DATABASES

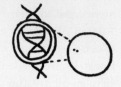

The #BlackLivesMatter social movement stems from many social forces. There is, of course, explicit and implicit racial bias among law enforcement officers that causes racialized police violence. Technology also plays an important role in explaining how the issue of police violence became so big so quickly. First, social media allow what might have been local incidents to compile together into a national awareness—not to mention acting as an organizing tool for actual protests. Perhaps the most important technological innovation contributing to the concern about racialized police brutality, however, is the cell phone camera. Urban theorist Jane Jacobs (1961) once talked about the "eyes on the street" as the primary means by which order was kept in cities. That is, there simply were not enough police to enforce good behavior at all times in all places, so informal watching of our neighbors along with social sanctions is what really kept order, according to Jacobs. Today, cell phones on the street likely matter most—at least when it comes to policing the policers. Has racialized police violence gotten worse or are we simply more aware of it now that almost every citizen has a handy-dandy camera at hand? Technology reveals—and may ultimately help resolve—a racial problem. One of the most debated policies around police behavior is the implementation of body cameras on police to keep records of interactions.

As long as race matters, seemingly "neutral" technology will be inflected with racialized power relations. Take another example: forensic DNA databases—the stuff of TV courtroom drama. Today, when people are taken into custody by law enforcement in most jurisdictions, a sample of DNA is taken from them. This DNA is then available to compare with all other criminal cases that contain DNA data. Many of the stories in the media are about DNA exonerating—often years later—wrongly convicted individuals. The Innocence Project started in 1992 at Cardozo Law School pioneered the movement to initiate appeals of flimsy convictions based on often overlooked biological samples. And the success of the Innocence Project, along with its heart-wrenching tales of wrongful imprisonment, seems to suggest that civil libertarians should welcome this new era of forensic science. This would seem to have a racial-equality-producing effect by countering other forms of bias (say, by juries) in the criminal justice system.

On the side of prosecutors, DNA has also been a boon where it has been available at a crime scene or obtained from a rape kit. Now suspects can be definitively matched to the scene of the crime via blood or semen, for instance. At first blush, then, it seems that DNA in the courtroom is an unalloyed good: It reduces error in an otherwise error-ridden system that relies on fallible human testimony and other less "scientific" approaches to establishing perpetrator identities.

But like most technologies, forensic genetics has a tendency to reproduce existing inequalities. If you are caught because you have a prior conviction and your bodily fluids at the scene of a new crime match those that are on file, that is unfortunate for you, but it is hard to make a case that it is inherently or systematically unfair. People who have committed prior crimes are more likely to be caught than those who are not in the system. However, if your brother or mother has been genotyped by law enforcement, even if you have led a squeaky-clean life until now, then you are also more likely to be fingered by your genetic fingerprint. That is, your DNA will identify you as a first-degree relative of your sibling. And that information, plus a little detective work, is almost as good as you, yourself, appearing in the data set. DNA fingerprinting can even identify cousins or grandchildren, although with less certainty. So if your relatives are more likely to have been registered in the database, you are more likely to be located, even if you yourself have no priors. Of course, in this case, the unfairness lies not in the fact that you were tripped up by your DNA but rather in the fact that the person who committed a crime who comes from a more advantaged background and thus does not have relatives in the database gets away with murder (literally or figuratively). Add in the sort of class or race stratification in the criminal justice system that is thought to exist, and you have a perfect storm by which DNA amplifies existing inequalities. In the United Kingdom, for example, 1 in 4 Black children over the age of 10 have their DNA in a database, while only 1 in 10 White children do (Doward, 2009). Multiply that out to their relatives, and boom, a technology that gets a lot of press for exonerating wrongly convicted minorities suddenly does more to add to the disproportionality in the system.

Conclusion

When you look at race using the sociological imagination, you'll recognize that it's hardly a cut-and-dried issue. You'll see the historical social construction of ideas and identities. You'll see the present-day realities—sometimes monstrosities—of an aspect of our lives so often called a myth or fiction. And you'll be equipped to look at the changing nature of race and race relations that will affect your future.

HOW SEGREGATED ARE YOU?

In recent decades, the United States has undergone what some scholars call "the Big Sort," whereby we have segregated ourselves by political views (think red state versus blue state) and clustered into communities of like-minded people. But as we separate into different communities by lifestyle and belief systems, does that mean that we also live in more racially homogenous social worlds? There is some debate about the overall trends of racial segregation. By some measures, America today is actually less integrated across racial lines than it was 30 years ago; by others, it is more so. It all depends on how we measure the phenomenon.

TRY IT!

Put your hometown's zip code into American Fact Finder at **data.census.gov**. (If you aren't from the United States, use the zip code where your college is based or pick your favorite five-digit number.) From the list of data sets, choose a recent estimate of racial and ethnic origin—a good one is the DP05 American Community Survey's "Demographic and Housing Estimates."

   Then compare the racial/ethnic diversity of your community to that of the country overall. Follow the same instructions above, except instead of your zip code, search for "United States" and pull up the same data set you used to measure the diversity in your community. I'll plug in my NYC zip code in the greater Princeton area:

RACE / ETHNICITY	PERCENTAGE
WHITE	75.0
BLACK OR AFRICAN AMERICAN	4.5
AMERICAN INDIAN AND ALASKA NATIVE	0.1
ASIAN	9.4
NATIVE HAWAIIAN AND OTHER PACIFIC ISLANDER	0.0

RACE / ETHNICITY	PERCENTAGE
SOME OTHER RACE	3.7
TWO OR MORE RACES	7.3
HISPANIC OR LATINX (OF ANY RACE)*	13.7

*Remember that the U.S. Census Bureau does not consider "Hispanic" or "Latinx" as racial categories. That's why most data sets include a breakdown of racial origin (e.g., White, African American, Asian), and a separate breakdown of Latinx or Hispanic origin.

THINK ABOUT IT

Is your hometown more racially homogenous than the national average? How do you think the results would change if you zoomed into your specific neighborhood or zoomed out to a wider view such as your metropolitan area or state?

The American Community Survey includes data over five years. Compare the diversity of your community today and five years ago. Is yours a community in transition?

10

WE THINK OF THE FAMILY
AS A HAVEN IN A HARSH WORLD,
BUT IN FACT, INEQUALITY
BEGINS AT HOME.

ELDEST

MIDDLEBORNS

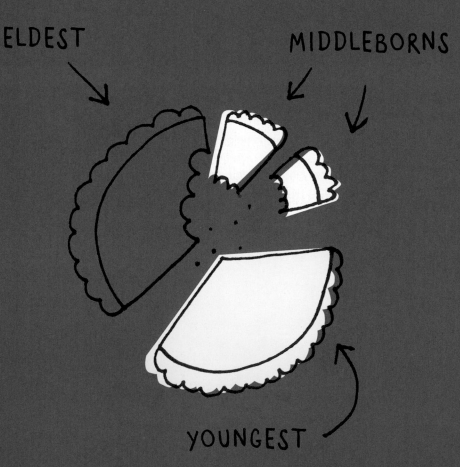

YOUNGEST

Family

The first time I had kids, I was pretty much right on time, so to speak. My eldest was born when I was 28 years old. That's about two years shy of the mean age at first birth in 1998, the year she was born. If you consider education level, then I actually had my first child six years younger than the typical man with a college degree. It may be TMI, but she was conceived the old-fashioned way (though not in the back of a Chevy, as the saying goes). When she was born prematurely and spent several weeks in the neonatal intensive care unit, I was panicked. While I had my mother to turn to for advice, none of my friends had kids yet. We figured it all out day to day—literally.

Fast-forward over two decades, and I just had my third child weeks shy of my fiftieth birthday. Before he was conceived, I wondered if I was making a big mistake. After all, as a social scientist I knew all about the research on age and happiness. Namely, happiness steadily declines throughout adulthood, reaching its lowest point around the mid-forties before starting a steady climb. Was it merely a coincidence that the decline corresponded to the prime years of raising kids and that the rise started when most folks became empty nesters? Was I going to miss out on late adulthood happiness by pressing the fertility reset button?

Meanwhile, his conception could not have been more different from the almost unplanned nature of my first. It took two years of in vitro fertility treatment, including two failed embryo implantation attempts, before my wife found herself with child. Reproductively speaking, I was trying to have a child at an advanced paternal age, and the presence of certain neurological and psychological conditions such as schizophrenia in offspring rises with the dad's age. Schizophrenia lowers life expectancy by 15 to 25 years, so I don't think I was alone among parents in my desire to minimize the chances my child would get it. Because this correlation is stronger in sons than in daughters, we decided to do what we could to reduce this sort of risk by testing each five-day blastocyst that we (or rather, the lab) had created to determine its sex. Those first two failed attempts at pregnancy involved the female embryos, leaving us with only frozen males to implant. We held our breath and tried. It worked.

I reassured myself with studies arguing that most of the increased risk of such conditions results not from the aging process of older men's sperm (which do accumulate more mutations with each decade of life) but from adverse selection—to use the technical term. Namely, men who don't have their first child until age 40 or 50 are different than men who manage to reproduce at, say, age 30. They themselves have more genetic risk for psychopathology. That is, men with mental health or neurological issues are more likely to have kids later in life. The apparent effect of older dads was (mostly) not from the aging process, but from the logic of dating and mating—older first-time dads were more likely to have problems, even if reaching a threshold to be diagnosable.

Since I had been a first-time dad at a much younger age, I hoped my son would not be at a substantially higher risk for schizophrenia than his brother, who was born almost 20 years before. Instead, my worries (for I always worry) turned to other issues. How long would I live? As much as this third child would enjoy a more comfortable and economically secure life than his older siblings did—given that I am more financially secure than I was at 28—he would by definition have me around for much less time than they did. I hesitated to look at the life tables provided by the Social Security Administration, but they indicated that I could expect 30 more years of life, if I were an average American male. That's all he would get of me. And I would need to stay employed—if possible—for 22 of those 30 years in order to see him through college. Additionally, how different would this son's childhood be from that of his brother?

My youngest niece started swiping screens before age one, and by 14 months she managed to call up her favorite Peppa Pig videos on her brothers' iPhones. Moreover, a friend recently signed up his *newborn* daughter for a Gmail account and started cc'ing her on all e-mail threads that involved her (such as brunch plans) so that she'd have a concrete record of some of her preverbal experiences. I hadn't considered these issues with my first child, but the world had changed even over the course of my lifetime.

As lifespans lengthen and age at first birth continues to climb, it turns out that I am at the leading edge of a growing group of older parents—many of whom probably share some of these same worries. Over 9 percent of births today are to fathers over the age of 40 and about 1 percent of births are to dads over the age of 50. Women, as well, are extending their fertility careers, with many having children well into their forties—partly thanks to the increased use of in vitro fertilization (IVF). As adolescence creeps up through the twenties, such childbearing at older ages is perhaps inevitable, even if it requires an assist from technology.

I can report that while many of my worries have not abated, at least one has: Though I am exhausted and can't even believe I went through this sort of extended sleeplessness back when I needed more hours abed on account of being younger, my happiness does seem to be rising, despite (or because of) the new addition to the household. Of course, not regretting your kids is one of the strongest social norms in modern society, so you may not believe me. But I'm telling you, sociologist to sociologist, it's true. (Though you should definitely ask me again when he's a teenager asking to borrow the car keys.)

By the end of this chapter you'll be able to:

- Describe different forms of marriage and family.
- Identify features of the contemporary family that differ from previous historical periods.
- Analyze the gendered implications of the idealized nuclear family and its effects on women in particular.
- Describe the various ways actual families can differ from the idealized, traditional image of the family.

Family Forms and Changes

❚ Describe different forms of marriage and family.

Why do we fall for the people we do? At first thought, this question might seem simple. You start by envisioning the personal qualities of your lover, perhaps something to do with physique, personality, sense of humor, or charm. If you take a step back and really try to think about it, you might admit to more practical reasons as well, such as physical proximity, shared language, and financial security—those everyday factors vital to functioning relationships. If you take yet another step back, you face the larger question of mate selection: the phenomenon of human partnering patterned by history, culture, and law.

Viewing your love life as the product of social norms may feel unromantic, but consider the host of cultural and legal codes prohibiting you from partnering with, say, your 14-year-old first cousin. In Victorian England or a modern-day Bedouin tribe, a man's 14-year-old first cousin might be a perfectly good match. Historically, interracial partnerships have also been prohibited. In 1961, when President Barack Obama's parents got married, 22 different states still outlawed marriage between a White and nonwhite person. Then in *Loving v. Virginia* (1967) the U.S. Supreme Court unanimously

ENDOGAMY

marriage to someone within one's social group.

EXOGAMY

marriage to someone outside one's social group.

MONOGAMY

the practice of having only one sexual partner or spouse at a time.

struck down America's antimiscegenation laws. (See Chapter 9 for a discussion of the one-drop rule.) Similar laws, aimed at maintaining White "racial purity," existed in South Africa during apartheid as well as in Nazi Germany. In the contemporary world, ethnically mixed couples are hardly shocking, but 60 years ago in the United States, they were almost unthinkable. When a culture maintains either legal or normative sanctions against people marrying outside their race, class, or caste, we call it a rule of endogamy, meaning marriage from within. To some extent, we all practice endogamy—that is, on some level people tend to hook up with similar people, because it makes for easier relations if you and your partner share a social group. In other parts of the world, such as India, historically people haven't had much of a choice: The caste system of India relies on a rigid adherence to endogamy (see Chapter 7).

In much of the contemporary Western world, exogamy, or marriage to someone outside one's social group, is legally possible, if not always culturally acceptable. Consider the following unlikely pair: the African American son of a steel mill worker and the only child and sole heir of a mega-millionaire, White, chart-topping rock-and-roll star. The 1994 union of Michael Jackson and Lisa Marie Presley lasted less than two years but serves as an example of a couple who transgressed social, class, and racial groups. However, by the time they met and fell for each other, they were already both celebrities and social equivalents, despite the gulf between their backgrounds. What does their shared social status say about endogamy and exogamy? Total exogamy—that is, when people from completely different social categories get together—is rare.

The Lovings embrace at a press conference the day after the Supreme Court ruled in their favor in *Loving v. Virginia*, June 13, 1967.

In addition to codes of endogamy and exogamy, another basic social structure governs your love life: how many partners you're expected to have. In societies that practice monogamy, a person can partner with only one other. In societies that practice polygamy, people have more than one sexual partner or spouse at a time. (See Chapter 8 for a more thorough discussion of a wide range of sexual practices.) Polygamy can take the form of a woman having several husbands, called polyandry, as happens in some rural areas of Asia. Alternatively, a man can take several wives, called polygyny, the most common form of polygamy, practiced in many contemporary Islamic and African cultures. Although the Mormon Church outlawed polygamy in 1890, some Mormon splinter groups, called fundamentalists, continue the practice of one man supporting several families at the same time (Lee, 2006).

If one day someone asks why you fell for your special someone, keep in mind that the answer could be quite long and sociologically involved. Cultural norms and state regulations play a fundamental, if invisible, role in your love life. These factors first set the limits as to who is even available on your romantic horizon. Once you find that person (or those persons, for you polygamists), your next move will be to form a relationship with them, probably in the shape of a family. But just how might that family look?

MALINOWSKI AND THE TRADITIONAL FAMILY

In the post–World War II era in the United States, the nuclear family—the idealized model of a male breadwinner, a female homemaker, and their dependent children that populated 1950s television shows—emerged as the dominant, normative, and mythical model for domestic life. It was dominant, because indeed many Americans took to it; in the 1950s, 86 percent of children lived in two-parent families, and 60 percent of children were born into homes with a male breadwinner and a female homemaker (Coontz, 2001). It was normative, because it has been hailed, then and now, as the proper form for families, the way things ought to be. Finally, the taken-for-grantedness of the nuclear family is mythical, because its existence represents not a natural, timeless, or universal approach to family arrangements but one that appeared in specific historical contexts.

In the sociological imagination, this version of the family looks less like a universal norm and more like an ideological construct, and an unusual one at that, which arose out of the unique social structural conditions of the 1950s. That is, the 1950s nuclear family model deviates from both its predecessors and its successors, yet many of us still idealize this model and miss it terribly. By studying cross-cultural variation in family forms, we'll find that this allegedly "normal" family is not always the dominant model. By unpacking the historical development of the nuclear family model and its subsequent unraveling, we'll come to recognize that this form of family does not represent a universal ideal. Regardless of what kind of family ties you may deem worth forging, worth loving, and worth defending, as a sociologist your job will be to study all family forms without prejudgment.

In prior centuries, some scholars assumed that the very institution of the nuclear family had developed in Western societies and had not "yet" emerged in some other populations. However, in 1913, Bronislaw Malinowski put to rest a long-standing family debate among anthropologists about the universal existence of families. Scholars had argued that traditional tribal societies couldn't possibly have family units because of their egregious non-discriminating sexual promiscuity. Malinowski (1913), based on his research among Australian Aboriginals (who seemed to have sex with everyone), suggested that these natives did, in fact, form familial arrangements. They

POLYGAMY

the practice of having more than one sexual partner or spouse at a time.

POLYANDRY

the practice of having multiple husbands simultaneously.

POLYGYNY

the practice of having multiple wives simultaneously.

maintained a central place, the equivalent of a hearth and home, where the family gathered, and they bestowed feelings of love, affection, and care on each family member. Thus the dispute was settled: The family was accepted as a universal human institution for most of the twentieth century, a notion that continues to endure today.

Moreover, Malinowski argued that the family, in addition to being a universal phenomenon, fulfilled the necessary task of child rearing in society. The influential structural-functional sociologist Talcott Parsons would expand on this notion in the 1950s. As we learned in Chapter 8, according to Parsons, the traditional nuclear family, consisting of a mother and father and their children, was a functional necessity in modern industrial society, because it was most compatible with fulfilling society's need for productive workers and child nurturers. And so the nuclear family reigned supreme, timeless, and universal. (Note that although the traditional family is a particular form of the nuclear model, in this chapter we will use the two terms synonymously.)

The problem with these functionalist arguments is that even if one social institution seems to perform some function for society, the function is not necessarily performed only by that particular institution. A functional need is not sufficient cause for the development of an institution, especially not when other kinds of institutions can perform the function just as well. But when you have Western blinders on, as most social scientists following Malinowski did, seeing anything other than the kind of family life you expect to see becomes difficult. When properly fitted with your sociological lens, however, you can make the familiar strange, and you'll find some colorful variation among familial arrangements.

Take the Munduruku villagers of South America, for instance. They give new meaning to the hearth-and-home feature of Malinowski's universal family. Munduruku men and women live in separate houses at different ends of their village; they eat separate meals; they sleep apart. In fact, they meet up with each other only to have sex (Collier et al., 1997). Among the Na people of southwestern China (also known as the Mosuo to outsiders), who have managed to retain much of their distinctive culture despite war, Communism, and the onset of quasi-capitalism, the institution of marriage doesn't exist. The Na do not have any practice like it, nor do they put much thought into fatherhood. Children grow up with uncles rather than fathers as the primary males in the home. Sex occurs in the middle of the night, when men visit women for sexual encounters ranging in duration from one-night stands to lifelong relationships (Booth, 2017). No social restrictions limit who can partner with whom. Property is passed down through the maternal line. The Na manage just fine, reproducing from generation to generation and maintaining a stable farming economy that has recently been bolstered by Chinese tourism (people fascinated by the so-called "kingdom of women"). What are the long-term consequences of the Na's particular arrangements?

NUCLEAR FAMILY

familial form consisting of a father, a mother, and their children.

Families come in all different forms. What are some of the ways that family groups can differ from culture to culture? For instance, how does an extended family in the United States (top) differ from the Na in China (middle) or Zambian families in Africa (bottom)?

It turns out that, whereas in most patrilineal societies females are more risk-averse than males, among the Na, that pattern flips: Na girls tend to be the greater risk-takers (Liu & Zuo, 2019). Otherwise, their outcomes don't seem all that different from those in most subsistence farming societies.

If the Na take hands-off fatherhood to the extreme, women in present-day Zambia implode our notions of caring motherhood. Zambian mothers don't nurture their daughters in the way Westerners would expect. When a Zambian girl needs advice, she seeks out an older female relative as a confidante in preference to her mother (Collier et al., 1997). Western culture has always defined mothers' "essential" nature as nurturing and being connected to offspring, presumably ordained by women's biological birthing functions. However, the traditions of motherhood in Zambian culture suggest that a mother's unconditional warmth, despite the rhetoric, does not necessarily reflect a biological given.

THE FAMILY IN THE WESTERN WORLD TODAY

Even the modern Western family comes in a variety of forms. The typical American family today does not always resemble the versions so often idealized in 1950s television shows. In addition to nuclear families, one needs to count the extended family—kin networks that extend outside or beyond the nuclear family. Families with no children also exist (for instance, couples that become "empty nesters" after their children move out), as do two-wage-earner families (dual-income families), single-parent families, blended stepfamilies, and adopted families, to name just a few possibilities. Although the traditional family was the dominant model for a majority of people living in the 1950s, it never described home life for all Americans, and it's increasingly losing its edge today as families take on new shapes and sizes.

EXTENDED FAMILY

kin networks that extend outside or beyond the nuclear family.

In 2021, less than 20 percent of families consisted of two married parents with children and with the husband as the sole earner (Bureau of Labor Statistics, 2022c). According to the Census Bureau, 73.24 percent of American households are shared by a married couple, and 26.75 percent of households are headed by just one person (U.S. Census Bureau, 2020i, 2020j).

In the face of soaring divorce rates, the 1950s-style way of life is indeed becoming a historical artifact. Nowadays, although the exact figure varies considerably from study to study, approximately 43 to 46 percent of all marriages end in divorce (Schoen & Canudas-Romo, 2006). This statistic doesn't seem to discourage too many people, though, because three of four divorced men and two of three divorced women try their hand at marriage again. But alas, the second time around has about the same rate of failure as the first, and those marriages are even more likely to hit the skids (Coontz, 2010). Although divorce seems to have skyrocketed since the 1950s, the divorce rate has actually increased steadily since the nineteenth century, as the practice became less and less of a social and religious taboo. Divorce rates have stabilized over the past decade or so, with about 90 percent of marriages making it to the five-year mark and 70 percent making it to 15 years; then, another 1 percent of marriages dissolve each year after that, whether by divorce or death.

Rising divorce rates in the United States have not put marriage in any danger of extinction. Eventually, about 80 percent of young adults will likely get married at some point if current projections hold, while men are more likely than women to remarry after a divorce (Hendi, 2019; Vespa et al., 2013).

Given the increased incidence of divorce and remarriage, families are taking on new shapes and sizes, such as single-parent and blended arrangements (Figure 10.1). As of 2013, about 15 percent of children in America lived in a blended family (Pew Research Center, 2014), which reconfigures the aftermath of divorce into step-relations. (We'll have more to say about the effect of divorce on children later.) Cohabitation, living together in an intimate relationship without formal legal or religious sanctioning, has also emerged as a socially acceptable arrangement; roughly 24 percent of never-married Americans between 25 and 34 years old live together without marriage. Within three years, though, 58 percent will be married, 19 percent will have broken up, and 23 percent will still be cohabiting (Copen et al., 2013). Many cohabiters believe that living together without marrying lowers the chances of future divorce. It's the commonsense notion that living together

COHABITATION

living together in an intimate relationship without formal legal or religious sanctioning.

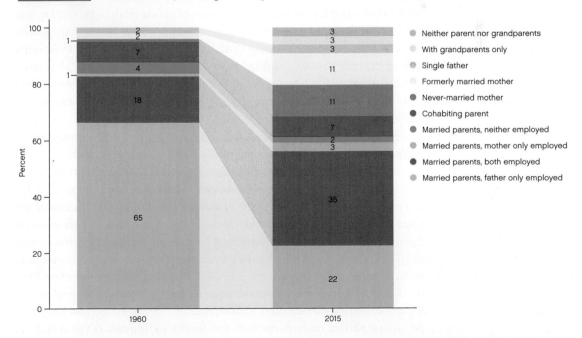

FIGURE 10.1 Work–Family Living Arrangements of Children, 1960 and 2015, Ages 0–14

Legend:
- Neither parent nor grandparents
- With grandparents only
- Single father
- Formerly married mother
- Never-married mother
- Cohabiting parent
- Married parents, neither employed
- Married parents, mother only employed
- Married parents, both employed
- Married parents, father only employed

SOURCE: Cohen, 2017.

provides a sample of married life and informs and improves the couple's future marriage. On the opposite side of the debate, conservative supporters of "family values" point to studies showing a higher divorce rate in the long term among couples who cohabit before marriage than those who don't (Rosenfeld & Roesler, 2018) or those who cohabit before engagement specifically (Rhoades et al., 2009). Conservative Christian counselors advise that "living in sin" sets up a rockier road for a marriage, but the higher divorce rate probably reflects selection bias: Most people who cohabit are open to premarital sex, which also means they are less likely to see divorce as sinful.

Single women with children head 21 percent of American households, while 15 percent of women remain child-free (Livingston, 2015, 2018). Women tend to have children at a later age than ever before—now averaging 26 years, up from 21 in the 1970s (Martin & Osterman, 2019). Women have also started delaying marriage for even longer, tying the knot at a median of 28.6 years old compared to 20.5 in 1947 (U.S. Census Bureau, 2021a). The age when a woman has her first baby varies by subgroup: White professional women, on average, postpone motherhood even longer. Another interesting new twist in American families is the rapid rise in the number of twins. Between the years 1980 and 2016, the number of twin births nearly doubled, from 68,339 to 133,155 births, and triplet and other higher-order multiple births increased by a staggering 3.1 times, from 1,337 to 4,123 (Martin et al., 2017), though this trend has stabilized and even experienced slight declines over the last few years (Martin et al., 2019). This rise has taken place almost entirely among White women. As professional White women increasingly delay childbearing, their biological chances of giving birth to twins rise, and the more widespread use of fertility treatments, which increase the likelihood of a multiple birth (Martin et al., 2010), have compounded this trend. Indeed, the rate of use of assisted reproductive technology (ART) has risen rapidly. As of 2015, 1.7 percent of all live births were the result of some form of ART—a number that is sure to steadily rise over the foreseeable future (Sunderam et al., 2018).

Now, let's take a look at adoption. From 2011 to 2015, approximately 0.7 percent of women 18–44 years old had ever adopted a child, while about 1.2 percent of these women were actively pursuing adoption (Ugwu & Nugent, 2018). International adoptions, which had been climbing since the 1980s, peaked at 22,000 in 2004 and are now falling fast. In 2021, only 1,622 children were adopted from foreign countries, due in part to more rigorous qualifications required of new parents by foreign countries, as well as UN-sanctioned adoption bans on countries like Guatemala (U.S. Department of State, 2022). Meanwhile, in 2012, the Hague Convention on Protection of Children and Co-operation in Respect of Intercountry Adoption (Hague Adoption Convention), an international treaty, stated that domestic adoptions should be pursued first and foremost. Indeed, many countries that used to serve as sources for U.S. international adoptions are now shutting their doors. For example, Ethiopia banned foreign adoptions in 2018 (Hosseini, 2018).

Single-parent families, historically the result of death or desertion, are on the rise as more parents never marry or end up divorced. In 1960, 9.1 percent of U.S. children lived with just one parent; by 1986, that number was 23.5 percent; by 2020, it was 25.5 percent, with 21 percent of all children living in single-mother families (U.S. Census Bureau, 2021g). Single-parent families are also becoming more common worldwide; currently, approximately 14 percent of all families around the globe are headed by women (Chamie, 2016).

Keeping It in the Family: The Historical Divide between Public and Private

| Identify features of the contemporary family that differ from previous historical periods.

Given the enormous cross-cultural and even within-cultural variation among family forms, you may be wondering how and why the so-called traditional family ever came to be the standard marker of normalcy. The short answer is that the family developed alongside modernity, state formation, and the rise of the modern economy. For starters, *traditional family* is a misleading term; this family structure does not characterize all tradition so much as it reflects the 1950s. The "standard" nuclear model of stay-at-home mom and working father deviates from American family arrangements both 50 years before it and 50 years after. It was a historically specific model in a unique era, in which many White city-dwellers moved to the suburbs, married young, and raised three or four children. To recreate this trend in the twenty-first century has actually become nearly impossible: With just a high-school education, an average 30-year-old White man in the 1950s could earn enough at his manufacturing job to buy a median-priced home on 15 percent of his salary (Coontz, 2001). Today, with just a high-school education, an average 30-year-old man is likely to be tenuously positioned in the service sector, making about $15 an hour and probably lacking employer-provided health insurance. Along with money, a number of values set the 1950s apart. As Stephanie Coontz notes in *The Way We Never Were: American Families and the Nostalgia Trap* (1992), people long for the sense of simplicity, wholesomeness, and ease that 1950s families like those portrayed in popular TV shows of the time seemed to enjoy.

PREMODERN FAMILIES

In the preindustrial family of the nineteenth century, each household unit operated like a small business—that is, as a miniature family economy. It was a site for both production and consumption, where work was done in the home and the home was a working unit. Families made and used their own food, clothes, and goods, and there was little if any surplus wealth.

Families tended to live near their kin and thus could get help and support from their kinship networks, strings of relationships between people related by blood and co-residence (i.e., marriage). Preindustrial communities didn't have huge savings banks, insurance companies, payday lenders, or government agencies to help in hard times; that was the role of family. For example, a down-and-out uncle might have a failed crop of wheat one summer. He could call in an IOU from his luckier cousin across the village, borrowing some of his crop and setting off a reciprocal exchange of food, clothing, and child care. Such families would have a grapevine structure where more lateral kinship ties endured than vertical ones (usually, no more than three generations of one family were alive at a time). Communities cooperated in a noncash economy, using a barter system to swap goods. There was no significant accumulation of goods, no savings, no wealth, and not much beyond what individuals needed to survive. There was also minimal division of labor between the sexes, such that men were involved

KINSHIP NETWORKS

strings of relationships between people related by blood and co-residence (i.e., marriage).

Preindustrial families, such as these settlers, operated like a small business. The home was a site for work, and the entire family was involved.

in child care, and women and children often performed the same manual labor as men. Indeed, in the preindustrial family, children were thought of as "small adults," as Philippe Ariès argued in 1962. They didn't warrant any special treatment or consideration, and childhood was hardly the nurturing period we think of today. In fact, some scholars argue that the whole notion of childhood, or children's special needs, is a relatively recent invention, as is that of motherhood as a full-time occupation. Both have emerged only since the middle of the nineteenth century and have been made possible through industrialization, the rise of the cash economy, formal schooling, and the establishment of privacy in the family.

THE EMERGENCE OF THE MALE BREADWINNER FAMILY

With the Industrial Revolution, the realms of the public and private— previously intertwined as one in the working family—split into separate spheres of work and home, as men left household production for wage work in factories. Families stopped being productive mini-economies for the barter system and instead became strictly sites for consumption. Out went household spinning and weaving, and in came the factory-made sweater. Food, clothing, furniture, decorations, appliances, cosmetics, pharmaceuticals: If you can name it, the family probably consumed it.

Specifically, women made the choices of what and how much their families would consume. Furthermore, "women's work"—namely, tending the home and raising children—became relegated to the private, *unpaid* domestic sphere, leading most middle-class women to rely on a man's wages. All the extra money in the new wage economy passed through the hands of women, who remained in charge of running the home and doing the shopping. Such functions might seem like a move toward women "wearing the pants" in the family, but they, in fact, provided a point of emergence for a new form of gender inequality. Women were in charge of spending the family's money, not earning it, and in our society, work for money is the most highly valued form of labor. Women's work was the unpaid management of the home, and this distinction established unequal positions for men and women in society. At the very least, a man had the chance to spend his wages before they ever reached the other members of his family, and women's financial freedom outside of household obligations became inherently limited.

These structural changes had far-reaching results. First, a gendered division of labor arose in the household, where women now were in exclusive charge of maintaining the home and rearing children. Second, as the mobility of families searching for paid labor opportunities increased, they became separated from their kinship networks. Family structures changed from grapevine forms to "beanpole" families, in which kinship ties are vertical. Because people didn't live near their siblings, aunts, and uncles, they could depend only on their children and parents who lived with them. As

This nineteenth-century painting illustrates the Victorian feminine domestic ideal. How did the Industrial Revolution transform the division of labor between men and women?

life expectancies increased, up to five generations may have been alive at any given time, but lateral ties (such as those existing between cousins) weakened because of the longer distances separating these kin.

The beanpole family structure is particularly taxing on women today, who, because of delayed childbirth, are likely to find that their parents need assistance just as their own children leave home. As a result of declining fertility and longer life expectancies, the U.S. population is growing older, so the problem of elder care (and its disproportionate impact on women) will only get worse. In 2021, the median age in the United States was 38.8 years (U.S. Census Bureau, 2022g). A recent survey found that 10 percent of respondents over age 50 reported providing more than 200 hours of informal care to folks (outside their home) in the past year. Women bore most of the burden, but men did 40 percent of that care. We are in the middle as compared to other wealthy countries in this regard (Bauer, 2019). Our government's relatively low support for elder care (Medicare does not cover long-term care, for instance) is balanced out by the fact that we have one of the youngest populations in the developed world.

A third fallout of the new cash economy and the resulting split between public and private realms was the creation of the cult of domesticity, the notion that true womanhood centers on domestic responsibility and child rearing. During the first half of the twentieth century, ideas sprang up surrounding woman's true nature—ideas meant to support her newly created role as housewife, including the notion that women, more than men, have innate emotional qualities required to provide warmth and comfort. According to this ideology, women's "natural" domesticity both better suits them for home life and serves a necessary role in the survival of society. Women, so the argument goes, ensure that the home remains a safe haven in the otherwise cold seas of capitalist enterprise. As breadwinners, men struggle in the dog-eat-dog commercial world, whereas women provide the emotional shelter that anchors private life in human sentiment, emotion, care, and love.

FAMILIES AFTER WORLD WAR II

By the 1950s, the idealized model of the nuclear family was mostly attainable only by White middle- and upper-class families (see the discussion of racial and ethnic differences in family structure later in the chapter). Most men's earnings were simply not great enough to afford a stay-at-home wife and dependent children. The gap between ideal and real narrowed as real wages (wages adjusted for inflation) increased in the 1950s, making the patriarchal tradition of a male breadwinner and a female homemaker a feasible arrangement for a greater number of families. Still, many nonwhite, non-middle-class families and individuals were excluded from the prosperity of the 1950s (see Chapter 9), and women worked outside the home throughout history, especially nonwhite women.

During the post–World War II economic boom, the manufacturing economy thrived with unionized jobs, real living wages, government housing subsidies, and job-training programs. It was a period of great optimism for good reasons: The Depression was over; America and its allies had won the war; and the United States was now dominant on the world's economic stage. White Americans moved en masse to the suburbs—often to homes that required little to no down payment. Meanwhile, many women quit their jobs and returned to cultivating domesticity full-time; the divorce rate dropped to just over one in four marriages; and fertility rates soared during this "baby boom."

As family scholars point out, however, these trends in families were atypical. Although the divorce rate dipped in the 1950s, it had been on the rise since the end of the nineteenth century, so modern appeals to return to an age when divorce did not exist ring somewhat hollow. Furthermore, the fertility boom following World War II represented an unusual spike in family size, which had otherwise been on the decline since well before the turn of the century. What's more, the 1950s were also an era of rampant teen pregnancies: The teenage birthrate was twice as high in 1957 as in the 1990s. Compared to the 1990s, pregnant teens in the postwar era had less access to

Textile factory workers in 1949. Why did many women leave their jobs after World War II?

abortion, so when they bore children, they more often got married. In fact, the 1950s marked the twentieth century's youngest national average for age at time of marriage—an average of 20 and 22 years old for women and men, respectively. Finally, the decline in women's workforce participation represented a dip in an otherwise upward trend, especially given women's labor power during World War II (when women worked as temporary replacements for men serving in the armed forces).

Although the period was an anomaly in many ways, we tend to look back fondly (and sometimes bitterly) to the 1950s family as the normal and "right" way for families to be. But Stephanie Coontz (2001) found that while children's well-being and family economic security were at an all-time high toward the end of the 1960s, it was also a time of tumultuous struggle for racial and sexual equality. What, then, do we really miss?

The Gendered Nuclear Family

| Analyze the gendered implications of the idealized nuclear family and its effects on women in particular.

Since the 1970s, American men and women have been caught up in what Kathleen Gerson (1985) calls a "subtle revolution" in our way of organizing work and home, even as we fantasize about an imagined time gone by. Women's participation in the labor force has soared, whereas fertility rates have plummeted. By the end of the 1970s, more women were in, rather than out of, the labor force for the first time. In 1950, approximately 30 percent of women worked outside the home; that number more than doubled to 60 percent by 1999 (Francis, 2005). In 2020, the labor force participation rate for women was 56.2 percent (Bureau of Labor Statistics, 2022j; Figure 10.2).

At the same time, birthrates have dropped, sinking from a baby boom to a baby bust. In the mid-1950s, the birthrate was about 106.2 births per 1,000 women. That rate had dropped to just 62.9 in 1980 and to 59.1 as of 2018 (Martin et al., 2019). The National Center for Health Statistics reports that marriage rates since the 1960s have also declined, and many adults are postponing marriage until later in life. With the rising divorce rate, marriage looks less and less like the stable force in women's lives compared to the postwar era. In fact, by 2007, more Americans age 15 and older were single than married for the first time in a century. The result is that the cult of domesticity is out of the picture for most women, and daughters since the 1970s have increasingly departed from their mothers' paths.

FIGURE 10.2 Women in the Labor Force, 1970–2022

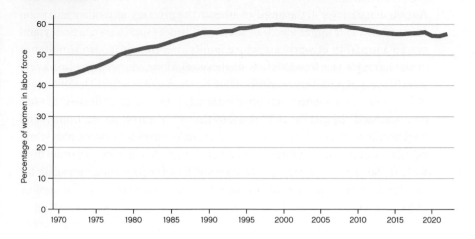

SOURCE: Bureau of Labor Statistics, 2022f.

The gender revolution in work and family is probably here to stay and with notable effects on children. Research study after research study has hinged on one basic question: Is maternal employment good, bad, or neutral for kids? There's no shortage of hypotheses. A study published in *Child Development* (Brooks-Gunn et al., 2003) suggests that having a working mother in one's early years can result in lower cognitive achievement and increased behavioral problems for a child. Yet another study published in the prestigious journal *Science* (Chase-Lansdale et al., 2003) claims the opposite: For moms with lower income levels, leaving kids in day care to enter the workforce is beneficial. Hundreds of studies fall on both sides of the argument, with mothers' employment being either disastrous or advantageous to their children. Family situations are just too complex and diverse to generalize. Perhaps, then, this mishmash of results is a consequence of asking the wrong question. Maybe we should instead ask, "How does maternal employment affect children differently within the family?"

In *The Pecking Order* (Conley, 2004), I found that when a mother worked while raising her children, the adult daughters and sons eventually attained jobs that were more or less equivalent and made about the same income. But in families with a stay-at-home mom, the gender gap widens. When the mother does not work and thus cannot provide a same-sex parental role model in terms of career choices, daughters fare far worse than sons, earning roughly $8,000 less a year than their brothers later in life. And without a working-mother role model, daughters are 15 percent less likely to graduate from college than their brothers (whereas in the general population, more women than men earn college degrees).

A FEMINIST "RETHINKING OF THE FAMILY"

As noted in Chapter 4, the family serves as the primary unit of socialization for most of us. If larger forces in the social order (such as wage policy and gender inequality at work) structure family life, then it is also simultaneously a site for the reproduction of these relations. As we have just seen, whether or not a mother works outside the home may affect the outcomes of her sons and daughters differently. Sarah Fenstermaker Berk (1985) has characterized the family as a "gender factory" of sorts, where women and men learn to take on distinct roles paralleling the divide between public and private spheres. The family teaches people how to "do gender" in conformity with social rules. Sociologist Marjorie DeVault (1991) shows in *Feeding the Family* that family ties are constructed through women's acts of shopping, preparing meals, and serving them. In everything from the planning of menus to accommodating a child's dislike of lima beans, women are doing gender. As Barbara Risman (1998) notes, "It is at home that most people come to believe that men and women are and should be essentially different." In the act of traditional marriage itself, rituals are gender-stratified: Brides are given away by their fathers, and they take their husband's last name in patrilineal custom.

The idealized cult of domesticity, although a historical and cultural anomaly among many possibilities, has had powerful and lasting effects on many women's family ideals. Feminist consciousness, raised in the 1960s, led many women to question the ideology of domesticity, finding it "stultifying, infantilizing, and exploitative" of women (Stacey, 1987). In 1963, the feminist writer Betty Friedan led the assault against the limits of being a homemaker with her classic *The Feminine Mystique*. She writes in the introduction:

> The problem lay buried, unspoken, for many years in the minds of American women. It was a strange stirring, a sense of dissatisfaction, a yearning that women suffered in the middle of the twentieth century in the United States. Each suburban housewife struggled with it alone. As she made the beds, shopped for groceries, matched slipcover material, ate peanut butter sandwiches with her children, chauffeured Cub Scouts and Brownies, lay beside her husband at night—she was afraid to ask even of herself the silent question—"Is this all?" (Friedan, 1997, p. 15)

Sociologists elaborated on Friedan's invocation, claiming that power truly distinguishes the head of the family. The family, as they see it, is a battleground for the power to make collective decisions on everything from who does the laundry to what neighborhood to live in to what college fund to invest in. This conflict exists, argues sociologist Jessie Bernard in *The*

Future of Marriage (1972), even in the comfortable living rooms of traditional nuclear families. Take, for instance, the tensions that arise from the different ways that household members spend money. In studies of welfare recipients, women have been known to spend a greater portion of their welfare benefits on children than fathers do. And in a study of Japanese American families, working wives tended to keep their earnings separate from their husbands' income, and even secret, to preserve their autonomy to spend it how they—and not their husbands—chose (Glenn, 1986).

Furthermore, money is not all the same within the family; rather, the incomes of husbands, wives, and children are earmarked in distinctive ways. Women's earnings tend to be spent on extras, so-called luxury items, or otherwise nonessential expenses. Their money is devalued as "fun money." Men's earnings, on the other hand, are earmarked for essentials. When sociologist Margaret Nelson (1990) interviewed working wives, one woman explained, "What he makes there is mainly like insurance, taxes, and all that. What I make usually goes for food, clothing—whatever I find necessary . . . or just to take the kids once a week to Middlebury and blow it," so even a household's income has gendered connotations. As Viviana Zelizer (2005) notes, the distinctions between household incomes help protect a man's status and sense of masculinity when a wife also takes on a breadwinner role in dual-income families. In this way, feminist rethinking of the family urges us not to view the family as a necessarily cohesive, unified whole but to recognize that the family does not exist outside of the sphere of socially structured gender relations. And as gender relations change, so also do family forms. As women become less financially dependent on men, for example, more equality slowly develops in other areas of their relationships. Or does it?

Betty Friedan in 1967, advocating for the addition of an equal rights clause for women in the New York State Constitution.

THE CHORE WARS: SUPERMOM (HAS TO) DO IT ALL

One of the main representations of gender within the family takes the form of the unpaid labor that needs to be done at home. In the case of housework and the chore wars, gender remains a salient social force that shapes family life. The cult of domesticity lingers on, such that even though women make up almost half of the workforce (46.8% in 2022), domestic duties, such as housework and child care, still fall disproportionately on their shoulders (Bureau of Labor Statistics, 2023; Francis, 2005). Women return from the office to take up what Arlie Hochschild (1989) calls the second shift: Women take responsibility for housework and child care, which includes everything from cooking dinner to doing laundry, bathing children, reading bedtime stories, and sewing Halloween costumes. Despite women's gains in the public realm of work, the revolution at home has, as Hochschild described it, stalled.

SECOND SHIFT

women's responsibility for housework and child care—everything from cooking dinner to doing laundry, bathing children, reading bedtime stories, and sewing Halloween costumes.

Within a two-career household, parents spend their at-home time on separate—and unequal—tasks. One study from 1965 to 1966 found that working women averaged three hours each day on housework, whereas men put in a meager 17 minutes. When it comes to leisure activities, however, men surpass their working wives. Working fathers watch an hour more of television per day than working mothers. They also sleep a half hour longer (Hochschild, 2003). The resulting "leisure gap" can brew hostilities between exasperated, exhausted wives and their unresponsive husbands.

Using national studies on time use from the 1960s and 1970s, Hochschild counted the hours that women and men put in on the job in addition to their time spent on housework and child care. She determined that women worked roughly 15 hours longer each week than men (Hochschild, 2003). After 52 weeks, women have worked 780 hours more than men—that's an extra month! While the gap in unpaid work has shrunk since the 1960s, it has remained more or less the same over the past decade (Figure 10.3). Women over the age of 15 spend 5.7 hours every day on housework, child care, and elder care, while men over 15 years of age spend just 3.6 hours daily (Hess et al., 2020).

Recent research shows how and when this gendered division of labor arises. Before the birth of the first child, men exhibit higher total work hours than women: They tend to work more paid hours and also do a relatively equitable share of housework. But after the birth of children, the division of labor in the home changes, both because men do less of the child-care work and because, at the same time, they reduce their non-child-care housework. In total, before becoming parents, married men spend about three additional hours doing all forms of work (jobs and housework) compared to women, but after the birth of a child, women do about six hours more work than men (Yavorsky et al., 2015).

FIGURE 10.3 Trends in Housework and Child Care since 1965

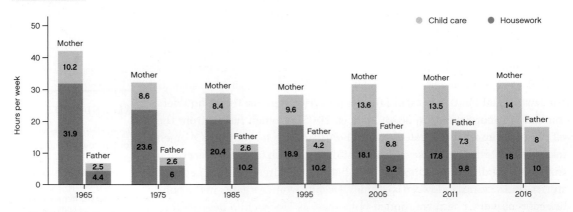

SOURCES: Parker & Livingston, 2018; Pew Research Center, 2013.

The division of labor in the home refers to not just who does how much but also who does what. As Viviana Zelizer (2005) shows, housework tasks are patterned around gender. When men do housework, their contribution is referred to as "helping out around the house," and their wives zealously thank them. Women who have "helping" husbands in the home consider themselves extremely lucky. Many men, however, never report feeling lucky or extremely thankful when their wives do the housework. And women *run* the household; they don't simply "help out."

In addition, men are typically in charge of outdoor, stereotypically masculine activities, whereas women disproportionately do the work inside. Even cooking is broken down by gender: Men more often cook the meat for a meal when they share work in the kitchen. Men also have more control over when they help out, because they are more likely to be in charge of chores that don't require completion on a daily basis, such as changing the oil in the family car or mowing the lawn. Women are more likely to be locked into a fixed and harried housework routine: pick up the kids from day care, cook dinner, wash the dishes, bathe the kids, and put the baby to bed (Zelizer, 2005).

Yet another male advantage in the division of household labor is that men get to do more of what they like to do, while women are often stuck with the most undesirable chores, such as scrubbing toilets and ironing. The time fathers spend on domestic labor is more likely to be spent with their children, which is usually more enjoyable and satisfying than doing chores. In a recent interview with me, sociologist Jennifer Senior pointed out how much more parenting today's dads are doing: "Dads spend three times as much time with their kids today as their fathers spent with them. So they're not trying to imitate their mothers or their fathers. They're trying to imitate their wives . . . they are not slackers at all. In spite of all the differences within the house, they are really doing way more than they ever saw and ever had modeled for them" (Conley, 2015b). Not only is the time that dads spend with kids more enjoyable than scrubbing pans or other household drudgery, but studies consistently also find that men who share child rearing and housework have happier marriages, better health, and longer lives (Kimmel, 2000). As

DIGITAL.WWNORTON.COM/YOUMAYASK8

To see an interview with Jennifer Senior, go to
digital.wwnorton.com/youmayask8

best-selling author and pediatrician Dr. Spock (1998) put it, "There is no reason why fathers shouldn't be able to do these jobs as well as mothers." Furthermore, studies show that when left to their own devices, men are perfectly fine housekeepers, cooks, and primary parents (Gerson, 1993).

Neoclassical economists typically look at a member's power in the family as a direct expression of that member's utility to the family unit, usually measured in terms of income. In such a formulation, money talks, and whoever earns the bacon doesn't have to cook it; however, women's income goes only so far in increasing their power in the family. The more a wife contributes to the household income, the more her husband is likely to share, or "help out" with, the second shift. That trend seems to fit the bacon theory. But as soon as the wife's earnings start to overtake the husband's, he drops out of the shared domestic equation, leaving the entire second shift up to her (Bittman et al., 2003). Furthermore, when women earn more than their husbands, the perceived insult to masculinity may make for a tense home environment. Men, it seems, are usually not eager to let anyone else wear the proverbial pants in the household.

The capitalist value system in the United States contributes to the power difference between inside and outside labor. The entrepreneur Don Aslett, who built a business around domestic cleaning services, told one sociologist, "The whole mentality out there is that if you clean, you're a scumball" (Ehrenreich, 2001). In kinder words, household labor is unpaid labor, and in a capitalist economy, it seems pretty, well, worthless. For another, housework has been construed historically as women's work. A housewife, measured against modern criteria for success such as salaries, pensions, benefits, bonuses, and promotions, is just a housewife. Feminists in the 1960s argued that housework should be fairly compensated, because without a woman's labor, the American workforce would not be able to keep going (Ellen, 2014; Scalise, 2014; Shulevitz, 2016). This "reproductive labor" argument stressed the value of social reproduction: All the activities and tasks that women performed daily kept their working husbands' lives running smoothly. Still, unpaid domestic work has not yet triggered broader policy discussions around the way housework functions in the U.S. economy. For example, the federal government still offers no guarantee of paid maternity (or paternity) leave.

It also takes marginalization to appreciate the center, as Christopher Carrington's study of gay couples in San Francisco demonstrates. Blumstein and Schwartz (1983) have suggested that an egalitarian division of labor exists more commonly in the households of gay and lesbian couples. But as Carrington (1999) notes, they also pay much more care and attention to their household chores, spending about two times as long on cleaning as heterosexual couples. The explanation? Homosexual couples see housework as a means of legitimating their households; thus it is a more central, validating activity for them than it is for the typical working wife. Even as same-sex couples have become more societally accepted, their more egalitarian division of household labor has appeared to persist (Bauer, 2016; Brewster, 2015). This trend suggests that egalitarianism may not just be an effort to gain legitimacy but, rather, is a reflection of the attitudes of those who decide to enter into a same-sex marriage or is a result of the psychological effect of being in such a household or, perhaps, simply reflects the more equal labor market positions of such spouses.

Many women juggle full-time jobs with caring for their children and running their home with little help from their spouses. According to Arlie Hochschild, what are the consequences of the supermom strategy?

If, as sociologists argue, the burden of the second shift falls on working mothers in dual-income families, we might expect some nasty consequences. Indeed, Hochschild found that in response to the stalled revolution, some women tried to do it all. This is the supermom strategy. She cooks, she cleans, she climbs the career ladder, all while being a devoted parent and loving partner. Supermoms, of course, don't really exist, but a perpetual myth maintains that some women can do it all, and if other women can't, it's a result of some personal flaw.

Women who buy into the supermom myth burn out quickly, and typically their marriages absorb the shock. In one study, Hochschild (1989) found that married women are more likely than men to think about divorce (30 percent of married women have considered divorce versus 22 percent of men). Women are also likely to give a more comprehensive list of reasons for wanting a divorce. In her interviews of dual-income families, Hochschild encountered bitter women, fed up with doing all the work, and puzzled men, confused over their wives' hostilities or bitter themselves at begrudgingly having to help out more.

Because women still earn less than men, about $0.81 for every dollar that a man earns, a disproportionate financial shock hits women after a divorce (Hegewisch & Williams-Baron, 2017). Given the rampant threat of divorce, some women bite the second-shift bullet, just letting the hostilities simmer. Other women manage by cutting household corners where they can, allowing the dust to pile up and skimping on the children's evening story time. For them, hostilities linger beneath a growing sense of parental guilt.

By contrast, in households in which men and women genuinely share the second shift, marriages are much more likely to be stable and happy ones. Studies (e.g., that conducted by Michael S. Kimmel in 2000) have found that when men share the housework, working wives experience less stress. Barbara Risman (1998) calls these "fair families," where husbands and wives equally split the roles of breadwinner and homemaker. In fair families, couples honor an ideology of gender equality, and both men and women benefit from such an arrangement. Women win the self-respect that comes with being economically independent, and they respond by regarding marriage less as a necessity and more as a voluntary, love-based relationship. Men, by sharing the breadwinner burden, feel less stressed and freer to find jobs they enjoy. Perhaps most important, Risman speculates about a uniqueness in these sharing couples: They are more often close friends.

WHEN HOME IS NO HAVEN: DOMESTIC ABUSE

Family life is not always the warm, nurturing environment that appears on prime-time television, where moms and dads stand ready with hugs, siblings crack jokes, and grandma is strict but well intentioned. Abuse, neglect, and manipulation happen across all familial relationships: Sibling "rivalry" becomes physically aggressive, husbands and wives with powerful tempers hit and control one another, adult children plunder their elderly parents' life savings. The most frequent form of family violence is sibling on sibling (Eriksen & Jensen, 2006). But before you assign all the blame for your current low self-esteem on that time your brother walloped you upside the head with a shoe, note that the strongest two predictors of sibling-on-sibling violence are dads with short tempers and moms who get physical with punishment (Eriksen & Jensen, 2006). Is it really your brother's fault that he learned how to solve problems by mimicking dad's anger management strategy and piggybacking on mom's heavy hand of authority? This monkey-see, monkey-do explanation has had a long history in the study of domestic violence.

Broad social factors like poverty, single-parent households, and low levels of educational attainment are associated with higher levels of all types of domestic abuse. Situational stressors can also contribute to violence in the family. For example, studies have found that during the pandemic-related lockdowns—when much of our routines and mobility were curtailed, and many members of families were suddenly home all the time together—domestic violence rose by over 8 percent (Piquero et al., 2021).

When violence occurs within a couple, it's often called intimate partner violence (IPV). One in four women and one in ten men have been raped, physically attacked, and/or stalked by an intimate partner at some point in their lives (National Coalition Against Domestic Violence, 2020). In a study of 10,018 homicides for women over age 18: "Over half of all homicides (55.3%) were IPV-related; 11.2% of victims of IPV-related homicide experienced some form of violence in the month preceding their deaths, and argument and jealousy were common precipitating circumstances" (Petrosky et al., 2017).

A relatively new field of study investigates physical, verbal, and financial abuse intentionally or unintentionally perpetrated against people (usually family members) who are at least 57 years old. Estimates suggest elder abuse is not particularly widespread; one-year prevalence (that is, a statistical measure of how frequently these problems occur within a given 12-month period) was 4.6 percent for emotional abuse, 1.6 percent for physical abuse, 0.6 percent for sexual abuse, 5.1 percent for potential neglect, and 5.2 percent for current financial abuse by a family member (Acierno et al., 2010). The impact of mistreatment in intimate relationships can have serious and long-lasting financial, health, and emotional consequences for individuals, families, and communities.

Variations from the Ideal Nuclear Family

| Describe the various ways actual families can differ from the idealized, traditional image of the family.

AFRICAN AMERICAN FAMILIES

For millions of American households, the idealized traditional family *as depicted in 1950s television* never even came close to being a lived reality. For African American families, who throughout history have combined work and family, the split between the public and private spheres has never made much sense. Neither has the ideal of exclusive, "isolationist" motherhood made sense for women lacking the resources that allow for full-time homemaking. More often, Black and poor women have come to rely on extrafamilial female networks in order to manage child-care and work responsibilities (Stack & Burton, 1994). If the average American woman has two shifts, then the typical Black American mother has three, because she is more often the primary or only breadwinner. This greater importance of women in the Black family has unfortunately been conflated with "backward" female domination or matriarchy.

Social scientists in the 1960s made heavy use of the matriarchal thesis to explain social problems in the African American community. In *The Negro Family: The Case for National Action* (1965), Daniel Patrick Moynihan found that 25 percent of Black wives outearned their husbands versus only 18 percent of White wives. This "pathological" matriarchy, Moynihan argued, undercuts the role of the father in Black families and leads to all sorts of problems later in life, such as domestic violence, substance abuse, crime, and degeneracy. You name it, the matriarch caused it. The root of matriarchy, Moynihan asserted, dated back to the days of slavery, which reversed roles for men and women and continued to haunt African Americans up to the time of his report. Moynihan's image of the Black matriarch as domineering lays blame on African American families for social ills such as stagnating wages, single motherhood, high divorce rates, and lower school achievement. The matriarch is also a powerful reminder to all women of just what can go wrong when women challenge the patriarchal decree that they be submissive, dependent, and feminine. The Moynihan report's prescription for the social problems of Black people was just this: Black women should aspire to the cult of true (White) womanhood.

Scholars like W. E. B. Du Bois had argued all along, however, that African American female-headed families were the outcome, rather than the cause, of racial oppression and poverty. In 1987, William Julius Wilson graphed a "marriageable Black male index," which highlighted the scarcity of employed, nonincarcerated Black men (fewer than 50 marriageable Black men per 100 Black women back then). In such a context, if Black women didn't work to pay the rent, put food on the table, and take care of the kids, who would? As Elaine Kamplain has pointed out, African American mothers were "damned if they worked to support their families and damned if they didn't" (Hochschild, 2003).

Matriarchy is one of many misreadings that social critics have imposed on the Black family. When critics hold fast to the idealized concept of the nuclear family, they are likely to see any model that differs from the traditional yardstick as deviant. The sociologist's trick is to view the traditional family, in which a heterosexual couple lives together with their dependent children in a self-contained, economically independent household, as just one of many potential family forms. After all, this particular kind of family evolved from the socially constructed separation of home and work—a separation rooted in the upper classes—and the experiences of most African American families stray from that norm. In fact, asserts Patricia Hill Collins (1990), women of color have never fit this model. Collins looks at the family with a different set of lenses—what she calls an Afrocentric worldview—that allows for alternative concepts of family and community. One instance of this worldview is more of a collective effort with strong neighborhood support: the "it takes a village" model described in Chapter 10 on the culture of poverty.

Identifying the traditional family as a specific historical phenomenon that has rarely applied to Black families enables us to analyze the Black community's unique characteristics in a less judgmental manner. African American communities tend to have an expanded notion of kinship, as denoted by the all-encompassing use of the words *brother* and *sister*. This linguistic

Many African American parents rely on extrafamilial community members to help raise children. What are some of the criticisms of the matriarchal thesis?

tendency and dense social network may have developed out of Blacks' historical experience with slavery. Because slaves were separated from their biological families at the auction block by White owners, they adapted by expanding the definition of *family* from immediate bloodlines to racial ones. Under slavery, Black men and women occupied indistinct work roles, often performing the same labor side by side in plantation fields. The legacy of their shared labor was incompatible with a nuclear family, a model predicated on the differentiation between male and female spheres (Collins, 1990).

As a result of segregation throughout the twentieth century, the particular African American notions of community and family continued to endure. But after World War II, the manufacturing economy took a downturn and many Black workers, employed by shrinking industries, found themselves at risk of economic marginalization. Marital rates among Blacks have been in decline since the 1960s, and female-headed households have been on the rise among both the poor and middle classes. Kathryn Edin's ongoing research in poor African American communities has found a consistent interest in the elements that constitute family life, such as having children and getting married, although poor-quality schools, lack of jobs, and (sometimes) substance abuse make it difficult to undertake a traditional progression of dating, love, marriage, and childbearing. Childbearing often precedes marriage, but unlike common stereotypes of indifferent cads interested primarily in sex, fathers-to-be are often excited about becoming parents and tend to strengthen their commitment to the baby's mother. Unfortunately, parenting the same child (or children) may not be enough to hold these couples together until they feel financially secure enough to marry. Black children (50.8 percent) and Hispanic children (29.1 percent) were more likely to live with a single parent than non-Hispanic White children (18.1 percent) or Asian children (9.7 percent) (U.S. Census Bureau, 2021g). This statistic reflects, in part, the high rates of unemployment and incarceration and low rates of education among Black men.

LATINX FAMILIES

According to the U.S. Census Bureau (2020d), Latinxs are the largest minority group in America, making up 18 percent of the U.S. population. The U.S. Census Bureau (2022b) defines Latino as "a person of Cuban, Mexican, Puerto Rican, South or Central American, or other Spanish culture or origin regardless of race." Latinxs also live all over the United States, although they have clustered on the West Coast and in the South and Midwest (Hernandez et al., 2007). Given the diverse origins and geography of Latinxs, how can we make general claims about the Latinx family? Sociologists don't all agree that such a thing exists or that a generic Latinx identity is even imaginable (Santa Ana, 2004). But there are a few common threads that run through many Latinx families. Their strong family ties make family a top priority for many Latinxs—so important, in fact, that individual Latinxs often define their self-worth in terms of their family's image and accomplishments (Ho, 1987). Like African American families, Latinx families act as safety nets, and members take seriously their responsibilities to help one another, even in long chains of needy extended relations (Skogrand et al., 2004). They have a strong sense of community and allegiance to family (Hurtado, 1995). For example, so many Latinx immigrants send remittances, or money, to family members back home that remittances are now one of the largest sources of cash in the Mexican and many other Central American economies.

Traditional rules of gender and authority also loom large in Latinx culture. Women listen to their men, and children to their elders, in a clear-cut hierarchy. This should make sense to anyone who's taken a Spanish language class (or studied any other Romance language). The heavy use of titles and ranks in the everyday vocabulary shows that respect and formality are crucial (DeNeve, 1997). Most Latinx families are also shaped by a tradition of devout Catholicism. Combine high religiosity with the importance of family honor and you soon recognize a few tendencies: high rates of marriage and relatively low rates of divorce, high rates of marriage at a young age, and a lot of babies born out of wedlock. This third outcome may seem contradictory, but think about it: If a young Latinx does have premarital sex and becomes pregnant without a marriage prospect in sight, she's less likely than her African American or White peers to have an abortion, a worse breach of Catholic culture than an out-of-wedlock birth. Add to that a tight-lipped stance on discussing sex at home, the dwindling of preventive sex education, and the difficulty (not to mention the embarrassment) teens face trying to get their hands on effective and affordable birth control, and you end up with a lot of babies born to single Latinx moms. In 2020, about 52.8 percent of all Latinx babies were born to unwed mothers, compared with 28.4 percent of non-Hispanic White babies (those numbers are still lower than the nearly 70.4 percent of African American babies born outside of marriage) (Centers for Disease Control and Prevention, 2020b).

ASIAN AMERICAN FAMILIES

While the diverse "Asian American" label applies to people with origins from Pakistan to the Philippines, this group shares some commonalities. Overall, like Latinxs, Asian Americans are much more likely to be immigrants than U.S. residents from other racial groups. As a result, two-thirds (66 percent) speak a language other than English at home (they may also speak English at home). They also are more likely to live in multigenerational households—that is, with grandparents, parents, and children; 27 percent of Asian Americans live in such family arrangements compared to 19 percent

of U.S. residents overall (Budiman & Ruiz, 2022). By 2055, they are projected to be the largest immigrant group in the country. As a result of these
demographic trends, among Asian American families, the children—who
often speak English better than their older relatives at home—commonly
take on the role of "language broker" (*The Language Brokers (Audio)*, 2017).
The language broker acts as the family interpreter and public face with
teachers, bankers, doctors, and other institutional representatives. There
is a debate about the impact of this role. Some kids seem to suffer higher
rates of depression from the burden, for example. Meanwhile, others thrive
with the responsibilities, becoming skilled and confident at interacting with
authority figures in society.

FLAT BROKE WITH CHILDREN

The lack of support for single motherhood in America puts single mothers
and their families at a greater risk for experiencing poverty, so the higher
rates of single-parent families in nonwhite communities create more significant challenges for them. In a thin welfare state with widening economic gaps between the rich and the poor, single mothers must often decide
between mothering and work. Single mothers rely on a combination of welfare, family, friends, luck, and creativity to make ends meet. At any given
point in the past few decades, half of all mothers raising children by themselves have relied on welfare to get by. In contrast to the media myth of the
"lazy welfare mother" who watches television and buys filet mignon with
her food stamps, many of these mothers work hard (often off the books)
and desperately want to escape poverty. Welfare critics might be surprised
to read *Making Ends Meet: How Single Mothers Survive Welfare and Low-Wage
Work* (1997), in which sociologists Kathryn Edin and Laura Lein find that all
single mothers prefer self-reliance to welfare dependency. In fact, a majority
get off the welfare rolls in two years, and hardly any stay on welfare for more
than eight years.

In their study of 379 mothers across four U.S. cities, Edin and Lein
traced what happens when poor single mothers are faced with the choice
between welfare and work. The word *choice* here is misleading because it
implies freedom, as though these women can easily move from dependency
to self-sufficiency. However, because single mothers are often unskilled or
semiskilled and have less education than average, their employment options
are limited to low-wage work that rarely provides benefits.

Edin and Lein found that mothers on welfare could cover about three-
fifths of their expenses. In low-wage jobs, they faced a larger gap between
earnings and expenses, in part to cover the costs of transportation, child-care
arrangements, increased rent, and fewer food stamps. (Both the food stamp
program and federal housing program consider income when determining
benefits; even a father's child support can translate into a rent increase for

a single mother.) This system makes a savings account virtually impossible for welfare recipients to maintain and is arguably the real culprit behind the trap of dependency. In fact, leaving welfare for work substantially increases these women's expenses, such that they can cover only two-thirds of those expenses on low wages alone. One working mother voiced her frustrations:

> Ask any politician to live off my budget. Live off my minimum wage job and just a little bit of food stamps—how can he do it? I bet he couldn't. I'd like him to try it for one month. Come home from work, cook dinner, wash clothes, do everything, everything, get up and go to work the next day, and then find you don't have enough money to pay for everything you need. (Edin & Lein, 1997, p. 149)

Barbara Ehrenreich, a sociologist and writer, tried to make ends meet with low-wage work in 1998. That was a year in which the Preamble Center for Public Policy estimated that the odds against a typical welfare recipient's landing a job at a living wage were about 97 to 1. Nationwide, it took an average hourly wage of $8.89 to afford a one-bedroom apartment. Currently, the federal minimum wage is $7.25, which amounts to a full-time yearly salary of $15,080. Only approximately 1.4 percent of workers paid hourly make the minimum wage or less, but about 42 percent plug away for less than $15 an hour, and Ehrenreich wanted to figure out just how they did it (Bureau of Labor Statistics, 2022a; Ehrenreich, 2001; Rodgers & Novello, 2019).

Ehrenreich traveled the country working for $6 or $7 an hour as a waitress, hotel maid, and Walmart sales clerk. At these low wages, she had to pay high rates for rent by the week (because she lacked the required one-month security deposit). She had to eat for less than $9 a day, a budget that at best included canned beans, fast food, or noodle soup microwaved at a convenience store, and she supplemented this diet by sponging junk food from charities. All the while, Ehrenreich prayed for her health to keep up (low-wage jobs are often physically taxing), gave up clothes shopping, and juggled two or more jobs. She still could not afford to live off of her wages:

> I grew up hearing over and over, to the point of tedium, that "hard work" was the secret of success: "Work hard and you'll get ahead" or "It's hard work that got us where we are." No one ever said that you could work hard—harder than you ever thought possible—and still find yourself sinking ever deeper into poverty and debt. (Ehrenreich, 2001, p. 220)

Most welfare recipients live with few extras, often in neighborhoods with high poverty concentration and elevated crime rates. Yet politicians and voters alike worry about the cycle of dependency, the so-called welfare trap, and taxpayers deeply resent any person, real or perceived, who gets a free ride. Welfare critic Charles Murray, author of the conservative classic *Losing Ground* (1984), believes that welfare moms stain the very moral fabric that holds the country together. As he sees it, all economic support should be pulled from under the feet of single mothers to keep poor women and teens from having babies for whom they cannot care.

The 1996 Personal Responsibility and Work Opportunity Reconciliation Act, the national welfare reform enacted during the Clinton administration, didn't go as far as Murray would have liked, but it did make into policy the sentiment common among taxpayers that it was time for lazy welfare moms to get their act together, learn self-sufficiency, and take responsibility for themselves. But responsibility can take on several, often conflicting, meanings for mothers. Faced with either welfare or low-wage work, single mothers find that the government's definition of responsibility is narrowly defined as wage work. In *Flat Broke with Children: Women in the Age of Welfare Reform* (2003), Sharon Hays shows that many of these women are forced to take low-paying jobs with no future and little career stability. As a result, they are frequently driven to marry for financial support. All too often, Hays finds, single mothers (and their children) end up in poverty, homeless, or seeking alternatives to get by, including illicit sources of income.

Single mothers' paid labor often requires that they sacrifice responsible parenthood. By forcing welfare moms to enter the workforce while not providing adequate child care, the government encourages women to abandon their children in an unsupervised home. To the single mothers Hays interviewed, real responsibility meant taking care of and supervising their children, looking after their health, and providing them with a safe home environment. According to Hays, for the most desperate women in America, being a responsible

Jill Lawrence is a single mother in South Dakota. Like many of the single mothers that Sharon Hays has written about in *Flat Broke with Children*, she struggles to raise her son and make ends meet on her own.

worker requires being an irresponsible mother. To manage this tension between being a good worker or a good mother, single mothers may shoot for the nearly impossible strategy of self-reliance, but in reality they often end up depending on cash assistance from family or boyfriends. They barter with sisters, cousins, and kindly neighbors. They also take side jobs (again hiding their income to avoid rent increases or food stamp ineligibility) or go to relief agencies, although this last option proves too humiliating for most to bear. As a last resort, some single mothers turn to criminal activity such as prostitution or drug dealing, where the earnings are high but the moral costs "rob them of the self-respect they gained from trying to be good mothers" (Edin & Lein, 1997).

THE PECKING ORDER: INEQUALITY STARTS AT HOME

By now, you can see that there's no universal family form and that plenty of gender inequality exists in American families. But you might still think that, at least when it comes to the children, the home (no matter who makes up a family) is a haven of equality, altruism, and infinite love in an otherwise harsh world. In *Haven in a Heartless World* (1977), Christopher Lasch paints a rosy portrait of domestic life. To him, the home really is a shelter where workers seek refuge from the cold winds of a capitalist public sphere. The family provides a sacred, intimate privacy, managed by a caring woman who shields male workers from "the cruel world of politics and work." Building on the socially constructed split between the public and private spheres, this idea of the family as insulated from the outside world is deeply entrenched in America.

However, as you might have guessed by now, such ideas give a misleading sense of the family as a harmonious unit, its members altruistically sacrificing for one another to forge a healthy, hearty, and loving private world. As I found while researching my book *The Pecking Order* (Conley, 2004), a compelling but largely invisible struggle also takes place in the home. In each American family, there exists a pecking order among siblings—a status hierarchy, if you will—that can ignite the family with competition, struggle, and resentment. Parents often abet such struggles, despite their protestations that they "love all their children equally."

Let me illustrate with the story of a future president, William Jefferson Blythe IV, born to a 23-year-old widow named Virginia. Childhood was rough for young Bill, especially after his mother married Roger Clinton, a bitter alcoholic who physically abused his wife. In 1962, when Bill was 16, Virginia finally left Roger, but by then there was another Roger Clinton in the family, Bill's younger half-brother. Although they were separated by 10 years, were only half-siblings, and ran in very different circles, the brothers were close. As Bill's political fortunes rose, Roger's prospects first stagnated and then sank. He tried his hand at a musical career, worked odd jobs, and eventually began dealing drugs. In 1984, the Arkansas state police informed then governor Bill Clinton that his brother was a cocaine dealer under investigation. After a sting operation, which the governor did not obstruct, Roger was arrested. You might be wondering, as Clinton biographer David Maraniss (1995) has, "How could two brothers be so different: the governor and the coke dealer, the Rhodes scholar and the college dropout?" Since the Clinton brothers represent a single case, we cannot draw any definitive conclusions: Different scholars might point to the genetic differences between the two (especially given they were only half-siblings), to spending the first four years of his life in the relative stability of his grandparents' home that gave Bill a leg up that Roger lacked, or perhaps the large shadow cast by Bill's success that contributed to Roger's addictions and legal problems. All of these factors (or none of them) could explain their different life trajectories.

To be sure, a pair of brothers who are, respectively, a former president and an ex-con is a fairly extreme example. But the basic phenomenon of sibling differences in success that the Clintons represent is not all that unusual. In fact, in explaining economic inequality in America, sibling differences represent more than half of all the differences between individuals. What do sibling disparities as large as these indicate? If asked to explain why one brother succeeded while the other failed miserably, most people would point to different individual characteristics, such as work ethic, responsibility, personal motivation, and discipline. To account for a sibling's failures, people again tend to cite personal reasons, such as "a bad attitude," "poor emotional or mental health," or most commonly, "lack of determination" (Conley, 2004).

Other people will grapple for an explanation by suggesting the role of birth order. The commonly held idea is that firstborns are naturally more driven and successful, if just because they are most favored by their parents. But this is still a form of individual explanation—something unique to the psychology of the sibling—that fails to take into account the role of sociological factors. For example, in families with two kids, birth order doesn't matter that much. Firstborns don't have too much advantage over one younger sibling. Slightly less than one-fourth of U.S. presidents were firstborns, about what we would expect from chance. Birth position matters only in the context of larger families and limited resources. When family resources are stretched thin, love really does become a pie, as they say. The children born first or last into a large family seem to fare better socioeconomically than those born in the middle. Middle kids feel the effects of a shrinking pie, as they tend to be shortchanged on resources like money for college and parental attention (Cáceres-Delpiano, 2006).

Taken as a whole, the facts about intrafamily stratification present a much darker portrait of American family life. Sure, we want to think of the home as a haven in a heartless world, but inequality starts at home. These statistics also pose problems for media stories and politicians concerned with the erosion of the idealized nuclear family. In fact, they hint at a trade-off between economic opportunity and stable, cohesive families. The family is, in short, no shelter from the cold winds of capitalism; rather, it is part and parcel of that system.

A pecking order emerges during the course of childhood. It both reflects and determines siblings' positions in the overall status ordering that occurs within society. It is not just the will of parents or the "natural" abilities of children (or lack thereof); the pecking order is conditioned by the swirling winds of society, which in turn envelop the family. Furthermore, sibling disparities are much more common in poor families and single-parent homes than in rich, intact families. In fact, when families have limited resources, the success of one sibling often generates a negative backlash among the others. As the parents unwittingly put all their eggs—all their hopes and dreams—into just one basket, the other siblings inevitably are left out in the cold. Americans like to think that their behavior and destiny remain solely in their own hands. But the pecking order, like other aspects of the social fabric, ends up being shaped by social forces.

DIVORCE

Throughout this chapter we have examined the idealization of monogamous marriage as a key characteristic of American culture. Sociologist Andrew Cherlin writes in *The Marriage-Go-Round: The State of Marriage and the Family in America Today* (2009) about how the idealized conception of marriage currently helps delay age at first marriage and otherwise shapes contemporary American marital patterns. He finds a paradox. On the one hand, Americans value marriage very highly—85 to 90 percent of us will eventually get married. On the other hand, America has the highest divorce rate of any comparable Western country. How does Cherlin explain this love–hate relationship? He suggests that both the drive to get married and the desire to divorce are rooted in our collective past,

> all the way to the Colonial days when marriage was the nexus of civil society that the early settlers established. It's very important here. . . . We want to be married. At the same time though, we're very individualistic, and that has deep cultural roots too. Think about the saying "Go West, young man." Think about the rugged individual. We're individualists. And so we want to be married, but

we evaluate our marriages in very personal terms. Am I getting the personal growth that I need out of my marriage? And if you think the answer is no, you feel justified in leaving. (Conley, 2009k)

Social science research over the past couple of decades has struggled to establish just how high rates of divorce alter the social fabric. Figure 10.4 illustrates the divorce rate in America since 1920. Adding a layer to the American marriage paradox, it turns out that the most politically and religiously conservative states have the highest rates of divorce: "The states with the top ten divorce rates, eight out of ten of those voted for John McCain in the 2008 election. All ten voted for George Bush in the 2004 election" (Conley, 2009k). Cherlin explains that personal economics, not personal values, may end up contributing to rocky marriages. The states with high divorce rates are relatively poor; a sizable number of their citizens struggle to find jobs with decent wages, which compromises the ideal vision of family as a haven protected from crass financial concerns. Couples who cannot provide themselves a middle-class lifestyle may begin to question the utility of marriage in the first place. They face all of the responsibility of looking out for each other without the means to live the ideal lifestyle to which they aspire. Cherlin also notes that younger people have even more difficulty finding good jobs because they have less work experience, which may delay their marriage plans (Conley, 2009k). Young couples may live together and even have children together, but they hold off on long-term personal relationships until after they have established long-term financial relationships with reliable employers.

FIGURE 10.4 U.S. Divorce Rate, 1920–2021

SOURCES: Centers for Disease Control and Prevention, 2021a; National Center for Health Statistics, 2017; U.S. Census Bureau, 2010b.

DIGITAL.WWNORTON.COM/YOUMAYASK8

To see an interview with Andrew Cherlin, go to
digital.wwnorton.com/youmayask8

Much of the debate about divorce follows the children of divorced parents through their educational careers and into their adult relationship choices. The moral and political debate surrounding the long-term consequences of divorce has largely treated its effects as uniform for all offspring. In *The Pecking Order* (Conley, 2004), I paint a more nuanced picture, in which circumstances and context widely vary the impact of divorce on kids—even those in the same family. Everything from the timing of the divorce to a parent's hostility can influence a kid's educational attainment, future earnings, and socioeconomic success. Blanket condemnations of divorce are therefore dangerously naive, as are those who say that it's no big deal.

For example, in their best seller *The Unexpected Legacy of Divorce* (2000), Judith Wallerstein and colleagues claim that divorce almost universally damages children's self-esteem and developmental trajectories. Based on interviews with about 50 offspring of divorced parents, they conclude that adult children of divorce suffer from higher rates of depression, endure low self-esteem, and have difficulties forming fulfilling, lasting relationships of their own.

Sociologist Linda Waite and columnist Maggie Gallagher echo this view in *The Case for Marriage: Why Married People Are Happier, Healthier, and Better Off Financially* (2000). (The title, in this case, says it all.) They claim that married parents provide better homes for their children than divorced ones because they have more money and time to spend on the children, enjoy stronger emotional bonds with them, have more social capital (connections) that will be helpful to their children's chances for success, and are physically and mentally healthier. By contrast, they say, divorced families manifest more child abuse, neglect, and delinquency, and the children will probably attain less education.

On the flip side of the debate, other research suggests a less calamitous future for the children of single-parent families, indicating that children from divorced households generally do not do much worse than other kids. In *For Better or for Worse: Divorce Reconsidered* (2002), psychologists E. Mavis Hetherington and John Kelly argue that the children of divorce, for the most part, do adjust well to the new reality. Under some conditions, but certainly not all, divorce produces in kids more stress and depression and lower future socioeconomic success. Continued parental conflict and role reversals in which children "play parent," for example, make divorce potentially destructive. In other cases, however, parents who leave a high-conflict marriage probably spare their children from ongoing family feuds, hostilities, or abuse. At least one study shows that kids from high-conflict marriages that stay together may do worse than kids from high-conflict marriages that break up (Morrison & Coiro, 1999).

Too often, political debates carelessly pick up social science research as simple sound bites. Saying kids from divorced families fare worse than kids from intact families is one thing; saying that divorce *caused* those worse outcomes is quite another matter. That is, we can't really know for sure that had those parents stayed together, the kids would have been better off. We can only say that high levels of parental conflict are bad—with or without divorce in the picture.

BLENDED FAMILIES

As should be clear by this point, the dynamics involved in maintaining a family (both as a whole and in terms of the individual relationships within it) are complicated. This complexity increases drastically when two family units are integrated. As stated on **helpguide.org**, "To a child who does not belong to one, stepfamily may suggest Cinderella's family or the Brady Bunch." However, if you are part of a blended family or know someone who is (there's a good chance you do, given that one-third of the children in the United States now fall into this category), you understand that neither extreme reflects reality. As divorce becomes more common, so does the blended family form. Two people meet, fall in love, get married, have kids—we'll call them family A. Then they decide to split. Another pair does the same (family B). Some time later, Mom A encounters Dad B, and the process repeats. The result is a blended family or stepfamily, with stepparents, stepchildren, and sometimes stepsiblings. Blended families result from not only divorce but also death. When either partner dies, remarriage is not uncommon. According to the 1990 U.S. Census, 3.6 percent of grooms and 10 percent of brides had previously lost a spouse (Kreider & Ellis, 2011).

In fact, in his book, Cherlin estimates that more than a quarter of American children today experience at least two maternal partner changes, and more than 8 percent experience three or more. Some developmental psychologists worry about this dynamic, as it impacts children's ability to form trusting, stable ties with adult figures in their lives (Espejo et al., 2006). Others see children as robust and more or less adaptable to most changes that come their way.

MULTIRACIAL FAMILIES

MISCEGENATION

the technical term for interracial marriage, literally meaning "a mixing of kinds"; it is politically and historically charged, and sociologists generally prefer the term *exogamy* or *outmarriage*.

Gays have not been the only ones who have faced obstacles to legal marriage. The technical term for interracial marriage is miscegenation, which literally means "a mixing of kinds." This term, however, is politically and historically charged and, as such, should be used with a high degree of caution. Sociologists and other social scientists generally prefer the term *exogamy* or *outmarriage*.

Considering the history of race relations in the United States (see Chapter 9), the idea as well as the legality of interracial marriages and families has unsurprisingly been cause for controversy. Although interracial marriage was never illegal at the federal level, from 1913 to 1948, 30 states enforced antimiscegenation laws. Many of these laws lasted until 1967, when the Supreme Court finally declared them unconstitutional, reversing the restrictions in 16 remaining states.

We have undoubtedly come a long way since 1967. One year after the Supreme Court ruling in 1968, a Gallup poll revealed that 80 percent of Americans were opposed to Blacks and Whites getting married. By 2009, that number had dropped to 17 percent (Wang, 2012). However, attitudes toward exogamy in the United States vary greatly by location, religion, and a host of other factors. And, of course, such polls capture only expressed attitudes, subject to social desirability bias, not actual behavior (i.e., actual intermarriage rates).

In 2015, 17 percent of new marriages were between people of different races or ethnic groups. Asian Americans had the highest rate of outmarriage at 29 percent, followed by 27 percent of Hispanics, 18 percent of Blacks, and 11 percent of Whites (Bialik, 2017). These percentages significantly change when gender is taken into account. For example, 36 percent of Asian American

American families are increasingly looking like the family pictured here. How are attitudes about multiracial families changing?

women marry someone outside of their race, unlike Asian American men who have only a 21 percent rate of outmarriage. Black men have a 24 percent rate of outmarriage versus Black women's rate of 12 percent.

IMMIGRANT FAMILIES

Immigrants—today arriving mostly from Latin America and Asia—face a unique set of challenges in forming and sustaining families. Aside from the difficulty of the immigration process itself, in which it can take years to reunify spouses and siblings through visa sponsorships, families who migrate to America tend to be poorer and larger and to hold fewer educational credentials. For instance, about 9.1 percent of people born in the United States have less than a high-school degree, while the same is true for 28.8 percent of people born abroad (Ryan & Bauman, 2016). What's more, the gaps between natives and immigrants who have not obtained citizenship or who are undocumented are even larger. There are more than four times as many noncitizens who have less than a high-school degree (or equivalent) compared to those born in the United States, while those native households make about $14,000 (or about 25 percent) more in earnings (Ryan & Bauman, 2016). These socioeconomic disparities are exacerbated by the reality that an overwhelming proportion of immigrants live in expensive cities on the East and West Coasts, like Los Angeles and New York (López & Bialik, 2017). Because of these resource gaps, undocumented immigrants face a particularly daunting set of challenges in providing for their families and obtaining safe, stable, and affordable housing.

Most Americans nowadays delay forming families until they receive college degrees and earn more money precisely because of the difficulties of having children with fewer resources. Yet though we might expect immigrant families to form and stay together less often because of these challenges, the opposite is true. Immigrants tend to start families regardless of their educational attainment or income, with the poor marrying and having children at a similar rate as their peers with higher socioeconomic status (Qian, 2013). About a quarter of immigrants have never been married, while that's true for more than a third of native-born populations (Ryan & Bauman, 2016). And in terms of keeping the family unit intact, the gaps are similarly big—about 77.9 percent of foreign-born children live with married parents, compared to 65 percent of natives (U.S. Census Bureau, 2022d).

Why do families facing greater socioeconomic, geographic, and linguistic challenges manage to form and sustain themselves better than U.S. natives? While some propose a different set of cultural norms—for example, a greater emphasis on family ties and the necessity of social support to get ahead in America—immigration policy itself likely contributes to the structure of immigrant families. Even though the process is difficult, current immigration policy favors family-based reunification rather than education level or labor market skills (Kandel, 2018). So, while the Republican Party made immigration a key issue in the 2016 election (and beyond) and sought to put an end to family-based immigration policy in particular (not to mention separating detainee families from their parents for a period), foreign-born populations actually show a greater tendency to live out the kinds of mid-twentieth-century nuclear family arrangements to which many political conservatives often express a desire to return.

GAY, LESBIAN, AND TRANSGENDER FAMILIES

Marriage, divorce, remarriage. Stepfamilies, blended families, sperm and egg donors incorporated into family narratives. Another family arrangement on the rise is same-sex couples. At present, same-sex marriages are legal in an increasing number of countries, including the United States and about half of Europe. As for LGBT parenting, research consistently finds that lesbian and gay parents are at least as successful as heterosexuals in producing well-adjusted, successful offspring (APA, 2005; Stacey, 1997).

However, until recently homosexual unions faced fierce opposition. In 1996 President Clinton signed into federal law the Defense of Marriage Act (DOMA), which stipulated that federally recognized marriages had to be heterosexual and that states where gay marriage was previously illegal were not required to recognize same-sex marriages conducted in states where it was legal. DOMA was struck down in 2013, and the Supreme Court effectively legalized same-sex marriage across the United States in 2015.

An old joke goes, "Gays and lesbians getting married—haven't they suffered enough?" That is, if homosexual couples want to marry, why not just let them do it? Opponents of gay marriage—many of whom are strongly religious, "social values" conservatives—argue that nontraditional familial arrangements will wreak social havoc. Let gays get married, so the argument goes, and you effectively destroy the family. Once the family goes, look out—the next step is chaos, no moral order. Furthermore, opponents of gay marriage claim that the purpose of a family is to procreate and raise children into functioning adults, and this is determined by biology. Because gay marriage does not produce the biological children of both parents, such people believe that it is not functional, right, or natural.

According to research, views are steadily shifting. In 1996, only 27 percent of Americans supported gay marriage. By 2021, those numbers had flipped with 70 percent supporting gay marriage. Young people are the strongest supporters of same-sex marriage, with 84 percent of young adults, 72 percent of middle-aged adults, and 60 percent of older adults supporting same-sex marriage (NPR, 2021b).

Families with one or more transgender parents have also challenged conservative notions of how a family "should" look. Transgender individuals lag behind gays and lesbians in terms of societal acceptance (see Chapter 8),

 # EXPANDING MARRIAGE

When the poet Elizabeth Barrett Browning wrote, "How do I love thee? Let me count the ways," little did she know that a century and a half later the list would extend into the hundreds—at least for married couples. As of 2004, the U.S. General Accounting Office had identified more than 1,000 legal rights and responsibilities attendant to marriage (Shah, 2004). The era of big government clearly still has an influential hold on family policy.

These rights and responsibilities range from the continuation of water rights upon the death of a spouse to the ability to take funeral leave. And that's just the federal government. States and localities have their own marriage provisions. New York State, for example, grants a spouse the right to inherit a military veteran's peddler's license. And Hawaii extends to spouses of state residents lower fees for hunting licenses. No wonder gay and lesbian activists put such a premium on access to marriage rights. Some gay marriage advocates want all spousal rights immediately and will settle for nothing less. Others take an incremental approach, aiming to secure first the most significant domestic partner rights, such as employer benefits like health care.

But with all the divorces and blended families, it's unclear if our current legal system is

best suited to the task of serving families' needs. Perhaps we'd be better off by breaking down or unbundling the marriage contract into its constituent parts. Then, applying free-market principles, we could allow each citizen to assign the various rights and responsibilities now connected to marriage as they see fit. In addition to employer benefits, some of the key marital rights include the ability to pass property and income back and

Jeanne Fong (left) and Jennifer Lin, a same-sex couple from San Francisco, celebrate during a marriage equality rally in Washington, DC.

forth tax-free, spousal privilege (i.e., the right not to testify against one's husband or wife), medical decision-making power, and the right to confer permanent residency to a foreigner, just to name a few. The mutual responsibilities of marriage include parenthood—a husband is the legal father of any child born to his wife regardless of biological paternity—and some shared legal liability under civil law. Why not allow people to parcel out each of these marital privileges?

Take my own first marriage as a case in point: My ex-wife is a foreigner who applied for citizenship, and her marriage to me made that possible. Marrying a foreigner is not uncommon: In 2021, 8 percent of women getting married for the first time were entering a mixed-nativity marriage (U.S. Census Bureau, 2021d). As the law now stands, as a straight American man, I theoretically could become a green card machine. As long as I can convince the overstretched Department of Homeland Security that my penchant for falling in love with foreign women is genuine, I can divorce and remarry as many times as I like, obtaining permanent residency for each of my failed loves along the way. Is this fair to the many Americans who can't sponsor aging grandparents or, in some cases, even parents? Or is it even fair to the vast majority of Americans who are happy marrying other Americans and may not want to see the country fill up with all my exes?

Instead, why not give all Americans the right to sponsor one person in their lifetime—a right that they could sell, if they so desire? This right would mean that if I wanted to marry a Kenyan after divorcing an Australian, I could, but I would need to purchase, perhaps on eBay, the right to confer citizenship from someone else who didn't need it. Similarly, why not let all Americans name one person (other than their lawyer, priest, or therapist) who can't be forced to testify against them

in court? This zone of privacy could be transferred over the course of a lifetime, perhaps limiting such changes to once every five years.

While we are at it, how about allowing each of us to choose someone with whom we share our property, with all the tax (and liability) implications that choice would imply? We might even allow parenthood to become contractual and in multiples greater than two by letting people name individuals they want to be the co-parents to their biological children, even if that means a kid ends up with three or four parents, none of whom is married to any of the others. This freedom would help grandparents, for instance, to have the legal right to act on behalf of the grandchildren in their care.

We could go down the long list of rights and responsibilities embedded in the marriage contract. Ideally, most people would choose one person in whom to vest all these rights, but everyone would have the freedom to decide how to configure their domestic, business, legal, and intimate relationships in the eyes of the law.

Other people have proposed changing marriage by making it more flexible. Some queer activists continue to argue that the law should recognize a variety of households, from conjugal couples to groups of elderly people living collectively, as "legal families." But they have not specified the rights that should go along with such arrangements or addressed the problems and paradoxes that might arise if legal rights and responsibilities were extended to groups of more than two. Unbundling marital rights would achieve the same end without creating new inequities based on group size.

It might also take some of the vitriol out of the marriage debate. Marriage itself could stay in church (or in Las Vegas, as the case may be). And each couple could count their own ways to love.

Two married women greet their eight-year-old daughter after school in Ridgefield, Washington, in 2017. How have attitudes toward gay and lesbian families changed?

but the trend lines point similarly toward tolerance. There is, as of yet, no reliable data on how many families include transgender parents, but best estimates put the figure at less than 1 percent.

Even as legal and normative restrictions have eased in recent years, LBGT families face other obstacles. For example, many "face restrictions on caregiving and medical decision-making" and are more likely to suffer from a lack of health insurance (MAP et al., 2012b). Children of color are more likely to be raised in LBGT families, perhaps experiencing discrimination on two fronts: race and stigma around the sexuality of their parents. Further, these children are more often raised in de facto arrangements with aunts and uncles, grandparents, or other relatives. A lack of legal recognition of such relationships causes problems for caretaking of children (MAP et al., 2012a).

Conclusion

By now you should be wary of any social institution that people view as "natural." You should be skeptical of any family arrangement deemed more functional than any other, and you should hold the traditional family at a critical distance, especially considering the experiences of women, African Americans, gays and lesbians, the poor, the mainstream, and the marginalized.

Under the "postmodern family condition," as Judith Stacey (1996) calls it, clear rules no longer exist in our complex, diversified, and sometimes messy postindustrial society. Gone are the ruling days of the family structure idealized in the 1950s. Families today take on many shapes and sizes that best fit their members' needs, and they are defined not by blood ties but by the quality of relationships. Let us count the ways . . .

MAKING INVISIBLE LABOR VISIBLE

Building on the ideas introduced by Arlie Hochschild's book *The Second Shift* (1989), in recent years commentators have talked about "invisible" domestic labor—work that happens at home that is often unacknowledged and unpaid.

TRY IT!

Think about all the work a parent or caregiver did when you were growing up, and consider the economic value of that labor. Caregivers often seem like Uber drivers who chauffeur kids, act as health aides, or function as short-order cooks—how much was that worth per week? Here are some estimates to get you started:

TASK	NATIONAL AVERAGE
UBER DRIVER	$4 PER 15-MINUTE RIDE
BABYSITTER / CARETAKER	$12 PER HOUR
SHORT-ORDER COOK	$5 PER MEAL
HOUSE CLEANER	$10 PER ROOM
HOMEWORK TUTOR	$20 PER HOUR

WORK PROVIDED BY PARENT OR CARETAKER	AMOUNT WORTH PER WEEK
_____	_____
_____	_____
_____	_____

For simplicity's sake, you could use minimum wage in your state for any tasks not defined above.

TOTAL AMOUNT

$ _____

THINK ABOUT IT

So, have you broken out your checkbook to pay your mother, father, or other primary caregiver for all those years of uncompensated labor on your behalf? Think about your family and others you know well: Who typically does this unpaid labor? Is it equally borne by all adults in the family? Does it break down along gender lines? Or age? Or by task (Dad is chauffeur and Mom is short-order cook, for example)? How do you feel about the social division of unpaid labor in your family as it compares to the typical American household?

Glossary

A

absolute poverty the point at which a household's income falls below the necessary level to purchase food to physically sustain its members.

achieved status a status into which one enters; voluntary status.

affirmative action a set of policies granting preferential treatment to a number of particular subgroups within the population—typically, women and historically disadvantaged racial minorities.

agricultural revolution the period around 1700 marked by the introduction of new farming technologies that increased food output in farm production.

alienation a condition in which people are dominated by forces of their own creation that then confront them as alien powers; according to Marx, the basic state of being in a capitalist society.

alternative social movements social movements that seek the most limited societal change and often target a narrow group of people.

altruistic suicide suicide that occurs when one experiences too much social integration.

androgynous neither masculine nor feminine.

animism the belief that spirits are part of the natural world, as in totemism.

anomic suicide suicide that occurs as a result of insufficient social regulation.

anomie a sense of aimlessness or despair that arises when we can no longer reasonably expect life to be predictable; too little social regulation; normlessness.

Anthropocene a term proposed to mark our current epoch when human activity has been the dominant influence on the climate and environment.

anthropogenic climate change changing temperatures, weather patterns, frequencies of extreme weather events, sea level rises, glacier and snow-cap depletions, and other changes to the earth's climate due to the effects of industrialization and other human activities.

ascribed status a status into which one is born; involuntary status.

authority the justifiable right to exercise power.

B

bisexual an individual who is sexually attracted to both genders/sexes.

boundary work work done to maintain the border between legitimate and nonlegitimate science within a specific scientific discipline or between legitimate disciplines.

bourgeois society a society of commerce (modern capitalist society, for example) in which the maximization of profit is the primary business incentive.

bourgeoisie the capitalist class.

broken windows theory of deviance theory explaining how social cues impact whether individuals act deviantly—specifically, whether local, informal social norms allow deviant acts.

bureaucracy a legal-rational organization or mode of administration that governs with reference to formal rules and roles and emphasizes merit-based advancement.

C

capitalism an economic system in which property and goods are primarily privately owned; private decisions determine investments; and competition in an unfettered marketplace primarily determines prices, production, and the distribution of goods.

case study an intensive investigation of one particular unit of analysis in order to describe it or uncover its mechanisms.

caste system a religion-based system of stratification characterized by no social mobility.

causal relationship the idea that one factor influences another through a chain of events; such a dynamic differs from two associated or correlated factors, which may appear to vary together but could both vary due to chance or a third factor.

causality the notion that a change in one factor results in a corresponding change in another.

charismatic authority authority that rests on the personal appeal of an individual leader.

churches religious bodies that coexist in a relatively low state of tension with their social surroundings; they have mainstream, "safe" beliefs and practices relative to those of the general population.

cisgender describes people whose gender corresponds to their birth sex.

citizenship rights the rights guaranteed to each law-abiding citizen in a nation-state.

civil rights the rights guaranteeing a citizen's personal freedom from state interference, including freedom of speech and the right to travel freely.

class system an economically based hierarchical system characterized by cohesive oppositional groups and somewhat loose social mobility.

classical model model of social movements based on a concept of structural weakness in society that results in psychological disruption of individuals.

coalescence the second stage of a social movement, in which resources are mobilized (i.e., concrete action is taken) around the problems outlined in the first stage.

code switch to flip fluidly between two or more languages and sets of cultural norms to fit different cultural contexts.

coercion the use of force to get others to do what you want.

cohabitation living together in an intimate relationship without formal legal or religious sanctioning.

collective action action that takes place in groups and diverges from the social norms of the situation.

collective resistance an organized effort to change a power hierarchy on the part of a less powerful group in a society.

color-blind racism the view that racial inequality is perpetuated by a supposedly color-blind stance that ends up reinforcing historical and contemporary inequities, disparate impact, and institutional bias by "ignoring" them in favor of a technically neutral approach.

Communism a political system in which the means of production are shared through state ownership and in which rewards are tied not to productivity but to need, supposedly leading to a classless society.

comparative research a methodology by which two or more entities (such as countries), which are similar in many dimensions but differ on one in question, are compared to learn about the dimension that differs between them.

conflict theory the idea that conflict between competing interests is the basic, animating force of social change and society in general.

conformist an individual who accepts both the goals and the strategies that are considered socially acceptable to achieve those goals.

congregation a group of people who gather together, especially for worship.

consumerism the steady acquisition of material possessions, often with the belief that happiness and fulfillment can thus be achieved.

contagion theory theory of collective action claiming that collective action arises because of people's tendency to conform to the behavior of others with whom they are in close contact.

content analysis a systematic analysis of the content rather than the structure of a communication, such as a written work, speech, or film.

contradictory class locations the idea that people can occupy locations in the class structure that fall between the two "pure" classes.

convergence theory theory of collective action stating that collective action happens when people with similar ideas and tendencies gather in the same place.

corporate crime a particular type of white-collar crime committed by the officers (CEOs and other executives) of a corporation.

corporation a legal entity unto itself that has a legal personhood distinct from that of its members— namely, its owners and shareholders.

correlation or association when two variables tend to track each other positively or negatively.

counterculture a large cultural group defined in opposition to the ideologies, values, and norms of the mainstream culture.

credentialism an overemphasis on credentials (e.g., college degrees) for signaling social status or qualifications for a job.

crime the violation of laws enacted by society; formal deviance.

critical race theory a legal theory that asserts that race is not natural but rather is socially constructed in order to oppress nonwhites and that racism is inherent in U.S. legal institutions.

cult religious movement that makes some new claim about the supernatural and therefore does not easily fit within the sect–church cycle.

cult of domesticity the notion that true womanhood centers on domestic responsibility and child rearing.

cultural capital the symbolic and interactional resources that people use to their advantage in various situations.

cultural lag the time gap between the appearance of a new technology and the words and practices that give it meaning.

cultural relativism taking into account the differences across cultures without passing judgment or assigning value.

cultural scripts modes of behavior and understanding that are not universal or natural.

culture the sum of the social categories and concepts we operate within in addition to beliefs, learned behaviors, and practices; everything but the natural environment around us.

culture jamming the act of turning media against themselves.

culture of poverty the argument that poor people adopt certain practices that differ from those of middle-class, "mainstream" society in order to adapt and survive in difficult economic circumstances.

culture shock doubt, confusion, or anxiety arising from immersion in an unfamiliar culture.

culture war a conflict between distinct cultures within a given society.

D

deductive approach a research approach that starts with a theory, forms a hypothesis, makes empirical observations, and then analyzes the data to confirm, reject, or modify the original theory.

democracy a system of government wherein power theoretically lies with the people; citizens are allowed to vote in elections, speak freely, and participate as legal equals in social life.

denomination a big group of congregations that share the same faith and are governed under one administrative umbrella.

dependent variable the outcome the researcher is trying to explain.

deterrence theory philosophy of criminal justice arising from the notion that crime results from a rational calculation of its costs and benefits.

dialectic a two-directional relationship, following a pattern in which an original statement or thesis is countered with an antithesis, leading to a conclusion that unites the strengths of the original position and the counterarguments.

dialectic materialism a notion of history that privileges conflict over economic, material resources as the central struggle and driver of change in society.

dictatorship a form of government that restricts the right to political participation to a small group or even to a single individual.

discrimination harmful or negative acts (not mere thoughts) against people deemed inferior on the basis of their racial category, without regard to their individual merit.

divide et impera the role of a member of a triad who intentionally drives a wedge between the other two actors in the group.

domination the probability that a command with specific content will be obeyed by a given group of people.

double consciousness a concept conceived by W. E. B. Du Bois to describe the behavioral scripts, one for moving through the world and the other incorporating the external opinions of prejudiced onlookers, which are constantly maintained by African Americans.

dramaturgical theory the view (advanced by Erving Goffman) of social life as essentially a theatrical performance, in which we are all actors on metaphorical stages, with roles, scripts, costumes, and sets.

dyad a group of two.

E

education the process through which academic, social, and cultural skills are developed.

egoistic suicide suicide that occurs when one is not well integrated into a social group.

elastic ties social connections that display the repeated interactions characteristic of strong ties while maintaining a degree of protective social distance (i.e., not knowing more than a first name, if that).

elite–mass dichotomy system a system of stratification that has a governing elite, a few leaders who broadly hold power in society.

embeddedness the degree to which indirect ties (i.e., friends of friends) reinforce social relationships.

emergence the first stage of a social movement, occurring when the social problem being addressed is first identified.

emergent norm theory theory of collective action emphasizing the influence of keynoters in promoting new behavioral norms.

emotional labor managing emotions and their outward expression to meet the expectations of a job, especially in service sector work and in female-dominated occupations.

endogamy marriage to someone within one's social group.

epigenetics chemical regulation of gene activity that may be switched "on" or "off" in response to environmental influence.

equality of condition the idea that everyone should have an equal starting point.

equality of opportunity the idea that everyone has an equal chance to achieve wealth, social prestige, and power because the rules of the game, so to speak, are the same for everyone.

equality of outcome the idea that each player must end up with the same amount regardless of the fairness of the "game."

essentialist arguments explaining social phenomena in terms of natural, biological, or evolutionary inevitabilities.

estate system a politically based system of stratification characterized by limited social mobility.

ethicalism the adherence to certain principles to lead a moral life, as in Buddhism and Taoism.

ethnicity one's ethnic quality or affiliation. It is voluntary, self-defined, nonhierarchical, fluid and multiple, and based on cultural differences, not physical ones per se.

ethnocentrism the belief that one's own culture or group is superior to others and the tendency to view all other cultures from the perspective of one's own.

ethnography a qualitative method of studying people or a social setting that uses observation, interaction, and sometimes formal interviewing to document behaviors, customs, experiences, social ties, and so on.

ethnomethodology literally "the methods of the people"; this approach to studying human interaction focuses on the ways in which we make sense of our world, convey this understanding to others, and produce a shared social order.

evangelicals members of any Christian denomination distinguished by four main beliefs: the Bible is without error, salvation comes only through belief in Jesus Christ, personal conversion is the only path to salvation (the "born again" experience), and others must also be converted; they proselytize by engaging with wider society.

exchange mobility mobility resulting from the swapping of jobs.

exogamy marriage to someone outside one's social group.

experimental methods methods that seek to alter the social landscape in a very specific way for a given sample of individuals and then track what results that change yields; they often involve comparisons to a control group that did not experience such an intervention.

extended family kin networks that extend outside or beyond the nuclear family.

F

face the esteem in which an individual is held by others.

family wage a wage paid to male workers sufficient to support a dependent wife and children.

fatalistic suicide suicide that occurs as a result of too much social regulation.

feminism a social movement to get people to understand that gender is an organizing principle in society and to address gender-based inequalities that intersect with other forms of social identity.

feminist methodology a set of systems or methods that treats women's experiences as legitimate empirical and theoretical resources, that promotes social science for women (think public sociology, but for a specific half of the public), and that takes into account the researcher as much as the overt subject matter.

feudalism a precapitalist economic system characterized by the presence of lords, vassals, serfs, and fiefs.

formal social sanctions mechanisms of social control by which rules or laws prohibit deviant criminal behavior.

free rider problem the notion that when more than one person is responsible for getting something done, the incentive is for each individual to shirk responsibility and hope others will pull the extra weight.

functionalism the theory that various social institutions and processes in society exist to serve some important (or necessary) function to keep society running.

fundamentalists religious adherents who follow a scripture (such as the Bible or Qur'an) using a literal interpretation of its meaning.

G

game theory the study of strategic decisions made under conditions of uncertainty and interdependence.

gender a social position; behaviors and a set of attributes that are associated with sex identities.

gender roles sets of behavioral norms assumed to accompany one's status as masculine, feminine, or other.

generalizability the extent to which we can claim our findings inform us about a group beyond the one we studied.

generalized other an internalized sense of the total expectations of others in a variety of settings—regardless of whether we've encountered those people or places before.

genocide the mass killing of a group of people based on racial, ethnic, or religious traits.

glass ceiling an invisible limit on women's climb up the occupational ladder.

glass escalator the accelerated promotion of men to the top of a work organization, especially in feminized jobs.

global warming rising atmospheric concentrations of carbon dioxide and other greenhouse gases, resulting in higher global average temperatures.

grassroots organization a type of social movement organization that relies on high levels of community-based membership participation to promote social change; it lacks a hierarchical structure and works through existing political structures.

H

hegemonic masculinity the condition in which men are dominant and privileged, and this dominance and privilege is invisible.

hegemony a condition by which a dominant group uses its power to elicit the voluntary "consent" of the masses.

heteronormativity the idea that heterosexuality is the default or normal sexual orientation from which other sexualities deviate.

hidden curriculum the nonacademic and less overt socialization functions of schooling.

historical methods research that collects data written from reports, newspaper articles, journals, transcripts, television programs, diaries, artwork, and other artifacts that date back to the period under study.

homosexual the social identity of a person who has sexual attraction to and/or relations with people of the same sex.

human capital the skills, knowledge, and experience possessed by a person or group that can yield economic benefits.

hypothesis a proposed relationship between two variables, usually with a stated direction.

I

I one's subjective sense of having consciousness, agency, action, or power.

ideology a system of concepts and relationships; an underlying explanation of phenomena in society; a framework of causes and effects.

income money received by a person for work, from transfers (gifts, inheritances, or government assistance), or from returns on investments.

independent variable a measured factor that the researcher believes has a causal impact on the dependent variable.

inductive approach a research approach that starts with empirical observations and then works to form a theory.

informal deviance minor violations of social norms that may or may not be punished.

informal social sanctions the usually unexpressed but widely known rules of group membership; the unspoken rules of social life.

in-group another term for the powerful group, most often the majority.

innovator social deviant who accepts socially acceptable goals but rejects socially acceptable means to achieve them.

institutional racism institutions and social dynamics that may seem race-neutral but actually disadvantage minority groups.

interest group an organization that seeks to gain power in government and influence policy without campaigning for direct election or appointment to office.

international state system a system in which each state is recognized as territorially sovereign by fellow states.

interpretive sociology a type of scholarship in which researchers imagine themselves experiencing the life positions of the social actors they want to understand rather than treating those people as objects to be examined.

intersectionality the idea that it is critical to understand the interplay between social identities such as race, class, gender, ability status, and sexual orientation, even though many social systems and institutions (such as the law) try to treat each category on its own.

isomorphism a constraining process that forces one unit in a population to resemble other units that face the same set of environmental conditions.

K

kinship networks strings of relationships between people related by blood and co-residence (i.e., marriage).

L

labeling theory the belief that individuals subconsciously notice how others see or label them, and their reactions to those labels over time form the basis of their self-identity.

large group a group characterized by the presence of a formal structure that mediates interaction and, consequently, status differentiation.

legal-rational authority authority based on legal, impersonal rules; the rules rule.

M

macrosociology a branch of sociology generally concerned with social dynamics at a higher level of analysis—that is, across the breadth of society.

master status one status within a set that stands out or overrides all others.

material culture everything that is a part of our constructed, physical environment, including technology.

matrix of domination intersecting domains of oppression that create a social space of domination and, by extension, a unique position within that space based on someone's intersectional identity along the multiple dimensions of gender, age, race, class, sexuality, location, and so on.

Matthew effect a term used by sociologists to describe the notion that certain scientific results get more notoriety and influence based on the existing prestige of the researchers involved.

me the self perceived as an object by the "I"; the self as one imagines others perceive one.

mechanical or segmental solidarity social cohesion based on sameness.

media any formats, platforms, or vehicles that carry, present, or communicate information.

mediator the member of a triad who attempts to resolve conflict between the two other actors in the group.

medicalization the process by which problems or issues not traditionally seen as medical come to be framed as such.

megachurch typically, a conservative Protestant church that attracts at least 2,000 worshipers per week.

meritocracy a society where status and mobility are based on individual attributes, ability, and achievement.

microsociology a branch of sociology that seeks to understand local interactional contexts; its methods of choice are ethnographic, generally including participant observation and in-depth interviews.

middle class a term commonly used to describe those individuals with nonmanual jobs that pay significantly more than the poverty line—though this is a highly debated and expansive category, particularly in the United States, where broad swaths of the population consider themselves middle class.

midrange theory a theory that attempts to explain generalizable patterns of behavior that are neither all-encompassing of society as a whole nor focused on very particular groups or individuals.

Milgram experiment an experiment devised in 1961 by Stanley Milgram, a psychologist at Yale University, to see how far ordinary people would go to obey an authority figure.

miscegenation the technical term for interracial marriage, literally meaning "a mixing of kinds"; it is politically and historically charged—sociologists generally prefer the term *exogamy* or *outmarriage*.

modernity social relations characterized by rationality, bureaucratization, and objectivity as well as individually created by nonconcentric, but overlapping, group affiliations.

monogamy the practice of having only one sexual partner or spouse at a time.

monopoly the form of business that occurs when one seller of a good or service dominates the market to the exclusion of others, potentially leading to zero competition.

morbidity illness in a general sense.

mortality death.

N

narrative the sum of stories contained in a set of ties.

natural experiment something that takes place in the world that affects people in a way that is unrelated to any other preexisting factors or their characteristics, thereby approximating random assignment to treatment or control groups.

nonmaterial culture values, beliefs, social norms, and ideologies.

normal science science conducted within an existing paradigm, as defined by Thomas Kuhn.

normative view of science the notion that science should not be affected by the personal beliefs or values of scientists but rather should follow objective rules of evidence.

norms how values tell us to behave.

nuclear family familial form consisting of a father, a mother, and their children.

O

offshoring a business decision to move all or part of a company's operations abroad to minimize costs.

oligopoly the economic condition that exists when a handful of firms effectively control a particular market.

one-drop rule the belief that "one drop" of Black blood makes a person Black, a concept that evolved from U.S. laws forbidding miscegenation.

ontological equality the philosophical and religious notion that all people are created equal.

operationalization how a concept is defined and measured in a given study.

organic solidarity social cohesion based on difference and interdependence of the parts.

organization any social network that is defined by a common purpose and has a boundary between its membership and the rest of the social world.

organizational culture the shared beliefs and behaviors within a social group; often used interchangeably with *corporate culture*.

organizational structure the distribution of power and authority within an organization.

other someone or something outside of oneself.

out-group another term for the stigmatized or less powerful group, the minority.

P

panopticon a circular building composed of an inner ring and an outer ring designed to serve as a prison in which the guards, housed in the inner ring, can observe the prisoners without the detainees knowing whether they are being watched.

paradigm the framework within which scientists operate.

paradigm shift or scientific revolution when enough scientific anomalies accrue to challenge the existing paradigm, showing that it is incomplete or inadequate to explain all observed phenomena.

paradox of authority although the state's authority derives from the implicit threat of physical force, resorting to physical coercion strips the state of all legitimate authority.

parenting stress hypothesis a paradigm in which low income, unstable employment, a lack of cultural resources, and a feeling of inferiority from social class comparisons exacerbate household stress levels; this stress, in turn, leads to detrimental parenting practices such as yelling and hitting, which are not conducive to healthy child development.

participant observation a qualitative research method that seeks to uncover the meanings people give their social actions by observing their behavior in practice.

party a group that is similar to a small group but is multifocal.

patriarchy a nearly universal system involving the subordination of femininity to masculinity.

perverse incentives reward structures that lead to suboptimal outcomes by stimulating counterproductive behavior; for example, it is argued that welfare—to the extent that it discourages work efforts—has perverse incentives.

pluralism the presence and engaged coexistence of numerous distinct groups in one society.

political participation an activity that has the intent or effect of influencing government action.

political party an organization that seeks to gain power in a government, generally by backing candidates for office who subscribe (to the extent possible) to the organization's political ideals.

political process model model of social movements that focuses on the structure of political opportunities; when these are favorable to a particular challenger, the chances are better for the success of a social movement led by this challenger.

political rights the rights guaranteeing a citizen's ability to participate in politics, including the right to vote and the right to hold an elected office.

politics power relations among people or other social actors.

polyandry the practice of having multiple husbands simultaneously.

polygamy the practice of having more than one sexual partner or spouse at a time.

polygyny the practice of having multiple wives simultaneously.

population an entire group of individual persons, objects, or items from which samples may be drawn.

positivism the approach to sociology that emphasizes the scientific method as an approach to studying the objectively observable behavior of individuals irrespective of the meanings those actions have for the subjects themselves.

positivist sociology the approach to sociology that emphasizes the scientific method as an approach to studying the objectively observable behavior of individuals irrespective of the meanings of those actions for the subjects themselves.

postmodernism a condition characterized by the questioning of the notion of progress and history, the replacement of narrative with pastiche (i.e., a collage of existing ideas) or imitation of other work in the service of satire or subversion, and multiple, perhaps even conflicting, identities resulting from unconnected affiliations.

postmodernity social relations characterized by a questioning of the notion of progress and history, the replacement of narrative with pastiche, and multiple, perhaps even conflicting, identities resulting from disjointed affiliations.

power the ability to carry out one's own will despite resistance.

prejudice thoughts and feelings about an ethnic or racial group, which lead to preconceived notions and judgments (often negative) about the group.

premodernity social relations characterized by concentric circles of social affiliation, a low degree of division of labor, relatively undeveloped technology, and traditional social norms.

primary deviance the first act of rule breaking that may lead to a new label of "deviant," thus influencing how people think about and act toward you.

primary groups social groups, such as family or friends, composed of enduring, intimate face-to-face relationships that strongly influence the attitudes and ideals of those involved.

primordialism Clifford Geertz's term to explain the strength of ethnic ties because they are fixed and deeply felt or primordial ties to one's homeland culture.

productivity enhancing economic activities that increase the total economic value available to society.

profane the things of mundane, everyday life.

proletariat the working class.

Q

qualitative methods methods that attempt to collect information about the social world that cannot be readily converted to numeric form.

quantitative methods methods that seek to obtain information about the social world that is already in or can be converted to numeric form.

R

race a group of people who share a set of characteristics—typically, but not always, physical ones—and are said to share a common bloodline.

racialization the formation of a new racial identity by drawing ideological boundaries of difference around a formerly unnoticed group of people.

racism the belief that members of separate races possess different and unequal traits.

rationalization a never-ending process of ordering or organizing.

rebel an individual who rejects both traditional goals and traditional means and wants to alter or destroy the social institutions from which he or she is alienated.

recidivism when an individual who has been involved with the criminal justice system reverts to criminal behavior.

redemptive social movements social movements that target specific groups but advocate for more radical change in behavior.

reference group a group that helps us understand or make sense of our position in society relative to other groups.

reflection theory the idea that culture is a projection of social structures and relationships into the public sphere, a screen onto which the film of the underlying reality of social structures of a society is projected.

reflexive spirituality a contemporary religious movement that encourages followers to look to religion for meaning, wisdom, and profound thought and feeling rather than for absolute truths on how the world works.

reflexivity analyzing and critically considering our own role in, and effect on, our research.

reformative social movements social movements that advocate for limited social change across an entire society.

relative poverty a measurement of poverty based on a percentage of the median income in a given location.

reliability the likelihood of obtaining consistent results using the same measure.

religion a system of beliefs, traditions, and practices around sacred things; a set of shared "stories" that guides belief and action.

religious experiences an individual's spiritual feelings, acts, and experiences.

rent seeking economic activities that aim to move value from one person or company to another without increasing value.

representative sample the idea that a particular slice of social observation—a sample of survey respondents, an ethnographic research site such as an organization, or a batch of social media posts—captures in an accurate way the larger set (or universe) of those phenomena that it is meant to stand in for.

research methods approaches that social scientists use for investigating the answers to questions.

resocialization the process by which one's sense of social values, beliefs, and norms are reengineered, often deliberately, through an intense social process.

resource dilution model hypothesis stating that parental resources are finite and that each additional child gets a smaller amount of them.

resource-mobilization theory model of social movements that emphasizes political context and goals but also states that social movements are unlikely to emerge without the necessary resources.

retreatist one who rejects both socially acceptable means and goals by completely retreating from, or not participating in, society.

reverse causality a situation in which the researcher believes that A results in a change in B, but B is actually causing A.

revolutionary social movements social movements that advocate the radical reorganization of society.

risk society a society that both produces and is concerned with mitigating risks, especially manufactured risks (ones that result from human activity).

ritualist an individual who rejects socially defined goals but not the means.

role the duties and behaviors expected of someone who holds a particular status.

role conflict the tension caused by competing demands between two or more roles pertaining to different statuses.

role strain the incompatibility among roles corresponding to a single status.

routinization the clear, rule-governed procedures used repeatedly for decision making.

routinization or institutionalization the final stage of a social movement, in which it is institutionalized and a formal structure develops to promote the cause.

S

sacred holy things endowed with special status and often used for worship and kept separate from the profane; the sacred realm is unknowable and mystical, so it inspires us with feelings of awe and wonder.

sacred canopy Peter Berger's term to describe the entire set of religious norms, symbols, and beliefs that expresses the most important thing in life—namely, the feeling that life is worth living and that

reality is meaningful and ordered, not just random chaos.

sample the subset of the population from which you actually collect data.

scientific method a procedure involving the formulation, testing, and modification of hypotheses based on systematic observation, measurement, and/or experiments.

scientific racism nineteenth-century theories of race that characterize a period of feverish investigation into the origins, explanations, and classifications of race.

second shift women's responsibility for housework and child care—everything from cooking dinner to doing laundry, bathing children, reading bedtime stories, and sewing Halloween costumes.

secondary deviance subsequent acts of rule breaking that occur after primary deviance and as a result of your new deviant label and people's expectations of you.

secondary groups groups marked by impersonal, instrumental relationships (those existing as a means to an end).

sects or sectarian groups high-tension organizations that don't fit well within the existing social environment; they are usually most attractive to society's least privileged—namely, outcasts, minorities, or the poor—because they downplay worldly pleasure by stressing otherworldly promises.

secularism a general movement away from religiosity and spiritual belief toward a rational, scientific orientation; a trend adopted by industrialized nations in the form of separation of church and state.

segregation the legal or social practice of separating people on the basis of their race or ethnicity.

self the individual identity of a person as perceived by that same person.

service sector the section of the economy that involves providing intangible services.

sex the perceived biological differences that society typically uses to distinguish males from females.

sex role theory Talcott Parsons's theory that men and women perform their sex roles as bread-winners and wives/mothers, respectively, because the nuclear family is the ideal arrangement in modern societies, fulfilling the function of reproducing workers.

sexism a form of prejudice that occurs when a person's sex or gender is the basis for judgment, discrimination, or other differential treatment against that person.

sexual harassment an illegal form of discrimination revolving around sexuality that can involve everything from inappropriate jokes to sexual "barter" (where victims feel the need to comply with sexual requests for fear of losing their job) to outright sexual assault.

sexuality desire, sexual preference, and sexual identity and behavior.

sick role concept describing the social rights and obligations of a sick individual.

small group a group characterized by face-to-face interaction, a unifocal perspective, lack of formal arrangements or roles, and a certain level of equality.

social capital the information, knowledge of people or things, and connections that help individuals enter, gain power in, or otherwise leverage social networks.

social class or socioeconomic status (SES) an individual's position in a stratified social order.

social cohesion social bonds; how well people relate to each other and get along on a day-to-day basis.

social construction an entity that exists because people behave as if it exists and whose existence is perpetuated as people and social institutions act in accordance with widely agreed-on formal rules or informal norms of behavior associated with that entity.

social control mechanisms that create normative compliance in individuals.

social Darwinism the application of Darwinian ideas to society—namely, the evolutionary "survival of the fittest."

social deviance any transgression of socially established norms.

social equality a condition in which no differences in wealth, power, prestige, or status based on nonnatural conventions exist.

social institution a complex group of interdependent positions that, together, perform a social role and reproduce themselves over time; also defined in a narrow sense as any institution in a society that

works to shape the behavior of the groups or people within it.

social integration the extent to which you are integrated into your social group or community.

social media technologies that allow users to produce, share, and consume media in a variety of formats.

social mobility the movement between different positions within a system of social stratification in any given society.

social movement collective behavior that is purposeful and organized (but not ritualized) and that seeks to challenge or change one or more aspects of society through institutional and extra-institutional means.

social movement organization a group developed to recruit new members and coordinate participation in a particular social movement; these groups also often raise money, clarify goals, and structure participation in the movement.

social network a set of relations—essentially, a set of dyads—held together by ties between individuals.

social regulation the number of rules guiding your daily life and, more specifically, what you can reasonably expect from the world on a day-to-day basis.

social rights the rights guaranteeing a citizen's protection by the state.

socialism an economic system in which most or all of the needs of the population are met through non-market methods of distribution.

socialization the process by which individuals internalize the values, beliefs, and norms of a given society and learn to function as members of that society.

socioeconomic status an individual's position in a stratified social order.

sociological imagination the ability to connect the most basic, intimate aspects of an individual's life to seemingly impersonal and remote historical forces.

sociology the study of human society

soft power power attained through the use of cultural attractiveness rather than the threat of coercive action (hard power).

specialization the process of breaking up work into specific, delimited tasks.

state as defined by Max Weber, "a human community that (successfully) claims the monopoly of the legitimate use of physical force within a given territory."

status a recognizable social position that an individual occupies.

status hierarchy system a system of stratification based on social prestige.

status set all the statuses one holds simultaneously.

status-attainment model approach that ranks individuals by socioeconomic status, including income and educational attainment, and seeks to specify the attributes characteristic of people who end up in more desirable occupations.

stereotype threat when members of a negatively stereotyped group are placed in a situation where they fear they may confirm those stereotypes.

stigma a negative social label that changes others' behavior toward a person and therefore alters that person's own self-concept and social identity.

straight-line assimilation Robert Park's 1920s universal and linear model for how immigrants assimilate: they first arrive, then settle in, and achieve full assimilation in a newly homogenous country.

strain theory Robert Merton's theory that deviance occurs when a society does not give all of its members equal ability to achieve socially acceptable goals.

stratification the hierarchical organization of a society into groups with differing levels of power, social prestige, or status and economic resources.

street crime crime committed in public and often associated with violence, gangs, and poverty.

strength of weak ties the notion that relatively weak ties often hold hidden value because they yield new information.

structural functionalism a theory in which society's many parts—institutions, norms, traditions, and so on—mesh to produce a stable, working whole that evolved over time; best embodied by Talcott Parsons.

structural hole a gap between network clusters, or even two individuals, if those individuals (or clusters) have complementary resources.

structural mobility mobility that is inevitable from changes in the economy.

subaltern a subordinate, oppressed group of people.

subculture the distinct cultural values and behavioral patterns of a particular group in society; a group united by sets of concepts, values, symbols, and shared meaning specific to the members of that group and distinctive enough to distinguish it from others within the same culture or society.

supernatural compensators promises of future rewards, such as salvation or eternity in heaven.

survey an ordered series of questions intended to elicit information from respondents.

symbolic ethnicity a nationality, not in the sense of carrying the rights and duties of citizenship but in the sense of identifying with a past or future nationality. For later generations of White ethnics, it is something not constraining but easily expressed, with no risks of stigma and all the pleasures of feeling like an individual.

symbolic interactionism a micro-level theory in which shared meanings, orientations, and assumptions form the basic motivations behind people's actions.

T

Taylorism the methods of labor management, introduced by Frederick Winslow Taylor to streamline the processes of mass production, in which each worker repeatedly performs one specific task.

tertius gaudens the member of a triad who benefits from conflict between the other two members of the group.

theism the worship of a god or gods, as in Christianity, Islam, and Hinduism.

theory an abstracted, systematic model of how some aspect of the world works.

tie the connection between two people in a relationship that varies in strength from one relationship to the next; a story that explains our relationship with another member of our network.

total institution an institution in which one is totally immersed and that controls all the basics of day-to-day life; no barriers exist between the usual sphere of daily life, and all activity occurs in the same place and under the same single authority.

tracking a way of dividing students into different classes by ability or future plans.

traditional authority authority that rests on or appeals to the past or traditions.

transgender describes people whose gender does not correspond to their birth sex.

triad a group of three.

U

underclass the notion, building on the culture of poverty argument, that the poor not only are different from mainstream society in their inability to take advantage of what society has to offer but also are increasingly deviant and even dangerous to the rest of us.

union an organization of workers designed to facilitate collective bargaining with an employer.

union busting a company's assault on its workers' union with the hope of dissolving it.

upper class a term for the economic elite.

V

validity the extent to which an instrument measures what it is intended to measure.

value-added theory theory claiming that certain conditions are required for a social movement to coalesce and achieve a successful outcome.

values moral beliefs.

Verstehen German for "understanding." The concept of *Verstehen* comes from Max Weber and is the basis of interpretive sociology.

W

wealth a family's or individual's net worth (i.e., total assets minus total debts).

welfare state a system in which the state is responsible for the well-being of its citizens.

white coat effect the phenomenon wherein a researcher's presence affects her subjects' behavior or response, thereby disrupting the study.

white-collar crime offense committed by a professional (or professionals) against a corporation, agency, or other institution.

Bibliography

Aboim, S. (2016). *Plural masculinities: The remaking of the self in private life.* New York: Routledge.

Abrutyn, S., & Mueller, A. S. (2014). Are suicidal behaviors contagious in adolescence? Using longitudinal data to examine suicide suggestion. *American Sociological Review, 79*(2), 211–27.

Acemoglu, D., & Restrepo, P. (2018, January). Artificial intelligence, automation and work (NBER Working Paper No. 24196). National Bureau of Economic Research. Retrieved from www.nber.org/papers/w24196.

Acemoglu, D., & Robinson, J. A. (2006). *Economic origins of dictatorship and democracy.* New York: Cambridge University Press.

Acemoglu, D., et al. (2001, December). The colonial origins of comparative development: An empirical investigation. *The American Economic Review, 91*(5), 1369–401.

Acierno, R., et al. (2010). Prevalence and correlates of emotional, physical, sexual, and financial abuse and potential neglect in the United States: The National Elder Mistreatment Study. *American Journal of Public Health, 100*(2), 292–97.

Action Against Hunger. (2022). World hunger: Key facts and statistics. Retrieved from www.actionagainsthunger.org /world-hunger-facts-statistics.

Ad Council. (2018). Texting and driving prevention. Retrieved from www.psacentral.org/campaign/Texting _and_Driving_Prevention.

Adida, C. L., et al. (2010). Identifying barriers to Muslim integration in France. *Proceedings of the National Academy of Sciences USA, 107*(52), 22384–90.

Aguirre, B. E., et al. (1998). A test of the emergent norm theory of collective behavior. *Sociological Forum, 13*(2), 301–20.

Ahmad, F. B., et al. (2022). Provisional drug overdose death counts. National Center for Health Statistics. Retrieved from www.cdc.gov/nchs/nvss/vsrr/drug-overdose-data .htm#citation.

Alexander, K., et al. (2001). Schools, achievement and equality: A seasonal perspective. *Educational Evaluation and Policy Analysis, 23*(2), 171–91.

Allen, F. A. (1981). *The decline of the rehabilitative ideal: Penal policy and social purpose.* New Haven, CT: Yale University Press.

Allen, J. T. (1973). Designing income maintenance systems: The income accounting problem (paper no. 5). *Studies in Public Welfare.* Washington, DC: Government Printing Office.

Amenta, E. (2006). *When movements matter: The Townsend Plan and the rise of Social Security.* Princeton, NJ: Princeton University Press.

American Civil Liberties Union. (2013). The war on marijuana in Black and White. Retrieved from www.aclu .org/files/assets/aclu-thewaronmarijuana-rel2.pdf.

American Medical Association. (2022, December 16). AMA offers 10 health recommendations for new year. Retrieved from www.ama-assn.org/press-center/press-releases/ama -offers-10-health-recommendations-new-year-0.

American Psychological Association. (2005). Lesbian & gay parenting. Retrieved from www.apa.org/pi/lgbt /resources/parenting-full.pdf.

Ammerman, N. T. (2005). *Pillars of faith: American congregations and their partners.* Berkeley: University of California Press.

Anderson, E. (1999). *Code of the street: Decency, violence, and the moral life of the inner city.* New York: Norton.

Anderson, J. L. (2009). The most failed state: Letter from Mogadishu. *The New Yorker, 85*(41), 64.

Appiah, Kwame Anthony. (2020). The Case for Capitalizing the B in Black. *The Atlantic.* Retrieved from www.theatlantic .com/ideas/archive/2020/06/time-to-capitalize-blackand -white/613159.

Arias, E., et al. (2021). Provisional life expectancy estimates for January through June, 2020. In NVSS Vital Statistics Rapid Release. Retrieved from www.cdc .gov/nchs/data/vsrr/VSRR10-508.pdf.

Ariès, P. (1965). *Centuries of childhood: A social history of family life.* New York: Vintage. (Original work published 1962.)

Armstrong, E. A., & Bernstein, M. (2008). Culture, power, and institutions: A multi-institutional politics approach to social movements. *Sociological Theory, 26*(1), 74–99.

Armstrong, E. A., et al. (2012). Accounting for women's orgasm and sexual enjoyment in college hookups and relationships. *American Sociological Review, 77*(3), 435–62.

Arnold, M. (1869). *Culture and anarchy.* London: Smith, Elder.

Arum, R. (2003). *Judging school discipline: The crisis of moral authority.* Cambridge, MA: Harvard University Press.

Arum, R., & Shavit, Y. (1995). Secondary vocational education and the transition from school to work. *Sociology of Education, 68*(3), 187–204.

Asch, S. E. (1956). Studies of independence and conformity: A minority of one against a unanimous majority. *Psychological Monographs, 70*(9, Whole No. 416).

Associated Press. (2022, March 8). New Zealand changes its tack on surging COVID-19 cases. NPR. Retrieved from www.npr.org/2022/03/08/1085095406/new-zealand -changes-tack-on-surging-covid-19-cases.

Attanasio, O., et al. (2013). The evolution of income, consumption, and leisure inequality in the US, 1980– 2010. In C. Carroll et al. (Eds.), *Improving the measure of consumer expenditures* (pp. 100–140). Chicago: University of Chicago Press.

Auletta, K. (1981, November 16). I—the underclass. *The New Yorker*, p. 63.

Australian Catholic University. (2008). Principles of inclusive curriculum. Retrieved from www.acu.edu .au/__data/assets/pdf_file/0019/103735/Principles_of _Inclusive_Curriculum.pdf.

Australian Human Rights Commission. (1997, April). *Bringing them home: Report of the national inquiry into the separation of Aboriginal and Torres Strait Islander children from their families*. Retrieved from www.hreoc.gov .au/social_justice/bth_report/report/index.html.

Autor, D. H., et al. (2013). The China syndrome: Local labor market effects of import competition in the United States. *American Economic Review, 103*(6), 2121–68. Retrieved froxm www.aeaweb.org/articles?id=10.1257 /aer.103.6.2121.

Ayres, I., & Unkovic, C. (2012). Information escrows. *Michigan Law Review, 111*(2), 145. Retrieved from https://repository.law.umich.edu/mlr/vol111/iss2/1.

Bacher-Hicks, A., et al. (2021). Proving the school-to-prison pipeline: Stricter middle schools raise the risk of adult arrest. *Education Next, 21*(4), 52–57.

Bacolod, M. (2017). Skills, the gender wage gap, and cities. *Journal of Regional Science, 57*(2), 290–318.

Bailey, M. J., & Dynarski, S. M. (2011). Inequality in postsecondary education. In G. J. Duncan & R. J. Murnane (Eds.), *Whither opportunity? Rising inequality, schools, and children's life chances* (pp. 117–32). New York: Russell Sage Foundation.

Baker, D. C. (2005, May 26). Church hosts " drive-thru" Sunday services. *Quad-City Times*. Retrieved from www .qctimes.com/articles/2005/05/26/local/export93493 .txt.

Baker, J. H. (1977). Politics, paradigms, and public culture. *Journal of American History, 84*(3), 894–99.

Baker, J. O. (2015). *American secularism: Cultural contours of nonreligious belief systems*. New York: NYU Press.

Baker, M. G., et al. (2020). Successful elimination of Covid- 19 transmission in New Zealand. *The New England Journal of Medicine*. Retrieved from www.nejm.org/doi/full /10.1056/NEJMc2025203.

Bakshi, A. (2003). Potential adverse health effects of genetically modified crops, part B. *Journal of Toxicology and Environmental Health, 6*, 211–55.

Baldus, D. C., et al. (1998). Racial discrimination and the death penalty in the post-*Furman* era. *Cornell Law Review, 83*, 1638. Retrieved from www.lawschool.cornell .edu/research/cornell-law-review/upload/baldus.pdf.

Baltzell, E. D. (1958). *Philadelphia gentlemen*. New York: Free Press.

Banerjee, N. (2005, December 30). Going to church to find a faith that fits. *The New York Times*, pp. 1a, 18. Retrieved

from www.nytimes.com/2005/12/30/us /teenagers-mix-churches-for-faith-that-fits.html.

Barber, K. (2016). *Styling masculinity: Gender, class, and inequality in the men's grooming industry*. Brunswick, NJ: Rutgers University Press.

Barth, E. A. T., & Noel, D. L. (1972). Conceptual frameworks for the analysis of race relations: An evaluation. *Social Forces, 50*, 333–48.

Bashshur, R. L., et al. (2000). Telemedicine: A new health care delivery system. *Annual Review of Public Health, 21*(1), 613–37.

Bast, J. (2008, May 5). Controversy arises over lists of scientists whose research contradicts man-made global warming scares. The Heartland Institute. Retrieved from https://webarchive.loc.gov/all/20080919220421 /http://www.heartland.org/policybot/results .html?artId%3D23207.

Bauer, E. (2019). Eldercare: How does the United States stack up? *Forbes*. Retrieved from www.forbes.com/sites /ebauer/2019/08/28/eldercare-how-does-the -united-states-stack-up/#425f2c96bc96.

Bauer, G. (2016). Gender roles, comparative advantages and the life course: The division of domestic labor in same-sex and different-sex couples. *European Journal of Population, 32*(1), 99–128.

Bauluz, L., et al. (2021). Top 1% versus bottom 50% wealth shares in Western Europe and the US, 1910–2020. Retrieved from https://wir2022.wid.world/chapter-4.

Bear, C. (2008, May 13). American Indian school a far cry from the past. *Morning Edition*. National Public Radio.

Bearman, P. S., & Brückner, H. (2001). Promising the future: Virginity pledges and the transition to first intercourse. *American Journal of Sociology, 106*(4), 859–912.

Bearman, P. S., et al. (2004). Chains of affection: The structure of adolescent romantic and sexual networks. *American Journal of Sociology, 110*(1), 44–91.

Beauvoir, S. de. (1952). *The second sex*. New York: Knopf.

Beck, U. (1992). *Risk society: Towards a new modernity* (Mark Ritter, Trans.). London: Sage.

Becker, H. S. (1953, November). Becoming a marihuana user. *American Journal of Sociology, 59*, 235–43.

Becker, H. S. (1963). *Outsiders: Studies in the sociology of deviance*. New York: Free Press.

Belley, P., & Lochner, L. (2007, October). *The changing role of family income and ability in determining educational achievement* (NBER Working Paper No. 13527). National Bureau of Economic Research. Retrieved from www.nber .org/papers/w13527.

Bender, C. J. (2007). Touching the transcendent: Rethinking religious experience in the sociological study of religion. In N. Ammerman (Ed.), *Everyday religion: Observing modern religious lives* (pp. 201–19). New York: Oxford University Press. Retrieved from www.oxfordscholarship .com/oso/private/content/religion/9780195305418/p050. html#acprof-9780195305418-chapter-11.

Benedict, R. (1934). *Patterns of culture*. New York: Mentor Books.

Berbrier, M. (2000). The victim ideology of White supremacists and White separatists in the United States. *Sociological Focus, 33*, 175–91.

Berger, P. L. (1967). *The sacred canopy: Elements of a sociological theory of religion.* Garden City, NY: Anchor Books.

Berk, R. A., et al. (2003). The legalization of abortion and subsequent youth homicide: A time series analysis. *Analyses of Social Issues and Public Policy, 3*(1), 45–64.

Berk, S. F. (1985). *The gender factory: The apportionment of work in American households.* New York: Plenum Press.

Bernard, J. S. (1972). *The future of marriage.* New York: World Publishers.

Berry, B. (1963). *Almost White.* New York: Macmillan.

Bertrand, M., & Mullainathan, S. (2004). Are Emily and Greg more employable than Lakisha and Jamal? A field experiment on labor market discrimination. *American Economic Review, 94*(4), 991–1013.

Besecke, K. (2007). Beyond literalism: Reflexive spirituality and religious meaning. In N. Ammerman (Ed.), *Everyday religion: Observing modern religious lives* (pp. 169–86). New York: Oxford University Press. Retrieved from www.oxfordscholarship.com/oso/private/content/religion/9780195305418/p009.html.

Bialik, K. (2017, June 12). Key facts about race and marriage, 50 years after *Loving v. Virginia.* Pew Research Center. Retrieved from www.pewresearch.org/fact-tank/2017/06/12/key-facts-about-race-and-marriage-50-years-after-loving-v-virginia.

BiopharmaDive. (2018, November 29). Memorial Sloan Kettering scandal raises questions for pharma's biggest corporate boards. Retrieved from www.biopharmadive.com/news/memorial-sloan-kettering-scandal-raises-questions-for-pharmas-biggest-corp/540750.

Birnbaum, E. (2018). Hate crimes up for the third year in a row: FBI. *The Hill.* Retrieved from https://thehill.com/policy/national-security/416418-hate-crimes-up-for-third-year-in-a-row.

Bittman, M., et al. (2003). When does gender trump money? Bargaining and time in household work. *American Journal of Sociology, 109,* 186–214.

Bivens, J. & Kandra, J. (2022). CEO pay has skyrocketed 1,460% since 1978. Economic Policy Institute. Retrieved from www.epi.org/publication/ceo-pay-in-2021.

Bixler, M. T. (1992). *Winds of freedom: The story of the Navajo code talkers of World War II.* Darien, CT: Two Bytes.

Black, D. A., et al. (2017). The Methuselah effect: The pernicious impact of unreported deaths on old-age mortality estimates. *Demography, Springer.* Population Association of America (PAA), *54*(6), 2001–24.

Black megachurches surge. (1996). *Christian Century, 113*(21), 686–87. Retrieved from www.christiancentury.org.

Blanchard, R., & Bogaert, A. F. (1996). Homosexuality in men and number of older brothers. *American Journal of Psychiatry, 153,* 27–31.

Blanton, C. K. (2000). "They cannot master abstractions, but they can often be made efficient workers": Race and class in the intelligence testing of Mexican Americans and African Americans in Texas during the 1920s. *Social Science Quarterly, 81*(4), 1014–26.

Blau, P. M., & Duncan, O. D., with collaboration of A. Tyree. (1967). *The American occupational structure.* New York: Wiley.

Blažun, H., et al. (2012). Impact of computer training courses on reduction of loneliness of older people in Finland and Slovenia. *Computers in Human Behavior,*

28(4), 1202–12. Retrieved from www.sciencedirect.com/science/article/pii/S0747563212000350?via%3Dihub#!.

Bleakley, A., et al. (2018). How patterns of learning about sexual information among adolescents are related to sexual behaviors. *Perspectives on Sexual and Reproductive Health, 50*(1), 15–23.

Bloom, D. E., & Canning, D. (2004). *Global demographic change: Dimensions and economic significance.* No. w10817. National Bureau of Economic Research. Retrieved from www.nber.org/papers/w10817.

Blum, B. (2018, June). The lifespan of a lie? *Medium.* Retrieved from http://medium.com/s/trustissues/the-lifespan-of-a-lie-d869212b1f62.

Blumer, H. (1969). *Symbolic interactionism: Perspective and method.* Englewood Cliffs, NJ: Prentice-Hall.

Blumstein, P. W., & Schwartz, P. (1983). *American couples: Money, work, and sex.* New York: Morrow.

Bobo, L. (1989). Keeping the linchpin in place: Testing the multiple sources of opposition to residential integration. *Revue Internationale de Psychologie Sociale, 2,* 306–23.

Bobo, L., et al. (1997). Laissez-faire racism: The crystallization of a kinder, gentler, antiblack ideology. In S. A. Tuch & J. K. Martin (Eds.), *Racial attitudes in the 1990s: Continuity and change* (pp. 15–42). Westport, CT: Praeger.

Bogaert, A. F. (2006). Biological versus nonbiological older brothers and men's sexual orientation. *Proceedings of the National Academy of Sciences USA, 103*(28), 10771–74.

Bogle, K. A. (2008). *Hooking up: Sex, dating and relationships on campus.* New York: NYU Press.

Booth, B. (2015, April 16). How much would you pay to get your kid into Harvard? CNBC. Retrieved from www.cnbc.com/2014/11/10/is-a-college-planner-really-worth-it.html.

Booth, H. (2017). The kingdom of women: The society where a man is never the boss. *The Guardian.* Retrieved from www.theguardian.com/lifeandstyle/2017/apr/01/the-kingdom-of-women-the-tibetan-tribe-where-a-man-is-never-the-boss.

Bordo, S. (1990). Feminism, postmodernism, and gender skepticism. In L. J. Nicholson (Ed.), *Feminism/postmodernism* (pp. 133–56). New York: Routledge.

Bourdieu, P. (1977). Cultural reproduction and social reproduction. In J. Karabel & A. H. Halsey (Eds.), *Power and ideology in education* (pp. 487–511). New York: Oxford University Press.

Bowen, W. G., & Bok, D. (1998). *The shape of the river: Long-term consequences of considering race in college and university admissions.* Princeton, NJ: Princeton University Press.

Bowles, S., & Gintis, H. (1976). *Schooling in capitalist America: Educational reform and the contradictions of economic life.* New York: Basic Books.

Bozorgmehr, M., et al. (1996). Middle Easterners: A new kind of immigrant. In R. Waldinger & M. Bozorgmehr (Eds.), *Ethnic Los Angeles* (pp. 347–78). New York: Russell Sage Foundation.

Bradberry, L. A. (2016). The effect of religion on candidate preference in the 2008 and 2012 Republican presidential primaries. *PlOS One, 11*(4), e0152037. Retrieved from www.ncbi.nlm.nih.gov/pmc/articles/PMC4820110.

Bradley, M. B., et al. (1992). *Churches and church membership in the United States, 1990.* Atlanta: Glenmary Research Center.

Brainard, J. (2020). Scientists are drowning in COVID-19 papers. Can new tools keep them afloat? *Science Mag.* Retrieved from www.sciencemag.org/news/2020/05/scientists-are-drowning-covid-19-papers-can-new-tools-keep-them-afloat.

Brame, R., et al. (2014). Demographic patterns of cumulative arrest prevalence by ages 18 and 23. *Crime and Delinquency, 60,* 471–86.

Brandon, R. (2015, December 1). Mark Zuckerberg and Priscilla Chan to donate 99 percent of their Facebook fortune. The Verge. Retrieved from www.theverge.com/2015/12/1/9831554/mark-zuckerberg-charity-45-billion.

Brandow, M. (2008). *New York's poop scoop law: Dogs, the dirt and due process.* West Lafayette, IN: Purdue University Press.

Brewster, M. E. (2015). Lesbian women and household labor division: A systematic review of scholarly research from 2000 to 2015. *Journal of Lesbian Studies, 21*(1): 47–69.

Bridges, T., & Pascoe, C. J. (2014). Hybrid masculinities: New directions in the sociology of men and masculinities. *Sociology Compass, 8*(3), 246–58.

Bromwich, J. E. (2017, August 7). Minnesota governor calls mosque attack a "criminal act of terrorism." *The New York Times.* Retrieved from www.nytimes.com/2017/08/07/us/minnesota-mosque-explosion.html.

Brooks-Gunn, J., et al. (2003). Maternal employment and child cognitive outcomes in the first three years of life: The NICHD study of early child care. *Child Development, 73*(4), 1052–72.

Brubaker, R. (1992). *Citizenship and nationhood in France and Germany.* Cambridge, MA: Harvard University Press.

Brückner, H., & Bearman, P. S. (2005). After the promise: The STD consequences of adolescent virginity pledges. *Journal of Adolescent Health, 36,* 271–78.

Brulle, R., & Dunlap, R. (2021). A sociological view of the effort to obstruct action on climate change. *American Sociological Association.* Retrieved from www.asanet.org/footnotes-article/sociological-view-effort-obstruct-action-climate-change.

Bryk, A., et al. (1993). *Catholic schools and the common good.* Cambridge, MA: Harvard University Press.

Buchmann, C., et al. (2006). The growing female advantage in higher education: The role of family background and academic achievement. *American Sociological Review, 71*(4), 515–41.

Budge, S. L., et al. (2013). Anxiety and depression in transgender individuals: The roles of transition status, loss, support, and coping. *Journal of Consulting and Clinical Psychology, 81*(3), 545–57. Retrieved from www.ncbi.nlm.nih.gov/pubmed/23398495.

Budiman, A., & Ruiz, N. G. (2022, October 10). Key facts about Asian Americans, a diverse and growing population. Pew Research Center. Retrieved from www.pewresearch.org/fact-tank/2021/04/29/key-facts-about-asian-americans.

Bureau of Justice Statistics. (2020). Total correctional population. Retrieved from https://bjs.ojp.gov/data/key-statistics#citation--0.

Bureau of Labor Statistics, U.S. Department of Labor. (2007). Working and work-related activities done by men and women in 2007. *American Time Use Survey.* Retrieved from www.bls.gov/tus/current/work.htm#a1.

Bureau of Labor Statistics, U.S. Department of Labor. (2013). Table 19: Persons at work in agricultural and non-agricultural industries by hours of work. Retrieved from www.bls.gov/cps/cpsaat19.htm.

Bureau of Labor Statistics, U.S. Department of Labor. (2019a). Median usual weekly earnings of men and women, 2010 to 2018. *The Economics Daily.* Retrieved from www.bls.gov/opub/ted/2019/median-usual-weekly-earnings-of-men-and-women-2010-to-2018.htm.

Bureau of Labor Statistics, U.S. Department of Labor. (2019b). Time spent in leisure activities in 2014, by gender, age, and educational attainment. Retrieved from www.bls.gov/opub/ted/2015/time-spent-in-leisure-activities-in-2014-by-gender-age-and-educational-attainment.html.

Bureau of Labor Statistics, U.S. Department of Labor. (2020a). Average hours employed people spent working on days worked by day of week. Retrieved from www.bls.gov/charts/american-time-use/emp-by-ftpt-job-edu-h.htm.

Bureau of Labor Statistics, U.S. Department of Labor. (2020b). Employment characteristics of families, 2019. Retrieved from www.bls.gov/news.release/pdf/famee.pdf.

Bureau of Labor Statistics, U.S. Department of Labor. (2020c). Labor force statistics from the Current Population Survey. Retrieved from https://data.bls.gov/PDQWeb/ln.

Bureau of Labor Statistics, U.S. Department of Labor. (2020d). Labor force statistics from the Current Population Survey: Household data, not seasonally adjusted, A-36. Unemployed persons by age, sex, race, Hispanic or Latino ethnicity, marital status, and duration of employment. Retrieved from www.bls.gov/web/empsit/cpseea36.htm.

Bureau of Labor Statistics, U.S. Department of Labor. (2020e, March). Women in the labor force: A databook. Retrieved from www.bls.gov/opub/reports/womens-databook/2021/home.htm.

Bureau of Labor Statistics, U.S. Department of Labor. (2021a, September 9). Educational attainment for workers 25 years and older by detailed occupation. Retrieved from www.bls.gov/emp/tables/educational-attainment.htm.

Bureau of Labor Statistics, U.S. Department of Labor. (2021b). Employed persons by detailed occupation, sex, race, and Hispanic or Latino ethnicity. Retrieved from www.bls.gov/cps/cpsaat11.htm.

Bureau of Labor Statistics, U.S. Department of Labor. (2021c, April 21). Employment projections. Retrieved from www.bls.gov/emp/chart-unemployment-ear.

Bureau of Labor Statistics, U.S. Department of Labor. (2021d). BLS Reports. Highlights of women's earnings in 2020. Sep 2021. Retrieved from www.bls.gov/opub/reports/womens-earnings/2020/home.htm#:~:text=Earnings%20by%20age%20group,54%2C%20with%20earnings%20of%20%24977.

Bureau of Labor Statistics, U.S. Department of Labor. (2021e). Labor force characteristics by race and ethnicity, 2020.

Retrieved from www.bls.gov/opub/reports/race-and
-ethnicity/2020/home.htm

Bureau of Labor Statistics, U.S. Department of Labor. (2021f).
29-1229 Physicians, All Other. Retrieved from www.bls
.gov/oes/current/oes291229.htm#nat

Bureau of Labor Statistics, U.S. Department of Labor.
(2022a). Characteristics of minimum wage workers, 2021.
Retrieved from www.bls.gov/opub/reports/minimum
-wage/2021/home.htm#:~:text=Among%20those%20
paid%20by%20the,of%20all%20hourly%20paid%20
workers.

Bureau of Labor Statistics, U.S. Department of Labor.
(2022b). Chart 1. Union membership rates by state, 2022
annual averages. Retrieved from www.bls.gov/news
.release/pdf/union2.pdf.

Bureau of Labor Statistics, U.S. Department of Labor.
(2022c). Employment characteristics of families—2021.
Retrieved from www.bls.gov/news.release/pdf/famee
.pdf.

Bureau of Labor Statistics, U.S. Department of Labor.
(2022d). Employment situation— August 2022. Retrieved
from www.bls.gov/news.release/pdf/empsit.pdf.

Bureau of Labor Statistics, U.S. Department of Labor.
(2022e). Labor force participation of mothers and fathers
little changed in 2021, remains lower than in 2019.
Retrieved from www.bls.gov/opub/ted/2022/labor-force
-participation-of-mothers-and-fathers-little-changed
-in-2021-remains-lower-than-in-2019.htm.

Bureau of Labor Statistics, U.S. Department of Labor.
(2022f). Labor force participation rate—women. Retrieved
from https://fred.stlouisfed.org/series/LNS11300002.

Bureau of Labor Statistics, U.S. Department of Labor.
(2022g). A look at paid family leave by wage category
2021. Retrieved from www.bls.gov/opub/ted/2022
/a-look-at-paid-family-leave-by-wage-category-in-2021
.htm.

Bureau of Labor Statistics, U.S. Department of Labor.
(2022h). Median earnings for women in 2021 were 83.1
percent of the median for men. Retrieved from www.bls
.gov/opub/ted/2022/median-earnings-for-women-in
-2021-were-83-1-percent-of-the-median-for-men.htm.

Bureau of Labor Statistics, U.S. Department of Labor. (2022i,
July 19). Usual weekly earnings of wage and salary
workers. Retrieved from www.bls.gov/news.release
/pdf/wkyeng.pdf.

Bureau of Labor Statistics, U.S. Department of Labor. (2022j).
Women in the labor force: A databook. Retrieved from
www.bls.gov/opub/reports/womens-databook/2021
/home.htm.

Bureau of Labor Statistics, U.S. Department of Labor. (2023)
Labor force statistics from the current population survey.
Retrieved from www.bls.gov/cps/cpsaat11.htm

Bush, G. W. (2001, August 11). The president's radio address.
Retrieved from www.govinfo.gov/content/pkg/PPP-2001
-book2/html/PPP-2001-book2-doc-pg956.htm.

Burt, R. (1992). *Structural holes*. Cambridge, MA: Harvard
University Press.

Burton, C. (2014). Suburban student raises $25K in 24 hours
for college tuition. ABC Eyewitness News. Retrieved from
http://abc7chicago.com/education/suburban-student
-raises-$25 k-in-24-hours-for-college-tuition/176216.

Butler, J. (2002). *Gender trouble*. Routledge.

Butler, J. (2006). *Precarious life: The powers of mourning and
violence*. New York: Verso Books.

Cáceres-Delpiano, J. (2006). The impacts of family size on
investment in child quality. *Journal of Human Resources*,
41(4): 738–54.

Calhoun, C. (2002). *Dictionary of the social sciences*. New
York: Oxford University Press.

Callan, T., et al. (1993). Resources, deprivation and the
measurement of poverty. *Journal of Social Policy*, 22, 141–72.

Cantril, H. (1941). *The psychology of social movements*. New
York: Wiley.

Card, D., et al. (2008). Tipping and the dynamics of
segregation. *Quarterly Journal of Economics*, 123(1), 177–218.

Carlyle, T. (1971). Chartism. In *Selected writings*. A. Shelston
(Ed.). Harmondsworth: Penguin Books. (Original work
published 1839.)

Carnevale, A. P., et al. (2014). The college payoff: Education,
occupations, lifetime earnings. Washington, DC:
Georgetown University, Center on Education and the
Workforce. Retrieved from https://cew-7632.kxcdn
.com/wp-content/uploads/2014/11/collegepayoff
-complete.pdf.

Carpiano, R. M., et al. (2006). Social inequality and health:
Future directions for the fundamental cause explanation
for class differences in health. Paper presented at the
Russell Sage Foundation conference Social Class: How
Does It Work?, New York.

Carrington, C. (1999). *No place like home: Relationships and
family life among lesbians and gay men*. Chicago: University
of Chicago Press.

Case, A., & Deaton, A. (2015). Rising morbidity and mortality
in midlife among White non-Hispanic Americans in
the 21st century. *Proceedings of the National Academy of
Sciences USA*, 112(49), 15078–83. Retrieved from www
.pnas.org/content/112/49/15078.full.

Casey, N. (2020). College made them feel equal. The virus
exposed how unequal their lives are. *The New York Times*.
Retrieved from www.nytimes.com/2020/04/04
/us/politics/coronavirus-zoom-college-classes.html.

Center for Climate and Energy Solutions. (2022, December
1). Global manmade greenhouse gas emissions by sector,
2013. Retrieved from www.c2es.org/content
/internationalemissions/#:~:text=CO2%20accounts%20
for%20about%2076,are%20expressed%20in%20
CO2%2Dequivalents.

Centers for Disease Control and Prevention. (2012). Reported
cases and deaths from vaccine preventable diseases,
United States, 1950–2011. Retrieved from www.cdc
.gov/vaccines/pubs/pinkbook/downloads/appendices/g
/ases&deaths.pdf.

Centers for Disease Control and Prevention. (2015). Health,
United States, 2014: With special feature on adults aged
55–64. Retrieved from www.cdc.gov/nchs/data/hus
/hus14.pdf#016.

Centers for Disease Control and Prevention. (2017a). Health,
United States, 2016: With chartbook on long-term trends
in health. Retrieved from www.cdc.gov/nchs/data/hus
/hus16.pdf#053.

Centers for Disease Control and Prevention. (2017b).
Diagnoses of HIV infection in the United States and
dependent areas, 2017. Table 19b. Retrieved from www
.cdc.gov/hiv/pdf/library/reports/surveillance/cdc-hiv
-surveillance-report-2017-vol-29.pdf.

Centers for Disease Control and Prevention. (2018a). Substance use and sexual risk behaviors among youth. Retrieved from www.cdc.gov/healthyyouth/substance-use/pdf/dash-substance-use-fact-sheet.pdf.

Centers for Disease Control and Prevention. (2018b). Table 4. Life expectancy at birth, at age 65, and at age 75, by sex, race, and Hispanic origin: United States, selected years 1900–2017. Retrieved from www.cdc.gov/nchs/data/hus/2018/004.pdf.

Centers for Disease Control and Prevention. (2019). Trends in the prevalence of sexual behaviors and HIV testing national YRBS: 1991–2019. Retrieved from www.cdc.gov/healthyyouth/data/yrbs/factsheets/2019_sexual_trend_yrbs.htm.

Centers for Disease Control and Prevention. (2020a). Antidepressant use among adults: United States, 2015–2018. Retrieved from www.cdc.gov/nchs/products/databriefs/db377.htm#:~:text=%2C%202009%E2%80%932018.-,Summary,in%20both%20men%20and%20women.

Centers for Disease Control and Prevention. (2020b). Births: Final data for 2020. Retrieved from www.cdc.gov/nchs/data/nvsr/nvsr70/nvsr70-17.pdf.

Centers for Disease Control and Prevention. (2020c). Reproductive health: Infant mortality, 2020. Retrieved from www.cdc.gov/reproductivehealth/maternalinfanthealth/infantmortality.htm.

Centers for Disease Control and Prevention. (2021a). Provisional number of marriages and marriage rate: United States, 2000-2021. Retrieved from www.cdc.gov/nchs/data/dvs/marriage-divorce/national-marriage-divorce-rates-00-21.pdf.

Centers for Disease Control and Prevention. (2021b). Youth Risk Behavior Survey: Data Summary & Trends Report. Retrieved from www.cdc.gov/healthyyouth/data/yrbs/pdf/YRBS_Data-Summary-Trends_Report2023_508.pdf.

Centers for Disease Control and Prevention (2022). Table A. Expectation of life, by age, Hispanic origin and race, and sex: United States, 2020. Retrieved from www.cdc.gov/nchs/data/nvsr/nvsr71/nvsr71-01.pdf.

Centers for Medicare & Medicaid Services. (2021). NHE fact sheet. Retrieved from www.cms.gov/Research-Statistics-Data-and-Systems/Statistics-Trends-and-Reports/NationalHealthExpendData/NHE-Fact-Sheet#:~:text=NHE%20grew%209.7%25%20to%20%244.1,Gross%20Domestic%20Product%20(GDP).

Cesarini, D., et al. (2016). Wealth, health, and child development: Evidence from administrative data on Swedish lottery players. Quarterly Journal of Economics, 131(2), 687–738. Retrieved from https://academic.oup.com/qje/article/131/2/687/2606947.

Cesarini, D., et al. (2017). The effect of wealth on individual and household labor supply: Evidence from Swedish lotteries. American Economic Review, 107(12), 3917–46.

Chamie, J. (2016, October 15). 320 million children in single-parent families. Inter Press Service. Retrieved from www.ipsnews.net/2016/10/320-million-children-in-single-parent-families.

Chase-Lansdale, P. L., et al. (1997). Neighborhood and family influences on the intellectual and behavioral competence of preschool and early school-age children. In J. Brooks-Gunn et al. (Eds.), Neighborhood poverty. Vol. 1 (pp. 79–118). New York: Russell Sage Foundation.

Chase-Lansdale, P. L., et al. (2003). Mothers' transitions from welfare to work and the well-being of preschoolers and adolescents. Science, 299(5612), 1548–52.

Chauncey, G. (1994). Gay New York: Gender, urban culture, and the makings of the gay male world, 1890–1940. New York: Basic Books.

Chaves, M. (2002, summer). Abiding faith. Context Magazine, 1(2).

Chaves, M., & Higgins, L. M. (1992). Comparing the community involvement of Black and White congregations. Journal for the Scientific Study of Religion, 31(4), 425–40.

Chen, Y., et al. (2020). The roots of health inequality and the value of intra-family expertise. NBER Working Paper No. 25618.

Chenoweth, E., & Stephan, M. J. (2011). Why civil resistance works: The strategic logic of nonviolent conflict. New York: Columbia University Press.

Cherlin, A. J. (2009). The marriage-go-round: The state of marriage and the family in America today. New York: Knopf.

Chetty, R., & Hendren, N. (2015). The impacts of neighborhoods on intergenerational mobility: Childhood exposure effects and county level estimates. Retrieved from www.equality-of-opportunity.org/images/nbhds_paper.pdf.

Chetty, R., Hendren, N., & Katz, L. F. (2015). The effects of exposure to better neighborhoods on children: New evidence from the moving to opportunity experiment. Retrieved from www.equality-of-opportunity.org/images/mto_paper.pdf.

Child Trends Data Bank. (2018). Violent crime victimization: Indicators of child and youth well-being. Retrieved from www.childtrends.org/indicators/violent-crime-victimization.

Chirot, D. (1985). The rise of the West. American Sociological Review, 50, 181–95.

Chodorow, N. (1978). Reproduction of mothering: Psychoanalysis and the sociology of gender. Berkeley: University of California Press.

Chorev, N. (2007). Remaking U.S. trade policy: From protectionism to globalization. Ithaca, NY: Cornell University Press.

City Observatory. (2020). America's least (and most) segregated areas: 2020. Retrieved from https://cityobservatory.org/most_segregated2020.

City of Detroit. (2019). The next step: Detroit aims to be free of residential blight by the end of 2024. Retrieved from https://detroitmi.gov/news/next-step-detroit-aims-be-free-residential-blight-end-2024.

Clark, A. (2005, January 7). Frequent flyer miles soar above sterling. The Guardian. Retrieved from www.theguardian.com/money/2005/jan/08/business.theairlineindustry.

Clark, G. (2014). The son also rises: Surnames and the history of social mobility. Princeton, NJ: Princeton University Press.

Clifton, R. A., et al. (1986). Effects of ethnicity and sex on teachers' expectations of junior high school students. Sociology of Education, 59(1), 58–67.

Cloward, R., & Ohlin, L. (1960). Delinquency and opportunity. New York: Free Press.

Cohen, P. N. (2017). Families are changing—And staying the same. Educational Leadership, 75(1), 46–50. Retrieved from www.terpconnect.umd.edu/~pnc/EdLead17.pdf.

Colby, S. L., & Ortman, J. M. (2015, March). Projections of the size and composition of the U.S. population: 2014–2060. *Current Population Reports*. Retrieved from www.census.gov/content/dam/Census/library/publications/2015/demo/p25-1143.pdf.

Coleman, J., & Hoffer, T. (1987). *Public and private high schools*. New York: Basic Books.

Coleman, J., et al. (1966). *Equality of educational opportunity*. Washington, DC: US Government Printing Office.

Coleman, J., et al. (1982). *High school achievement: Public, Catholic and private schools compared*. New York: Basic Books.

CNN. (2022, July 17). Federal judge temporarily blocks Biden administration from protecting transgender students and workers in 20 states. Retrieved from www.cnn.com/2022/07/17/politics/biden-administration-transgender-protections-lawsuit-tennessee/index.html.

Collier, J., et al. (1997). Is there a family? New anthropological views. In R. N. Lancaster & M. di Lionardo (Eds.), *The gender/sexuality reader: Culture, history, political economy* (pp. 71–81). New York: Routledge.

Collins, P. H. (1990). Work, family, and Black women's oppression. In *Black feminist thought: Knowledge, consciousness and the politics of empowerment* (pp. 45–68). New York: Routledge.

Collins, R. (1971). Functional and conflict theories of educational stratification. *American Sociological Review*, 36(6), 1002–19.

Collins, R. (1979). *The credential society: A historical sociology of education and stratification*. New York: Academic Press.

Conger, R., et al. (1992). A family process model of economic hardship and adjustment of early adolescent boys. *Child Development*, 63, 526–41.

Conger, R., et al. (1994). Economic stress, coercive family process and developmental problems of adolescence. *Child Development*, 65, 541–61.

Conley, D. (1999). *Being Black, living in the red: Race, wealth, and social policy in America*. Berkeley: University of California Press.

Conley, D. (2001). Capital for college: Parental assets and postsecondary schooling. *Sociology of Education*, 74, 59–72.

Conley, D. (2004). *The pecking order: Which siblings succeed and why*. New York: Pantheon Books.

Conley, D. (2009a, October 8). Interview with Mitchell Duneier. New York.

Conley, D. (2009b, October 8). Interview with Duncan Watts. New York.

Conley, D. (2009c, August 8). Interview with C. J. Pascoe. 104th Annual Meeting of the American Sociological Association. San Francisco.

Conley, D. (2009d, August 8). Interview with Paula England. 104th Annual Meeting of the American Sociological Association. San Francisco.

Conley, D. (2009e, August 9). Interview with Victor Rios. 104th Annual Meeting of the American Sociological Association. San Francisco.

Conley, D. (2009f, October 8). Interview with Devah Pager. New York.

Conley, D. (2009g, October 8). Interview with Jeffrey Sachs. New York.

Conley, D. (2009h, August 9). Interview with Michael Hout. 104th Annual Meeting of the American Sociological Association. San Francisco.

Conley, D. (2009i, August 9). Interview with Jen'nan Read. 104th Annual Meeting of the American Sociological Association. San Francisco.

Conley, D. (2009j, August 9). Interview with Jennifer Lee. 104th Annual Meeting of the American Sociological Association. San Francisco.

Conley, D. (2009k, August 8). Interview with Andrew Cherlin. 104th Annual Meeting of the American Sociological Association. San Francisco.

Conley, D. (2009l, August 8). Interview with Stephen Morgan. 104th Annual Meeting of the American Sociological Association. San Francisco.

Conley, D. (2009m, August 9). Interview with Frances Fox Piven. 104th Annual Meeting of the American Sociological Association. San Francisco.

Conley, D. (2009n, October 8). Interview with Alondra Nelson. New York.

Conley, D. (2009o, August 8). Interview with John Evans. 104th Annual Meeting of the American Sociological Association. San Francisco.

Conley, D. (2009p, August 8). Interview with Doug McAdam. 104th Annual Meeting of the American Sociological Association. San Francisco.

Conley, D. (2011a, August 21). Interview with Allison Pugh. 106th Annual Meeting of the American Sociological Association. Las Vegas, NV.

Conley, D. (2011b, August 21). Interview with Annette Lareau. 106th Annual Meeting of the American Sociological Association. Las Vegas, NV.

Conley, D. (2011c, August 21). Interview with David Grusky. 106th Annual Meeting of the American Sociological Association. Las Vegas, NV.

Conley, D. (2011d, August 21). Interview with Shamus Khan. 106th Annual Meeting of the American Sociological Association. Las Vegas, NV.

Conley, D. (2011e, August 21). Interview with Nitsan Chorev. 106th Annual Meeting of the American Sociological Association. Las Vegas, NV.

Conley, D. (2013a, August 12). Interview with Julia Adams. 108th Annual Meeting of the American Sociological Association. New York.

Conley, D. (2013b, August 12). Interview with Michael Gaddis. 108th Annual Meeting of the American Sociological Association. New York.

Conley, D. (2013c, August 12). Interview with Ashley Mears. 108th Annual Meeting of the American Sociological Association. New York.

Conley, D. (2013d, August 12). Interview with Mario Luis Small. 108th Annual Meeting of the American Sociological Association. New York.

Conley, D. (2013e, August 12). Interview with Matthew Desmond. 108th Annual Meeting of the American Sociological Association. New York.

Conley, D. (2013f, August 12). Interview with Susan Crawford. 108th Annual Meeting of the American Sociological Association. New York.

Conley, D. (2014a, November 19). Interview with Shamus Khan. New York.

Conley, D. (2014b, September 17). Interview with Fadi Haddad. New York.

Conley, D. (2014c, September 24). Interview with Marc Ramirez. New York.

Conley, D. (2014d, November 5). Interview with Amos Mac. New York.

Conley, D. (2014e, November 26). Interview with Delores Malaspina. New York.

Conley, D. (2014f, October 8). Interview with Adeel Qalbani. New York.

Conley, D. (2014g, October 22). Interview with Andy Bichlbaum. New York.

Conley, D. (2015a, February 25). Interview with Asha Rangappa. New York.

Conley, D. (2015b, February 2). Interview with Jennifer Senior. New York.

Conley, D. (2015c, March 5). Interview with Adam Davidson. New York.

Conley, D. (2015d, February 4). Interview with Jennifer Jacquet. New York.

Conley, D. (2015e, April 8). Interview with Zephyr Teachout. New York.

Conley, D. (2019a, August 10). Interview with Stacey Torres. New York.

Conley, D. (2019b, August 10). Interview with Jacqueline Stevens. New York.

Conley, D. (2019c, August 10). Interview with Kevin Lewis. New York.

Conley, D. (2020a, July 23). Interview with Morgan Levine. New York.

Conley, D. (2020b, July 23). Interview with Daniel Belsky. New York.

Conley, D. (2020c, August 11). Interview with Maria Abascal. New York.

Conley, D., & Bennett, N. G. (2000). Is biology destiny? Birth weight and life chances. *American Sociological Review, 65*(3), 458–67.

Conley, D., & Glauber, R. (2006). Parental educational investment and children's academic risk: Estimates of the impact of sibship size and birth order from exogenous variation in fertility. *Journal of Human Resources, 41*(4), 722–37.

Conley, D., & Heerwig, J. (2011). The war at home: Effects of Vietnam-era military service on postwar household stability. *American Economic Review, 101*(3), 350–54.

Conley, D., & Rauscher, E. (2013, December). The effect of daughters on partisanship and social attitudes toward women. *Sociological Forum, 28*(4), 700–718.

Conley, D., et al. (2003). *The starting gate: Birth weight and life chances.* Berkeley: University of California Press.

Conley, D., et al. (2007). *Africa's lagging demographic transition: Evidence from exogenous impacts of malaria ecology and agricultural technology* (NBER Working Paper No. 12892). National Bureau of Economic Research.

Connell, C. (2010). Doing, undoing, or redoing gender? Learning from the workplace experiences of transpeople. *Gender & Society, 24*(1), 31–55.

Connell, R. (1987). *Gender and power.* Stanford, CA: Stanford University Press.

Cooley, C. H. (1909). *Social organization: A study of the larger mind.* New York: Scribner's.

Cooley, C. H. (1922). *Human nature and the social order.* New York: Scribner's. (Original work published 1902.)

Coolidge, C. (2011, September 16). Christian goods big seller for Wal-Mart. *ABC News.* Retrieved from http://abcnews.go.com/Business/story?id=86290&page=1#.Tt-3dXPZuoA.

Coontz, S. (1992). *The way we never were: American families and the nostalgia trap.* New York: Basic Books.

Coontz, S. (Ed.). (2001). *Historical perspectives on family diversity. Shifting the center: Understanding contemporary families.* Mountain View, CA: Mayfield.

Coontz, S. (2010). How to make it work this time. *The New York Times,* Room for Debate section. Retrieved from www.nytimes.com/roomfordebate/2010/12/19/why-remarry/how-to-make-a-second-marriage-work.

Copen, C. E., et al. (2013, April 4). First premarital cohabitation in the United States: 2006–2010 National Survey of Family Growth. *National Health Statistics Reports, 64.* Retrieved from www.cdc.gov/nchs/data/nhsr/nhsr064.pdf.

Corman, H., & Mocan, N. (2005). Carrots, sticks, and broken windows. *Journal of Law and Economics, 48*(1), 235–66.

Corman, H., et al. (2022). Effects of welfare reform on household food insecurity across generations. *Economics & Human Biology, 45,* 101101. Retrieved from https://doi.org/10.1016/j.ehb.2021.101101.

Cornell, S. (1988). *The return of the native: American Indian political resurgence.* New York: Oxford University Press.

Cornell, S., & Hartmann, D. (1998). Fixed or fluid? Alternative views of ethnicity and race. In *Ethnicity and race: Making identities in a changing world* (pp. 39–71). Thousand Oaks, CA: Pine Forge Press.

Correll, S. J., et al. (2007). Getting a job: Is there a motherhood penalty? 1. *American Journal of Sociology, 112*(5), 1297–1339.

Coser, L. A. (1957). Social conflict and the theory of social change. *British Journal of Sociology, 8*(3), 197–207.

Costello, E. J., et al. (2003). Relationships between poverty and psychopathology: A natural experiment. *Journal of the American Medical Association, 290,* 2023–29.

Council on Criminal Justice. (2022). Pandemic, social unrest, and crime in U.S. cities. Retrieved from https://counciloncj.org/mid-year-2022-crime-trends.

Covenant House. (n.d.). Sleep out to end youth homelessness. Retrieved from www.covenanthouse.org/helping-homeless/sleep-out.

Covert, B. (2011, March 8). Prepare for a possible "womancession." National Public Radio. Retrieved from www.npr.org/2011/03/08/134357162/the-nation-prepare-for-a-possible-womancession.

The COVID Tracking Project. (2021). COVID-19 is affecting Black, Indigenous, Latinx, and other people of color the most. *The Atlantic.* Retrieved from https://covidtracking.com/race.

Crenshaw, K. (1989). Demarginalizing the intersection of race and sex: A Black feminist critique of antidiscrimination doctrine, feminist theory and antiracist politics. *University of Chicago Legal Forum, 1989*(8): 139–167.

Croucher, K., & Romer, W. (2007). Inclusivity and curriculum design. *Guide to Teaching and Learning in Archaeology 6.* Higher Education Academy.

Crouse, J., & Trusheim, D. (1988). The case against the SAT. *Public Interest, 93,* 97–110.

Currie, D. H. (1999). *Girl talk: Adolescent magazines and their readers.* Toronto: University of Toronto Press.

Dahrendorft, R. (1958). Toward a theory of social conflict. *Journal of Conflict Resolution, 2*(2), 170–83.

Daminger, A. (2019). The cognitive dimension of household labor. *American Sociological Review, 84*(4), 609–33.

Dart, J. (2001, February 28). Hues in the pews: Racially mixed churches an elusive goal. *Christian Century.* Retrieved from http://hirr.hartsem.edu/cong/articles _huesinthepews.html.

David, E. (2015). Purple-collar labor: Transgender workers and queer value at global call centers in the Philippines. *Gender & Society, 29*(2), 169–94.

Davidson, J. D., et al. (1995). Persistence and change in the Protestant establishment, 1930–1992. *Social Forces, 74*(1), 157–75.

Davis, A. & Mishel, L. (2014). CEO pay continues to rise as typical workers are paid less. Economic Policy Institute. Retrieved from www.epi.org/publication/ceo-pay -continues-to-rise.

Davis, F. J. (1991). *Who is Black? One nation's definition.* University Park: Pennsylvania State University Press.

Davis, G. F. (2003). American cronyism: How executive networks inflated the corporate bubble. *Contexts, 2*(3), 34–40.

Davis, K. (1940). Extreme social isolation of a child. *American Journal of Sociology, 45*, 554–65.

Davis, K., & Moore, W. E. (1945). Some principles of stratification. *American Sociological Review, 10*(2), 242–49.

Davis, L. (2011). Race, gender, and class at a crossroads: A survey of their intersection in employment, economics, and the law. *Journal of Gender, Race & Justice, 14*(2).

Dawkins, R. (2006). *The God delusion.* Boston: Houghton Mifflin.

Death Penalty Information Center. (2020a). Executions by race and race of victim. Retrieved from https:// deathpenaltyinfo.org/executions/executions-overview /executions-by-race-and-race-of-victim.

Death Penalty Information Center. (2020b). Innocence Database. Retrieved from https://deathpenaltyinfo.org /policy-issues/innocence-database.

Death Penalty Information. (2021). Executions in 2021. Retrieved from https://deathpenaltyinfo.org/executions /2021.

Death Penalty Information. (2022a). Executions in 2022. Retrieved from https://deathpenaltyinfo.org/executions /2022.

Death Penalty Information Center. (2022b). Exonerations by race. Retrieved from https://deathpenaltyinfo.org /policy-issues/innocence/exonerations-by-race.

DellaCava, F. A., et al. (2004). Adoption in the U.S.: The emergence of a social movement. *Journal of Sociology and Social Welfare, 31*(4), 141–60.

DeNeve, C. (1997, winter). Hispanic presence in the workplace. *The Diversity Factor, 14*–21.

DeParle, J. (2004). *American dream: Three women, ten kids and a nation's drive to end welfare.* New York: Viking.

Desmond, M. (2016). *Evicted: Poverty and profit in the American city.* New York: Crown.

Desmond, M. (2023). *Poverty, by America.* New York: Crown.

DeVault, M. (1991). *Feeding the family: The social organization of caring as gendered work.* Chicago: University of Chicago Press.

De Vos, G., & Wagatsuma, H. (1966). *Japan's invisible race: Caste in culture and personality.* Berkeley: University of California Press.

DiAngelo, R. (2018). *White fragility: Why it's so hard for white people to talk about racism.* Boston: Beacon Press.

Dill, J. S., et al. (2016). Does the "glass escalator" compensate for the devaluation of care work occupations? The careers of men in low-and middle-skill health care jobs. *Gender & Society, 30*(2), 334–60.

Dillon, M., & Wink, P. (2003). Religiousness and spirituality: Trajectories and vital involvement in late adulthood. In M. Dillon (Ed.), *Handbook of the sociology of religion* (pp. 179–89). Cambridge, UK: Cambridge University Press.

DiMaggio, P. J., & Powell, W. (1983). The iron cage revisited: Institutional isomorphism and collective rationality in organizational fields. *American Sociological Review, 48*, 149.

Dinnerstein, L., et al. (1996). *Natives and strangers: A multicultural history of Americans.* New York: Oxford University Press.

Doran, K. M., et al. (2013, December 19). Housing as health care—New York's boundary-crossing experiment. *New England Journal of Medicine, 369*, 2374–77.

Doucouliagos, C., & Laroche, P. (2003). What do unions do to productivity? A meta-analysis. *Industrial Relations, 42*(4).

Doward, J. (2009, August 8). "Racist bias" blamed for disparity in police DNA database. *The Guardian.* Retrieved from www.theguardian.com/politics /2009/aug/09/police-dna-database-black-children.

Downey, D. B. (1995). When bigger is not better: Family size, resources, and children's educational performance. *American Sociological Review, 60*(5), 746–61.

Doyle, D. H. (1977). The social functions of voluntary associations in a nineteenth-century American town. *Social Science History, 1*(3), 333–55.

DPA. (2013, May 16). Palestinian smugglers deliver KFC to Gaza. *Haaretz.* Israel. Retrieved from www.haaretz .com/news/middle-east/palestinian-smugglers-deliver -kfc-to-gaza-1.524370.

Drape, J. (2005, October 30). Increasingly, football's playbooks call for prayers. *The New York Times.* Retrieved from www.nytimes.com/2005/10/30/sports/football /increasingly-footballs-playbooks-call-for-prayer.html.

Du Bois, W. E. B. (1903). *The souls of Black folk.* Paris: McClurg.

Du Mez, K. K. (2020). *Jesus and John Wayne.* New York: Liveright. Retrieved from https://wwnorton.com /books/9781631495731.

Duncan, G. (2016, December 19). When a basic income matters most. Economic Security Project. Retrieved from https://medium.com/economicsecproj/when-a-basic -income-matters-most-d90d093458a3.

Duncan, G., et al. (1994). Economic deprivation and early childhood development. *Child Development, 65*(2), 296–318.

Duncan, G. J., et al. (2005). Peer effects in drug use and sex among college students. *Journal of Abnormal Child Psychology, 33*(3), 375–85. Retrieved from www.gse.uci .edu/person/duncan_g/docs/11peerdrugs.pdf.

Duneier, M. (1999). *Sidewalk.* New York: Farrar Straus & Giroux.

Duneier, M., et al. (2014). *The urban ethnography reader.* New York: Oxford University Press.

Durkheim, É. (1951). *Suicide: A study in sociology* (G. Simpson & J. A. Spaulding, Trans.). New York: Free Press. (Original work published 1897.)

Durkheim, É. (1972). The forced division of labor. In A. Giddens (Ed.), *Selected writings* (p. 181). Cambridge, UK: Cambridge University Press. (Original work published 1893.)

Durkheim, É. (1995). *The elementary forms of religious life* (K. E. Fields, Intro. & Trans.). New York: Free Press. (Original work published 1917.)

Durkheim, É. (1997). *The division of labor in society* (L. A. Coser, Intro.; W. D. Halls, Trans.). New York: Free Press. (Original work published 1893.)

Dyer, G. (1985). *War.* New York: Crown.

Easterly, W., & Levine, R. (2002). *Tropics, germs, and crops: How endowments influence economic development* (NBER Working Paper No. W9106). National Bureau of Economic Research.

Eck, D. L. (2006). From diversity to pluralism. In *On common ground: World religions in America* [CD-ROM]. Cambridge, MA: The Pluralism Project.

Economist Intelligence Unit. (2023, June 22). Democracy index 2022: Frontline democracy and the battle for Ukraine. Retrieved from https://pages.eiu.com/rs/753 -RIQ-438/images/DI-final-version-report.pdf.

Economic Policy Institute. (2020). Wages for the top 1% skyrocketed 160% since 1979 while the share of wages for the bottom 90% shrunk. Retrieved from www.epi .org/blog/wages-for-the-top-1-skyrocketed-160-since -1979-while-the-share-of-wages-for-the-bottom-90 -shrunk-time-to-remake-wage-pattern-with-economic -policies-that-generate-robust-wage-growth-for-vast -majority.

Economic Policy Institute. (2022). CEO pay has skyrocketed 1,460% since 1978. Retrieved from www.epi.org /publication/ceo-pay-in-2021.

Economist, The. (2018, February 3). All must have degrees: Going to university is more important than ever for young people. Retrieved from www.economist.com /news/international/21736151-financial-returns-are -falling-going-university-more-important-ever.

Edgell, P., et al. (2006). Atheists as "other": Moral boundaries and cultural membership in American society. *American Sociological Review, 71*(2), 211–34.

Edgell, P., et al. (2017). From existential to social understandings of risk: Examining gender differences in nonreligion. *Social Currents, 4*(6), 556–74. Retrieved from https://doi.org/10.1177/2329496516686619.

Edgerton, R. (1995). "Bowling alone": An interview with Robert Putnam about America's collapsing civic life. *American Association for Higher Education Bulletin, 48*(1).

Edin, K., & Lein, L. (1997). *Making ends meet: How single mothers survive welfare and low-wage work.* New York: Russell Sage Foundation.

Edwards, B., & McCarthy, J. D. (2004). Resources and social movement mobilization. In D. A. Snow, S. A. Soule, and H. Kriesi (Eds.), *The Blackwell companion to social movements* (pp. 116–52). Malden, MA: Blackwell Publishing.

Ehrenreich, B. (2001). *Nickel and dimed: On (not) getting by in America.* New York: Metropolitan Books.

Eisenberg, D., et al. (2013, November). Peer effects on risky behaviors: New evidence from college roommate assignments. *Journal of Health Economics, 33*, 126–38.

Eisenbrey, R. (2007, June 20). *Strong unions, strong productivity: Snapshot for June 20.* Economic Policy Institute. Retrieved from www.epi.org/content.cfm /webfeatures_snapshots_20070620.

EITC (2022). EITC Participation rate by states tax years 2012 through 2019. Retrieved from www.eitc.irs.gov/eitc -central/participation-rate-by-state/eitc-participation -rate-by-states.

Elder, G., et al. (1995). Linking family hardship to children's lives. *Child Development, 56*, 361–75.

Ellen, B. (2014). Paid housework? No one'll clean up from that idea. *The Guardian.* Retrieved from www.theguardian .com/commentisfree/2014/mar/08/paying-for-housework -domestic-women-men.

Engels, F. (1878, May– July). *Herrn Eugen Dühring's Umwälzung des Sozialismus* in the supplement to *Vorwärts.*

Engzell, P., et al. (2021). Learning loss due to school closures during the COVID-19 pandemic. *Proceedings of the National Academy of Sciences of the United States of America, 118*(17). Retrieved from https://doi.org/10.1073 /pnas.2022376118.

Entwisle, D. R., & Alexander, K. L. (1992, February). Summer setback: Race, poverty, school composition, and mathematics achievement in the first two years of school. *American Sociological Review, 57*(1), 72–84.

Environmental and Energy Study Institute. (2022, June 9). Issue brief: The growth in greenhouse gas emissions from commercial aviation (2019, revised 2022). Retrieved from www.eesi.org/papers/view/fact-sheet-the-growth-in -greenhouse-gas-emissions-from-commercial-aviation.

Environmental Performance Index. (2022). 2022 EPI results. Retrieved from https://epi.yale.edu/epi-results/2022 /component/epi.

Epistemological modesty: An interview with Peter Berger. (1997, October 29). *The Christian Century.* Retrieved from www.christiancentury.org/article/epistemological -modesty.

Epstein, C. F. (1988). *Deceptive distinctions: Sex, gender, and the social order.* New Haven, CT: Yale University Press.

Eriksen, S., & Jensen, V. (2006). All in the family? Family environment factors in sibling violence. *Journal of Family Violence, 21*(8), 497–507.

Erikson, K. (2005). *Wayward Puritans: A study in the sociology of deviance* (rev. ed.). Boston: Pearson/Allyn & Bacon. (Original work published 1966.)

Eskenazi, B., et al. (2002). The association of age and semen quality in healthy men. *Human Reproduction, 18*(2), 447–54.

Espejo, E. P., et al. (2006). Stress sensitization and adolescent depressive severity as a function of childhood adversity: A link to anxiety disorders. *Journal of Abnormal Child Psychology, 35*, 287–99.

Espenshade, T. J., & Chung, C. Y. (2005). The opportunity cost of admission preferences at elite universities. *Social Science Quarterly, 86*(2), 293–305.

Espenshade, T. J., et al. (2004). Admission preferences for minority students, athletes, and legacies at elite universities. *Social Science Quarterly, 85*(5), 1422–46.

Essman, E. (2007). The American people: Social classes. *Life in the USA: The complete guide for immigrants and*

Americans. Retrieved from www.lifeintheusa .com/people/socialclasses.htm.

European Commission. (2022). CO_2 emissions of all world countries. Retrieved from https://edgar.jrc.ec.europa .eu/report_2022.

European Economic and Social Committee. (2021). Collective bargaining in the EU: It takes two to tango. Retrieved from www.eesc.europa.eu/en/news-media/news /collective-bargaining-eu-it-takes-two-to-tango.

Evans, J. (2002). *Playing God? Human genetic engineering and the rationalization of public bioethical debate.* Chicago: University of Chicago Press.

Eyerman, R. (2001). *Cultural trauma: Slavery and the formation of African American identity.* Cambridge, UK: Cambridge University Press.

Fadiman, A. (1997). *The spirit catches you and you fall down: A Hmong child, her American doctors, and the collision of two cultures.* New York: Farrar, Straus, & Giroux.

Fagan, J., et al. (2003, March 31). Reciprocal effects of crime and incarceration in New York City neighborhoods. *Fordham Urban Law Journal, 30,* 1551–602.

Faruqee, H., & Mühleisen, M. (2003). Population aging in Japan: Demographic shock and fiscal sustainability. *Japan and the World Economy, 15*(2), 185–210.

Faughnder, R. (2016, March 26). Faith-based films are building followings at the box office. *Los Angeles Times.* Retrieved from www.latimes.com/entertainment /envelope/cotown/la-et-ct-faith-based-movies-20160325 -story.html.

Fausto-Sterling, A. (2000). *Sexing the body: Gender politics and the construction of sexuality.* New York: Basic Books.

Federal Bureau of Investigation. (2003). *Facts and figures 2003.* Retrieved from www.fbi.gov/libref/factsfigure/wcc.htm.

Federal Bureau of Investigation. (2021a). Rate of homicide offenses by population. Retrieved from https://cde.ucr.cjis .gov/LATEST/webapp/#/pages/explorer/crime/crime-trend.

Federal Bureau of Investigation. (2021b). Rate of violent crime offenses by population. Retrieved from https://cde.ucr .cjis.gov/LATEST/webapp/#/pages/explorer/crime/crime -trend.

Federal Deposit Insurance Corporation. (2021). 2021 FDIC national survey of unbanked and underbanked households. Retrieved from www.fdic.gov/analysis/household-survey /index.html.

Federal Reserve Board. (2021). *Report on the economic well-being of U.S. households in 2021.* Retrieved from www .federalreserve.gov/publications/2021-economic -well-being-of-us-households-in-2020-dealing-with -unexpected-expenses.htm

Ferber, A. L. (1999). *White man falling: Race, gender, and White supremacy.* Lanham, MD: Rowman & Littlefield.

Ferran, L. (2009, December 31). Megachurch asks for nearly $1M in 48 hours: Pastor Rick Warren of Saddleback Church asks members for $900,000 before New Year. *Good Morning America. ABC News.* Retrieved from http://abcnews.go.com/GMA/church-asks-mil-48-hours /story?id=9455589.

Fetter, J. H. (1995). *Questions and admissions: Reflections on 100,000 admissions decisions at Stanford.* Stanford, CA: Stanford University Press.

Figlio, D. N. (2005). *Boys named Sue: Disruptive children and their peers* (NBER Working Paper No. W11277).

National Bureau of Economic Research. Retrieved from http://palm.nber.org/papers/w11277.

Figlio, D. N. (2007, September). Boys named Sue: Disruptive children and their peers. *Education Finance and Policy, 2*(4), 376–94.

Fillinger, K. (2013). Megachurches by the numbers. *Christian Standard.* Retrieved from http://christianstandard.com /2013/05/megachurches-by-the-numbers.

Finke, R., & Stark, R. (1992). *The churching of America, 1776–1990: Winners and losers in our religious economy.* New Brunswick, NJ: Rutgers University Press.

Finkelstein, A., et al. (2022). Heterogeneity in damages from a pandemic. Retrieved from https://doi.org/10.3386 /w30658.

Finn, J. D., et al. (2005). Small classes in the early grades, academic achievement, and graduating from high school. *Journal of Educational Psychology, 97*(2), 214–23.

Fischer, C., & Hout, M. (2006). How Americans prayed: Religious diversity and change. In C. Fischer & M. Hout (Eds.), *A century of difference: How America changed in the last one hundred years* (pp. 186–211). New York: Russell Sage Foundation.

Fischer, C. S., et al. (1996). *Inequality by design: Cracking the bell curve myth.* Princeton, NJ: Princeton University Press.

Fischer, P. M., et al. (1991, December). Brand logo recognition by children aged 3 to 6 years: Mickey Mouse and Old Joe the Camel. *Journal of the American Medical Association, 266,* 3145–48.

Flora, C. (2013). *Friendfluence: The surprising ways friends make us who we are.* New York: Anchor Books.

Foer, J. S. (2009). *Eating animals.* New York: Little, Brown.

Folbre, N. (1987). *A field guide to the U.S. economy.* New York: Pantheon Books.

Forbes. (2020). Profile: Bill Gates. Retrieved from www .forbes.com/profile/bill-gates/#b084484689f0.

Ford, H., & Crowther, S. (1973). *My life and work, by Henry Ford.* New York: Arno Books. (Original work published 1922.)

Fordham, S., & Ogbu, J. (1986). Black students' school success: Coping with the "burden of acting White." *Urban Review, 18,* 176–206.

Foss, R. J. (1994). The demise of homosexual exclusion: New possibilities for gay and lesbian immigration. *Harvard Civil Rights– Civil Liberties Law Review, 29,* 439–75.

Foster, D. (2006, February 19). Mind over splatter. *The New York Times.* Retrieved from www.nytimes.com/2006 /02/19/opinion/mind-over-splatter.html.

Foucault, M. (1977). *Discipline and punish: The birth of the prison.* New York: Pantheon Books.

Foucault, M. (1978). *The history of sexuality.* New York: Pantheon Books.

Fox News. (2017, May 10). Top 13 highest grossing faith films. Retrieved from www.foxnews.com/entertainment /2017/05/10/top-13-highest-grossing-faith-films.html.

Francis, D. R. (2005, November). Changing work behavior of married women. *NBER Digest.* Retrieved from www.nber .org/digest/nov05/w11230.html.

Frank, R. H. (2007). *Falling behind: How rising inequality harms the middle class.* Berkeley: University of California Press.

Franklin, J. H. (1980). *From slavery to freedom* (5th ed.). New York: Knopf.

Fredrickson, G. M. (2002). *Racism: A short history.* Princeton, NJ: Princeton University Press.

Freedman, J. O. (2003). *Liberal education and the public interest.* Iowa City: University of Iowa Press.

Freeman, C. E. (2004, November 19). *Trends in educational equity of girls and women: 2004* (NCES 2005-016). U.S. Department of Education, National Center for Education Statistics. Washington, DC: U.S. Government Printing Office. Retrieved from http://nces.ed.gov/pubsearch /pubsinfo.asp?pubid=2005016.

Freeman, R. B. (2007, February 22). *Do workers still want unions? More than ever* (Briefing Paper No. 182). Economic Policy Institute, Agenda for Shared Prosperity. Retrieved from www.sharedprosperity.org/bp182.html.

Friedan, B. (1997). *The feminine mystique.* New York: Norton. (Original work published 1963.)

Friedman, M. (1970, September 13). A Friedman doctrine— The social responsibility of business is to increase its profits. *The New York Times Magazine.* Retrieved from http://select.nytimes.com/gst/abstract.html?res= F10F11 FB3E5810718 EDDAA0994 D1405B808 BF1D3&scp= 1&sq = The+ social+ responsibility+ of+ business+ is+ to+ increase + its+ profits&st=p.

Frogner, B. K., et al. (2018). Physical therapy as the first point of care to treat low back pain: An instrumental variables approach to estimate impact on opioid prescription, Health Care Utilization, and Costs. *Health Services Research, 53*(6), 4629–4646. Retrieved from https://doi .org/10.1111/1475-6773.12984.

Frost, J. (2017, May 25). *The meaning and measurement of secularization—there's research on that.* Retrieved from https://thesocietypages.org/trot/2017/05/25/measuring -secularization.

Fryer, R. G., Jr. (2010, August 10). *Racial inequality in the 21st century: The declining significance of discrimination* (NBER Working Paper No. 16256). National Bureau of Economic Research. Retrieved from www.nber.org/papers/w16256.

Fuchs, V. (1967). Redefining poverty and redistributing income. *Public Interest, 8,* 88–95.

Gallup. (2021). How religious are Americans? Retrieved from https://news.gallup.com/poll/358364/religious-americans .aspx#:~:text=According%20to%20an%20average%20 of,with%20a%20specific%20religious%20faith.

Gallup. (2022a). Belief in God in U.S. dips to 81%, a new low. Retrieved from https://news.gallup.com/poll/393737 /belief-god-dips-new-low.aspx.

Gallup. (2022b). How many Americans believe in God? Retrieved from https://news.gallup.com/poll/268205 /americans-believe god.aspx.

Gallup. (2022c). U.S. approval of labor unions at highest point since 1965. Retrieved from http://news.gallup .com/poll/398303/approval-labor-unions-highest -point-1965.aspx.

Gamm, G., & Putnam, R. D. (1999). The growth of voluntary associations in America, 1840–1940. Patterns of social capital: Stability and change in comparative perspective, Part II. *Journal of Interdisciplinary History, 29*(4), 511–57.

Gamoran, A., & Mare, R. D. (1989). Secondary school tracking and educational inequality: Compensation, reinforcement or neutrality? *American Journal of Sociology, 94*(5), 1146–86.

Ganna, A., et al. (2019). Large-scale GWAS reveals insights into the genetic architecture of same-sex sexual behavior. *Science, 365*(6456), eaat7693.

Gans, H. (1979a). *Deciding what's news: A study of* CBS Evening News, NBC Nightly News, Newsweek *and* Time. New York: Vintage.

Gans, H. (1979b). Symbolic ethnicity: The future of ethnic groups and cultures in America. *Ethnic and Racial Studies, 2,* 1–19.

Ganz, M. (2004). Why David sometimes wins: Strategic capacity in social movements. In J. Goodwin & J. M. Jasper (Eds.), *Rethinking social movements: Structure, meaning, and emotion* (pp. 177–98). Lanham, MD: Rowman & Littlefield.

Garfinkel, H. (1967). *Studies in ethnomethodology.* Englewood Cliffs, NJ: Prentice-Hall.

Garrett, J. T. (1994). Health. In M. B. Davis (Ed.), *Native Americans in the 20th century* (pp. 233–37). New York: Garland.

Garrow, D. (1968). *Bearing the cross: Martin Luther King, Jr. and the Southern Christian Leadership Conference—A personal portrait.* New York: Morrow.

Gately, G. (2005, December 31). A town in the spotlight wants out of it. *The New York Times.* Retrieved from www .nytimes.com/2005/12/21/education/a-town-in-the -spotlight-wants-out-of-it.html.

Gaustad, E. (1962). *Historical atlas of American religion.* New York: Harper & Row.

Gaventa, J. (1980). *Power and powerlessness: Quiescence and rebellion in an Appalachian valley.* Urbana: University of Illinois Press.

Geertz, C. (1973). *The interpretation of cultures.* New York: Basic Books.

Geiger, A. W. (2017). 5 Facts on how Americans view the Bible and other religious texts. Pew Research Center. Retrieved from www.pewresearch.org/fact-tank /2017/04/14/5-facts-on-how-americans-view-the-bible -and-other-religious-texts.

Gerson, K. (1985). *Hard choices: How women decide about work, career, and motherhood.* Berkeley: University of California Press.

Gerson, K. (1993). *No man's land: Men's changing commitments to family and work.* New York: Basic Books.

Gibson, C., & Jung, K. (2006). Historical census statistics on the foreign-born population of the United States: 1850 to 2000. U.S. Census Bureau. Retrieved from www.census .gov/population/www/documentation/twps0081 /twps0081.pdf.

Gieryn, T. F. (1999). *Cultural boundaries of science: Credibility on the line.* Chicago: University of Chicago Press.

Gilbert, D. (1998). *The American class structure in an age of growing inequality.* Belmont, CA: Wadsworth.

Gilligan, C. (1982). *In a different voice: Psychological theory and women's development.* Cambridge, MA: Harvard University Press.

Glaeser, E. L., & Ward, B. A. (2006). *Myths and realities of American political geography* (Harvard Institute of Economic Research Discussion Paper No. 2100). Retrieved from http://ssrn.com/abstract =874977.

Glass, J., & Jacobs, J. (2005). Childhood religious conservatism and adult attainment among Black and White women. *Social Forces, 84,* 555–79.

Glassner, B. (1999). *The culture of fear: Why Americans are afraid of the wrong things.* New York: Basic Books.

Glazer, N., & Moynihan, D. P. (1963). *Beyond the melting pot: The Negroes, Puerto Ricans, Jews, Italians, and Irish of New York City.* Cambridge, MA: MIT Press.

Glenn, E. N. (1986). *Issei, Nisei, war bride: Three generations of Japanese American women in domestic service.* Philadelphia: Temple University Press. Global Slavery Index. (2016). Global slavery index 2016 report. (3rd ed.). Retrieved from www.globalslaveryindex.org/download.

Glock, C., & Stark, R. (1965). *Religion and society in tension.* Chicago: Rand McNally.

Goel, S., Watts, D. J., & Goldstein, D. G. (2012, June). The structure of online diffusion networks. In *Proceedings of the 13th ACM conference on electronic commerce* (pp. 623–38).

Goffman, E. (1959). *The presentation of self in everyday life.* New York: Doubleday.

Goffman, E. (1961). *Asylums: Essays on the social situation of mental patients and other inmates.* New York: Doubleday Anchor.

Goffman, E. (1963). *Stigma: Notes on the management of spoiled identity.* Englewood Cliffs, NJ: Prentice-Hall.

GoFundMe. (2021). Giving report. Retrieved from www.gofundme.com/c/gofundme-giving-report-2021.

Goldberger, P. (1995, April 20). The gospel of church architecture, revised. *The New York Times*, pp. C1, 5. Retrieved from www.nytimes.com/1995/04/20/garden/the-gospel-of-church-architecture-revised.html?sq=+Megachurches%3A+User-friendly+architecture+&scp=1&st=cse.

Goldman, A. L., et al. (2018). Out-of-pocket spending and premium contributions after implementation of the Affordable Care Act. *JAMA Internal Medicine, 178*(3), 347–55.

Goodman, B. (2006a, April 17). People stand, the spirit walks: Easter at the Georgia Dome. *The New York Times.* Retrieved from www.nytimes.com/2006/04/17/us/17easter.html.

Goodman, B. (2006b, March 29). Teaching the Bible in Georgia's public schools. *The New York Times.* Retrieved from www.nytimes.com/2006/03/29/education/29bible.html.

Goodnough, A. (2020, February 14). Appeals court rejects Trump Medicaid work requirements in Arkansas. *The New York Times.* Retrieved from www.nytimes.com/2020/02/14/health/medicaid-work-requirements.html.

Goodstein, L. (2005, December 4). Intelligent design might be meeting its maker. *The New York Times.* Retrieved from www.nytimes.com/2005/12/04/weekinreview/intelligent-design-might-be-meeting-its-maker.html.

Goodstein, L. A. (2007, February 25). A divide, and maybe a divorce. *The New York Times*, p. 1. Retrieved from www.nytimes.com/2007/02/25/weekinreview/25goodstein.html.

Goodwin, J. (2006). *No other way out: States and revolutionary movements.* New York: Cambridge University Press.

Gordon, M. M. (1964). *Assimilation in American life: The role of race, religion, and national origins.* New York: Oxford University Press.

Gould, E. (2014). Why America's workers need faster wage growth—And what we can do about it. Economic Policy Institute. Retrieved from www.epi.org/publication/why-americas-workers-need-faster-wage-growth.

Gould, E. D., & Hijzen, A. (2016). Growing apart, losing trust? The impact of inequality on social capital. International Monetary Fund.

Gourevitch, P. (1998). *We wish to inform you that tomorrow we will be killed with our families: Stories from Rwanda.* New York: Farrar, Straus & Giroux.

GQ. (2014). 2 Chainz thinks this $5K toothbrush is going to knock your socks off. Retrieved from www.youtube.com/watch?v=TNcFWlNQMsY.

Gramsci, A. (1971). *Selections from the prison notebooks.* London: Lawrence & Wishart.

Grandey, A., et al. (2005). Must "service with a smile" be stressful? The moderating role of personal control for American and French employees. *Journal of Applied Psychology, 90*(5), 893–904.

Granovetter, M. (1973). The strength of weak ties. *American Journal of Sociology, 78*, 1360–80.

Granovetter, M. (1974). *Getting a job: A study of contacts and careers.* Chicago: University of Chicago Press.

Granovetter, M. (1978). Threshold models of collective behavior. *American Journal of Sociology, 83*(6), 1420–43.

Gray, K. F., & Cunnyngham, K. (2017). Trends in Supplemental Nutritional Assistance Program participation rates: Fiscal year 2010 to fiscal year 2015. Retrieved from https://fns-prod.azureedge.net/sites/default/files/ops/Trends2010-2015.pdf.

Gray, N., & Nye, P. S. (2001). American Indian and Alaska Native substance abuse: Co-morbidity and cultural issues. *American Indian and Alaska Native Mental Health Research, 10*(2), 67–84. Retrieved from www.ucdenver.edu/academics/colleges/PublicHealth/research/centers/CAIANH/journal/Documents/Volume%2010/10(2)_Gray_Substance_Abuse_67-84.pdf.

Green, E. L. (2017, December 15). DeVos delays rule on racial disparities in special education. *The New York Times.* Retrieved from www.nytimes.com/2017/12/15/us/politics/devos-obama-special-education-racial-disparities.html.

Greer, C. (2006, April). *Black ethnicity: Political attitudes, identity, and participation in New York City.* Institute for Social and Economic Research and Policy, Columbia University. Retrieved from www.iserp.columbia.edu/news/articles/black_ethnicity.html.

Grose, T., & Kallerman, P. (2015). The 1099 economy— Elusive, but diverse, and growing. *Bay Area Economy.* Retrieved from https://medium.com/@BayAreaEconomy/the-1099-economy-elusive-but-diverse-and-growing-bcc6f65694fe#.t39kzun5w.

Grosz, E. A. (1994). *Volatile bodies: Toward a corporeal feminism.* Bloomington: Indiana University Press.

Grundy, S. (2022). *Respectable: Politics and paradox in making the Morehouse man.* Berkeley: University of California Press.

Guardian, The. (2014, June 9). Computer simulating 13-year-old boy becomes first to pass Turing test. Retrieved from www.theguardian.com/technology/2014/jun/08/super-computer-simulates-13-year-old-boy-passes-turing-test.

Gurian, M., & Stevens, K. (2005). *The minds of boys: Saving our sons from falling behind in school and life.* San Francisco: Jossey-Bass.

Gusfield, J. (1986). *Symbolic crusade: Status politics and the American temperance movement* (2nd ed.). Champaign: University of Illinois Press.

Haber, A. (1966). Poverty budgets: How much is enough? *Asia Pacific Journal of Human Resources, 1*(3), 5–22.

Hacker, J. (2006). *The great risk shift: The assault on American jobs, families, health care and retirement and how you can fight back.* New York: Oxford University Press.

Hacking, I. (1999). *The social construction of what?* Cambridge, MA: Harvard University Press.

Hadaway, K. C., et al. (1993). What the polls don't show: A close look at U.S. church attendance. *American Sociological Review, 58,* 741–52.

Haley, A. (1976). *Roots: The saga of an American family.* New York: Doubleday.

Han, J. (2006). "We are Americans too": A comparative study of the effects of 9/11 on South Asian communities. Cambridge, MA: Discrimination and National Security Initiative, Harvard University. Retrieved from www.pluralism.org/affiliates/kaur_sidhu/We_Are_Americans_Too.pdf.

Haney López, I. F. (1995). White by law. In R. Delgado (Ed.), *Critical race theory: The cutting edge* (pp. 542–50). Philadelphia: Temple University Press.

Hankins, J. D. (2014). *Working skin: Making leather, making a multicultural Japan.* Berkeley: University of California Press.

Hannaford, I. (1996). *Race: The history of an idea in the West.* Washington, DC: Woodrow Wilson Center Press.

Hanson, T. L., et al. (1997). Economic resources, parental practices and children's well-being. In G. Duncan & J. Brooks-Gunn (Eds.), *Consequences of growing up poor* (pp. 190–238). New York: Russell Sage Foundation.

Hanushek, E. A., & Wößmann, L. (2006). Does educational tracking affect performance and inequality? Differences-indifferences evidence across countries. *The Economic Journal, 116*(510), C63–76.

Hanushek, E. A., et al. (1998). *Teachers, schools, and academic achievement* (NBER Working Paper No. 6691). National Bureau of Economic Research.

Hanushek, E. A., et al. (2005). *The market for teacher quality* (NBER Working Paper No. 11154). National Bureau of Economic Research.

Haraldsson, A., & Wängnerud, L. (2019). The effect of media sexism on women's political ambition: Evidence from a worldwide study. *Feminist Media Studies, 19*(4), 525–41.

Harding, S. (1987). *Feminism and methodology: Social science issues.* Bloomington: Indiana University Press.

Harris, A. R., et al. (2002). Murder and medicine: The lethality of criminal assault, 1960–1999. *Homicide Studies, 6,* 128.

Harris, D. R., & Sim, J. J. (2002, August). Who is multiracial? Assessing the complexity of lived race. *American Sociological Review, 67*(4), 614–27.

Harris, S. (2006). *Letter to a Christian nation.* New York: Vintage.

Hartmann, H. (1976). Capitalism, patriarchy, and job segregation by sex. *Signs, 1*(2), 137–69.

Hartmann, H. (1981). The unhappy marriage of Marxism and feminism. In L. Sargent (Ed.), *Women and revolution: A discussion of the unhappy marriage between Marxism and feminism* (pp. 1–43). Boston: South End Press.

Hasenfeld, Y., et al. (1987). The welfare state, citizenship, and bureaucratic encounters. *Annual Review of Sociology, 13,* 387–415.

Hashima, P. Y., & Amato, P. R. (1994). Poverty, social support and parental behavior. *Child Development, 65,* 394–403.

Haskell, K. (2004, May 16). Revelation plus make-up advice. *The New York Times.* Retrieved from www.nytimes.com/2004/05/16/weekinreview/ideas-trends-revelation-plus-makeup-advice.html.

Hawley, A. (1968). Human ecology. In D. Sills (Ed.), *International encyclopedia of the social sciences* (pp. 327–37). New York: Macmillan.

Hayford, S. R., & Morgan, P. S. (2008). Religiosity and fertility in the United States: The role of fertility intentions. *Sociological Forces, 86*(3), 1163–88.

Hays, S. (2003). *Flat broke with children: Women in the age of welfare reform.* New York: Oxford University Press.

Heckman, J. J., et al. (2016). Returns to education: The causal effects of education on earnings, health and smoking (NBER Working Paper 2291). National Bureau of Economic Research. Retrieved from www.nber.org/papers/w22291.

Hegewisch, A., & Williams-Baron, E. (2017, September 13). The gender wage gap 2016: Earnings differences by gender, race, and ethnicity. Institute for Women's Policy Research. Retrieved from https://iwpr.org/publications/gender-wage-gap-2016-earnings-differences-gender-race-ethnicity.

Heilbroner, R. L. (1999). *The worldly philosophers.* New York: Simon & Schuster.

Hendi, A. S. (2019). Proximate sources of change in trajectories of first marriage in the United States, 1960–2010. *Demography, 56,* 835–62.

Hendricks, M. (1993, November 10). Is it a boy or a girl? *Johns Hopkins Magazine.*

Henley, J. (2018, January 12). Money for nothing: Is Finland's universal basic income trial too good to be true? *The Guardian.* Retrieved from www.theguardian.com/inequality/2018/jan/12/money-for-nothing-is-finlands-universal-basic-income-trial-too-good-to-be-true.

Henwood, B. F., et al. (2012). Substance abuse recovery after experiencing homelessness and mental illness. *Journal of Dual Diagnosis, 8*(3), 238–46.

Henwood, B. F., et al. (2013, December). Permanent supportive housing: Addressing homelessness and health disparities? *American Journal of Public Health, 103*(S2), S188–92.

Herdt, G. H. (1981). *Guardians of the flutes: Idioms of masculinity.* New York: McGraw-Hill.

Hernandez, D. J., et al. (2007, April). *Children in immigrant families in the U.S. and 50 states: National origins, language, and early education* (Research Brief Series Publication #2007–11). Albany, NY: Child Trends and the Center for Social and Demographic Analysis, SUNY.

Herring, C., & Henderson, L. (2016). Wealth inequality in Black and White: Cultural and structural sources of the racial wealth gap. *Race and Social Problems, 8,* 4–17.

Herrnstein, R. J., & Murray, C. (1994). *The bell curve: Intelligence and class structure in American life.* New York: Free Press.

Hess, C., et al. (2020). Providing unpaid household and care work in the United States: Uncovering inequality [dataset]. Institute for Women's Policy Research. Retrieved from https://iwpr.org/wp-content/uploads/2020/01/IWPR-Providing-Unpaid-Household-and

-Care-Work-in-the-United-States-Uncovering
-Inequality.pdf.

Hetherington, E. M., & Kelly, J. (2002). *For better or for worse: Divorce reconsidered.* New York: Norton.

Heyrman, C. L. (1997). *Southern cross: The beginnings of the Bible Belt.* New York: Knopf.

Hitchens, C. (2007). *God is not great: How religion poisons everything.* New York: Twelve Books.

Ho, M. K. (1987). *Family therapy with ethnic minorities.* Newbury Park, CA: Sage.

Hobbes, T. (1981). *Leviathan.* New York: Penguin Books. (Original work published 1651.)

Hochschild, A. R. (1983). *The managed heart: Commercialization of human feeling.* Berkeley: University of California Press.

Hochschild, A. R. (1989). *The second shift: Working parents and the revolution at home.* New York: Viking.

Hochschild, A. R. (1997). *The time bind: When work becomes home and home becomes work.* New York: Metropolitan Books.

Hochschild, A. R. (2003). *The commercialization of intimate life: Notes from home and work.* Berkeley: University of California Press.

Hodkinson, P. (2002). *Goth: identity, style and subculture.* New York: Berg.

hooks, b. (1984). Black women: Shaping feminist theory and feminism: A movement to end sexist oppression and the significance of the feminist movement. In *Feminist theory from margin to center* (pp. 1–17). Boston: South End Press.

Horowitz, J., et al. (2017, March 23). Americans widely support paid family and medical leave, but differ over specific policies. Pew Research Center. Retrieved from www.pewsocialtrends.org/2017/03/23/americans-widely -support-paid-family-and-medical-leave-but-differ -over-specific-policies.

Horwitz, A. V., & Wakefield, J. C. (2007). *The loss of sadness: How psychiatry transformed normal sorrow into depressive disorder.* New York: Oxford University Press.

Hosseini, B. (2018, February 3). Ethiopia bans foreign adoption. CNN. Retrieved from www.cnn.com/2018/01/11 /africa/ethiopia-foreign-adoption-ban/index.html.

Hout, M. (1983). *Mobility tables: Quantitative applications in the social sciences.* Beverly Hills, CA: Sage.

Howe, L. K. (1977). *Pink collar workers: Inside the world of women's work.* New York: Putnam.

Howes, C., & Olenick, M. (1986). Family and child influences on toddlers' compliance. *Child Development, 26,* 292–303.

Howes, C., & Stewart, P. (1987). Child's play with adults, toys, and peers: An examination of family and child care influences. *Developmental Psychology, 23,* 423–30.

Hoxby, C. (2000, August). *Peer effects in the classroom: Learning from gender and race variation* (NBER Working Paper No. 7867). National Bureau of Economic Research.

Hsin, A. (2009). Parent's time with children: Does time matter for children's cognitive achievement? *Social Indicators Research, 93*(1), 123–26.

Hughes, B. T., et al. (2022). Occupational prestige: The status component of socioeconomic status. *PsyArXiv.* Retrieved from https:psyarxiv.com/6qgxv.

Humphries, J. E., et al. (2019). Does eviction cause poverty? Quasi-experimental evidence from Cook County, IL (No. w26139). National Bureau of Economic Research.

Hurtado, A. (1995). Variations, combinations, and evolutions: Latino families in the United States. In R. E. Zambrana (Ed.), *Understanding Latino families: Scholarship, policy, and practice* (pp. 40–61). Thousand Oaks, CA: Sage.

Iannaccone, L. R. (1997). Skewness explained: A rational choice model of religious giving. *Journal of the Scientific Study of Religion, 36,* 141–57.

Iannoccone, L. R., et al. (1995). Religious resources and church growth. *Social Forces, 74,* 705–31.

Ichihara, M. (2006). Making the case for soft power. *SAIS Review, 26*(1), 197–200.

Idler, E. L. & Benyamini, Y. (1997). Self-rated health and mortality: A review of twenty-seven community studies. *Journal of Health and Social Behavior, 38*(1), 21–27.

Ikeda, H. (2001). Buraku students and cultural identity: The case of a Japanese minority. In K. Shimahara (Ed.), *Ethnicity, race, and nationality in education: A global perspective* (pp. 81–100). Mahwah, NJ: Erlbaum.

Imbens, G. W., et al. (2001). Estimating the effect of unearned income on labor earnings, savings, and consumption: Evidence from a survey of lottery players. *American Economic Review, 91*(4), 778–94.

Inequality.org. (2022). Updates: Billionaire wealth, U.S. job losses and pandemic profiteers. Retrieved from http://inequality.org/great-divide/updates-billionaire -pandemic.

Inglehart, R., & Baker, W. (2000, February). Modernization, cultural change and the persistence of traditional values. *American Sociological Review, 65*(1), 19–51.

Institute for Family Studies. (2020, September 1). Fewer American high schoolers having sex than ever before. Retrieved from http://ifstudies.org/blog/fewer-american -high-schoolers-having-sex-than-ever-before.

International Bottled Water Association. (2020). Bottled water consumption shift. Retrieved from https://bottledwater.org/bottled-water-consumption -shift.

International Labour Organisation. (2022). Collective bargaining coverage rates around the world. Retrieved from https://ilostat.ilo.org/topics/collective-bargaining.

International Monetary Fund. (2023). GDP per capita, current prices. Retrieved from www.imf.rg/external/datamapper /NGDPDPC@WEO/OEMDC/ADVEC/WEOWORLD.

Ireland, S. (2020, May 16). Revealed: The world's most (and least) religious countries based on religious beliefs 2020. *CEOWORLD Magazine.* Retrieved from https://ceoworld .biz/2020/05/16/revealed-the-worlds-most-and-least -religious-countries-based-on-religious-beliefs-2020.

Isaacs, H. (1975). *Idols of the tribe: Group identity and political change.* New York: Harper & Row.

Jackson, P. (1968). *Life in classrooms.* New York: Holt, Reinhart, & Winston.

Jacobi, T., & Schweers, D. (2017, April 11). Female Supreme Court justices are interrupted more by male justices and advocates. *Harvard Business Review.* Retrieved from https://hbr.org/2017/04/female-supreme-court-justices -are-interrupted-more-by-male-justices-and-advocates.

Jacobs, J. (1961). *The death and life of great American cities.* New York: Random House.

Jacobs, J., & Gerson, K. (2004). *The time divide: Work, family, and gender inequality.* Cambridge, MA: Harvard University Press.

Jacobson, M. F. (1998). Anglo-Saxons and others, 1840–1924. In *Whiteness of a different color: European immigrants and the alchemy of race* (pp. 39–90). Cambridge, MA: Harvard University Press.

Jacquet, J. (2016). *Is shame necessary? New uses for an old tool.* New York: Vintage Books.

Jacquet, J. (2022). The playbook: How to deny science, sell lies, and make a killing in the corporate world. New York: Pantheon.

James, G. (2003, June 29). Exurbia and God: Megachurches in New Jersey. *The New York Times*, pp. 1, 17. Retrieved from www.nytimes.com/2003/06/29/nyregion/exurbia-and -god-megachurches-in-new-jersey.html.

James, S. A., et al. (1987). Socioeconomic status, John Henryism, and hypertension in Blacks and Whites. *American Journal of Epidemiology, 126,* 664–73.

James, W. (1982). *The varieties of religious experience.* New York: Penguin. (Original work published 1903.)

Jencks, C., & Phillips, M. (Eds.). (1998). *The Black-White test score gap.* Washington, DC: Brookings Institution Press.

Jencks, C., et al. (1972). *Inequality: A reassessment of the effect of family and schooling in America.* New York: Basic Books.

Jenkins, A. (2011). Participation in learning and wellbeing among older adults. *International Journal of Lifelong Education, 30*(3), 403–20. Retrieved from www .tandfonline.com/doi/full/10.1080/02601370.2011.570876.

Jenkins, D., et al. (2018, April). What we are learning about guided pathways. Community College Research Center. Retrieved from https://ccrc.tc.columbia.edu/publications /what-we-are-learning-guided-pathways.html.

Jenson, A. R. (1969). How much can we boost IQ and scholastic achievement? *Harvard Educational Review, 39,* 1–123.

Johnson, B. D., et al. (2005). The rise and decline of hard drugs, drug markets, and violence in inner city New York. In A. Blumstein (Ed.), *The crime drop in America* (pp. 164–206). Cambridge, UK: Cambridge University Press.

Johnson, E. R., et al. (2016). Extreme weight-control behaviors and suicide risk among high school students. *Journal of School Health, 86*(4), 281–87.

Johnson, L. (1998). Proposal for a nationwide war on the sources of poverty. In P. Halsall (Ed.), *Internet modern history sourcebook.* Retrieved from www.fordham.edu /halsall/mod/1964 johnson-warpoverty.htm. (Original speech presented March 16, 1964.)

Johnston, D. C. (2005, June 5). Richest are leaving even the rich far behind. *The New York Times.* Retrieved from www.-nytimes.com/2005/06/05/national/class/HYPER -FINAL.html?scp=1&sq=Richest%20are%20leaving%20 even%20the%20rich%20far%20behind&st=cse.

Jones, N., et al. (2021). 2020 Census illuminates racial and ethnic composition of the country. U.S. Census Bureau. Retrieved from www.census.gov/library/stories /2021/08/improved-race-ethnicity-measures-reveal -united-states-population-much-more-multiracial.html.

Kaiser Family Foundation. (2022). An overview of Medicaid work requirements: What happened under the Trump and Biden administrations? Retrieved from www.kff .org/medicaid/issue-brief/an-overview-of-medicaid -work-requirements-what-happened-under-the-trump -and-biden-administrations.

Kandel, W. A. (2018, February 9). U.S. family-based immigration policy. Congressional Research Service. Retrieved from https://fas.org/sgp/crs/homesec/R43145 .pdf.

Kane, T. J. (1998). Racial and ethnic preferences in college admissions. In C. Jencks & M. Phillips (Eds.), *The Black-White test score gap* (pp. 431–56). Washington, DC: Brookings Institution Press.

Kanter, R. M. (1977). *Men and women of the corporation.* New York: Basic Books.

Kaplan, E. A. (2003, October 3–9). Black like I thought I was: Race, DNA, and a man who knows too much. *L. A. Weekly.* Retrieved from www.alternet.org/story.html?StoryID =16917.

Karen, D. (2002, July). Changes in access to higher education in the United States: 1980–1992. *Sociology of Education, 75*(3), 191–210.

Kashef, Z. (2003, February). Persistent peril: Why African American babies have the highest infant mortality rate in the developed world. *RaceWire.* Retrieved from www.arc .org/racewire/030210z_kashef.html.

Kasselstrand, I., et al. (2017). Institutional confidence in the United States: Attitudes of secular Americans. *Secularism and Nonreligion, 6,* 6.

Kelley, D. M. (1972). *Why conservative churches are growing: A study in sociology of religion.* San Francisco: Harper & Row.

Kelling, G. L., & Sousa, W. H., Jr. (2001). Do police matter? An analysis of the

Kessler-Harris, A. (1990). *A woman's wage: Historical meanings and social consequences.* Lexington: University Press of Kentucky.

KFF. (2022). COVID-19 cases and deaths by race/ethnicity: Current data and changes over time. Retrieved from www.kff.org/coronavirus-covid-19/issue-brief/covid-19 -cases-and-deaths-by-race-ethnicity-current-data-and -changes-over-time Figure 1.

Khan, S. R. (2010). *Privilege: The making of an adolescent elite at St. Paul's School.* Princeton, NJ: Princeton University Press.

Kilbourne, J. (1979). *Killing us softly: Advertising's image of women* [Motion picture]. Belmont, MA: Cambridge Documentary Films.

Killewald, A. (2013, August). Return to being Black, living in the red: A race gap in wealth that goes beyond social origins. *Demography, 50*(4), 1177–95. Retrieved from http://link.springer.com/article/10.1007/s13524 -012-0190-0.

Kim, S. (2001). Hegemony and cultural resistance. In N. J. Smelser & P. B. Baltes (Eds.), *International encyclopedia of the social & behavioral sciences.* New York: Elsevier.

Kimmel, M. S. (1996). *Manhood in America: A cultural history.* New York: Free Press.

Kimmel, M. S. (2000). *The gendered society.* New York: Oxford University Press.

Kinsey, A. C. (1948). *Sexual behavior in the human male.* Philadelphia: Saunders.

Klebanov, P. K., et al. (1994). Classroom behavior of very low birth weight elementary school children. *Pediatrics, 94*(5), 700–708.

Klein, N. (2000). *No logo: Taking aim at the brand bullies.* New York: Picador.

Klinenberg, E. (2002). *Heat wave: A social autopsy of disaster in Chicago.* Chicago: University of Chicago Press.

Klinenberg, E. (2013). *Going solo: The extraordinary rise and surprising appeal of living alone.* New York: Penguin.

Knafo, S. (2005, December 25). Praise the Lord and raise the curtain. *The New York Times*. Retrieved from www.nytimes.com/2005/12/25/nyregion/thecity/praise-the-lord-and-raise-the-curtain.html.

Knobel, D. T. (1986). *Paddy and the republic: Ethnicity and nationality in antebellum America*. Middletown, CT: Wesleyan University Press.

Kocchar, R., & Cilluffo, A. (2017). How wealth inequality has changed in the U.S. since the great recession, by race, ethnicity, and income. Pew Research Center. Retrieved from www.pewresearch.org/fact-tank/2017/11/01/how-wealth-inequality-has-changed-in-the-u-s-since-the-great-recession-by-race-ethnicity-and-income.

Koenig, H. G., et al. (1994). Religious practices and alcoholism in a southern adult population. *Hospital Communication Psychiatry*, 45, 225–31.

Kohn, M. L., & Schooler, C. (1983). *Work and personality: An inquiry into the impact of social stratification*. Norwood, NJ: Ablex.

Kozol, J. (1991). *Savage inequalities: Children in America's schools*. New York: Crown.

Kraybill, D. B. (Ed.). (1993). *The Amish and the state*. Baltimore, MD: Johns Hopkins University Press.

Kraybill, D. B., & Nolt, S. (1995). *Amish enterprise: From plows to profits*. Baltimore, MD: Johns Hopkins University Press.

Kreider, R., & Ellis, R. (2011). Number, timing, and duration of marriages and divorces: 2009. Current population reports, U.S. Census Bureau. Retrieved from www.census.gov/prod/2011pubs/p70-125.pdf.

Kremer, M., & Levy, D. (2008). Peer effects and alcohol use among college students. *Journal of Economic Perspectives*, 22(3), 189–206.

Krueger, A. B., & Whitmore, D. M. (2001). The effect of attending a small class in the early grades on college test-taking and middle school test results: Evidence from Project STAR. *Economic Journal*, 111(468), 1–28.

Krueger, A. B., & Zhu, P. (2002). *Another look at the New York City school voucher experiment* (NBER Working Paper No. 9418). National Bureau of Economic Research.

Krugman, P. (2005, September 16). Not the new deal. *The New York Times*. Retrieved from www.nytimes.com/2005/09/16/opinion/not-the-new-deal.html.

Kuhfeld, M., et al. (2020). Projecting the potential impact of COVID-19 school closures on academic achievement. *Educational Researcher*, 49(8), 549–565. Retrieved from https://doi.org/10.3102/0013189x20965918.

Kuhn, T. (1962). *The structure of scientific revolutions*. Chicago: University of Chicago Press.

Kulick, D. (1998). *Travesti: Sex, gender, and culture among Brazilian transgendered prostitutes*. Chicago: University of Chicago Press.

Kuruvil, M. C. (2006, September 3). 9/11: Five years later. Typecasting Muslims as a race. *San Francisco Chronicle*. Retrieved from www.sfgate.com/cgi-bin/article.cgi?f=/c/a/2006/09/03/MNG4FKUMR71.DTL.

Kurzman, C. (2002, December). Bin Laden and other thoroughly modern Muslims. *Contexts Magazine*, 1(4), 13–20.

Laal, M., & Salamati, P. (2012). Lifelong learning: Why do we need it? *Procedia—Social and Behavioral Sciences*, 31, 399–403. Retrieved from www.sciencedirect.com/science/article/pii/S1877042811030023.

Ladders. (2021). Research: Remote work now accounts for nearly 15% of all high paying jobs. Retrieved from www.theladders.com/press/research-remote-work-now-accounts-for-research-remote-work-now-accounts-for-nearly-15-of-all-high-paying-jobs.

Laidley, T., et al. (2019). New evidence of skin color bias and health outcomes using sibling difference models: A research note. *Demography*, 56(2), 753–62.

Lamont, M. (1992). *Money, morals, and manners*. Chicago: University of Chicago Press.

Landau, E. (2012, July 30). Why polio hasn't gone away yet. CNN. Retrieved from www.cnn.com/2012/07/27/health/polio-eradication-efforts/index.html.

The Language Brokers (Audio). (2017, December 14). Retrieved from https://he.utexas.edu/hdfs-news-list/the-language-brokers-audio.

Landsbergis, P. A., et al. (2014). Work organization, job insecurity, and occupational health disparities. *American Journal of Industrial Medicine*, 57(5), 495–515.

Langlois, D. E., & Zales, C. R. (1992). Anatomy of a top teacher. *Education Digest*, 57(5), 31–34.

Laqueur, T. (1990). *Making sex: Body and gender from the Greeks to Freud*. Cambridge, MA: Harvard University Press.

Lareau, A. (1987). Social class differences in family-school relationships: The importance of cultural capital. *Sociology of Education*, 60, 33–85.

Lareau, A. (2002). Invisible inequality: Social class and child-rearing in Black families and White families. *American Sociological Review*, 67, 747–76.

Lareau, A. (2003). *Unequal childhoods: Class, race, and family life*. Berkeley: University of California Press.

Lareau, A. (2011). *Unequal childhoods: Class, race, and family life, with an update a decade later*. Second Edition. Berkeley: University of California Press.

Lareau, A., et al. (2006, July). *Social class and children's time use* (working paper). College Park: University of Maryland, Department of Sociology.

Lasch, C. (1977). *Haven in a heartless world: The family besieged*. New York: Basic Books.

Latour, B., & Woolgar, S. (1979). *Laboratory life: The social construction of scientific facts*. Los Angeles: Sage.

LeBon, G. (2002). *La psychologie des foules*. (*The crowd: A study of the popular mind*.) Mineola, NY: Dover. (Original work published 1895.)

Lee, F. R. (2006, March 28). "Big Love": Real polygamists look at HBO polygamists and find sex. *The New York Times*. Retrieved from www.nytimes.com/2006/03/28/arts/television/28poly.html.

Legewie, J., & Fagan, J. (2019). Aggressive policing and the educational performance of minority youth. *American Sociological Review*, 84(2).

Legislative Analyst's Office. (2020). Overview of federal COVID-19 research funding. Retrieved from https://lao.ca.gov/Publications/Report/4230.

Leiter, J. (1983). Classroom composition and achievement gains. *Sociology of Education*, 56(3), 126–32.

Leland, J. (2004, May 16). Alt-worship; Christian cool and the new generation gap. *The New York Times*. Retrieved from www.nytimes.com/2004/05/16/weekinreview/ideas-trends-alt-worship-christian-cool-and-the-new-generation-gap.html.

Lempers, J. D., et al. (1989). Economic hardship, parenting and distress in adolescence. *Child Development*, 60, 25–39.

Lenski, G. (1961). *The religious factor: A sociological study of religion's impact on politics, economics, and family life*. New York: Doubleday.

Leswing, K. (2015). A Yelp-sponsored study says Google is making your search results worse. *Business Insider*. Retrieved from www.businessinsider.com/a-yelp -sponsored-study-says-google-is-making-your-search -results-worse-2015-6.

Levitt, S. D. (2004). Understanding why crime fell in the 1990s: Four factors that explain the decline and six that do not. *Journal of Economic Perspectives, 18*(1), 163–90.

Levitt, S. D., & Dubner, S. J. (2005). *Freakonomics: A rogue economist explores the hidden side of everything*. New York: Morrow.

Lewis, A. E. (2004). *Race in the schoolyard: Negotiating the color line in classrooms and communities*. New Brunswick, NJ: Rutgers University Press.

Lewis, A. E., & Diamond, J. B. (2015). *Despite the best intentions: How racial inequality thrives in good schools*. New York: Oxford University Press.

Lewis, C., et al. (1992). Sex stereotyping of infants: A re-examination. *Journal of Reproductive and Infant Psychology, 10*, 53–61.

Lewis, O. (1966). The culture of poverty. *Scientific American, 215*(4), 19–25.

Lieberson, S. (1961). A societal theory of race and ethnic relations. *American Sociological Review, 26*, 902–10.

Lieberson, S., & Mikelson, K. S. (1995). Distinctive African American names: An experimental, historical, and linguistic analysis of innovation. *American Sociological Review, 60*, 928–46.

Lieberson, S., et al. (2000). The instability of androgynous names: The symbolic maintenance of gender boundaries. *American Journal of Sociology, 105*(5), 1249–87.

Lien, T. (2018, February 19). Uber class-action lawsuit over how drivers were paid gets green light from judge. *The Los Angeles Times*. Retrieved from www.latimes.com /business/technology/la-fi-tn-uber-class-action-20180219 -story.html.

Lindstedt, N. (2017). Shifting frames: Collective action framing from a dialogic and relational perspective. *Sociology Compass, 12*(1).

Liu, E. M., & Zuo, S. X. (2019). Measuring the impact of interaction between children of a matrilineal and a patriarchal culture on gender differences in risk aversion. *PNAS, 116*(14), 6713–19. Retrieved from www.pnas .org/content/116/14/6713.

Livingston, G. (2015, May 7). Childlessness falls, family size grows among highly educated women. Pew Research Center. Retrieved from www.pewsocialtrends .org/2015/05/07/childlessness.

Livingston, G. (2018, April 25). The changing profile of unmarried parents. Pew Research Center. Retrieved from www.pewsocialtrends.org/2018/04/25/the-changing -profile-of-unmarried-parents.

Lleras-Muney, A. (2005). The relationship between education and adult mortality in the United States. *Review of Economic Studies, 72*, 189–221.

Locke, J. (1980). *Second treatise of government*. Indianapolis: Hackett. (Original work published 1690.)

López, G., & Bialik, K. (2017, May 3). Key findings about U.S. immigrants. Pew Research Center. Retrieved from www.pewresearch.org/fact-tank/2017/05/03/key -findings-about-u-s-immigrants.

Lorber, J. (1994). *Paradoxes of gender*. New Haven, CT: Yale University Press.

Lucas, S. R. (1999). *Tracking inequality: Stratification and mobility in American high schools*. New York: Teachers College Press.

Lucas, S. R., & Good, A. D. (2001). Race, class, and tournament track mobility. *Sociology of Education, 74*, 139–56.

Lui, M. (2004). Doubly divided: The racial wealth gap. In C. Collins et al. (Eds.), *The wealth inequality reader*. Cambridge, MA: Economic Affairs Bureau.

Lukes, S., & British Sociological Association. (2005). *Power: A radical view*. New York: Palgrave Macmillan. (Original work published 1974.)

Luo, M. (2006, April 16). Evangelicals debate the meaning of "evangelical." *The New York Times*, pp. 4, 5. Retrieved from www.nytimes.com/2006/04/16/weekinreview /evangelicals-debate-the-meaning-of-evangelical.html.

Mack, J., & Lansley, S. (1985). *Poor Britain*. London: Allen & Unwin.

MacKinnon, C. (1983). Feminism, Marxism, method and the state: Toward feminist jurisprudence. *Signs: Journal of Women in Culture and Society, 8*, 635.

MacLeod, J. (1995). *Ain't no makin' it: Aspirations and attainment in a low-income neighborhood*. Boulder, CO: Westview Press. (Original work published 1987.)

Malinowski, B. (1913). *The family among the Australian Aborigines*. London: University of London Press.

Malmberg, B., et al. (2008). Productivity consequences of workforce aging: Stagnation or Horndal effect? *Population and Development Review, 34*, 238–56.

Maltz, M. D. (2001). *Recidivism*. Orlando, FL: Academic Press. (Original work published 1984.) Retrieved from www.uic .edu/depts/lib/forr/pdf/crimjust/recidivism.pdf.

Manza, J., & Uggen, C. (2006). *Locked out: Felon disenfranchisement and American democracy*. New York: Oxford University Press.

Maraniss, D. (1995). *First in his class: The biography of Bill Clinton*. New York: Simon & Schuster.

Marcin, J. P., et al. (2016). Addressing health disparities in rural communities using telehealth. *Pediatric Research, 79*(1), 169–76.

Marmot, M., & Wilkinson, R. G. (Eds.). (1999). *Social determinants of health*. New York: Oxford University Press.

Martin, J. A., & Osterman, M. J. K. (2019). Is twin childbearing on the decline? Twin births in the United States, 2014–2018. National Center for Health Statistics, CDC: Brief No. 351, October 2019. Retrieved from www .cdc.gov/nchs/products/databriefs/db351.htm#section_3.

Martin, J. A., et al. (2010). Births: Final data for 2008. *National Vital Statistics Report, 59*(1). Retrieved from www.cdc.gov/nchs/data/nvsr/nvsr59/nvsr59_01.pdf.

Martin, J. A., et al. (2015). Births: Final data for 2013. *National Vital Statistics Reports, 64*(1). Retrieved from www.cdc .gov/nchs/data/nvsr/nvsr64/nvsr64_01.pdf.

Martin, J. A., et al. (2017). Births: Final data for 2015. *National Vital Statistics Reports, 66*(1). Retrieved from www.cdc .gov/nchs/data/nvsr/nvsr66/nvsr66_01.pdf.

Martin, J. A., et al. (2018). Births: Final data for 2016. *National Vital Statistics Reports, 67*(1). Retrieved from www.cdc.gov/nchs/data/nvsr/nvsr67/nvsr67_01.pdf.

Martin, J. A., et al. (2019). National vital statistics reports: Births, final data for 2018. Retrieved from www.cdc.gov/nchs/data/nvsr/nvsr68/nvsr68_13-508.pdf.

Martin, J. T., & Nguyen, D. H. (2004). Anthropometric analysis of homosexuals and heterosexuals: Implications for early hormone exposure. *Hormones and Behavior, 45*(1), 31–39.

Martineau, H. (1837). *Theory and practice of society in America.* London: Saunders & Otley.

Martineau, H. (1838). *How to observe morals and manners.* London: Charles Knight.

Marx, A. W. (1998). To bind up the nation's wounds: The United States after the Civil War. In *Making race and nation: A comparison of South Africa, the United States, and Brazil* (pp. 120–57). Cambridge, UK: Cambridge University Press.

Marx, K. (1932). Estranged labor. In *Economic and Philosophical Manuscripts of 1844.* Retrieved from www.marxists.org/archive/marx/works/1844/manuscripts/labour.htm. (Original work published 1844.)

Marx, K. (1978). Contribution to the critique of Hegel's philosophy of right: Introduction. In R. Tucker (Ed.), *The Marx-Engels reader* (pp. 53–65). New York: Norton. (Original work published 1844.)

Marx, K. (1999). Critique of the Gotha programme. *Marxists internet archive.* Retrieved from www.marxists.org/archive/marx/works/1875/gotha/index.htm. (Original work published 1890–91.)

Marx, K., & Engels, F. (1998). *The Communist manifesto.* New York: Penguin Group. (Original work published 1848.)

Massey, D. S. (1995). The new immigration and ethnicity in the United States. *Population and Development Review, 21,* 631–52.

Massey, D. S., & Denton, N. A. (1993). *American apartheid: Segregation and the making of the underclass.* Cambridge, MA: Harvard University Press.

Maus, J. (2012). It's the 20th anniversary of critical mass: What it meant to Portland then and now. Bikeportland.org. Retrieved from http://bikeportland.org/2012/09/28/its-the-20th-anniversary-of-critical-mass-what-it-meant-then-and-now-in-portland-78129.

Mayer, S. (1997). *What money can't buy: Family income and children's life chances.* Cambridge, MA: Harvard University Press.

McAdam, D. (1982). *Political process and the development of Black insurgency, 1930–1970.* Chicago: University of Chicago Press.

McBean, A., et al. (2004). Differences in diabetes prevalence, incidence, and mortality among the elderly of four racial/ethnic groups: Whites, Blacks, Hispanics, and Asians. *Diabetes Care, 27*(10), 2317–24.

McCammon, S. (2017). Christian teen magazine "Brio" returns with a "Biblical worldview." NPR. Retrieved from www.npr.org/2017/04/19/524518993/christian-teen-magazine-brio-returns-with-a-biblical-worldview.

McCarthy, J. D., & Zald, M. N. (1973). *The trend of social movements in America: Professionalization and resource mobilization.* Morristown, NJ: General Learning Press.

McCarthy, J. D., & Zald, M. N. (1977). Resource mobilization and social movements: A partial theory. *American Journal of Sociology, 82*(6), 1212–41.

McCoy, J. (2022, January 18). What happens when democracies become perniciously polarized? Carnegie Endowment for International Peace. Retrieved from https://carnegieendowment.org/2022/01/18/what-happens-when-democracies-become-perniciously-polarized-pub-86190.

McCullough, M., & Smith, T. (2003). Religion and health: Depressive symptoms and mortality as case studies. In M. Dillon (Ed.), *Handbook of sociology of religion* (pp. 190–206). Cambridge, UK: Cambridge University Press.

McDonald, M. P. (2020). 2020 November general election turnout rates. Retrieved from www.electproject.org/2020g.

McDonald, M. P., & Popkin, S. L. (2001). The myth of the vanishing voter. *American Political Science Review, 95*(4), 963–74.

McGregor, P. P. L., & Borooah, V. K. (1992). Is low spending or low income a better indicator of whether or not a household is poor: Some results from the 1985 Family Expenditure Survey. *Journal of Social Policy, 21*(1), 53–69.

McGuire, M. (2007). Embodied practices: Negotiation and resistance. In N. Ammerman (Ed.), *Everyday religion: Observing modern religious lives* (pp. 187–200). New York: Oxford University Press.

McIntosh, P. (1988). *White privilege and male privilege: A personal account of coming to see correspondences through work in women's studies.* Wellesley, MA: Wellesley College Center for Research on Women.

McIntosh, P. (1989). White privilege: Unpacking the invisible knapsack. *Peace and Freedom Magazine.* Retrieved from https://psychology.umbc.edu/wp-content/uploads/sites/57/2016/10/White-Privilege_McIntosh-1989.pdf.

McKenna, P. (2016, December 27). 2016: How Dakota pipeline protest became a Native American cry for justice. *InsideClimate News.* Retrieved from https://insideclimatenews.org/news/22122016/standing-rock-dakota-access-pipeline-native-american-protest-environmental-justice.

McLeod, J. D., & Shanahan, M. J. (1993). Poverty, parenting and children's mental health. *American Sociological Review, 58,* 351–66.

McMillan, C. (2011, July 14). State budget shortfall forces UC fee increase for 2011 [press release]. University of California Office of the President. Retrieved from http://newsroom.ucla.edu/stories/uc-regents-vote-tuition-increase-210662.

Mead, G. H. (1934). *Mind, self, and society from the standpoint of a social behaviorist.* C. W. Morris (Ed.). Chicago: University of Chicago Press.

Mead, M. (1928). *Coming of age in Samoa.* New York: Morrow.

Mechanic, D., & Meyer, S. (2000). Concepts of trust among patients with serious illness. *Social Science and Medicine, 51*(5), 657–68.

Meier, R. F. (1982). Perspectives on the concept of social control. *Annual Review of Sociology, 8,* 35–55.

Meighan, R. (1981). *A sociology of educating.* New York: Holt, Reinhart & Winston.

Melucci, A. (1989). Nomads of the present: Social movements and individual needs in contemporary society. New York: Vintage.

Merton, R. (1938). Social structure and anomie. *American Sociological Review, 3,* 672–82.

Merton, R. (1949). Discrimination and the American creed. In R. M. MacIver (Ed.), *Discrimination and national welfare;*

a series of addresses and discussion (pp. 99–126). New York: Institute for Religious and Social Studies.

Meyer, D. S. (2007). *The politics of protest: Social movements in America*. New York: Oxford University Press.

Michels, R. (1915). *Political parties: A sociological study of the oligarchical tendencies of modern democracy* (E. Paul & C. Paul, Trans.). New York: Hearst's International Library.

Miele, F. (1995). For whom the bell curve tolls: Interview with Charles Murray. *Skeptic, 3*(2), 34–41. Retrieved from www.prometheism.net/articles/interview01.html.

Milbank, Q. (2005). The compression of morbidity. *The Milbank Quarterly, 83*(4), 801–23.

Milkie, M. A., et al. (2015). Does the amount of time mothers spend with children or adolescents matter? *Journal of Marriage and Family, 77*(2), 355–72.

Milkman, R. (2006). *LA Story: Immigrant workers and the future of the US labor movement*. New York: Russell Sage Foundation.

Milkman, R. (2007). Unions fight for work and family policies. In D. S. Cobble (Ed.), *The sex of class: Women transforming American labor* (pp. 63–80). Ithaca, NY: Cornell University Press.

Miller, C. C. (2015, May 26). When family-friendly policies backfire. *The New York Times*. Retrieved from www.nytimes.com/2015/05/26/upshot/when-family-friendly-policies-backfire.html.

Milloy, C. (2017, August 22). Want to see proof of institutional racism? Let weed open your eyes. *The Washington Post*. Retrieved from www.washingtonpost.com/local/want-to-see-proof-of-institutional-racism-let-weed-open-your-eyes/2017/08/22/099b7740-8751-11e7-a94f-3139abce39f5_story.html?utm_term=.abaaae83946b.

Mills, C. W. (1959). *The sociological imagination*. New York: Oxford University Press.

Mills, C. W. (2000). *The power elite*. New York: Oxford University Press. (Original work published 1956.)

Milo, R., & Phillips, R. (2018). The biomass distribution on Earth. *Proceedings of the National Academy of Sciences of the United States of America, 115*(25), 6506–11.

Mishel, L., & Schieder, J. (2017). CEO pay remains high relative to the pay of typical workers and high-wage earners. Economic Policy Institute. Retrieved from www.epi.org/files/pdf/130354.pdf.

Mishel, L., & Shierholz, H. (2013, August 21). *A decade of flat wages: The key barrier to shared prosperity and a rising middle class*. Economic Policy Institute. Retrieved from www.epi.org/publication/a-decade-of-flat-wages-the-key-barrier-to-shared-prosperity-and-a-rising-middle-class.

Mishel, L., & Wolfe, J. (2019, August 14). CEO compensation has grown 940% since 1978. Economic Policy Institute. Retrieved from www.epi.org/publication/ceo-compensation-2018.

Missouri Economic Research and Information Center. (2022). Cost of living data series: 2022. Retrieved from https://meric.mo.gov/data/cost-living-data-series.

Mohamed, B. (2018, January 3). New estimates show U.S. Muslim population continues to grow. Pew Research Center. Retrieved from www.pewresearch.org/fact-tank/2018/01/03/new-estimates-show-u-s-muslim-population-continues-to-grow.

Mohamed, B., & Sciupac, E. P. (2018, January 26). The share of Americans who leave Islam is offset by those who become Muslim. Pew Research Center. Retrieved from www.pewresearch.org/fact-tank/2018/01/26/the-share-of-americans-who-leave-islam-is-offset-by-those-who-become-muslim.

Monaghan, T. (1990, August). The thrill of poverty. *Harpers Magazine*, p. 22.

Montesquieu, C., Baron de. (1899). *The spirit of the laws*. (Vols. 1–2; T. Nugent et al., Trans.). New York: Colonial Press. (Original work published 1748/1750.)

Moore, B. (1993). *Social origins of dictatorship and democracy: Lord and peasant in the making of the modern world*. Boston: Beacon Press. (Original work published 1966.)

Morgan, P. L., et al. (2017). Replicated evidence of racial and ethnic disparities in disability identification in U.S. schools. *Educational Researcher, 46*(6): 305–22.

Morning, A. (2004). *The nature of race: Teaching and learning about human difference*. (Unpublished doctoral dissertation). Department of Sociology, Princeton University, Princeton, NJ.

Morris, A. (1984). *The origins of the civil rights movement*. New York: Free Press.

Morris, A. (2004). Reflections on social movement theory: Criticisms and proposals. In J. Goodwin & J. M. Jasper (Eds.), *Rethinking social movements: Structure, meaning, and emotion* (pp. 233–46). Lanham, MD: Rowman & Littlefield.

Morris, E. W., & Perry, B. L. (2016). The punishment gap: School suspension and racial disparities in achievement. *Social Problems, 63*(1), 68–86. Retrieved from www.researchgate.net/publication/289687063_The_Punishment_Gap_School_Suspension_and_Racial_Disparities_in_Achievement.

Morrison, D. R., & Coiro, M. J. (1999). Parental conflict and marital disruption: Do children benefit when high-conflict marriages are dissolved? *Journal of Marriage and the Family, 61*, 626–37.

Moulds, J. (2020). Gig workers among the hardest hit by coronavirus pandemic. Retrieved from www.weforum.org/agenda/2020/04/gig-workers-hardest-hit-coronavirus-pandemic.

Mounk, Y. (2022, December 5). The doom spiral of pernicious polarization. *The Atlantic*. Retrieved from www.theatlantic.com/ideas/archive/2022/05/us-democrat-republican-partisan-polarization/629925.

Movement Advancement Project, Family Equality Council, Center for American Progress. (2012a, January). *LGBT families of color: Facts at a glance*. Retrieved from www.lgbtmap.org/lgbt-families-of-color-facts-at-a-glance.

Movement Advancement Project, Family Equality Council, and Center for American Progress. (2012b, March). *Obstacles and opportunities: Ensuring health and wellness for LGBT families*. Retrieved from www.lgbtmap.org/obstacles-and-opportunities-ensuring-health-and-wellness-for-lgbt-families.

Moynihan, D. P. (1965). *The Negro family: The case for national action*. Washington, DC: Office of Policy Planning and Research, U.S. Department of Labor.

Mueller, A. S., et al. (2015). Suicide ideation and bullying among U.S. adolescents: Examining the intersections of sexual orientation, gender and race/ethnicity. *American Journal of Public Health, 105*(5), 980–85. Retrieved from https://ajph.aphapublications.org/doi/pdf/10.2105/AJPH.2014.302391.

Muraki, I., et al. (2013, August 29). Fruit consumption and the risk of type 2 diabetes: Results from three prospective longitudinal cohort studies. *British Medical Journal, 347.*

Murnane, R. J., et al. (2005). Learning why more learning takes place in some classrooms than others. *German Economic Review, 6*(3), 309–30.

Murphy, C. (2015). Most Americans believe in heaven . . . and hell. Pew Research Center. Retrieved from www.pewresearch.org/fact-tank/2015/11/10/most-americans-believe-in-heaven-and-hell.

Murphy, S. L., et. al. (2021). Mortality in the United States, 2020. National Center for Health Statistics. Retrieved from www.cdc.gov/nchs/products/databriefs/db427.htm.

Murray, C. (1984). *Losing ground: American social policy, 1950–1980.* New York: Basic Books.

Murray, C. (2016). *In our hands: A plan to replace the welfare state.* Lanham, MD: Rowman & Littlefield.

Murray, C. (2020). *Human diversity: The biology of gender, race, and class.* London: Hachette.

Mustanski, B. S., et al. (2005, March). A genomewide scan of male sexual orientation. *Human Genetics, 116*(4), 272–78. Retrieved from http://mypage.iu.edu/~bmustans/Mustanski_etal_2005.pdf.NAACP. (2019). Criminal justice fact sheet. Retrieved from https://naacp.org/resources/criminal-justice-fact-sheet.

Nanda, S. (1999). *Neither man nor woman: The hijras of India* (2nd ed.). New York: Wadsworth.

NASA. (2022a). Goddard Institute for Space Studies (GISS), Global Land-Ocean Temperature Index. Retrieved from https://climate.nasa.gov/vital-signs/global-temperature.

NASA. (2022b). What's the difference between climate change and global warming? Retrieved from https://climate.nasa.gov/faq/12/whats-the-difference-between-climate-change-and-global-warming.

Nash, J. M. (2000, July 31). This rice could save a million kids a year. *Time, 156*(5). Retrieved from http://content.time.com/time/magazine/article/0,9171,997586-6,00.html.

Nason-Clark, N. (2000). Making the sacred safe: Woman abuse and communities of faith. *Sociology of Religion, 61*(4), 349–68.

Natanson, H. (2017, June 5). Harvard rescinds acceptances for at least ten students for obscene memes. *The Harvard Crimson.* Retrieved from www.thecrimson.com/article/2017/6/5/2021-offers-rescinded-memes.

National Center for Education Statistics. (2019). Characteristics of children's families. Retrieved from https://nces.ed.gov/programs/coe/indicator_cce.asp.

National Center for Education Statistics. (2020). The condition of education 2019 (NCES 1990–2019): Mathematics performance. Retrieved from https://nces.ed.gov/fastfacts/display.asp?id=514.

National Center for Education Statistics. (2021a). Tuition costs of colleges and universities. Retrieved from https://nces.ed.gov/fastfacts/display.asp?id=76.

National Center for Education Statistics. (2021b, May). Undergraduate enrollment. Retrieved from https://nces.ed.gov/programs/coe/indicator/cha.

National Center for Education Statistics. (2022a, May). Immediate college enrollment rate. Retrieved from https://nces.ed.gov/programs/coe/indicator/cpa.

National Center for Education Statistics. (2022b, May). Undergraduate retention and graduation rates. Retrieved from https://nces.ed.gov/programs/coe/indicator/ctr/undergrad-retention-graduation.

National Center for Health Statistics. (2017). National marriage and divorce rates 2000–16. Centers for Disease Control and Prevention, National Vital Statistics System. Retrieved from www.cdc.gov/nchs/data/dvs/national_marriage_divorce_rates_00-16.pdf.

National Center for Science Education. (2019). Creation science bill in Indiana. Retrieved from https://ncse.ngo/creation-science-bill-indiana.

National Coalition Against Domestic Violence. (2020). Domestic violence. Retrieved from https://assets.speakcdn.com/assets/2497/domestic_violence-2020080709350855.pdf?1596828650457.

National Collegiate Athletic Association. (2022). Board of Governors updates transgender participation policy. Retrieved from www.ncaa.org/news/2022/1/19/media-center-board-of-governors-updates-transgender-participation-policy.aspx.

National Highway Traffic Safety Administration. (2021). Table 2: Fatalities by person type and in large-truck-related crashes and police-reported alcohol-involved crashes; by person's race; and in speeding-related crashes by NHTSA region, as a percentage of total fatalities, 2019–2020. Retrieved from https://crashstats.nhtsa.dot.gov/Api/Public/ViewPublication/813118.

National Philanthropic Trust. (2018). Charitable giving statistics. Retrieved from www.nptrust.org/philanthropic-resources/charitable-giving-statistics.

Nature. (2020, December 16). How a torrent of COVID science changed research publishing—in seven charts. Retrieved from www.nature.com/articles/d41586-020-03564-y.

Nelson, A. (2011). *Body and soul: The Black Panther Party and the fight against medical discrimination.* Minneapolis: University of Minnesota Press.

Nelson, M. K. (1990). *Negotiated care: The experience of family day care providers.* Philadelphia: Temple University Press.

Nermoe, K. (2018). Millenials: The "wellness generation." Retrieved from https://news.sanfordhealth.org/sanford-health-plan/millennials-wellness-generation.

New York State Division of Parole. (2007, September). *New York State parole handbook* (NYSPH). Retrieved from http://parole.state.ny.us/Handbook.pdf.

New York Times. (2022, September 23). A shift in crime. Retrieved from www.nytimes.com/2022/09/23/briefing/crime-rates-murder-robberies-us.html.

New University. (2021). UC system votes to increase undergraduate tuition. Retrieved from https://newuniversity.org/2021/08/01/uc-system-votes-to-increase-undergraduate-tuition/#:~:text=This%20is%20the%20first%20tuition,undergraduates%20beginning%20in%20fall%202022.

Nguyen, V. (2017). Fact sheet: Long-term support and services. AARP Public Policy Institute. Retrieved from www.aarp.org/content/dam/aarp/ppi/2017-01/Fact%20Sheet%20Long-Term%20Support%20and%20Services.pdf.

Nicholas, R. W. (1973). Social and political movements. *Annual Review of Anthropology, 2,* 63–84.

Niebuhr, G. (1995, April 18). The gospels of management. The minister as marketer: Learning from business. *The New York Times*, p. 1. Retrieved from www.nytimes.com /1995/04/18/us/megachurches-second-article-series -gospels-management-minister-marketer-learning.html.

Niebuhr, H. R. (1929). *The social sources of denominationalism*. New York: Holt.

Nissle, S., & Bshor, T. (2002). Winning the jackpot and depression: Money cannot buy happiness. *International Journal of Psychiatry in Clinical Practice*, 6(3), 183—86.

NORC-ABIM Foundation (2021). Public & physician trust in the U.S. health care system. Retrieved from https:// buildingtrust.org/public-physician-trust-in-the-u-s -health-care-system.

NPR. (2020). Money tracker: How much Trump and Biden have raised in the 2020 election. Retrieved from www .npr.org/2020/05/20/858347477/money-tracker-how -much-trump-and-biden-have-raised-in-the-2020 -election.

NPR. (2021a, February 15). Immigration hard-liner files reveal 40-year bid behind Trump's census obsession. Retrieved from www.npr.org/2021/02/15/967783477/immigration -hard-liner-files-reveal-40-year-bid-behind-trumps -census-obsession.

NPR. (2021b). A record number of Americans, including Republicans, now support same-sex marriage. Retrieved from www.npr.org/2021/06/09/1004629612 /a-record-number-of-americans-including-republicans -support-same-sex-marriage.

Nussbaum, P. (2006, January 21). A global ministry of "muscular Christianity." *The Washington Post*. Retrieved from www.washingtonpost.com/wp-dyn/content/article /2006/01/21/AR2006012100284_pf.html.

Nye, B. A., et al. (1994). Small is far better. *Research in the Schools*, 1(1), 9—20.

Nye, J. (1990). Soft power. *Foreign Policy*, 80, 153—71.

Oakes, J. (1985). *Keeping track: How schools structure inequality*. New Haven, CT: Yale University Press.

Oakley, A. (1972). *Sex, gender, and society*. London: Maurice Temple Smith.

O'Barr, W. (1995). *Linguistic evidence: Language, power and strategy in the courtroom*. San Diego, CA: Academic Press.

O'Connor, L. (2013, September 21). California universities come up with crazy crowdfunding scholarship idea. *Huffington Post*. Retrieved from www.huffingtonpost.com /2013/09/20/uc-promise-for-education-n_3965021.html.

O'Connor, N. (2009, April). Hispanic origin, socio-economic status, and community college enrollment. *Journal of Higher Education*, 80(2), 121—45.

Office of Disease Prevention and Health Promotion. (2020). Immunization and infectious diseases. Retrieved from www.healthypeople.gov/node/3527/data-details .%C2%A0Accessed.

Ohtake, F., & Shintani, M. (1996). The effect of demographics on the Japanese housing market. *Regional Science and Urban Economics*, 26(2), 189—201.

Okahana, H., & Zhou, E. (2017). Graduate enrollment and degrees: 2006 to 2016. Council of Graduate Schools. Retrieved from http://cgsnet.org/ckfinder/userfiles /files/CGS_GED16_Report_Final.pdf.

Oliver, M., & Shapiro, T. (1995). *Black wealth, White wealth: A new perspective on racial inequality*. London: Routledge.

Orfield, G. (1996). Turning back to segregation. In G. Orfield & S. E. Eaton (Eds.), *Dismantling desegregation: The quiet reversal of* Brown v. Board of Education (pp. 1—22). New York: New Press.

Orfield, G., et al. (2016, May 16). *Brown at 62: School segregation by race, poverty and state*. Civil Rights Project/Proyecto Derechos Civiles. Retrieved from https://civilrightsproject.ucla.edu/research/k-12 -education/integration-and-diversity/brown-at-62 -school-segregation-by-race-poverty-and-state/Brown -at-62-final-corrected-2.pdf.

Organisation for Economic Co-operation and Development. (2021). Poverty rates in OECD countries as of 2021. Retrieved from www.statista.com/statistics/233910 /poverty-rates-in-oecd-countries.

Organization for Economic Co-operation and Development. (2022). Parental leave systems, PF2.1.A. Retrieved from www.oecd.org/els/soc/PF2_1_Parental_leave_systems.pdf.

Orr, A. H. (2007). A mission to convert. *The New York Review of Books*, 54(1). Retrieved from www.nybooks.com /articles/19775.

Orshansky, M. (1963). *Children of the poor* (Social Security Bulletin). Washington, DC: U.S. Department of Labor.

Ortner, S. (1974). Is female to male as nature to culture? In M. Z. Rosaldo & L. Lamphere (Eds.), *Woman, culture, and society* (pp. 67—88). Stanford, CA: Stanford University Press.

Oster, E. (2022). *The family firm: A data-driven guide to better decision making in the early school years* (Vol. 3). New York: Penguin.

Our World in Data. (2019). Causes of death in children under five years old, World, 2019. Retrieved from Causes of death in children under five years old, World, 2019 (ourworldindata.org).

Oyêwùmí, O. (1997). *The invention of women: Making an African sense of Western gender discourses*. Minneapolis: University of Minnesota Press.

Padgett, D. K. (2007, May). There's no place like (a) home: Ontological security among persons with serious mental illness in the United States. *Social Science & Medicine*, 64(9), 1925—36. Retrieved from www.ncbi.nlm.nih.gov /pubmed/17355900.

Pager, D. (2003a). Blacks and ex-cons need not apply. *Contexts*, 2(4), 58—59.

Pager, D. (2003b). The mark of a criminal record. *American Journal of Sociology*, 108(5), 937—75.

Paik, A., et al. (2016). Broken promises: Abstinence pledging and sexual and reproductive health. *Journal of Marriage and Family*, 78(2), 546—61.

Pareto, V. (1983). *The mind and society* (A. Livingston, Ed.; A. Bongiorno & A. Livingston, Trans.). New York: AMS Press. (Original work published 1935.)

Pareto, V., & Finer, S. E. (1966). *Sociological writings*. New York: Praeger Sociology.

Pariser, E. (2011). *The filter bubble: How the new personalized web is changing what we read and how we think*. New York: Penguin Press.

Parker, I. (2007, July 30). Our far-flung correspondents: Swingers. *The New Yorker*. Retrieved from www .newyorker.com/reporting/2007/07/30/070730fa _fact_parker.

Parker, K., & Livingston, G. (2018, June 13). 7 facts about American fathers. Pew Research Center. Retrieved from

www.pewresearch.org/fact-tank/2017/06/15/fathers
-day-facts.

Parkin, F. (1982). *Max Weber*. London: Tavistock.

Parsons, E. F. (2005). Midnight rangers: Costume and
performance in the Reconstruction-era Ku Klux Klan.
Journal of American History, 92(3), 811.

Parsons, T. (1951). *The social system*. Glencoe, IL: Free Press.

Pascoe, C. J. (2007). *Dude, you're a fag: Masculinity and
sexuality in high school*. Berkeley: University of California
Press.

Patillo, M. (2007). *Black on the block: The politics of race and
class in the city*. Chicago: University of Chicago Press.

Payne, C. (2013, August 1). Fertility forecast: Baby bust is
over, births will rise. *USA Today*. Retrieved from www
.usatoday.com/story/news/nation/2013/08/01/usa-total
-fertility-rate/2590781.

PBS. (2000, February 22). Lost tribes of Israel. *Nova*.
Retrieved from www.pbs.org/wgbh/nova/transcripts
/2706israel.html.

Pearson, B. Z. (1993). Predictive validity of the Scholastic
Aptitude Test (SAT) for Hispanic bilingual students.
Hispanic Journal of Behavioral Sciences, 15(3), 342–56.

Perkins, C. (1997). Age patterns of victims of serious violent
crime. Department of Justice, Office of Justice Programs,
Bureau of Justice Statistics. Special Report, NCJ-162031.

Perlman, J., & Parvensky, J. (2006). *Denver Housing First
Collaborative: Cost benefit analysis and program outcomes
report*. Denver: Colorado Coalition for the Homeless.
Retrieved from www.denversroadhome.org/files
/FinalDHFCCostStudy_1.pdf.

Perrow, C. (2007). *The next catastrophe: Reducing our
vulnerabilities to natural, industrial, and terrorist disasters*.
Princeton, NJ: Princeton University Press.

Perry, G. (2013). *Behind the shock of the machine: The untold
story of the notorious Milgram psychology experiments*. New
York: New Press.

Petrosky, E., et al. (2017). Racial and ethnic differences
in homicides of adult women and the role of intimate
partner violence—United States, 2003–2014. *Morbidity
and Mortality Weekly Report, 66*(28), 741–46.

Pew Forum on Religion and Public Life. (2015). US public
becoming less religious. Retrieved from www.pewforum
.org/2015/11/03/u-s-public-becoming-less-religious.

Pew Research Center. (2011a). Muslim American survey.
Retrieved from www.people-press.org/2011/08/30
/section-1-a-demographic-portrait-of-muslim
-americans.

Pew Research Center. (2011b, July 26). Pew Research Center's
social & demographic trends. Wealth gaps rise to record
highs between Whites, Blacks and Hispanics. Retrieved
from http://pewresearch.org/pubs/2069/housing-bubble
-subprime-mortgages-hispanics-blacks-household
-wealth-disparity.

Pew Research Center. (2011c, April 5). Multi-race Americans
and the 2010 Census. Retrieved from www
.pewsocialtrends.org/2011/04/05/multi-race-americans
-and-the-2010-census.

Pew Research Center. (2013). Modern parenthood study:
Parental time use table. Retrieved from www
.pewresearch.org/data-trend/society-and-demographics
/parental-time-use.

Pew Research Center. (2014). Less than half of U.S. kids
today live in a "traditional" family. Retrieved from

www.pewresearch.org/fact-tank/2014/12/22/less-than
-half-of-u-s-kids-live-in-a-traditional-family.

Pew Research Center. (2015). U.S. public becoming less
religious. Retrieved from www.pewforum.org/2015
/11/03/u-s-public-becoming-less-religious.

Pew Research Center. (2017a). Demographic portrait of
Muslim Americans. Retrieved from www.pewresearch
.org/religion/2017/07/26/demographic-portrait-of
-muslim-americans.

Pew Research Center. (2017b). Most people say they have
achieved the American dream, or are on their way to
achieving it. Retrieved from www.pewresearch
.org/fact-tank/2017/10/31/most-think-the-american
-dream-is-within-reach-for-them/ft_17-10-31
_americandream_demographic.

Pew Research Center. (2019). In US, decline of Christianity
continues at rapid pace. Retrieved from www.pewforum
.org/2019/10/17/in-u-s-decline-of-christianity
-continues-at-rapid-pace.

Pew Research Center. (2020). The global God divide.
Retrieved from www.pewresearch.org/global
/2020/07/20/the-global-god-divide.

Pew Research Center. (2021a). 16% of Americans say they
have ever invested in, traded or used cryptocurrency.
Retrieved from www.pewresearch.org/fact-tank/2021
/11/11/16-of-americans-say-they-have-ever-invested-in
-traded-or-used-cryptocurrency.

Pew Research Center. (2021b). About three-in-ten U.S. adults
are now religiously unaffiliated. Retrieved from www
.pewresearch.org/religion/2021/12/14/about-three-in
-ten-u-s-adults-are-now-religiously-unaffiliated.

Pew Research Center. (2021c, April 7). Internet/broadband
fact sheet. Retrieved from www.pewresearch.org
/internet/fact-sheet/internet-broadband.

Pew Research Center. (2021d). The size of the U.S. Jewish
population. Retrieved from www.pewresearch
.org/religion/2021/05/11/the-size-of-the-u-s-jewish
-population.

Pew Research Center. (2022a, April 20). COVID-19 pandemic
pinches finances of America's lower- and middle-income
families. Retrieved from www.pewresearch.org/social
-trends/2022/04/20/covid-19-pandemic-pinches
-finances-of-americas-lower-and-middle-income-families.

Pew Research Center. (2022b, April 20). How the American
middle class has changed in the past five decades.
Retrieved from www.pewresearch.org/fact-tank/2022
/04/20/how-the-american-middle-class-has-changed
-in-the-past-five-decades.

Phelan, C., & Link, B. G. (2005). Controlling disease and
creating disparities: A fundamental cause perspective.
Journals of Gerontology, 60B, 30, 31.

Phillips, D., et al. (1987). Child care quality and children's
social development. *Developmental Psychology, 23*, 537–43.

Phillips, M. E., et al. (2015, November 22). Transgender locker
room policy eludes school district facing government
sanctions under Title IX. Retrieved from www
.collegeandprosportlaw.com/uncategorized/transgender
-locker-room-policy-eludes-school-district-facing
-government-sanctions-under-title-ix.

Picchio, M., & van Ours, J. C. (2013). Retaining through
training even for older workers. *Economics of Education
Review, 32*, 29–48. Retrieved from www.sciencedirect
.com/science/article/abs/pii/S0272775712001100.

Pickert, K. (2014). University of California approves steep tuition hike. *Time*. Retrieved from http://time.com/3598249/university-of-california-tuition-hike.

Pierce, J. L. (1995). *Gender trials: Emotional lives in contemporary law firms*. Berkeley: University of California Press.

Pierné, G. (2013). Hiring discrimination based on national origin and religious closeness: Results from a field experiment in the Paris area. *IZA Journal of Labor Economics*, 2(4). Retrieved from https://izajole.springeropen.com/articles/10.1186/2193-8997-2-4.

Pilkington, D. (1996). *Follow the rabbit-proof fence*. St. Lucia, Australia: University of Queensland Press.

Piquero, A. R., et al. (2021). *Domestic violence during COVID-19: Evidence from a systematic review and meta-analysis*. National Commission on COVID-19 and Criminal Justice. Retrieved from https://build.neoninspire.com/counciloncj/wp-content/uploads/sites/96/2021/07/Domestic-Violence-During-COVID-19-February-2021.pdf.

Pisetsky, E. M., et al. (2008). Disordered eating and substance abuse in high-school students: Results from the Youth Risk Behavior Surveillance System. *International Journal of Eating Disorders*, 41(5), 464–70.

Piven, F. F., & Cloward, R. A. (1988). *Why Americans don't vote: And why politicians want it that way*. Boston: Beacon Press.

Plath, S. (1971). *The bell jar*. New York: Harper & Row. (Original work published 1963.)

Pollan, M. (2006). *The omnivore's dilemma: A natural history of four meals*. New York: Penguin Press.

Poorman, E. (2018, January 14). Why does America still have so few female doctors? *The Guardian*. Retrieved from www.theguardian.com/commentisfree/2018/jan/14/why-are-there-still-so-few-female-doctors.

Popken, B. (2022, January 11). Management and workers are divided over returning to the office. *NBC News*. Retrieved from www.nbcnews.com/business/economy/full-return-work-dead-experts-say-remote-only-growing-rcna11323.

Portes, A. (1969). Dilemmas of a golden exile: Integration of Cuban refugee families in Milwaukee. *American Sociological Review*, 34, 505–18.

Portes, A., & MacLeod, D. (1996). Educational progress of children of immigrants: The roles of class, ethnicity and school context. *Sociology of Education*, 69(4), 255–75.

Portes, A., & Zhou, M. (1993). The new second generation: Segmented assimilation and its variants. *Annals of the American Academy of Political and Social Science*, 530, 74–96.

Portes, A., et al. (1985). After Mariel: A survey of the resettlement experiences of 1980 Cuban refugees in Miami. *Estudios Cubanos* (Cuban Studies), 15, 37–59.

Posner, R. A. (1992). *Sex and reason*. Cambridge, MA: Harvard University Press.

Powell, B., & Steelman, L. C. (1990). Beyond sibship size: Sibling density, sex composition, and educational outcomes. *Social Forces*, 69(1), 181–206.

Public Religion Research Institute. (2021). The 2020 census of American religion. Retrieved from www.prri.org/research/2020-census-of-american-religion.

Public Religion Research Institute. (2022). Figure 1. The American religious landscape in 2022. Retrieved from www.prri.org/research/2020-census-of-american-religion.

Putnam, R. D. (2000). *Bowling alone: The collapse and revival of American community*. New York: Simon & Schuster.

Qaim, M., & Zilberman, D. (2003). Yield effects of genetically modified crops in developing countries. *Science*, 299, 900–902.

Qian, Z. (2013, September 11). Divergent paths of American families. US2010 Project. Retrieved from https://s4.ad.brown.edu/Projects/Diversity/Data/Report/report09112013.pdf.

Quadagno, J. (1987). Theories of the welfare state. *Annual Review of Sociology*, 13, 109–28.

Quadagno, J. (1996). *The color of welfare: How racism undermined the war on poverty*. New York: Oxford University Press.

Rafalow, M. H. (2020). *Digital divisions: How schools create inequality in the tech era*. University of Chicago Press.

Radway, J. (1987). *Reading the romance: Women, patriarchy, and popular literature*. Chapel Hill: University of North Carolina Press.

Rahman, Q., et al. (2003). Sexual orientation–related differences in prepulse inhibition of the human startle response. *Behavioral Neuroscience*, 117(5), 1096–102.

Rainwater, L. (1974). *What money buys: Inequality and the social meanings of income*. New York: Basic Books.

Ralli, T. (2005, September 5). Who's a looter? In storm's aftermath, pictures kick up a different kind of tempest. *The New York Times*. Retrieved from www.nytimes.com/2005/09/05/business/05caption.html.

Read, J. (2008, February). Muslims in America. Retrieved from http://contexts.org/articles/fall-2008/muslims-in-america.

Reardon, S. F. (2013, May). The widening income achievement gap. *Educational Leadership*, 70(8), 10–16. Retrieved from http://nppsd.fesdev.org/vimages/shared/vnews/stories/525d81ba96ee9/SI%20-%20The%20Widening%20Income%20Achievement%20Gap.pdf.

Reardon, S. F., et al. (2012, August 3). Race, income, and enrollment patterns in highly selective colleges, 1982–2004. Center for Education Policy Analysis, Stanford University. Retrieved from https://cepa.stanford.edu/sites/default/files/race%20income %20%20%26%20 selective%20college%20enrollment %20august%20 3%202012.pdf.

Reaves, E. L., & Musumeci, M. (2015). Medicaid and long-term services and supports: A primer. KFF. Retrieved from www.kff.org/medicaid/report/medicaid-and-long-term-services-and-supports-a-primer.

Reddy, G. (2005). *With respect to sex: Negotiating hijra identity in South India*. Chicago: University of Chicago Press.

Reimer, S. (2016). It's just a very male industry: Gender and work in UK design agencies. *Gender, Place & Culture*, 23(7), 1033–46.

Reskin, B., & Roos, P. (1990). *Job queues, gender queues*. Philadelphia: Temple University Press.

Reyes, J. W. (2007). Environmental policy as social policy? The impact of childhood lead exposure on crime. *The B.E. Journal of Economic Analysis & Policy*, 7(1).

Rhoades, G., et al. (2009). The pre-engagement cohabitation effect: A replication and extension of previous findings. *Journal of Family Psychology*, 23(1), 107–11.

Rich, A. (1980). Compulsory heterosexuality and lesbian existence. *Signs: Journal of Women in Culture and Society, 5*, 631–60.

Ringen, S. (1987). *The possibility of politics.* New York: Oxford University Press.

Rios, V. (2011). *Punished: Policing the lives of Black and Latino boys.* New York: NYU Press.

Risman, B. J. (1998). *Gender vertigo: American families in transition.* New Haven, CT: Yale University Press.

Rockoff, J. E. (2004). The impact of individual teachers on student achievement: Evidence from panel data. *The American Economic Review, 94*(2), 247–52.

Rodgers, W. M., & Novello, A. (2019). Making the economic case for a $15 minmum wage. The Century Foundation. Retrieved from https://tcf.org/content/commentary /making-economic-case-15-minimum-wage/?agreed=1.

Ronis, S. D., et al. (2017). Urban telemedicine enables equity in access to acute illness care. *Telemedicine and e-Health, 23*(2), 105–12.

Roof, W. C. (1989). Multiple religious switching. *Journal for the Scientific Study of Religion, 28*, 530–35.

Rosaldo, M. Z. (1974). Woman, culture and society: A theoretical overview. In M. Z. Rosaldo & L. Lamphere (Eds.), *Woman, culture, and society* (pp. 17–42). Stanford, CA: Stanford University Press.

Rose, A., & LeBlanc, P. (2022, May 26). Oklahoma GOP governor signs anti-transgender bathroom bill into law. CNN. Retrieved from www.cnn.com/2022/05/25 /politics/oklahoma-anti-transgender-bathroom-law -signed-stitt/index.html.

Rosenbaum, J. E. (1980). Track misperceptions and frustrated college plans: An analysis of the effects of track perception in the National Longitudinal Survey. *Sociology of Education, 53*(2), 74–88.

Rosenbaum, J. E., with L. S. Rubinowitz. (2000). *Crossing the class and color lines: From public housing to White suburbia.* Chicago: University of Chicago Press.

Rosenfeld, J., & Kleykamp, M. (2009). Hispanics and organized labor. *American Sociological Review, 74*(4), 916–37.

Rosenfeld, M. J., & Roesler, K. (2018). Cohabitation experience and cohabitation's association with marital dissolution. *Journal of Marriage and Family, 81*(1), 42–58.

Rosenhan, D. L. (1973). On being sane in insane places. *Science, 179*, 25–58.

Rosenthal, R., & Jacobson, L. (1968). *Pygmalion in the classroom: Teacher expectation and pupils' intellectual development.* New York: Rinehart & Winston.

Rosenzweig, M. R. (1982). Educational subsidy, agricultural development and fertility change. *Quarterly Journal of Economics, 97*(1), 67–88.

Roser, M., & Ortiz-Ospina, E. (2019). Global extreme poverty. Retrieved from https://ourworldindata .org/extreme-poverty#:~:text=In%201990%2C%20 there%20were%201.9,were%20living%20in%20 extreme%20poverty.

Rothstein, J. M. (2004). College performance predictions and the SAT. *Journal of Econometrics, 121*(1–2), 297–317.

Rousseau, J.-J. (2004). A dissertation on the origin and foundation of the inequality of mankind. In *Discourse on inequality.* Whitefish, MT: Kessinger Publishing. (Original work published 1754.)

Rowe, J. W., & Kahn, R. L. (1997). Successful aging. *The Gerontologist, 37*(4), 433–40.

Rowntree, B. S. (1910). *Poverty, a study of town life.* London: Macmillan.

Rubin, G. (1975). The traffic in women: Notes on the "political economy" of sex. In R. R. Reiter (Ed.), *Toward an anthropology of women* (pp. 157–210). New York: Monthly Review Press.

Rumsfeld, D. H., & Myers, R. (2002, February 12). DoD news briefing [Speech transcript]. U. S. Department of Defense. Retrieved from https://archive.ph/20180320091111 /http:/archive.defense.gov/Transcripts/Transcript.aspx.

Ruggles, P. (1990). *Drawing the line: Alternative poverty measures and their implications for public policy.* Washington, DC: Urban Institute Press.

Ryan, C. L., & Bauman, K. (2016, March). Educational attainment in the United States: 2015. Population characteristics. U.S. Census Bureau. Retrieved from www.census.gov/content/dam/Census/library /publications/2016/demo/p20-578.pdf.

Sacerdote, B. (2001). Peer effects with random assignment: Results for Dartmouth roommates. *Quarterly Journal of Economics, 116*.

Sachs, J. D. (2001). *Macroeconomics and health: Investing in health for economic development.* Report of the Commission on Macroeconomics and Health. Geneva: World Health Organization.

Sadker, D., et al. (2009). *Still failing at fairness: How gender bias cheats girls and boys in school and what we can do about it.* New York: Scribner.

Sadker, M., & Sadker, D. (1994). *Failing at fairness: How America's schools cheat girls.* New York: Touchstone.

Samuels, A. (2015). Rachel Dolezal's true lies. *Vanity Fair.* Retrieved from www.vanityfair.com/news/2015/07.

Sander, T. H., & Putnam, R. D. (2010). Still bowling alone? The post-9/11 split. *Journal of Democracy, 21*(1), 9–16.

Santa Ana, O. (2004). Is there such a thing as Latino identity? *American Family: Journey of Dreams.* Retrieved from www.pbs.org/americanfamily/latino2.html.

Saroyan, S. (2006, April 16). Christianity, the brand. *The New York Times.* Retrieved from www.nytimes.com /2006/04/16/books/christianity-the-brand.html.

Savas, G. (2016). Gender and race differences in American college enrollment: Evidence from the education longitudinal study of 2002. *American Journal of Educational Research, 4*(1), 64–75.

Sawyer, K., et al. (2016). Queering the gender binary: Understanding transgender workplace experiences. In T. Kollen (Ed.), *Sexual orientation and transgender issues in organizations* (pp. 21–42). Cham, Switzerland: Springer.

Sawyer, L. (2017, January 28). Waconia woman crawls back from the "dead." *Star Tribune.* Retrieved from www .startribune.com/waconia-woman-crawls-back-from -the-dead/412049283.

Sawyer, W., & Wagner, P. (2019). Mass incarceration: The whole pie 2019. Retrieved from www.prisonpolicy .org/reports/pie2019.html.

Sawyer, W., & Wagner, P. (2022). Mass incarceration: The whole pie 2022. Prison Policy Initiative. Retrieved from www.prisonpolicy.org/reports/pie2022.html.

Scalise, I. M. (2014, January 26). Lo stato riconosca a casalinghe un salario e una vera pensione. *La Repubblica.* Retrieved from www.repubblica.it/economia/2014/01/26

/news/bongiorno_lo_stato_riconosca_salario_a
_casalinghe-76954421.

Schackner, B. (2002, September 27). College course focuses on the wealthy minority. *Post-Gazette*. Retrieved from www.post-gazette.com/localnews/20020929wealthy6 .asp.

Schacter, J., & Thum, Y. M. (2004). Paying for high-and low-quality teaching. *Economics of Education Review, 23*(4), 411–30.

Scharf, S. A., & Flom, B. A. (2010, October). Report of the fifth annual national survey on retention and promotion of women in law firms. National Association of Women Lawyers. Retrieved from www.aauw.org/learn /research/upload/NewVoicesPayEquity_NAWL.pdf.

Scheitle, C., & Dougherty, K. (2010). Race, diversity, and membership duration in religious congregations. *Sociological Inquiry, 80*(3), 405–23.

Scherrer, K. S., & Pfeffer, C. A. (2017). None of the above: Toward identity and community-based understandings of (a)sexualities. *Archives of Sexual Behavior, 46*(3), 643–46.

Schippers, M. (2016). *Beyond monogamy: Polyamory and the future of polyqueer sexualities.* New York: NYU Press.

Schlosser, E. (2001). *Fast food nation: The dark side of the all-American meal.* Boston: Houghton Mifflin.

Schoen, R., & Canudas-Romo, V. (2006). Timing effects on divorce: 20th century experience in the United States. *Journal of Marriage and Family, 68*(3), 749–58.

Sciolino, E. (2004, October 22). France turns to tough policy on students' religious garb. *The New York Times*. Retrieved from www.nytimes.com/2004/10/22/world /europe/france-turns-to-tough-policy-on-students -religious-garb.html.

Scott, D. W. (2021). U.S. membership decline and the rhetoric of the global church. *United Methodist Insight*. Retrieved from https://um-insight.net/in-the-church/umc-global -nature/us-membership-decline-and-the-rhetoric-of -the-global-church.

Seelye, K. Q. (2005, May 16). *Newsweek* apologizes for report of Koran insult. *The New York Times*, p. A1. Retrieved from www.nytimes.com/2005/05/16/world/asia /newsweek-apologizes-for-report-of-koran-insult.html.

Segers, G. (2020). Asked why Black Americans are killed by police, Trump responds, "So are White people." *CBS News*. Retrieved from www.cbsnews.com/news/trump -black-americans-killed-police-so-are-white-people.

Setoodeh, R. (2006, March 20). Troubles by the score. *Newsweek*. Retrieved from www.msnbc.msn.com/id /11788171/site/newsweek.

Shah, D. (2004). *Defense of Marriage Act: An update.* Washington, DC: U.S. General Accounting Office.

Shaheen, J. G. (1984). *The TV Arab.* Bowling Green, OH: Bowling Green State University Popular Press.

Shapiro, D., et al. (2016). Time to degree: A national view of the time enrolled and elapsed for associate and bachelor's degree earners [signature report 11]. Herndon, VA: National Student Clearinghouse Research Center. Retrieved from https://nscresearchcenter.org/wp-content /uploads/SignatureReport11.pdf.

Sharkey, P. (2010). The acute effect of local homicides on children's cognitive performance. *PNAS, 107*(26), 11733–38. Retrieved from www.pnas.org/content/107/26/11733.

Sheff, E. (2014). The polyamorists next door: Inside multiple-partner relationships and families. Lanham, MD: Rowman & Littlefield.

Sheler, J. (2001, October 29). Muslim in America. *U.S. News & World Report*, pp. 50–52.

Sherkat, D. E. (1991). Leaving the faith: Testing theories of religious switching using survival models. *Social Science Research, 20*, 171–87.

Sherkat, D. E. (1998). Counterculture or continuity? Competing influences on baby boomers. Religious orientations and participation. *Social Forces, 76*, 1087–115.

Sherkat, D. E., & Ellison, C. G. (1999). Recent developments and current controversies in the sociology of religion. *Annual Review of Sociology, 25*, 363–94.

Shierholz, H., et al. (2022). Latest data release on unionization is a wake-up call to lawmakers. Economic Policy Institute. Retrieved from www.epi.org/publication /latest-data-release-on-unionization-is-a-wake-up-call -to-lawmakers.

Shiva, V. (1992a). Recovering the real meaning of sustainability. In D. E. Cooper & J. A. Palmer (Eds.), *The environment in question: Ethics in global issues* (pp. 187–93). London: Routledge.

Shiva, V. (1992b). Women's indigenous knowledge and biodiversity conservation. In G. Sen (Ed.), *Indigenous vision* (pp. 205–14). New Delhi: Sage.

Shiva, V. (2002). *Water wars: Privatization, pollution and profit.* Cambridge, MA: South End Press.

Shiva, V. (2004). Turning scarcity into abundance. *Yes! Magazine*. Retrieved from www.yesmagazine.org/article .asp?ID=698.

Shore, B. (1998). *Culture in mind: Cognition, culture, and the problem of meaning.* New York: Oxford University Press.

Shore, L. (2017, January 3). Gal interrupted, why men interrupt women and how to avert this in the workplace. *Forbes*. Retrieved from www.forbes.com/sites /womensmedia/2017/01/03/gal-interrupted-why-men -interrupt-women-and-how-to-avert-this-in -the-workplace/#437dd01217c3.

Shulevitz, J. (2016, January 8). It's payback time for women. *The New York Times*. Retrieved from www.nytimes.com /2016/01/10/opinion/sunday/payback-time-for-women .html.

Shulman, J., & Bowen, W. G. (2002). *The game of life: College sports and educational values.* Princeton, NJ: Princeton University Press.

Silva, T. J. (2017). Bud-sex: Constructing normative masculinity among rural straight men that have sex with men. *Gender & Society, 31*(1), 51–73.

Silverglate, H. (2011). *Three felonies a day: How the feds target the innocent.* New York: Encounter Books.

Simmel, G. (1900). *Philosophie der Geldes* (The philosophy of money). Leipzig: Duncker & Humblot.

Simmel, G. (1950). Quantitative aspects of the group. In K. Wolff (Comp. and Trans.), *The sociology of Georg Simmel* (pp. 87–180). Glencoe, IL: Free Press.

Singer, N. (2017, May 13). How Google took over the classroom. *The New York Times*. Retrieved from www .nytimes.com/2017/05/13/technology/google-education -chromebooks-schools.html?mcubz=0&_r=0.

Singh, A., et al. (2022). Covid-19 learning loss and recovery: Panel data evidence from India. Retrieved from https://doi.org/10.3386/w30552.

Singleton, C. R., et al. (2016). Decomposing racial disparities in obesity prevalence: Variations in retail food environment. *American Journal of Preventative Medicine, 50*(3), 365−72.

Skocpol, T. (2004). Civic transformation and inequality in the contemporary United States. In K. Neckerman (Ed.), *Social inequality* (pp. 731−69). New York: Russell Sage Foundation.

Skocpol, T., & Amenta, E. (1986). States and social policies. *Annual Review of Sociology, 12,* 131−57.

Skogrand, L., et al. (2004, July). Understanding Latino families: Implications for family education. *Family Resources.* Retrieved from http://extension.usu.edu /diversity/files/uploads/Latino02-7-05.pdf.

Smedley, A. (1999). *Race in North America: Origin and evolution of a worldview.* Boulder, CO: Westview Press.

Smelser, N. (1962). *Theory of collective behavior.* New York: Free Press.

Smith, A. (2003). *The wealth of nations.* New York: Penguin. (Original work published 1776.)

Smith, B. H. (2009). *Natural reflections: Human cognition at the nexus of science and religion.* New Haven, CT: Yale University Press.

Smith, J. R., et al. (1997). Consequences of living in poverty for young children's cognitive and verbal ability and early school achievement. In J. G. Duncan & J. Brooks-Gunn (Eds.), *Consequences of growing up poor* (pp. 132−89). New York: Russell Sage Foundation.

Snow, D. A., et al. (1986). Frame alignment processes, micromobilization, and movement participation. *American Sociological Review, 51*(4), 464−81.

Snow, D., et al. (2014). The emergence, development, and future of the framing perspective: 25+ years since "frame alignment." *Mobilization: An International Quarterly, 19*(1), 23−46.

Snowden, F. M. (1983). *Beyond color prejudice: The ancient view of Blacks.* Cambridge, MA: Harvard University Press.

Snyder, S., & Evans, W. (2002). *The impact of income on mortality: Evidence from the Social Security notch* (NBER Working Paper No. W9197). National Bureau of Economic Research. Retrieved from www.nber.org/papers/w9197.

Snyder, S. E., & Evans, W. N. (2006). The effect of income on mortality: Evidence from the Social Security notch. *Review of Economics and Statistics, 88,* 482−95.

Snyder, T. D., & Tan, A. G. (2005). *Digest of education statistics, 2004* (NCES 2006-005). US Department of Education, National Center for Education Statistics. Washington, DC: U.S. Government Printing Office.

Sokal, A., & Bricmont, J. (1999). *Fashionable nonsense: Postmodern intellectuals' abuse of science.* London: Picador.

Sommers, C. H. (2000). *The war against boys: How misguided feminism is harming our young men.* New York: Simon & Schuster.

Sorokin, P. (1959). *Social and cultural mobility.* New York: Free Press. (Original work published 1927.)

Sorokin, P., & Lunden, W. A. (1959). *Power and morality: Who shall guard the guardians?* Boston: Porter Sargent.

Sotoudeh, R., et al. (2019). Effects of the peer metagenomic environment on smoking behavior. *Proceedings of the National Academy of Sciences, 116*(33), 16302−307.

Spencer, H. (1967). *The evolution of society: Selections from Herbert Spencer's* Principles of Sociology (R. L. Carneiro, Ed.). Chicago: University of Chicago Press. (Original work published 1898.)

Spencer, M. B., et al. (1987). Double stratification and psychological risk: Adaptational processes and school achievement of Black children. *Journal of Negro Education, 56*(1), 77−87.

Spiegel, A. (Producer). (2006, December 15). Shouting across the divide, act one: Which one of them is not like the other? [Radio broadcast]. *This American Life.* Retrieved from www.thisamericanlife.org/Radio_Episode.aspx ?episode=322.

Spock, B. (1998). *Baby and child care.* New York: Pocket Books. (Original work published 1946.)

Spohn, C., & Holleran, D. (2002). The effects of imprisonment on recidivism rates of felony offenders: A focus on drug offenders. *Criminology, 40*(2), 329−58.

Spurlock, M. (Director). (2004). *Super size me* [Motion picture]. United States: Sony Pictures.

Spurlock, M. (Host). (2005, June 29). Muslims and America [Television series episode]. In J. Chinn et al. (Producers), *30 days.* Los Angeles, Bluebush Productions LLC.

Stacey, J. (1987). Sexism by a subtler name? Postindustrial conditions and postfeminist consciousness in the Silicon Valley. *Socialist Review, 96,* 7−28.

Stacey, J. (1996). *In the name of the family: Rethinking family values in the postmodern age.* Boston: Beacon Press.

Stacey, J. (1997). Neo-family-values campaign. In R. N. Lancaster & M. di Lionardo (Eds.), *The gender/sexuality reader: Culture, history, political economy* (pp. 453−72). New York: Routledge.

Stack, C. B. (1974). *All our kin: Strategies for survival in a Black community.* New York: Harper & Row.

Stack, C. B., & Burton, L. M. (1994). Kinscripts: Reflections on family, generation and culture. In E. N. Glenn et al. (Eds.), *Mothering: Ideology, experience, and agency* (pp. 33−44). New York: Routledge.

Stark, R., & Bainbridge, W. S. (1985). *The future of religion: Secularization, revival, and cult formation.* Berkeley: University of California Press.

Stark, R., & Bainbridge, W. S. (1987). *A theory of religion.* Toronto: Lang.

Stark, R., & Finke, R. (2000). *Acts of faith: Explaining the human side of religion.* Berkeley: University of California Press.

Steele, C. M., & Aronson, J. (1995). Stereotype threat and the intellectual test performance of African Americans. *Journal of Personality and Social Psychology, 69*(5), 797.

Steele, C. M., & Aronson, J. (1998). Stereotype threat and the test performance of academically successful African Americans. In C. Jencks & M. Phillips (Eds.), *The Black-White test score gap* (pp. 401−27). Washington, DC: Brookings Institution Press.

Steelman, L. C., & Powell, B. (1985). The social and academic consequences of birth order: Real, artifactual or both? *Journal of Marriage and the Family, 47*(1), 117−24.

Steelman, L. C., & Powell, B. (1989). Acquiring capital for college: The constraints of family configuration. *American Sociological Review, 54*(5), 844−55.

Steinberg, L., & Monahan, K. C. (2007). Age differences in resistance to peer influence. *Developmental Psychology, 43*(6), 1531−43.

Steinberg, S. (1974). *The academic melting pot.* New York: McGraw-Hill.

Stephens-Davidowitz, S. (2022). *Don't trust your gut: Using data instead of instinct to make better choices.* New York: Bloomsbury Publishing.

Stewart, J. B. (2015, July 16). Convictions prove elusive in "London Whale" trading case. *The New York Times.* Retrieved from www.nytimes.com/2015/07/17/business /figures-in-london-whale-trading-case-escape-the -authorities-nets.html.

Stokes, B. (2017). Public divided on prospects for the next generation. Pew Research Center. Retrieved from www .pewglobal.org/2017/06/05/2-public-divided-on -prospects-for-the-next-generation.

Stone, D. A. (1994). Making the poor count. *American Prospect, 17,* 84–88.

Strings, S. (2019). *Fearing the Black body: The racial origins of fat phobia.* New York: New York University Press.

Subbaraman, N. (2021). NIH reverses Trump-era restrictions on fetal-tissue research. *Nature.* 2021, April 16.

Sunderam, S., et al. (2018). Assisted reproductive technology surveillance—United States, 2015. *Morbidity and Mortality Weekly Report, 67*(3), 1–28.

Sykes, J., et al. (2014, October 10). Dignity and dreams. *American Sociological Review, 80*(2), 243–67.

Tavernise, S. (2016, April 22). U.S. suicide rate surges to a 30-year high. *The New York Times.* Retrieved from www .nytimes.com/2016/04/22/health/us-suicide-rate -surges-to-a-30-year-high.html.

Taylor, K. (2014, October 27). How buying beer paid me $4,000 a month for college. *Daily Finance.* Retrieved from www.dailyfinance.com/2014/10/27/how-buying-beer -paid-me-4-000-a-month-for-college.

Taylor, P., & Urwin, P. (2001). Age and participation in vocational education and training. *Work, Employment, and Society, 15*(4), 763–79. Retrieved from www.cambridge .org/core/journals/work-employment-and-society /article/age-and-participation-in-vocational-education -and-training/9AF153573EDDB7F59C2800B05512B596.

Tett, G. (2010). Road map that opens up shadow banking. *Financial Times.* Retrieved from www.ft.com/intl/cms/s/0 /1a222bf4-f33d-11df-a4fa-00144feab49a.html #axzz3x3F5SrvG.

Tharps, Lori L. (2014). The case for black with a capital b. *The New York Times.* Retrieved from https://www.nytimes .com/2014/11/19/opinion/the-case-for-black-with-a -capital-h.html.

Thinggaard, C. K., et al. (2009). Perceived age as clinically useful biomarker of ageing: Cohort study. *BMJ, 339.* Retrieved from https://doi.org/10.1136/bmj.b5262.

Thomas, E. (2005, May 23). How a fire broke out. *Newsweek.* Retrieved from www.msnbc.msn.com/id/7857407/site /newsweek.

Thomas, W. I., & Thomas, D. S. (1928). *The child in America: Behavior problems and programs.* New York: Knopf.

Thomeer, M. B., et al. (2022). Racial and ethnic disparities in mental health and mental health care during the COVID-19 pandemic. *Journal of Racial and Ethnic Health Disparities.* Retrieved from https://doi.org/10.1007 /s40615-022-01284-9.

Thurow, L. (1970). *Investment in human capital.* Belmont, CA: Wadsworth.

Tinkler, J. E. (2013). How do sexual harassment policies shape gender beliefs? An exploration of the moderating effects of norm adherence and gender. *Social Science Research, 42*(5), 1269–83.

Tocqueville, A. de. (1835). *Democracy in America.* Retrieved from http://xroads.virginia.edu/~HYPER/DETOC/toc _indx.html.

Todd, M. A., & Goldman, N. (2013). Do interviewer and physician health ratings predict mortality? A comparison with self-rated health. *Epidemiology, 24*(6), 913–20.

Torres, N. G. (2017, December 19). More than 37,000 Cubans face deportation orders. *The Miami Herald.* Retrieved from www.miamiherald.com/news/nation-world /world/americas/cuba/article190571369.html.

Torrey, E. F. (2005, May 10). Deinstitutionalization: A psychiatric "Titanic." PBS. Retrieved from www.pbs .org/wgbh/pages/frontline/shows/asylums/special /excerpt.html.

Treisman, R. (2019). FBI reports dip in hate crimes, but rise in violence. NPR. Retrieved from www.npr.org/2019 /11/12/778542614/fbi-reports-dip-in-hate-crimes-but -rise-in-violence.

Troller-Renfree, S. V., et al. (2021).The impact of a poverty reduction intervention on infant brain activity. *Psychological and Cognitive Sciences, 119*(5), 1–8.

Truth, S. (1851). Ain't I a woman? Speech delivered at the Women's Convention in Akron, Ohio. National Park Service. Retrieved from www.nps.gov/articles/sojourner -truth.htm.Tufekci, Z. (2017). *Twitter and tear gas: The power and fragility of networked protest.* New Haven, CT: Yale University Press.

Turkewitz, J. (2018, January 4). For Native Americans, a "historic moment" on the path to power at the ballot box. *The New York Times.* Retrieved from www.nytimes.com /2018/01/04/native-american-voting-rights.html.

Turner, R., & Killian, L. M. (1987). *Collective behavior* (3rd ed.). Englewood Cliffs, NJ: Prentice-Hall.

Tyson, K., et al. (2005). It's not "a Black thing": Understanding the burden of acting White and other dilemmas of high achievement. *American Sociological Review, 70*(4), 582–605.

Ugwu, C., & Nugent, C. (2018). Adoption-related behaviors among women aged 18–44 in the United States: 2011–2015. National Center for Health Statistics, Centers for Disease Control and Prevention. Retrieved from www.cdc.gov /nchs/products/databriefs/db315.htm.

Unah, I., & Boger, J. C. (2001, April 16). *Race and the death penalty in North Carolina.* Retrieved from www.common -sense.org/pdfs/NCDeathPenaltyReport2001.pdf.

UNICEF. (2021). Billions of people will lack access to safe water, sanitation, and hygiene in 2030 unless progress quadruples warn WHO, UNICEF. Retrieved from www .unicef.org/press-releases/billions-people-will-lack -access-safe-water-sanitation-and-hygiene-2030-unless.

UNICEF. (2022a). Under-five mortaliy. Retrieved from http://data.unicef.org/topic/child-survival/under-five -mortality.

UNICEF. (2022b). Where are we on education recovery? Retrieved from www.unicef.org/media/117626/file /Where%20are%20we%20in%20Education%20 Recovery?.pdf.

United Methodist Church. (2023). The United Methodist Church online directory & statistics. *UMData*. Retrieved from www.umdata.org/UMFactsHome.aspx.

United Nations. (2001, May 17). Poverty biggest enemy of health in developing world, secretary-general tells World Health Assembly [Press release]. Retrieved from www.un.org/News/Press/docs/2001/sgsm7808.doc.htm.

U.S. Census Bureau. (1993). We the first Americans. U.S. Department of Commerce Economics and Statistics Administration. Retrieved from www.census.gov/apsd/wepeople/we-5.pdf.

U.S. Census Bureau. (2010a). Data profile highlights, population finder fact sheet. 2006–2008 American Community Survey 3-year estimates. Retrieved from http://factfinder.census.gov/servlet/ACSSAFFFacts?_sse=on.

U.S. Census Bureau. (2010b). 2012 statistical abstract: Income, poverty, & wealth. Retrieved from www.census.gov/compendia/statab/cats/income_expenditures_poverty_wealth.html.

U.S. Census Bureau. (2012). Table 4: Percent distribution of household net worth, by amount of net worth and selected characteristics: 2011. Retrieved from www.census.gov/people/wealth.

U.S. Census Bureau. (2017a). 2017 national population projections tables: Main series. Table 6. Race and Hispanic origin by age group. Retrieved from www.census.gov/data/tables/2017/demo/popproj/2017-summary-tables.html.

U.S. Census Bureau. (2017b). Poverty status in the past 12 months by sex by age (American Indian and Alaska native alone). 2016 American Community Survey 1-year estimates. Retrieved from https://factfinder.census.gov/faces/tableservices/jsf/pages/productview.xhtml?pid=ACS_16_1YR_B17001C&prodType=table.

U.S. Census Bureau. (2017c, March 16). Supplemental poverty measure. Retrieved from www.census.gov/topics/income-poverty/supplemental-poverty-measure/about.html.

U.S. Census Bureau. (2019). America's foreign born in the last 50 years. Retrieved from www.census.gov/programs-surveys/sis/resources/visualizations/foreign-born.html.

U.S. Census Bureau. (2020a). Demographic characteristics for occupied housing units. Retrieved from https://data.census.gov/cedsci/table?q=tenure&tid=ACSST1Y2018.S2502&t=Owner%2FRenter%20%28Tenure%29&vintage=2018.

U.S. Census Bureau. (2020b). Hispanic by country of origin. Retrieved from https://data.census.gov/cedsci/table?q=hispanic%20by%20country%20of%20ori-gin&hidePreview=false&tid=ACSDT1Y2018.B03001&vintage=2018.

U.S. Census Bureau. (2020c). Hispanic by region. Retrieved from https://data.census.gov/cedsci/map?q=hispanic%20by%20region&tid=ACSDP1Y2018.DP05&t=Hispanic%20or%20Latino&vintage=2018&hidePreview=false&cid=DP05_0071PE&layer=VT_2018_040_00_PY_D1&mode=selection.

U.S. Census Bureau. (2020d). Hispanic or Latino by specific origin. Retrieved from https://data.census.gov/cedsci/table?q=hispanic%20by%20country%20of%20origin&hidePreview=false&tid=ACSDT1Y2018.B03001&vintage=2018.

U.S. Census Bureau. (2020e). Median income in the past 12 months (in 2018 inflation-adjusted dollars). Retrieved from https://data.census.gov/cedsci/table?q=median%20family%20income&tid=ACSST1Y2018.S1903&t=Income%20%28Households,%20Families,%20Individuals %29%3AHousehold%20and%20Family&vintage=2018.

U.S. Census Bureau. (2020f). People reporting ancestry. Retrieved from https://data.census.gov/cedsci/table?q=arab&tid=ACSDT1Y2018.B04006&vintage=2013.

U.S. Census Bureau. (2020g). Selected characteristics of the foreign-born population by period of entry into the United States. Retrieved from https://data.census.gov/cedsci/table?q=foreign%20born%20african%20americans&hidePreview=false&tid=ACSST1Y2018.S0502&t=Foreign%20born%3ABlack%20or%20African%20American&vintage=2018.

U.S. Census Bureau. (2020h). Table: Detailed race. Retrieved from https://data.census.gov/cedsci/table?q=asian&hidePreview=false&tid=ACSDT1Y2010.B02003&t=Asian&vintage=2018.

U.S. Census Bureau. (2020i). Table F1: Family households, by type, age of own children, age of family members, and age of householder. Retrieved from www2.census.gov/programs-surveys/demo/tables/families/2019/cps-2019/tabf1-all.xls.

U.S. Census Bureau. (2020j). Table HH-4: Households by size, 1960 to present. Retrieved from www2.census.gov/programs-surveys/demo/tables/families/time-series/households/hh4.xls.

U.S. Census Bureau. (2021a, November 29). Census Bureau releases new estimates on America's families and living arrangements. Retrieved from www.census.gov/newsroom/press-releases/2021/families-and-living-arrangements.html#:~:text=In%202021%2C%2034%25%20of%20adults,20.5%2C%20respectively%2C%20in%201947.

U.S. Census Bureau. (2021b). Educational attainment: American Community Survey 1-year estimates subject tables. Retrieved from https://data.census.gov/table?q=College+degree&tid=ACSST1Y2021.S1501.

U.S. Census Bureau. (2021c). Educational attainment in the United States: 2021 Table 3. Retrieved from www.census.gov/data/tables/2021/demo/educational-attainment/cps-detailed-tables.html.

U.S. Census Bureau. (2021d). Foreign-born people are older when they first marry, less likely to remarry than native-born. Retrieved from www.census.gov/library/stories/2021/05/marital-histories-differ-between-native-born-and-foreign-born-adults.html.

U.S. Census Bureau. (2021e). Hispanic or Latino origin by specific origin. 2021: ACS 1-year estimates detailed tables. Retrieved from https://data.census.gov/table?q=hispanic+by+country+of+ori-gin&tid=ACSDT1Y2021.B03001.

U.S. Census Bureau. (2021f). Income and poverty in the United States: 2020. Retrieved from www.census.gov/library/publications/2021/demo/p60-273.html.

U.S. Census Bureau. (2021g). Percentage and number of children living with two parents has dropped since 1968. Retrieved from www.census.gov/library/stories/2021/04/number-of-children-living-only-with-their-mothers-has-doubled-in-past-50-years.html.

U.S. Census Bureau. (2021h). Place of birth for the foreign-born population in the United States. 2021: ACS 1-year estimates detailed tables. Retrieved from https://data.census.gov/table?q=B05006&tid=ACSDT1Y2021.B05006.

U.S. Census Bureau. (2021i). QuickFacts. Retrieved from www.census.gov/quickfacts/fact/table/US/PST045221.

U.S. Census Bureau. (2021j) Table AVG1: Average number of people per household, by race and hispanic origin, marital status, age, and education of hourseholder. Retrieved from www.census.gov/data/tables/2021/demo/families/cps-2021.html.

U.S. Census Bureau. (2021k). Table HH-4. Households by size: 1960 to present. Retrieved from www.census.gov/data/tables/time-series/demo/families/households.html.

U.S. Census Bureau. (2022a). 2019 data show baby boomers nearly 9 times wealthier than millennials. Retrieved from www.census.gov/library/stories/2022/08/wealth-inequality-by-household-type.html.

U.S. Census Bureau. (2022b, April 15). About the Hispanic population and its origin. Census.gov. Retrieved from www.census.gov/topics/population/hispanic-origin/about.html.

U.S. Census Bureau. (2022c). Census Bureau releases new educational attainment data. Retrieved from www.census.gov/newsroom/press-releases/2022/educational-attainment.html.

U.S. Census Bureau. (2022d, April 13). Children living with at least one foreign-born parent more likely to live with two parents than children with native-born parents. Census.gov. Retrieved from www.census.gov/library/stories/2022/02/over-quarter-of-children-lived-with-at-least-one-foreign-born-parent.html#:~:text=While%20the%20majority%20of%20children,new%20U.S.%20Census%20Bureau%20report.

U.S. Census Bureau. (2022e). Current Population Survey, 2021 and 2022 Annual Social and Economic Supplements (CPS ASEC). Retrieved from www.census.gov7/content/dam/Census/library/visualizations/2022/demo/p60-277/figure2.pdf.

U.S. Census Bureau. (2022f). In Puerto Rico, no gap in median earnings between men and women. Retrieved from www.census.gov/library/stories/2022/03/what-is-the-gender-wage-gap-in-your-state.html#:~:text=In%202020%2C%20women%20earned%2083,gap%20is%20narrowing%20but%20continues.

U.S. Census Bureau. (2022g). Nation continues to age as it becomes more diverse. Retrieved from www.census.gov/newsroom/press-releases/2022/population-estimates-characteristics.html.

U.S. Census Bureau. (2022h). Number in poverty and poverty rate using the official poverty measure: 1959 to 2021. Retrieved from www.census.gov/content/dam/Census/library/visualizations/2022/demo/p60-277/figure1.pdf.

U.S. Census Bureau. (2022i). Poverty in the United States: 2021. Retrieved from www.census.gov/content/dam/Census/library/publications/2022/demo/p60-277.pdf.

U.S. Department of Agriculture. (2018). Supplemental Nutrition Assistance Program: Participation and costs, 1969–2017. Retrieved from www.fns.usda.gov/pd/supplemental-nutrition-assistance-program-snap.

U.S. Department of Education, National Center for Education Statistics. (2019). Program for the International Assessment of Adult Competencies (PIAAC). Retrieved from https://nces.ed.gov/pubs2019/2019179.pdf.

U.S. Department of Health and Human Services (2015). Dietary guidelines for Americans 2015–2020. Retrieved from http://health.gov/dietaryguidelines/2015/guidelines.

U.S. Department of Health and Human Services. (2023). U.S. federal poverty guidelines used to determine financial eligibility for certain federal programs. Retrieved from https://aspe.hhs.gov/poverty-guidelines.

U.S. Department of the Interior, Indian Affairs. (2018). Frequently asked questions: What is the Bureau of Indian Education? Retrieved from www.bia.gov/frequently-asked-questions.

U.S. Department of Justice, Civil Rights Division. (2007). *Enforcement and outreach following the September 11 terrorist attacks*. Retrieved from www.usdoj.gov/crt/legalinfo/discrimupdate.html.

U.S. Department of State, Bureau of Consular Affairs. (2022). Adoption statistics. Retrieved from https://travel.state.gov/content/travel/en/Intercountry-Adoption/adopt_ref/adoption-statistics.html.

Usher, N. (2014). *Making news at the* New York Times. Ann Arbor: University of Michigan Press.

Van Nieuwerburgh, S. (2022). The remote work revolution: Impact on real estate values and the urban environment. *National Bureau of Economic Research*. Retrieved from www.nber.org/papers/w30662.

Varon, J. (2004). *Bringing the war home: The Weather Underground, the Red Army faction, and revolutionary violence in the sixties and seventies.* Berkeley: University of California Press.

Vars, F. E., & Bowen, W. G. (1998). Scholastic Aptitude Test scores, race, and academic performance in selective colleges and universities. In C. Jencks & M. Phillips (Eds.), *The Black-White test score gap* (pp. 457–79). Washington, DC: Brookings Institution Press.

Ventola, C. L. (2011). Direct-to-consumer pharmaceutical advertising: Therapeutic or toxic? *Pharmacy and Therapeutics*, 36(10), 669–74, 681–84.

Verba, S., et al. (2004). Political inequality: What do we know about it? In K. M. Neckerman (Ed.), *Social inequality* (pp. 635–66). New York: Sage.

Verdier, H. (2016). DTR: Define the relationship — Swipe right for Tinder's first podcast. *The Guardian*. Retrieved from www.theguardian.com/tv-and-radio/2016/dec/15/dtr-define-the-relationship-swipe-right-for-tinders-first-podcast.

Vespa, J., et al. (2013). America's families and living arrangements: 2012. Population characteristics. U.S. Census Bureau. Retrieved from www.census.gov/prod/2013pubs/p20-570.pdf.

Vestal, S. (2017, December 1). Rachel Dolezal remains unabashadly Rachel Dolezal. *The Spokesman-Review*. Retrieved from www.spokesman.com/stories/2017/dec/01/shawn-vestal-rachel-dolezal-remains-unabashedly-ra.

Virupaksha, H. G., et al. (2016). Suicide and suicidal behavior among transgender persons. *Indian Journal of Psychological Medicine*, 38(6), 505–9.

Voas, D., & Chaves, M. (2016). Is the United States a counterexample to the secularization thesis? *American Journal of Sociology, 121*(5), 1517–56.

Vogl, T., & Freese, J. (2020). Differential fertility makes society more conservative on family values. *Proceedings of the National Academy of Sciences of the United States of America, 117*(14), 7696–7701.

Wade, L. (2017). *American hookup: A new culture of sex on campus.* New York: Norton.

Wall, A. (2012). Gubernatorial electons, campaign costs, and winning governors. Council of State Governments. Retrieved from http://knowledgecenter.csg.org/kc /content/gubernatorial-elections-campaign-costs -and-winning-governors.

Waite, L., & Gallagher, M. (2000). *The case for marriage: Why married people are happier, healthier, and better off financially.* New York: Doubleday.

Wallerstein, J., et al. (2000). *The unexpected legacy of divorce.* New York: Hyperion.

Wang, W. (2012, February 16). The rise of intermarriage. Pew Research Center, Social and Demographic Trends. Retrieved from www.pewsocialtrends.org/2012/02/16 /the-rise-of-intermarriage.

Wang, X., et al. (2021). Adoption of delivery services in light of the COVID pandemic: Who and how long? *Transportation Research Part A: Policy and Practice.* Retrieved from www.sciencedirect.com/science/article /pii/S0965856421002676#ab005.

Ward, J. (2015). *Not gay: Sex between straight White men.* New York: NYU Press.

Warren, E. (2007). Unsafe at any rate. *Democracy: A Journal of Ideas, 5.* Retrieved from www.democracyjournal.org /article2.php?ID=6528&limit=0&limit2=1500&page=1.

Warren, E., & Tyagi, A. W. (2003). *The two-income trap: Why middle-class mothers and fathers are going broke.* New York: Basic Books.

Warren, J. W., & Twine, F. W. (1997). White Americans, the new minority? Non-Blacks and the ever-expanding boundaries of Whiteness. *Journal of Black Studies, 28*, 200–18.

Washington, E. (2008). Female socialization: How daughters affect their legislator fathers. *American Economic Review, 98*(1), 311–32.

Washington State Department of Health. (2020). Department of Health releases new COVID-19 data tied to occupation, industry. Retrieved from www.doh.wa.gov/Newsroom /Articles/ID/1255/Department-of-Health-releases-new -COVID-19-data-tied-to-occupation-industry.

Watts, D. (2003). *Six degrees: The science of a connected age.* New York: Norton.

Watts, D. J. (2011). *Everything is obvious:* Once you know the answer. New York: Currency.

Weber, M. (1946). *From Max Weber: Essays in sociology.* H. H. Gerth & C. W. Mills (Eds. & Trans.). New York: Oxford University Press.

Weber, M. (1968). *Economy and society: An outline of interpretive sociology.* G. Rothe & C. Wittich (Eds.). (E. Fischoff et al., Trans.). New York: Bedminster Press. (Original work published 1922.)

Weber, M. (2003). *The Protestant ethic and the spirit of capitalism.* Oxford: Blackwell. (Original work published 1904.)

Weber, M. (2004). *The vocation lectures: Science as a vocation, politics as a vocation.* D. S. Owen et al. (Eds.). Indianapolis: Hackett.

Wegener, B. (1991). Job mobility and social ties: Social resources, prior job, and status attainment. *American Sociological Review, 56*(1), 60–71.

Welsh, B. C., & Farrington, D. P. (2004). Surveillance for crime prevention in public space: Results and policy choices in Britain and America. *Criminology and Public Policy, 3*(3), 497–526.

West, C., & Zimmerman, D. H. (1975). Sex roles, interruptions and silences in conversation. In *Language and sex: Difference and dominance* (pp. 105–29). Stanford, CA: Stanford University Press.

West, C., & Zimmerman, D. (1987). Doing gender. *Gender & Society, 1*(2), 125–51.

West, L. A., et al. (2014). 65+ in the United States: 2010. U.S. Census Bureau. Retrieved from www.census.gov /content/dam/Census/library/publications/2014 /demo/p23-212.pdf.

Whitbeck, L. B., et al. (1991). Family economic hardship, parental support, and adolescent self-esteem. *Social Psychology Quarterly, 54*, 353–63.

Whitehead, A. L., & Perry, S. L. (2022). *Taking America back for God.* Oxford University Press. Retrieved from https://global.oup.com/academic/product/taking -america-back-for-god-9780197652572?lang=en&cc=us#.

White House. (2022). The U.S. economy and the global pandemic. Figure 3-3. Real GDP by country. 2022. Economic Report of the President. Retrieved from www.whitehouse .gov/wp-content/uploads/2022/04/Chapter-3-new.pdf

Widman, L., et al. (2016). Parent-adolescent sexual communication and adolescent safer sex behavior. *JAMA Pediatrics, 170*(1), 52–61. Retrieved from https://jamanetwork.com/journals/jamapediatrics /article-abstract/2468100.

Wilcox, W. B. (1999). *Religion and paternal involvement: Product of religious commitment or American convention?* Paper presented at the Annual Meeting of the American Sociological Association, Chicago.

Wilcox, W. B. (2004). *Soft patriarchs, new men: How Christianity shapes fathers and husbands.* Chicago: University of Chicago Press.

Wilensky, H. L. (1974). *The welfare state and equality: Structural and ideological roots of public expenditures.* Berkeley: University of California Press.

Wilkerson, I. (2020). *Caste: The origins of our discontents.* New York: Random House.

Williams, C. (1995). *Still a man's world: Men who do women's work.* Berkeley: University of California Press.

Williams, C. (2013). The glass escalator, revisited. *Gender & Society, 27*(5), 609–29.

Williams, S. (2005). Million dollar blocks. Public service announcement [Digital presentation]. Columbia University, Spatial Information Design Lab. Retrieved from www.spatialinformationdesignlab.org/movie.php?url =MEDIA/PSA_01.avi.

Willis, P. (1981). *Learning to labor: How working class kids get working class jobs.* New York: Columbia University Press. (Original work published 1977.)

Wilson, J. Q., & Kelling, G. L. (1982). Broken windows: The police and neighborhood safety. *The Atlantic Monthly, 249*(3), 29–37.

Wilson, W. J. (1978). *The declining significance of race: Blacks and changing American institutions.* Chicago: University of Chicago Press.

Wilson, W. J. (1987). *The truly disadvantaged: The inner city, the underclass, and public policy.* Chicago: University of Chicago Press.

Wilson, W. J. (1996). *When work disappears: The world of the new urban poor.* New York: Knopf.

Winant, H. (2001). *The world is a ghetto: Race and democracy since World War II.* New York: Basic Books.

Wing, W., et al. (1985). The Black/White mortality crossover: Investigation in a community-based study. *Journal of Gerontology, 40*(1), 78−84.

Wingfield, A. H. (2009). Racializing the glass escalator: Reconsidering men's experiences with women's work. *Gender & Society, 23*(1), 5−26.

Wirth, L. (1938). Urbanism as a way of life. *American Journal of Sociology, 44*(1), 1−24.

Witte, J. F. (1998). The Milwaukee voucher experiment. *Educational Evaluation and Policy Analysis, 20*(4), 229−51.

Woo, H., & Zajacova, A. (2016). Predictive strength of self-rated health for mortality risk among older adults in the United States: Does it differ by race and ethnicity? *SAGE Journals, 39*(7), 879−905.

World Bank. (2002). Global partnership to eliminate riverblindness. Retrieved from www.worldbank.org/afr/gper.

World Bank. (2019). Indicators: Age dependency ratio (% of working-age population). Retrieved from https://data.worldbank.org/indicator/SP.POP.DPND?most_recent_value_desc=true.

World Bank. (2020a). CO_2 emissions (metrics tons per capita). Retrieved from https://data.worldbank.org/indicator/EN.ATM.CO2E.PC?most_recent_value_desc=false.

World Bank. (2020b). Sex ratio at birth. Retrieved from https://data.worldbank.org/indicator/SP.POP.BRTH.MF?end=2020&start=2020&view=map.

World Health Organization. (2019). Poliomyelitis: Key facts. Retrieved from www.who.int/news-room/factsheets/detail/poliomyelitis.

World Health Organization. (2022). HIV: Global situation and trends. Retrieved from www.who.int/data/gho/data/themes/hiv-aids.

World Health Organization. (2023). Life expectancy at birth (years). Retrieved from www.who.int/data/gho/data/indicators/indicator-details/GHO/life-expectancy-at-birth-(years).

World Inequality Lab. (2022). World Inequality Report 2022. Retrieved from https://wir2022.wid.world/chapter-4.

World Inequality Report (2022). Executive summary. Retrieved from https://wir2022.wid.world/executive-summary.

World Population Review. (2022). Median income by country. Retrieved from https://worldpopulationreview.com/country-rankings/median-income-by-country.

Worldometer. (2022). Life expectancy of the world population. Retrieved from www.worldometers.info/demographics/life-expectancy.

Wuthnow, R. (1998). *Loose connections: Joining together in America's fragmented communities.* Cambridge, MA: Harvard University Press.

Wyler, G. (2014, May 6). NYC's newest megachurch is more popular than Jesus. *Vice.* Retrieved from www.vice.com/en_us/article/8gd8jp/hillsong-nyc-more-popular-than-jesus.

Yano, Y., et al. (2017). Racial differences in associations of blood pressure components in young adulthood with incident cardiovascular disease by middle age. *JAMA Cardiology, 2*(4), 381−89.

Yavorsky, J. E., et al. (2015). The production of inequality: The gender division of labor across the transition to parenthood. *Journal of Marriage and the Family, 77*(3), 662−79.

Young, M. P. (2002). Confessional protest: The religious birth of U.S. national social movements. *American Sociological Review, 67,* 660−88.

Zelizer, V. A. (2005). *The purchase of intimacy.* Princeton, NJ: Princeton University Press.

Zenith USA. (2018). Top 30 global media owners 2017. Retrieved from www.zenithusa.com/top-30-global-media-owners-2017.

Zernike, K. (2006, April 23). College, my way. *The New York Times.* Retrieved from www.nytimes.com/2006/04/23/education/edlife/zernike.html.

Zill, N. (1988). Behavior, achievement, and health problems among children in stepfamilies: Findings from a national survey of child health. In E. M. Hetherington & J. Arasteh (Eds.), *Impact of divorce, single parenting and stepparenting in children* (pp. 325−68). Hillsdale, NJ: Erlbaum.

Zill, N., et al. (1991). *The life circumstances and development of children in welfare families: A profile based on national survey data.* Washington, DC: Child Trends.

Zimbardo, P. (1971). *Stanford prison experiment: A simulation study of the psychology of imprisonment conducted at Stanford University.* Retrieved from www.prisonexp.org.

Zimbardo, P. (2007). *The Lucifer effect: Understanding how good people turn evil.* New York: Random House.

Zimbardo, P. (2018). Philip Zimbardo's response to recent criticisms of the Stanford Prison Experiment. Retrieved from www.prisonexp.org/response.

Zimmer, R. W., & Toma, E. F. (2000). Peer effects in private and public schools across countries. *Journal of Policy Analysis and Management, 19*(1), 75−92.

Zimmerman, D. H., & West, C. (1975). Sex roles, interruptions and silences in conversation. In B. Thorned & N. Henley (Eds.), *Language and sex: Difference and dominance* (pp. 105−29). Rowley, MA: Newbury House.

Zuckerman, P. (2009). Atheism, secularity, and well-being: How the findings of social science counter negative stereotypes and assumptions. *Sociology Compass, 3*(6), 949−71.

Zukin, S. (2003). *Point of purchase: How shopping changed American culture.* New York: Routledge.

Zurio, G. A., et al. (2020). World Christianity and mission 2021: Questions about the future. *International Bulletin of Mission Research, 45*(1), 15−25. Retrieved from https://journals.sagepub.com/doi/full/10.1177/2396939320966220.

Zwick, R. (2002). *Fair game? The use of standardized admissions tests in higher education.* New York: Routledge.

Zwick, R., & Sklar, J. C. (2005). Predicting college grades and degree completion using high school grades and SAT scores: The role of student ethnicity and first language. *American Educational Research Journal, 42*(3), 439−65.

Credits

TEXT

CHAPTER 8: Jackson, Elliot. 2017. "'Have You Ever Reconsidered Being Transgender?' Answer by Elliot Jackson," Quora. com. Last modified September 30, 2017. https://www.quora.com /Have-you-ever-reconsidered-being-transgender. Reprinted by permission of the author.

FIGURES AND TABLES

CHAPTER 2: Figure 2.3: Used with permission of Cengage Learning, from Babbie, Earl R. 2007. *The Practice of Social Research*. Belmont, CA: Thomson Wadworth; permission conveyed through Copyright Clearance Center, Inc.

CHAPTER 5: Figure 5.3: Originally from Asch, S.E. 1956. "Studies of independence and conformity: I. A minority of one against a unanimous majority." *Psychological Monographs* 70, no. 9: 1-70. https://doi.org/10.1037/h0093718. **Figures 5.5 and 5.6:** Used with permission of University of Chicago Press, from Bearman, Peter S., James Moody, and Katherine Stovel. 2004. "Chains of affection: The structure of adolescent romantic and sexual networks." *American Journal of Sociology* 110, no. 1: 44-91; permission conveyed through Copyright Clearance Center, Inc.

CHAPTER 7: Figure 7.1: From *World Inequality Report 2022*, coordinated by Lucas Chancel, Thomas Piketty, Emmanuel Saez, Gabriel Zucman, with a Forward by Esther Duflo and Abhijit Banerjee, Cambridge, Mass.: The Belknap Press of Harvard University Press, Copyright © 2022 by the World Inequality Lab. Used by permission. All rights reserved. **Table 7.1:** From Hughes, Bradley T., Sanjay Srivastava, Magdalena Leszko, and David M. Condon. 2022. "Occupational Prestige: The Status Component of Socioeconomic Status." PsyArXiv. September 28. https://doi.org/10.31234/osf.io/6qgxv. This article is available under a Creative Commons Attribution 4.0 International license. https://creativecommons.org/licenses /by/4.0/. **Table 7.2:** From Featherman, David L., and Robert Mason Hauser. 1978. *Opportunity and Change*. New York: Academic Press. Reprinted by permission of the authors.

CHAPTER 9: Table 9.1: From Gordon, Milton M. 1964. *Assimilation in American Life: The Role of Race, Religion, and National Origins*. New York: Oxford University Press. Copyright © 1964. Reproduced with permission of the Licensor through PLSclear.

CHAPTER 10: Figure 10.1: Figure "Work-Family Living Arrangements of Children, 1960 & 2012" by Philip Cohen. Reprinted by permission of the author.

PHOTOS

FRONTMATTER: p. ix: AP Photo/Paul Sakuma; **p. x:** CBS/ Photofest; p. xi: Emmanuel Dunand/AFP/Getty Images; **p. xii:** Ammentorp Photography/Alamy Stock Photo; **p. xiii:** AP Photo/Jacquelyn Martin; **p. xiv:** imageBROKER/Alamy Stock Photo; **p. xv:** Bettmann//Getty Images; **p. xvi:** John Birdsall/ Alamy Stock Photo

CHAPTER 1: Page 5: Gjon Mili/The LIFE Picture Collection/ Shutterstock; **p. 7:** Miramax/Photofest; **p. 10 (left):** AP Photo/ Paul Sakuma; **p. 10 (right):** Sunday Times/Moeletsi Mabe/ Shutterstock; **p. 13:** Courtesy of Erica Rothman/Nightlight Productions and Dalton Conley; **p. 15 (left):** Spencer Platt/ Getty Images; **p. 15 (right):** Mario Tama/Getty Images; **p. 18 (left to right):** SuperStock, GRANGER, and Sarin Images/ GRANGER; **p. 19 (left to right):** Private Collection/Bridgeman Images, GRANGER, and Temple de la Religion de l'Humanite, Paris, France/Bridgeman Images; **p. 20 (left to right):** George Rinhart/Corbis via Getty Images and Bettmann/Getty Images; **p. 21 (left to right):** Bibliotheque Nationale, Paris, France/ Bridgeman Images, GRANGER, Bentley Historical Library/ The University of Michigan, and Underwood Archives/UIG/ Shutterstock; **p. 22 (left to right):** GRANGER and ullstein bild/GRANGER; **p. 23 (left to right):** GRANGER, GRANGER, Sarin Images/GRANGER, and Pictorial Parade/Getty Images; **p. 24 (left to right):** From the Collections of the University of Pennsylvania Archives, Robert W Kelley/The LIFE Picture Collection/Shutterstock, Fritz Goro/The LIFE Picture Collection/ Shutterstock, Sarah Lee/eyevine/Redux, and Carl Wagner/ KRT/Newscom; **p. 25 (left to right):** Jeff Morgan 14/Alamy Stock Photo, Bob Pepping/KRT/Newscom, Gado Images/ Alamy Stock Photo, Courtesy of Duncan Watts, Jason Jones/ Lake Shore Photography, Amir Levy/The New York Times/ Redux, and Dan Komoda; **p. 29:** George Rinhart/Corbis via Getty Images; **p. 31:** Bettmann/Getty Images; **p. 34:** Bob Krist/

Getty Images; **p. 35:** Fox Photos/Getty Images; **p. 37:** Courtesy of Erica Rothman/Nightlight Productions and Dalton Conley; **p. 38:** Visions of America LLC / Alamy Stock Photo.

CHAPTER 2: Page 48: Courtesy of Erica Rothman/Nightlight Productions and Dalton Conley; **p. 53:** AP Photo/Nati Harnik; **p. 63:** Alfred Eisenstaedt/The LIFE Picture Collection/Shutterstock; **p. 64:** AP Photo/Julie Jacobson; **p. 65:** Hansel Mieth/The LIFE Picture Collection/Shutterstock; **p. 66:** dpa picture alliance/Alamy Stock Photo; **p. 67:** Jack Guez/AFP/Getty Images; **p. 69:** Courtesy of Erica Rothman/Nightlight Productions and Dalton Conley; **p. 71:** Ovie Carter; **p. 75:** Education & Exploration 3/Alamy Stock Photo.

CHAPTER 3: Page 82: Monica Schipper/Getty Images for American Express; **p. 84 (top left):** Efrain Padro/Alamy Stock Photo; **p. 84 (top right):** Orhan Cam/Shutterstock; **p. 84 (bottom left):** JLImages/Alamy Stock Photo; **p. 84 (bottom right):** Werner Forman/Universal Images Group/Getty Images; **p. 86 (top):** GRANGER; **p. 86 (bottom):** RMN-Grand Palais/Art Resource, NY; **p. 88 (left):** Artiom Photo/Shutterstock; **p. 88 (center):** Graham Prentice/Alamy Stock Photo; **p. 88 (right):** Rudy Sulgan/Getty Images; **p. 93:** Library of Congress; **p. 94:** Klaas Slot/Shutterstock; **p. 96 (left):** dpa picture alliance/Alamy Stock Photo; **p. 96 (right):** Christian Kober/Robert Harding World Image; **p. 97:** Everett Collection Historical/Alamy Stock Photo; **p. 99 (left):** Universal History Archive/UIG via Getty Images; **p. 99 (center):** Everett Collection; **p. 99 (right):** CNN via Getty Images; **p. 100:** AP Photo/Bill Hudson; **p. 103:** Cyberstock/Alamy Stock Photo; **p. 106:** Bettmann/Getty Images; **p. 107 (top):** CBS/Photofest; **p. 107 (bottom):** Eric Liebowitz/©FX/Courtesy Everett Collection; **p. 109:** Kypros/Shutterstock; **p. 110 (left):** AP Photo/Dave Martin; **p. 110 (right):** Chris Graythen/Getty Images; **p. 112:** Chronicle/Alamy Stock Photo; **p. 114:** Courtesy of Erica Rothman/Nightlight Productions and Dalton Conley; **p. 116:** Marmaduke St. John/Alamy Stock Photo; **p. 117 (left):** Adbusters; **p. 117 (right):** Adbusters; **p. 118:** Theo Wargo/Getty Images.

CHAPTER 4: Page 127: Jose Luis Pelaez/Iconica/Getty Images; **p. 130:** David Grossman/Alamy Stock Photo; **p. 132:** Manuel Ruiz Díaz de Rivera/Alamy Stock Photo; **p. 134:** Red Images LLC/Alamy Stock Photo; **p. 137:** Courtesy of Erica Rothman/Nightlight Productions and Dalton Conley; **p. 138:** Courtesy of Erica Rothman/Nightlight Productions and Dalton Conley; **p. 142:** Scott Olson/Getty Images; **p. 144 (top left):** AP Photo/Chris Pizzello; **p. 144 (top right):** John Ricard/FilmMagic/Getty Images; **p. 144 (bottom):** Emmanuel Dunand/AFP/Getty Images; **p. 145:** Mark Peterson/Redux; **p. 146:** Courtesy of Erica Rothman/Nightlight Productions and Dalton Conley; **p. 150:** Kevork Djansezian/REUTERS/Newscom; **p. 152 (left):** AP Photo/Patrick Semansky; **p. 152 (right):** © CNAC/MNAM/Dist. RMN-Grand Palais/Art Resource, NY. © 2018 The Pollock-Krasner Foundation/Artists Rights Society (ARS), New York; **p. 155 (top left):** Michael Dwyer/Alamy Stock Photo; **p. 155 (top right):** Eric Vidal/AFP/Getty Images; **p. 155 (bottom):** STEPHANIE MCGEHEE/REUTERS/Newscom; **p. 156:** 20th Century Fox/Photofest; **p. 159:** Piotr Redlinski/The New York Times/Redux; **p. 161:** AP Photo/Steve Meyers.

CHAPTER 5: Page 166: Kim Hong-Ji/REUTERS/Newscom; **p. 168:** Mark Leong/Redux; **p. 171:** Cavan Images/Alamy Stock Photo; **p. 173 (left):** MBI/Alamy Stock Photo; **p. 173 (right):** PYMCA/UIG via Getty Images; **p. 174:** VARLEY/SIPA/Newscom; **p. 179:** redsnapper/Alamy Stock Photo; **p. 181:** Courtesy of Erica Rothman/Nightlight Productions and Dalton Conley; **p. 182:** Courtesy of Erica Rothman/Nightlight Productions and Dalton Conley; **p. 183:** Lee Celano/The New York Times/Redux; **p. 184:** Richard Perry/The New York Times/Redux; **p. 185:** Brandon Pollock/The Courier via AP; **p. 186:** Doug Pensinger/Getty Images for AFL; **p. 187:** Courtesy of Erica Rothman/Nightlight Productions and Dalton Conley; **p. 188:** AP Photo/The Ledger Independent, Terry Prather; **p. 189:** AP Photo/Patriot-News, Paul Chaplin; **p. 191:** Ammentorp Photography/Alamy Stock Photo; **p. 199:** keith morris/Alamy Stock Photo.

CHAPTER 6: Page 204: Courtesy of Erica Rothman/Nightlight Productions and Dalton Conley; **p. 208 (left):** © British Library Board/Robana/Art Resource, NY; **p. 208 (right):** Bettmann/Getty Images; **p. 209:** AP Photo/David J. Phillip; **p. 210 (left):** Bettmann/Getty Images; **p. 210 (right):** Bettmann/Getty Images; **p. 211:** Three Lions/Getty Images; **p. 212:** AP Photo/Greg Wahl-Stephens; **p. 215:** Pacific Press Service/GRANGER — All rights reserved; **p. 219 (top left):** Jack Hollingsworth/Corbis; **p. 219 (top right):** Luis Alvarez/Getty Images; **p. 219 (bottom left):** Seth Wenig/REUTERS/Newscom; **p. 219 (bottom center):** Kathy deWitt/Alamy Stock Photo; **p. 219 (bottom right):** Joseph Scherschel/The LIFE Picture Collection/Shutterstock; **p. 222:** Ruth Fremson/The New York Times/Redux; **p. 223:** Allied Artists/Photofest; **p. 224:** Steve Dietls/Coup D'Etat/Sandbar/Abandon/Ifc/Kobal/Shutterstock; **p. 225:** AP Photo; **p. 228:** Courtesy of Erica Rothman/Nightlight Productions and Dalton Conley; **p. 231:** Timothy A. Clary/AFP/Getty Images; **p. 237:** Courtesy of Erica Rothman/Nightlight Productions and Dalton Conley; **p. 238:** Q. Sakamaki/Redux; **p. 240:** Chronicle/Alamy Stock Photo; **p. 242:** Bettmann/Getty Images; **p. 245:** Brant Ward/San Francisco Chronicle/Polaris; **p. 246:** Courtesy of Erica Rothman/Nightlight Productions and Dalton Conley.

CHAPTER 7: Page 259: Courtesy of Erica Rothman/Nightlight Productions and Dalton Conley; **p. 261:** Photo12/UIG via Getty Images; **p. 263:** AP Photo/Themba Hadebe; **p. 266:** © Ted Streshinsky/CORBIS/Corbis via Getty Images; **p. 267:** Ben Stechschulte/Redux; **p. 269:** Will Burgess/REUTERS/Newscom; **p. 271:** Farooq Naeem/AFP/Getty Images; **p. 272:** AP Photo/Steve Coleman; **p. 275:** B.O'Kane/Alamy Stock Photo; **p. 278:** AP Photo/Jacquelyn Martin; **p. 284:** Courtesy of Erica Rothman/Nightlight Productions and Dalton Conley; **p. 285:** Q. Sakamaki/Redux; **p. 288:** Katherine Taylor/The New York Times/Redux; **p. 289:** GRANGER.

CHAPTER 8: Page 294: © Doug Hoke/The Oklahoman/USA TODAY NETWORK; **p. 297:** Dotted Yeti/Shutterstock; **p. 299:** FO Travel/Alamy Stock Photo; **p. 300:** Courtesy of Erica Rothman/Nightlight Productions and Dalton Conley; **p. 303:** Marvin Joseph/The Washington Post via Getty Images; **p. 304 (left):** Erin Baiano/The New York Times/Redux; **p. 304 (right):** PYMCA/UIG via Getty Images; **p. 310:** The Advertising Archives; **p. 312:** AP Photo/Noah Berger; **p. 314:** Courtesy of Erica Rothman/

Nightlight Productions and Dalton Conley; **p. 316:** ClassicStock/ Alamy Stock Photo; **p. 319:** Associated Press; **p. 320:** Library of Congress; **p. 322:** AP Photo/Greg Smith; **p. 324:** Ashmolean Museum, University of Oxford, UK/Bridgeman Images; **p. 326:** University Archives and Records Center, University of Pennsylvania; **p. 327:** Jason Szenes/UPI/Newscom; **p. 328:** imageBROKER/Alamy Stock Photo; **p. 331:** Courtesy of Erica Rothman/ Nightlight Productions and Dalton Conley.

CHAPTER 9: Page 344: The Ohio State University Billy Ireland Cartoon Library & Museum; **p. 347:** Brad Rickerby/ REUTERS/Newscom; **p. 350:** SPL/Science Source; **p. 351:** © Hulton-Deutsch Collection/CORBIS/Corbis via Getty Images; **p. 352:** Courtesy of Dr. Bhagat Singh Thind Spiritual Science Foundation; **p. 353:** Keith Bedford/The New York Times/ Redux; **p. 355:** Patsy Lynch/MediaPunch/Alamy Stock Photo; **p. 356:** Simon Rawles/Alamy Stock Photo; **p. 357:** Courtesy of Erica Rothman/Nightlight Productions and Dalton Conley; **p. 358:** REUTERS/Alamy Stock Photo; **p. 360:** Ralph Orlowski/ Getty Images; **p. 365:** Library of Congress; **p. 370:** National Archives; **p. 371:** Bettmann//Getty Images; **p. 372:** Bettmann/ Getty Images; **p. 374:** Reuters/Newscom; **p. 378:** Jonathan Ernst/Reuters/Newscom; **p. 379:** Mario Villafuerte; **p. 381:** Jim West/agefotostock; **p. 385:** AP Photo/The Sun Herald, Sean Loftin; **p. 389:** Courtesy of Erica Rothman/Nightlight Productions and Dalton Conley; **p. 390:** Courtesy of Erica Rothman/Nightlight Productions and Dalton Conley; **p. 391:** Courtesy of Erica Rothman/Nightlight Productions and Dalton Conley.

CHAPTER 10: Page 400: Francis Miller/The LIFE Picture Collection/Shutterstock; **p. 403 (top):** Jenny Acheson/ Getty Images; **p. 403 (middle):** Courtesy of Tami Blumenfield; **p. 403 (bottom):** Jenny Matthews/Alamy Stock Photo; **p. 408:** GRANGER; **p. 410:** Louis Edmond Pomey/Fine Art Photographic/Getty Images; **p. 411:** Bert Hardy/Getty Images; **p. 415:** Everett Collection/Newscom; **p. 417:** Courtesy of Erica Rothman/Nightlight Productions and Dalton Conley; **p. 419:** Maskot/Getty Images; **p. 422:** Ozier Muhammad/ The New York Times/Redux; **p. 426:** AP Photo/Morry Gash; **p. 428:** Stephan Gladieu/Getty Images; **p. 432:** Courtesy of Erica Rothman/Nightlight Productions and Dalton Conley; **p. 434:** John Birdsall/Alamy Stock Photo; **p. 437:** Alex Wong/ Getty Images; **p. 439:** Amanda Cowan/The Columbian via AP.

Index

African cultures, polygamy and, 400
African immigrants, 349, 382
Afro-Caribbeans, 382
Afrocentric worldview, 422
Age of Exploration, 83–84, 350
aging, 234; "aging in place," 180–81; parenting and, 397–98; sex and, 335–36, 338; sexuality and, 335–36, 338
Alaskan Natives, *388–89*
Alger, Horatio Jr., 291, *291*
Alien Land Act, 366–67
Allen, Frank, 242
Alphabet, 113–14, 115
Altria, 15–16, *15*
altruistic suicide, *214*, 215–16, *215*
"ambiguous" genitalia, surgical reassignment and, 299–300
American Community Survey, 76
"American dream," trope of, 89
American Indians, *388–89*
American Psychiatric Association (APA), 328–29, 331
American Psychological Association, 328–29
American Revolution, 381
American Sociological Association, 72
American sociology, 27–30
Amish, 188–89, *188*, *189*
analysis, *51*, *60*; units of, 77
Anderson, Elijah, 88, 378
androgyny: definition of, 300–301; names and, 306–7
Angel, *107*
Anglos, 379. *See also* Whites
anomie, 26, 216–17, 235, 236
anomie suicide, *214*, 216–17
anonymity, social media and, 157
anthropology, 38–39
anti-Black ideology, 362
anti-immigration sentiment, 345, *346*
anti-isomorphism, 197
anti-Japanese stereotypes, World War II and, 108–9
antimiscegenation laws, 399–400, 434
anti-Muslim hate crimes, 359, 360
anti-Semitism, 354
apartheid, 91, 176, 377, 400
Apple, 114

application, *60*
Arab Americans, 359, 360
Arabian Peninsula, 385
Arabs, 359, 385; Christian, 359; stereotypes and, 360, 385
aristocracy, 196
Aristotle, 350
Arizona, Native Americans in, 380
Arnaz, Desi, *107*
Arnold, Matthew, 85–87
Aronson, Joshua, 365
artificial intelligence, 102, 126
ascending vertical social mobility, 282
Asch, Solomon, 175–76, *175*
Asch test, 175–76, *175*
ascribed status, 144
asexuality, 331
Asia, 287–88. *See also specific countries; specific countries and regions*
Asian American families, 424–25
Asian American men, outmarriage and, 435
Asian American women, outmarriage and, 434–35
Asian immigrant families, children as "language brokers" in, 425
Asian immigrants, 424–25
Asians/Asian Americans, 345, 384–85, *388–89*; growing population of, 389, 390, 391; high average socioeconomic status of, 384; as "model minority," 385, 391; multi-generational households and, 424–25; rates of outmarriage, 434–35; stereotypes and, 108–9; symbolic ethnicity and, 348; unemployment and, 384
assets, 264
assimilation, 367, 379; attitude reception, 368; behavior reception, 368; Black immigrants and, 382; civic, 368; cultural, 368; Gordon's stages of, 368t; identification, 368; Irish immigrants and, 345; marital, 368; vs. pluralism, 369–71; stages of, 368t;

straight-line assimilation, 368; structural, 368
assisted reproductive technology (ART), 406
association, 51. *See also* correlation
attention-deficit hyperactivity disorder (ADHD), 138–39
attitude reception assimilation, 368
"audience studies," 101
audit studies, 363
Australia, Aboriginals in, *271*, 401–2
authoritarianism, 104
authority: in Latinx families, 424; masculinity and, 314
Baartman, Saartje, *112*
"baby boom," 411
baby names, gender and, 306–7
backstage arenas, 149, 160
"bacon theory," 418
Baek, Bliss, *159*
Bailar, Schuyler, *305*
Ball, Lucille, *107*
Barber, Kristen, 303, 306
Barth, Ernest, 369
"bathroom bills," 296, *296*
Baumann, Shyon, 306
Beane, Billy, 197
Bearman, Peter, 190, 194
Beauvoir, Simone de, 321
Becker, Howard, 221–23
Bedhraj Mata, 302
behavior reception assimilation, 368
Belgium, 376–77
belief systems, 83, 89. *See also* values
Belizeans, 382
Belmont Report, 75
Benedict, Ruth, 92
Benite, Zvi Ben-Dor, 41
Bentham, Jeremy, 241–42
Berbrier, Mitch, 388
Berk, Sarah Fenstermaker, 414
Bernard, Jessie, 414–15
Bernier, François, 351
Beyonce, 118, *118*, 144
Biden, Joe, 185–86
Biden administration, locker room and bathroom policy and, 305
"the Big Sort," 396

Coontz, Stephanie, 407–8, 412
Copernicus, Nicolaus, 90
corporate boards, 196
corporate censorship, 114
corporate crime, 231–32
corporate culture, 195
"corrective" genital surgery, 299–300
correlation, *51*; vs. causation, 51–55; charge of spuriousness and, *54*; definition of, 51
correspondence studies, 363
Cortés, Hernán, *86*
Coser, Lewis, 32, 267
counterculture, 96–97, *97*
Counter-Reformation, 36, 38
Couric, Katie, 81
covenants, racially restrictive, 366
COVID-19 pandemic: crime rates and, 234–35; domestic abuse and, 420; mask mandates, 205–6; mask-wearing and, 139, 154, 205–6; socialization affected by, 139; upper class and, 257–58
Craft, Ellen, 377–78
Cranston, Alan, 158
credentialism, 11–13, *12t*
Crenshaw, Kimberlé Williams, 324
crime, 230–35; corporate, 231–32; crime rate, 232–35, *232*, *234*; definition of, 205; deterrence theory of crime control, 235–36; internet and, 160; recidivism and, 236–37; street crime, 230–31; white-collar, 231–32; "zero tolerance" policies and, 229
crime rates: COVID-19 pandemic and, 234–35; drop in, 233–34, 237; explanations for falling, 233–34; interpreting, 232–35, *232*, *234*; police involvement and, 237; rise with COVID-19 pandemic, 234–35
crime reduction, 230–31, 235–47; deterrence theory of crime control, 235–36; recidivism and, 236–37
criminalization, policing and, 204
criminal justice system, 242; executions by race, *247*;

mechanical social sanctions and, 211–13; organic social sanctions and, 211–13; prisons and, *238*, *242*, *244–45*, *245*; punishment and, 242; rehabilitation and, 242; segregation and, 375–76; size of U.S. prison population, *243*; socialization and, 133
criminal records, 227–28; African Americans and, 227–28; race and, 363; stigma of, 227–28, 237, 363; Whites and, 227–28
criminals, rehabilitation of, 212
Crisis magazine, *29*
critical race theory, 356–57, *357*, 387
cross-disciplinary studies, 48
cross-race gentrification, 59
cross-sectional surveys, 62–63
crowdfunding, *185*, *186*
Cruz, Ted, *357*
cryptocurrencies, 165–66, *166*
Cuba, 383–84
Cubans, 382, *382*, 383–84
cult of domesticity, 410, *410*; African Americans and, 422; definition of, 410; disappearance of, 412; effects of, 414; lingering on of, 415; questioning of, 414; race and, 422
cultural anthropology, 39
cultural assimilation, 368
cultural differences, 84–85, *84*
cultural effects, 89–90
cultural lag, 87
cultural norms, love life and, 399–401
cultural production, media and, 102
cultural racism, in Germany, *362*
cultural relativism, definition of, 92
Cultural Revolution, in China, 255
cultural scripts, 93
cultural sociology, 26, 27
culture: alternative practices and, 84–85; as aspiration to ideal forms, 86–87; belief systems, 83; class and, 88; cultural scripts, 93; culture jams, 117–18; defining, 83–87; gender and, 88; high vs. low, 84–85; ideality and, 85–87;

ideologies, 83; material vs. nonmaterial, 87–99; media and, 80–123; vs. nature, 83–84; race and, 88; racism and, 362; social structures and, 98–99; studying, 92–93; symbolic, 93–95; symbolic representations, 83; technology and, 83
culture jamming, 117–18, *117*, 120
culture lag, technology and, 87
culture shock, 88
culture war, 97
Currie, Dawn, 112
Dahrendorf, Ralf, 32, 267
Dakota Access Pipeline, protests against, 381
Dalits (Untouchables), 272, 273
Damiens, Robert-François, 239, 240, *240*, 241
Daminger, Allison, 317
Damore, James, 307–8
"dark web," 165
Darwin, Charles, 49, 353
data: data collection, 59–68, 77; data processing, *60*; politics and, 75–76
dating apps, 335, 393
David, Emmanuel, 312
Davis, F. James, 355
Davis, Kingsley, 267
day care. *See* child care
Dayton, Mark, 359
death penalty, 211–13, 243; African Americans and, 246–47; DNA testing and, 247; Latinx and, 247; opponents of, 211–12; race and, 246–47, *247*; Whites and, 246–47
death row, 246–47
"deceptive distinctions," 306, 309
Declaration of Independence, 268
deductive approach, 50, *51*
Defense of Marriage Act (DOMA), 436
"define-the-relationship" (DTR) conversation, 335
Delaware, abolition of death penalty in, 247
demographics, socialization and, 134–35
Denton, Nancy, 374
DeParle, Jason, 135

268−69; of outcome, 270−71 (*see also* equal opportunity); social equality, 263; standards of, 267−71

equal opportunity, 89

equal pay laws, 317

equity inequality, 366, *367*

erectile dysfunction (ED), 336

Erikson, Kai, 232

essentialism, 298−99, 309, 362, 369

Essman, Elliott, 258

estate system, 271, 272

Ethereum, 165, *166*

ethical standards, professional associations and, 72

ethics of social research, 68−75

Ethiopia, 407

ethnicity, 27; cultural, 347; cultural theories of, 355; definition of, 347; "ethnic honor," 349; ethnic identification, 369; ethnic ties, 369; fluidity of, 369; Hispanics and, 383; Irish descent and, 346−47; Latinxs and, 383, *383*; planar, 347; power and, 347; vs. race, 347, *383*; social mobility and, 253−54; studies of, 27; symbolic, 348−49, *349*

ethnocentrism, 85, 351

ethnography, 48, 70

ethnomethodology, 155−57, 322−23

Europe: development of, 285−88; social mobility in medieval, 254. *See also specific countries*

European Commission, 198

European Union (EU), 198−99. *See also* Europe; *specific countries*

Evans, Phyllis, *64*

evolutionary biology, 40

examining, 241, 242

exchange mobility, 283

executions, 239, 240; collective vengeance and, 211−12; by race, *247*; in Texas, 212−13. *See also* capital punishment

exogamy, 400, 434

experimentation, 67−68

experimenter effects, 68

exploitation, 275, 350

extended family, definition of, 404

extractivism, 285

extrafamilial female networks, African American families and, 421, *421*, 422

"eye for an eye" mentality, 240

"eyes and ears of the street," 207, 394

face, 149−51; saving, 150−51

Facebook, 102, 103, 113−14, 187

face-to-face interaction, 172−73, 174, 175; civic engagement and, 185−86; decline of, 183−90

factory work, *411*. *See also* labor

facts, 33

faculty, tenured vs. adjunct, 277, *277*

"fair families," 419−20

Fair Sentencing Act, 364

family/families, *134*, 396−441; adoption and, 406−7; African American, 421−23, *422*; after World War II, 410−12; alternative concepts of, 422; Asian American, 424−25; birth order and, *396*; blended, 405−6, 433; child-free, 406; expanded notion of, 422−23; extended, 404; family forms and changes, 399−406, *403*; family life, 27; feminist "rethinking of the," 414−15; gay, lesbian, and transgender, 436−39, *439*; as "gender factory," 414; immigrant, 435−36; inequality within, 428−30; intrafamily stratification, 428−30; Latinx, 423−24; male breadwinner, 401−4, 409−10; modernity and, 407; multiracial, 434−35, *434*; Na people, 402, 404; nuclear, 401−4, 422−23, 424; nuclear family, 407, 410−11; pecking order and, 428−30; premodern, 408−9, *408*; as primary groups, 175; public/private divide and, 407; single motherhood, 406, 425−28, *426*, *428*; single-parent, 405−6, 407; socialization and, 134−38; traditional, 401−4, 407, 422−23, 424, 439; in the Western world, 404−7;

White masculinist ideal of, 324; work and, *405*. *See also* family structure

family policy, 437−38

family separations, by ICE, 246

family structure: child rearing and, 402; class and, 407, 410−11; consumption and, 409; division of labor and, 409−10; divorce and, 404−5, 406; "fair families," 419−20; functionalist argument and, 402; gender revolution in, 412−13, *413*; gender roles and, 414; Industrial Revolution and, 409; Japanese Americans and, 415; male breadwinner family, 404; Munduruku villagers, *403*; Munduruku villagers and, 402; Na people, *403*; power and, 414−15, 418; public/private divide and, 409; race and, 407, 410−11; reproduction of gender inequality in, 414; spending of money and, 415; "subtle revolution" in, 412; tribal societies and, 401−2; women and, 412−13, 414−15; in Zambia, *403*, 404

"family values," 406

family violence, 420−21

Fascism, 91

fascism, 36, 38

fatalistic suicide, 217

Fausto-Sterling, Anne, 299−300

favelas, *250−51*

FBI (Federal Bureau of Investigation), 231

Federal Housing Administration (FHA), 375

federal prison reform, under Trump, 243

fellatio, 326

female orgasm, 298

female subordination: capitalism and, 321−22; explanations for, 320−21

femininity, 146−48, 300−301; names and, 306−7; performance of, 322−23; psychoanalytic theories and, 319

feminism, 325; definition of, 307; feminist consciousness, 414;

gender relations, 40

gender revolution, in work and family, 412–13, *413*

gender roles, 338; childhood and, 145–46, *145*; definition of, 145; family structure and, 414; in Latinx families, 424; peers and, 146–47; social constructionism and, 322–23; socialization and, 145–46, *145*; theories of socialization and, 145; toys and, *145*

gender socialization, 308–9; gender differences and, 308–10; psychoanalytic theories and, 319

gender stereotypes, tokenism and, 314

general deterrence, 235–36

generalizability, 58, 65

generalized other, 28, *131*, 132

General Social Survey (GSS), 62–63

genocide, 376–77

gentrification, 59

geography, development and, 286

Germany, cultural racism in, *362*

Gerson, Kathleen, 412

gestures, 151–52

ghettos, 373–74. *See also* residential segregation

Gilbert, Dennis, 258

Gilligan, Carol, 309

Giuliani, Rudy, 115, 229

given gestures, 152

given-off gestures, 152

glass ceilings, 313–15, *314*

glass escalators, 315–16

Glassner, Barry, 110

Glazer, Nathan, 369

global inequality, 285–88

globalization, 39, 285

Goel, Sharad, 104

Goffman, Erving, 33, 148–52, 157; on acceptance, 378; dramaturgical theory and, 322–23; on masculinity, 303; total institutions and, 238–39, *238*

Goldman Sachs, 280, 281

Goldstein, Daniel, 104

Google, 113–14, 115–16, *116*, 198; gender diversity at, 307–8; Google+, 114; Google

Classroom, 115–16; Google Docs, 115; women at, 308

Gordon, Milton, 368, 368t

goth culture, 95–96, *95*

Gramsci, Antonio, 91, 92, 108

Granovetter, Mark, 178, 179, 196

Great Britain. *See* United Kingdom

Great Depression, 411

"great man" histories, 37

Great Migration, 27, 346, 374, 377

Great Recession, 165, 310, 365–66

Greece, ancient, 326, *326*, 328, 350

greetings, *155*

Grindr, 335

Grooms, Richard, *212*

gross domestic product (GDP) per capita, *288*

Grosz, Elizabeth, 299

group conformity, 175–76

groups, 26, 164–201; bifocal, 174; complexity and, 171–72, *172*; multifocal, 174; networks and, 177–90; size of, 171–72, *172*; unifocal, 173. *See also* social groups

Grundy, Saida, 305–6

Guevara, Ernesto "Che," 219, *219*

Gulf of Tonkin Resolution, 101

gun control laws, policy and, 67

Gutenberg, Johannes, 100

Guthrie, Doug, 39

Hacker, Jacob, 261

hackers, 160

Haddad, Fadi, 138–39, *138*

Hague Convention on Protection of Children and Co-operation in Respect of Intercountry Adoption (Hague Adoption Convention), 406–7

Haitian slave revolt, 36, 38

Haley, Alex, 349

Ham, curse of, 350–51

Hamme, Kimberly, *189*

happiness, 397, 399

hara-kiri, 215, *215*

Harding, Sandra, 72

Harlem Renaissance, 377

Harper's Weekly Magazine, 345, *346*

Harris, David R., 158

Hart, Owen, 161

Hartmann, Heidi, 321–22

Harvard University, 304, *305*

Hawaii, as "majority minority" state, 391

Hays, Sharon, 427, 428

Hays Code, 105, 106–7

Heerwig, Jennifer A., 158

Hegel, Georg Wilhelm Friedrich, 265–66

hegemonic masculinity, 303–6

hegemony, 108; definition of, 91; as mother of all ideologies, 91–92

Herdt, Gilbert, 326

Herrnstein, Richard J., 31

heteronormativity, 320, 330, 331–32

heterosexuality, "compulsory heterosexuaity," 327

heterosexuals, 176

Hetherington, E. Mavis, 432–33

Higgensen, Vy, *355*

high culture, vs. low culture, 84–85

higher education: credentialism and, 11–13, 12t; financial benefits of, 5; true costs and returns of, 8–10. *See also* college(s)

hijab, 360

hijra community, in India, *301*, 302

Hippocrates, 350

hiring patterns, race and, 365

Hispanics, 382, *383*, *388–89*; ethnicity and, 383; mass incarceration and, 243; rates of outmarriage, 434–35; by region of origin, *382*; U.S. Census and, 383, *390*; U.S. Hispanic population by region of origin, *382*. *See also* Latinxs

historically black colleges and universities (HBCUs), 305–6

historical materialism, 22–23

historical methods, 63, *63*

history, 36–38

Hitchcock, Alfred, 107

Hitler, Adolf, 36–37, *36*, 38

Hmong, 384

Hobbes, Thomas, 19

Hobbs, Allyson, 378

Hochschild, Arlie, 312, 415, 416, 419, 440

Hodkinson, Peter, 96

Moss, Kate, 119
motherhood: Black women and, 324; motherhood penalty, 316–17
mothering, reproduction of, 319
Moynihan, Daniel Patrick, 369, 421–22
Ms. Magazine, 113
multiculturalism, 370
multigenerational households, Asian Americans and, 424–25
multinational corporations, 196, 285
multiple births, 406
multiracial families, 434–35, *434*
Multiracial March on Washington, 390
multiracial people, *388–89*, 389, 390. *See also* interracial relationships
Munduruku villagers, 402, *403*
Murray, Charles, 31, 427
Muslim Americans, 347, 359, 360
Muslims, 359, 385; racialization of, 359–60; stereotypes and, 360
Mussolini, Benito, *36*
nadle identity, 301, 302
Nakamoto, Satoshi, 165
names, 118–19; African American and, 118–19; androgyny and, 306–7; femininity and, 306–7; gender and, 306–7; masculinity and, 306–7; occupation and, 253–54
Nanda, Serena, 302
Na people, 402, *403*, 404
Napoleonic Code, 213
narrative, definition of, 177
National Association for the Advancement of Colored People (NAACP), *29*, 30, 372, 378, 382
National Association for the Advancement of White People (NAAWP), *387*, 388
National Center for Health Statistics, 412
National Collegiate Athletic Association (NCAA), 304, 305
National Commission for the Protection of Human Subjects of Biomedical and Behavioral Research, 75

National Democratic Party, *362*
nationality, racism and, 362
National Longitudinal Study of Adolescent Health, 190
National Opinion Research Center, University of Chicago, 62–63
National Origins Act of 1924, 346
National Research Council, 389
National Survey of Sexual Health and Behavior, 336
nationhood, citizenship and, 66
Native Americans, 379–81, *380*; 2008–9 financial crisis and, 365–66; colonialism and, 89; diseases and, 380; European settlers and, 379–80; political organization of, 380–81; on reservations, 380; social problems facing, 380; structural racism and, 365–67; wealth and, 365–66. *See also* American Indians; *specific groups*
Native Hawaiians, *388–89*
naturalization law, 345–46
natural selection, 353
nature, vs. culture, 83–84
nature–behavior relationship, 299
nature–nurture debate, 160
Navajo "code talkers," 380
Navajoland (Diné Bikéyah), 380
Navajo society, three genders in, 301–2
Nazi experimentation, 75
Nazi Germany, 354, 372, 400
Nazis, 346
NBC, 102
Nebraska, abolition of death penalty in, 247
"neighborhood associations," 374
neighborhood watch groups, 207
Nelson, Alondra, 96–97
Nelson, Margaret, 415
netroots political groups, 187
networks: macro-level studies, 199; micro-level studies, 199; network analysis, 199; network analysis in practice, 190–95; networking events, *179*; network position, 190
New Deal, 63, 66
New France settlers, 253–54

New Guinea, 326
New Hampshire, abolition of death penalty in, 247
"new immigration," 369
new institutionalism, 197
New Jersey, abolition of death penalty in, 247
New Mexico: abolition of death penalty in, 247; as "majority minority" state, 391; Native Americans in, 380
New Moon Girls, 113
new racism, 360–63
Newsweek, 102
New York State: abolition of death penalty in, 247; Asian Americans in, 384; marriage equality and, 437
New York State Constitution, proposal for equal rights clause for women in, 415
New York State Parole Handbook, 241
New York Times, 121
Nichols, Nichelle, 107
Nixon, Richard, 199, 372
Noah, biblical story of, 350–51
Noel, Donald, 369
nonbinary identity, 206, 299–300, 304–5
non-college graduate, *10*
non-European immigration, 369–71, *370–71*
nonheteronormativity, 331–32
nonmaterial culture, unpacking, 87–89
non-monogamy, 332
nonverbal communicaton, 152, 154–55
nonwhiteness, 354, 362
nonwhites, 390; 2008–9 financial crisis and, 365–66; structural racism and, 365–67; wealth and, 365–66. *See also* minorities; *specific groups*
"normal science" model of sociology, 42. *See also* positivism
normative regulation, peer groups and, 140
norms: "breaching experiments," 156; breaching of, 156–57, *156*, 161; conformity and, 175–76; definition of, 89–90; internalization of, 132–33; masking

Putnam, Robert, 183–87, *184*
Quadagno, Jill, 63, *63*, 66
Quakers, 232
qualitative methods, 41–42, 43, 49–50, 58–59, 70
quantitative methods, 41–42, 43, 49, 58–59
queer, 331–32
queer theory, 322–23
race, 27, 342–97; addiction and, 221–22; based on physical difference, 347; biology and, 342; capitalism and, 246–47; capital punishment and, 246–47, *247*; citizenship and, 345–46, 354; consequences of, 342; criminalization of addiction and, 221–22; criminal records and, 363; critical race theory, 356–57; cult of domesticity and, 422; cultural theories of, 355; culture and, 88; definition of, 344, 347; discrimination and, 360–63, 371–76; DNA testing and, 356–58; in early modern world, 350–53; essentialism and, 362; vs. ethnicity, 347, *383*; family structure and, 407, 410–11; as fluid and changeable category, 344; in France, 363; future of, 389; hierarchy and, 347; hiring patterns and, 365; history of concept of, 347, 349–58; housing discrimination and, 363–64; incarceration and, 375–76; inequality and, 347; as instrument of oppression, 356; intersectionality and, 357; Latinxs and, 383, *383*; media representations and, 111–12, *112*; myth of, 344–49; pay discrepancies and, *311*; physical differences and, 350; politics of making out and, 106–7; power and, 347; prejudice and, *358*, 360–63, *360*; property values and, 363–64, 374; questions on U.S. Census, *390*; racial conflict, 376–77; realities of, 344, 358–67; segregation and, 371–76; sentencing laws and, 364; single-parent families

and, 423; as social construction, 356; social construction of, 343–44; social safety net and, 66; socioeconomic status (SES) and, 70, 289–90; sociological imagination and, 344; twentieth-century concepts of, 353–58; U.S. Census and, 390, *390*; wealth inequality and, 290–91
"race-neutral" rhetoric, 362
race privilege, 323–25
race relations: changing, 389–93; technology and, 393
race riots, *373*, 377
racial bias, technology and, 394–95
racial conflict, 376–77
racial differences, climate and, 352
racial discrimination, 363. *See also* discrimination
racial dissimilarity, index of, *375*
racial diversity, tolerance of, 206
racial groups, in United States, 379
racial hegemony, 362
racialization, 348, 359–60
racial progress, 357
"racial purity," 400
racial realities, 358–67
racial thinking, 351
racism, 203–4; as central to organization of society, 356; color-blind racism, 362; cultural, *362*; culture and, 362; definition of, 346; discrimination and, 357, 361–62, *361*; experience of, 357; history of, 345; institutional, 363–65; institutional bias and, 357; manifestations of, 357; in the media, 108–11, *109*, *110*; microaggressions and, 357; nationality and, 362; negative effects of, 109; new racism, 360–63; prejudice and, 361–62; scientific, 351; structural, 363–67
radical feminism, 321–22
radio, 100
Rae, Issa, 81–82, *82*, 117, 120–21
Rae Diop, Jo-Issa, 81. *See also* Rae, Issa

Ramirez, Marc, 236–37, *237*
Rangappa, Asha, 13, *13*, 14
Rauscher, Emily, 134
Read, Jen'nan, 359, *359*
Reagan, Ronald, 372, 425
reality, 77; construction of, 124–63; social construction of, 28, 152–60
Reardon, Sean, 290
rebels, 219, *219*
recidivism, 236–37, 238, 244
recording technology, 100–101
Reddit, 157
Reddy, Gayatri, 302
redlining, 366, 375
reference groups, 176
reflection theory, 98, 98–99, 104
reflexivity, 68
refugees, *362*
regimenting, 241, 242
rehabilitation, 212, *212*, 236; incarceration and, 236–37; prison and, 236–37; punishment and, 240
reliability, definition of, 58
religion, 90, 91
remarriage, 405, 433
representation, 85–86, *86*
representative sample, definition of, 62–63
"reproductive labor" argument, 418
reproductive technologies, 406
Republican Party, 76, 436
research: conducted with humans, 72; golden rules of, 72–73
research 101, 50–55
research cycle, *51*
researcher, role of, 68
researcher responsibility, 68–74
researchers: experimenter effects and, 68; informed consent and, 73; objectivity and, 71–72; power and, 71–72; responsibilities of, 68–74; role of, 70
research methods, 77; case studies, 65; choosing your method, 58–68, *60*; of comparative research, 66; comparative research, 63; content analysis, 63, 67; data collection, 59–68; definition of, 49; experimentation,